Matthew Fo
Father of O

MAURY
PATHFINDER OF THE SEAS

Matthew Fontaine Maury, Father of Oceanography

A Biography, 1806–1873

JOHN GRADY

McFarland & Company, Inc., Publishers
Jefferson, North Carolina

Frontispiece: Matthew Fontaine Maury was the last Confederate honored along Richmond's Monument Avenue. Robert E. Lee, Jefferson Davis, J. E. B. Stuart, and Thomas Jackson are the other Confederates recognized along this historic street. In 1996, a monument honoring Arthur Ashe, an African American tennis star born in Richmond, was dedicated. Photograph by the author.

LIBRARY OF CONGRESS CATALOGUING-IN-PUBLICATION DATA

Grady, John.
Matthew Fontaine Maury, Father of Oceanography : a biography, 1806–1873 / John Grady.
p. cm.
Includes bibliographical references and index.

ISBN 978-0-7864-7821-7 (softcover : acid free paper) ∞
ISBN 978-1-4766-1808-1 (ebook)

1. Maury, Matthew Fontaine, 1806–1873. 2. Oceanographers—United States—Biography. 3. Oceanography—History. I. Title.

GC30.M4G73 2015
551.46092—dc23
[B] 2014044930

BRITISH LIBRARY CATALOGUING DATA ARE AVAILABLE

Printed in the United States of America

McFarland & Company, Inc., Publishers
Box 611, Jefferson, North Carolina 28640
www.mcfarlandpub.com

Acknowledgments

Producing this work has been a long journey for me that started when I drove past Lake Maury near the Mariners' Museum on my way to work in the late summer of 1976. I have many people to thank for their encouragement and assistance over the years.

I start with my family—my wife, Lillian, who, in order to push this work to completion, took to the keyboard to fix manuscript formatting problems and also proofread, and my daughter Katherine Anne, who probably wondered as a child why the family was going to these strange places and calling them vacations. My first wife, Anne Penn Chew Born Grady, who died in November 1992, strongly believed in this project and accompanied me on a number of these vacation-research trips to Central Virginia; the Shenandoah Valley; Sewanee and Nashville, Tenn.; Philadelphia; Chapel Hill, Raleigh, and Durham, N.C.; and Charleston and Columbia, S.C., especially when she was in graduate school at the University of South Carolina.

I thank Dr. William N. Still, Jr., who, over the years, inspired me to continue and read many parts of this work in its different incarnations. I would be remiss if I did not thank Dr. David Winkler, Dr. Jan Herman, Dr. Steven Dick, Dr. Martin Gordon, Dr. John Coski, Waite Rawls, Teresa Roane, and Dr. Amanda Foreman for their assistance.

There could never be thanks enough for the librarians and archivists at the Library of Congress, the National Archives, the Department of the Navy Library, the Smithsonian Institution, the Library of Virginia, the Virginia Historical Society, the Museum of the Confederacy, the University of Virginia, Virginia Tech, Virginia Military Institute, Washington and Lee University Library and Archives, West Virginia University Library and Archives, the University of the South, the Tennessee State Library, and Hagley Museum, who helped me sift through the puzzle of Maury's complex life.

Table of Contents

Preface

Matthew Fontaine Maury is long overdue for a fresh look at his contributions to the United States and Confederate navies, nineteenth-century maritime exploration, the quest for a National Weather Service, the building of the Naval Observatory, the charting of the oceans, and the birth of a new science—oceanography. He wielded power in Washington for decades. In the breakup of the Union, he lost that power even in the Confederacy and a son, spent years in exile, and died with a thwarted dream.

Frances Leigh Williams's *Matthew Fontaine Maury: Scientist of the Sea*, the last comprehensive biography of this scientific visionary, was published fifty years ago. The latest and more limited work was published eleven years ago. Key differences exist between my work and these biographies. This book

- examines Maury and the leading American scientific figures of the mid-nineteenth century engaged in political and bureaucratic turf battles for money, power, and prestige in a broader manner than Patricia Jahns's 1961 work, which focused on Maury and Joseph Henry at the Smithsonian; details the split between "popularizers" and "pure scientists" to control James Smithson's bequest to the United States; and explores the scientific jealousy that metastasized over his appointment to head the National Observatory and his success in brokering the first successful maritime international conference that led to worldwide recognition and honors;
- acknowledges rather than denies Maury's keen interest in politics and string-pulling with the leading national political figures of his time, not simply within the Navy Department, i.e., John Tyler, James K. Polk, Abel Parker Upshur, John C. Calhoun, Henry Clay, John Quincy Adams, Sam Houston, John Bell, T. Butler King, and Charles Conrad (often key allies

in the United States and Confederate governments); and John Clayton, Thomas Hart Benton, Jefferson Davis, Judah Benjamin, and Stephen Mallory (often key opponents in both governments on the major issues of their time);

- contrasts the financial perils Maury's family experienced with those of his grandparents and parents and how those perils drove a writing career that made him wildly popular in the United States and overseas before and after the Civil War; explains how he resurrected his naval career by detailing the festering ills in the Navy following an accident that left him lame; describes how he rode his popularity into becoming the Confederates' most influential polemicist in the South and Europe and immigration cheerleader for Maximilian after the war;
- plumbs the depth of opposition to Maury inside the Navy led by Samuel F. DuPont, Charles Davis, and James Gilliss—much of it arising from the turf battles that Maury, Henry of the Smithsonian, Alexander Dallas Bache of the Coast Survey, and Benjamin Peirce of Harvard so heatedly engaged in over the observatory's direction—and later his resigning his commission to side with Virginia following its vote for secession, and in their eyes becoming a traitor;
- repositions Maury vis-à-vis his family's long interest in faraway lands as Huguenot exiles in the seventeenth century in Ireland and later Virginia and American Western exploration through the Loyal Land Company of Albemarle County, Virginia; as a rival to Great Britain's naval power; as a champion of American business and maritime interests—especially with and through the sons of the original "Yankee traders" and the merchants who dominated the American Geographical and Statistical Society in New York to expand the Navy's role in protecting commerce;
- examines Maury's religiosity, which is bonded to his family's Huguenot experience, its exiles from France and the British Isles, and his own exile from the United States during and after the Civil War; his insistence in his writing and lectures on including divine inspiration in his discoveries and findings and their theological setting; his iron ties to the Episcopal Church in the South and the Anglican Church in Great Britain, influencing his career as an American scientific celebrity and, later, educator; and the deep conviction in his own righteousness in his work and against all critics, a trait shared with his paternal grandfather, the Rev. James Maury, Thomas Jefferson's last teacher as a boy and a plaintiff in the "Parson's Cause" case in colonial Virginia;

- redirects attention to Maury's limiting civilian American scientists' role, especially in exploration, by focusing on the Navy's priorities of navigation and ocean charting by bolstering the commercial aspects of these missions; his lifelong interest in naval warfare technology, perfecting electronically detonated land and marine mines for the Confederacy, buying and building commerce raiders in Great Britain and France, and seeing himself—as lame as he was and as far removed from service afloat as any naval officer—in command of one of the most modern raiders in taking the war to the Union;
- sheds new light on Maury's interactions with Maximilian, erstwhile emperor of Mexico, with the naval officer tantalizingly offering the Habsburg monarch a way to retake California using Confederate sympathizers there (e.g., former Senator William Gwin) and buying the seized "Birkenhead Rams" potentially to attack San Francisco during the Civil War; and
- confronts Maury's racial beliefs in pre– and post–Civil War America as a Southern nationalist like James D. B. DeBow and an officer ashore immediately after the Nullification Crisis and Nat Turner's slave revolt in Virginia with a politically active family; his constant looking to expand slavery even to Brazil's Amazon basin as a "safety valve" for the South and to preserve it in post–Civil War Mexico; and predicting, in his postwar *Physical Survey of Virginia*, that newly freed slaves in the Old Dominion would move to the Gulf Coast rather than stay, a migration that never occurred.

Prologue: The Last Crusade

In 1872, Matthew Fontaine Maury, one of America's best-known scientists, was nauseated, suffering from bleeding ulcers and using crutches to hobble about his Virginia home. Yet he felt driven to leave that small house on a college campus to address the men who worked the truck and dairy farms outside Boston, the very people who once had put a price on his head. If his strength held, Maury intended to ride the cars to St. Louis, where the dry goods merchants, bankers, and hard-scrabbling farmers of the Mississippi Valley would gather to hear the old master tell how the scientifics, schoolmen all, cared not a whit for men of the soil. Then, if providence smiled, the pathfinder of the seas would come back east to rally the merchants, bankers, shippers, and farmers of Virginia to *the* cause. It would be another crusade, maybe his last, for a national weather service.[1]

Knowing what the weather was, had been, and might be could take some of the risk out of planting. It would allow the meanest man who survived the Civil War to rise. Knowledge collected from observers in every whistle-stop flashed over telegraph wires and could warn of battering hail on ripening wheat or sing of sweet rains on newly planted tobacco and cotton. These landsmen-observers would be akin to the sailing masters Maury had used a quarter of a century earlier.[2]

As always in Maury's professional life, there was Joseph Henry, secure inside his castle in the capital, defending the Smithsonian's prerogatives. To the secretary, Maury was a trickster. Henry and the schoolmen saw themselves as building American science, rigorous and precise in procedure. Henry, the schoolmen, and Maury all claimed to be the truest disciples of Alexander von Humboldt, the nineteenth-century German naturalist.[3]

But who was the truly anointed?

In a faraway age, these Americans—notably Maury, Henry, Alexander

Dallas Bache of the Coast Survey, and Benjamin Peirce of Harvard—joined on works as grand as mapping the stars and as picayune as identifying a rock's minerals. By the early 1850s, the schoolmen left scant room for savants wearing naval uniforms.[4]

As Bache wrote, "I have had an interview with Maury who while he declares himself very friendly and anxious [to] do justice in all cases is rather I think indefinite in his views of scientific ethics."[5]

Ethics proved a minefield for all these men.

After all, Maury built the great National Observatory in Washington. From inside its walls, this officer's influence stretched far beyond navies into the great trading companies and banking houses.

Who was Matthew Fontaine Maury? A scientist? A charlatan?

In becoming "a useful man" on the world stage, Maury first focused light on the rotten ills of a clique-ridden Navy; charted pathways through the oceans; bested the Admiralty in securing the fastest, safest trading routes to India; helped bind the old and new worlds with the laying of the transatlantic cable; advocated most forcefully Southern rights in a troubled union; and preached American Manifest Destiny from the frozen wastes of the Arctic to treacherous waters south of Cape Horn. In the ebb of his life, he revolutionized warfare in perfecting electronically detonated mines.[6]

As with his scientific pursuits, Maury's eagerness to go to the public in person and in print on the questions of the day riled powerful men in business, politics, and the United States, Confederate, and Royal navies. They dismissed him as the "Man on the Hill."[7]

Over his career, Maury found himself afoul of Jefferson Davis, as a senator from Mississippi, as a cabinet member, and as president of the Confederacy, and Stephen R. Mallory, as chairman of the Senate Naval Affairs Committee and as secretary of the Confederate Navy.[8]

Through all the struggles over the political, social, and scientific questions of his time, Maury, however, had had his share of allies among the powerful; but now, in the early 1870s, they, too, were in eclipse or in the grave.

President John Tyler long championed Maury and used his ideas to overhaul the Navy in the 1840s and, later, to embarrass the "Cotton Kings"—Davis and Mallory—as a member of the Confederate Congress.[9]

Likewise, the 1860 presidential candidate John Bell steadfastly supported Maury. The same can be said of Sam Houston, who won for Maury his acting midshipman's warrant and three decades later salvaged his naval career on the Senate floor.[10]

Those men—and those old battles over the route of the transcontinental railroad, the opening of the Amazon to American slaveholders, the defense of the Great Lakes, the isthmian crossing, the building of commerce raiders for the Confederacy, and the creation of a "New Virginia" in Mexico—were now only stories in crumbling newspapers, twice-told tales in taverns in 1872.

Through those battles in the long-running wars of his life, Maury found comfort in the songs of David, especially Psalm 107:

> They who sailed the sea in ships,
> trading on the deep water,
> These saw the works of the Lord and his wonders in the abyss.[11]

Like older brother John, Maury took to the Navy, a life far removed from the foundering farms of his parents. The sea, with its wonders and mysteries, was the stage for his energies, his work, and his ambitions.

By September 1872, Maury's time was passing like the sands in the hourglasses he once turned aboard the *Vincennes* as it circumnavigated the globe. Yet he intended to give the last full measure of his spirit.

1. God's Wandering Children

Far from the sea, hard in a thick forest of scrub pine and oak in Spotsylvania County, Virginia, stood the stone house where Matthew Fontaine Maury was born January 14, 1806. The high winter sun barely pierced the thick pine canopy surrounding the site, and pools of water left by melted snow or the more frequent ice storms turned rusty black. The rocky, rolling 103 acres were the property that Richard Maury, Matthew's father, bought from "Light Horse Harry" Lee, Robert E. Lee's father, in 1797.[1]

Life for Matthew's mother, Diana Minor Maury, on the edge of the Wilderness, a tangled landscape known now as a Civil War battlefield, was a far cry from that of her childhood home at "Topping Castle" on the North Anna River in Caroline County. Life for Matthew's father, Richard Maury, on that same land echoed the straitened circumstances of his birth as the twelfth child of the brilliant but poor the Rev. James Maury of Albemarle County.[2]

The soaring language of the English church was the family's bulwark. Although the Maurys and the Fontaines worshipped in the Episcopal Church of the United States, and before that in the Church of England and Ireland, the roots of their beliefs ran deep among France's persecuted Protestants. The Maurys and the Fontaines were Huguenots, forced into exile when Louis XIV repealed the Edict of Toleration. By Richard's children's adulthood, their stories were a collected popular chronicle of a people determined to keep "that pure reformed religion" in foreign lands.[3]

In 1715, John Fontaine, a veteran of British wars with Spain, sailed for the New World. That same year his sister, Mary Anne, married fellow Huguenot Matthew Maury. The voyage set the stage for the Fontaines and Maurys in North America.[4]

With its capitol, Bruton Parish Church, and the few buildings of the College of William and Mary, Williamsburg had replaced the pestilential

Jamestown as the capital sixteen years before Fontaine arrived. Despite the trappings of British power, for most of the year Williamsburg was a sleepy village of fifteen hundred.

Instead of immediately scouring the countryside for suitable lands to cultivate, John, the soldier-adventurer, enlisted in Lieutenant Governor Alexander Spotswood's expedition across the mountains. The Indians had been subdued by disease, war, and treaty throughout Tidewater, all of eastern Virginia below the rivers' fall lines. Now was the time—before the French canoed into the Ohio and Mississippi River valleys, or the Germans and Scotch-Irish from Pennsylvania lumbered in crude wagons into the Shenandoah Valley—to discover new sources of furs and skins and iron and coal and to investigate the stories of gold in the runs and possess it all.[5]

Spotswood, who had arrived in Virginia in 1710 with his mistress Katherine Russell, embodied his family: "I endure that I may secure." He endured over the burgesses in completing the Italianate "Governor's Palace" with its distinctive cupola and four towering chimneys. He was John Fontaine's kind of man.[6]

In Fontaine's spirited account, Spotswood and sixty-three young adventurers with servants, fourteen rangers, and four Indian guides toasted their Hanoverian monarch on an American mountaintop. In more than four hundred miles of wanderings, they didn't find the Seven Cities of Cibola, but land unclaimed by other Europeans was its own treasure.[7]

As the years passed, the patient and disciplined Spotswood built a fanciful estate—Enchanted Castle—in what was long called The Wilderness. There, he developed a vine culture, mined iron and coal, and built postal roads for the colony. All required patience, discipline, and the willingness to diversify.[8]

Back in the governor's palace, Spotswood dubbed these young gallants "Knights of the Golden Horseshoe" and awarded each a shoe made of gold for their mounts. Fontaine had found a path into Virginia society.[9]

Though Virginia's Tidewater remained a "half-cleared land studded with stumps and skeletons of giant trees, old fields disappearing under a ragged regrowth," it was a gambler's den of land, a commodity so scarce in the British Isles that talk of it rattled reasonable men's rationality.[10]

When news at last arrived from Fontaine, Matthew Maury was so excited that he sailed immediately from Ireland in early 1718, leaving behind his then-pregnant wife, Mary Anne Fontaine Maury. Maury's excitement must have been tempered by the long ocean crossing and the search ashore for his kinsman. But once he found Fontaine, he was as taken with the King William County property as his brother-in-law.

Maury did not pause. With laborers building his house, he returned for his wife and their newborn son, James. Upon their arrival in King William, the Maurys named their rustic plantation Fontainebleu—a bow to their French heritage.[11]

James Maury, Matthew and Mary Anne's son, proved an exceptional student. As an adolescent, he taught at the preparatory school of William and Mary, and James Blair, the college president, recommended young James cross the Atlantic to study for the ministry.[12]

Following ordination in Great Britain, James Maury stood in line with his Fontaine forebears—an academic and a man of God. When he returned, he wed Mary Walker, the daughter of a physician and adventurer from neighboring King and Queen County.[13]

As Tidewater lands played out or were encumbered by inheritance, the established church moved with young planters like Peter Jefferson into the Piedmont. An estimated 130 miles from Williamsburg and "planted close under the southwest mountains," James Maury preached the gospel of the Church of England in the sprawling Fredericksville Parish. The traveling "to baptize & marry & bury" over the primitive roads and traces of the Piedmont and mountains took its toll. He lamented his "Intervals of Leisure & Repose are as short, as they are rare."

Like James Fontaine, his grandfather, in Dublin, James Maury founded a school and enrolled his son; Jefferson's son Thomas, one of the younger Maury's closest boyhood friends; Dabney Carr, later Jefferson's brother-in-law; and James Madison, a cousin of the president with the same name and first Anglican bishop of Virginia. "In a log house below the Southwest Mountains [Jefferson and other students] received at an impressionable age personal instruction from a sound scholar who was aware of the niceties of language and the beauties of literature." Jefferson, who spent two years living with the Maurys before enrolling at William and Mary, recalled the reverend as "a correct classical scholar" who impressed upon him the value of literature and the study of nature.[14]

Here was James Maury, a cleric, educator, and pathfinder in faith and knowledge. Although he was proficient in Greek and Latin, he belittled the teaching of "dead languages." He wrote that most of his charges "ought to be instructed as soon as possible in the most necessary branches of useful, practical knowledge."[15]

Being a pastor and an educator, James Maury exerted influence over the colony's most ambitious men. While John Fontaine took to the march, Maury shaped a vision of what new lands could be. He, like many members of his vestry—Jefferson, Joshua Fry, his father-in-law Thomas Walker, and Meriwether Lewis's grandfather—established the Loyal Company in 1749. His grandson, Matthew Fontaine Maury, made turning that vision into reality his life's work.[16]

In the mid–1760s, a nervous peace was in place with the French stay-behinds in Canada, Indiana, and Illinois, and a few Spanish clustered along the Mississippi to the Gulf of Mexico and Florida.

The 1763 Treaty of Paris proved of little help financially to Great Britain's oldest North American colony. What followed was worse. The Royal Proclamation of October 1763 barred expansion west of the Appalachians. Virginians, like the Reverend Maury, felt they had been stabbed in the back. This was the very reason they had gone to war.[17]

The war with France and the Indians left the Virginia planters in greater debt than usual. Adding to their burden were the poor harvests of 1755 and 1758. To ease their plight, the legislature passed emergency acts allowing debts to be paid in currency or tobacco notes and set the price of a pound of tobacco at the artificially low level of two pence. The market price was about six pence. Planters naturally took the two-pence option.

The Anglican clergy were outraged. They demanded their sixteen thousand pounds of tobacco, as guaranteed by statute. Thirty-five of the seventy Anglican priests in Virginia gathered in a convention to demand their due. To them, this was another example of the legislature's daring to put itself ahead of Parliament and the king, like their outrageous attempt to control the College of William and Mary.

Because the 1758 law did not have a clause saying when the emergency act was to start—with royal confirmation or the day it was passed—the clergymen sent their case to the Board of Trade for a decision. There the Rev. John Camm, supported by the bishop of London and the archbishop of Canterbury, won a ruling invalidating the law, but not from its inception.

Matters didn't end there. Lieutenant Governor Francis Fauquier became outraged when Camm, a professor at William and Mary, accompanied by several witnesses, showed him a copy of the ruling. Fauquier accused the minister of breaking the seals of an official document intended for him alone. Although he let the relief act lapse as had his predecessor, Robert Dinwiddie, the lieutenant governor left reimbursement to the courts, expecting they would rule that the clergy had no grounds, because the law had lapsed.[18]

As a clergyman, Maury believed like Camm that the burgesses had cheated them. Since the first cases foundered in York and King William counties, he sued Thomas Johnson, the collector of the parish levies, for the difference between the two pence paid under the act and the six pence market price. His attorney, Peter Lyons, thought Maury's chances better if he filed in Hanover County, rather than Louisa, where the collector lived, served on the county court, and was a burgess.

When the suit was filed, the Rev. Patrick Henry, the vicar of St. Paul's in Hanover County, took a proprietary interest in the case. In the small world of Piedmont society, the Henry brothers were church and state in Hanover. When the interests of both intersected as they did during the wild days of George Whitefield's preaching in the mid–1740s, the brothers felt duty-bound to contain the "religious Phrenzy" of the revivalists.

Patrick's position in the county was obvious by his long education and ordination. Although John was well educated, he took "a traditional shortcut on the road to wealth and power" in Virginia by marrying above his station. By 1763, he was a judge, a powerful man in handling the local affairs.

In November 1763, Lyons carried the first round when Presiding Judge Henry ruled the law invalid and ordered a jury be selected to determine the amount owed Maury. The collector's attorney then resigned, and Judge Henry's son Patrick took over the case. His uncle cautioned young Henry against "saying hard things of the clergy" at the session.

Although court days brought crowds to enjoy the spectacle, the numbers milling about the single-story brick courthouse were larger than usual. On the day of the trial in December, men of property excused themselves when the sheriff tried to press them into jury duty. "Hence he went among the vulgar herd" of New Light dissenters (followers of evangelical preachers such as Jonathan Edwards) like the bricklayer Samuel Morris and Roger Shackleford (who had little use for the Reverend Henry), deists, and disgruntled Hanover County planters for jurymen. Lawyer Henry pronounced the jury "honest men."

Once the veniremen were picked, there was a scramble for seats. William Wirt, Patrick Henry's first biographer, claimed twenty or so of the colony's Anglican clergymen were inside the court that day. Those in clerical robes and the men of property who could not squeeze into the small chamber battled with the vulgar herd to hold spots near the doorway to hear what was said.

For a corpulent man who went about in measured stride, Lyons moved swiftly this day by calling two tobacco dealers to establish the price of leaf in the late spring of 1759. As he finished, he admonished the jury to remember the clergy's good deeds in the community and rested Maury's case. The "honest men" or "vulgar herd" were now primed for the "hard things."

The young Henry declared, "The Act of 1758 had every characteristic of a good law." Drawing upon the oratorical skills he learned from the evangelical preachers that so enraptured his mother, he said, "A King by disallowing acts of this salutary nature, from being the father of his people, degenerated into a tyrant and forfeits all right his subjects' obedience."

Lyons shouted: "The gentleman had spoken treason."

Taking the course the Reverend Henry feared he would, the twenty-seven-year-old, self-taught lawyer shot back for an hour that the clergy's challenge to Virginia's law made them "enemies of the community." Finishing, Henry said Maury and his coplaintiff "deserved to be punished by signal severity" as "rapacious harpies."

Out for only five minutes, the jury awarded Maury one penny in damages. The verdict stunned the clergymen. Lyons was on his feet offering motions to set aside the decision to no avail. John Henry had lost control of his courtroom. The only recourse open to Maury was to take the case to the General Court in Williamsburg, far away from the boisterous crowd that hoisted Henry on their shoulders and marched in glee toward a tavern.

With this defeat as an example of the vagaries of life, Maury instilled in his descendants a deep fear of debt. There also now showed a darker side to this brilliant man's legacy: self-righteousness. A century later, many powerful men viewed Matthew Fontaine Maury in this light.

The verdict affected James Maury instantly. His ever-expanding family needed to be fed, clothed, and educated, but there was now even less to go around than before. Into those severe circumstances three years later Richard Maury, Matthew Fontaine's father, was born.[19]

In 1769, the impoverished James Maury died, and his oldest son, Matthew, took over his church and school. The primogeniture and entail traditions were as strong in the Piedmont as they were in the Tidewater and Great Britain. There was little for the younger Maury sons but to keep faith in God and try their luck in planting.

The Minor family's Virginia roots went back to the seventeenth century clandestine trade with Europe. Maindort Doodes, a Dutch sea captain, settled first near Norfolk sometime between 1639 and 1650, and fit peaceably into the trading and Chesapeake Bay planting community. In 1671, the Virginia General Assembly naturalized father and son as Englishmen.[20]

Doodes, the sea captain's son who adopted Minor as the family name, found the usual course to prosperity for Virginia planters congenial. He and his progeny married into other landholding families like the Cooks, the Vivians, and the Carrs; increased their estates; crossed and recrossed rivers while all the time buying, selling, and leasing lands and slaves; and passed on what they had in buildings, lands, and slaves to their children. Following one rule, the oldest son got the most—if not all. Theirs were the lives of the Tidewater plantocracy. Along the way, the men usually garnered positions of trust in the church and county, and a few went to Williamsburg as burgesses. The women had children, plenty of children. If a spouse died, they remarried and went on with life, clearing and exhausting land as they went.[21]

For decades, the Minors held steady to prosperity's course.

Then came John Minor II, born November 18, 1735, the inheritor of Topping Castle on the North Anna River in Caroline County. The maternal grandfather of Matthew Fontaine Maury wore the badges of colonial achievement: vestryman and magistrate. He also proudly wore the badges of the Revolution: member of the county committee of correspondence, organizer of a militia company, and present at Lord Cornwallis's surrender at Yorktown in 1781.

From his marriage with Elizabeth Cosby of Louisa County came children. One was named Diana, who, on January 18, 1792, brought to her marriage to a young man of good family, Richard Maury, her love and a large dowry.[22]

When Matthew Fontaine was born, six Maury children—Mary, John, Walker, Matilda, Betsy, and Richard Launcelot—lived in the stone house near the Rappahannock River. While they prayed, played, studied, and did their chores, the Maury children could not know how their father worried over his growing debts.[23]

On the surface the future looked bright in 1797 when Richard bought for a little more than sixty-six pounds the acreage that included the house with an outdoor cook house and kitchen and cabins for slaves. To better his chances, Richard also leased another 323 acres from Henry "Light Horse Harry" Lee. The rent was due Christmas Day, payable in cash or with 1,000 pounds of tobacco. They tilled the lands that made Alexander Spotswood a wealthy man. Spotswood diversified; Maury stuck with tobacco.[24]

Matters seemed under control three years later when Diana inherited some slaves upon her father's death. Land clearing in the tangled second growth forest was easier, but there was a troubling caveat in her father's will, as appeared in other prosperous planters' final testaments.

Although Diana's father provided her with slaves, he put the rest of her inheritance into trust with John and Launcelot Minor, her brothers, as administrators. This was consistent with the laws of entail that barred sale of an inheritance without a higher lord's approval. In this way, Richard's lack of cash and crop could not consume what the Minor family had accumulated.

By 1808, the debts were a plague of locusts. The Maurys, like many planters, cleaved off twenty-four acres they owned and another fifty-five and a half acres they leased. For this transaction on February 13, they received $155 from their in-law Edward Herndon.[25]

Richard Maury paid off his most pressing debts and gambled the rest on another crop of tobacco. Within two years he lost that as well. When Diana's brother John, a successful lawyer in Fredericksburg, visited in the summer of 1810, the realities were obvious. Whatever John said and however Richard took it, the facts were that the creditors held all the cards.

By August 1, under pressure, Richard signed an indenture placing his holdings in trust. The reasons were spelled out at the Spotsylvania Courthouse "for the purpose of paying and satisfying all the just debts of the said Richard Maury."[26]

Where Richard clung to the appearances of prosperity—after all, he had twelve slaves—the trustees moved to silence the creditors. Instead of hacking off more acreage, the trustees—John Minor, William Maury, and John Herndon—took the safest route for cash, one used by Jefferson: they sold the slave Isaiah.

It was only the start.

The trustees knew that when one part of the family hurt they all ached. They were particularly concerned about the boys. Richard's sons had to be set upon paths to provide for themselves. John, the oldest, chafed at the idea of becoming a farmer, and the trustees, especially John Minor, thought it unlikely that he would be any more successful at raising tobacco than his father. He therefore appealed to President Jefferson to remember kindly his teacher's grandson. On March 8, 1809, John Maury, barely in his teens, was appointed an acting midshipman in the Navy. For the other boys, the appointment could have momentous, life-changing consequences—if they so chose. John was embarking on a life that showed all the children, especially Matthew, that the world could be one of adventures like those of Fontaine, a Knight of the Golden Horseshoe, and John Maury, heading to sea.[27]

New failures in the fields spawned new debts. Compounding his financial problems was the trade embargo with Great Britain, dramatically cutting exports. In the home there was little peace. Dick's, Matthew's, and little Charles's boisterousness and chatter proved especially irksome to their father.

Only Abram Maury's letters of good available acreage for cotton in Tennessee provided Richard with a note of hope. Although his family's name was well known, Richard didn't have the option of petitioning the Virginia legislature for a special lottery as Jefferson did to pay off his debts. But if Richard could sell his remaining holdings, he would be free of this gnarled land, and, better yet, free of the trustees and out of the reach of the Old Dominion's courts. Richard was determined to make one last attempt to seize control of his family's destiny.[28]

Despite his father's achievements, the Reverend Maury's poverty left the younger sons like Richard with little choice of station. He was a planter, a farmer really, literate but losing its family's hold on their place in pre–Revolutionary Virginia. With his mounting debts, Richard was flirting with jail. He had to look no further than to his landlord, Lee, who was jailed in Spotsylvania County in 1809 as a debtor.[29]

With Diana recovering from the birth of their ninth child, Catherine Ann, in May 1810, Richard let his hope—distilled into a scheme—be known. Now he wanted to uproot her from everything and everyone she knew and move seven hundred miles westward onto the frontier.

Through the hazy burning days of summer, Richard grew more rigid that the family's only hope was to flee to Tennessee. No matter what the trustees said, the debts were his and not theirs. Only by mid–September did the trustees agree to allow yet another gamble on selling what was left to pay for the move.

The seventy-nine acres remaining went to Nathaniel Gordon on September 22, 1810, for three hundred dollars. If Richard thought his troubles ended with a filing with the county clerk, the confessed debtor was very wrong. He had to endure one more humiliation in the state of his birth.

Because Diana approved the sale at home and not before witnesses or in a public setting, the Spotsylvania County Court refused to accept Richard's word that all was proper. It sent emissaries to the Maury home. This was the equivalent of Henry's denunciation of his grandfather as being one of the "rapacious harpies." Whatever her true feelings were, Diana told the appointees she approved the sale.[30]

In the early fall, the Maurys piled all the goods they could carry into a twelve-foot-long wagon and set out on their journey. The children walked along or, like Matthew, rode on their older brothers' and sisters' shoulders westward.

Progress was slow. In Salem, Virginia, on the front range of the Appalachians, there were stables, blacksmiths, and buggy and wagon repair shops. In the hamlet's taverns, like the Globe, or the Mermaid Hotel, were spread the tales of the dangers in crossing the Watauga, Holston, Clinch, and French Broad rivers and confronting the mountains, whose peaks looked like waves on the ocean.

Out of the Roanoke Valley, the jarring wagon ride through the narrow passes was made rougher by hard winds blowing thick dust or sinking the overloaded wagon as rain mired the roads. A dozen miles a day was considered a success. At the end of those long days, the Maurys camped by streams, cooked what they had, and tried to rest.

As the hours of daylight dwindled, Richard drove relentlessly toward the stagecoach road between the Middle and North Forks of the Holston until they crossed into Tennessee with the hope for a life free of debt, courts, and trustees. Markers now counted down mileage to Nashborough (Nashville). From the village on the Cumberland River, the Maurys traveled eighteen gently rolling miles to Franklin, the home of his influential cousin, Abram. Richard Maury, unlike Moses, entered his Promised Land.[31]

2. Becoming a Useful Man

The cost of moving left the Virginia Maurys as straitened in the Tennessee bluegrass as they had been east of the Blue Ridge. Land near Franklin, the Promised Land, was going for about four dollars an acre, and Richard, even with the advice of Abram Maury, could not afford to buy, and for now did not turn to the trustees for money. Instead, in 1811, he leased property two miles southeast of Franklin from Alexandria Ewing.[1]

On the property was a dwelling, and Diana quickly turned it into a home built on strong religious values. There, she and Richard taught Matthew and the younger children their prayers and the lessons of the Episcopal Church. As they had with the older children, the Book of Common Prayer with a heavy dose of the Psalms were the cornerstones of their lessons. Religious instruction here was especially important to them, because there was no nearby Episcopal church. In time, life settled into a routine for the transplanted Virginia farmers.[2]

John, now sixteen, did not stay ashore long on half pay when his Navy tour ended. He signed on as first officer with a shipmate from the forty-four-gun frigate *United States* and fellow Virginian, William Lewis.

As fitted as they were for naval service, the pair—despite their differences in age—found life aboard a merchantman tedious. A graduate of William and Mary, Lewis wrote that to be successful in business "a man must drudge a little, and the devil of it is that we in the navy are almost unfit by our habits for this drudgery."[3]

The two wanted a shot at wealth in the China trade, not the drudgery of commerce. When John's merchantman, the *Pennsylvania Packet* with a crew of twenty-five and six guns, got underway in 1811, peace between Great Britain and the United States was being sorely tested.

As the Napoleonic wars dragged on, tensions also ran high along thousands of miles of ill-defined North American border. As far away as the Pacific Coast, the two nations snarled at each other over control of the fur trade and refitting stations for whaling fleets.[4]

In 1812, congressional "War Hawks" led by Speaker Henry Clay of Kentucky and John C. Calhoun of South Carolina—young men on the make—were building a Navy to challenge the British squadrons patrolling the Atlantic coast and outfitting an Army—primarily militiamen—to liberate Canada, believed to be a simple march away.[5]

They raced bills through Congress to strengthen land fortifications of major ports from New York to New Orleans. The War Hawks likewise ordered twenty- to thirty-men crewed gunboats to bolster coastal defenses. Langdon Cheves, the South Carolinian chairing the House Naval Affairs Committee, demanded frigates with multiple guns. "The God of Nature did not give to the United States a coast of two thousand miles in extent, not to be used."[6]

For these brash young Southerners and Westerners, there were to be no more humiliations such as that inflicted on Commodore James Barron. Four years before, the British man-of-war *Leopard* had fired more than twenty shots into the frigate *Chesapeake*, leaving more than twenty sailors dead or wounded.

Excellent designs; hiring the wrights needed to build ships, private subscriptions in hand; and congressional appropriations on the way did not put American warships to sea. The American fleet in 1811 consisted of three frigates and a brig in Newport, Rhode Island; two frigates and some sloops or brigs in Norfolk, Virginia; and a frigate and a brig carrying a diplomat across the Atlantic to France. Five other brigs were split among Charleston, South Carolina; New Orleans, Louisiana; and Lake Ontario. Five more frigates were "laid up in ordinary," needing overhaul. By contrast, 121 British warships were on station in North America.[7]

By June, the country again was at war with Great Britain.[8]

Even though the Maurys were hundreds of miles from the fighting, concerns over their oldest son's safety added to the family's continuing worries over finances. In 1813, Diana told her brothers, the administrators of her inheritance, that Richard needed one thousand dollars to buy a two-hundred-acre farm about six miles northwest of Franklin.

Although the Minor brothers were leery of letting Richard control so much money, they accepted the judgment of Abram Maury, who had moved from Lunenburg County, Virginia, that the price was fair. But the brothers again took to the courts and their legal paper bonds. The money was available to buy the cotton farm, which would be held in trust by John and Launcelot Minor for Richard and Diana's children. The father and mother were only "to occupy, cultivate and use said tract of land." This Promised Land was not one of milk and honey—but cotton and, yes again, courts.[9]

On the occupied acreage, they erected a log house and built furniture to replace the beds and cabinets they sold when fleeing Virginia. Diana Maury had kept her silver service, and the presence of slaves kept up pretenses. The children—ever resilient—adapted to their new home and surroundings.

As a child in Williamson County, Matthew Fontaine Maury did what boys of his time in that place did. He swam in the West Harpeth River, rode through the fields with his brothers, and hunted. The games and hunts passed time but did not leave the boy thrilled or enriched. Matthew, more than the others, had that itching curiosity about the larger world.[10]

When he arrived in Williamson County in the summer of 1814, John was back in the service of his beleaguered country, full of grand tales of being marooned on an island unimaginably distant to anyone living in Richard Maury's home, a war, and a lucky escape from the British intent on clearing the American menace from the Pacific. His most eager listener was his little brother Matthew. John was the first of the four towering figures who shaped Matthew Fontaine Maury's life.[11]

John Maury's adventures began with the return voyage of the *Pennsylvania Packet* from China in search of sandalwood in Polynesia. Oriental cabinetmakers believed its insect-repelling scent perfect for their delicate work. The risk to life in harvesting the sandalwood on hostile atolls was great, but the profits were immense when sold on the Asian mainland.

To reap those profits, Lewis sent John Maury, his executive officer, and a party of four seamen ashore on Nukuhiva Island in the Marquesas to begin the hunt. Lewis then set out to scout other cargo to move about the Pacific.

Nukuhiva is a lushly beautiful island with a long white beach, green valleys, three-thousand-foot mountains, bountiful breadfruit trees, and plenty of sandalwood. It was also dangerous. The shore party came upon a heavily tattooed English beachcomber named Wilson, who spoke the native language well. The American needed his skills if they were to succeed.

The hunt for sandalwood was over quickly, but the harvesting required time, helping hands, and strong backs. To help, Maury befriended Happa tribal chief Gattenewa. This bought the mariners peace with his people, but put them at knife's point against his enemies, the Typees. In a series of lightning raids, the Typees, immortalized by Herman Melville, killed three of the seamen. John Maury's life was at great risk.

When the *Pennsylvania Packet* arrived in China, Lewis learned that the United States was at war, and he knew better than to test the Royal Navy or

British privateers on the open seas. He stayed put. Marooned, the teenaged John Maury had no idea that a far larger war was unfolding in the Pacific.

As weeks passed into months, Maury and the other survivor, a man named Baker, worked to improve their chances of survival. The castaways built a hut in the coconut palms that provided shelter and a vantage point to stay clear of attack and scan the sea for rescue.[12]

But it would be more than a year and a half before the sails of any vessel hove into view. When the rescuers at last arrived, they did not sail alone. Behind the first ship, flying an American flag, Maury and Baker could see other smaller vessels. The two scrambled from their perch and paddled out to the largest ship, *Essex*, a thirty-two-gun frigate.

When Maury and Baker drew alongside the American flotilla, *Essex*'s crew took no chances with these long-haired, sunburned men, as "naked as any of [the islanders] and refused to let them board." Captain David Porter had warned his crew, "Let the fate of many who have been cut off by the savages of the South Sea Islands be a useful warning to us." The sailors had to make their ships ready for overhaul and secure themselves against the British and ashore against "savages of the South Sea islands." Only later, back on shore, did a former shipmate, Stephen Decatur McKnight, recognize Maury.[13]

McKnight told Maury about the war, *Essex*, and its prizes. The now battle-tested squadron had come to the Marquesas to repair, refit, and resume the fight. The young officer took Maury to Porter, a Revolutionary War veteran, who tapped the teenaged Virginian as executive officer of *Essex Junior*, one of the prizes.

Although the American commander had crewmen and prisoners available, Porter needed additional hands to work on his ships. With beachcomber Wilson translating, John Maury, who knew the tribal climate of the island all too well, won the cooperation of a third tribe, the Taiis, in supplying and refitting the fouled vessels. The price for the Americans came in breaking a longstanding taboo.

Until Porter's time, Westerners had refrained from taking sides in tribal fighting. At the same time, the Westerners had kept their own wars off the islands. The past of thirty years' standing was not prologue for Porter. The first taboo to go was neutrality. Porter, who watched his brother die in his arms as a prisoner during the Revolution, required tribal allies and a refuge in a larger war. The second taboo now teetered. He trained the Taiis to fire cannons, pistols, and muskets; when Happa raiders destroyed some breadfruit trees, the American commander had his allies haul cannons up the steep mountains to control the passes.[14]

Porter was not through bringing American order to Nukuhiva. When his offer to buy hogs and fruit as a way to end the raids was rejected, he ordered Lieutenant John Downes to lead a punitive expedition of sailors, marines, and Taiis against the Happas. In late October 1813, with a flash of muskets and pistols, the sailors and Taiis overwhelmed the spear-throwing and rock-heaving Happas.

With the Happas cowed, the Typees, the tribe that almost annihilated Maury's shore party, dared Porter to come after them. The commander was as determined as a duelist to break the Typees. For three wearying days, the allies dragged heavy equipment up and down mountains. When Porter had position, he pounced. After the attack, Porter saw "a long line of smoking ruins now marked our traces from one end to the other; the opposite hills were covered with unhappy fugitives."[15]

In the full flush of triumph, the American commodore annexed the islands to the United States. In the ceremony on the beach, Maury signed the proclamation that was sent to President James Madison telling him of his newest lands and its principal settlement, Madisonville. The second taboo had been pushed over the cliff by a piece of paper.

John Maury's tale had more drama to come.

In early December 1813, the flotilla's "decks were filled with hogs, cocoa nuts and bananas" from the islanders "who seemed anxious that the Americans should want for nothing, that it was in their power to supply." Porter wanted a showdown with whatever warships his majesty and war cabinet sailed to this far end of the world. With that in the commander's mind, John Maury sailed with the *Essex* and its fleet of prizes toward Valparaiso, Chile, the closest port to the southern passage.[16]

The British and the Americans were sailing steadily toward the encounter that Porter wanted. *Essex*, with forty 32-pound carronades and six long 12-pounders, and *Essex Junior*, with its eight 24-pound carronades and two long 9-pounders, arrived at the Chilean port on February 3, 1814.

At the time, Chile and, indeed, large parts of North America and the whole of Central and South America were in turmoil, wracked by a political earthquake that began on the Iberian Peninsula. The first tremor came in 1807 when a French army invaded Spain, an ostensible ally, marching for Portugal to seize its fleet to invade Britain.

Under the protection of British warships, Maria I, her son John, and the royal court sailed the Portuguese navy to its largest colony, Brazil, and reestablished the empire's court there.[17]

From Spain, Bonaparte wanted the corridor to Portugal, as well as treasure, to continue fighting, soldiers, and more ships. With one hundred thousand French soldiers occupying the corridor, Napoleon forced Charles IV and Ferdinand, his son and heir, to abdicate. He then installed his brother Joseph as king. With a new crown upon another Bonaparte's head, Great Britain now considered Spain under its ousted rulers an ally.[18]

The aftershocks were felt in Washington. Who was in control of the Spanish colonies—the Bonapartists; the old monarchists; or revolutionaries like Jose San Martin, Simon Bolivar, and Bernardo O'Higgins? What did this mean for the United States' newly acquired Louisiana Territory? Desperate for answers, the Jefferson and Madison administrations sent a number of travelers-scientists-diplomats southward.

Like many parts of the old Spanish empire, some in Chile—especially in the Catholic clergy—supported the removed monarchy. A few colonials backed Joseph Bonaparte's regime with its promising constitution. And then there were the true revolutionaries, like O'Higgins, the son of a royally appointed governor, who wanted to sever all ties with Spain. Determining who was who in Chile was as tricky a matter as determining tribal intentions in Nukuhiva. Instead of a beachcomber, Porter had Joel Poinsett, one of the traveler-scientist-diplomats now in Valparaiso to put into context men and events.[19]

On February 7, Porter hosted the governor, influential residents of Valparaiso, and their families to a gala aboard his flagship. After the Chileans departed at midnight, *Essex Junior*'s lookouts spotted two British warships—*Phoebe* and *Cherub*—closing in on the city. As soon as the message was received, Porter signaled the crewmen ashore to return. Within ninety minutes, *Essex* was ready.

The next morning, the British captain provocatively sailed between *Essex* and *Essex Junior*. Porter remained cool. *Phoebe* drifted out of the range of *Essex*'s guns while *Cherub*, the smaller warship, positioned itself near *Essex Junior*. As it turned out, Porter and the British captain, James Hillyar, knew each other from service in the Mediterranean. "You have no business where you are," Porter shouted. The British stayed. For almost two months, the standoff continued; as winter approached, time favored the British.[20]

On March 28, flying an ensign proclaiming "Free Trade and Sailors' Rights," Porter tried to make his break, but a quick-moving squall took out *Essex*'s main top mast. *Phoebe* and *Cherub*, flying ensigns proclaiming, "God, Our Country, and Liberty; Traitors Offend Both," firing furiously fast closed in on Porter. Hundreds of civilians watching from the city's heights saw the battle unfold. The British gunnery was devastating, and so was the Americans' forcing *Cherub* out of the battle. "Our decks were now strewn with dead and the cockpit filled with wounded," Porter wrote and John Maury likely recounted.

An estimated 155 Americans were dead, and seventy, including Porter, were taken prisoner in the two-hour melee. *Essex* had been sunk, but *Essex Junior* escaped the carnage. Hillyar, Porter, and Poinsett arranged for the care of the wounded and to have *Essex Junior* return Porter and the other survivors to the United States as parolees.[21]

What John likely didn't tell his eager little brother was the price of Porter's glory. Among the wounded were boys, some slightly older than Matthew, like the thirteen-year-old David Glasgow Farragut, also from Tennessee, but now bloodied and bruised after a very large wounded sailor knocked him off a ladder and fell on top of him. John likely recounted how Farragut, seeing his pig taken as a prize by a British sailor, wrestled him for it and won. The boy later wrote that this "in some degree wiped off the disgrace of our capture."[22]

For now, John's tales were over. He was on his way to Lake Champlain as the "new races of Goths" threatened to cut New York and New England off from the rest of the country.[23]

In the years after the War of 1812, Matthew Fontaine Maury begged his father to send him to Harpeth Academy in Franklin, like his brother Dick, rather than the field school he was attending. Academies varied widely in age of the students and even from master to succeeding master in curriculum. As Joseph Kett wrote, "The broad age span common to most academies was not the result of prolonged education but of a combination of late starts and random attendance stretched out over a number of years, with sizable gaps between sessions attended and with attendance in a given year rarely embracing more than a month or two."[24]

Those facts mattered not a whit to Matthew. He was eager to learn, as he was earlier fascinated by a shoemaker's notations with an awl that introduced the boy to mathematics. The primitive field school and home schooling in the Bible and the Book of Common Prayer whetted his appetite for a more formal education, as his grandfather had once offered.

For months Matthew's pleas fell on deaf ears. One day in 1818 while climbing a tree, he lost his hold and crashed to the ground. Dick raced home for help. When the others arrived, Matthew was not moving. He was alive, but his back was seriously injured and he had bitten through his tongue.[25]

During that slow recovery, Richard relented and allowed Matthew to enroll. As in many academies, the route to learning for Matthew, his cousin

Alex Maury, and his lifelong friend William C. S. Ventress began with Latin grammar, measured the way of the Greek classics, and walked the path of moral instruction. While moral instruction was expected, this was not the practical education Grandfather Maury had urged upon the young. As Matthew matured, it would not be the practical education he would advocate for future naval officers; as he closed out his days, it certainly would not be the practical education he would struggle to create for young men in Reconstruction Alabama, Tennessee, and Virginia.

When the Rev. Gideon Blackburn left Harpeth in December 1821, Maury was introduced to the new headmaster, James Hervey Otey, who became the second figure dramatically influencing his life. As a grown man, honored across the world for his achievements, Maury turned to Otey in times of personal, professional, and political crisis for advice. Otey, a graduate of the University of North Carolina, shook up the academy's curriculum. He had the boys studying mathematics, navigation, surveying, English grammar, and geography. Maury recalled fondly "these Tennessee school days when the air was filled with castles."[26]

James Hervey Otey, pictured here as an Episcopal clergyman, was a towering influence in Maury's life. To Maury, Otey always remained his "preceptor," whose counsel he sought in times of personal and professional crisis (courtesy University of the South Archives).

It was an education nurtured by the third towering figure in Maury's life, his older cousin Abram. Abram Maury commanded respect not only from his transplanted Virginia relatives but from the men and women working the far-flung farms and plantations of the bluegrass and in the important town beyond its size he established—Franklin. The town was home at one time or another to Thomas Hart

Benton, Sam Houston, and John Bell—men who shaped the politics of "Manifest Destiny" and whom Maury trumpeted in his writings.

Otey reigned in the classroom, and across the road, Abram Maury offered Matthew the plantation's books on science and mathematics and the use of his maps. During the winters, Abram let the boy, who called him uncle, stay at Tree Lawn, so the teenager did not have to journey six miles each way to school and back in the cold and dark. The kindness and interest in his future led Matthew to want to emulate the elder Abram as he never did with his father. Otey sailed the boy into the world of ideas, science, and their intersection with moral instruction. Abram, by his example, drive, and concern, became the beacon of a good life—"the useful man."[27]

There was soon a fourth man Maury took as a role model. Again he was a teacher at Harpeth. He remained a confidante of Maury's until his death. The friendship between Maury and William C. Hasbrouck survived forty years as well as being on opposite sides in the Civil War.

When Otey left to study for the Episcopal ministry in June 1823, Hasbrouck became headmaster. Hasbrouck, as James Maury had with Thomas Jefferson, Dabney Carr, and James Madison, saw that Matthew Fontaine had far greater capacity for a career beyond raising cotton, owning slaves, and running a plantation. But as with all the children of Richard Maury, there was the question of money. Money—more accurately the lack of it—was the overriding issue in Richard's life. To hold on to what he precariously had, Richard needed all hands, and that included Matthew's.[28]

John's life showed the Navy was an avenue of escape. There was an even better avenue—one that offered a boy a free education and an adventurous life. It was on bluffs overlooking the Hudson River in New York State.

When Matthew learned from his Tennessee cousin Abram Poindexter Maury about the Military Academy's emphasis on mathematics and science, he was thrilled, but an appointment, usually through the parents' beseeching a political sponsor, was needed. In Franklin, then, there were plenty of men who could sponsor Matthew, but Richard Maury had no intention of having a second strong-backed son leave the Tennessee cotton fields.

Hasbrouck, who was from New York, continued to encourage Matthew to keep the military academy in mind. "But the bare mention of the wish put my father in a rage. I abandoned the idea therefore." Maury only changed his tactics.[29]

In the summer of 1824, the Maury family was devastated by the news that John, again sailing under Porter's command as his flag-captain, had died from yellow fever and had been buried at sea off the Virginia Capes. When he became ill, John, a lieutenant, was returning to Norfolk carrying Porter's reports and to obtain supplies for the squadron. The twenty-eight-year-old officer left behind a wife, Eliza, and two sons, William and Dabney.[30]

The anguish over the loss and deep concern for John's family tautened Richard's resolve that Matthew not follow in John's footsteps. Matthew's resolve to leave, however, grew stronger daily.

Inside the academy, Matthew savored his first taste of what a different life could be. At Harpeth, the teen was helping teach the younger boys; in Maury's words he was "a regular amateur assistant." There, he continued receiving strong support to further his education, and Headmaster Hasbrouck put his money where his mouth was. As Maury later wrote, "He had just drawn $500 in a lottery.... And no doubt in my eyes also, the $500 seemed like the old woman's empty barrel of meal in the Bible, perfectly inexhaustible."[31]

Maury, for whatever reason, turned down the offer.

On January 2, 1825, Abram Maury died; and relatives, friends, political allies, planters, and land speculators from near and far gathered to pay homage. The young Maury put into words his deep feelings about Abram when he vowed then "to make myself a useful man." The Navy appeared the fastest route to that goal. If his father would not approach the leaders of the community for their endorsements for the Military Academy, the boy seized the day for himself. He used the friend of a friend's relative approach to get his way. The necessary middleman was Sam Houston, the district's congressman.[32]

It was common then and required now that any application for the Navy carry the recommendation of at least one leading citizen to attest to the young man's character. Maury's carried none but his own when it arrived in Houston's hands. As irregular as the application was, Houston endorsed it and sent it to the Navy Department.

On the congressman's recommendation, orders were cut February 1, 1825, and with that Matthew Fontaine Maury became an acting midshipman. Unknown to a young man on the Tennessee frontier, the Navy did not limit its accessions or force retirements. It also was not building many ships or even manning some in the fleet. The chosen route could be as precarious as those trails the family trod through the Virginia mountains.

Those were not concerns of Matthew. Bubbling over with enthusiasm, he wrote Ventress: "My Dad and Mom say I shall not go; but you can guess whether I will or not." By now, Richard's grief over John's death was compounded by his anger over Matthew's deviousness. Maury left no record of rages between father and son, but it was clear the two wills clashed until the day the adolescent left.[33]

As Matthew told a relative, Rutson Maury, fifteen years later, "As I had proceeded without consulting him, he determined to leave me to my own resources."[34]

Diana tried brokering peace, but, at best, she achieved a fitful truce. The next few months were extremely painful for all living on the farm off Blazer Road. Solidifying his intent to leave, Matthew arranged to buy a horse from Sanford Allen, an overseer, for seventy-five dollars, promising payment when he arrived in Washington and received his travel pay.

"The bitterest pang I felt on leaving home was parting with my brother Dick, two years my senior. We two had hitherto been inseparable."[35]

Separate, they did. Matthew was following in John's footsteps off a debt-ridden farm, out to sea, and into a world he believed filled with promise. His chosen course was to be a "useful man" like Abram Maury, who had opened his heart and home to a very young cousin, facts Matthew never forgot.

3. Citizen of Virginia

From the outset the journey toward a new life for Matthew Fontaine Maury became a twisting odyssey. Too filled with his own optimism and lacking experience, he tried to move—always forward, but sometimes sideways. He paid prices that he didn't realize for each landmark event and his decisions on that journey. Along the way, he survived tests of his frontier upbringing, found peace in a family whose roots were as deep in Central Virginia as they were broad in Central Tennessee, met the great love of his life, Ann Hull Herndon, and sailed into the Navy returning an aging Revolutionary War hero to France.

At Laurel Hill, near Fredericksburg, Virginia, he stayed with his father's oldest sister, Elizabeth, married to Edward Herndon, the successful planter who had bought some of Richard's land years before. The couple, then in their sixties, cared for an orphaned niece, Ann Hull Herndon, and nephew, Brodie S. Herndon. At their meeting in 1825, the auburn-haired, fourteen-year-old girl was taken by Maury, whom she likened to "the young shepherd David."[1]

Fredericksburg and Spotsylvania County teemed with Maurys and Minors, and life for the Virginia family members centered on their plantations near the Rappahannock River and their trade and businesses in the bustling town. From the river's fall line, Fredericksburg's wharves shipped grain and tobacco to Europe, and goods and fine clothes from the continent and Great Britain were hauled inland to the planters. On its streets stood a slave auction block, not far from James Monroe's law office. The town, which sat astride Virginia's main north-south overland trading route, had changed much since George Washington had spent his boyhood near there, and even since Monroe had practiced law in its courts. Commemorating its role in the Revolution, Fredericksburg was one of many communities that hosted the Marquis de Lafayette on his sentimental return journey in 1824.

As pleasant as the interlude at Laurel Hill was, Maury had fifty miles to go. He sold the horse, Fanny, and was persuaded to take money from the Herndons to cover his remaining expenses.[2]

In June 1825, the Navy Department was housed in a two-story, classically façaded building near the White House, itself rebuilt after the British burned it in 1814. Thirty clerks, such as Maury's cousin, Richard B. Maury, labored on the first floor. The secretary, the auditor, and the three Navy commissioners—the service's most senior uniformed officers—were on the second.

Calling on a cabinet secretary in his office was not an everyday occurrence, especially for a young man from Tennessee. Samuel Southard, who had served under Presidents Monroe and John Quincy Adams, was the civilian head of a small navy in manpower and ships. When he made his call, the confident Maury had several "ins" with Southard: his brother's service, his cousin's working in the building, and another relative, Fontaine Maury, then "high in favor with the government." Southard also shared the same geographical roots as the acting midshipman. He knew many of Maury's relatives, like the prosperous Herndons and Minors.[3]

In his office, Southard explained that the letter was one of appointment. Nonetheless, the secretary told Maury that he was to be paid for his 750-mile journey at a rate of fifteen cents per mile. For now, that would be all the money he was to receive from the department. The secretary also cautioned the Tennessean about taking his acting warrant seriously. Before parting, Southard, an able man, stressed that Maury's first six months were a test of his fitness for naval service. Maury took those words to heart.[4]

Living in his cousin Richard's house and meeting John's widow and two children there, Maury was in limbo until he received an assignment. All he could do was wait and distract himself by seeing the capital's sights. In his wanderings, he went to the Navy Yard and admired the newly constructed *Brandywine* that "looks as if made for execution." The ship originally named *Susquehanna* was a "frigate of the first class" with fifty-four guns.

What Maury did not know was that the warship, with its rounded stern, had been a rushed job to meet Lafayette's sailing schedule. To have it ready on time, sails from *Congress* were borrowed, as were boats from the frigate *Potomac* and masts, spars, and hawsers from other ships in the yard. Even after its late June launch, workers waited for the special furniture, curtains, and fixtures for the marquis's cabin.[5]

On July 9, 1825, Maury could hardly believe his luck when he opened his orders. Maury was to "proceed to Washington and report to Captain T. Tingey for duty on board the *Brandywine*," renamed for Lafayette's first battle, and was to return the nobleman to France.

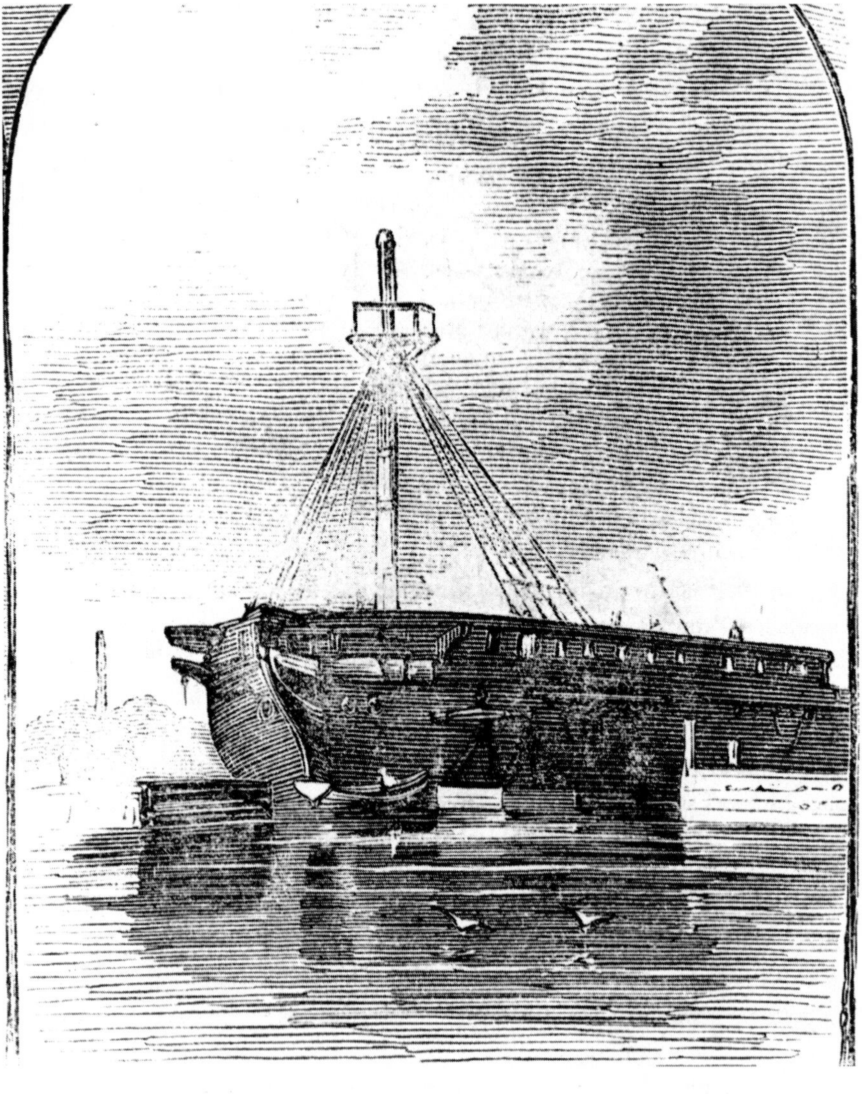

The USS *Brandywine* was Maury's first sea-duty assignment, and for its maiden voyage took the Marquis de Lafayette back to France after his triumphal tour of the United States in 1825 (courtesy the Naval History and Heritage Command).

How Maury received those orders is not clear. Maybe his cousin Richard, soon to be the Navy's register, or another relative intervened, but Matthew was an extremely lucky young man. Dozens of anxious parents—many with strong political and naval connections—had pulled every string they could to have their sons appointed for that singular voyage. All told, he was one of twenty-six midshipmen aboard the ship, which normally carried eleven.[6]

Lucky though Maury was, the one hundred dollars he had in travel money was not enough to outfit him for active service. He could not ask his father for money, even if Richard's finances were brighter. The parting had not been smooth. He turned to Ventress for a loan of two hundred dollars. Maury bought his dress and undress uniforms, blue wool cloth jacket with six brass buttons on each lapel, half boots, sword, thick winter coat, quadrant, and a copy of Bowditch's *American Practical Navigator*.[7]

When he boarded on August 13, 1825, Maury reminded himself to "make everything bend to my profession." Then, the acting midshipman in his white ducks, vest, and blue pea jacket was hustled along the upper deck, down a companionway, onto the gun deck, and down another companionway to the steerage, reeking from odors rising from the bilge. Only two eight-by-twelve-inch portholes provided ventilation. Furniture, equipment, and uniforms were crammed into every nook and cranny. Sleeping was done in hemp hammocks.[8]

In those close confines, Maury joined a number of talented young men from deeply connected families. They included William F. Irving, nephew of author Washington Irving; Samuel Barron, son of the late Commodore James Barron; William Francis Lynch, who became a lifelong friend; and William Radford, stepson of the explorer William Clark.[9]

Where did this grandson of Thomas Jefferson's teacher fit? In Christopher McKee's study of the Navy's early officer class, Maury was slightly older but with a similar background to many other acting midshipmen. Before *Brandywine* weighed anchor, experienced midshipmen, like Barron, explained the bells and watch-standing. They also taught the language of the sea and drills on deference to authority, the necessity of carrying out commands promptly, and saluting properly. Lastly, they showed the "landsmen" how to climb the rigging, handle the ship, go to general quarters, man the guns, and, when ready, how to pass down an order.[10]

Where did the midshipmen fit on a warship? While considered a class of officers, meriting "in an especial degree their fostering care," the ship's carpenter, boatswain, gunner, master's mate, and sailing master outranked them.[11]

That was Maury's small world when Captain Charles Morris, who had been seriously wounded in the battle between *Constitution* and *Guerriere* in the War of 1812, stepped aboard. A decade after the war ended, the Navy leadership was full of veterans who had sailed against Barbary and Caribbean pirates, Revolutionary France, and the British. They brought those experiences—good and bad—to their commands, facts the acting midshipmen were to learn.

Brandywine was at anchor near the mouth of Chesapeake Bay, and the five-hundred–man crew was readying the ship for its maiden voyage. They had already buried one crewman on the short sail from the Navy Yard. Now, everything from gunpowder to sugar was to be in its place, and everything in its place was to be secured.[12]

September 8 was windy and rainy. The warship's yards were manned with crewmen, and Marines stood at attention on deck as a barge carrying Lafayette and Southard approached. Seven times the frigate's guns rent the air. Adding to the moment was a passing steamboat from Baltimore filled with more well-wishers and Revolutionary War veterans giving one last yell of thanks to the sixty-seven-year-old Frenchman.

On the deck were generals, mayors, and naval officers, including David Glasgow Farragut, and dignitaries like George Washington Parke Custis, the first president's adopted son and future father-in-law of Robert E. Lee, enjoying *Brandywine*'s band and bidding Lafayette bon voyage.[13]

In the next day's spectacular dawn, *Brandywine*'s sails flapped in a brisk breeze, its rigging groaned slightly, and its prow bobbed up and down on the tidal flow as it set sail. Entering the bay, the ship was "traversing the centre of a brilliant rainbow, one of whose limbs appeared to rest on the Maryland shore and the other on that of Virginia." By 2 p.m., it was past the Virginia Capes, and Morris asked Lafayette where he wanted to land. "My heart feels a strong desire to present myself in the first instance to those who received my farewell with such kindness, when I last year left my country," he said in directing the American to Le Havre.[14]

Once *Brandywine* entered the Gulf Stream, the rougher seas sickened Lafayette and the midshipmen. Worse yet, the ship was fast taking on water. The pumps worked futilely to staunch fifteen-to-twenty-four inches of sea-water rushing into the holds every ten minutes. After consulting with Lafayette about returning to port, Morris ordered two thousand pounds of iron shot, used for ballast, cast overboard. With the ship rising in the heavy seas, crewmen hurried below deck to seal the leaks.

For the midshipmen, the rough seas left an aftertaste even more bitter than salt water. Spilled turpentine fouled their sugar barrel. The lesson learned was there is a price to pay when everything has not been secured.[15]

As each day at sea broke, drums sounded, sentries fired their guns, and the boatswain and mates piped, "All hands ahoy." The crew, under a midship-man's supervision, holystoned the deck before breakfast. Each evening, weather permitting, the band's drummers beat the sound to quarters. The crew dressed, stowed hammocks, and manned battle stations. Midshipmen like Maury called each gun crew's roll, and the dozen sailors answered, not by name, but by duty—"first loader." Then they exercised the guns.[16]

While there was a routine for duties and ample time to talk about their superior officers, there was none for midshipmen's education. "Larking got the better of Bowditch and study." That bothered Maury deeply.

Even with sailing master Elisha Peck teaching navigation, and despite the French party's high opinion of shipboard training, the midshipmen were not receiving "a competent knowledge even of the art of shipbuilding, the higher mathematics, and astronomy; the literature which can place our officers on a level of polished education with the officers of other maritime nations." In short order, Maury's bother boiled over into a crusade to throw overboard this catch-as-catch-can training.[17]

By 10 p.m., the sole voices were those of the sentries answering each bell on the half hour with an "all's well, all's well" over the sounds of wind in the rigging, the slapping of waves against the hull, and watch-standers' shoes and officers' boots pacing the deck.

The routine was broken only on Sundays for the readings of the *Act for the Better Governance of the Navy* and the divine service, drawn from the Book of Common Prayer, whose familiar cadences surely comforted this religious young man.[18]

At the parting ceremony in Le Havre, midshipmen cried as they presented Lafayette a silver urn as a token of their appreciation. Emotions ran so high that Francis H. Gregory, the ship's senior lieutenant, faltered in expressing the nation's affection for the general. Acting on impulse, a sailor snatched the flag from the ship's stern and presented it to Lafayette. "It will always testify to all who may see it, the kindness of the American nation toward its adopted and devoted son," he said to the cheers of the men in the yards.[19]

Naval life's harsher realities set in once Lafayette departed. The restriction on flogging was lifted as the ship refitted at Isle of Wight. Ashore, some officers toured Carisbrooke, where Charles I was imprisoned before his execution, and others went to Portsmouth to prowl the quarterdeck of *Victory*, Lord Nelson's flagship at Trafalgar. There was also time for midshipmen like Maury to meet young women, like Meg Bailey, the daughter of a jurist. She invited the shy young man to accompany her to London, but it was an offer he could not accept. *Brandywine* was ready to weigh anchor.[20]

Bound for Gibraltar, Maury grew tired of the roughhousing midshipmen—despite their social, political, and naval pedigrees. If the Navy wouldn't provide for his education, the one-time "regular amateur assistant" at Harpeth Academy would do it for himself. He plunged into Norie's *Epitome of Navigation.* He looked for more nautical works when he was on the island. As McKee wrote, "The commanding officer's commitment to education and study was key. When he made clear that these were a high priority, teachers could be attracted and midshipmen's motivation heightened." Maury found the commanders' commitment to broad education lacking.[21]

On the island, Maury mingled with Arabs from North Africa, Spaniards, and the British. He drank in these sights, these sounds, these encounters. In time, they were as important as the nautical works he devoured on board ship. *Brandywine* now joined *North Carolina*, *Constitution*, and *Erie* in sailing to Minorca, the American Navy's winter anchorage near the Barbary Coast in the Mediterranean. By early December, the American sailors in Port Mahon were chasing women, downing flagons of wine, and losing their pay and shirts on the island's gaming tables. Fights and occasional duels were growing common among "young men still in the process of establishing personal identities." Maury, who was sending half his pay to his family, tamely entertained himself by riding donkeys in the surrounding hills and treating himself to dinners of partridge imported from Africa.[22]

Captain Todd Patterson's charge upon taking command was to restore discipline, but the charge did not extend far enough to educate midshipmen. A hero in his own right, he had commanded the gunboat fleet that had battled to hold back the British invasion of the Gulf Coast. He had failed at that but had fought on. With the British army forcibly ashore, he had ordered sloop *Louisiana* and schooner *Carolina* on the Mississippi River to rake the British positions. When they had tried to push past Andrew Jackson's Tennesseans, New Orleans' militia, and Jean Lafitte's smugglers on January 8, *Louisiana*'s guns had provided the enfilading fire that had repulsed the invasion.

When Patterson's task was complete, he turned the ship over to Captain George Read, who accompanied Lafayette to his home. Read's orders were to sail *Brandywine* back to the United States. Not wasting any time, Maury resumed his studies. "If I went below only a moment or two and could lay hands upon a dictionary or any book, I would translate a sentence, or even word, that I did not understand, and fix it in my memory to be reflected upon when I went on deck." For him, it was a routine as regular as the ship's.[23]

Brandywine's maiden voyage proved a success for its builders, its crew, and Maury. Farragut praised the ship as "perhaps the fastest vessel in the world." And Maury, despite the Navy, learned the basic skills of seamanship from Peck and its underpinnings in Bowditch and Norie, and gleaned lessons of how three captains commanded a ship.[24]

The midshipman's discipline—the better side of his steel will—paid off. When he landed in New York, Commodore Isaac Chauncey, another of the naval heroes of the War of 1812, handed the young man his warrant, backdated to February 1, 1825. An excited Maury wrote Southard to accept the warrant and described himself as "Born in Virginia, Appointed from Tennessee, Citizen of Virginia."[25]

4. Lessons for a Lifetime

In New York's harbor during the summer of 1826, Matthew Fontaine Maury began his life's work. The clamor of commerce, the movement of produce from farms on the Great Lakes via the Erie Canal, the arrival of fine goods from Great Britain, France, and China, and the emerging coastal trade in cotton and American manufactures stirred his curiosity. Here, every "thought, word, look, and action of the multitude seemed to be absorbed by commerce."[1]

Through July and into August at the New York Navy Yard, *Brandywine* built toward its full complement of 480 men and officers. A few midshipmen were shipmates on his first voyage. But more men kept boarding—replacements for deserters, invalided sailors, the dead, and those whose enlistments expired while in the Pacific. Commodore Jacob Jones found the crowding in *Brandywine* and *Vincennes*, about to make its maiden voyage, despicable. His appeal for relief was turned down by the Board of Commissioners, the senior officers administering the service's daily operations, which he recently had left in Washington.[2]

Aboard *Brandywine* this time, Maury was a naval officer of junior rank and part of a major naval mission—relieving the Pacific Squadron. Along the western coast of South America, it was an era of revolution, counterrevolution, coups, and countercoups. Enforcing the Monroe Doctrine was the ship's mission. "We could not see any portion [of former Spanish colonies] transferred to any other power with indifference," were the president's words. The reality was that the squadron was more a presence than a show of force.[3]

British Foreign Minister George Canning, possessing an unmatched navy, issued his own warning to France and Spain especially about having new designs on Central and South America. He reminded the Russians that Britain and the United States had great economic interests in the American Northwest.[4]

When back at sea, Maury again suffered the Navy's system of educating

Maury's service aboard the sloop of war USS *Vincennes* in the Navy's first circumnavigation of the globe provided him with a wealth of experiences that he drew on extensively in his writings (courtesy the Naval History and Heritage Command).

young officers. The instructor, a Spaniard named Inocencia De Soto, was so weak, "We therefore voted both teacher and grammar a bore, and committing the latter to the deep, with one accord, we declared in favor of the Byronical method." The young men preferred to learn Spanish from the lips of young women in Valparaiso, Lima, or Guayaquil.[5]

While the floating schoolhouse proved intellectually barren, Jones provided valuable lessons in command. After one sailor either toppled or jumped overboard and another fell from the mizzen top, the captain halved the noontime whiskey ration. His discipline was as clear as the Caribbean when he banned the drunken celebration of Neptune in crossing the equator. The midshipmen were fortunate enough also to have able officers such as Senior Lieutenant John H. Aulick and Lieutenant Thomas A. Dornin, born in Ireland but living in Fredericksburg, to model themselves after.[6]

Reaching Rio de Janeiro in late October, the crews of the two American warships beheld a beautiful white beach stretching in a long curve to the east, and beyond it grassy lowland backing into lush coastal hills—Sugar Loaf and Corcovado.

To the Americans, Brazil was exotic. The Princeton-educated chaplain from *Vincennes*, a man of wide experience in the Pacific islands, was surprised by what he saw. "Were I an inhabitant of the city, there would be times at which I should tremble, in the fear of witnessing the development of a tragedy like that of Santo Domingo," he said, referring to the successful and bloody slave revolt in Haiti at the turn of the nineteenth century.[7]

The beautiful setting belied the crisis the Americans had sailed into at the continent's richest and largest city. A few weeks after the ships' arrival, the guns in the fortifications at each corner of the rough parallelogram that bounded Rio were menacingly in play when *Macedonian*, a third American warship with Maury's cousin Alex, entered the harbor.

Captured from the British, this was the flagship of the Brazil Squadron. On November 14, the Brazilians, without warning, closed the port. In doing so, the Brazilians reminded the American Navy that imperial law required ships to dot the i's and cross the t's in this harbor. It was also payback for an earlier affront.[8]

In 1824, crewmen of *Franklin* whose enlistments had ended demanded their discharge in Brazil, but Charles Stewart, the American captain, needed able bodies to bring his ship back. So without waiting for clearance and over the men's objections, he put all to sea. In the wake of the hasty departure, stories floated about Rio for two years, embellished with each telling how *Franklin*'s sailors were pressed back into American service.

When American consul Condy Raguet told Jones of the port's closing, the captain answered bluntly, "I have to inform you [the American consul] that I shall go to sea tomorrow, if the weather will permit." Raguet reminded Jones that an emperor ruled Brazil, who could bring all the guns in the harbor to bear if Jones tried to leave without clearance. For the time being, Jones stayed.

Day passed to night. Guns on ships were aimed at guns in forts. Watches changed on the ships; new sentries were posted on the forts. Day passed to night twice more. Who would blink as Raguet made the American case to leave?[9]

On November 17, the Brazilians, acting as if nothing had happened, ended the standoff. The consul noted his "most entire approbation" of Jones's refusal to be intimidated.[10]

Now the squadron pressed southward past the windswept British-controlled Falklands. Ice gathered on the masts and coated the decks. Sailors and officers wrapped themselves like mummies as the warships beat through the young ice toward Cape Horn.

At the tip of South America, "Men of war strike part of their armament into the hold; get their anchors between decks; send up stump masts; bend the storm sails; and secure their spars with preventer rigging, as they get near the tempestuous region." What followed was seventeen days of winds coming "from every point of the compass," before the ships reached the safety of the Pacific on Christmas.[11]

After the battering of the ship and crew in the riotous seas, Valparaiso seemed like a small paradise of single-story brick houses with tile roofs. Maury was curiously silent on his first impressions of the city so central to John's tale of epic struggle. Quiescent as he was, for Maury, the irony of his being in the Chilean port had to have been magnified during a holiday celebration. The Americans toasted the New Year with the captain and officers of *Cambridge*, a Royal Navy vessel.[12]

Commodore Isaac Hull's *United States*, a forty-four-gun frigate, arrived at last on January 6, and schooner *Dolphin* thirteen days later. *Brandywine*'s and *Vincennes*'s midshipmen soon led details, as Maury did January 9 on *Columbia*, a brig, to work on the arriving ships. At the same time, replacements gathered their gear to move aboard their next ship. As busy as they were, there was almost a month's break between the turmoil of Cape Horn and weighing anchor to sail up the coast toward Callao, a rowdy city of four thousand inhabitants. Callao was the port through which the tin, gold, and silver—the wealth of the Incas—had flowed for centuries to Spain.[13]

All that had changed the year before Maury and shipmates raised the Peruvian port. When the city had surrendered to Simon Bolivar in January 1826, Spain's last foothold on South America was gone. John Maury's experience had been with revolutionaries like Bernardo O'Higgins, who had fought to liberate a country. Matthew Fontaine Maury's experience would be with revolutionaries, including O'Higgins, Jose de San Martin, and Bolivar, who fought on to unite a continent.

The fight was on. Maury wrote to Otey: "After a little bloodshed one party decided in favor of [Bolivar] and permitted the other, called the rebels, to leave the country: they have since joined the Peruvians" in the mountains near the old Incan capital of Cuzco.[14]

Eight miles from Callao lay Lima, built almost two hundred years earlier by the Spanish. Despite a decade of revolution and a series of devastating earthquakes, the Creole oligarchy moved about the capital in luxury coaches to enlightened salons in New World palaces and enjoyed the city's many theaters and opera houses. Maury's less serious side soon showed itself in the capital of sixty thousand. As he happily reported, the midshipmen passed "time quite pleasantly here among the Spanish ladies."[15]

Outside Lima's walls was a forbidding desert stretching into the Andes where the mineral riches lay. To the uninitiated Americans, it was an eye-opening experience to see wealthy Europeans enjoying life, and the blacks, Mestizos, and Indians paying the price for revolutionary freedom. Maury left no record on the dichotomy or resemblance to the slaveholding South.[16]

On March 9, Maury was transferred to *Vincennes* under the command of William Bolton Finch. As the Adams administration was leaving office, Secretary Samuel Southard wanted to follow up on an earlier mission to the Marquesas, Tahiti, and Hawaii commanded by Thomas ap Catesby Jones and sent new orders to *Vincennes*.[17]

Shortly before Independence Day, Finch announced to the assembled company that the "most beautiful vessel of her class" was to become the first American warship to circumnavigate the globe. With *Vincennes*'s broader orders, Finch handpicked several officers, including Dornin, to join the ship. Also added was the observant the Rev. Charles Stewart as chaplain. Maury was about to receive a lifetime of intellectual capital and connections as part of this historic voyage.[18]

Vincennes officers' first test of discipline came at Nukuhiva in the Marquesas, the island on which castaway John Maury had been marooned. As the twenty-four-day crossing ended, Maury, more than the others, strained to see the mountains where the sandalwood grew. From the deck, all could see the palm trees and "the naked figures of the islanders and their rude and extravagant gestures and vociferations, exhibiting man in the simplest state of his fallen nature."[19]

Unlike David Porter, Finch, like Jones, welcomed a heavily tattooed Happa chief and his family aboard with great ceremony on July 29. The islanders and the Americans invoked the name of Porter, or Opoti as he was called, in exchanging greetings. "They think that Porter is king of all the world; they venerate his name," another visitor wrote.[20]

A few days later, Stewart and Maury went by canoe to Hakapaa on the coast. On the heights, Typee warriors, wearing peaked bird feathered bonnets, sported spears and clubs, and shouted defiance. This day, the whoops, spears, and war clubs were to menace, not fight.[21]

Each day ashore, the sailors, as Porter's and Jones's had, contrasted their lives with the islanders': "Here were bread and fruit grown upon trees without cultivation, and hogs and fowls increase and fatten without care—where the climate has never dictated the necessity of clothing, it is not surprising that they take the world easy, and prefer singing and dancing away a lifetime to adapting the customs and cares of civilization."[22]

On the islands, it was customary to hold a tribal figure to guarantee the safe return of a landing party. So near the end of *Vincennes*'s intended stay, a Happa chief remained aboard ship as an American search party hunted the kidnappers of three Happa children. When the sailors returned, having rescued two of them, Maury, who had picked up some of the islanders' language, was selected to return the chief, Gattenwa, to his family. As the men talked, their connection became obvious. Gattenwa "was the firm and fast friend of my brother. He had saved his life. He was then old. He ... offered me his scepter, his own wife and the daughter of a neighboring chief if I would remain." As flattered and likely flustered as Maury was by the chief's offer, he politely declined.[23]

Shortly before *Vincennes* departed for Tahiti, Finch invited a number of Happa chiefs aboard for a short cruise. Becalmed in water too deep for an anchor but being pushed "by the swell of the sea" toward the rocks below Tower Bluff, the crew using spars fought what seemed inevitable. "Every face was pale with agitation and the silence of the grave hung over the ship." The Happas feared for their lives even if they survived the rocks. The "great man-of-war canoe" was now in Typee waters. The crewmen and islanders pondered their fate until a "breath of air" from the land caught the topsail and slowly carried Vincennes out to sea. All were nervously relieved.[24]

At the final feast, Finch ordered a fireworks display. These Americans, although arriving on a warship, preached a gospel of mutually beneficial trade and an end to cannibalism. The islanders said they understood. Porter had been like a god. Jones had given them certificates of friendship to show to American ship captains. Now there was Finch and his crew talking about treating all visitors hospitably.[25]

Trade was a gospel Finch preached throughout the Pacific. Although the Navy did not arrive with the first traders and whalers or even the missionaries and consuls, expanding American trade and protecting American interests was the service's mission. To Maury, Finch came to embody the better attributes of a senior naval officer. He spoke the mind of his nation for peace and commerce with clarity and purpose. Although not a giant like John Maury, Abram Maury, James Hervey Otey, and William Hasbrouck had been to Matthew the boy, Finch's influence on Maury was substantial, especially on what the Navy must do.

Seven hundred miles away on August 17, with a ceremony filled with regal pomp and naval tradition, Finch greeted the young Tahitian Queen Pomare and her maids of honor. During private talks, the monarch reaffirmed assurances she had given Jones of safety for shipwrecked Americans and recognition of American consuls. Finch had what he wanted.[26]

Vincennes now entered the most critical part of its voyage among the islands. In mid–October, the ship called in the Sandwich Islands or, as they were coming to be known, the Hawaiian Islands. To the United States, these islands were more important than the Marquesas and Tahiti. American-flagged ships and whalers wintered here, and the islands were stopping points in the China trade. The grievances the American Navy came to redress also were more pronounced here: The soaring private debts of tribal leaders, the harboring of deserters, and rocketing ransom demands for kidnapped seamen. The Hawaiians and the missionaries on the islands had their own grievances to redress with the Americans.[27]

Honolulu was then a community of between 7,000 and 9,000, and between 150 and 200 Americans lived in "the little thatch-hut village" that was the islands' capital. The Americans there were of two minds, the mammon of the business community and the fierce God of the missionaries led by Hiram Bingham.[28]

The Hawaiians greeted *Vincennes* exuberantly. If the tension in Rio de Janiero's harbor when *Brandywine* called had been taut but quiet, any tension in Oahu was drowned out in a prolonged exchange of gunfire salutes. The Americans' "landing, consequently, was attended, at least, with noise enough."[29]

A festive charade continued inside "a fine spacious, thatched building of peculiarly nice Hawaiian workmanship." In the palace, the Americans presented sixteen-year-old King Kamehameha III, his regent Queen Kaahumanu, the widow of his grandfather, and family with gifts from President John Quincy Adams of gloves, a silver vase, and silver goblets.[30]

Finch also presented the Hawaiians with a letter in which the president apologized for the behavior of an American officer, Lieutenant John "Mad Jack" Percival, commanding *Dolphin*. Percival's men, drunk and angry, and accompanied by equally drunk and angry whalers, had rioted ashore over the "taboo" placed by the regents at the missionaries' instigation forbidding women to come aboard the ship for sex. In the ensuing melee, they had threatened Boki, the governor of Oahu, and his party in a saloon, disrupted a church service, and chased the minister, umbrella-wielding Bingham, into his house.[31]

Maury was quiet about what came next. Stewart was not. Using two Protestant missionaries—one of whom was Bingham—as his interpreters, Finch asked for a private audience with the king and Boki. From Jones's reports, the Americans knew the British were courting the governor.

The British had taken the king's parents and Boki to London as royal guests in 1824 in expectation of signing an alliance with the islanders. Shortly after landing, virtually the whole party of Hawaiians had been stricken with measles. They had had no immunity to this common European and American childhood disease. Before they could meet with King George IV, the twenty-seven-year-old monarch and twenty-two-year-old queen had died, and the others were slowly recovering. Yet Boki and the others in the royal party had stayed.[32]

King George had told Boki the islanders must learn to read and write to remain Great Britain's friend. British and the more numerous American missionaries were teaching them to do just that. But with an eye on his own interests, the governor had become deeply suspicious of the missionaries' and king's long-range intent in the islands.[33]

Finch said the American merchants wanted the debts settled with scarce sandalwood to keep peaceful relations. Was Finch, despite his government's apology, another Percival from "the mischief-making man-of-war" or Jones "the kind-eyed chief"?[34]

When the Americans left the palace, the king called his chiefs together. How much was properly owed? he asked. In the back of their minds, the chiefs and the king knew the Americans, including their navy, were not going to disappear. In short order, hadn't three American warships under three captains entered Honolulu's spacious harbor? They were more persistent than the British.

The Hawaiians wrangled among themselves on a counteroffer. They had little room to maneuver. The chiefs agreed to settle the debts—in sandalwood. Although it meant mounting an expedition to New Hebrides, they agreed to pay fifty thousand dollars to close out their accounts.[35]

The Americans were not through with the Hawaiians. As long as there had been seamen, there had been deserters, and as long as there had been the sick, halt, and lame recovering ashore in foreign ports, there had been demands for ransom for their return. These were the issues Finch next took up with the islanders.

In the long-term view of the United States' relations with Hawaii, missing seamen were more important than settling old debts by profligate monarchs and chiefs. The United States wanted this: Hawaiians would not harbor American deserters in the brothels of Oahu or on the outer islands, and they would not demand ransoms for sailors brought ashore for treatment and recuperation. The king agreed. Diplomatically and commercially, the mission was on course.[36]

Maury took away another lesson as well, and it was the lesson Boki had taken away in London. With Stewart and often through Stewart's eyes, the midshipman saw American missionaries propagating the Gospel in paradise.

If the whalers, merchantmen, and traders were dying to win treasure, these men and women, many from the hardness of New England, were ready to die for the islanders' salvation. But the missionaries also posed a different challenge when they claimed moral authority in political and business matters.

On the whole, Maury came to see them as an untapped resource for scientific research "not only in Turkey and China, but in all other heathen or pagan lands."[37]

After leaving Oahu, the sloop sailed for days with steady winds to China. If the crew settled into the routine of fair winds and following seas, they were reminded on Christmas Eve of the perils of nineteenth-century voyaging. Rains, winds, and seas bruited the ship: "Both main topmast studding sail, the halyards were by accident let go (in rain shower), the studding sail went overboard, the gear and boom broke and the sail lost, in the effort to recover the sail, John Beaty, became entangled in some of the rigging attached to it and had his foot taken off just above the ankle."[38]

During the dreadful week that ensued, fishing junks twice rammed the sloop. Each time the vessels successfully freed themselves, *Vincennes*'s men hurried repairs to staunch the flow of sea water into the holds. With Beaty, a foot lost, the rest of the crew tired from fighting the seas, and the sloop groaning from the beating of waves and wind, *Vincennes* at last dropped anchor off Macao on January 1, 1830. When the anchor held fast, *Vincennes* became the first American warship to call in China in more than a decade.[39]

In 1557, the Portuguese, maritime descendants of Prince Henry the Navigator, had established a foothold on the island just off the Ancient Kingdom. They had clung to that hilly strip of rock like lichen for centuries. It wasn't much, but for the Portuguese, whose empire had long since fallen into eclipse, something was better than nothing. They leased the one-mile-wide by three-mile-long island from the Chinese, and on it, the Portuguese rented homes to the families of European and American merchants.[40]

Upon arrival, Finch alerted the American consul in Canton, seventy miles away and where most trading was conducted, that he would be contacting businessmen such as J. R. Sturgis, Samuel Russell, W. H. Low, and J. R. Latimer. This was the most important stop on *Vincennes*'s voyage.

If *Vincennes* couldn't ascend the Pearl River, the master commandant and some of his best men could. After thirty-nine days at sea, he selected thirteen officers, including Maury, to journey to the American factories. They traveled through a mystical world. Wooden sluice gates controlled the river's flow past high earthen banks protecting mile after mile of rice paddies. In the middle distance, pagodas rose majestically. This side trip became Maury's shared experience with the China traders in Boston, especially Robert Bennet Forbes, one of the earliest Americans calling in Canton, and in New York. He would exploit that common denominator for the Navy and himself.[41]

At Whampoa, a dozen miles below Canton, hundreds of vessels from Great Britain, France, Sweden, and the United States waited. They could go no farther up the Pearl. It was a bottleneck of imperial proportions for foreign vessels. Moving constantly about the anchorage were Chinese merchants' and smugglers' schooners, barges, junks, and lighters to take cargo and visitors to the Cantonese factories. To entertain the traders ashore and sailors afloat, there were the Chinese "flower boats"—floating brothels.[42]

In Canton, the Chinese had another set of rules, every bit as restrictive as those ritualized for Macao and Whampoa. The court kept all foreigners close to their factories (warehouses) outside the city's walls. Inside the factories—three-story-high buildings fronting the river and extending back three hundred to four hundred feet with narrow walkways through their centers—was a boisterous babel of trade in sandalwood, rice, teak, silk, spices, tea, chinaware, and furs, the "starting point of the foreign commerce of the United States."

Americans, particularly New Englanders, had been trading with China, India, and the islands of the East Indies since the republic's founding. No longer constrained by the British trade laws and staying clear of the British and French war fleets patrolling the Caribbean, Americans sailed around the Cape of Good Hope, up the coast of Africa, passing Portuguese-held Madagascar and the French naval and trading outpost Ile de France, now Mauritius, toward India and China. "This trade helped to build up the fortunes of the first merchant princes of America."[43]

Shortly thereafter, a triangular trade developed between the American Atlantic Coast in sending supplies for trappers and goods for the Indians on the Columbia River in exchange for pelts and furs to be sold in Canton. With the profits, the Yankee traders bought tea and silk back to be sold in American ports.

All these American merchants demanded the Navy's presence.[44]

The businessmen emphasized that the American Navy's continuing presence was a necessary demonstration to the Europeans, particularly the British, that the United States meant to protect its commercial interests in the Far East. In a letter to the businessmen, Finch asked for more information on the scope of the Chinese trade to justify the continuing presence in his official report.[45]

United States' naval presence was the businessmen's refrain in Finch's meetings with other American merchants from the Philippines to the Spice Islands. In Manila, for example, the American merchants explained how they were trying to expand the thirty-year-old trade they had with Canton. They told Finch that the Philippine capital, though still Spanish-ruled, could become an American shipping point to newly independent Mexico.[46]

The merchants restated the facts. Spain had collapsed as a maritime power after Trafalgar. The trade numbers were in the Americans' favor. From twenty-nine United States vessels calling in Manila in 1828 and none leaving that year, thirty-three called the next year, and twenty left with sugar, indigo, sappan-wood, rice, and cigars. The Americans believed they were destined to be the new "treasure fleet." These were lessons Maury took to heart as *Vincennes* set out for its longest stint at sea without a port call.[47]

The dutiful student at Harpeth was bending all to his profession. In the two-month Indian Ocean passage, Maury "went through a course of study commencing with the rudiments of Euclid and extending to the higher mathematics of LaPlace."[48]

During this time, too, Maury may have risked his career in an unlikely confrontation with Finch. As told by his daughter Diana, while dining in the captain's cabin, the older man offered Maury liquor to drink, but the midshipman politely refused. Finch was making an offer of conviviality, and it was not easily turned aside. Finch was the captain, after all; Maury had not even passed his midshipman's examination. What followed was half-comic in appearance, but deeply serious for the young man. Finch "rising from his seat, approached glass in hand, to push him further, [Maury] dashed the glass to the floor, and turning on his heel, left the cabin." There could be a very high price indeed demanded for such impertinence. Captains had long memories, and midshipmen had few rights, as junior officers serving later under Charles Wilkes discovered on another circumnavigation of the globe by an American warship.[49]

Finch was not Wilkes. In his daughter's account, whatever anger boiled in Finch over Maury's impertinence steamed away either in a long night's sleep or sober recollection of the midshipman's value as a future officer. Maury again was lucky. Capetown would not be a courtroom.

After fifty-six days at sea, *Vincennes* anchored off Capetown. Here again, as in Brazil, Chile, and Peru, Maury learned how the Napoleonic wars had changed the world. To keep its sea lanes open to India, Australia, and China, Great Britain had seized the Cape Colony from the Dutch in 1806 for a second and final time. The takeover was so complete that the governor's tea was brought to him exclusively by the British East India Company from China.[50]

Off *Vincennes*, Maury toured the seventeenth century Dutch-built castle that dominated the harbor, walked through the well-tended 120-acre gardens of flowers, fruits, and vegetables—divided by a mile-long oak-shrouded promenade—started by the Dutch East India Company, and visited the nearby wineries to sample the colony's main export. As pleasant a break as it was for all, Finch had one more long leg of sailing.[51]

On the final turn toward home, the sloop called May 1 at St. Helena, the British-controlled island where Napoleon was exiled following Waterloo. The governor general entertained Maury and other officers at Longwood House, little changed since the deposed emperor had died there nine years earlier. From the house, the visitors went to his tomb. "A plain iron railing of eight feet square encloses the tomb, which is covered by a plain stone slab without inscriptions." Close to the tomb stood three willows "weeping and bowing over it," and a spring gurgled in the glen—a surprisingly peaceful setting for a man whose life had been spent waging global war. The irony was not lost on Maury.[52]

Finch's report on the voyage guided Maury's thinking and writing over the years. While not commanding a voyage of discovery, Finch reported success in demonstrating America's coming of age as a naval and commercial power:

> The *Vincennes* voyage will seem to correct a very general and common error—that is an easy one to a vessel and of duration to be computed with precision. Neither is the fact. None is more trying to a ship's hull, qualities, rigging and spars; and only such vessel, as is most perfect, ought to undertake it.
>
> The winds are not to be relied upon, with any confidence, either as to the actual points which they may blow, when or whence to be met with; or as to their strength and continuance.

Finch's report highlighted another dimension to Maury's development as a naval officer:

> The opportunity, which has been enjoyed by the officers, of personal acquaintance with places, inspection of coasts and ports, and the knowledge acquired as to the stores, supplies and refreshment to be obtained are considerations of weight in the event of war, may avail the nation greatly.[53]

Maury spent the most productive years of his life correcting that general and common error by charting the winds and seas to give mariners the confidence they needed to sail and merchants to trade anywhere. He seized the opportunity to acquaint himself with far-off lands and weighed what he had experienced when his country next went to war.

There was another closer family analogy and parallel. Matthew shared the intellectual curiosity of his paternal grandfather, James Maury, but his scholarly circumstances were that of his father—a younger son of a financially strapped younger son. In Matthew's life, there was no Rev. James Blair to send him to Great Britain to further his formal education. "If a whaling ship was Melville's Yale," warships were supposed to be Maury's Harvard. They never were—formally.[54]

The most serious drawback of experiencing, gathering, and analyzing this wealth of data from his voyages was that he did it on his own. Maury did not have the benefit of the rigor of a university education—as did his cousin Abram Poindexter Maury and his contemporaries like Alexander Dallas Bache, Jefferson Davis, Robert E. Lee, and Joseph Johnston, through the United States Military Academy—to test his analyses. His critics would use Maury's lack of formal education to excoriate his work.[55]

On June 8, *Vincennes* took aboard a New York harbor pilot and by late afternoon was at the quarantine station for inspection. Finch's ship passed and within an hour was in the harbor. With well-wishers on two steamboats cheering on the officers and men, the anchor was paid out, and the band began "Hail Columbia, happy land!" After nearly four years at sea, Maury was back in the United States.[56]

Ashore he needed to get matters straight with his family, especially his father in Tennessee. He also needed to secure his position in the Navy, a service where promotions were as slow as the funeral dirge at an old captain's passing.

5. The Siren's Song

During the months after leaving *Vincennes*, Matthew Fontaine Maury wondered if he had heard the siren's song in his brother's stories. He mentioned leaving the Navy for an Indiaman, a merchant vessel plying Far Eastern waters. For his five years in the Navy, Maury was only a midshipman, having spent much of his time huddled on the gun deck swinging in a hammock over the bilge.

In his twenties, there were gaps in his life: The breach with his father needed to be closed, and he longed for the sparkling blue-eyed Ann Hull Herndon. As he rested at the Herndon's plantation, Laurel Hill in Central Virginia, the nineteen-year-old sang ballads to him, and he shared stories of places he had seen.[1]

Likely to ease the tensions that might surround his long-delayed return to Franklin, Maury arranged to travel with his brother John's family, to make the arrival a homecoming: a son long at sea and John's wife and two of Richard's and Diana's grandchildren; the old test of wills might be stowed away in familial attention lavished on the young Maurys.

Whatever fears Maury harbored, he had been a dutiful son, regularly sending his parents money to help keep the Tennessee cotton farm off the financial rocks. Diana and Richard were proud of their son. As often as he had asked John to share his memories about life at sea, Maury brought to his parents, brothers, sisters, friends, and teachers his own tales of faraway places: Berbers in North Africa, Gattenwa in the Marquesas, to mention two.

Now, in their home (his home, too) he put aside the long hours of watch standing and reliving the terror of being rammed in tempestuous seas. He relaxed with his family and childhood friends, including his preceptor, James Hervey Otey, now an Episcopal priest and faithful correspondent with the young midshipman. Maury treasured this homecoming.[2]

In September, Maury returned eastward, but tarried in Spotsylvania. He spent a month again with Ann in the sweet prelude to courtship. The time with her took his mind off what lay ahead in New York.[3]

The school at the New York Navy Yard proved as pitiful as the seagoing classroom on *Brandywine*. Outside the classroom window were constant lessons in the maritime arts, lessons as valuable as the ones learned on the Pearl River in China. "The information that I wanted I knew not where to seek. The consequence was that I had to search for grains of knowledge among bushels of chaff," he wrote. Maury struggled in a sea where most senior officers had their dogmas on navigation and discipline, as inviolate as the commandments handed to Moses.[4]

The midshipman, who wanted more than old tenets, was closing on his March 3, 1831, date of the examination to determine his naval future. The examinations tested memory as much as knowledge. In 1819, Commodore William Bainbridge, president of the first Board of Commissioners, created the examination to test junior officers on "rigging and stowing a ship, the management of artillery at sea, arithmetic, geometry, trigonometry, navigation and the mode of making astronautical calculations for nautical purposes." In 1831, the examination covered the same ground, discouraged originality, and rewarded rote learning. Maury's biggest question was "why" in his study, a question the Navy rarely asked.[5]

For a time, Maury stayed in the confines of seamanship and Bowditch on navigation, algebra, Spanish, Euclid, and McClure's *Spherics*, but as New York fall passed into winter, he yearned for the "professional studiousness" that Thomas Truxtun, an early nineteenth-century navy leader, had extolled more than thirty years before.

Probably because he was older at twenty-five than many midshipmen and demonstrated a commitment to study, Maury's request to work on his own was granted. In his cousin Richard's home in Georgetown, Maury focused on advanced astronomy and mathematics. He now understood LaPlace's mathematical analysis of Isaac Newton's theories on gravitational astronomy—fundamental to mastering navigation. As at Harpeth Academy, Maury taught other midshipmen what they needed to know and why.

Not all Maury's hours near the Capitol were spent studying and tutoring. Also in Georgetown for a time was Ann, his "Nannie." Their romance flowered like the first daffodils of spring.[6]

Still, there was the examination. As Maury wrote, "He who repeats 'by heart' the rules of Bowditch, though he does not understand the mathematical principles involved in one of them, obtains a higher number from the Board than he who, skilled in mathematics, goes to the blackboard and, drawing diagrams can demonstrate every problem in navigation."[7]

On examination day, Maury went to the blackboard. Rote was rewarded. At the end, he was ranked twenty-seventh out of the forty midshipmen tested that day. The ranking grated on Maury for the rest of his life. For him, it was proof of the Navy's hidebound approach to education. But he had passed.[8]

As Maury awaited orders, a condition as common as ships in ordinary, his heart drove him to be with "gentle Nannie." As he wrote, "Our greatest happiness often depends upon a word, the glance of an eye, the tone of the voice, or what is more expressive ... the manner."[9]

Ah, "the manner," the headiness of love, caused Maury, the ardent suitor, to finally propose marriage, and Ann accepted. The courtesy of telling other family members was observed, but no date for the ceremony was set. He knew his finances were not strong enough to provide a comfortable home for a wife and the children who were expected to follow. He had learned that much from his parents' struggles. He wondered more and more if he should seek a more profitable civilian career.[10]

Before he made that decision, Maury received orders to report as sailing master on *Falmouth*, a sloop. The orders crystallized Maury's thinking. He knew the Navy and its ways. The same could not be said about making a living ashore. If he took those orders, exactly how long the couple would be separated depended upon the readiness of ships, the seas, and the winds—all too variable for a man and woman deeply in love to know. Three years was common. As he left, Maury presented Ann with a seal with the single word *Mizpah* on it. The salutation means: "The Lord watch between thee and me when we are absent one from the other."[11]

The sailing master, originally a warrant officer not in the line of promotion, directed the officer of the deck in setting course and the amount of sail to be carried. He also was the captain's spokesman on navigation, precisely the duty needed for promotion. Seamanship, as Maury knew, was what the Navy prized even more than rote learning.

Back in New York, he scoured South Street, looking for information on the winds and currents of the oceans he would transit. Yet, for all the ships that passed in and out of New York harbor and the hundreds of logs that were kept aboard them over the years, Maury, the untested sailing master, found little to guide him. He would have to rely on his brother officers.

In this regard, Maury was fortunate to serve under Francis H. Gregory, the officer so overcome by emotion when Lafayette had left *Brandywine*. There was also Lieutenant Thomas Dornin, who prepared the sloop for sea; Lieutenant Elisha Peck, former sailing master on *Brandywine;* and Lieutenant William W. S. Ruschenberger, a surgeon who had sailed with Maury aboard *Brandywine* in 1826 onto the Pacific station.[12]

At sea, Dornin, the senior lieutenant, comparable to the executive officer, daily personified to Maury how an officer could get much from his crew. Dornin wrote, "Seamen can easily be encouraged to entertain a pride for dress; and where they are kept clean you are sure of a clean ship; all this can be obtained without half the flogging, which is generally deemed necessary to arrive at such a desirable object; stopping grog is a quick and efficient way [of] achieving your object."

Maury also learned the value of a quick-acting captain halving the spirit ration following the deaths of two sailors on the passage from New York to Rio de Janeiro. Dornin's advice and Captain Jacob Jones's action were contrasts from many other officers' prescriptions. Men like Franklin Buchanan placed great faith in the whip to keep discipline at sea.[13]

Life at sea, even without the threat of a whip, could be capricious. As *Falmouth* continued southeastward from Rio de Janeiro, the rigging was covered with snow. Ice grated against the hull. The cold, wet weather and churning seas were exacting their price among the 232 men aboard. By the time the ship reached Cape Horn, twenty sailors were on the sick list, and others complained of rheumatism, as well as liver and bowel problems. "Everything in the ship was wet for the last 30 days—that is our clothing and bedding."[14]

Maury's severest test lay in rounding Cape Horn. He had watched gales batter a British ship as it unsuccessfully tried to pass. Maury noted everything he could about the battened-down *Falmouth*'s progress: "The barometer has not been found to be of much practical utility off Cape Horn.... Here the mercury below the mean height of lower latitudes, becomes very unsteady, falling and rising several inches in a few hours."[15]

Like Nathaniel Bowditch, in his small cabin drawing on the confidence bred of experience, Maury worked on his record of the passage. Later, when he was satisfied that what he had written was valuable, Maury sent his polished notes and designs for a device to determine longitude more accurately to Benjamin Silliman, the editor of the *American Journal of Science and Arts* in New Haven. For Maury, writing for the leading scientific journal of his day seemed as natural as working navigation problems on a blackboard in an examination room or solving mathematical equations on round shot aboard a warship. If the senior Navy did not prize learning, Maury by this act showed he did. The young officer's work and style appealed to Silliman, who published "On the Navigation of Cape Horn" in July 1834.[16]

While at sea, Maury began preliminary work on a book to explain the fundamental mathematics of navigation, but he had too few materials aboard for serious research, and the duties of a sailing master were such that his free time was limited. Where Bowditch labored on, Maury paused. The notes needed time to mature, as did Maury. Although he needed more experience to complete the larger work, Gregory rewarded Maury's diligence by making him an acting lieutenant.[17]

The memory of the long struggle his parents and the Rev. James Maury had had with debts gnawed at him when he tried to pick a wedding date. Maury felt that when he returned the Herndons, Ann's guardians, would press him to embark on a different career—as a teacher, a clergyman, or merchant—to provide for a wife and family in "the battle of life."

As before his temporary promotion, Maury helped his parents financially. In addition, Maury lent his brother Dick three hundred dollars. "At such a time a youth will oftentimes feel his heart sink within him from the mere weight of despondency. This is a time when the wisdom of the saw 'Tis wise and brave to hope the best' is needed."[18]

Personal finances and the future remained unsettled when Maury was assigned to the schooner *Dolphin* in Callao as executive officer on August 21, 1833. During this time, he wrote, "At a moderate calculation, I will not be a captain continuing the same for 25 years." Time far from a dear love passed no faster even with different duties. Several months later, he was cheered by orders moving him to the frigate *Potomac*, returning to the United States on November 22, 1833.[19]

Potomac had an experienced crew, commanded by John Downes. Having survived the battle with the British off Valparaiso, Downes was completing the second circumnavigation of the globe by an American warship. If Maury's experiences aboard *Vincennes* were largely peaceful, Downes and his men had other orders in addition to showing the flag.

In February 1831, East Indian pirates had killed three American merchantmen and plundered the Salem, Massachusetts-based *Friendship*. Although President Andrew Jackson had ordered negotiations first to arrest the murderers and destroy any vessel and weapons used in the attack, Downes reasoned that since a year had passed, talks with the Malays were pointless. He planned to come ashore in force.

With 250 sailors and Marines accompanying him, Downes attacked Quallah Battoo. As at Nukuhiva, the islanders armed with javelins and darts were no match for the more modernly equipped Americans. The raiders from the sea raced through the town, destroying what they could and looking for cargo stolen from *Friendship*, and then smashed the port's fortifications. When the Americans were through on that Sunday, about one hundred Malays were dead. Only the ship's medicine chest was recovered at the cost of two American lives.

The next day, before departing, Downes ordered the ship's guns turned on the smoldering town to send a message different from Finch's. It was a message as old as the United States Navy itself. The Navy protected American lives and American commerce—with force, if necessary. The wardroom must have dissected Downes, and their actions during those two days and again before and after Maury came aboard.[20]

Gathering all the reports he could about the attack and keeping careful notes of *Potomac*'s voyage was Jeremiah N. Reynolds, an Ohio newspaperman whom Downes had brought aboard as his secretary. Maury shared much with the journalist beyond what happened in Sumatra and the ports of call both made in Rio de Janeiro, Capetown, Macao, Canton, Honolulu, and Tahiti. Maury offered his extensive notes on the whalers working in the "unknown west." Reynolds passed along his tale of a great white whale he named "Mocha Dick."[21]

As welcome as this voyage back to the United States promised to be, Maury's time aboard *Potomac* was full of emotional and physical perils. Fittingly enough, it started in Valparaiso. The Chilean port city became the stage for a nineteenth-century romantic melodrama involving the younger Maury. The triangle involved Señorita Manuela Poma, a "very lovely, pure, intellectual and refined person"; a jilted Chilean army officer; and Maury.

The first act was played out on February 9, 1834, the day before *Potomac* was to sail for Cape Horn. On the sloop's deck, the distressed Chilean officer demanded to know why Señorita Poma had rebuffed his proposal of marriage and "destroyed all hopes of happiness." In his story, the Chilean lamented how the young woman had said "her affections were already engaged" by the American naval officer. For the Chilean it was a storm of unrequited love and wounded pride. For Maury it was a rain of continued assurances that all was proper between him and the young woman. Back and forth they went. Maury never changed his story of propriety and respect. With his ship ready to leave, Maury's assurances finally mollified the army officer.

The story did not end there.

"Most young men would have thought the conquest of a lady's affections but slight cause of regret and rather a feather in their cap, but Maury was exceedingly distressed and his distress was evidently genuine," one of his friends recalled.

In the drama's second act, Maury wrote Señorita Poma, explaining that there was nothing between them. He remained troubled over the incident. The passed midshipman questioned himself repeatedly on what impressions he had left with the young woman.[22]

The turmoil in Maury's personal life was now matched by the icy murkiness of the South Atlantic. Life aboard ship after rounding Cape Horn was a deadly contest of weather against vessel and crew in a cold sea. The sailing was rough in thick, cold fog. During long days with little visibility, the frigate felt its way through a field of ice until stove by an iceberg, but the damage was controlled. All watch-standers, drenched and numbed, strained their eyes, knowing they were in greater danger than they had been when they took on the Sumatran pirates. At last, the weather broke; when it did, *Potomac* beat fast for safety.[23]

If Maury thought Boston, *Potomac*'s American port of debarkation in late May 1833, would be a haven, the third act opened as the ship was being readied for a gala "Welcome Home" evening hosted by Downes and his wife. Then Maury learned that Manuela Poma had died of consumption. The anxiety he felt in leaving Valparaiso was born anew. Maury wondered as long as he lived if the young woman had created the story of their affair because she didn't want the Chilean officer to know how ill she was.[24]

Under that shroud, on May 27 Maury set out to begin a life with his "first and only love." For a time, he pushed aside the questions of finances and career. Maury wanted love and stability in his life. Of that, he was sure.

6. The Ever-Changing Sea of Life

Gathered in the parlor of Laurel Hill on July 15, 1834, were Maurys, Minors, and Herndons to celebrate the long-delayed marriage of the twenty-eight-year-old naval officer and his auburn-haired bride, a "beautiful and accomplished lady of Virginia." The hesitations Matthew Fontaine Maury had had about the couple's finances were washed away in the name of love. In fact, the exuberant groom was so taken by the moment that he gave the Rev. Edward C. McGuire his last twenty dollars.[1]

For Maury, the summer should have been a celebration of the heart with his new wife and an exercise of the mind for his book on navigation. The money Maury had coming to him then was $450 he claimed in back pay, his half pay for being ashore, and, in a pinch, the $300 he had loaned his brother Richard.[2]

As in his life so often, finances intruded.

Amos Kendall, one of Andrew Jackson's trusted lieutenants, rejected the claim for $450, challenging the amount of time Maury served as an acting lieutenant and the date on which he reverted to half pay.

In January 1835, disregarding the auditor's political power, Maury wrote former Navy Secretary Samuel Southard, "An officer has dared to question an act of Mr. Kendall's and to appeal from the decision of a clerk.... Must I call upon my friends to conciliate, and to use their influence with the honorable secretary, solicit this claim as a boon?" At Maury's request, Dick repaid the loan, with interest. Even in tightened circumstances, he returned the unexpected interest payment.[3]

With Dick's money in hand and half pay arriving, the newlyweds lodged in Fredericksburg with the daughter of his uncle, Abraham, and father of Maury's mentor in Tennessee.

In the bedroom of the two-story frame house, Maury had the space, resources, and time to do research for his book, all in short supply aboard ship: "At this time, I am closely occupied with my nautical book. I hope that it shall be ready by the spring, provided my labors are not interrupted by a call into active service from the Navy Department.... Of this work, I am by no means a speculative visionary."[4]

In view of his age, Maury was a man on a precipice. He was married, likely with children in his and Nannie's future and all the time and resources they were to demand. He, too, was deeply committed to producing a superior book on navigation—a signal of bending all to his profession.

If Maury's "university days" were his at-sea assignments, these next few years became independent studies of Virginia's and the United States' politics. This was a crucial decade for Maury. He made connections then, usually through extended family that stood him in good stead for decades as an officer, as a public figure, and as a writer.

From his experiences at sea, Maury's world view was broader than that of his family. But they all were men and women of their times—socially, politically, and economically. By the mid–1830s, these Virginians, as provincial as they might seem now, had survived perils of their own—the country's largest slave revolt and the gravest threat to the Union to date.

The nation during this time also appeared more violent—rioting against Mormons and Catholics, as just one example. To many Americans, the first attempted presidential assassination in January 1835 "was only one more indication that something was terribly amiss [that] needed attention and healing."[5]

White America (and the black slaves some of those whites owned) was a country on the move, and Virginians were leading continental imperialism. Abram Maury and Richard Maury had struck out for Tennessee, and George Rogers Clark and Henry Clay for Kentucky. Now others, Stephen F. Austin, western land speculator, and Sam Houston, who fought alongside Jackson in the Creek War, were "gone to Texas." In the nation's first sixty years, more than 375,000 Virginians pulled up stakes for another chance in another place—the bluegrass west of the Appalachians, the Ohio River Valley, Missouri, Alabama, Mississippi, and Mexico's "Promised Lands."[6]

As a congressman, John Floyd hectored administrations to control this vast territory—by squatting, by force, or by negotiation. He reminded all that Sergeant Charles Floyd, his cousin, had died in Mandan country as a member of Meriwether Lewis and William Clark's expedition. He reasoned aloud that Virginia had blazed the trail to the western ocean and owned it. The proof was self-evident. Lewis and Clark were two Army officers from Virginia who had commanded the adventure on orders from one of the Rev. James Maury's prized pupils, Jefferson.[7]

Floyd cared not that "plain old Robert Gray," an original Yankee trader in sea otter pelts to China, had established the first United States claim to the Columbia River basin a decade before the Corps of Discovery arrived. President George Washington, with Secretary of State Jefferson's knowledge, had authorized it. The British and their trading companies had given both claims short shrift.[8]

Americans were entering a new age of revolution—industrial, mechanical, and technological—in the 1830s. Along the waterways of New England the economy was changing from one of village artisans to urban industrial laborers. Manufacturing soon altered how federal revenue laws—tariffs—were employed. During Jackson's presidency, they shielded New England mill owners from European competition and provided money to run the federal government. By the late 1820s, cotton growers who sold their crop northward decried the "abomination" of the tariff in favoring one section over another. South Carolina's irritation bordered on rebellion.[9]

Historic activities like agriculture, too, were revolutionized with the patenting of Rockbridge County's Cyrus McCormick's "Virginia Reaper" in 1834. With John Deere's forged plow three years later, wheat harvests in Virginia's Shenandoah Valley were being shipped to Richmond's behemoth flour mills to dominate the international flour trade instead of being consumed locally.

Nowhere was the new age of revolution more apparent than in transportation. By 1807, Robert Fulton's steam-powered *Clermont* plied the Hudson River from New York to Albany. In besting river current and tidal flow, cargo and passengers went up the river almost as easily as they came down. After the War of 1812, there were hundreds of steamboats racing each other up river from New Orleans on the Mississippi to the falls of the Ohio at Louisville and westward up the Missouri and onto the Great Plains.[10]

The transportation revolution fired Maury's imagination. From 1826 onward, Maury's ferry crossings from the Navy Yard in Brooklyn to New York and his walks about lower Manhattan made real to him the spectacular growth of the city.

Tied to New York's piers were hundreds upon hundreds of steamboats, transatlantic sailers, coastal carriers, and lighters. The city by the mid–1820s eclipsed Boston in the China trade. Looking eastward, regularly scheduled passenger service on mail packets was offered between New York and Liverpool.

New York pushed aside Philadelphia to become the capital of an economic empire running the length of the Erie Canal and then from Buffalo across the Great Lakes. Capturing the inland trade, in turn, made New York the nation's most important port.

Of more import to Maury's eye, cotton told a bigger story best. As Maury saw, bales from the Sea Islands and the new Southwest were being loaded on ships bound for New England—developing the coastal trade—and Great Britain and France, expanding international trade.[11]

When Maury returned from sea duty, Virginia was embarked on a futile effort to best New York by linking Richmond to its western counties on the Ohio River. Wearing blinders, legislators, using a survey by Chief Justice John Marshall before the War of 1812, saw only the success of the 363-mile-long Erie Canal in making Manhattan's and New York State's fortunes. The legislature repeatedly ignored Virginia's geography in trying to build a canal over "a longer distance through more mountainous terrain" than any other such venture in the nation.[12]

The legislature's commitment of five hundred thousand dollars in 1831 has been singled out as the prime reason "Virginia failed to advance commercially and industrially with anything like the speed that might reasonably have been expected." Each vote to forge on left Norfolk's deep water harbor in a position "which never came close to realizing its potential." Like the legislators, Maury in his writings could not say "no more" for the canal.[13]

Focused on the canal and Richmond, the state's leaders largely missed the future. As John Quincy Adams's term ended and the Erie Canal neared completion, Charles Carroll of Carrolton, the last surviving signer of the Declaration of Independence, turned the first spade of earth in the building of the Baltimore and Ohio Railroad.

By the 1830s, people "welcomed the steam locomotive as a heaven-sent deliverance from the tyranny of distance." In a decade that ended in double financial panics, the United States had 3,200 miles of track, as "much as the total canal mileage" and "more than twice the track in all Europe."[14]

When Virginians thought about where railroads should go, they most often looked north and south. Sure, upstart Baltimore and Maryland had their grandly named westward looking track and even more boastful "National Road" linking the Potomac River at Cumberland, Maryland, to Virginia's Wheeling on the Ohio River. But Virginia's bet was on the bateaux of the James River and Kanawha Canal. For its main north–south rail line, the Old Dominion settled for a more prosaic name and smaller ambitions: the Richmond, Fredericksburg, and Potomac.[15]

When Maury identified himself as a citizen of Virginia, he committed himself to the state of his birth. As busy as he was, Maury drank in the politics of his times with the same enthusiasm that he demonstrated in learning about Great Britain, France, the Napoleonic wars, Latin America, the southern tip of Africa, and China. Here, family and friends were his pathfinders.[16]

Nat Turner's slave rebellion, the "Southampton Insurrection," in the late summer of 1831, and the long-running "Nullification Crisis" that began with the "Tariff of Abominations" three years earlier, left Virginians shaken.[17]

Turner's rebellion was "an alarm bell which roused the entire South." Like the slave revolts of Gabriel Prosser outside Richmond and Denmark Vesey in Charleston, Turner and his sixty conspirators believed "an identifiable divine force [was] guiding the rebellion" in southeastern Virginia. In less than two days, fifty-five whites, mostly women and children, were massacred by hatchet, ax, razor, dagger, sword, or gun.[18]

When the armed and frightened militia companies and slave patrols finally got their bearings in Southampton County, they tore apart shacks and barns and rooted through fields and forests hunting down Turner's band. "No one [white or black] could enter a district after dark without danger of being killed or arrested under suspicion of inciting rebellion among the slaves."[19]

Fear was contagious. In Virginia, faraway Fredericksburg beseeched the governor for protection. Suppressing a slave revolt as major as Turner's was imagined to be was taken as seriously in Jackson's Washington as it was in Floyd's Richmond. The War Department ordered five companies of regulars, at least one coming from as far away as New York, to the huge but unfinished Fortress Monroe in Hampton Roads to restore order in southeastern Virginia. From Delaware to the Carolinas, federal troops were sent to pacify whites.[20]

By then, the three thousand militiamen, deputized posses, and slave patrollers were in a blood frenzy. Most of Turner's accomplices were quickly seized. Blacks in the wrong place at the wrong time also were rounded up. Some were held for trial. More were killed on the spot and their severed heads placed on poles. Very few were set free.[21]

Finally, after a month-long manhunt, Turner was captured hiding in a copse close to the spot where his insurrection began.[22]

On November 11, he and three accomplices were hanged. When doctors received the body, they dissected it as expected. But instead of burying or burning the corpse, Turner's body and parts, including his skull, were apparently passed hand to hand among Southampton slaveholders. Turner dead was as feared as Turner alive. Parents in Virginia scolded recalcitrant children, raising Turner's specter—a bogeyman—to keep them in line.[23]

Floyd cast about for scapegoats after Turner's capture. He confided to his diary, "The whole of that Massacre is the work of these Preachers [from the free black population of the District of Columbia] as daily intelligence informs me." In what became a litany assailing incendiary troublemakers for the next three decades, Floyd also blamed "Yankee pedlars and traders," like Lewis and Arthur Tappan, "Northern preachers" and "our females and of the most respectable [class who] were persuaded that it was piety to teach negroes to read and write" to understand scripture. He soon added Quakers, Dunkers, Mennonites, and some Baptists to his list of dangerous white agitators. Even more shocking, literate black men believed "all men were born free and equal," Floyd explained in a letter to the governor of South Carolina.[24]

Where Floyd and other Virginians scoured the earth and hell looking for the devil's agents, Mary Minor Blackford, one of Maury's cousins, wailed liked Cassandra and called for repentance. To her, Turner's rampage was retribution for the sin of slavery. Few white Virginians shared that view.[25]

After the insurrection was forcibly put down, Floyd, surprisingly, planned to encourage the legislature to pass a gradual emancipation bill. Most of Maury's relatives and in-laws believed in gradual emancipation and transporting the freed slaves to Africa as supporters of the American Colonization Society. A few, notably the Blackfords, took to heart former President Madison's warning against considering slaves "mere property."

But following a visit from Calhoun and cries of outrage from the governors of South Carolina and Georgia, and Great Britain's announcement that it was freeing its West Indian slaves, Floyd reconsidered. The governor's new silence did not stop the debate in the state Capitol. In the end, the largest slaveholding sections—the east and south of the James River—prevailed. Slavery stayed.[26]

If transporting "excess slaves" to Africa was more and more out of the question by the mid–1830s, then "selling slaves south," especially "boys and girls, about the age of puberty" to the Carolinas, Georgia, and the Gulf Coast, was becoming the approved way to provide an economic lifeline to planters and a "safety valve" for the state.[27]

As the threat of a slave revolt receded, the growing political crisis over the tariff, the "Nullification Crisis," became a defining public moment for Maury's generation.

What to do about menacing federal laws had obsessed an earlier generation of Virginians—Thomas Jefferson, then John Adams's vice president, and James Madison, a principal architect of the Constitution. The embattled Virginia Republicans claimed the Alien and Sedition Acts were "leveled against the right of freely examining public characters and measures and of free communication among the people." To High Federalists, it was libel, sedition, and, if unchecked, treason.

Jefferson and Madison decried the acts' selective enforcement in Federalist-dominated courts. As proof, they had to look no further than Justice Samuel Chase's behaving as another prosecutor in the Richmond libel trial of rabble-rousing writer James Callender. They believed their strongest bulwark against an overzealous judiciary lay in state legislatures their party controlled. Their constitutional basis was the Tenth Amendment.[28]

The Kentucky Resolution, secretly written by Jefferson, declared the acts "void and of no force" within the state's boundaries. The vice president wanted to ensure there was no misunderstanding of his intent, so he inserted the word "nullification." The more temperate legislature struck Jefferson's term from the bill. Virginia's never included the word. With both resolutions adopted, the Virginia Republicans wishfully believed they had a platform on which to stand.[29]

The excesses of the French Revolution, French meddling, French officials' soliciting bribes, and a quasi war waged on the high seas led nine Northern states to reject the resolutions outright. Four Southern states chose to do nothing.

Yet, in two years, the political landscape changed dramatically. The excesses of the High Federalists in the judiciary, like Chase, proved too egregious for a new majority to ignore. They elected a Republican Congress, Jefferson president, and Madison became secretary of state.[30]

But nullification, and by implication, secession continued to smolder.

Like Jefferson and the Kentucky Resolution, John C. Calhoun, Adams's vice president, wrote willingly but secretly a detailed argument denouncing the sectional bias of the 1828 tariff. With its severely restricted franchise, the leaders of the least democratic of the states, like Governor James Hamilton, George McDuffie, and Robert Barnwell Rhett, turned Calhoun's thesis into a rail against an all-powerful federal juggernaut. The South Carolinians had caught lightning in a Deep South struggling through a time of depressed cotton prices.[31]

To Hamilton, McDuffie, and Rhett, each more radical than Calhoun, the Virginians like John Floyd and John Tyler appeared to be so many Hamlets. Hamilton called a state convention that overwhelmingly passed an ordinance of nullification and proposed South Carolina secede. He then moved to raise a volunteer force to defend the state, buy arms to enforce the ordinance, and demand the federal government return the state-built Citadel to South Carolina.[32]

Step by step, the federal and state governments appeared headed toward armed confrontation. The War Department replaced Charleston-based troops with two companies from Fortress Monroe and ordered more artillery units to South Carolina. With General Winfield Scott now in Charleston on an "inspection tour," all regular Army officers were ordered to renew their oaths to the federal constitution. Following suit, the Treasury Department sent more revenue cutters and customs collectors to South Carolina. Unionists with Joel Poinsett, the onetime adventurer-diplomat, as a leader warned the Nullifiers there would be blood in the streets if South Carolina seceded. Jackson offered Poinsett five thousand muskets for his secret Washington Societies and access to federal arsenals.

Incoming Governor Robert Hayne received the legislature's approval to raise a force of twelve thousand volunteers—thirty-five hundred of whom were to be a "corps of mounted minutemen" able to "concentrate on Charleston" quickly. In a tit-for-tat check on loyalty, all South Carolina civil and military officers were to take an oath to obey and enforce the nullification ordinance.[33]

By December 1832, federal guns at Fort Moultrie on Sullivan's Island and Castle Pinckney off Charleston's Battery and those aboard *Natchez* and *Experiment* were pointed at the city. The Nullifiers targeted Castle Pinckney, where the collector of the port and other federal officials were to retreat for safety if violence erupted.

An angry Jackson sought congressional approval to use force to carry out federal law.[34]

Publicly, Virginia's political elite took a middle stance. The commonwealth sent Benjamin Watkins Leigh as a "peace commissioner" to tone down the rhetoric. Instead, the volume boomed louder. Privately, Floyd wrote, Jackson was "determined to wage war upon a sovereign state, because I knew he was not a patriot but a tyrant."[35]

After the secretary of war ordered more reinforcements to Charleston, Floyd sent the General Assembly without comment the South Carolina nullification ordinance and Jackson's proclamations to uphold federal laws, using force if necessary, across the Union.

Virginia legislators prayed that delay could defuse the crisis. They named a select committee to study future relations with the federal government. Weeks later, the committee's pox-on-both-your-houses report denounced the tariff, praised South Carolina, if not its methods, and finger-wagged against the use of force by either side. Virginia's Hamlets were trying to have their cake with the Union and eat it with the Carolinians. But Virginia had shown a way out.[36]

Moderates across the South took heart that bloodshed could be avoided if their legislators adopted Virginia's approach. Lawmakers in slaveholding states now qualified their support for the Carolinians until "this dress rehearsal for civil war passed into history."[37]

As the crisis wound down, Jackson fumed privately: "The coalition between Calhoun, Clay Poindexter & the Nullifiers in the South—intend to blow up a storm on the subject of the slave question." Jackson was right in fingering slavery for poisoning national politics, but the question refused to go away. An older Maury helped see to that.[38]

During the day back inside his own home, Maury's energies, confidence, and capacity for work were poured into his book. In February 1835, before the "speculative visionary" had a publisher, he wrote Boston booksellers: "Such a work as this purports to be is much required in the service of our country. It is elementary and designed for the use of those who are being educated for the merchant, as well as for the naval service."[39]

Maury understood marketing.

On April 30, 1835, keeping to his rigid schedule, Maury sent the finished manuscript to Key and Biddle, a Philadelphia publishing house. Like the expectant father he was, Maury fretted over each day's post until the Philadelphians agreed to publish the book. As the Maurys celebrated that good news, Ann delivered their first child, Elizabeth, on June 25, 1835.[40]

With the baby, the Maurys needed more room, and they rented a house with a yard on Charlotte Street between Princess Anne and Prince Edward streets in Fredericksburg. Even in a new house and with new responsibilities, Maury remained without orders and was dying for more word from Philadelphia. This was the first but not the last time he thought only the worst could have happened in his dealings with a publisher. By mid–October, he could wait no longer and traveled alone northward to midwife his manuscript. This leaving wife and children behind for weeks, months, years at a time became common practice for Maury—in and out of the Navy.[41]

Though no longer the capital and eclipsed by New York as a trading center, Philadelphia was a bustling city of maritime business, banking, and insurance in the 1830s. It remained the city of the American enlightenment, the place where Meriwether Lewis, Jefferson's private secretary, received scientific training from the American Philosophical Society before setting out for the Pacific Coast.

More to the point, Philadelphia was expensive. For a passed midshipman, living on forty dollars a month with a wife and child to support in Virginia, he could barely afford a garret's rent and a cheese-and-cracker diet. Once there,

Maury threw himself into the painstaking work of checking and double-checking. Going over the proofs, especially the 174 pages of mathematical tables, was laborious, but these were the details that made his work singular. And he staked his future on their accuracy.

In a letter to Dick, Maury wrote, "You must bear in mind that this is the first nautical work of science that has ever come from the pen of a naval officer and upon its merits I intend to base a claim for promotion. Such a case has no precedent." He daydreamed that the book would guarantee his promotion to lieutenant with ten years of service.[42]

On April 29, 1836, Key and Biddle applied for a copyright on *A New Theoretical and Practical Treatise on Navigation by M. F. Maury, passed midshipman, U.S. Navy.*[43]

An elated Maury left for Washington to meet with Mahlon Dickerson, secretary of the Navy, and the president himself, if possible, to show off his work and claim his lieutenancy. Although Maury was using his cousin Abram's Tennessee political connections, he was beating fast against the wind. He later claimed the president was favorably inclined, but the "very old granny secretary" said, "The work brought with it its own reward."

Despite the secretary's ordering the book be put in ships' libraries, Maury never forgave Dickerson. The twin hopes of promotion and longevity pay turned out to be as elusive as the tobacco tithe owed his grandfather. It was also not the last time Maury overvalued his service to the Navy.[44]

Taking some of the sting out of the situation was the public applause he received for his contribution to nautical science. Early praise came from Bowditch and Alexander Dallas Bache, the great grandson of Benjamin Franklin and a prominent Philadelphia educator. George Bache, serving in the Navy, seconded his older brother's accolade.

Silliman's Journal noted that the officer is "already favorably known to the public for his contributions to science, and the work before us amply sustains his character as an officer well grounded in the varied learning demanded in his profession."

Edgar Allan Poe, in the *Southern Literary Messenger*, wrote that the "time is coming when, imbued, with a taste for science and a spirit of research, [Navy officers] will become ardent explorers of the regions in which they sojourn."[45]

The reception among the naval officers brought praise from Maury's former commander Francis Gregory and Robert F. Stockton in a joint note, as well as Cadwallader Ringgold, O. H. Perry, William B. Shubrick, Raphael Semmes, and former shipmate surgeon W. P. Ruschenberger.[46]

Writing later, Samuel F. DuPont summed up the Navy's reactions:

> [T]he value of a class book like yours preparing to teach the young officer the theory of one branch of his profession, which makes his mind with some tincture of science and raise him above the blind and ignorant workers of mechanical problems, cannot be better appreciated by those in the profession.[47]

In his book as in the original article, Maury acknowledged Bowditch, LaPlace, and Ferdinand Hassler, the Swiss-born scientist who headed the United States Coast Survey. His work covered algebra, geometry, logarithms, and trigonometry, the study of spheres, as well as astronomy and navigation. It demonstrated Maury's strength—synthesis—and then "placed within the reach of every student."[48]

In June 1836, Maury's long-awaited promotion arrived, but without credit for a decade of back service or orders. Although his half pay was increased, Maury again needed ways to supplement his income. "I fill up an allotted portion of my leisure time with the study of mineralogy and geology," he wrote. He craved the public stage. On May 13, 1836, in an address to the Geological and Mineralogical Society in Fredericksburg, Maury said, "Every pebble and every mineral have order and arrangement—they are the reflectors in which the geologist sees the wisdom of God."[49]

The mineral that most interested Maury that spring, however, was gold. Above the falls of the Rappahannock, small mines with large ambitions operated in Spotsylvania County. The East was peppered with similar regions, and they attracted investors interested in the big strike and engineers like Paris-trained T. G. Clemson, Calhoun's son-in-law.

To supplement his Navy half pay and royalties, Maury served on the board of the United States Gold Mine. The mine occupied a choice location near the river, and the Rappahannock Canal crossed its property. In the summer of 1836, he accepted an offer to become its superintendent. Maury seemed to be launching a career ashore away from the pettiness of auditors and slights of secretaries.[50]

The first gold operation in Spotsylvania employed about fifty men. The gold, rarely found in large pieces, was "concealed entirely in the quartz." To extract it, water turned huge wooden, iron-covered wheels, crushing the quartz. The quartz was placed with mercury in large receptacles and agitated. Through distilling, only the gold remained.

That summer an intrigued Benjamin Silliman with his son and Eli Whitney journeyed from New Haven to see the workings of the Virginia gold fields. He was shocked by what he saw: "The strong arms of athletic black men were employed to crush the quartz for us in heavy iron mortars, preparatory to the washing for gold; they also broke the quartz from the veins." The Yale professor concluded his account with this observation: "Slavery, begun in wrong, is sustained by cruel despotism." Maury never viewed slavery in those lights.

When the New Englanders left, Maury was concerned about making the operations more efficient and more profitable. As he later wrote for Silliman's publication: "The metallurgical process of obtaining gold in Virginia, is by no means perfect, in every stage through which it passes, from the stamps to 'blowing off' of the quicksilver, there is a wasteful loss of both metals."[51]

Throughout the summer, a steam engine drained the mine to open a fourth vein, which like the others "run through the whole length of the company's lands" of 450 acres.[52]

In its best weeks, the mine took in about six hundred dollars in gold, enough to keep going but not investors' hoped-for riches. Maury thought there would be more profit in extracting the abundant iron ore found on the site, as colonial lieutenant governor Spotswood had. Yet gold was in the company's name, and the search for more (and easily reachable) gold was to continue.

To raise capital for a planned 1837 expansion, the company sent out circulars for a bond issue. The timing could not have been worse. The nation was tumbling into a deep financial panic following the protracted battle over the rechartering of the Second National Bank of the United States. During this time Maury was offered a promotion to chief engineer. The tender was tempting, but what the future held ashore was cloudy, as investors began guarding what they had, and state banks struggled to survive.[53]

7. The Exploring Expedition Fiasco

As Matthew Fontaine Maury plotted his way into the Navy over his father's stern objections in 1825, the course of what became his life's work was being spelled out in detail in Washington. John Quincy Adams's first State of the Union message envisioned highways from Washington to New Orleans and canals grander than the Erie, a national university, an observatory like the 130 "lighthouses of the sky" operating in Europe, a school to prepare future naval officers for service, and great "voyages of discovery" in the manner of the British, the French, and the Russians. Over the course of the next half century, Maury left his imprint in all these areas—sometimes for the better and sometimes not.[1]

Nothing forged Maury's career as a naval officer more than the "voyages of discovery," especially the first that took years to mount and split the Navy's officer corps into competing cliques. What looked golden was dross. For Adams's "voyages of discovery," like the ones he had urged upon President James Monroe to find new killing grounds for New England whalers, the president had the talents of Jeremiah Reynolds, Maury's *Potomac* civilian shipmate, to rouse public and congressional support. He also had an able secretary of the Navy, the man who had lectured Maury on his duties as an acting midshipman. Samuel Southard approached Reynolds to sound out whalers and sealers on the benefits of a "Southern Ocean" expedition, knowing well what they would say.[2]

Adams's call for a great exploration of the Antarctic and South Seas moldered on Capitol Hill and inside the Navy Department for most of the eight years that Andrew Jackson held the White House. During much of this time, Maury was at sea, slowly advancing as a junior officer through the ranks.

As his second term was ending, Jackson's belated interest in the Oregon coast was barely enough to rouse Mahlon Dickerson—the "old granny"—into twisting congressional arms to pay for it. The secretary had no clear idea of what he expected from such an expedition—advancement of the Navy, creation of a truly American science, or development of the nation's commercial interests.[3]

Titian Ramsey Peale, a scientist later picked for the expedition, attributed the president's change of mind to his desire to carry out James Smithson's bequest "to found an institution for the increase and diffusion of knowledge." The president's interest could best be defined as thwarting British ambitions from California to Nootka Island off present-day British Columbia.[4]

Although money was appropriated, men and ships were not put to sea. Instead, the highest levels of the Navy—uniform and civilian—embarked on a two-year voyage of bickering. Who should command? What should be surveyed? Why are civilians coming aboard? Does naval discipline apply to them? Scientific résumés flooded Dickerson's office. In response, he turned to his first love—gardening—to escape.[5]

Jackson finally ordered Thomas ap Catesby Jones to take command. The president had known Jones since the Battle of New Orleans and knew he had recent experience in the Pacific, vital for such an undertaking.

Jones figured he needed five vessels, led by frigate *Macedonian* for the mission. At the time, there was no set procedure for selecting subordinate commanders and the other officers for a squadron. So, as was customary, Jones picked Josiah Tattnall, Charles H. Bell, A. B. Pinkham, and Thomas A. Dornin, Maury's naval mentor, and submitted the list to the secretary and the Board of Commissioners for expected routine approval.[6]

Dickerson balked and told Jones to consider Charles Wilkes, who headed the Depot of Charts and Instruments, and Alexander Slidell, because they were senior to some officers on Jones's list. In addition, Dickerson, the president of the Columbian Institute for the Promotion of Arts and Sciences and a member of the American Philosophical Society, pointed out the men's scientific strengths. The secretary then went down the hall to "the old captains" for their views. The Board of Commissioners likewise favored Wilkes and Slidell for all Dickerson's reasons, and these two officers could keep the civilian "scientifics" under control and, better yet, off the ships.[7]

For now, the matter of putting the scientifics aboard was peripheral. Jones insisted his choices were the right ones. Dickerson, having stirred the pot, maintained golden silence, but the old captains busied themselves whispering their disapproval to the White House and Congress.[8]

Through all this back-and-forth in Washington, Maury looked at his naval career differently. He knew that with more than two years without a sea assignment his career could be ending. But Dornin gave him a glimmer of hope. Jones wanted the young lieutenant in a scientific capacity, an idea that appealed to Maury's sense of himself.

After Maury concluded his affairs with the United States Gold Mine in the summer of 1836, he visited Jones at his home in Fairfax County, Virginia. What Jones said excited Maury. "I am dying in the expectation of orders," Maury wrote. Jones asked for Maury as Dornin's executive officer aboard storeship *Relief*.[9]

As was his nature, Maury could not resist analyzing and reanalyzing the situation. He worried about using warships in a scientific undertaking. To Dornin, he wrote, "I am not without my fears that it falls through and prove an abortion."[10]

An abortion, the expedition almost was. Dickerson was being "cautious not to attempt too much business in a day" as the old captains' rancor dripped through the officer corps like acid. Maury wrote, "I have a foreboding that no good is to come of this expedition under its present arrangement, better no arrangement. The officers are at loggerheads among themselves." Yet Maury did not seek reassignment.[11]

Back inside the secretary's office, Dickerson did not budge on naming Wilkes and Slidell as ship commanders. He now dipped well below the level of command when he sent Dornin three lieutenants, two of whom held date of rank higher than Maury. This meant that Maury, who had been "first lieutenant," or the executive officer, was reduced to being just another member of the wardroom. Maury wrote Dornin, "What reason can he [Dickerson] have why I should not be ordered. And why keep me both in uncertainty as to whether I shall go or not."[12]

Expecting to sail in the fall, the Maurys planned to give up the lease on their house and have Ann and daughter Betty stay with relatives, but as the impasse continued, those plans were shelved. Uncertainty was the only constant.

In the spring of 1837, Maury was transferred to *Macedonian*. The largest ship in the Navy could berth the "Scientific Corps" and their collections, and protect "our whalers and traders," but the expedition's mission remained undefined. To the lieutenant, this was the proverbial straw that broke the camel's back. He angrily wrote his cousin Ann, saying he was requesting furlough so "I might not be subject to the control of the imbecile secretary and his minions—both of whom I have offended in times gone by for daring to report some of their misdemeanors to their master the president."[13]

Foremost among his reasons were his standing as a very junior officer aboard the expedition's flagship and the birth of the Maurys' second child. The cool-headed Dornin told Maury that the transfer really meant he was to be the expedition's astronomer. When Maury heard that news from someone he trusted, the lieutenant realized he could not have carved out a better assignment if he had written the orders himself.[14]

In renewing his vow to bend all to his profession, Maury set off to study under Professor Walter R. Johnson, who was to lead the expedition's study of magnetism. His observatory in Philadelphia's Rittenhouse Square then also housed much of the equipment for the expedition.[15]

After completing his studies in October, Maury stopped to see Dickerson. The secretary assured the lieutenant that he was about to sign the papers to make the appointment of Maury as astronomer official.[16]

Back in Fredericksburg, the lieutenant wrote Dickerson suggesting that the astronomer also measure tides, currents, and winds, and check latitudes and longitudes of newly discovered islands "and on any other subjects of general interest to the navigator and which may serve to guide mariners in the navigation of whatever seas the expedition shall visit." These were all areas designated for other officers, such as Lieutenant James Glynn, who had seniority over Maury.[17]

Outside the Navy, the secretary consulted with scientific groups. Those talks prompted even more civilian résumés to be sent to the Navy Department, a fact the secretary abhorred. But Dickerson probed away without counsel from two of the nation's prominent scientists. During this time, Alexander Dallas Bache, newly named president of Girard College in Philadelphia, and Joseph Henry of Princeton were touring Great Britain. Dickerson sorely missed their advice. Civilian scientists continued viewing the expedition as "the most ambitious scientific reconnaissance since Napoleon's expedition to Egypt discovered the Rosetta Stone."[18]

The uniformed Navy didn't think that broadly. "Maury and other officers were becoming suspicious of the close relationship Dickerson had with the scientific community in planning operations," causing more delays.[19]

The dithering scientifics were only part of Jones's problem. Inside the Navy, Wilkes dillydallied with the captain's requests to turn over the chronometers and other instruments needed for the expedition. In early November 1837, Jones exploded and ordered Maury to get the instruments from Wilkes. "There is no occasion for detaining the chronometers twenty days longer at Washington to obtain Lieutenant Wilkes' rates of those delicate instruments, for they must all be tested by new ratings after they are returned to this place and put on board the respective vessels, and as this indispensable preliminary may require several weeks, at this season," Jones wrote.[20]

Maury was only partially successful. Wilkes, in his contempt for Jones, had left the instruments in storage in New York. An angrier Jones then ordered Wilkes, whom he begrudgingly accepted as a commander, not to take the brig *Porpoise* to sea until all the instruments were in the expedition's hands.

For more than a year and a half, Jones was whipsawed by the impertinence of officers like Wilkes, the backstabbing of the old captains, and the second-guessing of Dickerson. The secretary, however, had one more turn of the screw to discomfit Jones. That came in the expedition's sailing orders. Dickerson ordered him to have at least two subordinates certify and seal every document made in the expedition. Jones felt his integrity impugned.[21]

Jones offered to withdraw, and as an afterthought, the captain added in a letter to Dickerson that he had recently been ill. Seizing upon that, the secretary, with unseemly haste, accepted Jones's resignation on December 6.[22]

The secretary shopped the command around the Navy. He went to William Shubrick, Lawrence Kearny, Matthew C. Perry, and Francis Gregory, and all refused. The continued delays over mission, command, and the financial crisis sweeping the country threatened to sink the expedition.[23]

President Martin Van Buren, who as Jackson's vice president was well aware of the fiasco in the making, turned to Joel Poinsett. The secretary of war met with Adams, now a congressman, to review the predicament. The former president was in a cantankerous mood: "All I want to hear about the exploring expedition was, that it sailed." With that ringing in his ears, the South Carolinian stormed through the sea service, interviewing officers, including Maury, to elicit names of possible expedition commanders.[24]

Poinsett, who had stared down his home state's Nullifiers, was not concerned with the niceties of naval rank; he wanted competence. Maury wrote that he felt Poinsett wanted him to command, but the lieutenant didn't push his own name forward. Instead, Maury listed himself at the bottom as the most junior lieutenant and "preserved my integrity." The secretary's written legacy is silent on Maury assuming command.[25]

Poinsett, brooking no more delay, put the arrogant Wilkes in command. He immediately scaled back the mission to charting the seas, astronomy, and navigation—the Navy's interests, while paring the Scientific Corps from thirty-two to eight. When the appointment was announced, Maury asked to be relieved. Although he said he did this so the new commander could pick his own officers, as Jones wanted, the battle for control of the chronometers cast a pall over all future relationships. If he were being honest, Maury was also jealous and soon was calling Wilkes "a cunning little Jacob" and a "sinecurist."[26]

In Fredericksburg, Maury was "hanging by the eyelids." He had lost a major opportunity to advance his naval career, and the bitter aftertaste of the "confused state of the exploring expedition" stuck in his craw. To Maury, the affair was symptomatic of the Navy's ills. He recalled how his independence was slapped down with a middling ranking on his midshipman's examination. Now his scientific ambitions were corked. Maury blamed Dickerson, the man who appeared to single-handedly stymie his career and the careers of dozens of creative officers.[27]

The lieutenant again took up his pen, this time for the newspaper press, to publicly detail the rot. Maury, using the pseudonyms of Harry Bluff and Will Watch in the *Richmond Whig*, was not a pioneer in taking his frustrations with the Navy public. Franklin Buchanan and Samuel F. DuPont had sailed the same course.

"Harry Bluff is exciting a good deal of attention in the Navy," Maury wrote in the summer of 1838. "It is noticed abroad that a past captain is the gentleman. But Harry taking advantage of the rapier remains snugly enclosed [in anonymity]." Maury asked his New York cousins, the sons of the "Old Consul," to keep his identity as the author secret, but to pass the articles around the city's business community. The naval reform articles will be examined in Chapter 8.[28]

For all the problems he found in the service, Maury thought of himself as a naval officer. He had put aside his venture into mining, a decision made easier by the financial panic. But his next orders were pedestrian, serving under Lieutenant James Glynn in surveying Wilmington, North Carolina; Beaufort, South Carolina; and spots along the Georgia coast for a new naval yard. It was a far cry from serving as the astronomer for the exploring expedition.

If coast surveying was what he had to do, Maury wanted to be assigned to the more prestigious Coast Survey. From his research for his book, Maury knew the high place Ferdinand Hassler occupied in nautical science, if not in congressional esteem. In 1839, he twice applied for duty in "the prosecution of your great work along the coast," but the superintendent apparently never answered Maury's letters.[29]

Another possible but interesting assignment came from Dornin, who wanted to survey the Columbia River to solidify American claims to Oregon. With characteristic vigor, Maury wrote his New York relatives asking for more information about the Pacific Northwest. Nothing came of Dornin's effort, either. Wilkes conducted the survey and launched inland explorations through what are now the states of Oregon and California as part of his expedition.[30]

So Maury, as ordered, went to sea under the command of a former rival in the expedition. The survey's first phase was completed in two months. Because the next phase was to include surveys on the Sabine River in newly independent Texas, a sturdier ship was needed. To this end, workmen were outfitting brig *Consort* in New York, preparing for a fall departure.

Back in Fredericksburg on leave, news of his parents' declining health commanded Maury's attention. He and Ann were prepared to take in his parents, but getting the older couple to Virginia would be too difficult with colder weather approaching. Maury headed westward to arrange for their care through the winter with his sister, Betsy, now Mrs. Kemp Holland, at her home near Memphis. When the family business in Tennessee was complete, Maury left for New York. The journey took several months, and when it ended his naval career and his body were left severely crippled.[31]

On October 17, 1839, Maury rode inside a stagecoach bound for Chillicothe, Ohio. The stage was to stop there and then go on to Wheeling, Virginia. Nine people were already aboard, but at Lancaster, the agent took on three more passengers, including a woman. Maury gave up his seat inside and joined two other men and the driver on top.

The stage continued over the western slope of the Appalachians toward Somerset on a cloudy night. There, the horses were changed, and the coach was back on the rolling road shortly after midnight. The turnpike in southern Ohio was under construction, and the driver set off on the road's shoulder. As he urged the team forward, the right wheels sank deeper and deeper into the soft earth of a small rise. The driver tried to ease the stage onto the safer, beaten track, but it was too late. The top-heavy stagecoach rolled over. Maury crashed to the ground.[32]

Somerset, the closest town, was too small for a hospital, and Maury was too grievously injured to be taken to Zanesville or Lancaster for treatment. The best that could be done was to get him to former wagoner Jake Breakhill's roadside inn, the Hotel Phoenix. There, a doctor in haste improperly set the right thigh bone. Maury endured more excruciating pain when the bone was broken again and reset, again without anesthetic. Days later, Dr. G. W. Boerstler, the family physician of former United States Senator Thomas Ewing, examined Maury and said that recovery would take three or four months.[33]

In later examinations, doctors determined that Maury had torn the ligaments of the knee cap and fractured the thigh bone as well as the kneecap itself. The lieutenant understood his Navy career now was in as much jeopardy as *Potomac* had been in the ice fields of the South Atlantic and *Vincennes* off the breakers in Nukahiva.

A self-composed prayer may have eased his mind, but the crippled officer had to hire a thirteen-year-old boy to nurse him until help could come from his family. His wife, Ann, tried to come to his side but was taken ill and forced to return to Fredericksburg. At last, John Minor, his mother's nephew, found Maury in an ill-heated room with a cracked looking glass and "a striped rag here called carpet, the office of which is to secrete dust."

Through prayer and John's attention, Maury was more accepting of what became a seventy-day recovery at the grungy hotel: "Nature is a wondrous kind and providence whose servant she is marvelous in his ways, but when damages have been as extensive as mine have been it takes her a long time to repair them and to get everything properly fitted in its place again."[34]

The "fracture box" bound to his leg was changed periodically with John Minor's help: "In this shield, I expect to travel and weather out the winter." On Christmas 1839, he wrote, "We have a fine snow for sleighing; I hope it will hold, traveling will be much more easy and much less fatiguing."[35]

When he was strong enough in January 1840, Maury and John Minor started by sleigh for New York, but by the time they arrived in the city, *Consort* had departed. Maury tried putting the best face he could on his circumstances: "It is of opinion that I have a tolerable use of the leg, but it will be two or three years for it [to heal]."[36]

"Ifs" defined his position. If Maury was so badly injured that he could not go to sea, the Navy could terminate his service and let his cries for compensation be lost in the torrent of other such pleas. If he could go to sea, then the life he fought so hard to start in the Navy could resume. What if he had stayed in Fredericksburg as a mining engineer? Was there a future in writing? Had Maury been broken in "bending everything to my profession?" What about Ann and the children?

The future was as foreboding as a winter storm sky.

8. Survival Ashore

While in Fredericksburg convalescing from 1839 to 1842, Matthew Fontaine Maury found an audience for his writings among the men who devoured Virginia politics and business. His readers were the slave handlers, tobacco auctioneers, and the warehousemen of Shockhoe Bottom, the flour merchants who commanded the trade between Richmond and Rio, the bankers and the up-country traders who dreamed of building a canal linking the James River to the Ohio River Valley.[1]

For these men, life revolved around Richmond, a city that forged iron in the Tredegar Works and laws in Jefferson's Capitol. By 1840, this city had been home to George Wythe, Jefferson's ill-fated law professor, to Edgar Allan Poe, the erratic writer and editor, and to John Marshall, the steadiest jurist.

Maury's readers were deeply concerned about their city's future and their own, following the Panic of 1837. Without credit or specie, they saw canal and railroad companies failing. State-supported "internal improvements" and state banks stalled or busted. They had seen the facade of "family" stripped away from slavery in Nat Turner's rebellion. Their political loyalties had been ripped apart into Jackson and anti–Jackson factions during the near civil war of the Nullification Crisis.

In their vanguard stood the gaunt John Tyler, whose family was used to political power. Tyler found a most useful vehicle to defend himself politically in the newly launched *Southern Literary Messenger* in the city. By Tyler's side was Judge Abel Parker Upshur, a rising political figure from the Eastern Shore. Upshur used the Richmond magazine to proclaim slavery "as a great positive good." Joining them as contributors was Maury.[2]

Maury's first writing on naval reform had appeared in a Richmond newspaper, which set the stage for his later contributions to the more influential periodical. In 1838, angered over his treatment in the South Seas Exploring and Surveying Expedition and before his crippling accident, Maury launched his first broadsides of naval reform, using the *Richmond Whig and Public Advertiser* as his gun deck. It is necessary to recap some of them for their later impact on the service and the attitudes of the time.[3]

The long delays in getting the expedition underway, the turmoil over its command, the role of civilian "scientifics," the shoving aside of the secretary of the Navy for the secretary of War to move the ships out of port, the clogged promotion ladder all were newspaper topics before Maury, but his articles struck the right chord at the right time. Writing under the names Harry Bluff and Will Watch, Maury personified the "naval reform" movement.[4]

Predictably, his earliest target was the secretary of the Navy, Mahlon Dickerson, whom Maury referred to derisively as "that imbecile old man." Maury added that Jackson's secretary was not the only civilian official crippling the Navy. "For the last 10 years, the Navy Department has been cursed with secretaries."[5]

In his next piece, Maury blasted the Board of Commissioners, the sea service's senior governing officers, over Navy spending. "What has become of the 7 million per annum which have been appropriated for the naval service? They certainly have not been expended on sea-going ships."[6]

That set the stage for Will Watch's troubling tale of *Ohio 74*, the nation's most powerful warship. "Can anybody but the secretaries tell why ships after making a single cruise are laid up—not merely to undergo some trifling repair ... but laid up for years? ... The millions that have been squandered in this way would have erected all the cannon foundries that the Navy required."[7]

Being forcibly ashore, the naval officer made his move to win Tyler's and Upshur's supporters. More practically, since his Navy career was on hold, he needed money for his growing family. In the January 1839 issue of the *Messenger*, Maury's first defining piece as a Southern nationalist, "Direct Trade with the South," led the periodical. The young man who had witnessed New York's rise to preeminence wrote, "In a geographical point of view, Norfolk would appear to be best suited for *the port* or emporium for the United States, but Virginia has slept upon her natural advantages." Here was his challenge to New Orleans' cotton shippers and maritime interests in his home state to recapture the coastal trade and, by doing so, win the transatlantic trade. Cotton was the nation's leading export, and the South grew cotton. As with naval reform, building the commercial strength of the South over New York became a lifetime and, ultimately, futile crusade of Maury's.[8]

After that piece appeared, Maury returned to his critique of the Navy. The long period of peace between 1815 and the arrival in 1841 of Upshur as secretary was largely an era of hoary thinking in the Navy. As secretaries came and went, the presidentially appointed Board of Commissioners—"old captains," all—stayed, discarding new ideas like bilge.[9]

In the *Southern Literary Messenger*, Maury addressed four themes in his "Scraps from the Lucky Bag" series: rank, midshipmen's education, shipbuilding and overhaul, and placement of the fleet.

For a naval officer following the War of 1812, there was no more pressing issue than rank. Not only were the higher echelons creaking with age—the same men Maury once had so admired—the service had fewer grades in which to promote its officers than foreign navies or its sister force, the Army. There were no limits on accessions, even for line officers. At the same time, line officers such as Maury doubly resented efforts of doctors, pursers, etc., in trying to secure for themselves naval rank, thus further clogging the promotion ladder. Donald Chisholm summed up Maury's examination of the Navy's problems of ships, organization, and personnel to his penchant for efficiency and economy: "Over the previous thirty years the navy had built ships and added and subtracted officers without regarding the proper relationship between them."[10]

Rank was the iceberg's tip of naval problems: "Why should not the Navy officer be taught to plan the model of your ship; and submitting his plan and drawings have the privilege also of superintending the construction of his castle—the fort in which he is to sink or swim?"[11]

Maury wanted midshipmen taught gunnery, ship and squadron tactics, and the necessity of discipline both to sail and fight the vessel. His midshipmen would also learn foreign languages, and not in "Lord Byron's" style, as he did—from the lips of a young woman in a foreign land. "For the Navy officer, whose calling takes him to all countries and among all people, no plan of education can be complete unless it contains at least one of three languages, French, Spanish or German." As Christopher McKee noted, "These were not customarily part of the navy's program of formal shipboard instruction." Yet the Navy's officers sailed to lands where those were the languages of commerce, diplomacy, and science.[12]

By May 1841, Maury wrote, "The building of officers ... is quite of as much importance as the building of ships." These were subjects that he had thought deeply about while at sea, grew frustrated over when ashore, and wanted to change for years.

In his articles, Maury called for a flow of officers through the grades, limiting accessions to vacancies, size the officer corps for the size and kinds of ships in the fleet, promote at set times in grade, require formal education of junior officers, and develop a grade structure similar to the Army's.[13]

As troubled as he was about the internal operations of the Navy, Maury's public was more interested in how its money was lost in shipbuilding and repair. Through 1840 and 1841, he struck at the Navy's "prodigal expenditure of the public money." The lieutenant feasted on the reports of former Secretary Mahlon Dickerson and Captain John Rodgers, the president of the Board of Commissioners. If they claimed that the Navy was well governed, then the cold numbers of repairs running twice as high as building showed them out of touch. Maury deemed the pair incompetent.

Ship construction had its own problems. In the *Whig*, Maury pointed out that Congress set aside $385,000 to build and outfit one ship in the seventy-four-gun Ohio class. Using the Navy's reports, Maury exposed a staggering overrun in which the service claimed "to build one of those line-of-battle ships, the *Ohio*, and to fit her for her first cruise, has instead of less than $385,000, actually cost from first to last, more than $887,000; and that too, exclusive of 'provisions and clothing'!"

In the Navy's record keeping, Maury found it impossible to fix where the overrun had occurred. Words like *building* and *equipping* meant different things in the Navy; the Senate resolution giving the go-ahead for the service's largest warship did not differentiate between those two terms. To the Navy, *building* meant keel, hull, masts, spars, boats, rigging, sails, and guns. *Equipping* meant furnishing—the provisions and clothing. So the Navy then mixed its own figures together and came up with the $500,000 overrun.[14]

Labor costs, when they could be identified as Maury did with work on *Boston* and *Lexington*, were equally outrageous. "According to a well-established rule among shipbuilders, the cost proper of labor for building sloops-of-war is about one-half the cost of the materials used ... though the rates here exhibited defy in this, as they do in other respects, all limits of rule or ratio."

To end such abuses, Maury proposed replacing the board with departments: "Must stronger proof be brought against the Navy board, before legislators will perceive that it is at best a piece of marine mistletoe that is exhausting the Treasury and billing the Navy?"[15]

In these articles, the lieutenant wrote while tensions ran high over unsettled boundaries with Canada from the Atlantic to the Pacific. It was also when Mexico disputed thousands of miles of its boundaries with breakaway Texas and the United States. War fever was contagious, and Maury caught it.

Adopting yet another pseudonym, Union Jack, for jingoism, Maury advocated building a naval depot at Memphis: "By the revolution which the powers of steam are effecting in the means of maritime warfare, the Mississippi boatmen will be the navy in the next war, what our Marblehead seamen were in the last." He also wanted a strong military presence at Chicago on the Great Lakes: "We sit quietly and behold England at work on the Lakes. She is erecting fortifications and in violation of a solemn treaty, is strengthening herself there."[16]

With that noted, Maury wrote, "The long line of boundary from the waters of the Mississippi to those of the Pacific is unsettled and is rapidly rising into importance. England is said to have her eyes on the two Californias; but the declaration long since made known to the world, that the United States would not prevent on this continent the future colonization of any European power remains to be tested."[17]

As troublesome as relations with Mexico became, replacing Mexican authority in California with British rule was unacceptable to Americans who believed in the Monroe Doctrine and Manifest Destiny.

Thomas White, the editor/publisher of the *Southern Literary Messenger*, loved the sparks Maury's articles set off, and in May 1840, he journeyed from Richmond to talk personally with the lieutenant. The editor was looking not only for more articles, but also a copy of the *Navy Register*, the roster of officers, to use in an almanac. Whether White secured the register from Maury is not clear, but the fires from the debate in his magazine spread to Washington and the arrival of a new Whig administration.[18]

We need to step back four years from that visit and see Maury now ashore completing his work on navigation. As noted earlier, these were formative years for Maury, then in his early to mid-thirties, politically, as well as personally and professionally. Virginians such as Upshur and Tyler and a former Virginian, William Henry Harrison, were emerging then from the Nullification Crisis to play critical roles nationally. The South Carolina fire-eaters were, for now, dormant volcanoes.

The national political figure key to Maury's future for the next quarter century was Tyler. Tyler's defection from the party of Thomas Jefferson and Andrew Jackson into the Whig Party was marked by a caveat after resigning his Senate seat. He really was not a Whig.[19]

The Oppositionist or Whig Party strategy, if it could be called that, for the 1836 campaign was to offer differing slates of presidential and vice presidential candidates across the nation and even in an individual state. These candidates were believed to have enough local or regional appeal and Electoral College strength to deny Martin Van Buren the presidency.[20]

Although with reduced majorities from Jackson's two campaigns, Van Buren prevailed. His good fortune ended there. If John Quincy Adams had been cursed by machinations in the House of Representatives that had put him in the White House, the "Little Magician" from New York was cursed with financial and economic catastrophe. The Age of Jackson was setting.[21]

As the 1840 campaign developed, Harrison put on a rustic veneer of hard cider and a log cabin in the Old Northwest. The facts were very different. He was born to a wealthy Charles City County family on one of Virginia's most historic plantations, Berkeley—a Tyler neighbor; he was educated at Hampden-Sydney College; and studied medicine in Richmond. His father, Benjamin, as the chairman of the Continental Congress's committee of the whole, introduced the resolution calling for independence, signed the Declaration, and served as Virginia's last Revolutionary War governor.[22]

Despite Harrison's and Tyler's coming from the same Virginia county and having fathers who had governed the commonwealth, to the public the Whigs appeared to have balanced the ticket regionally. "Tippecanoe," as Harrison was called for his battle with the Indians there, evoked the opening of the West to small farmers, not a Virginia plantation with dozens of slaves working tobacco fields.

Going repeatedly to the court house and the post office in Fredericksburg tracking the election was Maury. How and if he voted is not known, but clearly he favored Harrison and Tyler. Maury wrote about Van Buren's victory in Virginia, "Ephraim is joined to his idols, let him alone" in the national Whig landslide. The party had little time to celebrate its victory.[23] A month after the sixty-eight-year-old Harrison delivered a ninety-minute inaugural address without hat and overcoat on a blustery March day, he was dead of pneumonia.

Downing a quick breakfast at his plantation home after learning of Harrison's death, Tyler, now fifty-one, took to his horse. Thus began the "accidental presidency" of John Tyler. The rise of Upshur and the resurrection of Matthew Fontaine Maury's naval career were near.[24]

Tyler had to make his own decision on how to proceed. Even with his split with Jackson over executive power, Tyler knew from his term as governor the severe limitations of having a weak executive. He jettisoned Harrison's notion of running the executive by cabinet consensus. The next move was politically more complex. Tyler also had to ensure that the legislative branch, particularly Henry Clay, whom he admired, understood that he was not an "acting president" bound to Whig Party promises.[25]

When Clay understood that, he was bent on putting Tyler in a position where he could not govern. On September 11, 1841, all cabinet officers except Secretary of State Daniel Webster submitted their resignations. Clay wanted to force Tyler to resign as well, but the president did not take the bait. A four-year scramble over cabinet secretaries and vetoes was on.

Tyler asked George Badger to stay on as Navy secretary to deal with the most pressing issues of expanding the West Indies Squadron and building a Home Squadron to defend Charleston, Norfolk, New York, Boston, and the North Atlantic fisheries. But when the cabinet showdown unfolded, Badger submitted his resignation after seven months in office. That proved a boon for Maury.[26]

In July 1841, Maury's fig leaf of anonymity disappeared when a "Brother Officer" praised the lieutenant as the author of the "Scraps from the Lucky Bag" series: "All the numbers of these productions contained interesting and valuable information. Of great literary merit, they abound in sound suggestions, wonderful developments, and in innumerable evidences of great ability and patriotism." Maury stepped willingly onto the public stage.[27]

Following Badger's departure, the series even produced a boomlet for the lame Maury as secretary of the Navy, a fact noted by Brother Officer and pushed by White at the *Southern Literary Messenger* and the *National Intelligencer*, the leading Whig publication in Washington, and Senator John C. Calhoun. Tyler had his own ideas. He first approached Navy Captain Robert F. Stockton from New Jersey, who declined. Tyler then turned to Upshur.

In shark-infested political waters with almost a whole cabinet to fill, Tyler wanted men he could trust. The newly inaugurated president turned to John C. Spencer, a New York politician and veteran of the War of 1812, to be his secretary of war. With Webster remaining at State to conclude boundary talks with Great Britain, the president had the principal members of a war cabinet in office.[28]

For Maury, his writings helped stave off bouts of anxiety and generated needed income. "My panacea for ennui is the pen," he wrote. During this time, "brother officers" kept him abreast of the Navy's condition, while his New York relatives, Rutson and Mat Maury, fed him information on maritime trade, especially cotton brokering.[29]

Maury's financial worries eased when Ohio Senator Thomas Ewing successfully argued the Virginian's case against the stage coach company. The $2,325 Maury was awarded helped cover the loans he received from his New York relatives and welcome the family's third child, Richard Launcelot, born in October 1840. At the same time, he and Ann also took into their home the widow and two children of Richard B. Maury, the cousin who had treated them so well in Washington.[30]

Despite his growing reputation as a writer, Maury wanted to return to active naval service. He asked to index court-martial proceedings, but the request was rejected. Navy doctors twice examined Maury in 1840, once in Fredericksburg and then in Washington. Although Maury's leg showed improvement, he was granted a $12.50 per month pension retroactive to the time of the accident. While in Washington for the second physical, Maury applied to Secretary James K. Paulding for hydrographic duty, but the secretary, a writer himself, thought Maury, the naval officer, was unfit for the least demanding sea duty. The apostle of reform was beached as the congressional debates on the Navy's ills began.[31]

Throughout his career in Virginia politics, Upshur was even more a marble statue state's rights conservative than Tyler. When he became Navy secretary, Upshur turned the service upside down and inside out.

The Virginian was intent on rebuilding the department, incorporating what he had learned from Maury on promotions and education; Captains Thomas ap Catesby Jones on preparedness; Matthew C. Perry on steam propulsion; Stockton on innovation; Charles Stewart on rank and responsibility; and Marine Colonel Archibald Henderson on the corps' value to the fleet. From them and his brother Lieutenant George Upshur and Captain Beverly Kennon came this chorus: Do away with the Board of Commissioners, increase the size of the fleet, bring on steam, and open up the ranks for promotion of younger, more vigorous officers.

When Van Buren was defeated in 1840, Whigs who supported Harrison peppered the Navy Department for appointments. The Whigs were not immune from "to the winner belongs the spoils" politics of the Jackson and Van Buren administrations. The patronage requests for midshipmen's appointments, coupled with endorsements from heavyweight sponsors such as New York's William Henry Seward, Virginia's Henry Wise, and Webster, became a paper storm that flooded the Navy building and only rose higher when Badger resigned.[32]

In exasperation, Upshur wrote, "If I cannot reform it altogether, I had better return to my life at Vaucluse [his home on Virginia's Eastern Shore]. But I will reform it or else the country shall know that I am not to blame for my failure."[33]

On December 4, 1841, Upshur, in a report to Tyler, cut to the heart of the Navy's problem: "It is in truth, not organized at all.... At present, a multitude of duties are imposed upon the head of the department, which any one of its clerks, could discharge as well as himself, but which, from their pressing nature, he is not permitted to postpone."

With a secretary freed from trivia, Upshur said the civilian head of the service could work "to increase the Navy as rapidly as the means at its disposal will admit." Using trade figures, he claimed, "In proportion, as other countries multiply the means by which they may annoy us, we ought in common prudence, to add to our own defenses, and to our means of resisting insult and injury."

From the Columbia River to Cape Horn, to the Hawaiian Islands, to the whaling grounds off Siberia, Japan, and China, America's Pacific trade was valued at $150 million. It was William Bolton Finch's *Vincennes* report writ large.

To protect that commerce, Upshur's Navy must be able to fight globally: "If these views be not altogether deceptive, the policy of increasing our Navy, without further delays is obvious."

The time for study was best spent on ironclad steam-powered warships. "We may thus acquire a cheap and almost imperishable naval force, while, at the same time, we afford encouragement to some of the most useful branches of our home industry," he wrote. By the end of Tyler's administration, *Mississippi* and *Missouri*, two paddlewheel steamboats, were authorized, as was the iron steam frigate *Michigan*, destined for Great Lakes duty.

Finally, Upshur, like the reformers, wanted to increase the number of naval ranks. Although he did not win approval of the admiral's rank, Congress did increase the number of captains' billets from 55 to 68; commanders from 55 to 96; and lieutenants from 288 to 328.[34]

In 1841, Louis M. Goldsborough, who later served with distinction in the Union Navy, wrote, "I perceive by the papers and by the new secretary's report to Congress that a reorganization of our Navy will, in all probability, take place shortly. God grant it!"[35]

The public's best-known spokesman for naval reform, Maury, remained on the beach. He wrote Upshur's predecessor, Badger, requesting sea duty, while admitting his "crippled condition." A little while later, the officer hoped to serve as Jones's flag lieutenant or chief aide in the Pacific Squadron. Jones told the lieutenant to remain in Fredericksburg until orders arrived. They never did.[36]

Although he was anxious to resume his Navy career, Ann and his friends were not. Led by Judge John Tayloe Lomax, three Fredericksburg physicians secretly wrote Upshur opposing Maury's return to active duty. With the doctors' letter and Lomax's note in one hand and Maury's request in the other, Upshur was on the horns of a dilemma.[37]

The secretary wrote asking Maury what his intentions were now. Although saying he was unaware of the letter or recommendation, Maury responded that he "be relieved from orders to sea."[38]

Now, the naval officer was forced to admit—in writing to a secretary who sought his counsel—that he was unfit for the most important task of his commission, duty at sea in a time of pending war. Admitting defeat publicly, as his father had, was humiliating.

Each sunrise reminded Maury that his leg was not healing quickly. Ashore, he no longer had the option of running the United States Gold Mine. The promise of a writing career was there, but was it a profession lucrative enough to support his family? "Sometimes, I have a notion to take to books and be learned, but then such vast fields and prairies and wastes and seas of unexplored knowledge appear on the horizon. My ignorance sickens at the prospect. I am reminded of how little; very little I do know.... I'll content myself with cultivating a few little patches of knowledge. What shall they be: Shall they be light and heat, storms and currents, ship-building or ship-sailing, steam or trajectiles?"[39]

9. In Washington in a Scientific Post

For all his bombast over New York's commercial dominance, Great Britain's high-handedness in searching American vessels for slaves, and his latest offerings as "Union Jack" on protecting the southern Atlantic coast, Matthew Fontaine Maury's writings on naval reform, his book on navigation, and his recent election as a corresponding member of the National Institution for the Promotion of Science mixed into a cocktail that salvaged his naval career.

Maury's request "to be relieved from orders to sea" did not prove fatal. The Virginians in national power—John Tyler and Abel Parker Upshur—could find a place for one of their own, especially after Upshur began overhauling the Navy Department, a move Maury applauded in the January 1842 issue of the *Southern Literary Messenger.*[1]

At the Tyler administration's request, Congress authorized a reorganization of the department while waiting for another bill to write the regulations dumping the board for five bureaus, answering directly to the secretary. For Maury, the creation of the Bureau of Ordnance and Hydrography offered—from a distance—an avenue to return to active duty. His lecture on trolling the ocean's bottom to produce "useful and new charts" of the American seaboard fit naturally the bureau's mission.

But the volatile Charles Wilkes, commanding the exploring expedition, was technically the man in charge of the Navy's charts and instruments. Indeed, they remained in Wilkes's possession. A hesitant Maury wrote, "I have been often urged to get this place but have invariably declined to take any steps towards it on the ground that it is in Wilkes' house, and the Navy Board being in his interest, I should be *a locein temens* [ocean in fear] till his return."[2]

Maury knew Lieutenant James M. Gilliss, commanding the depot in

Wilkes's absence, was not content with being a caretaker of nautical instruments. With the backing of the "old captains" and Upshur, he lobbied Congress for $25,000 to build a "small observatory." His choice of the word "small" masked the Navy's ambitions to grab the scientific prize of the decade. In that quest, Gilliss saw encouraging signs in an 1841 House report that favored the Navy controlling the observatory.[3]

Gilliss reported, "My aim was higher. It was to place an institution under the management of naval officers, where, in the practical pursuit of the highest known branch of science, they would compel an acknowledgment of abilities hitherto withheld from the service." If the Army had its academy and a firm grip on the nation's major engineering endeavors, naval officers like Gilliss, who was becoming a favorite of the scientifics, and Maury wanted their service's control of any national observatory. It was too important to be left in the hands of the indecisive schoolmen.[4]

The Navy's lusting for the observatory was opposed in and out of the government. For one, Martin Van Buren's Secretary of War Joel Poinsett, who well knew the Navy's penchant for pettiness, thought the National Institute, a forerunner of the Smithsonian Institution, should control it.

In secret talks with Gilliss, Senator W. C. Preston, another South Carolinian, discussed what was to be done with Smithson's bequest, and the observatory surfaced in the conversations. Preston was opposed to using the bequest for an observatory, but wanted the money controlled by the institute. When the legislation was signed, the Navy had a permanent Depot of Charts and Instruments and an observatory. "No one yet considered the naval observatory a national observatory."[5]

Fifty miles from Washington, Maury could only speculate about what was happening in the Capitol. Likewise, Maury also was largely in the dark as to how the necessary final bill covering the expansive naval reform agenda of Tyler and Upshur would fare.

Even without Wilkes lurking offstage, Maury at first spurned the idea of "pulling wires for one's own advancement" to head the Depot of Charts and Instruments. But when he learned the position could be filled by a civilian, Maury wrote, "I will do all I can to prevent it." He sent a coy letter to Upshur, saying if a hydrographical bureau were created he wanted to be considered for a position in it.[6]

Gilliss, surprisingly was not in a much better position than Maury in charting his career. At the very moment that Gilliss aimed for the moon and asked for the stars, Wilkes abruptly brought him and the Navy back to earth. Now in New York after being gone for four years, he told the service to have its equipment and offices out of his Washington residence by the end of June 1842. He needed a place to work on the expedition's findings.

The lieutenant rushed to find temporary lodgings for the depot, which he did at 2422–2424 Pennsylvania Avenue, but this was not enough. He had to keep on scrambling—for a job—because on June 29, 1842, the noticeably limping Matthew Fontaine Maury reported with orders from Upshur to take command.[7]

Exactly why Upshur tapped Maury then remains a guess. The secretary certainly was familiar with the lieutenant's writings. Upshur also knew that Thomas ap Catesby Jones, a man the secretary respected, had requested the admittedly lame officer to serve as his flag lieutenant. The secretary finally had correspondence from Maury saying he wanted to return to active duty. It proved to be the clean sweep of the new broom. The commissioners were going, the bureaus were coming, and so was Maury. To smooth Maury's way in Washington, Upshur sent Gilliss on an overseas shopping mission for the observatory.[8]

With a rival dispatched, in the thick summer's heat, handling the minutiae of a tiny command ashore, Maury was where he wanted to be: on active duty ashore and assigned scientific duties in the nation's capital.

Maury came to his post at the dawn of the American age of exploration. Who knew where "Manifest Destiny" would lead next: All of Mexico or only half? Cuba? Central America? The Amazon basin? These were political questions that Southern navalists like Tyler, John Calhoun, Representative T. Butler King of Georgia, and others pondered, questions that a strong Navy could answer in keeping the British abolitionist lion caged. Maury's writings would crystallize their thinking in protecting slavery.[9]

Upshur, in his 1841 report to the president, and Maury, in his writings in the *Southern Literary Messenger*, agreed wholeheartedly with the original Yankee traders. Trade "ought to feel that it is safe wherever that flag is displayed."[10]

The secretary and the invalided officer drew the same lessons for the Navy closer to home. Until the War with Mexico, the Pacific Northwest Coast from today's Vancouver, British Columbia, to the California border drew increasing attention from presidents and their secretaries of war and the Navy.[11]

Maury's writings then and Upshur's next report were in synchronization over the American future there. In this case they were supported by Secretary of War John Spencer's proposal to build forts from Council Bluffs, Iowa, to the mouth of the Columbia River.

The Treaty of Ghent had ended the War of 1812, but left possession of the Pacific Northwest unsettled. The United States and Great Britain had agreed in 1818 to accept the forty-ninth parallel as the boundary from the Atlantic Coast to the Rocky Mountains. West of that range, the two nations agreed to a ten-year joint occupancy arrangement from the forty-second parallel north.

In fall 1836, Cambridge-bred Nathaniel Wyeth's accounts caused President Andrew Jackson to order William A. Slocum as his personal representative to the Willamette Valley. The president used Slocum's accounts to prod his Navy secretary, Mahlon Dickerson, to have the Wilkes expedition expand its mission from new seal and whale hunting grounds and a far southern continent to survey the south, central, and north Pacific.[12]

The lure of fertile land at little or no cost was sorely tempting to struggling families, adventurers, and political warhorses. By the summer of 1842, the first emigrant wagon train led by Doctor Elijah White set out on the two-thousand-mile journey from Missouri. A few days behind them was John Charles Fremont, who left Washington in May on an Army exploring mission cloaked in secrecy. To his father-in-law, Missouri Senator Thomas Hart Benton, who had steered the appropriation through Congress, it was a mission as important as Lewis and Clark's.

Long a skeptic of the Navy's worldwide ambitions, Benton was committed to opening the West to settlers and their families, but not planters and their slaves. While John Jacob Astor kept the journals of his government-aided explorations secret to ward off competitors in the early nineteenth century, Benton welcomed publicity about Fremont's mission when completed.[13]

With Fremont back in St. Louis, the Missouri senator already turned to a new set of plans for Oregon. The senator needed the Army one more time, and in of all places, Benton found in the Navy's long-delayed exploring expedition the means to his end.

In the Army's Topographical Bureau, Benton found an ally. Reading the political terrain, Colonel John James Abert, the bureau's commander, ordered Fremont "to connect the reconnaissance of 1842 with the surveys of Commander Wilkes on the coast of the Pacific Ocean, so as to give a connected survey of the interior of our continent" and return eastward by the Oregon trail to demonstrate its usefulness. By this order, Abert took the bureau into "activities that ventured far beyond the realm of science into that of national politics." Maury absorbed those critical lessons for himself and the Navy.[14]

Before the Mexican-American War, when a United States warship sailed from the Washington Navy Yard down the Anacostia River to the Potomac, past George Washington's Mount Vernon, and on toward the Chesapeake Bay, the charts the captain used came from the Royal Navy. The Americans had great faith in the accuracy of those charts. They should. The British had used similar ones to sail a battle fleet up the river to take Alexandria and the Patuxent to sack the capital.[15]

The cliché "as safe as an Admiralty chart" rankled Upshur as it did Maury. In 1845, Maury reported, "As yet an American man-of-war cannot enter the Capes of Virginia or approach this city, the capital of the union without applying to the hydrographical office of England for a chart which to shape his course. The only charts of the northern lakes that we have are procured from the English and that through the courtesy of the admiralty office."[16]

By the 1840s the Admiralty's Francis Beaufort with the unflinching support of John Barrow, the long-serving senior civil servant, had reestablished British preeminence in maritime science. With support from the Royal Navy and the Indiamen, Beaufort returned Great Britain to the detailed surveying, comprehensive charting, and daring exploring that marked the age of James Cook and George Vancouver to support Great Britain's worldwide mercantile interests.

The more scientific work in the Royal Navy stopped during the long wars with revolutionary and imperial France and decades of European, Caribbean, and North American blockade duty. Almost fifteen years after Napoleon was exiled to St. Helena, the Royal Navy proceeded dead slowly into the era of Beaufort.[17]

While the duties Beaufort inherited in 1829 were similar to Maury's in Washington, their naval careers were markedly different. Beaufort had commanded a warship against France. He also had minutely charted the Turkish coast, which set the standard for the Royal Navy. Before his appointment, he mixed well in London society, sharing the company of scientists such as Davies Gilbert, the president of the Royal Society, and adventurers such as Sir John Franklin, the arctic explorer. When he was sent to the hydrography office, Beaufort was fifty-five and wrongly presumed on the downside of an honorable career. He was actually beginning a long Indian summer in expanding naval science.[18]

At the Admiralty, Beaufort meshed merchants' needs with an empire's. Along the way, he recorded the changing demands of navigation brought on by steam and added an observatory to his responsibilities. Throughout his tenure, he never lost a chance to use the Royal Navy to explore any spot on the globe in the name of the queen, the empire, trade, and science.[19]

By comparison, Maury had been off active duty recuperating from a stagecoach accident for more than two years when he took charge of the Depot of Charts and Instruments. He was almost twenty years younger than Beaufort when appointed and had never commanded any ship, barely even serving as "first lieutenant." He had done some surveying work along the southern coast of the United States, but was not in charge of the mission nor had he been selected for the more prestigious Coast Survey. Although he published several articles in scientific journals and a book on navigation, Maury was best known for his writings on naval reform. Later, Maury was handed an embryonic observatory and told to build a real one. Like Beaufort, however, he was keenly interested in naval exploration in the name of the republic, Manifest Destiny, commerce, and science.[20]

As Maury settled into his duties, he was ready to go public with the dirty secret of how weak the American charts were, even of its own coasts and tidal waterways. With new charts Maury first directly challenged the Admiralty.[21]

In late 1842, Captain William Crane, the first chief of the Bureau of Ordnance and Hydrography and Maury's immediate superior, ordered ship commanders to send to the depot complete navigational, hydrographic, and meteorological data using an abstract log or template devised by Maury. This was the base on which Maury could build the charts and interpret the old logs.[22]

In a September 1843 letter, Maury wrote Crane for permission to construct a new Atlantic chart:

> When it is considered how little we have done as a nation for navigation—that we at this moment are dependent on a foreign government even for the charts of our lakes and inland seas ... should induce us to publish and make available the errors of latitude and longitude, the existence or non-existence of shoals, etc., along our own sea.[23]

Crane, a combat-seasoned officer, was as eager as Maury to establish the United States Navy as a first-rate service. He offered Maury the civilian James P. Espy, newly appointed professor of mathematics in the Navy, to compile meteorological data to accompany the charts. Espy, known as the "storm king," did not stay long. Speeding his departure were his pending orders to sea, duty he wanted to avoid. His transfer to the Army's meteorological work was approved. Espy's leaving was the first (but not the last) of a civilian scientist from Maury's employ, and among the scientifics it raised questions about his competency to supervise the depot.

Without Espy, the depot launched its meteorological report in the *Army and Navy Chronicle* in January 1843. This was the opening chapter in Maury's most quixotic crusade—the building of a national weather service. It proved a nasty, brutish fight fueled by jealousy and inflamed by Civil War. It ended only when he was in his grave.[24]

Since arriving in Washington, Maury had dug through old logbooks. It was a quest similar to his as an untested sailing master scouring South Street bookstores for information on the South Atlantic, Cape Horn, and the Pacific. Many of the ships' logs were waterlogged or moldy. In others the writing was illegible. The logs covered too many voyages to too many different ports. The fact remained that the data were there, often in minute detail for each section; it needed to be teased out.[25]

As the Seminole War in Florida petered out, Maury's brother-in-law and fellow naval officer William Lewis Herndon arrived for duty at the depot. It made Maury's professional life brighter, if not easier. Because his family was not yet in Washington, their work days started between nine and ten and continued until one and two the next day, working on the logs. The question was how to unlock their secrets as to the fastest and safest routes from port to port.[26]

Sickness compelled his family to stay in Fredericksburg. Ann became seriously ill while pregnant with John Herndon Maury, who was born in October 1842. When she, the children, and his parents came to the capital in the fall, they would only have a short time together. Maury's father, the long-ailing Richard, died on January 30, 1843.

On February 11, he wrote his cousin Ann, "The doctor has said I was destroying myself with over much head work and in consequence I have had to hold up somewhat. But it is a hard case that one's brain will not stand the work of one's will."[27]

The burden did not become lighter as spring arrived. His mother, Diana Minor Maury, died on May 19, 1843. As he did throughout his life, Maury buried his grief in more work and more prayer.[28]

In that summer, the careful choreography of publicity that now marked Maury's endeavors—the letter to Crane, Crane's letter to the fleet, notice by Congress and the press—led to placing the blank charts on Navy ships and selected merchantmen, trolling widely for ever more data. He next asked the National Institute for the Promotion of Science in July 1843 for its support. As expected, the institute, of which Maury was a director, appointed a committee to invite Upshur, an institute member, to order the blank charts put on "all public cruisers" and any merchantmen who would take them.[29]

The *Southern Literary Messenger* reprinted Maury's speech in August:

> Such charts would be to the science of navigation, what that presenting a series of blank squares, and known in the merchant's counting house as the "German music chart" is to observations and facts in magnetism and meteorology.[30]

Despite Maury's and the Navy's push, completed charts were slow in arriving and often poorly done. Maury wrote his mentor, Captain Francis H.

Gregory, that ideally he wanted the tracks and dates of as many vessels as possible, the direction and force of wind daily, temperature of air and water, storm and Gulf Stream current data, position of icebergs and fields of seaweed, boundaries of the Sargasso Sea, suggested spots for lighthouses, and ideas on best routes, as well as corrections of errors in earlier charts. Realistically, he told Gregory, "As much as can be given will be thankfully received though it be simply the track of a vessel."[31]

From the Navy's Home Squadron, responsible for the Atlantic from the Newfoundland Banks to the Amazon, however, Maury directed:

> Each vessel should keep a careful record of the weather, the work performed at the end of each cruise to sea, forward an abstract of it, together with specimens of the soundings to the Navy Department that they may be lodged in the National Institute.[32]

The data were crucial to the accuracy of the Atlantic chart.

Maury's great energy was finally being focused. To him, hydrography was finding the shoals, rocks, and reefs to avoid the shipwrecks of the past. With accurate chronometers, now under his control, to determine longitude and way points, plotting the safe pathways through the seas was probable. Possible was a word, not a sailor's condition. He discarded maritime hearsay for serious study.

Yet, Maury simply told the depot's printers: "The work I have on hand may constitute the entering wedge to a regular systematic publication of charts. If so, there will be a constant employment of engravers."[33]

As yet, he lacked proof of how the charts were better than the Royal Navy's. His encyclopedic knowledge in collecting data was diffusing his intent. He needed to choose one route to study in depth. For now, Maury avoided making that decision, because the Navy was asking him to study the breadth of the heavens, as well as the secrets of the seas. He had bested Gilliss again.

10. The Navy and the Observatory

In Washington, before the leading lights of the nation in 1844, Matthew Fontaine Maury planned to deliver an address that would rank him among the nation's top scientists. It was his most far-reaching grab for attention and acclaim. However he justified the subject in his mind, there were bound to be repercussions with consequences. The address on "the Gulf Stream and Currents of the Sea" certainly caught the attention of Benjamin Franklin's great-grandson, Alexander Dallas Bache. The Philadelphia-born academic studied the Gulf Stream as his family inheritance and in his duties as newly appointed superintendent of the Coast Survey. For a time, Bache remained officially silent.[1]

As his health improved after a winter of illness, Maury tasted the sweetness of the first of the large ceremonial events he came to relish. The evening before the gathering's formal opening, Treasury Secretary John Spencer hosted a large reception for the keynote speaker, Senator Robert Walker of Mississippi; presiding officers of the sessions, including Senator Levi Woodbury of Connecticut and former President John Quincy Adams; presenters such as Maury and Bache, Walker's brother-in-law; and invited attendees in the department's spacious library.

All was not as harmonious as it seemed in the magnificent room. There were undercurrents of scientific jealousy over popularizers and amateurs versus professionals swirling about as rapidly as the political gossip over the annexation of Texas, the future of Oregon, and the coming presidential race. Tight knots of men in tight knots of self-interest and self-serving interest mingled after discussing control of the Smithson bequest.

The jealousy was expressed in asides and by absences. Former Secretary of War Joel Poinsett's drive to co-opt scientific groups into joining with his National Institute stalled when the Association of American Geologists and Naturalists declined to participate. It saw the meeting as an "attempt to upstage the Association or to absorb it completely." They were right on both counts. A number of those scientists stayed away.[2]

But the individual most noticeably absent was the nation's leading physicist, Joseph Henry at Princeton University. Although a member, he was openly skeptical about the institute's scientific value. Henry preferred distance from amateurs and charlatans.[3]

That night, hanging over everyone present was a pall of sadness and disbelief. So many things had been going disastrously wrong during the past few months in the Navy. What a change. Such a short time before, the Navy had appeared to be steaming into a golden age.

The host, Spencer, was a central figure in the story. His eighteen-year-old son, Philip, and two others had been convicted of fomenting mutiny on board training brig *Somers* as it returned from Africa. They had been summarily court-martialed and hanged from the ship's yardarm December 1, 1842, as an example.[4]

Shortly after learning of the executions, James Fenimore Cooper, who had served as a midshipman before the War of 1812 and written a popular history of the Navy in 1839, denounced Captain Alexander Slidell MacKenzie for not giving the accused the chance to testify in their own behalf. That was the spark. The critics had grumbled more loudly when MacKenzie was acquitted on murder charges in the case. Cooper had rushed into print a "Cruise of the *Somers*" pamphlet and his "Elaborate Review" attached to what were claimed to be transcripts of the court-martial.[5]

The pamphlet's popularity added fuel to the fire over the severity of naval discipline. The tragedy ironically rekindled congressional interest in a Naval Academy. A training ship for midshipmen did not adequately prepare them for a naval career. Only a school, an academy, on shore with a defined curriculum could, Maury argued.[6]

If the fallout from the "*Somers* Affair" were not enough trouble for the Navy, the absence at the reception of familiar faces such as former Navy Secretary Abel Parker Upshur and another of president John Tyler's closest friends and his spokesman in the House, Thomas W. Gilmer, was a reminder to many of how lucky they were to be alive.

A little more than a month earlier, many of the attendees had been among the two hundred guests invited aboard *Princeton*, the Navy's newest ship, for a cruise down the Potomac and a demonstration of its powerful twelve-inch guns. When one of the guns, "Peacemaker," exploded on the return upriver, Upshur; Gilmer; Navy Captain Beverly Kennon, chief of the Bureau of Construction; and Tyler's fiancée's father, David Gardiner, were killed instantly, and a score more wounded. Tyler, who had been below deck, escaped injury.[7]

Fingers pointed in every direction. Someone had to answer for this latest tragedy. The Navy was reeling.

In the audience the next day for the first session, elbow to elbow with the scientists, were cabinet members, diplomats, and congressmen on that April 1 to hear Tyler's brief remarks in Washington Presbyterian Church. Maury certainly was pleased when Walker said, "The names of Bache, Maury, Gilliss, Peirce, Lovering, and Bond are well known" in connection with astronomy. The dirty weather clashes with Bache, Henry, and Benjamin Peirce of Harvard over bureaucratic turf, the definition of who was a scientist and who was a charlatan, and personal and professional ethics had not risen to full fury.[8]

At thirty-eight, Maury was a short, balding man, growing stout and limping from a horrendous stagecoach accident. On April 2, like most other days, he pointedly was not wearing a naval uniform. When he came to the platform with Woodbury presiding, Maury delivered an address that flowed like a river to the sea.

Bowing to Franklin, he said:

> The Niagara is an "immense river descending into a plain." But instead of preserving its character in Lake Ontario as a distinct and well defined stream for several hundred miles, it spreads itself out, and its waters are immediately lost in those of the Lake? Why should not the Gulf Stream do the same? It gradually enlarges itself it is true; but instead of mingling with the ocean by broad spreading as the "immense rivers" descending into the Northern Lakes do, its waters, like a stream of oil in the ocean, preserve their distinctive character for more than 3,000 miles.[9]

Before this audience Maury ran with the current. The Gulf Stream demanded study not bound by bureaucratic lines between the Coast Survey and the Navy.

Bache's turn came the next day with Spencer, the cabinet member he answered to, presiding. The difference between Maury's tone and Bache's "On the Condition of Science in the United States and Europe" was profound. Maury wanted color and excitement with a call to action. Bache wanted proven facts and detachment.[10]

Henry wrote Bache, "What is to be done with the mass of diluvium which the Institute has drawn down on itself in an avalanche of pseudo-science?"[11]

At this time, the way public men's addresses were disseminated was through the press. As a writer, the Navy lieutenant well understood the process.

Once appearing in a publication, Maury created a ripple effect of widening interest as more newspapers or periodicals reprinted his speeches. Each reprinting gave the speechmaker another audience. If interest was great enough, these speeches were published as a pamphlet. The pamphlet might be printed as a memorial or petition in the *Congressional Globe.* In that way, public opinion was being shaped for legislative action. The lieutenant wanted action.

In May, Maury was back on a public stage, speaking before the independent-minded Association of American Geologists and Naturalists. The astronomer John Locke of Cincinnati, a former Navy surgeon and the inventor of a clock that was a major improvement over chronometers, sat in the chair. One of the secretaries was the younger Benjamin Silliman, following in his father's footsteps by editing the United States' most prestigious scientific journal. There, Maury said the Navy was ready to lead the way in gathering weather data from the land and the sea. Why wait? Some scientists bristled over Maury's claim on land meteorology. They cursed it as Navy empire building

Maury was delighted to be named to an association committee that, at his behest, asked, "All our cruisers, not only in the Atlantic, but in every sea, may be instructed to make and record observations as well upon the interesting phenomena." The petition's scope suited the lieutenant's ambitions. In studying the seas, Maury's tastes were always catholic, not parochial.[12]

The lieutenant's satisfaction over the association's endorsement was tempered by the reception its members gave his Number-One nemesis in the Navy, Charles Wilkes. He invited the group to the grand hall of the Patent Office to view the collections of the Exploring Expedition. Wilkes had learned an important lesson in dealing with a scientific audience. Two years before, a writer for the *Southern Literary Messenger* had lampooned the boring nature of his address to the National Institute. The writer, possibly Maury, who was a regular contributor, added, "From that time [the writer] distrusted [Wilkes's] ability to do justice to the work entrusted to him."

The savaging in the *Southern Literary Messenger* fit a pattern in the Tyler administration to diminish Wilkes's achievement. The political reasons for the cold shoulder were obvious. A Democratic administration had launched the expedition. It returned to "an intensely partisan atmosphere in which a Whig Congress battled an outcast Whig president." Who had time for the abrasive Wilkes?[13]

This time when Wilkes was through presenting his paper with illustrations on Antarctic ice, he invited the civilian scientists to his residence, the dwelling he had curtly told the Navy's Depot of Charts and Instruments to vacate. There, the geologists, among the very people Wilkes had tried to keep under control on the expedition, marveled at "the drawings of the artists and naturalists in the various departments of science, as well as of national costume and scenery." Maury likely was fuming.[14]

Maury's opinion shaping continued when the *Army and Navy Chronicle* reprinted his address in its May 23 issue. The *National Intelligencer* printed the association's proceedings. Of course, Silliman's *Journal*, where Maury had first published, printed the proceedings and major addresses like Maury's.[15]

As fulfilling as these spring days were for Maury, the *Somers* mutiny and the explosion aboard the *Princeton* were the most visible manifestations of the new crisis in civilian leadership facing the service. The crisis could be traced to Tyler's decision to move Upshur from the Navy Department to State when Daniel Webster had resigned.[16]

The week before the National Institute's 1844 meeting, John Young Mason, a federal judge in Virginia and a former chairman of the House Naval Affairs Committee, was confirmed as Navy secretary. Mason, the fourth man to hold the office since Maury had returned to active duty in 1842, had to replace Kennon and get the Navy back on its feet. He chose Charles Morris, regarded as one of the Navy's intellectual leaders.[17]

By the time Mason was in place, he found Captain Robert F. Stockton blaming John Ericsson, the man primarily responsible for the ship's design, its propulsion system, and the gun that didn't explode, for the disaster. He succeeded in blocking any payment to the Swede. Not to be outdone, Mason's old committee, House Naval Affairs, blocked spending on any follow-on Stockton vessels. For Congress, the Navy's internal review had not passed muster.

While not addressing the disaster directly, Mason ordered two officers to Britain and France to study ordnance in those navies. By spring 1845, a four-member board of senior captains recommended the Navy designate a frigate to train crews in safe handling of ammunition and establish uniform procedures of drill and have practice batteries ashore. To lock these in place, Lieutenant John Dahlgren was put in charge of all ordnance work at the Washington Navy Yard.[18]

Mason refused to retreat on Upshur's other areas of experimentation. He ordered Stockton to command a squadron in the Mediterranean. On the way to the station, he was to stop in Liverpool and take on the replacement for the Peacemaker that Stockton had ordered after the explosion.

In his first month as secretary, Mason brought Samuel Colt to the capital to demonstrate his "submarine battery" in the Anacostia River. (The experiment will be discussed in more detail in Chapter 16.) Finally, Mason, knowing Tyler's term was ending, wanted detailed reports on mines other than Colt's and the state of diving bells for harbor defense. A renewed sense of urgency rippled across the Navy.[19]

The story was different on Capitol Hill. By 1844, the Senate and the House had declared their interest in "retrenchment," bringing the federal government back to the first constitutional principles and cutting federal spending. For example, in the Naval Appropriations Act for the 1845 fiscal year, Congress set a manpower cap on the Navy to hold down costs. Mason struggled against the tide throughout his tenure.[20]

Astronomy in the mid–1840s was the growth science. Nations committed ever more resources to astronomical studies to satisfy expanding maritime commerce needs. Mariners needed fixed, accurate observations from land to know where they were on the seas. As important as astronomy was to the European great powers, the United States lagged far behind. There were only seven observatories in the United States.[21]

Talk about tapping a civilian to lead the Washington observatory was drowned out as the service's supporters battered Congress over the Navy's vital interests in astronomy. Before a decision was made over control of the observatory, there was jockeying for position inside the Navy. James Gilliss and Maury were the leading candidates for its superintendency.

Each had his strong points. Gilliss was more familiar with current astronomical work and had headed the Depot of Charts and Instruments. Maury had studied astronomy for the exploring expedition and was experienced in mathematics and hydrography. In addition, he was pushing the Navy to "Americanize" its charts, measure the Gulf Stream, and study the weather—part of the observatory's broad charter. Gilliss became the favorite among America's top scientists and many in the Navy. In September, an omen of how the wind was blowing came when Mason selected Maury's book on navigation as a standard text for midshipmen.[22]

When the secretary officially named Maury superintendent on October 1, neither could foresee the fortress the lieutenant would build on the seventeen-acre tract. Over the next seventeen years, inside those grounds on Twenty-Third Street between D and E Streets Northwest, Maury revolutionized maritime travel, led the charge for American naval exploration, and discovered "the key" to laying the transatlantic telegraph cable.

The observatory was the stage Maury used in carving out his unique profession of naval officer and scientist. He strutted about that stage—not as a crippled man—but as a proud and prickly man who bent everything to his profession. Maury, in his time, was seen in the same way as Hyman Rickover in the twentieth century. Both men's influence far transcended the Navy.[23]

The short walk the halt Maury took that day from the Depot of Charts and Instruments on Pennsylvania Avenue down Twenty-Third Street was the true beginning of a career that made him the sought-after and envied "Man on the Hill."[24]

From the outside and to outsiders that fall, the observatory was a handsome, if incomplete, structure. In the center was the dome, ready to scan the skies. Directly under the dome was a circular room with corridors leading into it from the east and west wings. To the south was another work area. To the north was the main entrance. Underground, but connected by a passageway to the main building, was a room to study magnetism.[25]

On October 8, 1844, Maury found as soon as he opened the door to the observatory that paint was sorely needed on the inside, and so was furniture and carpeting. Not even oil lamps, candlesticks, spittoons, washstands, and pitchers could be found on the Camp Hill site.[26]

If any work was to be done that fall, pens and inkstands had to be bought. If any work was to be done in the winter, a supply of coal had to be laid in.

"Bending all to my profession" then meant cleaning construction debris, buying elementary equipment, and assigning space for astronomy, hydrography, meteorology, and the charts and instruments being brought from Pennsylvania Avenue.[27]

For all, it was hop to from day one. "The top sides of the galleries consist of plank covered with earth, the dampness of the place and the want of free ventilation already show marks of decay and indicate that its progress in the wood ... will be sure and rapid.... Such a place cannot fail to be also extremely prejudicial to the health of the officers engaged in conducting these observations." His solution was to rebuild with stone or brick.[28]

Not only did he have to contend with a new building, a new mission, and a small staff, Maury also had to work with local officials in keeping the curious away.

Inside, Maury found he faced a far more serious problem than a curious public. Gilliss had followed custom in using cement made of sulfur to hold the metal stanchions of the astronomical instruments in their stone bases, but as the moist air from the Potomac marshes rose, the sulfur became corrosive. Now the instruments had to be dismounted and cleaned before they could, if ever, be used. It was a major setback.[29]

He then and always wanted a larger staff: "With the use of these instruments and a small increase in force which is already so beneficially employed here, much may be done that would prove itself not only useful and important to the Navy but would then in no small degree wipe away that which has been so often cast upon the country on account of the meagerness of its contribution to the general fund of nautical science." The plea went unanswered.[30]

Unlike the Congress, economy and retrenchment were not on Mason's agenda: they were not nouns in Maury's dictionary. He had an observatory and a name for himself as a scientific leader to build. Each season in those early years brought a new set of problems. During the winter, the basement furnace emitted gases, disrupting operations. After pondering the problem, Maury proposed heating the observatory by hot water. To do this, he added an outbuilding and pumped the heat back inside. His practical and innovative proposal was accepted, and the work was done for eight hundred dollars.[31]

With the weather warming, dust from outside construction became an irritant inside. Maury ordered the grounds sodded for one thousand dollars. By the summer, the twin miseries of mosquitoes and wispy fogs from the tidal marshes engulfed the grounds. Of these, he could only complain.[32]

Even if joint astronomical research on differences in longitude had to be delayed with Benjamin Peirce, the Harvard mathematician, and F. A. P. Barnard at the University of Alabama, he looked for other avenues of cooperation. In February 1845, he told the Royal Society that naval vessels must become "floating observatories" in continuing magnetic research to save sailors' lives.

This was especially true in the Polar Regions, where the magnetic poles differed from the geographic. "How many cases of shipwreck and disaster, ascribed to the effect of unknown drifts and currents, have been owing rather to false needles and misguiding compasses. Of British shipping 800 sailors [ships] and American 300, not to mention those of other nations are, it is roughly estimated annually lost at sea, and the number of human beings that perish in them cannot be told except by thousands."[33]

To reinforce his point, Maury urged insurance underwriters to demand that ship owners use the best available compasses. This trifling expense would be more than repaid as more ships arrived safely in port. What he said not only made sense but money. The underwriters joined Maury's chorus.[34]

In spring 1845, the superintendent received important backing to continue the observatory's study of magnetism when John Quincy Adams, then a congressman, explained its value to the recently appointed Navy secretary and fellow Massachusetts politician, George Bancroft. Although the former president felt snookered in having the Navy control the observatory, he was generally pleased with what he saw when he met Maury there. On parting, Adams asked to return to "look through the large refractor at the nebula in the sword of Orion."[35]

Fortunately, repairs were far enough along to let Adams have his view through the Equitorial, the most powerful telescope. Maury showed the seventy-eight-year-old congressman how each instrument was placed, explaining why they were placed where, and his plan to have two men at each instrument to make observations throughout the night. The hiatus that he had mentioned to Peirce and Barnard on astronomical work was over.[36]

As he spent more time as principal observer, Maury became more confident in his ability to teach others what must be done. As he had done as a teenager in Tennessee and a midshipman at sea, Maury threw himself into concentrated study. He pored over the writings of Friedrich George Wilhelm von Struve, director of the Russian observatory, and John and Sir William Herschel of Great Britain. As a recruiter, he wanted the best men in and out of the Navy for his staff. He approached William Bond of Dorchester, a maker of chronometers, about joining, but he did not want to leave Massachusetts. He did win over Joseph S. Hubbard of Harvard and added Ruel Keith to provide the necessary continuity in the observatory's work. His staff then consisted of three naval lieutenants, six passed midshipmen, and two civilian professors of mathematics. It would only grow incrementally over the years.[37]

For all his enthusiasm, Maury was never easy to work for. He pushed himself hard professionally and expected the same devotion to work—duty—that he had shown. He had demonstrated that when he had driven the staff of the Depot of Charts and Instruments relentlessly to unlock the secrets of the world's oceans. He did not let up at the observatory: "I know of no place in the navy either ashore or afloat where the duties are more arduous than those of the officers employed here. It is all hands every day, and watch and watch every clear night." He was becoming more like his father, sometimes harsh and usually demanding.[38]

While Maury's enthusiasm was infectious in official Washington, some astronomers, notably Peirce at Harvard, harbored grave misgivings about the naval officer's ability to establish the observatory on a sound scientific footing. He and Princeton's Henry wanted "an extended and uninterrupted program of observations" for the benefit of all astronomers and not simply the Navy.

The questions over who should be in charge of the observatory rose again like the wind in a new storm. And from that question, others followed. Had naval discipline driven James Espy away? Was the charter too broad in trying to make the observatory a center for research in too many of the physical sciences?[39]

Maury didn't want their questions or advice. The observatory was to "be out and out a Navy work." The critics did not understand the sea service's need to control the observatory. Inside the Navy, he sold a grandiose celestial scheme of cataloging 1,200 stars. "The intention is to make a contribution to astronomy worthy of the nation and the age, and so to execute the undertaking, that future astronomers in all time may say of it, such a star was not visible in the heavens at the date of the Washington Catalogue, because it is not there, and such a star that is now missing, was in the heavens because it is in that work."[40]

Like secretaries before him, Bancroft, whose tenure is most remembered for establishing the Naval Academy, copied Maury's words and ordered him to proceed. Maury branded the whispering campaign among civilian scientists about his competency as "the repetition of a practical libel."[41]

Maury's luck held. In December reports from Berlin and Rome reached the observatory that after twenty years Biela's Comet had been seen, and the observers in Washington now had something definite to search for on their nightly duties. As he scanned the sky on January 13, 1846, Maury witnessed the inconceivable. As the comet reached the point of least distance from the sun, it split in two. With relish, Maury rushed an article on his observations to the *Royal Astronomical Society Monthly.* Following on the heels of that, he published *The Astronomical Observations Made During the Year 1845 at the National Observatory under the direction of M. F. Maury, Lieutenant, United States Navy, Superintendent.*[42]

"We have beat Greenwich all hollow, there is not doubt; yet we shall do even better next time.... I have solved a problem that has often blistered my heart and proven that Navy officers are fit for something else than scrubbing decks at sea and tacking ships."[43]

As triumphant as 1845 was for Maury and the observatory, the pending war with Mexico drained away staff for all its projects. It pointedly reminded Maury that even with two decades of naval service he held low rank in a shore billet.

This was the war that should have been Maury's Barbary Coast, the Atlantic and Caribbean raids against pirates, and sea battles of the Revolution and the War of 1812. If service at sea was the sure way to promotion, then service at sea in a time of war was the sailing direction to higher honor among peers and greater acclaim from the public. He was of the age. He was of the experience. It was not to be. Like Charles Wilkes, completing the narrative of the exploring expedition, and John Dahlgren, toiling over naval ordnance, Maury remained ashore far from any action and far from command at sea. To his dying day, he believed that as crippled as he was, he could command a warship in combat.[44]

Yet, as his children remembered, Maury was an optimistic man and loving father even then. Once the family settled into life on the grounds in the superintendent's house, he greeted each morning by throwing open the shutters, and saying, "Let us let in the blessed light of the day."[45]

He followed the Bible's precept in his children's education. Maury's family life showed no separation between education and religion in the classroom, pew, or home. He began his children's lessons at the breakfast table. In Washington and later in England, he employed J. M. D. Meiklejohn, a Scotsman recommended to him by the head of the Royal Society, to educate his sons. This was not an age in the District of Columbia or in Virginia when free, public education for the youngest children was a priority. The hired tutor and the private academy for those who could afford them were as common in the mid-nineteenth century as they were when the Rev. James Maury had opened his school in Albemarle County a century before.[46]

He wrote, "As a general rule, I regard colleges, as at present conducted, as humbugs, and female seminaries as downright cheats." Years later in London, his first order of business was to arrange for his daughters' education. In raising his children, Maury rewarded energy, enthusiasm, and eagerness to learn. He punished indolence and skylarking.[47]

During the afternoons, when the brood was small, Maury took them on romps around the grounds, sometimes using his "Tennessee arm"—a pole on a crutch—to snatch a leaf for their examination, explaining nature and the divine plan. With the youngest, he let them pull on the ribbons of a Japanese dressing gown he wore—a gift from his friend Marin Jansen of the Dutch navy, as he led them around the superintendent's quarters. He was playing with them and teaching them about the places he visited and people he met. It was a device that he used near the end of his life as his family's fortunes were sinking in exile.[48]

In his geographies, started after the Civil War, Maury again talked to children, this time by the thousands, filling their lives as he had filled his children's with stories of distant lands. The slogans of Maury's life, *cur non* (Why not?) and *cui bono* (To whose benefit?), were particularly evident in his writings for children and his interest in education.

But Maury was a serious man, and he flashed that side of himself even to his children. Had not he as a boy begged his father for a chance at an education at Harpeth Academy? Had not he as an adolescent plotted to further his education at the Military Academy? Had not he spent hours at sea studying? He wanted them to be serious as well.

To make that point, Maury once burned a borrowed novel in front of his children's eyes. "Novel-reading is, to the student, what mint-juleps are to the tippler—most delightful and refreshing at the time, but serpents under the flowers at the end."[49]

Maury wanted his children not to think him "too severe," the judgment he had of his father. In the children's written accounts, they did not. The "too severe" epithet, however, was the judgment of Maury held by many men, especially civilians, who worked for him. The questions that Harvard's Peirce and others raised about Maury as a man, the Navy's often harsh discipline, and their roles in science were cudgels in the fight that bludgeoned American science before the Civil War.

11. A Most Uncivil War

Matthew Fontaine Maury did not need to be a weatherman to see the war clouds burst into a storm in April 1846. For months, he had beat war drums in the *Southern Literary Messenger* and the *Southern Quarterly*. He trumpeted confidence in the Navy as ready for a two-ocean conflict, be it against Great Britain over the Pacific Northwest and Alta California or Mexico over Texas and the New Mexico Territory and California.

He wanted command at sea.

There was the legacy of his brother John, who had fought the British in the Pacific and the Great Lakes and died chasing pirates in the Caribbean. One of John's sons, Dabney, whom Maury treated like his own, was to receive his commission from the Military Academy.

With his keen interest in public affairs and his proximity to the White House and the Capitol, Maury followed events in Texas, Mexico, and the Pacific Coast intently. Over a decade, he had come to know many of the era's leading political figures in a time of brinksmanship. A short while before Abel Parker Upshur, then Navy secretary, and his close political ally, President John Tyler, had saved Maury's naval career. Then-Senator John C. Calhoun, whose states rights' philosophy coursed through Upshur's veins, had recommended Maury as Navy secretary to Tyler. John Y. Mason, a former Virginia jurist but twice secretary of the Navy, championed Maury's wide-ranging scientific efforts at the newly founded observatory.

As noted earlier, Maury's family roots in Tennessee were a factor in his career from its start. There was Sam Houston and John Bell, as well as Thomas Hart Benton. Added to that list was President James K. Polk, who had served in Congress with Maury's cousin Abram and attended the University of North Carolina with Mason.

There were also two Massachusetts politicians playing key roles in Maury's career during this time. In his inaugural address, John Quincy Adams had called for a great naval exploring expedition and a national observatory. Democrat George Bancroft came into the Polk cabinet as Navy secretary; during his relatively short tenure Bancroft brought the Naval Academy into existence—a central point in Maury's writings on naval reform. The politicians used Maury for their ends, and Maury used them for his.

While offering his services in combat, Maury apparently did not pull any strings to win a ship's command. He had shown this hesitancy before in not pushing himself forward to command the Exploring Expedition.

When the Senate defeated the treaty between the United States and Texas Republic bringing it into the Union, Tyler and Calhoun, his secretary of state, adopted a course of action that almost guaranteed war with Mexico. "Stubborn, proud, and unpredictable," Tyler proposed annexing the republic with its consent to the United States. Instead of the two-thirds majority in the Senate needed for treaty ratification, Tyler needed simple majorities in both houses of Congress to approve the measure.[1]

That was how matters stood in the capitals of both North American republics as the presidential campaign of 1844 ended with Polk's victory. Like William Henry Harrison, Polk pledged to serve a single, four-year term. Without children and with a politically astute wife, Polk, whose industriousness could put Maury to shame, came into office determined to replace the protective tariff of 1842, establish an independent treasury, settle the Oregon boundary question with Great Britain, complete the annexation of Texas, and buy California. On Oregon, Texas, and California, Maury could have hewn the planks of the incoming administration's platform himself.

Texas was the more vexing question sectionally. From 1843 on, Adams, once an expansionist secretary of state, had damned the annexation and the spread of slavery for extending slavery. While many Whigs agreed with him, their mouths were usually closed in Congress when any petition concerning slavery arrived. Their muddle extended to the presidential campaign of 1844, when Henry Clay flip-flopped on rejecting annexation.

For years, Democratic representatives from the slaveholding states countered that Texas was a necessary "safety valve" against another murderous rebellion, like Nat Turner's. The expansion of slavery "safety valves" became constants in Maury's published work, including writings on Cuba, a slaveholding colony of Spain; Brazil, a slaveholding South American empire; and Mexico, where slavery had been abolished.

Trying to calm troubled waters, Mississippi Senator Robert Walker, Alexander Dallas Bache's brother-in-law, said in a "we're-all-in-it-together" speech that "Texas is but a part of the Mississippi Valley of which New York may be considered the head. The United States should possess the whole of this teeming region."[2]

With only a few days remaining in office, Tyler signed the resolution with a flourish and handed the gold pen to his young wife, Julia Gardiner Tyler, an enthusiastic expansionist. While Democrats expected Tyler to allow Polk the next move, the sitting president acted. He dispatched an envoy to Texas President Anson Jones with a copy of the resolution. It was Texas's turn to act.[3]

After his inauguration, Polk bought time by sending another rider with orders for the envoy to stop in place. Next, at a cabinet meeting, he stressed the point that delay played more and more into the hands of the British and French, who eyed Texas for themselves. With the Monroe Doctrine as a club and the promises of the winning campaign as a mace, he came away with its consensus to bring Texas into the Union. By March 10, Polk had the envoy on the road to Texas. Mexico had severed diplomatic relations with the United States four days earlier.[4]

The small coterie of Army and Navy officers in Washington, like Maury, wondered what was to happen next. Rumor and speculation had more currency than the few known facts. What passed among them was not idle gossip, no matter how speculative the talk. If war was to come, their lives and careers were on the line. Although holding out for diplomacy, Navy Secretary George Bancroft moved in spring 1845 to have the Home and Pacific Squadrons in place to "afford due protection to American property and persons and resist or punish any aggression of our rights."[5]

On July 4, 1845, the Texas Convention accepted annexation with the only dissenting vote being cast by Alexander Dallas Bache's father, Richard. Polk had the War Department order Colonel Zachary Taylor to move four thousand troops, half of the American Army, from Louisiana into Texas. He was to put the "army of occupation," as it was called, close to the disputed border to repulse any Mexican invasion. By late December, Texas was in the Union. In May, Taylor reported that fighting had begun.[6]

Polk cast aside any concerns that "all the powers of Christendom" would intervene in a United States war with Mexico. Like Maury in the *Southern Literary Messenger*, but with far more consequences for the nation, Polk told James Buchanan, his secretary of state, that "neither as a citizen nor as President would I permit or tolerate any intermeddling of any European Power on this Continent." Congress declared war.[7]

As reports of the fighting in Texas, Mexico, and California trickled into New Orleans and then sped like lightning over telegraph wires to the capital, the press created new heroes. The stories celebrated regular Army officers like Robert E. Lee and commanders of volunteers like Jefferson Davis for their exploits under fire. For a time, it was "a grand little war."

The Navy's contributions were more behind the scenes: sending landing parties ashore, raiding coastal installations, covering an amphibious assault, transporting troops, and blockading the Mexican coast. It was not the stuff of sagas. But for the generation of officers who rose to command in the war, like Matthew C. Perry, who succeeded Captain David Conner, it was a time to demonstrate their mastery of steam and skill at sail in combat. Perry and W. Branford Shubrick, his equally successful Pacific Coast counterpart, were masters of the new naval arts.[8]

The Navy's efforts were dramatic in the view of at least one junior Army officer, Dabney Maury. The lieutenant was part of a ten thousand-man invasion force off Veracruz. About him were "steam warships, troop transports, old three-decked ships-of-the-line, small packet steamers"—one hundred vessels in all—that filled the harbor.

Dabney Maury described the attack of the fifty specially designed broad-beamed and double-ended "surfboats," each carrying between fifty and sixty soldiers under their regimental colors, as "a glorious sight."[9]

Yet the easy victory so many Americans expected proved illusory. The Mexican army, larger than the American, offered determined resistance. Complicating matters for Taylor and Winfield Scott, guerrilla bands attacked extended supply lines and ambushed scouting patrols and squads and platoons separated from the main American columns. All the while sickness and disease took their toll on the invaders. War weariness set in.

Although Maury loved public attention for what he did, he never claimed a war record he had not earned. To his chagrin, Maury had his name added to the Mexican War pantheon of military figures and political powers in a book by Sarah Mytton Maury, an English in-law married to one of the Old Consul's sons.

> He is a man of science, equally well versed in the secrets of the sea and of the sky; an accomplished mariner, an admirable astronomer and mathematician and a superior author on many subjects; he writes excellent English.

"He is a great favourite with his brother officers, both for his ability and his kindly nature," she added. Despite his injury, she wrote, he "would instantly seize the boarding pike and cutlass and leap to the oar."

Although she now lived in Fredericksburg, Polk called her "a gossiping woman of a Foreign Country." Maury's critics, especially outside the Navy, had new fodder for their low views. The reality was that Maury's junior officers—younger and more able-bodied, like his brother-in-law William Lewis Herndon and the son of John Maury's former commander, David Dixon Porter—were being pulled from the observatory. They were not to be replaced soon.[10]

For whatever reason, the Navy's highest levels did not see Maury as leading a boarding party, commanding *Princeton*, *Mississippi*, or *Ohio* on blockade duty, seizing California, or securing Veracruz. They had chosen him to keep the young observatory producing. Maury more than ever needed civilian scientists to fill the gaps of staff. In early 1846, he was sent Sears C. Walker from the Central High School Observatory in Philadelphia, an institution once headed by Bache.

While in Philadelphia, Walker, a tempestuous and troubled man, had trained Joseph Hubbard, one of the civilian observers Maury credited in the observatory's astronomical publication the year before.[11]

Although deeply interested in science and mathematics, Maury was a naval officer, although rarely wearing his Navy uniform, and expected those working for him to follow orders as he had: unquestioningly. That lesson was drilled into him when he had first boarded *Brandywine*. Maury did not see how this approach flew in the face of his own restiveness over the by-the-book training the Navy called its midshipmen's education. He certainly did not grasp how this "follow orders" directive affected many civilians, especially headstrong ones like the Harvard graduate Walker.

Walker came to the observatory with his own baggage. By 1845, certain "commercial operations turned out disastrously and [left him] entirely bereft of means," historian William Jay Youmans noted. "The sense of defeat, the loss of luxuries at a time of life when habits have become fixed [Walker was forty then], together with anxiety for the future made the blow a hard one." In hindsight, the grating of the temperaments of Walker and Maury made an explosion inevitable. In a nation on the edge of war, with one serious man out of work and seemingly immediate prospects and another serious man knowing he was losing uniformed observers and directing an institution with a growing scientific and expanded military mission, their union at the observatory seemed preordained. It also seemed doomed.[12]

Early on, Walker's dual role at the observatory and as a paid Bache consultant benefited the observatory and the survey. They were cooperating in late 1846 in a venture using electric telegraph signals to determine fixed points in the United States, and Walker was one its leaders. The first successful tests were between the observatory and Central High School.[13]

Cooperation made sense in other ways as well. Maury had the astronomical equipment and trained observers, plus a prime location. Bache had money, the coastal longitude mission, and the survey's experience with precision instruments. There was no need for Bache to raise the character issue with Walker inside the observatory producing solid scientific work.[14]

On February 28, 1846, Maury gave Walker charge of the Equitorial "for the present." The lieutenant wanted the astronomer "to prepare for a regular series of observations upon double stars, clusters, nebulae and lunar occultations. The occultations will extend no farther than to stars of the sixth magnitude.... The observations of double and (multiple) stars will embrace, angle of position, color, magnitude, appearance and distance."[15]

Then, Maury, as with a midshipman, gave more minute instructions: "Angle of position will be recorded ... according to the quadrants always the larger star as the angular point ... exacting detailed as if writing to an untrained observer." Walker, who carried the title of assistant astronomer, bristled, but, being fresh to the job, did as he was told.[16]

In the fall, Maury gave Walker orders to study the newly discovered planet Neptune. Claims for the discovery were being made by Urbain Jean Joseph Le Verrier in Paris and Couch Adams at Cambridge University. To test the claims, Maury devised a mathematical model that might find an earlier discovery in the same area but one misidentified as a star. If correct, Maury would be advancing astronomical science and silencing his critics at the same time.

Whatever faults lay in Walker's personality, performing science was not one. On February 2, 1847, he found after much digging that Joseph Jérôme Lefrançois de Lalande in Paris had indeed catalogued findings on May 8 and May 10, 1795, in the same position but cited them as that of a fixed star. Hubbard confirmed Walker's work. The Europeans and Benjamin Peirce at Harvard were pursuing the same line of inquiry, so the race to publish the finding was furious.[17]

As Maury wrote John Y. Mason, back in office after Bancroft became the United States minister to Great Britain:

> A mathematical planet it certainly is, for it is the discovery of mathematics and has severed the ordinary rules: hitherto the telescope with its space penetrating power has discovered the planets and then referred them to mathematics, but in this case mathematics, a space penetrating power which has astonished the world, has taken the lead.[18]

Unlike Hubbard's and other scientists' in the astronomical publication of 1845, Walker's contributions and role went unmentioned. No matter how great the triumph was for the observatory, relations between the civilian scientist and the military superintendent were beyond repair. Within a month, Walker quit under pressure. As the lieutenant wrote mathematician Elias Loomis, Walker was "unwilling to comply with the rules of the office, as the officers do.... Mr. W., moreover, was a much better computer than observer; he could compute day in and day out but our night observations would knock him out."[19]

Maury then abruptly canceled the joint program on longitude. He claimed it "comes eminently under the province of the observatory." Poaching and turf protection were the order of the day. In retaliation and disregarding Congress's barring the survey from having an observatory, Bache established Seaton Station to continue the longitude project.[20] Tit for tat.

Maury vastly underestimated the effect of Walker's ouster in the larger scientific community, especially through his ties with Bache and Joseph Henry, soon to direct the Smithsonian Institution, and through his Harvard ties with Peirce.[21]

Here was the military discipline, especially naval discipline, canard personified in the handling of one middle-aged man with "special gifts." Here, too, in the same middle-aged man, was fresh fuel for a smoldering scientific and bureaucratic feud.

Walker found sanctuary with Bache. Fittingly, his new sinecure was directing the survey's longitude department. With Bache's encouragement, he went to Henry. What was important about the meeting was the material Walker brought along: an abstract of all his work at the observatory, including the hottest topic in astronomy—Neptune—and a major problem.[22]

The problem that Walker brought with him was more than anger at Maury; it was a matter of law. From the start, Congress said the observatory's work was to remain in its custody and under its control. This included the papers Walker had and any publication of those papers. He apparently did not care what the observatory's charter said. Walker wanted his "intense and unremitting" work recognized, and there were few better places to obtain this recognition than in prestigious international journals. Henry was in the ideal position to facilitate the publication of Walker's work and the observatory's findings.[23]

In late May 1847, Henry wrote Heinrich C. Schumacher, the editor of the *Astromische Nachrichten*, published in Altona, Germany, concerning Walker's work. Receiving such a letter was a tantalizing dessert to academics, and having Walker's observations come with it was an indescribable delicacy. Both Henry's letter and Walker's Neptune notes were printed in the journal.

"A memoir containing a full account of the investigation will be published in the course of the year in the *Transactions of the Smithsonian Institution* but as everything connected with the new planet is of special interest at the present time, this abstract may not be thought unacceptable to the readers of your valuable Journal," Henry wrote.

When Maury read Henry's letter preceding Walker's article, he was stunned. He first thought Henry's signature a forgery and said so in a letter to the secretary. Then Maury felt betrayed. How could Henry think of sending Walker's work to be published in a foreign country? What about the mutual pledges of support Henry and he had exchanged? What was the meaning of the sentence that the Smithsonian intended to publish Walker's work as well?

The lieutenant would not let the matter lie within the pages of a German astronomical journal and one letter to Henry. The poaching on the Coast Survey's mission, the Navy's winning control of the observatory, and Maury's appointment to head it were skirmishes. This was the flashpoint of the war that consumed American science for fifteen years. Maury was incensed that his celestial domain had been violated.[24]

Henry, normally a shy man, replied that he found Maury's first letter "unpleasant" and wanted to know "explicitly" what the complaint entailed.

On October 20, 1847, Maury fired back:

> I was unwilling to believe that your name had been printed from a genuine signation, because it was attached to articles in print which do myself and the observatory grievous wrong; articles which represent you as uniting with a disaffected subordinate of the observatory to injure it in the public estimation; as lending him the influence of your official character and position to appropriate without proper acknowledgment to the observatory its own labors.

Henry replied that he had "done no intentional or unintentional harm to the Observatory."[25]

Maury demanded an apology that "I under like circumstances would be willing to afford." The apology never came, and Walker's observations appeared in the Smithsonian's *Transactions*.[26]

From the mid–1840s to the firing on Fort Sumter in April 1861, Washington could be seen both as the seat of government and the nation's applied science center. What gave the three men who headed the centers and their institutions strength was continuity. As administrations came and went and Congresses convened and adjourned, the same three remained as superintendent of the National Observatory, superintendent of the Coast Survey, and secretary of the Smithsonian Institution. Their prominence shone in their public buildings—the observatory with its spacious grounds in Foggy Bottom, within easy walking distance of the White House and the Navy Department; the

Smithsonian with its turreted castle rising on the National Mall within sight of the Capitol, where the money was; and the survey's sprawling "barrack of a house" on the edge of Capitol Hill, where men of influence toiled and were, in turn, influenced.[27]

Bache, in particular, and Henry, to a lesser degree, abrogated to themselves, and to their friends, the mantle of belonging to an "elite corps" of pure scientists. The West Point–educated Bache put it bluntly in urging Henry to accept the position at the Smithsonian. "Science triumphs in you, my dear friend, and come you must. Redeem Washington. Save the great National Institution from the hands of charlatans."[28]

That advice was particularly apt. After all, Henry, then at Princeton, had recommended Bache for his position despite the opposition of the Treasury secretary, who controlled the survey. Henry then organized a campaign for Bache's appointment. If that failed as Ferdinand Hassler, the survey's first superintendent, lay dying, Bache relentlessly promoted himself for the job, tugging all his political ties to the Tyler administration.[29]

In Cambridge, Massachusetts, they found strong allies in Peirce and his brother-in-law, Navy Lieutenant Charles H. Davis, soon to head the *Nautical Almanac* office.

Over the years, Bache became the master of cliquishness. He courted friends in politics, such as Jefferson Davis, and academia, such as Peirce, and maritime research, such as Samuel F. DuPont, who together over cigars and brandy vowed to protect science's gates from infidels and magicians. They became the capital's "Lazzaroni," invoking the name of the Neapolitan masses who revolted against Austria in 1848.[30]

Not only would Maury not join them socially, he could not join them intellectually, in their estimation. Bache and Henry, who came from a dirt-poor background and was largely self-taught, knew few Navy men had formal training beyond high school. Its nascent academy was not the equivalent of West Point, the nation's premier engineering school. They judged it a trade school. As members of the Franklin Institute investigating the *Princeton* explosion in 1844, both saw the lack of rigor in the Navy's investigation.[31]

Maury clearly was not above empire-building himself. When Henry made it clear that the Smithsonian had little regard for the proprietary interests of the observatory, Maury felt freer to undercut the institution's mandate in studying the weather on land. He also intended to continue the Navy's research into the Gulf Stream, knowing those clashed with the Coast Survey's charter. To spite Bache publicly, Maury hired James Ferguson, recently fired from his position as a senior assistant at the survey. Adding greatly to the tensions was

Maury's vigorous advocacy of the Navy's repeated, but frustrated, attempts to take over the Coast Survey.[32]

Outside Washington, to astronomers like Peirce, Maury's public prominence was galling. Not only did he have all the faults ascribed to him by Henry and Bache, this naval officer was taking the nation's most important observatory who knew where. To the Harvard academic with his own deep religiosity, Maury's speech before the Virginia Historical Society in December 1848 proved beyond a doubt that the lieutenant was at best a lyricist and not a scientist.[33]

Maury said:

> At the dead hour of the night, when the world is hushed in sleep and all is still; when there is not a sound to be heard save the dead beat escapement of the clock, counting with hollow voice the footsteps of time in his ceaseless round, I turn to the Ephemeris and find there, by calculation, made years ago, that when the clock tells a certain hour which I never saw will be in the field of the telescope for a moment, flit through and then disappear.[34]

Most damning to the scientific purists and their allies in Congress was Maury's continued writings on national affairs, far outside the confines of even popular science. From his fortress above the Potomac, he called for canals in the Midwest and a naval coal depot in Chicago to protect the lower Great Lakes from British encroachment. The naval officer used the *Southern Literary Messenger* as his personal forum. It didn't end when the Mexican War ended. When gold was discovered in California, Maury's opinion was sought by shipping magnates on the easiest crossing of Central America and by congressmen on the best route for a transcontinental railroad, the provenance of the Army's Topographical Engineers. He was all over the political and economic agenda.[35]

By then, these three leaders of American science were engaged in a most uncivil war. As historian William Goetzmann wrote, "The great men who first brought forth respectable science in America were not always good men." This observation was surely true of Maury, Henry, and Bache.[36]

Yet through it all, Maury enjoyed good relations with many academics, especially those with a humanistic, traditional bent in the United States and Europe. From 1844 on, he encouraged the Rev. James Curley at Georgetown in building an observatory. Through Curley and other Jesuits, Maury developed contacts with astronomers and scientists across Europe that he exploited in later international studies of weather. Somewhat reluctantly, he shared data and collected samples from the Navy's exploring expeditions with "pure scientists" like Louis Agassiz, Jacob Whitman Bailey, and Benjamin Silliman, Jr.[37]

That was not all. In 1847, during some of the most perilous days of the Mexican War, Maury was invited to spend weeks traveling to Chapel Hill with President Polk and Secretary Mason, both graduates of the university. The invitation demonstrated Maury's prominence in the Navy secretary's eyes and his access to the nation's highest political circles. He went to Chapel Hill to receive an honorary Master of Arts degree. As pleasing as that was, Maury probably was miffed that "he was not deemed worthy of the Doctorate of Laws" that Peirce was to receive at a separate convocation.[38]

Politics were certainly evident during the events in Raleigh and Chapel Hill during that long spring week. Senator George Badger, Harrison's short-time secretary of the Navy, and Governor William A. Graham, a future Navy secretary—both Maury supporters—had considered not calling on Polk. The president, in his diary, denounced Badger as "a bitter partisan" and wrote "it was a matter of indifference" to him whether Badger called. Badger did not. On the other hand, Graham did, but the hour-long meeting was stiffly courteous.[39]

Maury and Graham, who served briefly in the Senate when Maury took over the Depot of Charts and Instruments, may have met then, but in Chapel Hill they became much better acquainted. Graham came away impressed with Maury's grasp of naval affairs and the United States' role in the world.[40]

Maury enjoyed his stay at the university, and he entertained many members of the faculty and staff that he met with his "sunny temper and genial manners," as well as an occasional risqué sea tale. He also didn't stay away from the Navy's business when in Chapel Hill. He interviewed J. Johnston Pettigrew, the valedictorian, for an open position of mathematics at the Naval Academy.[41]

During the North Carolina visit, the grandson of the Rev. James Maury also cemented his position with leaders of the American Episcopal Church, like William Mercer Green, the first bishop of Mississippi, which proved useful for decades at home and in Great Britain.

Green, longtime chaplain at the university and professor of belles lettres, had been a key figure in the decision by the Rev. James Otey, Maury's preceptor, to leave Harpeth Academy to become a clergyman. As the personal bonds grew stronger, Green, Otey, Maury, and President Polk's cousin Leonidas Polk, bishop of Louisiana, were pivotal figures in the founding of the University of the South at Sewanee, Tennessee, in the 1850s. They shared a vision of what the next generation needed to become leaders in their communities, their church, their states, their region, and the nation.[42] The Episcopal Church proved another means in Maury's rise and another way to prove himself a "useful man."

The situation in the observatory was another matter. During the summer of 1846, the draining effects of the war and Walker's firing stretched the observatory's resources almost to the breaking point. Long hours and dedication, even browbeating, were not enough to get the work done. The staff fell far behind in reducing the observations for publication. In a letter to Adams, Maury acknowledged that separating the *Nautical Almanac* from other observatory duties was now necessary. It was a move that added a new adversary, Charles Davis, to the ranks of the scientifics. They celebrated Davis's selection as a blow to Maury's power.[43]

Maury, however, tried to sound optimistic when he wrote Bancroft, "The spirit of the age with its upward and onward tendency has infused as much additional life and vigor into astronomy as in any other department whatever of science and knowledge." As much as he wanted to take science "upward and onward," Maury did not have the manpower to do it.[44]

Priorities had to be set, and separating the *Nautical Almanac*, a move approved by Maury, Bache, and Henry, proved only a start. Again, the move was similar to his father's forced cleaving of acreage and selling of slaves to halt his rush to fiscal ruin. When forced to choose, Maury instinctively turned his eyes down from the heavens toward the depths of the sea, and the success that forever had eluded his father became his, for a time, to savor.

While Maury was engaged in skirmishes over control and credit, he was not given his best chance to command in combat. This became a two-edged sword. Because he remained in Washington, he learned much about the politics of waging war that proved valuable later: Polk's distrust of Taylor and Scott and shifting war aims—take half or all of Mexico, and buy or seize Cuba on the troops' return—turned the fighting into "Polk's War." He also learned how Bancroft's foresight and Mason's execution in securing a "mosquito flotilla" and the importance of combined Army and Navy amphibious operations brought victory.[45]

The war's end put slavery front and center as a divisive political issue. In a ten-minute address, David Wilmot attached an amendment to an 1846 appropriations bill barring slavery from any territory taken from Mexico. Although the amendment didn't pass, it didn't die. Slavery, skirted as an issue in the 1840 presidential campaign and a factor but not the dominating issue of the 1844 race, was now the leading sectional issue confronting the two political parties. Maury's position was hardening on slavery as well. Like Abel Parker Upshur, the late secretary of the Navy, he saw it "as a positive good," a force for civilization.[46]

There, too, were the personal costs of "Polk's war." For the Maurys, the

Mexican War hinted at the personal price they would pay later. His nephew Dabney, whose landing had been unopposed, had his left arm shattered in a firefight. He took months to recover. Maury's brother-in-law, Kemp Holland, who served as Jefferson Davis's commissary officer in the Mississippi Rifles, died, like more than eleven thousand regulars and volunteers, of disease while returning from Monterrey. Summing up the pain of thousands, the old "War Hawk" Henry Clay, who lost his son Henry at Monterrey, railed against "this most unnecessary and horrible war" in his anguish. These were the ruins of war.[47]

12. Charting the Oceans and Finding Gold

After the war with Mexico, the observatory was viewed as one of the service's better shore assignments. Duty there in the 1840s was an assignment sought by the Navy's brightest young officers, even with its superintendent's reputation for long hours.[1]

"Hard work is glorious" was how Matthew Fontaine Maury put his invitation to William L. Whiting, who served with him on *Falmouth*. Tired of slavers, the British, sickness, and tropical heat on the Africa station, the officer now spent long hours deciphering logbooks of long-ago voyages in changeable Washington.[2]

Like many in his time, Maury loved mottoes. "Hard work is glorious" and *cur non* (Why not?) were appropriate for this man descended from generations of Protestant clergy and teachers. He had a third motto that more appropriately summed up his life's work: *cui bono*. When Maury spoke on the need to study the Gulf Stream in April 1844, he repeatedly asked the largest scientific gathering in America that Latin question. Loosely translated it means, "For whose benefit?"[3]

Now the superintendent of the National Observatory daily asked his staff the same curiously perverse question. The motto fit Maury's vision: the land, the sea, the air, the heavens, the Grand Architect's design. He was succumbing "to this escalatory temptation of related questions and related data, widening his field of vision." His critics warned that Maury lost focus in building "a complex scientific theory of earth-sea-air thermal relationship." He kept building that theory.[4]

Despite his protestations, the sea fascinated Maury.

Whiting wrote, "At first it was his intention to delineate the track of each vessel, but it soon became apparent that it was impossible to do so upon the scale adopted (one inch to one degree), and he resorted to the plan of tabulating the results only instead of making the track, which gave rise to the series of 'pilot' charts."[5]

As an institution, the observatory's hydrographical work, especially producing the charts, was further along than all others. In an 1847 letter to John Quincy Adams, Maury admitted: "Charts are to be corrected and compiled; and the undertaking has been commenced here of preparing wind and current charts of the three grand oceans, viz., the Atlantic, the Pacific and the Indian."

He added, "Books, if I may say so, impart information through the ear—these charts through the eye, and, therefore, in a manner and form much more condensed and available."[6]

The visual appeal was vital in wooing the reluctant maritime princes to accept his charts. The charts underlined the temperature of the water, used arrows to denote current, and the length of the arrow showed the strength in knots. Roman numerals denoted the degree of magnetic variation recorded, and colors represented the seasons in which a vessel had sailed. Maury made the raw data meaningful.[7]

An ecstatic Maury wrote: "The sheets already published and which have been sent to you have developed facts with regard to winds, which will probably reduce the average passage from the United States to Rio ten days or more. A fast sailing public cruiser is about to try this route."[8]

What seems obvious now was a chimera until then. Using the records of hundreds of voyages, Maury discovered pathways through dangerous seas, quickened trade, and increased safety. Here in a single place were the records of Navy ships, clippers, and merchantmen sailing from New York to Rio de Janeiro. Soon, there were charts from Norfolk, Virginia, to Callao, Peru—as important for the Navy's Pacific Squadron as any chart produced.[9]

After that came courses to the whaling grounds in the North Pacific. The observatory provided data on breeding and seasonal migration. He boasted that chart "will be of such practical importance to the whale men that they might well afford to give us a perpetual say in all their ships." In this chart, Maury was searching for the Northwest Passage. How else to explain the same breeds of whales being found in the North Atlantic and the North Pacific. The question prompted Maury to send the great German scientist Alexander von Humboldt the chart with an accompanying letter.[10]

All the observatory's exuberance was fine for watch-standers on public cruisers or even academics in Cambridge, Massachusetts, but for men whose fortunes rocked on the vagaries of the ocean, solid, incontestable evidence that even a counting house clerk at Fell's Point in Baltimore could digest was needed.

The proof came in a single sea lane tested by a merchantman bound from Baltimore to Rio de Janeiro. In the past, masters avoided the rocks, shoals, and currents of Cape St. Rogue, the bulge of Brazil closest to Africa, but risked becoming becalmed.

The observatory's staff's five-year investigation of its library of log books led Maury to proclaim that ships should hug the cape. "Stand boldly on, and if need be, tack and work by under the land" were his instructions.[11]

The vindication came in the voyage of *W. H. D. C. Wright* in February 1848. The usual sailing time from the Virginia Capes to Rio was fifty-five days, but following Maury's instructions, the bark under Captain John J. Jackson unloaded its cargo of flour in thirty-eight days. The return run with a cargo of coffee was made in thirty-seven. Stories of Jackson's bark whipped like a trade wind around the nation's seacoast coffeehouses and saloons.[12]

Soon enough, Robert Bennet Forbes, the China hand, and dozens of Atlantic Coast maritime merchants, underwriters, and shipbuilders realized the charts showed highways to gigantic treasure chests. Maury and the Navy were delivering on William Bolton Finch's promises to American merchants on Pacific Islands, in China, and in Africa.[13]

The interest Maury created in nautical science could not have come at a more propitious time. In 1848, two of the country's largest scientific societies—the National Institute for the Promotion of Science and the American Association of Geologists and Naturalists—finally merged, creating the American Association for the Advancement of Science.

In September 1848, at the association's inaugural session, Maury unveiled a plan to expand the collection of data to vessels of all nations, because the work "is not exclusively for the benefit of any nation." His reach of four years earlier had been puny in comparison.[14]

Endorsements by merchants like Forbes and scientists led Congress to authorize three ships for Maury's research, but money was only provided for one, *Taney*, to begin the Navy's oceanographic program.[15]

In 1848, Maury trumpeted his work:

> I have two other vessels which sailed together from New York, the one to China and the other to Rio. The Rio bound vessel was the better sailer, and their routes to the equator should have been the same. The dull vessel crossed the equator per this chart, the fast one pursued the old beaten track towards the coast of Africa, and the day she arrived at Rio her companion made St. Paul's island in the Indian Ocean!

Maury's charts eventually were published in six series, lettered A through F.[16]

Accompanying the charts were the *Sailing Directions*, essays in which Maury took special pride. Like the charts, they "are derived from the results of many thousand voyages and are, in fact, the combined experience of thousands of navigators." Each edition's essays covered more than seas and weather.

"The system of researches embraced by the Wind and Current Charts, therefore it would appear concerns the philosopher and the husbandmen, as well as the merchant and the statesmen." This aside was certainly an unsubtle jibe at Henry and the Army's surgeon general who kept close hold on weather data in the United States.[17]

After the war with Mexico, the need for the weather service never was greater and distribution never easier. The United States by force of arms had acquired half of Mexico and by negotiation the most promising half of the Oregon Territory. But the idea of Maury's amateurs collecting, tabulating, and instantaneously distributing their meteorological data on land via telegraph appalled Henry. Where Maury asked "why not," Henry answered, "Why?"[18]

The telegraph with lines from Boston to Charleston and from there to New Orleans gave war reporting and business transactions immediacy. But for the Navy, starting with Captain Charles Wilkes, and the Coast Survey from Sears Walker to Navy Lieutenant James Gilliss, there were more possibilities—scientific and military. Maury grasped what these developments meant for the observatory: weather reporting, determining longitude, and coastal defense. He recognized the communications revolution had far more potential than the one in transportation he so warmly applauded. (The effect of the telegraph will be examined in Chapter 16.)[19]

As he and his staff refined the charts through the 1840s and 1850s, Maury rode the crest of two other history-changing events. The first was the building of the long and narrow greyhounds of the sea—the American clipper ships. For the China trade of tea, spices, porcelains, and silks, the sleek freighters kept East Coast shipbuilders, shippers, merchants, and bankers busy and wealthy into the early 1850s. He was convinced that clippers, when "guided by the light of science," could maintain their edge over steamers in the long carrying trade.[20]

"Gold fever" was the second. In the early 1850s, clippers from New York raced each other over the fifteen thousand miles to San Francisco to win the California trade. Aboard the racers were all the expected nautical instruments, copies of Bowditch, and Maury's *Wind and Current Charts*.[21]

Sought since Andrew Jackson's term, California, won in the Mexican War, seemed a secondary prize to Oregon. In the flush of victory, Maury gathered information on which port was best for the Navy: San Diego, Los Angeles,

Monterey, or San Francisco Bay. The discovery of gold above Sacramento made that inquiry moot. San Francisco Bay was closest to Sutter's Mill; of course, it was best. It was the North American Callao and Lima, territory to be held at all costs. During the Civil War, the Navy continuously protected its San Francisco base to guard the "Treasure Fleet."[22]

The first news of the gold discovery at Sutter's Mill was carried by sailors to Hawaii, Sonora, Chile, Peru, China, and Australia. The rush from the West was on. An Australian prospector admired the "complete forest of masts—a sight well calibrated to inspire us with hope" as he sailed into San Francisco Bay. By nightfall, he reported only one officer and four apprentices remained aboard. The rest were off to the gold fields. When the report reached Oregon, two-thirds of the white men set off by land and sea to California's Sierra Nevada.[23]

When President James Polk heard the news, he added it to his State of the Union message, a sure way to silence his wartime critics. For any skeptics of Polk's claim, the physical proof—gold itself—was in the government's hands in Washington two days later.

Polk's announcement set thousands of vessels in motion, loaded with schemers and dreamers from the American Eastern Seaboard and, soon after, from Europe. As many as fourteen hundred vessels sailed to California by rounding Cape Horn in 1849 and 1850. Nothing like it had happened before. Maury's charts were a common denominator.[24]

The clippers were actually late arrivals in the boom. Even using Maury's charts, favorable winds, and following seas, and aboard a new ship, the voyage via Cape Horn was a long trial marked by brawling, drunkenness, and sexual promiscuity. It was a price landsmen willingly paid as time in purgatory. In the twelve months following Polk's announcement, 226 vessels sailed from New York City carrying almost twenty thousand people, all with gold fever.[25]

Ambitious men always knew time was money, and Maury was instrumental in showing them how to save time and make more money from the Gold Rush. The federal government and these merchant princes understood that the North American continent offered no shortcut, land-based answer to transferring gold from coast to coast. The fact was that, in 1850, railroad track had not crossed the Mississippi.

The great shipping merchants of New York, such as the Griswolds, A. A. Low & Brothers, Howland & Aspinwall—then the nation's largest import-export house—along with Cornelius Vanderbilt, would not wait for railroads to cross the continent or be outdueled in sailing around Cape Horn.

At the same time, the federal government was pressured to establish regular mail service, actually freight service, between the coasts, primarily by ship. To the newly created United States Mail Steamship Company on the Atlantic Coast and the Pacific Mail Steamship Company, the subsidized mail contracts were godsends.[26]

With the Mexican War history and relations with Great Britain on the Northwest Coast stable, there was little risk of converting paddlewheel steamers into auxiliary warships. Better yet for the companies, their captains, like David Dixon Porter, the son of John Maury's rescuer in the War of 1812, and later William Lewis Herndon, Maury's brother-in-law, were unlikely to don naval uniforms any time soon. Best of all, the Navy paid the captains' and past midshipmen's salaries, although the officers worked for the steamship companies.[27]

The benefits for the nation were that mail and bullion moved more quickly on the steamers to transfer points. The benefits for the Navy came in having officers familiar with steam propulsion on the high seas. On balance, the owners of the steamship companies were the winners.[28]

As with the Spanish conquistadors, the hunt was on to find the best transfer points in Central America. The Spanish had tried several paths across Panama, Nicaragua, and even Mexico. The mail contractors and merchants again turned to Maury. After studying the coasts of Mexico, Nicaragua, and Panama, Maury pointed to Panama. For decades the Navy had shipped new orders to ships in the Pacific Squadron over this route. It worked. Maury added, for now, they should use horses and mules to get from one ocean to the other, then build a railroad. A canal could come later.[29]

Maury lobbied for Panama in the July 1849 issue of *DeBow's Review* and the next month's *Southern Literary Messenger*, and he was not through pushing. As president of the Memphis Commercial Convention, he declared a canal across the isthmus was as necessary as a transcontinental railroad for the United States. Later, Secretary of State John Clayton claimed an isthmian canal as the surest way of keeping California and Oregon in the Union.[30]

The superintendent could not see from his new house on the observatory's grounds the crowding on both coasts and at the switching point from small boats to tired mules in Gorgona, Panama. He did not write about the toll that yellow fever, cholera, malaria, and "dissipation" took on the Americans like Jessie Benton Fremont, the daughter of influential Senator Thomas Hart Benton and wife of adventurer John Charles Fremont, waiting for passage.

Nor did Maury see the immense hurdles of moving locomotives from the United States and laying track through the mountainous jungles. Those were the concerns of other men with other talents like Collis P. Huntington, a California peddler on the rise. As in his selection of San Francisco, Maury provided vision through the validity of his office. In this, he followed his grandfather's lead in the Loyal Company.[31]

When gold fever broke in the mid–1850s, the breadth of Maury's charting work was more stunning than the take from thousands of grub-staked mines. As he wrote in his *Sailing Directions*,

> Havre is only 100 miles farther than Liverpool is from New York, and the great circle route to each from New York is nearly the same as far as Cape Clear in Iceland. Yet notwithstanding this, the Havre packets are, on the average, nine days longer on their passage than are the Liverpool packets. Neither the 100 miles of distance nor the difficulties of getting in and out of the channel can account for this difference. Neither does the difference owe to any superior sailing qualities of the Liverpool packets; what then can it be owing to? The conclusions are elicited from the facts contained in the records as to wind; weather and currents encountered during two and three thousand voyages to and fro at all seasons of the year may answer the questions, and in the answer bring Havre and New York a week closer together.[32]

As data trickled in on the Indian and Pacific oceans, Maury created better routes between Australia and New Zealand and Great Britain and collected logs of steamers moving from Australia to Panama. With the British Navigation Acts no longer in place, Maury saw an opportunity for the United States to win a share of the Australian bullion-carrying trade. He foresaw American-flagged clippers sailing around the Cape of Good Hope using the fierce westerlies close to Antarctica to cut one thousand miles on the Great Britain to Melbourne route and a broadening of trade with China and the Indies.

The Crimean War opened more opportunities for American Pacific traders. By the mid–1850s, Britain's merchant fleet—some converted to warships, others reconfigured as troop transports—was heavily engaged in supporting the one hundred thousand–man army around Sevastopol.

Within a year of the war's ending, Maury saw steamers from Melbourne crossing to Central America and transshipping gold across Panama, Honduras, Nicaragua, and Mexico for banks in New York and London.

As steamship operators saw "Forty-Niners" coming from New York and London, they predicted a new wave of "diggers" could be landed on the Atlantic and Gulf coast bound for the Australian gold fields. "I may say—though we don't run quite as fast as clippers do at times, yet we keep up a steady pace, which counts in the long run," one Australian ship's master chattily wrote Maury. Maury soon did the same charting on the Bombay run.[33]

In July 1853, Maury asked for $3,360 more to continue the oceanic work: "This excess arises chiefly in the estimates for publishing wind and current charts, hydrographical surveys &c." Maury indicated that he would return for more as data from the expeditions to the La Plata, North Pacific, and China arrived. As a Canadian publication noted approvingly, "The United States will be conducting physical researches in the Eastern seas, in Africa, in South America, and in the polar regions." The observatory under Maury had become *the* clearinghouse of this information. (The explorations will be examined in more detail in Chapter 13.)

For Maury, this was sweet revenge. In the decade before the Civil War, Maury and his small staff received wind, current, and sea data from hundreds of vessels. Charting errors were corrected immediately; new information was included rapidly. He added theories on currents and winds to the *Sailing Directions,* but just as easily discarded them when contradictory data emerged. Maury was no dogmatist when theories were toppled by facts. The charts and sailing directions grew each year until they had to be divided into two volumes in 1858–59.[34]

Hard work is glorious. *Cui bono? Cur non?*

13. Grand Explorations and Manifest Destiny

From the end of the Mexican War until 1861, Matthew Fontaine Maury used his reputation in maritime affairs to shepherd the Navy into a grand age of exploration. The American voyages publicly complemented the service's charts, demonstrations of greatness in commerce and naval power, if not "pure" science.[1]

The fifteen voyages he was involved with helped Maury salve his frustrations over the Charles Wilkes expedition in the early 1840s. While bound to a desk in Washington, the invalided officer "sailed the globe by proxy and pen."[2]

From the Dead Sea to the Amazon to the Arctic and the Antarctic, the Navy—often under Maury's spur, willing secretaries' assent, and sometimes businessmen with deep pockets—ordered ships and men to make known the world's "unknown regions." Until the Civil War, Maury did more than any one man to ensure that these expeditions were undertaken without the delay or fuzziness of mission that crippled Wilkes's expedition. In the words of historian Kenneth Hagan, Maury "was at the center of [the exploration aspect] of midcentury American naval globalism."[3]

William Lynch, a *Brandywine* shipmate, was the first of the American naval explorers inspired by Maury. These expeditions, even done in time of war, as Lynch's was of the Dead Sea, were what were expected of great nations and their navies. Maury and the secretaries of the Navy from John Y. Mason to James C. Dobbin could not have agreed more. The expeditions showed Congress that naval explorations were as valuable as the Army's topographical engineers' trailblazing the West.[4]

As in much of Maury's life, these explorations had goals beyond boosting national pride and showcasing the Navy's value. There was money to be made even in the Antarctic with new seal and whale hunting grounds.

There often was a darker side to Maury's expeditions. The good Southerner, Maury saw his grandest exploration—that of the Amazon—as opening a "safety valve" for American slavery. He returned to this theme often in his writings, public addresses, and involvement in a Southern rebellion against Northern economic domination.

As always with Maury, there was a religious side: Christianizing heathens, unlocking the divine plan of the universe, or retracing the steps of biblical figures in the Holy Land. Nowhere was his religious bent more clearly seen than in the Dead Sea expedition. The given scientific reason was to discover how far the Dead Sea was below the Mediterranean. The theological reason: discover the Garden of Eden.[5]

As Lynch wrote Secretary John Y. Mason in 1847, "This proposition pertains to a subject maritime in its nature and therefore peculiarly appropriate to your office; and it is involved in mystery, the solution of which will advance the cause of science and gratify the whole Christian world." To Maury, Lynch was less grand. "Please sit down with the *Navy Register* of officers before you and give me the result." The superintendent recommended fellow Virginians John Dale and Richmond Aulick for the expedition.

Although the expedition never received specific congressional approval, it had Mason's blessing with the proviso that Lynch receive Ottoman permission to explore. The ships had never been part of the buildup for war.[6]

From the start, the expedition did not go easily. Eden was not found, and Lynch's ship, *Supply*, ran out of provisions and water during its return to Malta in the end. Bottled inside Lynch was the experience of broiling heat in the day and shivering cold at night, paddling through harsh rapids at dusk, seeing the ruins of Jericho, floating effortlessly on the purplish Dead Sea, and the torment over Dale's death in Beirut of cholera.[7]

With Lynch suffering from depression over a shipmate's death and his own marital problems, Maury hailed the mission as done "to the glory of the Navy and the honor of the nation." He needed to peal the bells if he were to continue using naval explorations to burnish his own image. So he added the solid mortar of Christian belief:

> Seven-hundred dollars for a scientific exploration of the Dead Sea! There is not a village church in the land, where if the matter had been proposed, such a sum could not have been raised at once for the work.... [For all involved should receive] "Well done" of a Christian people, and the grateful acknowledgment of wise and good men everywhere.[8]

Lynch was temporarily buoyed, but he feared "much unkind criticism on our expedition, which had terminated so unhappily." He let more time slip by.[9]

Despite the superintendent's cheerleading, Lynch sank back into his gloom before, at long last, quietly sending his report to the Senate on February 3, 1849. For more than half a year, there was no reaction inside or outside the government. Then from New Haven came the recognition of an accomplishment of note. In November, Benjamin Silliman praised it in the *American Journal of Science and the Arts*.[10]

But this encouragement was not enough. Lynch delayed two years in turning an official report into a popular book, *Narrative of the U.S. Expedition to Explore the Dead Sea and the River Jordan*. The wait did not prove fatal.

Lynch had the meteorological observations, geological reconnaissance, botanical and ornithological reports, as well as trade data for Beirut and Jaffa required for the official report. Religious belief at last provided Lynch with reason to rise from his depression and chronicle the adventure.[11]

In the book, Lynch, a deeply religious man himself, tied what his party experienced to what the public knew from the Bible. He had explored the "Holy Land," and good Christians everywhere, as Maury had written, wanted to know what he found trekking through the land of David, Solomon, and Jesus.

For example, in describing a stream trickling toward the Jordan, Lynch wrote: "It was here that Jacob wrestled with the angel at whose touch the sinew of his thigh shrunk up." Or: "This ford, the bathing place of the Christian pilgrims, is consecrated by tradition as the spot where the Israelites passed over the Ark of the Covenant and where our blessed saviour was baptized by John."[12]

Greater scientific knowledge certainly was gained in the later Arctic explorations, but Lynch's was the pioneering journey that led Congress and the public to finance future adventures.[13]

The Arctic expeditions need their due—for how they were financed and what was learned. The first of these expeditions, named for Henry Grinnell, who underwrote the costs, in the search for the British explorer Franklin, was commanded by Lieutenant Edwin J. De Haven. "Considered an authority on meteorology," Maury called his aide, he was "the best man for the position."[14]

The superintendent next drafted a memorial for Moses Grinnell, Henry's father, to win congressional approval for the expedition. Using it himself, Maury successfully lobbied Kentucky Senator Henry Clay. His resolution detached officers and sailors to man the two ships and "give the vessels something like a naval and military discipline."

Maury urged Moses Grinnell to persuade his congressman brother to call on President Zachary Taylor for his backing. Taylor had twice received impassioned letters from Lady Jane Franklin asking American businessmen and the Navy to join in the search for her husband's 129-man expedition, but he passed the letters without comment to Congress. Grinnell chose not to make the call. That didn't stop Maury. Working inside the administration, he won Navy Secretary William Ballard Preston's backing to man the ships with Navy officers and crews.[15]

Following congressional approval, De Haven, a veteran of Wilkes's expedition, received two sets of orders, general ones orchestrated by Maury for the secretary's signature and very specific ones from Maury. Finding the remains of Franklin and his party was on the "to-do list" and good for publicity. Recording the meteorology of the Arctic was on the "must list," important to the Navy, and invaluable to whalers and seal hunters. Discovering the Northwest Passage by tracking whale migration would immortalize all involved.

In all these regards, Maury, De Haven, and the Navy were fortunate to have Elisha Kent Kane, a surgeon, detached from Coast Survey duty, as its medical officer. The short, slender man was already a war hero when he reported to De Haven. Seriously wounded by a lance while trying to deliver diplomatic dispatches to General Winfield Scott, Kane treated the other casualties in his party at his own peril. It was all in character.[16]

Kane's taste for adventure was extraordinary—climbing the Himalayas, exploring craters in the Philippines, venturing out to archaeological digs on the Upper Nile, and being stopped only by coastal fever from reporting back on West African slave markets. His dalliance with spiritualist Margaret Fox seemed the singular odd, out-of-character aspect for such a serious man. Only his health—the lingering effects of a childhood bout with rheumatic fever—was questionable.[17]

After the Navy Yard in Brooklyn completed its hardening work on the expedition's ships, Kane described them as still looking "more like a couple of coasting schooners than a national squadron." Nevertheless on May 20, 1850, six days after receiving his formal orders, De Haven was on course for Greenland. The contrast with the years of dithering over the Exploring Expedition was obvious. Maury was pleased.[18]

In Greenland, then, there were several British ships hunting for the remains of Franklin's party, and more were coming. The mix of mercantile vessels and Royal Navy warships all operating under separate commands was cumbersome. De Haven also understood his orders didn't encourage coordination. He was to search in a specific region off Greenland and from there sail northward—to look for the Northwest Passage.[19]

What De Haven hadn't expected so immediately was ice. Although it was summer, the ice was so thick it trapped his ships for three weeks. Time became a factor in De Haven's next decision. By late August, he and British Captain William Penny discovered evidence of encampments at Cape Riley and on Beechey Island. Because there was no indication where Franklin and his men went afterward, the parties agreed to split up.[20]

Again, the ice entrapped De Haven; that meant wintering over. Grinnell had stocked the ships' libraries with books on Arctic survival and exploration for a time such as this. Reading, while stimulating the crews' minds, did not fight off scurvy or growing depression from the continual darkness and killing cold. Going against accepted medical practice, Kane ordered daily exercise to keep the crew physically and mentally fit. He also increased rations to fight off scurvy and other illnesses. He kept the orders in place until the ice broke, and they worked.[21]

In the spring, De Haven set out again from Greenland. He had no better luck in the summer of 1851. "The frustrated De Haven abandoned the mission and headed for New York before facing another arctic winter," the American Philosophical Society wrote. Suffering from snow blindness, De Haven returned to the observatory "an almost forgotten man," according to the society. His career wound down quietly. For now, the Democratic-controlled Congress lost almost all interest in the Arctic and refused to pay for the publication of its results. This was bitter soup indeed for Maury and Kane.[22]

Naming a landfall after Grinnell and a channel after the superintendent was not enough for Maury. He would push on to find the Northwest Passage. Harpoons from whalers in Greenland were found in whales killed in the Bering Strait. Likewise, harpoons from whalers in the Pacific were pulled from whales taken in the North Atlantic. The search had to continue, again in the name of Franklin.[23]

The means to the end of future explorations during tight budget times was born in the same month that De Haven arrived in the United States. The New York–based American Geographical and Statistical Society proved the perfect vehicle to finance future expeditions. Maury understood that early on, accepting the society's offer to deliver its first keynote address. In the future when the government hesitated, the society became the conduit for Maury, its "strategic adviser," to employ for maritime exploration.[24]

The members were men of station and wealth. Henry Grinnell, the financier of the Franklin expeditions, became a longtime officer. John Aspinwall served as a vice president, and his partner John Howland in the Pacific Mail Steamship Company was an active member, as was the restless Cyrus Field, the driving force in the laying of the transatlantic telegraph cable. Important editors and writers were counted among its founders: George Bancroft, the historian, cabinet minister, and diplomat; Charles Dana, soon to be the editor of the *New York Sun*; Henry Raymond, founder of the *New York Times*; and Freeman Hunt, editor of the business publication *Hunt's Merchant Magazine*.

Kane, like Maury, was bursting to take another shot at the Arctic. To keep interest alive, Kane produced the very popular book *The U.S. Grinnell Expedition in Search of Sir John Franklin* and hit the lecture circuit, theorizing that Franklin had drifted into the "Open Polar Sea," Maury's Poliniya, the Northwest Passage.[25]

Maury's ambitions, Kane's eagerness, and the society's influence converged in "a mutuality of interest in naval exploration on the seafaring frontier." Kane's first official moves were toward the observatory and the society. The superintendent told his New York representative, George Manning, to send Kane the print of the Arctic to boost his fundraising efforts. Maury, who understood publicity's value, followed this up with an extensive report on the first expedition in the 1854 *Sailing Directions*.[26]

Grinnell was in for a second try.[27]

Kane was deft, determined, and diligent in his dealings with the scientific Lazzaroni and Congress. He had served in the Coast Survey, a plus with Alexander Dallas Bache. Kane's father, John, a federal judge, was active in the American Philosophical Society, another plus with Bache and Joseph Henry at the Smithsonian. The young man's promises of research in the Arctic with the proper equipment for meteorological observations won Henry over. Kane so differed from Maury that the Smithsonian secretary pledged more equipment than proposed for the first attempt, and the Coast Survey would do likewise. The endorsement of the American Philosophical Society followed. The Lazzaroni were on board.

When Congress ignored Representative Hamilton Fish's request for a second expedition, Navy Secretary John Pendleton Kennedy approved the transfer of provisions and kept Kane and his men on active duty in orders received in December 1852. No one publicly challenged the maneuver. Kane had successfully navigated the treacherous Maury-Henry-Bache-Democratic-Whig straits.[28]

When Kane set out from New York in May 1853, expectations were high. But as months went by with no word, fears of another lost party reached such intensity that a relief expedition was dispatched. Although Kane and his party were struggling, they were proceeding on their missions.

The meteorological record was meticulous. In addition, Kane, a superb artist, provided a powerful visual record that he intended to use for his published account of the expedition. At Maury's suggestion, Kane also took a camera along to record the expedition's day-to-day living, but the severe conditions overwhelmed nineteenth-century daguerreotype technology, and no pictures survived.

But the last mission, the one dearest to Kane's and Maury's hearts, crowned the expedition's achievements. As summer 1854 began, Kane sent a sledge party from their base northward. After days on the ice looking for the boundary between the ice on the land and ice on the water, William Morton, one of Kane's crew, and Hans Cristian, an Eskimo, reached the top of a 480-foot black cliff, later named Point Constitution. What they saw was "a boundless waste of water" stretching out forty miles toward the North Pole. There was "not a 'speck of ice.'" Along with the wind, the pair heard "the novel music of dashing waves" and surf beating on rocks, according to Kane.

For more than an hour and a half, on June 24, 1854, Morton flew the flag of *Peacock*, the sloop that had wrecked at the mouth of the Columbia River during Wilkes's expedition in De Haven's honor. "It was now the [*Peacock* ensign's] strange destiny to float over the highest northern land, not only of America, but of our globe," Kane wrote.[29]

If Lynch's was the groundbreaker, complete with religious overtones, and the second Grinnell expedition the most scientific, then William Lewis Herndon's was the most immediately influential.[30]

Although Perry's expedition to Japan is now better known, the 1851 exploration of the Amazon captured the nation's imagination. In the popular mind, Herndon and Lardner A. Gibbon wandered through a slave owners' paradise and a miners' Cibola.[31]

The Amazon expedition was particularly difficult to mount. Not only did the Brazilian authorities restrict the region to all but the British, but also the United States government and its Navy were distracted in the 1850s by out-of-control filibusterers like William Walker intent on seizing this Caribbean island or that Central America land.

The lieutenant needed new allies if the Amazon expedition were ever to get underway. In a New Orleans editor, James Dunwoody Brownson DeBow, Maury found one of his strongest. The filibusterers of the pen looked at the world in the same way—with the United States at its center, Europe and Asia off to the sides, and all the islands of the West Indies and countries of Latin America lying at the great republic's feet.[32]

The phrase *Manifest Destiny* now sounds like an echo from the past, but

Manifest Destiny in the 1850s stirred American souls. As DeBow wrote and Maury believed,

> We have a destiny to perform—a "manifest destiny" over old Mexico, over South America, over the West Indies and Canada. The Sandwich Islands are necessary to our eastern, as the isles of the Gulf to our western commerce. The gates of the Chinese empire must be thrown down by the men from Sacramento and the Oregon and the haughty Japanese tramples upon the cross be enlightened by the doctrines of republicanism and the ballot box.[33]

The decrees of a Latin American empire appeared as solid as manacles on Bahian slaves when viewed from a magazine office in New Orleans and the observatory grounds in Washington. But the Amazon's lure was too great to allow old decrees let grand opportunities slip by.

Maury's idea, approved by two secretaries, was to have Herndon and Gibbon, a passed midshipman, start in Peru on tributaries of the river and continue to Bolivia, then to come into the Amazon in Brazil. The two countries had recently opened the river to other nations, so their approval was expected. An important part of their mission to Peru and Bolivia in Maury's orders was sounding out the two governments about resettling American slaves in their countries.[34]

The superintendent thought the expedition could be done for three thousand dollars. He wrote Herndon with instructions of what he should do and what he should get from traders in the countries he visited. Again, Maury drew on William Bolton Finch's example on *Vincennes*. The superintendent also kept his brother-in-law posted on the slow shifting of the Navy's attention away from stopping filibusterers in Cuba, Mexico, and Nicaragua to opening the Amazon to American business and agriculture.

When the path through the Navy's bureaucracy cleared, the crippled Maury wrote Herndon, "Imagine myself by your side looking with your eyes at nature as she will display herself in her gorgeous and glorious kingdoms before you and listening with your ears to the answers to the various questions that you will propound to the 'lords of creation.'"[35]

The two took his advice to heart. Herndon suggested that Gibbon and his party start alone in Bolivia, while he embarked from Peru into a vast region of silver mines, lands that Maury had only surmised existed in his time in Lima. What Herndon found in the camps was hell on earth:

> There are no ladies—at least I saw none in society; and the men meet to discuss the mines, the probable price of quicksilver, and to slander and abuse each other. There seems to be no religion here even in form. The churches are mere barns, going to decay; and I saw no processions or religious ceremonies.[36]

Herndon and his men braved rapids and crocodiles, met more tough miners, and engaged European naturalists before reaching the sea.

> I fancy I can hear the crash of the forest falling to make room for the cultivation of cotton, cocoa, rice, and sugar, and the sharp shriek of the saw cutting into boards the beautiful and valuable woods of the country; that I can see the gatherers of India-rubber and copaiba redoubling their efforts, to be enabled to purchase new and convenient things that shall be presented at the doors of their huts in the wilderness; and even the wild Indian finding the way from his pathless forests to the steamboat depot to exchange his collections of vanilla, spices, dyes, drugs, and gums, for the things that would take his fancy—ribbons, beads, bells, mirrors, and gay trinkets.[37]

That was what Maury wanted. It was also what Raymond's *New York Times* had asked for. Unlike Lynch, Herndon wrote quickly and facilely, like Maury. It fit the superintendent's purpose of never letting Congress and the public forget what the Navy did for the nation.[38]

Writing under a variety of pseudonyms, including Inca, and quoting himself, Maury propounded the Amazon as the place where Southerners especially could "revolutionize and republicanize and Anglo-Saxonize that valley."[39]

Maury wrote, "Brazil should be invited into a negotiation by which American citizens should have the right of introducing their slaves into that empire and of holding real estate upon the same terms and conditions with the privileges of citizens and devising the same that Brazilian subjects have."[40]

Ideas that he bandied about parlors of Virginia plantations for years had solidified into speeches and magazine articles that proclaimed slavery must expand to preserve slavery.[41]

No matter what his antislavery Blackford relatives thought, Maury knew this expedition, his writings, and those of Herndon and Gibbon touched a responsive chord. Opening the Amazon became the "the question of the age" for Southerners, even more so than the future of Cuba. It also was a sure way to get around the Compromise of 1850's barring slavery in California, New Mexico, and Utah.[42]

"Men may talk about Cuba and Japan; but of all the diplomatic questions of the day, the free navigation of those majestic watercourses and their tributaries, is to this country the most interesting and most important. It surpasses them all. It is paramount," Maury wrote.[43]

Maury took to the stump as never before to sell the Amazon. He had used scientific gatherings to achieve political ends to support naval research in the past, but opening the Amazon cut across politics and commerce, regionalism, and nationalism. Other naval officers, such as Robert F. Stockton, had political ambitions, but none moved in and out of their roles as commissioned members of the federal armed forces not only to participate in but also lead popular movements as frequently as Maury. Only Winfield Scott and Zachary Taylor in the regular Army could best him in this regard.[44]

"For fifteen years, the Mississippi Valley seethed with the rivalries of competing towns and with the intrigues of promoters" over being the terminus of the transcontinental railroad, historian David Potter wrote. Ready to stir the cauldron was Maury in Washington. He only needed to be asked. The Southern commercial convention movement gave him orchestra halls for his Amazon idylls. At the 1849 Southern Commercial Convention in Memphis, the music he played was written in the Panic of 1837. Direct trade with foreign countries and the twin question of the future of the Amazon grew as articles of faith among Southern politicians, agriculturalists, and merchants.[45]

But how to break the North's grip on commerce and open Brazil? The answers for Maury and many men of his time lay in the Mississippi River Valley's vibrant cities. From Chicago heralded by Senator Stephen A. Douglas, St. Louis proclaimed by Senator Thomas Hart Benton to New Orleans promoted by Pierre Soule, these cities' politicians and businessmen had a lean and hungry look. Like the others, Memphis businessmen, flexing their muscles, saw their city as a river hub with steamboat access to the Gulf of Mexico and, with luck and guile, the city where the rails from the East met the rails from the West. They were ready to host a congress to address the South's economic concerns and their own dreams. They needed a public figure to preside over such a gathering. They chose Matthew Fontaine Maury, the maestro and visionary.[46]

Maury's love of the limelight burned especially brightly then. In the observatory, Maury, as early as June 1848, drafted resolutions for the convention's consideration. He wanted the secretary of war to estimate the cost of establishing steam communication between Memphis and the Pacific Coast, the secretary of the Navy to survey the coast of California and Oregon for a suitable dockyard site and placement of lighthouses, and the postmaster general to contract for "carrying a horse mail at least once a month" between San Francisco and Santa Fe.[47]

The superintendent launched a preconvention press campaign to win unanimity on big questions. Maury went so far, in the instance of the isthmian crossing, as to tell DeBow to shelve a pet project of New Orleans businessmen like Soule and Judah P. Benjamin. Maury called the survey of the Tehuantepec route through the Yucatan Peninsula of Mexico "shameful.... I look upon the Panama rail road as but a continuation of the California rail road."[48]

So as he pooh-poohed the idea of a Yucatan crossing, Maury ballyhooed New Orleans as another transcontinental railroad terminus: "If you stretch a string on a common terrestrial globe from Panama to China, you will find that it passes not far from New Orleans. Therefore when that railroad to the Pacific shall be built New Orleans will be the thoroughfare of travel between South America, California and China."[49]

When asked by Congress on the value of a transcontinental rail line, Maury quoted his grandfather's letter of 1756 of the interconnectedness of the West to the seaboard colonies. "Survey, survey, was the word then. I am sick of surveys," Maury wrote. "The paths through the mountains are known, so build."[50]

Over the next few years, Southern cities vied with one another to host these conventions. In 1852, Baltimore's merchants rammed through resolutions boosting the Maryland city's charms and commerce. If they expected Maury's endorsement, they misread the man. There, Maury spoke only about the Amazon: "Lay the foundation of direct trade and close commercial relations with Brazil and the Atlantic slopes of South America generally and with the Amazon in particular."[51]

Maury next took his Amazon gospel to Norfolk, where he preached the virtues of Virginia's opening a direct steamer line to Rio de Janeiro: "I have some friends who are now in the valley of the Amazon, exploring its resources and examining its capabilities for commerce, population and agriculture. Everything I have from them confirms to me more and more of the importance of this subject and also the necessity of the South moving promptly and energetically if she moves at all."[52]

Early on the *Southern Quarterly Review* saw all these conventions as producing only so many "windy resolutions." Maury's fixation on the Amazon and his other faraway interests—the isthmian crossing, the transcontinental railroad, etc.—were grandiose distractions that drained capital and energy from necessary local, state, and regional public works the South needed. The grueling work of securing capital to build this industry, improve that turnpike, lay more track of a standard gauge, etc., never materialized; that work proved critical if the South were to challenge Northern economic domination.[53]

In 1865, a few thousand beaten Confederates did pick up Maury's old song about a new Eden and moved to the Amazon rather than live in the occupied South. Maury chose not to go. Instead, he tried to entice other disaffected Southerners to come to a Habsburg-ruled Mexico.[54]

The convention movement died away, but Maury's visions of the Amazon's untapped riches and great explorations lived on. Secretary Kennedy was so taken by Maury that he proposed creating a naval scientific corps with its own line of promotion to reward the lieutenant.

The secretary wanted a corps of eighty officers independent of the regular Navy and answerable to him. These specialists would carry out all the hydrographical surveys and chart-making, improve naval ordnance, and supervise dockyards. Kennedy's proposal went nowhere. Several years later, Maury looked down his nose at the very idea of a naval scientific corps.[55]

The superintendent relished DeBow's commentary on his work as a navalist and as a Southern nationalist at the time: "No man's doing more for the sea interests than Lieut. Maury, and the South has no son more devoted to her advancement."[56]

14. Gauging the Politics of Weather

As a toddler, Matthew Fontaine Maury had seen his father, his brothers, and their slaves work from spring planting through hoped-for summer rains, and the long fall curing season, trying to conjure a sweet, choice tobacco crop from the hard, iron soil of the Virginia Wilderness. As an adolescent, he had toiled through the changing seasons with his family and their slaves trying to bring in enough cotton from the rich Tennessee bluegrass to stave off ruin for another year. And as a young man, Maury had been baptized in the winter rains of the Mediterranean, confirmed in the heat and dull winds of the tropics, anointed with ice in running the South Atlantic, blessed with afternoon showers in Pacific islands, and shriven for days in the Asian monsoons.

Maury was more taken by the weather than any Tidewater planter, hardscrabble Appalachian farmer, or old salt sailor. The *Wind and Current Charts* that the observatory produced from 1848 to 1861 were his continuing study of weather at sea. For the superintendent of the National Observatory, there were never enough data on the weather—afloat or ashore.[1]

In fact, by the 1850s, he angled to gather weather data on the land. Maury intended to run through, past, or around any obstacles the Smithsonian Institution and the surgeon general of the Army might throw in his way. To Maury, gathering weather and climatological information was not enough; publishing that information quickly and distributing it widely was the key. In that regard, neither the Smithsonian nor the Army felt rushed or moved.[2]

As his own schemes unfolded, Maury had to weather a personal fury unleashed by a onetime benefactor. In August 1851, Alexander Dallas Bache, the superintendent of the Coast Survey, said in his outgoing address as president of the American Association for the Advancement of Science:

> Our real danger lies now from a modified charlatanism, which makes merit in one subject an excuse for asking authority in others, or in all.... I remember well the chilling effect produced upon men, when you ... applied to a distinguished scientific writer, that he was not a "mere dry man of science." ... I have sometimes thought there was danger in the opposite.

The split at least five years in the making between "pure scientists" and "popular scientists" was now a chasm rent by jealousy. That year, Maury, a literary man whose writing Bache once lauded, was pointedly left off the association's meteorological committee.[3]

The speech and the snub spurred Maury on. Within two months, an inquiry from the British handed the lieutenant the necessary opening. The Royal Engineers modestly proposed taking meteorological observations from several foreign locations using standardized instruments.

The State Department sent the proposal to the cabinet departments for comment; as head of the observatory, Maury drafted the Navy's response. He immodestly proposed using an existing model for such study: the one he had devised for the Navy and American merchantmen. He had sped past the Smithsonian and the surgeon general:

> We must look to the sea for the rule, to the land for the exceptions. Therefore no general system of meteorological observations can be considered complete unless it embraces the sea as well as the land. The value of researches conducted at this office with regard to the meteorology of the sea was greatly enhanced by cooperation from the observatories on land.

By doing that, Maury resurrected the central idea from an aborted international project on sharing meteorological and magnetic data several years before. He also drew on Sir John Herschel, a fellow in the Royal Society, who commented, "Sea as well as land observations are, however, equally required for the effectual working out of these great physical problems."[4]

The superintendent next asked Abbott Lawrence, the United States minister in London, for the names of people to contact in Great Britain and then beseeched William Cabell Rives, the minister in Paris, to sound out the French about hosting an international meteorological conference in the summer of 1852.

Maury gave the naysayers and the go-slowers little chance to drag their feet. From the observatory, he wrote ministers from Europe, Asia, and Latin America on the benefits of cooperation in studying weather.[5]

He wrote Peter Parker, the minister and longtime missionary to China: "I am aware that the Chinese are a curious people, and that they are peculiarly averse to things generally which involve a departure from established usages and that therefore it may be useless to attempt to get them to act in concert with the rest of mankind in this matter." Nevertheless, he tried but failed to win the emperor's support.[6]

Maury moved at dervish speed at home as well. Captain Charles Morris, as head of the Bureau of Ordnance and Hydrography, strongly backed the "amendment" to the British proposal; so did Navy Secretary William Graham, a longtime Maury ally. "The suggestions for a more general and widely extended cooperation upon some uniform plan promises so many advantages that hopes may be reasonable indulged for its eventual adoption."

Each member of Millard Fillmore's cabinet was sent the instructions from the secretary of the Navy to have an international conference to "agree upon a system of meteorological observations which may be followed by meteorologists and navigators generally." His politicking paid off in December 1851, when Secretary of State Daniel Webster accepted the Navy's response as the American position.[7]

While he awaited ministerial response, Maury stormed Europe's scientists, especially Alexander von Humboldt, to push their governments to agree to a conference on weather. When the German, who became famous for exploring South America, endorsed the idea, the superintendent was jubilant. "It removes difficulties, breaks down obstacles, makes friends for the work and enlists many laborers for the field."[8]

As 1852 began, Maury faced the inevitable domestically and invited the cooperation of Joseph Henry, Bache, the Army, and other American scientists to set up the conference. Despite all the pushing and shoving from the Sears Walker debacle on, the superintendent truly needed Henry's endorsement. Maury asked that a joint letter be sent to the states' governors to encourage them to conduct weather observations similar to those being done in Massachusetts and New York. This would give the appearance of harmony on the American side. Maury added disingenuously that "I do not and cannot think for a moment of having anything to do with the observations on shore. I mean as I have done to confine myself exclusively to the sea."

For a time, Henry was quiet, possibly shocked by the speed with which Maury stampeded support at home and abroad for such an ambitious gathering. Nothing like this had been tried before, and there were too many questions to be answered before any institution—much less nation—could agree to such a gathering. The whole grandstanding idea was typical of Maury, the observatory, and the Navy. It also flew in the face of Henry's own more slender plans.[9]

The Smithsonian secretary earlier had sought British cooperation in studying North American weather, and such a large international conference as Maury wanted would divert the two nations' attention away from an essential continental project. Henry quietly launched his counterattack through the Royal Society in May 1852.[10]

Bache stated unequivocally that governments had no role in establishing, sponsoring, or even attending a meteorological conference. Any international gathering should be under the auspices of the American Association for the Advancement of Science and its British counterpart. That way Maury and his grand scheme could be ignored. No charlatans admitted.[11]

The surgeon general fell into skeptical line: "Our observers, many of them enlisted men acting under the supervision of the medical officers, are not competent to undertake any complicated system. Nor would their other various duties permit them to devote much extra time to such purposes. Consequently the aim of the department has been simplicity, both in the instruments employed and the mode of recording the results of the observations."[12]

In Great Britain, Colonel Edward Sabine, of the engineers and a secretary of the Royal Society, had in his hand Henry's letter. Sabine, recognized for his pioneering study of magnetism, took the letter back to his fellow officers. What was going on with the Americans? Amidst the confusion from the United States, the engineers opted out. The society suggested the British government cooperate in gathering weather information at sea.

The Americans were back squabbling among themselves. In late May 1852, Henry reminded Maury, "The proposition was that you should take charge of the dominion of the sea, that the Smithsonian Institution should collect observations from the eastern part of the United States, the surgeon general of the army from the western; and the British government from the northern part of the continent." Henry had Maury in check, but not mate.[13]

Despite the administration's backing, Maury was prepared to "abandon for the present at least that part of the 'universal system' which relates to the land." The accent remained on the phrase *for the present*.[14]

Maury clung to of the idea of an international conference. If the sea was his domain, then Maury would proceed with a conference on marine meteorology. In early spring 1853, he sent a new round of letters to the ministers of Russia, Britain, France, Holland, Prussia, Denmark, and Brazil, expanding on the benefits for trade that would come from such a gathering.

"A work of such a character in the middle of the nineteenth century may therefore commend itself to the attention of every intelligent navigator whatever the flag under which he may sail or whatever the character of the vessel, public or private in which he may serve."[15]

He expressed similar sentiments to Captain Henry James of the Royal

Engineers, saying, "What a spectacle! The idea of having merchantmen of all nations and men of war of all flags, as the prospect now seems to be, uniting together ... in a great field of philosophical research is certainly glorious."[16]

The British and French governments, sliding toward war in the Black Sea with Russia, paid little heed to the latest pleas from Washington. Tiny Belgium, however, offered to host the gathering. With that precarious foothold, Maury secured the permission of the new Navy secretary, James C. Dobbin, to convene the congress in Brussels on August 23. The risks of failure were high; only Denmark, the Netherlands, Sweden and Norway—minor powers all—said they would attend.

Maury kept the pressure on the Europeans: "Governments are slow to act, and I have not heard whether a majority of them will come into the proposition." One important government was not so slow to act. In St. Petersburg, events moved Maury's way. Newly installed in office, Grand Duke Konstantin Nikolayevich, the manager of Russia's Marine Ministry, was intrigued by the initiative and wanted more information.[17]

As a last act before leaving for Europe, Maury again invited France and Great Britain to attend. If that did not succeed, he intended to appeal directly to his British supporters to force Queen Victoria's government's hand. He then sailed for Liverpool with his two oldest daughters, Betty and Diana; Ellen Herndon, daughter of his brother-in-law; and Ellen Maury, the daughter of his cousin John Walker Maury, mayor of Washington, in tow.

In Liverpool, for decades the home of his uncle, the Old Consul, James Maury, Matthew Fontaine Maury addressed ship owners and underwriters. In the audience that day as the owners and underwriters pledged their support was Russian Captain-Lieutenant Aleksey Gorkovenko on Konstantin's orders.

The graduate of the imperial naval college was an officer experienced with meteorology. More importantly, Gorkovenko "had a good command of English," having translated Charles Dickens and Frederick Marryat for a Russian audience. He listened attentively to what Maury had to say.

After Maury finished, the Russian approached the American. Having won pledges from the British ship owners to share logbooks in exchange for the American charts, Maury gladly told Gorkovenko about his plans for Brussels. As the two talked about the Russians adopting his system of meteorological observations, Maury suggested they travel together and added that he was interested in coming to St. Petersburg when the conference ended.[18]

While the Russian news was positive, the news in Great Britain remained troublesome. Maury learned from Lord Wrottesley, soon to head the Royal Society, that the Commons supported participation, but the Admiralty balked.

Maury believed the way through the Admiralty lay in winning over more businessmen, especially in the city of London, to the cause. With Gorkovenko in this audience, too, Maury delivered an address on the importance of international cooperation in charting the winds and currents that electrified the brokers at Lloyd's. The most tantalizing aspect of the speech was Maury's assertion of the economic boom that would follow such a conference. As a letter in his support read, "It is impossible to overrate the amount of benefit that may be conferred on navigation and on the commerce of our nations by the unification of his *Theory of Wind and Currents* by means of systematic observations which he is laboring to establish. His views are broad and liberal, and his plan simple."[19]

Maury's drum beating and the insurers' chorus of unending support paid off. As he was to sail for Calais, the Royal Navy announced her majesty's government would send Captain Frederick W. Beechey, arctic explorer and member of the Board of Trade and Admiralty, to Brussels as its representative. Accompanying him would be a correspondent of Maury's, Captain Henry James of the Royal Engineers.

The French, not wanting to be isolated, agreed to send Alexander de la Marche, hydrographic engineer of Napoleon III's imperial navy. At last, the great European maritime powers—Britain, France, and Russia—were to be present. With war in the Crimea looming, how these three large European nations, represented by their navies, would work together was another matter.[20]

As acting superintendent, George Minor wrote before all the evidence was in, "Maury has met with a distinguished reception in Europe, particularly in England, and he will return home with a newly won garland around his brow."[21]

In Brussels, the only civilian attending, poet and mathematician Lambert Adolphe Jacques Quetelet, Belgium's royal astronomer, was chosen president of the congress. It was an omen of future accord. Maury, as the first speaker, promised his latest charts as a reward to all who participated in collecting and sharing data. His speech set the congress's agenda.

In the audience was Marin Jansen, representing the Netherlands, agreeing time and again with Maury. The superintendent had met the tall, very correct naval officer in Washington earlier. Both had overcome physical adversity—Maury his lameness and Jansen battling the aftereffects of his long service in the tropics. Building upon that useful meeting in Washington, this intense time in Brussels found Jansen and Maury moving from being acquaintances to becoming friends, and later trusted allies.

Point by salient point the conferees agreed on what kind of barometers, thermometers, and anemometers would be used. Next they had to hammer out what they wanted collected and when they wanted it done. During their two-week, nonstop session, the conferees built the standards for marine meteorology.[22]

The conferees insisted that, even in times of war, nations must continue gathering and sending data to Washington. "Though they may be enemies in all else, here they are to be friends," Maury added.

At the concluding banquet, the king of Belgium, Leopold I, saluted the conferees for making "every ship a floating observatory, a temple of science."[23]

Basking in success and with the four young women, Maury was off to meet von Humboldt in Berlin. When Maury called, the American found the German scientist studying the deep-sea soundings in the *Sailing Directions*. Maury was delighted. Although his proposed trip to Russia was postponed, Gorkovenko was not through with the superintendent. With Maury's encouragement, he journeyed to the United States "to make a close study of the American Fleet."[24]

More good news greeted Maury when he returned to Washington. Spain and Prussia joined the meteorological effort; Portugal, Hamburg, Bremen, Chile, and Brazil soon followed suit. In Britain, the government put Captain Robert FitzRoy, now of the Board of Trade and commander of the *Beagle* expedition, in charge of a special meteorological office.

All this was a heady brew for Maury. Maybe, just maybe, he could employ that international spirit of cooperation to study weather on land.

"So too with the meteorologists of the land; the great body of them also is made up of amateurs. But governments have their military posts, their lighthouses, and hospitals, institutions of higher learning, observatories and other public establishments ... where meteorological observations have already been instituted or where they may be instituted almost without cost," Maury said.[25]

In 1854, the time to strike for another international congress—this one on land meteorology—seemed at hand. The earlier opposition from the Royal Engineers and Army's surgeon general had evaporated. To keep Bache and Henry at bay, Maury suggested to the British that they lead the way.

Pressing the fight domestically, he wrote in *American Farmer:*

> If any officer of the government were authorized to say to the farmers, as I have to the sailors, here is the form of a meteorological journal, it shows you the observations that are wanted, the hours at which they are to be made, tells what instruments are required, and how they are to be used, take it, furnish the government with the observations and in return the government will discuss them and give you a copy

> of the result when published. He would have at once and without cost a volunteer corps of observers that would furnish him with all the data requested for a complete study of both agricultural and sanitary meteorology.[26]

He held out the dream that the Old World and the New World would soon share information through a transatlantic telegraph cable: "We shall have the whole surface of our planet covered with meteorological observers acting in concert."[27]

When Britain failed to lead because of the Crimean War, Maury was brought back to earth. Lamely, he suggested waiting until the reconvening of the international maritime congress four years away. He also felt that "jealousies among the so-called scientifics have prevented me from carrying out my plans as to another meteorological conference."[28]

Maury intended to keep fanning the domestic fires. He wrote Edmund Ruffin, a pioneering agriculturalist and Southern fire-eater:

> But this system of research with its teeming results is confined to the sea; therefore it may be asked by some farmers what have we landsmen to do with it? ... The germinations of the seed and the growth of the plant are but the display of meteorological force, the expression of atmospheric laws which when rightly understood cannot fail to confer upon agriculture and the well-being of the benefits as signal as the study of the movement of the same grand machine of the seas has conferred upon commerce and navigation.

To the Maryland Agricultural Society in 1855, Maury spelled out the advantages of sharing weather information: "The farmer you know is not interested in his own crops alone, but in those of his neighbor also; and knowledge of the prospect or state of the crop in England, France and other countries is as important for his own."[29]

Maury stumbled—not directly in combating his scientific critics, but in protecting himself in the Navy. By the fall of 1855, he was in a deep professional crisis that threatened his naval career and his position at the observatory. (The crisis will be discussed in Chapter 16.)

A chastened Maury wrote the editor of the *New York Tribune* in December 1855:

> The object I have in view is to cooperate with, not to work in opposition to the Smithsonian Institution, the meteorological department of the surgeon general of the army or any establishment whatever. The field is an immense one, and there is room without rivalry or opposition in it for all the laborers and all the talent that a dozen other systems can cull out.[30]

At no time before the Civil War were the differences between Maury and Henry over a national weather service so dramatically demonstrated as in 1856.

The superintendent, forcibly retired from naval service, probably thought himself in safe waters when he spoke before the United States Agricultural Society. Before the society was a resolution that called for the cooperation Maury advocated between land and sea observations. A second resolution called for one of the society's committees to press Congress to secure this cooperation.

"In the progress of discussing the observations thus obtained from the sea, we have arrived at that point at which observations on the land are found to be essential to a successful prosecution of the grand atmospherical machine," Maury said in his address.[31]

Maury denied that he offered a separate method from the Smithsonian's: "I have no doubt that the idea of rivalry in such a subject astonished my friend—if he will allow me so to call him—the distinguished Secretary of this institution, quite as much as it did myself."[32]

Henry, at least, before this audience, professed his appreciation of Maury's work, but the secretary insisted that the maritime study of weather was far different from what had to be done on the land. Already, he said, the Smithsonian had arranged for special equipment to be sent to selected places in the United States to ensure the accuracy of observations. Instead of proceeding with Maury's plan to teach farmers how to make the observations, Henry suggested that a committee of scientific men examine meteorology for agriculture.

Maury's call for the instantaneous transmission and dissemination of weather information was too much, Henry said, because, in effect, the superintendent was no scientist. On that point, Henry never yielded.[33]

As Maury wrote B. Franklin Minor, friend and cousin, "I had a regular scientific fight, and though the result was all I could have desired, yet it was utterly disgusting to encounter such miserable signs of jealousy and small feeling.... The two plans were no more rivals than the astronomical observatories which are opening up in various parts of the country." Where Maury saw linkages, Henry saw shoddiness.[34]

Maury was down, but not out. By late 1856, the Senate Agriculture Committee considered appropriating twenty thousand dollars to make daily weather observations and national reports for the observatory, not the Smithsonian.[35]

In efforts to defeat the bill, attacks on Maury's acumen were stepped up. As X wrote in the *Boston Atlas*, "Our scientific repute aboard may not be very high, but it is not quite so low as though entrusted to the 'Chief Hydrographer.' Let those be held responsible who keep him in office,—but not the seminaries of learning in the United States, nor those who give their attention to study."[36]

Henry won that round in the Senate, as he would later ones on the national weather service. The fight over the weather service was becoming an endless struggle in the press, at the lectern, in the Congress, and in one administration after another. Maury bristled, knowing that the Smithsonian received daily weather reports from around the nation. Snugly inside its castle was a map of the continent instantly updated on any changes—especially severe weather, but the public had to wait until the observations were published annually. Why wasn't this information given immediately to the men who could benefit from it? *Cui bono?*

In the capital, and trying to sidestep the parceling of meteorological duties in North America, Maury urged the Navy secretary to have lighthouse keepers along the Great Lakes make observations for a few minutes each day. The Lake Board of Underwriters, led by President E. P. Dorr, responded as enthusiastically as China trader Robert Bennet Forbes had a decade earlier. It was not enough.[37]

By 1858 and on the road for the national weather service cause, Maury gave twelve lectures in two weeks in Ohio. Two weeks later, he was back on the road along the Great Lakes and in the upper Midwest—Rochester, Cleveland, Indianapolis, Cincinnati, and Chicago, suffering through the cold, snow, the onset of rheumatism, and gout.

As always, there was a second purpose for these tours. He was counting on the $50 here and the $112 there for his family's future. His father's travails with debt and his own pressing needs when he was on half pay, especially during the "Plucking Board" squabble, were reminders of how tight circumstances could be. In this case in 1858, he was raising money to pay for his son Richard's education at the University of Virginia, and there were more children in line for the education he never received.[38]

Even trips to Alabama and Tennessee, although arousing popular support, were not enough to overcome Henry's strength in Congress.[39]

By the end of the 1850s, when the University of Virginia's Board of Visitors tendered Maury an offer in a "school of physical geography and agricultural science," he was tempted, but the public man in Washington was not yet ready for the academic life in Charlottesville. He had invested years in fighting to hold his rank in the Navy and position at the observatory.[40]

For Maury, there was so much to do in Washington, still the head of the observatory. The national weather service was now at the center of his concerns, and that old question, *Cui bono?*, was ever present. Why couldn't Henry see that? Even the splintering of the country did not fracture his belief that such a broad-based service was absolutely essential. Indeed, with the Civil War less than a year away, Maury wrote the governor of Ohio seeking his support to overcome "miserable scientific jealousies."[41]

Yet, Henry did not budge on using trained observers proceeding meticulously to collect data. Only the Civil War stopped the reports from coming in, the "wires from the north and west being so entirely occupied by public business that no use of them could be obtained for scientific purposes."[42]

Not surprisingly, that was not how Maury viewed the impasse. To Belgium's Quetelet, he wrote, "'The green eyed monster' is at work here in certain quarters and thus I am somewhat interfered with. I see at present no prospect of another conference of land co-operation, unless you on your side will inaugurate a system for Europe and shove us into it."

In his own defense, Maury added, "The true problem with which I have had to deal was to use my opportunities as to produce the greatest good to the greatest numbers. By the fruits of my labor, let me be judged."[43]

The fruits of his labor were bounteous. In the late 1850s, a reinvigorated Maury had more than 137,540 vessels, employing a million men and boys, all gathering the information that would shame the scientists who doubted the abilities of mariners to record weather.

"It is the largest fleet that has ever been seen to act in concert, for any purpose whatever, since the world began," he boasted, and its purpose was peaceful. Because of Maury's energy and persistence, "for the first time, the United States led the way in a branch of science," in spite of Bache and Henry.[44]

15. Some Fair Winds

For Matthew Fontaine Maury, 1855 was the year of tempests. As described in Chapter 14, he battled heavy squalls in the contest over a national weather service. It was also a year in which the red light of morning and fair winds propelled his writings to wide popular acclaim, but ended in a hurricane that almost swamped his naval career and laid waste to the observatory's science in support of the "Great Enterprise," the laying of the transatlantic telegraph cable. (These events will be discussed in the following chapters.)[1]

The red light of morning came in one of his shortest, but most important works, *Lanes for the Steamers Crossing the Atlantic*. It was an era of racing steamers across the Atlantic and steamboats up and down the rivers of America. Little concern was paid to safety. The October 1854 collision between the mail steamer *Arctic* and *Vesta* that claimed more than 350 lives in the foggy North Atlantic stunned Robert Bennet Forbes, Maury's longtime acquaintance from Boston.[2]

Forbes believed that lanes could be created to separate ships crossing the Atlantic that would not significantly add to the voyage's length, but dramatically increase safety. The superintendent and the staff pored over forty-six thousand days of observations from hundreds of ships. When they finished, Maury sketched "double track railway" lanes that were twenty to twenty-five miles wide. The lanes would be adjusted seasonally to keep captains and masters well away from icebergs and fogs. He noted that the lanes added only seventy-five miles to the voyage.

To Captain Charles Morris, his commanding officer, Maury wrote: "To set apart these lanes for the use of steamers requires the common consent of those who use that part of the sea in which they lie. The shipping interests of Boston and New York have received the proposition with favor. It is desirable to have the examples of the government also in furtherance of the plan."[3]

Maury wrote Forbes, his Boston associates, and New York merchants that the lanes were already printed on Navy charts, and that he was appealing to the Europeans to follow them. Most did, but the British, through Robert FitzRoy at the Board of Trade, agreed that the lanes were acceptable for paddle wheelers, but not screw steamers. For decades Great Britain held off adopting them.[4]

While this was an important work and signaled the red light of morning, popular acclaim was even more surely within Maury's grasp.

The fair winds of 1855 blew in from his Philadelphia publisher. E. C. and J. Biddle believed that the superintendent's knowledge of the sea contained in the *Sailing Directions,* articles in the *Southern Literary Messenger,* and other periodicals could be turned into a book, and they wanted to talk to him about such a venture. Maury pleaded the press of business in Washington and sent his nephew Dabney, an Army officer stationed in Philadelphia, instead. Before they were through, the publishers made sure Maury's nephew understood that if the superintendent did not write such a volume, then someone else could—using much of Maury's work from the public record—and that person would reap the financial benefits of what likely would be a very popular book.[5]

That was good enough for Maury. He now tested the marketing waters by suggesting to Navy Secretary James C. Dobbin that a work on the oceans could be a midshipman's textbook: "The researches which have been carried on at this office now for a number of years concerning the winds and currents and other phenomena bearing upon the commercial uses of the sea have led to the development of an amount of information sufficient in the opinion of Baron Humboldt to constitute a new department of science which he calls physical geography of the sea."[6]

The Biddles, who did the observatory's specialty printing, suggested that Harper and Brothers in New York handle Maury's book. Starting in the spring of 1854, Maury wrote *The Physical Geography of the Sea* on his own time. The lieutenant never possessed a fine hand, and his daughters, Betty and Diana, copied, criticized, and questioned the manuscript. Instead of disregarding what his children said, he encouraged them to be more exacting. By June, he was finished writing; by December, he was reading proof.[7]

Maury opened the *Physical Geography* with a description of the Gulf Stream that is one of the most memorable examples of his writing:

> There is a river in the ocean. In the severest droughts it never fails and in the mightiest floods it never overflows. Its banks and its bottom are of cold water, while its current is of warm. The Gulf of Mexico is its fountain, and its mouth is in the Arctic

Seas. It is the Gulf Stream. There is in the world no other such majestic flow of waters.[8]

Maury, the high-flying risk taker, wanted all ideas about natural science to be examined, challenged, debated, and refined. The superintendent could change them as necessary. As he wrote in a later edition, "True progress consists in the discovery of error as well as truth."[9]

In this book, he connected the layman to the ocean he could see and the invisible one that surrounded him—the atmosphere. From first to last, Maury used dozens of charts to show the reader the winds, ocean climates, and storms. Later editions honored men who made the study of the ocean their lives. Lieutenant John Mercer Brooke's work in determining the depth of the sea is lavishly recounted in discussing the transatlantic cable project.[10]

Here, in one book, were also the stories of the whalers, the findings of paths across the sea, the great explorations, and the weather over two-thirds of the earth.

In *The Physical Geography of the Sea*, Maury used not only the stylistic lessons gleaned from the King James Version of the Bible, but also stirred in religion and science. He was rendering the "natural order" of the "Almighty hand" as evident in the "harmonies of nature.... Whether of the land or the sea, the inhabitants are all His creatures, subjects of His laws and agents in His economy."[11]

What he wrote reflected his religiosity, one of the pillars of his life, and his commitment to educating himself and others, another pillar.

In a letter then, Maury wrote:

> The rule is never to forget who is the author of the great volume which nature spreads out before us, always to remember the same being is also the author the Book of Revelation holds up to us; and though the two worlds are entirely different, their records are equally true, and then they bear upon the same point as now and when they do, it is impossible that they should contradict each other. If the two cannot be reconciled, the fault is ours.[12]

Praise for *The Physical Geography of the Sea* was a zephyr, and the book went through five printings in its first year in the United States and was soon available in Europe. The great acclaim that came with this work seemed but another laurel for the man who brought nations together in peaceful research of the oceans. His popularity with the general public was soaring. Jules Verne kept a copy at his side as he wrote *Twenty Thousand Leagues Under the Sea*.[13]

In writing this book, Maury also helped establish ocean science as a field of study. His knowledge of currents, of winds, even of ships, made the work unmistakably his. By attaching Alexander von Humboldt's phrase *physical geography* to the title, Maury signaled this book was laden with concrete examples, such as the tides in the East Indies, drawn from data collected there, as well as Maury's ruminations about God and man. He was projecting himself as one of the world's practical and useful scientists.

Sir John Hershel, a prominent British astronomer; James P. Espy, the "Storm King" and former Maury colleague; and a few others challenged, even ridiculed, parts of the huge "strangely fascinating yet wildly disorganized book." But Maury had the satisfaction of being the trailblazer in gathering in one book so much data on the world's seas. In it, he "had confronted most of the basic questions that defined the new science."[14]

The fair winds seemed as steady as the trades. An enthused Senator Stephen R. Mallory of Florida pointed out that Maury, who because of his stage coach accident paid the price of shore duty by remaining a lieutenant, did the work of three men in Great Britain. The chairman of the Naval Affairs Committee proposed a new kind of "prize-money," the reward for capturing an enemy vessel in a time of war, for the lieutenant's *Wind and Current Charts*. The twenty-five thousand dollar prize was to be Maury's reward for "the energy that originality gives, and the excitement which is always attendant upon discovery and conscious progress towards the development of useful results." The Senate never acted on the request; indeed, within a few months, the Floridian likely wished he had never praised Maury's energy.[15]

The reason for the about-face was the latest hurricane of "naval reform" that Mallory spawned the year before. In that maelstrom, Maury, despite his scientific accomplishments, was seen as a superannuated lieutenant, clinging to one of the Navy's most prestigious billets. And in that sea state, the very integrity of the observatory's oceanic work was in danger of being undermined.

16. The Great Enterprise

Cyrus West Field was an extraordinarily energetic man on a lifelong quest for adventure, always doing. Like Matthew Fontaine Maury, Field came from a deeply religious family. The son of a Congregationalist minister, born in Stockbridge, Massachusetts, in 1819, was fond of mottoes. His came from John Bunyan's Puritan catechism, *Pilgrim's Progress*: "To know is a thing which pleaseth talkers and boosters; but to do is that which pleaseth God."[1]

Like many New Englanders, Field, the pleaser of God, gravitated to Manhattan in the mid–1830s, seeing in New York a "capital school." They found employment with earlier transplanted New Englanders, because "they are not afraid of work." Field's timing of the move was terrible.[2]

The Panic of 1837 left Field broke; the young man vowed that anyone who helped him then would be repaid in full—with interest. By 1851, Field was a leading merchant prince in the Gramercy Park realm of merchant princes. Among his neighbors were former coach maker Peter Cooper, the builder of "Tom Thumb," the first workable American locomotive and one of the nation's leading industrialists, and Chandler White, a longtime friend, and his brother David, a lawyer. Success, wealth, and prominence proved no cure for Field's restlessness. There always was more to do.[3]

Back in New York after a European grand tour, Field discovered the writings of "Inca" in the *National Intelligencer*. Here in black and white were Maury's tales of "a glowing wilderness and waste, which under the improvement and progress of the age, would soon be made to 'blossom as the rose.'" That caught Field's attention, so with renowned landscape artist Frederic Church as his companion, he trekked through the glowing wilderness, looking not for roses but new mining opportunities. Upon his return with "a flock of screeching parrots and a jaguar on a leash," Field needed a sounding board for an audacious idea. Maury was the man for that.[4]

Laying telegraphic cable across relatively narrow bodies of water had already been done. England and France were telegraphically connected in 1851. Telegraphy over great distances—like oceans—took money, planning, knowledge, and determination. Instead of weeks spent at sea, messages could be delivered in minutes or hours. From Maury, Field hoped in 1853 to obtain the oceanographic knowledge he needed to lay a seventeen hundred–mile transatlantic telegraph cable.[5]

At the same time, Field worked the problem of physics. There he ran headlong into the bitter feud between Joseph Henry of the Smithsonian and Samuel F. B. Morse, the artist-inventor, over who deserved credit for the telegraph.

Maury and the artist were linked in another way, other than through Henry's enmity. As Maury took up his Washington duties in 1842, Morse successfully stretched an electricity-carrying cable from Castle Garden to Governor's Island in New York Harbor, astonishing some spectators. Later that day, Samuel Colt demonstrated the potential of an electrical charge for harbor defense in blowing up a barge in the river. As the *New York Herald* wrote, "Bang! bang! bang!" as forty thousand spectators, including the secretary of war and Commodore Matthew C. Perry, the commandant of the New York Navy Yard, saw the aptly named *Volta* sink. Colt's application had eye-opening military applicability.[6]

In July 1853, when Field journeyed to Washington, Maury was preparing for the international meteorological conference in Brussels. As they met, the Navy's *Dolphin*, a research ship controlled by Maury, plumbed the Atlantic for a "telegraphic plateau." Without doubt, they talked about *Dolphin*'s mission and how its findings could help Field, shook hands, and parted. Their relationship was only beginning.[7]

Until the late 1840s, there was little need to know exactly how deep the ocean was at any one spot. Ships sailed on the water, not under it. Shoals, reefs, and rocks usually were close to islands or a mainland, not far out to sea. Once the building of a telegraphic link between North America and Europe appeared possible, the need for "blue water" soundings at depths of more than ten thousand feet gained importance.

The Coast Survey took soundings sixty miles off the shore of the United States and collected specimens from the bottom. The Navy gathered the same information from every ocean, and vessels under Maury's control were doing that. After Field's visit, the observatory had, in effect, been given the lead in researching what became popularly known as the "Great Enterprise." The enmity and jealousy that soured Alexander Dallas Bache's and Maury's relationship reached new depths of spite and calumny in Field's attempts to lay a transatlantic telegraph cable.[8]

What started with instructions to seventy-four-foot schooner *Taney* using winch and heavy wire to make soundings became an order from Secretary William Graham to all Navy vessels to help in "determining the shape of great oceanic basins."[9]

The usually inaccurate way of having a ship stop dead in the water for several hours in calm seas to take soundings ended when Passed Midshipman John Mercer Brooke, a Naval Academy graduate on the observatory's staff, created a device to measure depth and lift samples from the bottom.

Brooke's Patent Sounding Lead used a cannonball with a hole drilled through it, suspended on a line above a sampling tube. The momentum of dropping drove the tube into the seabed, and the lead fell away as the line slackened. Instead of hours, the thin line with tube could be rapidly hauled back into a small boat rather than a stopped-in-the-ocean warship or merchantman. The first test was made from *Dolphin*, under the command of Lieutenant Otway Berryman, on July 7, 1853. Berryman then took soundings every two hundred miles crossing and recrossing the Atlantic, hunting for the telegraphic plateau between Newfoundland and the Irish coast. His role in this drama would grow.[10]

Building on his earlier thesis in the *Bulletin of the National Institution*, Maury had a hunch about what would be found on the sea bottom:

> Between the two places is a plateau which seems to have been placed there expressly for the purpose of holding the wires of a submarine telegraph and of keeping them out of harm's way. It is neither too deep, nor too shallow. Yet it is so deep that the wires being once landed will remain forever beyond the reach of vessels, anchors, icebergs and drifts of any kind; and so shallow that the wires may be readily lodged upon the bottom.[11]

To Secretary James C. Dobbin, who came into office with Franklin Pierce's administration, Maury wrote:

> Had there been currents at the bottom these would have swept and abraded and mingled up with these microscopic remains the debris of the bottom of the sea, such as ooze, sand, gravel and other matter. But not a particle of sand or gravel was found among them. Hence the inference that those depths of the sea are not disturbed by either waves or currents.... The practicability of a submarine telegraph is proved.[12]

In 1854, the observatory published the *Bathymetrical Map of the North Atlantic Basin*, showing the sea floor with deep underwater trenches that Maury insisted was a telegraphic plateau. It was a very detailed answer to Field's questions on the oceans and the sea beds. Maury also assured Morse that the plateau was safe. In turn, Morse told Field he had "perfect faith" in the cable to safely cross the Atlantic.[13]

In David Dudley Field's dining room before 6 a.m., on May 8, 1854, a "million and a half dollars was subscribed to the new company." The partners agreed to proceed with a telegraph line from Newfoundland to New York as the first step. After tapping Cooper as president, some "of them went home and others sat down to breakfast." In Washington, the observatory was shutting down the night's astronomical work, and the Coast Survey and the Smithsonian were not yet open for business.[14]

From the start, Field offered Maury a financial stake in the enterprise, but the superintendent repeatedly turned it down. He said taking the offer would have "weakened my hands" in advocating the transatlantic telegraph.[15]

The lieutenant did make one request, one aimed at undercutting Bache: "I should like to have the promise of, at any rate, viz. that I shall have the right to first use of the telegraph for the purpose of determining longitude across the Atlantic. I want that promise from your board of directors in writing, so that there may be no difficulty when I come to claim its fulfillment."[16]

The board, under Cooper's signature, agreed.[17]

Maury was confident of the project's success in the summer of 1855: "This thing of a submarine cable across the Atlantic I consider one of the great problems of the age. My researches, you are aware, have done much to show the demonstration is possible. Indeed the company was founded upon the strength of our deep sea soundings, and the discovery of the great telegraphic plateau."[18]

Bache seethed. Adding insult to injury, the Navy and Maury published a pamphlet on new shipping routes in and out of New York. The rocks and reefs at Hell Gate had been Bache's first important project in that harbor. Again, Maury was poaching as he did on Gulf Stream research. Worse yet, Dobbin dusted off the old shibboleth of bringing the survey under Navy control. Maury's fingerprints were all over that.[19]

Bache, through influential allies in the Navy, went on the offensive. Among his allies were Samuel F. DuPont and Charles Davis, the Harvard-trained officer. Both played critical roles in an ensuing cabal to forcibly retire Maury. For DuPont, the problem with Maury was a professional one of having an old invalided lieutenant clinging to a young seagoing man's billet. For Davis, the problem with Maury was professional, similar to DuPont's, and deeply personal.[20]

One of the observatory's duties was to prepare the *Nautical Almanac and Ephemeris*, but when money to establish the office was delayed, Maury acceded to a plan allowing Davis, who was conducting Coast Survey work in Buzzards Bay in Massachusetts, to be appointed to the post in 1849. Among Maury's critics the appointment was hailed as a "serious defeat" for the observatory. Instead of staying in Washington and working under Maury's eye, Davis set up office in Cambridge, Massachusetts, to be closer to Benjamin Peirce, his mentor and brother-in-law, and to Harvard, his alma mater.[21]

At first, relations between Maury and Davis were cordial. The same could be said about Maury's initial encounters with Bache and Henry. For Davis, the breaking point came in an acerbic letter from Maury in early 1853:

> Pray don't go to the expense of doing up in gilt those Nautical Almanacs.... Nor need you take the trouble of having illuminated and done up in vellum that copy "Theoria Morus" that you are going to present to our library. We are not proud and will take them in sheets. But in plain English, when shall we have copies of the Nautical Almanac for distribution?[22]

Davis was as angry as Maury had been over the publication of the observatory's astronomical work in a German scientific journal. Maury's later apology was not enough. Now Davis had an idea on besting Maury that he shared with Bache. The ruse became known as the "Steamer Plan," a chess game of cabinet moves in taking ships and officers out of the observatory's control and into the Coast Survey's.

In the fall of 1855, shortly after Maury learned he had been retired from the Navy, Bache acted. The first step was to have Jefferson Davis, Pierce's secretary of war, persuade Dobbin to transfer screw steamer *Arctic* to the survey for a new sounding effort.[23]

Dobbin acted, but not as Bache and Davis anticipated. In a curious dispatch to the secretary of the Treasury, under whose authority the Coast Survey fell, he told James Guthrie he was returning Lieutenant Otway H. Berryman and Midshipman John S. Barnes to Navy duty and assigned the men to *Arctic*. But he kept the ship under his personal command, citing an 1849 law that gave the Navy the deep-sea sounding mission. But then, as Bache dreamed and Davis schemed, Dobbin permitted the Coast Survey to outfit the ship.[24]

After delivering a speech at the laying of the cornerstone of the Minnesota historical society's building in 1856, Maury met Field in New York to go over the cable project. There Maury discovered Dobbin's plans. An angry Maury asked Field to find out from the ship's officers what was going on. When questioned, Berryman readily gave Field a copy of Dobbin's orders.[25]

With each mile he traveled toward Washington, Maury was convinced that *Arctic*'s work fell under the observatory's control. The oceans were the observatory's domain. In its name, the great charting work was published.

Since 1849 in its *Taney*, the observatory was committed to "patient, attentive and laborious operations" in determining the depth of the oceans.[26]

As DuPont came to know, Dobbin could bend with the wind; on July 10, the secretary, after meeting with Maury, sent supplementary orders to Berryman. The log and specimens were to be sent to the observatory, and Berryman was "not to give any publicity to your observations, or their results before they have been communicated officially to the Department."

Dobbin did not change the ship's outfitting order or how it was to conduct its soundings. Because of the difference in equipment and techniques, contradictory data were assured, and a worried Maury told Field as much.[27]

Kinds of cable, new soundings, and interagency rivalry were not Field's immediate concerns. He was concentrating on winning extended financing from the British and American governments.

For all the furor that he was to cause, Berryman promptly sent his data to the observatory. As Maury checked and reexamined *Arctic*'s log against those taken earlier during Atlantic soundings and even the log against itself for soundings in the same region of the ocean, discrepancies were apparent.

By the end of October, Maury told Dobbin, "Most if not all of the work done in this vessel on this service has to be rejected." While the two likely wanted to keep the matter quiet, a cover-up could only last so long in a capital where tales such as these were politically valuable and interesting news.[28]

The shroud of secrecy over the discrepancies was lifted when a Washington newspaper article appeared in December.[29]

As the Fontaines and James Maury took to the pulpit, Matthew Fontaine Maury took to the press, scoring the chicanery he found in Berryman's work. The reality was that Maury was building a parallel defense to the one he constructed to restart his naval career. Using his position as superintendent, he said that neither the observer nor the reader of *Arctic*'s log could deduce the results of the ship's labors, because so many details were missing. "But this is not all, nor the worst; for when the different records had been turned over to the observatory from that vessel came to be compared with each other discrepancies the most glaring presented themselves," he added.[30]

For Field, the first order of business in early 1857 remained raising more money; in a rare instance of cooperation, Maury and Bache agreed to help. Field was lobbying Congress, with Bache's aid, to win seventy thousand dollars from the lame-duck Pierce administration to continue. Maury helped by telling Congress the best time to lay the cable was in July and August, avoiding the fogs and the drifting icebergs of the North Atlantic. Quick legislative action was imperative if an attempt was to be made that year, he said. The press took up the cause. Stories, drawings, and cutaway illustrations of how the cable looked from close-up and on the seabed were necessary ingredients for a busy page one. The company's promotional literature used an engraving of the "Telegraphic Plateau of Lieut. Maury" as a frontispiece to push the bill through Congress.[31]

While money was Field's focus, Maury's was again on *Arctic*. In late April, he went over point by point again with the businessman why he felt the newly named Atlantic Telegraph Company was wrong in trumpeting Berryman's findings as justification to proceed: "Now irrespective of any annoyance the company by giving currency to Berryman's work, has greatly embarrassed me in my researches, because now instead of going on simply to announce results, I am everlastingly required to reconcile them with Berryman's which are untrue."[32]

Field said simply that he never asked Berryman to cook the books. For the businessman, men, ships, and equipment had to be in place, because laying the cable was the matter at hand, not quibbling over plumbing the ocean.

Maury turned to Isaac Toucey, a former attorney general and now Navy secretary, asking for a board of "competent officers not connected with the observatory" to review *Arctic*'s soundings to see "whether they were properly made, faithfully recorded and how far they are entitled to credit."[33]

In July, Toucey appointed three members from the observatory staff to review *Arctic*'s soundings and their report, which not surprisingly agreed with Maury, but did nothing to silence Berryman's supporters, especially outside the Navy.

By then, the British government, a now nervous investor, dispatched *Cyclops* to make its soundings. Lieutenant Joseph Dayman followed Maury's procedures, and his findings were in line with the observatory's. The telegraph company, in its official account, officially credited Maury for his discovery of the "telegraphic plateau" and said it was the "only practicable route" between North America and Europe.[34]

For the moment, Berryman and the *Arctic* were hidden in the fog of publicity surrounding the Great Enterprise.

Through the summer, men, equipment, and ships moved into place. *Niagara*, the Navy's largest ship, and paddle-wheeler *Susquehanna* arrived in Ireland; waiting there were three British ships, *Agamemnon*, which was to lay twenty-five hundred nautical miles of the cable that Field favored, and *Leopard* and *Cyclops*. By August 5, the European end of the line was secured in Valentia, an island two and a half miles off Ireland, and *Niagara* led the way into the open sea.[35]

As the line went out, tests were run on the signal. With each mile, the cable's weight—the three coatings of insulating gutta-percha (a forerunner to rubber) alone weighed 206 pounds per nautical mile, strained the machinery, and a break occurred. One splicing was successful. The laying resumed, only to suffer a new break, almost four hundred miles out.[36]

An agonized Field returned to London in hopes of securing a vote to proceed. Morse, in London at the time, recommended the board delay for a year. This time, Field's arguments did not convince the directors.[37]

Naysayers on shore joined those criticizing Berryman's or the Navy's soundings. The transatlantic cable was a harebrained scheme based on suspect numbers.[38]

During the enforced lull, Maury continued vilifying Berryman's soundings. In the 1858 edition of the *Sailing Directions*, Maury used six pages to reprint *Arctic*'s abstract log, hacking off chunk by bloody chunk what he found in grievous error.[39]

Now in the public prints, he also offered the advice he privately gave Field on the kind of cable to use. Stout iron cable, Maury like Morse wrote, had failed in the line between Newfoundland and Cape Breton. "The true character of a cable for the deep sea is not that of an iron rope as large as a man's arm, but a single copper wire or facile of wires coated with gutta percha, pliant and supple and not larger than a lady's finger." Gutta-percha was chosen over rubber, because of its better insulating qualities.[40]

The fogs surrounding Berryman and the *Arctic* were dissipating rapidly following the appearance of Maury's new charts. Bache's assistant, W. P. Trowbridge, spoke before the American Association for the Advancement of Science in April, lauding *Arctic*'s soundings; though well received there, the speech, at first, created little stir.[41]

During the wait for the summer 1858 attempt, Maury suggested to Field using Labrador and Iceland as intermediate land points. But for Field, the project was too far along for such a revision. A lightened cable—though not as much as Maury desired—was to be laid in a continuous line between Newfoundland and Ireland.[42]

For this second attempt, *Agamemnon* and *Niagara* were to leave Plymouth, England, together July 21, and "the ships should proceed to a point midway between Trinity Bay and Valentia, there splice the cable and turn their bows east and west and proceed to their destinations."[43]

Once underway, the breaks happened again, and three hundred miles of cable was lost. Field returned to London to meet with Professor William Thomson, the inventor of the Kelvin scale of absolute temperature measurement.

Teaming up with the two was British physicist Michael Faraday to lobby Parliament for financial support and to beg the directors to continue. With the window of good weather narrowing, the board reluctantly approved another try.[44]

The ships set to sea again from Ireland on July 17. About noon on July 29, with the vessels at mid-ocean, the cable was spliced. *Niagara* headed westward for Trinity Bay, and *Agamemnon* eastward for Valentia.

Maury now harbored doubts. As he wrote C. Piazzi Smyth, the royal astronomer in Edinburg, on August 2: "I suppose the telegraphic fleets are again about joining hands at this time. I think it almost a pity, for it appears to me that success with such a cable is barely possible, scarcely probable."[45]

Despite Maury's doubts, on August 5, at about 6 a.m. Newfoundland time, both ships reached their destinations. The cable was taken to the telegraph houses on the two coasts, and, as reported from Canada, that station "received very strong electricity from the other side of the Atlantic." For more than a week, tests, including messages and measurements of current, were run between the stations. The line held, and the signals were strong.[46]

Queen Victoria sent the first official message across the ocean to President Buchanan on August 16. In response, Buchanan hailed the cable as "a bond of perpetual peace and friendship" between nations.[47]

As transmissions continued, invitations went out for a two-day celebration on September 1 and 2 in New York. Among the invitees from Washington were Maury, Bache, Henry, and Morse. While Maury, Bache, and Morse accepted, Henry did not. To Henry, not only was Maury's presence an affront, but Morse was a scientific charlatan and a thief.

The bickering among the scientifics was of little moment to a city, nations, and continents that wanted to hail a hero. Yet Cyrus West Field, the pilgrim making progress in a carriage up Broadway, was never so egocentric to believe the cable's success was solely his.

At the Metropolitan Hotel, Field praised his partners, the engineers and crews of the ships, as well as the two governments. Then turning to those men who helped without any compensation, Field lauded Faraday, Maury, Morse, Bache, and Thomson as "those never-to-be-forgotten philosophers." Toasts were offered in each philosopher's name, and for the tiniest moment, the scientific sniping was lost in the exultation of the crowd and the clinking of glasses.[48]

In nearby New Haven, Benjamin Silliman, Jr., the editor of the *American Journal of Science and Arts*, published Trowbridge's April address as Field was being honored. A reporter asked Maury for a response to the article. Although he had not seen the journal, he was galled by a statement claiming Berryman's work was more reliable than Dayman's. Trowbridge told the association and the journal repeated, "The idea of a 'Plateau' existing between Newfoundland and Ireland is not warranted it seems to me by any observations that have yet been made."[49]

Maury demanded to know how the Coast Survey had received Dayman's report. It appeared to be as clear-cut a case of interference as Henry's use of Sears Walker's astronomical abstracts. He dispatched an article to Silliman. "The superintendent of the Coast Survey has once before been rebuked by the Navy Department for laying improper hands upon the property of the observatory, intermeddling with its affairs and seeking to come between it and the public." But Silliman didn't use the piece.[50]

As with friendlier secretaries, Maury urged Toucey to force the Treasury Department to chastise Bache. At the same time Maury pointedly reminded the secretary that the observatory was to be the first user of the transatlantic telegraph to determine longitude, something the Coast Survey claimed as its right. He had the company's written agreement as proof.[51]

Never one to avoid a fight with Maury or the Navy, Bache, portraying himself as the defender of the sea service's integrity, wrote Treasury Secretary Howell Cobb:

> I learn that the arrangements which were in progress under the direction of the Coast Survey for using the Atlantic telegraph in the determination of longitude have been interrupted by Lieutenant Maury, the superintendent of that "lighthouse of the skies," which in General Jackson's time was simply a "Depot of Charts and Instruments." ... By whose sanction he made this arrangement I do not know, certainly it seems to me that he was stepping out of the proper line of his duty to forestall the action of another branch of public service.[52]

The war was on again. At Bache's request, the Smithsonian's Henry met with Cobb and his assistant, Philip Clayton, arguing that if Maury made the measurement of longitude, there "would be no certainty as to its correctness." Cobb agreed to back Bache.

Bache, taking no chances, next turned to Secretary of War Jefferson Davis to further stiffen Cobb's spine. Davis reported that Cobb "appeared gratified to learn how defensible the position of his bureau was, and hoped you would give the commander sharp pickle."[53]

In November, Maury, by then back on active duty and promoted to commander, wrote Toucey:

> He [Bache] sets himself up as the champion of the Navy—the guardian of its honor! I have always supposed that that was quite safe in the hand where the law has placed it. I allude to this part of that extraordinary letter only for the purpose of calling

> your attention to another instance of "impetuous intermeddlings" for which the superintendent of the Coast Survey is so famous.[54]

At the same time B. Franklin Minor, his cousin and friend, told Maury, "I suppose you are pretty well in for a fight. Lay on. I pray for you, for they are mean fellows—Bache and Berryman."[55]

They may have been "mean fellows," but the breaking of the cable ended this cockfight. After three months, the line went dead with the word *forward* as its epitaph. Recriminations flew across the ocean. Field was cursed as a stock manipulator, and the whole enterprise branded a hoax.[56]

A disappointed Field asked Maury, Bache, and Henry to serve on a board of advisers in July 1859. As before, Henry remained standoffish, but warned Bache about Maury's being "occupied in deciding on the propositions which are submitted to him relative to the telegraphic endeavour."[57]

The superintendent of the observatory directed Field back to their earlier correspondence and included a new map for a cable route using Iceland and Greenland as intermediate land points.[58]

Almost immediately, Field asked Maury the next question, "What kind of cable would you recommend the Atlantic Telegraph Co. to adopt?" likely knowing the answer.[59]

Through the year, Maury again advised Field to think of a cord and not a cable. The superintendent passed on the test results of Henry B. Rogers, who supplied Maury with the gutta-percha at the Washington Navy Yard. "The results were wonderful as two of the cords, not thicker than a lady's finger, and sustained over 1,900 pounds before parting."[60]

The parting of the Union put on hold the re-laying of the cable; when it was reestablished after the war, Maury's contributions were conspicuously omitted.

An anonymous writer in 1867 noted: "No mention is made by Mr. Field of the part borne in this important work by Maury, nothing of Brooke, and his sounding lead, and a faint but equivocal praise to the 'gallant lieutenant Berryman,' suggested no doubt by the fact that he had gone to his grave in the language of Dr. Field 'firm and loyal to the flag.'"[61]

17. Shipwreck and Salvation

The great personal storm that Matthew Fontaine Maury found himself in during 1855 swamped the arguments over the accuracy of the observatory's charts on the telegraphic plateau or over control of the Coast Survey, Navy research vessels, and naval officers. It included furious tempests over naval reform, the very issue that carried Maury to the superintendency of the Naval Observatory. But this time, instead of riding the winds, Maury was lashed by them.[1]

As early as 1853, James C. Dobbin, as had other Navy secretaries, wanted to create a retired list to open up promotions: "The great evil in our present system is, that neither merit, nor service, nor gallantry, nor capacity, but mere seniority of commission, regulates promotion and pay." He insisted a board of officers review service records, and its recommendations be sent to Congress and the president for approval: "Thus the president and the Senate, the appointing power, will be the removing power, and the apprehension of star-chamber persecution and being victimized by secret inquisition, now felt by some worthy officers, would be quieted."[2]

What was different about Dobbin's proposal was its timing—early in a new administration by a secretary uninterested in higher office. For the Navy, the last years of the Millard Fillmore administration had been consumed over flogging. Flogging certainly affected more men in the Navy, but the political stakes were dramatically higher when dealing with the service's officer class. They were not silent men.[3]

Over the years, Maury never lost his interest in naval reform and often wrote other officers sharing his concerns as he did in 1850 to Samuel F. DuPont and Florida Senator Stephen Mallory, chairman of the Senate Naval Affairs Committee.[4]

Having been tasked to examine the Navy's ills, DuPont wrote in early

1855, "It is pretty good as a résumé of the stagnant condition of the Navy—I expect to give it to Mr. Dobbin tomorrow, and I shall then feel that I have made my last effort for the reform of the Navy."[5]

The solution, in DuPont's eyes, lay not only in limiting admissions to the Naval Academy, but in setting age limits to ranks. Using that criterion, Maury, as a lieutenant, was clearly at risk. Dobbin read DuPont's report, adopted it, and went to work on Congress. With surprising quickness, both houses approved the Navy bill incorporating a fifteen-member retiring board February 28, 1855. In historian Donald Chisholm's words, "It was the most momentous officer personnel legislation since the Navy's founding."[6]

As DuPont wrote Charles H. Davis, the editor of the *Nautical Almanac*, in April, "We will have a fight afterwards, the issue of which the final results will depend."[7]

Navy Secretary James Dobbin, while praising Maury's work at the observatory, set in motion a top-to-bottom review of the department's officer personnel that led to Maury's forced retirement and by other actions threw into question the accuracy of the observatory's deep-sea soundings for the transatlantic telegraph cable (courtesy the Navy History and Heritage Command).

Even before the board was officially named, some likely members clustered in out-of-the-way offices, going over the *Navy Register*, marking R., F., D. by certain names. The initials stood for reserved—originally called retired—furloughed, or dropped. For years, a biographer of Franklin Buchanan noted that DuPont was talking about establishing a reserved list as early as 1850.[8]

DuPont told Davis, by then an enemy of Maury's, that the lieutenant must be shown that he could not keep his rank and superintendency. Being put on the reserved list was a recognition of Maury's condition of not being fit for duty afloat, DuPont reasoned. Henry Beaufort, Edward Sabine, and others in the navies of Britain and France had been so listed in pushing them into retirement.

As DuPont said of Maury, "He might write in his own person all the science and knowledge of Newton, LaPlace ... and be covered from the crown of his head to the soles of his feet, with geographical and cosmos medals and yet the board, if it be an honest one would have to reserve him." Lastly, DuPont asked, "Why should Maury, if he cannot go to sea, object?" He had not asked Maury.[9]

In early June, Dobbin announced the appointments to the board: William B. Shubrick, a captain, was to be president. Other captains were Matthew C. Perry, Charles S. McCauley, Cornelius K. Stribling, and Abraham Bigelow. The commanders were DuPont, Garrett J. Pendergast, Samuel Barron, Andrew H. Foote, and Buchanan. The lieutenants were John S. Missroon, Richard L. Page, Sylvanus W. Godon, William L. Maury, and James S. Biddle.[10]

From the time the board convened on June 20, DuPont kept scrupulous notes. For example, about Perry, he wrote, "I do not think he likes this work and winces under some fancied responsibility which may make him unpopular." DuPont, Buchanan, and others remained intent on cutting deadwood. "Mistakes will be made there can be no doubt. Yet those mistakes will not be in doing injustice to the individual, except in this way, that men equally culpable will be left."[11]

The official sessions were confined to 10 a.m. to 3 p.m., weekdays only. Long summer evenings and weekends gave DuPont time to repeat his message of "the necessity for this great reform" when the board members retired to the rooming house in which many of them lived.[12]

On July 26, the board completed its review of the records of 712 officers. Forty-nine were recommended to be dropped as incompetent or unworthy. Seventy-one were placed on the "reserved" list with leave-of-absence pay, and eighty-one on the "reserved" list with furlough pay.

DuPont conferred with Dobbin for several hours before the list was sent to President Franklin Pierce. After the president looked at it, he called the secretary, Shubrick, and DuPont to the White House. Once the decisions were explained, Pierce ordered Dobbin to carry out the recommendations.[13]

As DuPont wrote Maryland Congressman Henry Winter Davis, "The secretary of the Navy struck me as a man whose judgment, reason and pride, were all in the reform measure. He told me if he had done nothing else in this department, that one measure would satisfy his ambition. But while in this courageous mood, I could see him discover a bugaboo sitting in the corner in the shape of the public press."[14]

While vacationing in Albemarle County, Maury received his letter from Dobbin, dated September 18. It was similar to the letter Captain Charles Stewart, commissioned in the 1790s and commander of the Navy Yard at Philadelphia, received.[15]

> The board of naval officers who in their judgment should be placed on the "reserved sea list" on leave of absence pay, and the finding of the board having been approved by the president, it becomes my duty to inform you that, from this date, you are accordingly removed from the active "service list," and placed on the "reserved list" on leave of absence pay. You are, however, not detached from the naval authority. I avail myself of the authority of the law to direct that you continue on your present duty.

From the start, DuPont's intentions concerning Maury were obvious. No other officer was mentioned as often by name in any of his preboard communications. DuPont and others (like Davis, in Cambridge) wanted the aging lieutenant removed from active duty. Despite the scientifics' grousing, DuPont believed "the Navy generally appreciates Maury and his services." For now, the commander was not going after Maury's position at the observatory.[16]

In a number of letters to friends and Navy officials, Maury howled against this "cowardly inquisition." As he angrily stated, "It is a grievous error, a large public wrong to smother if not suppress altogether the hydrographical office of the Navy in this way."[17]

Maury's pen pricked at the split among board members, citing Perry's disavowal of the panel's action. About himself, Maury said the board never reexamined his leg, but instead looked only at a "few cases at the files of the Navy Department."[18]

Most telling, however, was Maury's dissection of the speed at which the board reached its decisions. Because all was done behind closed doors without official record, the board handed Maury the star-chamber argument Dobbin wanted to avoid.[19]

"We find that the board was not engaged in careful examination more than 28 days.... Thus they took 140 hours for this careful examination into the competency or ability to perform duties of 712 officers. This gives a little more than 10 minutes on the average to each officer," he wrote Dobbin on October 11.[20]

As Maury's anger beat on the Navy, DuPont wrote, "I hear Maury is going to fight—is furious and talks of civil suits. I hope Dobbin will walk him out of that observatory. He should not have the benefit of one clause of the law, while demurring at another part of it—and if he kicks against the board and the executive, he ought not to be employed by this administration."[21]

DuPont hit the nail squarely on the head. As long as Maury used his prestige as superintendent—and the observatory staff—he could stir the seas. Lieutenant Samuel Phillips Lee, second in command of the observatory, wrote, "Lists, confessedly, and mischievously erroneous are in circulation here and from them no considered opinion can be formed. But I know officially the action in regard to M. F. Maury. It fills me with astonishment and indignation.... The act is suicidal!"[22]

For his defense, Maury did not defer to rank. Although his title as superintendent was grandiose, his rank was only that of a lieutenant; Maury's letter demanding explanations for the board's action rankled superior officers.

Pendergast held to the official line of "the board's actions speak for themselves," while most, like Buchanan, refused to respond.

Biddle, however, gave Maury the real reason: "Since the year 1840, you have not performed any duty at sea and your service in a man of war dates still further back. A physical disability to perform the duties of a lieutenant at sea was clearly a cause for retirement under the law."

DuPont was dismissive: "The executive has shown that he attaches no such consequences [of official disgrace] to it, for whilst he approves of your removal from the active list, he has paid you the high compliment of retaining you in your present honourable and distinguished position in the naval observatory."[23]

Maury, who should have been celebrating the success of his new book, *Physical Geography of the Sea*, instead sent a second letter to Dobbin. "Is there anything I beg to know either among the files of the Department, or anywhere else within your knowledge to sustain such an imputation? If there be, I challenge its production and ask a lawful trial."[24]

In unabated fury, Maury wrote the Royal Navy's Frederick Beechey, "The officers who professed any devotion to science or who might become board with any professional accomplishments, except watching, going to sea, etc., were either dismissed, furloughed or put on the retired list and rendered ineligible to further promotion. So that here you have me, professionally with a black eye."[25]

To save his career, Maury had to rouse political support at home. The superintendent told former Tennessee governor and leading Whig Neill S. Brown: "Each member of the board will acknowledge himself if you could get him to lay his hand on his heart and say—to be as incapable of performing my duties on shore as it is possible for me to perform their duties at sea.... There has been foul play, and there has been a determination to hunt me down." He damned DuPont for personally benefiting by removing others for his own promotion.

Maury said he could not allow Brown, then serving in the legislature, to have the letter published, but "it is at your service in other respects." This meant Brown was free to show it around the state house, and that the legislature could instruct the state's senators in Washington to argue for Maury's reinstatement.[26]

Behind the scenes, DuPont labored to hold the secretary's resolve and keep his congressional allies, like Florida Senator Stephen R. Mallory, aboard the naval reform ship. Dobbin was bending in the political wind, as he did over the soundings for the transatlantic cable.

DuPont wrote Biddle and Davis, "The fight of the reform measure is going to be on Maury. He early accepted his retention on duty, the better to convert the observatory into a Malakoff tower to attack the board and manufacture public opinion.... But the truth is they are afraid of his popularity—the whole machinery of the observatory is at work, officers and all, writing slips and having them reproduced, writing puffs of himself, etc., in organizing eloquences." To DuPont, Maury was P. T. Barnum and a self-professed martyr. A longtime friend of Bache, DuPont enlisted the scientifics, who wanted the superintendent out of his fortress.

Heavy weather lay ahead.[27]

When Maury's family had arrived almost penniless in Franklin forty years before, John Bell had an established law practice in the Williamson County courthouse. Around the square, Bell looked out at the fast-growing county seat that Maury's cousin built. It was a town with more than its share of ambitious men, like Bell, Sam Houston, and Thomas Hart Benton. By the time Matthew Fontaine Maury won his Navy warrant through Houston's office, Bell had embarked on a political career that led to a presidential run in 1860.[28]

In 1856, Bell was Maury's Senate champion, and he was joined by Houston, a hero of Texas independence. Robert Toombs of Georgia, John Crittenden of Kentucky, and Robert Hale of New Hampshire also were to wield the star-chamber defense.

On the floor, these senators battled not only Mallory, but also John Clayton, of Delaware, a digging debater. Siding with them was Mississippi's Jefferson Davis, an ally of Bache and DuPont. He was joined by his colleague from Mississippi, Albert G. Brown, and Louisiana's Judah P. Benjamin.[29]

The 1856 chamber floor bloodletting especially galled Mallory. The year before he had warned the Senate it was not doing the easy thing in passing this overdue reform bill:

> It is almost impossible to pass through Congress anything that strikes at the root of the heart-burnings which are wearing the Navy out; and when you find men coming from all parts of the earth, men perfectly unknown to the Navy Department, whose names are looked upon by the clerks of the department as abstractions, a sort of John Does and Richard Roes, in the service, men of thirty-two years standing,

> who have not raised their hands in the service, whose characters are so bad in some instances that they cannot get a common bill for compensation through this body, and when we make the slightest attempt to place a hand upon them, we are met by objections. If this bill goes back to the House, filled as it is with the germ of excellence and improvement of the service, it fails.[30]

Mallory was correct about constituencies building for those ousted, even the incompetent, but the uproar unleashed over Maury's retirement was an event that even as acute a student of naval affairs as he could never have anticipated.

When Benjamin named Maury and used his leg injury as an example of why the board acted as it had, Bell leapt to his feet and said, "A few years afterward, he considered himself abundantly able and efficient to perform any duties to which he might be assigned afloat or ashore, and he made direct and earnest application to be assigned to sea service during the Mexican War, but was refused."

Benjamin beat the first of the tactical retreats: "As regards Lieutenant Maury's case, I, of course, withdraw as I said just now everything I stated in regard to it, though what I said is based upon what I deem to be reliable authority. I should not have referred to his name."[31]

Naming names and dredging up individual cases, followed by freshets of memorials from state legislatures lamenting sons grievously wronged, engulfed the Senate.

In late January, Maury sent Bell a corrected version of a Tennessee memorial calling for the superintendent's reinstatement. Virginia and others followed suit. With the new memorial in hand, Bell said, "He probably could not lead a boarding party and grapple an enemy ship with as much vigor and activity as if he were in full possession of his original vigor of body. But sir, many of the most gallant commanders who have distinguished themselves at sea have been in the same predicament.... The great Nelson himself, in his last great battle, had but one arm."[32]

Bell's mention of the British hero incensed Mallory. "Create, if you please, a scientific corps; place Lieutenant Maury at the head of it, and I would say nothing; he would then have his appropriate sphere. Mr. Maury's reputation as a civilian—call it what you please—would never awaken a throb in the heart of an American seaman." DuPont reveled, "Mallory belled the Maury cat."[33]

New Hampshire's Hale hauled up the service career of Davis, largely spent in the shadow of Harvard Yard. "How does he classify the preparation of the Nautical Almanac? Is that a naval duty?"[34]

The only zeal that Maury claimed his opponents had in this fight was for their own promotions. DuPont agreed with Maury on that. To Pendergast, he wrote, "The first thing to be done is to get those promotions confirmed—the battle will then be won and the Navy safe—the after proceedings will then be a guerrilla warfare and may be watered and controlled."[35]

Inside the Capitol, Mallory offered a compromise bill in which some forced retirement cases might be reviewed. At the same time, the Naval Affairs Committee demanded the board report on how members reached their findings. For the Senate, these two events were like the sighting of a lighthouse's beam by the crew of a ship lost at sea.

Maury saw vindication. The superintendent claimed Dobbin was in "ignominious retreat." After meeting with Dobbin, he believed the changes were a "give-in" to restoring him to active service. A little later, Bell asked Maury if the proposals were to his liking. DuPont, the secretary, and the board were now caught in the tidal wash of Maury's defenders. DuPont bitterly added that the secretary "caved in again" when it came time to strike down Maury. He wrote, "It's a dangerous thing to give advice to weak men."[36]

On March 11, Maury's supporters dissected the board's feathering of its own nest, especially Shubrick, a hero in the Mexican War, who moved from number seven on the promotion list to number two. On March 18, Houston blasted DuPont and the others as a "packed conspiracy to strike down chivalrous and gallant men." He added sarcastically: "All, or nearly all the principal men on the board had relatives who were benefited by it. It would be a pity to spoil a work so agreeable and family-like in its nature—a very great pity!"[37]

Houston compared DuPont to John Falstaff, both willing to swell tales of their own bravery. The Texas senator often returned to his theme of a Navy conspiracy to wrong Maury. Cabal, conspiracy, controversy.[38]

DuPont did not yet see the flood tide running in Maury's favor. He wrote Biddle, "I could not keep Mr. Clayton's hands off Maury, not for love of him, but for expediency. He has damaged him very severely." He delighted in Clayton's reading of Maury's disability certificate. "Where and from whom the old gentleman got this God only knows."[39]

But the screeching winds of assault-defense were dying after four months. "The Senate is very tired of the subject and nobody listens now," DuPont admitted.[40]

Inside the observatory with its instruments scanning the heavens, Maury remained dubious, especially over possibly being assigned to a scientific corps. What seemed a gleaming notion when proffered by John Pendleton Kennedy appeared tarnished dross when written by Mallory. In fact, Maury was writing friends in France and in Great Britain to find out how their nations recognized uniformed scientists and the kind of men such duty attracted. He had no regrets when the corps died on the Senate floor.[41]

On July 15, the Senate passed a bill amending the 1855 act. The secretary was to establish courts of inquiry to review the cases of those forcibly retired, but this time, the Senate instructed, accurate records be kept to prevent star-chamber decisions and star-chamber defenses.[42]

That ended half of the Senate's dilemma—if the House would go along with the compromise. Now, the Senate had to decide what to do about the promotion list. Three days later in executive session, it narrowly approved the promotions. As DuPont wrote Pendergast, "We were saved by the skin of our teeth, a majority of one or two!" To Biddle, he described the closed Senate session as "five hours of violence and vituperation."[43]

DuPont was not through on Capitol Hill. After all, Congress was a bicameral legislature, and the House did not have to march to the Senate's tune. In late July, DuPont and Biddle lobbied the House to kill the review courts. If the two chambers could not agree upon the bill's final language, then the 1855 act stayed in place. Better yet for DuPont personally, the Senate had the legislative say on promotions.[44]

"So we acted on one rule and the court of enquiry is to pass on our work and virtually condemn it by another rule! Those exacting words 'promptly and efficiently' and also ashore and afloat are nowhere in the amendatory act," DuPont wrote.[45]

Because the words "ashore and afloat" were not included, the implication was reinstatement for Maury. DuPont wrote, "I look upon it as the last struggle, and as I have said often before Providence has sustained us in every previous pinch when we were true to ourselves."[46]

Despite DuPont's forecast of divine assistance, the House approved the Senate bill in January 1857, and Pierce signed it in February.

When Isaac Toucey left the Senate to join James Buchanan's cabinet, he inherited the "courts of old men," the panels that were to review the removals of Maury and more than one hundred other Navy officers.[47]

John B. Minor, Maury's cousin and a law professor at the University of Virginia, was extremely concerned about these courts. He had read a pamphlet entitled "Cushing and the Court" claiming that the new attorney general, Caleb Cushing, held that every man appearing before these panels was under a cloud.[48]

Maury, by now very cautious, argued that these courts differed from courts-martial because there was no accusation against the officer. "I will try to get a little cool, for I must say this attempt or rather the idea of wrong that this pamphlet has impressed upon me, does make my blood boil." For whatever reason—staying cool or boiling blood—Maury didn't submit his request for review until April 1857.[49]

The next month, Toucey, a former attorney general himself, tried to speed the courts' progress by allowing the taking of depositions. Even this failed to accelerate the work, probably because the courts feared being brought before the Senate Naval Affairs Committee to explain how cases were decided.[50]

To escape summertime Washington and the speculation that surrounded the courts, Maury took his family to the Virginia mountains. This year there was not even peace in the Virginia highlands.[51]

Overarching all that summer and fall—from the dispute over the soundings for the transatlantic cable, to his continued naval career, and his position at the observatory—was Maury's deep grief over the loss at sea of his brother-in-law, William Lewis Herndon. From the ties of marriage, there developed between the two the deepest friendship. Herndon, the man to whom Maury entrusted the exploration of the Amazon, drowned after his paddlewheel steamer, the *Central America*, sank in a hurricane on September 8, 1857.

Herndon, like many naval officers who could not find billets in the sea service, had signed on with the busy mail steamers. His paddle-wheeler was one of the best known on the Atlantic run and credited with carrying one-third of the gold brought from California to New York. Its sinking with a loss of $1.6 million in gold "desperately needed in New York's constricted money market" is said to have sparked the Panic of 1857.[52]

In the late summer storm off South Carolina, the captain used all his seafaring skills in trying to save his ship and its passengers. The survivors hailed him as a hero.[53]

Maury wrote C. Piazzi Smyth, royal astronomer in Edinburgh, that the family mourned "her gallant commander, who stuck by her so gallantly and behaved so nobly was Mrs. Maury's brother and a very dear friend of my own."[54]

A grieving Maury asked Toucey, as he had Dobbin, how his fitness was being challenged. But the secretary's answer was equivocal. Maury, recalling the retiring board's actions and his cousin's warning, wrote Toucey anew: "Is it my fitness now? Is it my fitness as it appeared to the Navy board of '55 or is it my fitness at all times since I first entered the Navy? And in what respect morally, mentally, physically or professionally is it to be challenged.... What allegations have I to answer to?"

Maury, at fifty-one, was justifiably concerned. He knew that the courts, in some instances, questioned conduct "thirty odd years ago, when we were boys together."[55]

On the day before Thanksgiving, November 25, 1857, more than two years after the "Plucking Board" retired him, Maury was to have his hearing. He was given the names of the court members, but not an answer on how they were to judge his fitness. For the hearing, Commodore E. A. F. Lavalette was president; also sitting were Commodore Samuel Mercer and Captain Henry A. Adams. The judge advocate was Charles H. Winder, charged with keeping the now-required transcript.[56]

When the court convened at 10:30, Winder asked Maury if he wanted to challenge either the court or the judge advocate. Maury, acting as his own counsel, said he did not. Although witnesses had been summoned, none was present after the swearing in, and Lavalette then recessed the hearing until Friday.

In the court's second session, Captain Joseph Smyth, chief of the Bureau of Yards and Docks and who had known him since their days on *Potomac*, testified that Maury was capable of service "in all respects."

Next came Captain John H. Aulick, who knew Maury as a midshipman and praised his professional achievements since. Aulick described the fit service of other lame American and British officers he knew: "In the British service, [there were] Sir James Gordon and Sir George Collier, the last infinitely more lame than Lieutenant Maury. He commanded a fifty-gun ship, and although he used a stick and crutch he appeared to be very efficient." Maury was that kind of officer.

The day's last witness was Captain Robert B. Cunningham, who served with Maury on *Brandywine* and *Vincennes*. "I believe him qualified to command a ship or a squadron," he testified. This time, Winder, on cross-examination, asked whether the captain believed Maury capable of serving in war and peace. Cunningham said, "I do, under any circumstances."

Maury then put on the record that service at the observatory was considered naval duty. For the record, the judge advocate countered that Maury had applied for a disability pension of $12.50 per month and that Navy doctors' examinations in 1840 and 1841 had found him three-fourths disabled.

On Saturday, Maury called Navy surgeon W. S. W. Ruschenberger, who too knew him from *Brandywine* and *Falmouth*. Maury drew out from the surgeon the case of Plucking Board member Missroon, who was lame but on active duty. Winder challenged the surgeon, pointing out that he had not examined Maury. Ruschenberger said, "The fact that his condition has gone on improving to an extent not contemplated at that time—that he is enabled now to move about without crutches, or other artificial supports, justifies me in the opinion that his limb has recovered its tone and vigor to such an extent to enable him to perform efficiently his duty."

Maury's cousin, Dr. James Minor, said much the same, as did Maury's naval mentor, Captain Thomas Dornin, and Commander S. C. Rowan.

The court then ordered Ruschenberger and Minor to examine Maury and report back immediately their findings. After the examination Ruschenberger told the court, "I see no reason to change the opinion I have given in my testimony—on the contrary it has been confirmed by my examination I found the leg in a much better condition than I supposed." Minor agreed. Maury said in closing that he relied "with confidence upon the justice of the court."[57]

All Maury could do was wait. Toucey's reluctance to spell out the parameters of the court's questioning was disturbing. In addition, trouble could lurk behind a Senate cloakroom door. He had powerful friends, like Bell and Houston. He also had powerful enemies, like Davis and Mallory. Then, there was the Navy. On the retiring board sat giants of the sea service: Shubrick, Perry, and Buchanan, to mention three. Men used to command at sea were not used to being denounced on the Senate floor or in the press.[58]

Other signs were not encouraging. As Maury worked on the eighth edition of the *Sailing Directions*, Toucey's report to the president concentrated on the Navy's efforts to stop filibustering in the Caribbean and Central America. The observatory, so lavishly praised by earlier secretaries, was almost an afterthought, and the death of Herndon was officially ignored.[59]

Despite all that, the years of turmoil for Maury and the Navy ended quietly before Christmas. Buchanan sent the Senate Maury's nomination to be restored to the active list and promoted to commander. The Plucking Board was a Pierce administration mess; putting Maury back on active duty and raising his rank was one way of cleaning up a predecessor's flotsam and jetsam.

In early January 1858, Mallory quietly sent to the floor a favorable recommendation on Maury's restoration and promotion. The Senate unanimously approved it. On January 29, Toucey notified Maury of his recall to active duty and promotion effective September 14, 1855.[60]

From his fortress above the Potomac, Maury had weathered the deepest crisis in his life. From the 1840s onward, he fought to make the Navy's officer personnel system efficient. When others took the steps to do just that, Maury fought back with every power at his command. Chisholm wrote, "It was a curious turn of events."[61]

The Steamer Plan exposed the vulnerability of the observatory in its charting work. The Plucking Board proved that Maury was mortal. In the end, his victories in both affairs were pyrrhic, because even larger crises lay ahead. Those crises ended his naval career; tar brushed his name, tortured his soul, and sent him and his family into years of exile.

18. Wise and Good Counsels in Bedlam

As the 1860s began and the gulf between slaveholding and free states widened, the hunting down of demons was in full fury. The demons were visible to slaveholders and free-soilers alike in the rough justice of the Fugitive Slave Law, the ambiguity of the Kansas-Nebraska Act, the arming of Bleeding Kansas's bushwhackers, and the shipping crates filled with "Beecher Bibles" to keep the guerrilla war burning.

They were heard in treasonous whispers in the nation's capital. They were seen in the dispersal of the nation's army to chase Comanches in Texas and shadow Brigham Young's Latter Day Saints in the high desert. They were present in John Brown's raid to lead slaves to a new republic of freedom in the Virginia mountains. Finally, they raged in South Carolina's rush to secession. The travails of Nat Turner's rebellion and the Nullification Crisis were bearing poisonous fruit.

A day of fasting and humiliation, called for by President James Buchanan, could not stave off the rupturing of the Union.

William C. Hasbrouck, then a prominent New York attorney, wrote his former student that he was "ardently hoping the ... difficulties which threaten the nation may be averted by wise and good counsels." Hasbrouck, Matthew Fontaine Maury, and thousands of others tried to put meaning in Brown's attack on the Harper's Ferry arsenal. What they found were rising passions consuming "wise and good counsels."[1]

For Maury, his Southern nationalism showing and sounding like Governor John Floyd in the wake of Nat Turner's slave revolt, "The root of the evil lies in the preachings and the teachings of the Northern press, and pulpit, in the doings of the Northern politicians, the actions of Northern legislatures concerning slavery at the South—and not in the foray of John Brown that is only one of the offshoots from such seeds sowing, but which however as far as it goes has been torn off sub cortice."

He added, "Let the sons of Virginia do this: let them second the move of South Carolina at least as far as this, let them invite the people of the South to meet them at the council board upon the state of the South, and let them appoint as their counselor on the occasion such men from among them as ex-governors, or old judges, who are not only known to the public for their virtue and patriotism and moderation, but who are accustomed to speak in the name of the people and not with the voice of party."[2]

One of those "ex-governors" was Tyler, Maury's protector, living contentedly on his James River plantation, Sherwood Forest. Tyler believed the nation's disintegration—split first North and South, and then the Mississippi Valley from the Atlantic seaboard, and finally the Pacific Coast from the rest—was almost inevitable. Yet, a new governor of Virginia sent Tyler to Washington to help preserve the union.[3]

Hasbrouck, the hopeful teacher, might wish for peace and union, but the question was one of power. Maury, the keen student, understood that: "The balance of power of Europe was never so important to peace there as the balance of power between the North and the South is to domestic tranquility here."[4]

Particularly alarming to Southerners such as Maury was Congress's severing of Kansas from Nebraska, Washington from Oregon, and the Dakotas from Minnesota. For them, these acts set loose the demons to dilute the slave-holding states' power in the Senate.

But the sectional crisis, for the moment, remained in suspense as the free white male electorate headed to the polls in the fall of 1860 to elect a president, one-third of the Senate, and a House of Representatives. The presidential contest was a four-way race—Republican Abraham Lincoln, a one-term Whig congressman from central Illinois; Illinois Democratic Senator Stephen Douglas, the author of the Kansas-Nebraska Act; sitting Vice President John Breckinridge of Kentucky, endorsed by President James Buchanan and Southern Democrats; and Tennessee Senator John Bell, Maury's champion in the Plucking Board fight and the candidate of the newly formed Constitutional Union Party.

When it was clear that Lincoln had won, the Deep South was shocked. How could he have won? His party had not campaigned in the South. His "House Divided" speech in the 1858 senatorial campaign in Illinois was proof to slavery zealots that he was an abolitionist of the most extreme stripe. Virginia's governor, like his predecessor John Floyd, urged caution. Letcher repeated his call for a national peace conference. This time, his voice was heard.[5]

For South Carolina, black Republicans and abolitionists threatened slavery's existence on all fronts. In January 1860, well before the political conventions that rent the summer, C. G. Memminger, sent as a special representative, rendered the plainsong of secession in an address to the Virginia General Assembly: "Is it wise when we see a flame shining through every crevice, and ready to leap from every open window, is it wise to close the window, and fill up every gap and shut our eyes to the fact that the fire is raging within the building? It is not wise." In his accented English, the German-born emissary warned that South Carolina would seek "equality in the Union or she will seek independence out of it." He raised the specter of John Brown.[6]

Brown's raid was still a vivid memory to the legislators, but the Virginians opted only for more economic independence from the North, a course that Maury, tempering his Southern nationalism, then advocated.

Speaking for many, former governor and delegate John C. Rutherfoord said, "Let the other Southern states unite with us, then in the non-intercourse policy which this measure proposes to inaugurate in Virginia, and more than five-hundred million dollars will be annually kept back from Northern pockets." That was too small a step for Maury's taste.[7]

Maury wrote, "The real question at issue is a sectional one; and with the South, it is a question of empire. Increase, multiply and replenish the earth.... For that privilege the South is beginning to struggle. She must acquire it and exercise it as well as the North or she will be Africanized." It was the same question that troubled John Tyler's namesake son in his "Python" series in *DeBow's Review* and had haunted Judge Spencer Roane during the Missouri admission crisis forty years before.[8]

As he proposed new naval explorations, Maury could not hide his worries. In discussing the international venture to explore eight million square miles of Antarctica, he asked Lord Wrottesley, president of the Royal Society, to persuade the British government to take the lead in the exploration. "You go—we'll come," was all Maury could say.[9]

The work of the observatory was almost at a standstill. Maury asked Toucey for more money to keep the oceanographic work progressing, but the Panic of 1857 crippled federal revenue collection. As for the astronomical work, Maury had lost much of his interest in it. Even "the clocks, perfection in which almost is at the bottom of good work, were quite unfit for use."[10]

As Maury fretted over possible civil war, Ferdinand Maximilian of Austria sent the observatory a meteorological diary of his voyage to Latin America. Maury received the diary enthusiastically. In response, he cautiously inquired about serving with Maximilian should he come to Mexico as a ruler.

Why Maury sent out this feeler is not precisely known. Certainly, the growing sectional troubles disturbed him, but Maury also had more personal reasons. A new naval reform bill with another retiring board was in the hopper. Was he again a target?

To make matters worse, Senator Stephen Mallory, chairman of the Naval Affairs Committee and bloodied in the 1855 retiring board melee, questioned the appropriations bill for providing such luxurious accommodations for the superintendent of the observatory. A fresh start in Mexico was an option.[11]

The commander carried these political and personal concerns with him when he journeyed to Tennessee in the fall to deliver the keynote address at the laying of the cornerstone of the University of the South. His journey to Chapel Hill with President James K. Polk and Navy Secretary John Y. Mason years before and meeting the Rev. William Green laid the foundation for this signal event. Maury was now a recognized leader at the intersection of public affairs, education, and religion in the elites of the South. In the nineteenth century, "Success, power, and wealth in the United States had only one place of worship in the United States, the Episcopal Church," biographer James McGrath Morris wrote. Maury lacked only the wealth.

Maury was never more in his prewar element than at Sewanee. Here was an audience of five thousand intent on spreading knowledge and faith in their beloved South. Clothed in the academic garb of his honorary degrees, he marched in the long procession of bishops, including his preceptor, James Hervey Otey, and Leonidas Polk, a cousin of the former president; two hundred presbyters; and other honored speakers.

When his turn came, Maury recited the plan of the "Great Architect" contained in the *Benedicte*:

> In her services, she teaches her children in their songs of praise to call upon certain physical agents, principals in this newly-established department of human knowledge (physical geography) ... to bless, praise and magnify the Lord![12]

Such surety was necessary to survive chaos, and political chaos was spreading daily. Outwardly Maury's professional career seemed to be in full flower again. He was once more headed abroad to speak to Britain's most prestigious scientific societies. But inwardly, he wrestled with troubling fears. He twice wrote his son-in-law in October to secure his property—land and slaves—as best he could in this time of political uncertainty.[13]

"Apprehensions filled my mind today as I sat in church," he wrote Otey. "So instead of listening to the sermon, I was inquiring as to my duty and your duty, and duty of the quiet men of the country.... The answer was, stand forth and use your influence, your talent, if you have one or ten, for the right." Defining *right* was becoming more and more a dilemma.[14]

While in Great Britain, he met with scientific friends and discussed American politics and Antarctic exploration. He also consulted with navy colleagues, such as Marin Jansen of the Netherlands. Not even Maury's ensuing success in addressing the Royal Geographic Society and the British Association for the Advancement of Science tempered his fears. "Things at home look very squally. It will require the best exertions of our best men to save the union now," he wrote.[15]

Upon his return, Maury wrote a number of Southern men, the "quiet men," in hopes they could accept New Jersey as an honest broker of sectional differences. For Maury, the two states sympathetic to the South were logical choices as brokers through Robert F. Stockton in New Jersey and one of Tyler's sons in Philadelphia, a confidante of the Pennsylvanian Buchanan.

He wrote Stockton, "Though a Southern man born and bred, I do not pretend to speak for a single soul but myself. But as much as I love the union, I cannot shut my eyes to the fact that it cannot last long after the fact becomes patent that one group of states being parties to it, may use it to the prejudice of the other group, equal parties to it." Maury's pleadings with New Jersey and later Pennsylvania officials were like waving children's sparklers to the bomb blasts of war that followed.[16]

Maury also sounded out his trusted cousin Rutson Maury in New York on the latest version of nullification: "The *sine qua non* with it should be, in my judgment, the right of veto over any unfriendly legislation in Congress that the North may hereafter attempt," because "the South is blocked to expansion and that in itself is death." Rutson Maury shot back that this "ultimatum from the border states would never do," because "South Carolina wants everything their way."[17]

South Carolina, out of the Union before 1860 ended, had demanded control over all federal facilities inside its borders. As the tension mounted, white cockades, showing support for South Carolina, were sold on the streets of Washington. More troubling were the "Fire-eaters" driving Georgia, Florida, Alabama, Mississippi, Louisiana, and Texas to follow suit. This time, South Carolina was not alone in challenging federal authority, as it had been in the 1830s.[18]

In Richmond, at Letcher's insistence, the Virginia General Assembly called on the federal government and states to pause "while she and her sister states can institute negotiations." Letcher quoted Governor Floyd at the height of the Nullification Crisis to do all in Virginia's power to protect the rights of all the states through its coolness "united with prudence, wisdom, moderation and patriotism." Tyler personally won from Buchanan a delay in taking military action until Congress considered Virginia's call for a peace conference. How Lincoln and the new Congress already in session would react to a peace conference were unknowns.[19]

Sectional peace held that winter. Down Washington's F Street Northwest, in a former Presbyterian church now a large hall used for lectures, dances, readings, operas, and political gatherings near the Willard Hotel, 132 "old friends" and "old heroes" gathered at Letcher's call. The feeling that everything must be tried to save the Union drew prominent men, like Stockton; former Senator Thomas Ewing, who arranged for Maury's care following his crippling accident; the lawyer David Dudley Field, so instrumental in the laying of the transatlantic cable; and David Wilmot, the former Pennsylvania congressman who proposed barring slavery from all the territories seized in the war with Mexico.

As serious-minded as the delegates were, most came without clear instructions from their twenty-one state governments on what they were to do in Washington. By contrast, Virginia's Letcher and the legislature sent Tyler, James A. Seddon, and three others northward with very specific instructions.

Sitting in a chair overlooking the hall with a full-length picture of George Washington behind him, Tyler, the conference's president, noted: "Our ancestors probably committed a blunder in not being fixed upon every fifth decade for a call of a great convention to amend and reform the Constitution."[20]

Seddon, the "central figure of the convention," had a dark complexion and deep sunken eyes. Although in his forties, the former two-term Democratic congressman suffered from health problems that caused him to drop in and out of public life. Like many, Maury firmly believed "the continued existence for a slavocracy competing with free labor is boundless expansion."[21]

From the start, there was an undercurrent running through the gathering, no matter how noble their intentions, that the convention was flawed from the start. California, Oregon, Michigan, Wisconsin, and Minnesota had not sent any delegates. Distance could have been their excuse. More ominously, there were no conferees from the states that had seceded.[22]

After the convention opened, Maury met with Tyler. "I think I satisfied him that no parchment provision would stand," he wrote. Maury was correct.

Events away from Washington were testing how endangered peace was.

On the day the peacemakers convened, the federal Congress debated a bill from John Crittenden, the elderly Kentuckian, to restore the Missouri Compromise boundary line concerning slavery. Across the Potomac, Virginia voters elected a pro–Union majority to its convention considering secession. Joining colleagues from other Southern states that had seceded, Louisiana's John Slidell and Judah P. Benjamin resigned their Senate seats. Of more consequence that day, Jefferson Davis, who recently resigned his Mississippi Senate seat, was inaugurated in Montgomery, Alabama, as the first president of the Confederate States of America.[23]

Crittenden's bill and Virginia's instructions to protect slavery framed the convention's debate. Tyler warned attendees to rise above section as their forefathers had: "You have to snatch from ruin a great and glorious Confederacy." The delegates piled amendment on top of amendment in trying to agree on the wording of a proposed Thirteenth Amendment. The debate grew so heated at one point that Tyler had to prevent Stockton from physically attacking Maine Senator Lot Morrill when he savagely questioned the slaveholding states' delegates' integrity. The old men were in a bloody cockfight.[24]

Virginians, living between the states still in the Union and those now out, were nervous. The cautious Letcher stepped up his arms-shopping efforts. Ninety miles from Richmond to the southeast, rumors spread like marsh fires that the cannons of Fortress Monroe, overlooking Hampton Roads, were now turned landward. The rumors proved false.[25]

From Washington, Maury fired rocket after rocket of ideas at the state convention.

A sampling: North Carolina and Virginia should work jointly for peace. Admit that North and South were as different as France and England. Create a dual executive, as John C. Calhoun once had proposed, to protect regional rights. Maury temporarily dampened his Southern nationalism: "Many urge the immediate secession of Virginia as a point of honor.... I do not quite comprehend the system of ethics which enjoins Virginia on any such course of action." The first wave of secessionist sentiment washed over the Richmond convention and receded as peacefully as the short Atlantic chop along Lynnhaven Inlet.[26]

In Washington, seeking to break the deadlock and over the delegates' objections, Tyler arranged a preinauguration meeting with Lincoln. There, the president-elect said he would not start a war over slavery, but he expected the Constitution to be "respected, obeyed, enforced and defended." Compared to Andrew Jackson's bellicosity, Lincoln seemed conciliatory.[27]

If Lincoln's words were soothing, the newly seated, Republican-dominated

Congress's actions were not. Crittenden's attempt to hold a national referendum on his proposal died. With a number of seats now vacant because of Southern resignations, the remaining senators rejected the fuzzy ideas of "old men" on slavery, compromise, and peace on a 28–7 vote; the House, refusing to suspend the order of business, never considered the convention's proposals.[28]

As winter arrived, the guns in Charleston remained silent, allowing Major Robert Anderson to shift his troops from Fort Moultrie to Fort Sumter, an island in the middle of the harbor. The Confederate government in Montgomery announced that trade would not be hindered on the Mississippi, and postal service and telegraph communications would continue. The stock market responded optimistically.[29]

Under the watchful eye of well-positioned sharpshooters and with the protection of a District of Columbia militia purged of secessionists, Lincoln repeated his pledge to Tyler in his inaugural address: "You have no conflict without yourselves being the aggressors. You have no oath registered in heaven to destroy the government, while I have the most solemn one to 'preserve, protect and defend' it."[30]

Four days later, the president hosted the Army and Navy officers serving in Washington at a White House reception that Maury attended. The superintendent, wearing his full dress uniform with his ornate naval sword by his side, wanted to hear directly from Lincoln on the course his administration was charting in the crisis. But the occasion passed without any word from the president on his plans.[31]

Like many federal appointees and officers, especially military officers, Maury knew if fighting broke out he must tender his service without reservation to either the federal government, the state of his birth, or resign and remain neutral: "The line of duty, there, is to me clear—each one to follow his own state, if his own state goes to war; if not, he may remain to help on the work of reunion."[32]

How long Maury could put off making a decision was problematic. The superintendent, possibly remembering Gideon Welles from his service to the Navy during the War with Mexico, found him to be far better suited for his office than his predecessor Toucey, the "most corrupt and mean official I had ever known."[33]

In the opening days of the new administration, Maury sent the former Democrat Welles a letter explaining why the United States should participate in a new Antarctic exploration. Instead of responding, the Connecticut newspaperman was busily learning more about his officers' loyalties, leaning heavily

Maury wore his formal dress uniform and his ceremonial sword to his only meeting with President Lincoln in the spring of 1861. When he resigned his commission following Virginia's vote for secession, he left behind his sword and the keys to the observatory (courtesy the Naval History and Heritage Command).

on his friend and naval officer, Andrew Foote. He kept close watch on prominent Southern officers like Maury and David Dixon Porter, because they were "courted and caressed by the secessionists."[34]

Following the defeat of the peace convention's resolutions in Congress, Maury proposed the slaveholding "barrier states"—North Carolina, Tennessee,

Kentucky, and Virginia—be anointed peacemakers. "Their minds are not made up to it, and they are not yet ready to decide upon their course of action."[35]

In his reading of the political storm, Maury, the Southern nationalist, was fooled by his own wishful thinking that the North would offer major concessions as had happened so often in the past.

What Maury also misjudged was the rising tide in favor of secession in Richmond. Speaking on the steps of the Exchange Hotel, Tyler termed the resolutions sent to Congress a "poor, rickety, disconnected affair." The former president was convinced that "the time for deliberation had passed; it was now the time to act."

Speaking next as a delegate to the Virginia convention, Tyler said, "I look with fear and trembling to some extent at the condition of my country. But I do want to see Virginia united; I wish to see her carrying her head as she had it in former times."[36]

Word spread to Richmond that Secretary of State William Henry Seward, long a thorn in slaveholders' sides, assured Southerners still in the Union that the federal government would not defend Sumter. Seward invited George Summers to the White House to explain their intentions; but the prominent pro–Unionist from the state's far southwestern Kanawha County at the last moment backed off.

Alan Magruder, the lawyer brother of the new head of the Navy's Bureau of Ordnance and Hydrography, was the go-between in arranging the White House meeting with pro–Union delegate John B. Baldwin. Following breakfast on April 4, Baldwin, a far lesser light than Summers, set off first for Seward's residence. After some confusion at the door of the executive mansion, the Virginian was admitted, Lincoln answered that Seward spoke only for himself, and the president intended to resupply Anderson's troops. The president went on to say that he would not hand over any federal facilities, nor did he plan to recognize a rival government in Montgomery.

A flustered Baldwin said that any relief attempt would be met with gunfire, as had happened when the Buchanan administration had tried it. Gathering himself together, Baldwin warned that when that happened, Virginia "would be out in forty-eight hours." Lincoln said he didn't believe that possible. Baldwin said simply, "I did not come here to argue with you." The men talked a while longer, but Lincoln put nothing on the table to bring back to the convention.

After parting, Baldwin went to Alexandria and delivered what he believed was the "last speech" for the Union cause. When the convention heard Baldwin's report, the Unionist delegates were shocked. They wanted clarification—

from the president himself—and sent three more emissaries for a White House meeting. Delayed by high winds and rains, they arrived April 12. By then, the die was cast.[37]

Lincoln was handed his act of aggression by Jefferson Davis's cabinet's decision to attack. At 4:30 a.m. on April 12, as the battery of Charleston was lined by many of its finest citizens, the first cannon shots sailed toward Fort Sumter. Soon, firing began from other guns along the tip of the Peninsula and on the Sea Islands. The cannonading went on for thirty-three hours. Amid crumbling masonry, burning barracks, and magazines almost empty of ammunition, Anderson surrendered his command. In the first day of civil war, no one had been killed, and another piece of federal property had been seized.

Preserving, protecting, and defending the federal government now meant the call to arms. Lincoln called upon the governors to raise seventy-five thousand volunteers to put down the rebellion in South Carolina.[38]

On April 17, the Virginia convention, whipped along by former Governor Henry Wise's rants, voted secretly for secession. For weeks, Wise had plotted to overthrow the Letcher government and send Virginia militia to seize Harper's Ferry and the Navy Yard in Portsmouth, if the sitting governor balked at taking the state out of the Union. Although the state's voters were to have the final say in a referendum, the convention instructed Letcher to alert Davis in Montgomery and to notify the governors of the other slave states remaining in the Union of the convention's vote.[39]

Federal officials did not act quickly to protect and defend United States facilities in the Old Dominion. Within hours, Virginia forces controlled the arsenal and were securing the naval yard.

During these dizzying April days, Maury was alone at his house on the observatory grounds. Most of his family was in Fredericksburg. Now he had in his hand an offer of refuge in Albemarle if war should break out. There really was no longer any "if."

At work, Maury could rouse himself only in looking to the future of naval science, as he did when writing a Russian colleague that Antarctic research was necessary. A few weeks later, he forwarded his forty-four-page proposal to diplomats in Washington for their consideration. It was a by-the-book request. During that week, Maury arranged the publication of *The Barometer at Sea* and *The Southeast Trade Winds of the Atlantic*.[40]

On Saturday afternoon, April 20, George Magruder, a fellow Virginian, and Maury met with Welles, probably in his office off Seventeenth Street Northwest near the White House. What exactly the three men said during the half-hour session was not recorded, but the secretary could tell both were distraught over the rioting in Baltimore when troops from Massachusetts changed trains to come to Washington's defense. Welles believed well before the "unhappy state of affairs" in Baltimore that the pair were on the tipping point of resigning. Where Magruder then went is unknown, but Maury headed back to the observatory.[41]

At 3 p.m. Maury was completing a day like no other he had spent in the service of his country. He knew he could not again swear the oath of his commissioning, a requirement that Winfield Scott had demanded of his officers during the Nullification Crisis thirty years before and one surely to be imposed in a nation breaking up in civil war. In the observatory on that spring afternoon was a scene that his enemies—at the Smithsonian, the Coast Survey, the Congress, and the Navy—had awaited for years. The naval officer with three and a half decades in uniform behind him was ending his tour as superintendent. It was a change of command with neither bands nor flags. He first turned over the observatory and its property to Lieutenant William Whiting, the friend he had rescued from the Africa Station almost twenty years earlier. Then Maury handed Whiting the sword he had worn to his only meeting with Lincoln.

Next he submitted a simple letter of resignation, done in his own hand, to Thomas Harrison, his secretary, who knew it to be the superintendent's cup of hemlock.

> His Excellency
> Abraham Lincoln
> President of the United States
> I beg leave herewith to resign into your hands my commission as a commander in the Navy of the United States.
> Respectfully, etc.
> M. F. Maury[42]

Like Jefferson Davis, Stephen Mallory, and other members of Congress who had resigned, no one stopped the fifty-five-year-old limping, paunchy man as he rode in a hack from the observatory grounds. The man who had been too young for the second war with England and possibly too valuable at the observatory for the War with Mexico was leaving behind the fortress he had built and a naval career that had begun and now ended in Washington.

That evening, Magruder again met with Welles to hand over the keys to the "closed and abandoned" observatory. Someone had left the keys on his steps. When the secretary asked where Maury had gone, Magruder said presumably to Richmond.

One of the most influential men of the age was siding with his native

Virginia against the nation he had sworn to defend. Knowing that, as he did, made the parting all the more difficult, but Matthew Fontaine Maury kept traveling south that night to Richmond as Magruder had suspected.

In Washington shortly thereafter, Commander James Gilliss settled into Maury's duties and quarters. In his report on the astronomical and meteorological observations at the observatory, Gilliss wrote, "The prompt and unceasing efforts of Prof. Bache to supply the demands for information resulting from operations under his directions, and so indispensable to vessels of the navy, cannot be too highly appreciated." Maury's work in and for the Navy was sliding into eclipse.

A few days later, Magruder again reported to Welles to deliver personally his letter of resignation, still torn between the Navy he long served and Virginia. He later went into voluntary exile in Canada.

Instead of accepting Maury's, Magruder's, Franklin Buchanan's, Samuel Barron's, and others' letters of resignation, Welles ordered them all dismissed and stricken from the *Navy Register*.

In Magruder's place, he appointed John Dahlgren, a man fast becoming a favorite of Lincoln for his quick action in controlling the Washington Navy Yard during these perilous weeks, as head of a re-formed Bureau of Ordnance.[43]

19. The Heady First Spring of War

Virginia, then about the size of New England, was the most exposed of the Southern states when the Civil War began. On its borders, Kentucky declared itself neutral, Tennessee was split asunder, Maryland was in riot, and Ohio and Pennsylvania were poised to invade. Inside Virginia's borders, the western counties threatened armed revolt against the secessionists.

From Lincoln's election, Henry Wise, governor during the John Brown raid, wrote that the state convention should use the power of "resumption" to take over "all forts, arsenals &c." The question was: If the secessionists grabbed Fortress Monroe and Fort Norfolk, the Gosport Naval Shipyard, and the arsenal at Harper's Ferry, would Governor John Letcher hand them back? Southern Rights extremists talked darkly of a coup to install Robert L. Montague, the lieutenant governor, to take Virginia forcibly out of the Union.[1]

After Lincoln's call for volunteers to crush the revolt, Wise, not Letcher, told Virginia militia units to use the cover of night and seize the arsenal and shipyard. The units were already in train to the arsenal when Letcher consented. At the same time, workmen gathered menacingly outside the shipyard's walls. When the attacks began, federal forces destroyed what they could before retreating. Fortress Monroe on Old Point Comfort on the north side of Hampton Roads remained in Union hands.

Wise, acting like another Patrick Henry, hailed the seizures to the closed-door convention.[2]

The next day, Letcher approved the takeovers, but to keep order in Tidewater, he dispatched General William B. Taliaferro to Portsmouth to command militia forces there and to secure Fort Norfolk with its stores of 150,000 pounds of gunpowder. Accompanying the general was Commander Robert

Pegram and Lieutenant Catesby R. ap Jones, the first Virginia naval officers to resign their federal commissions, to inspect the shipyard.

At the foot of the Chesapeake Bay, Hampton Roads was one of the nation's most strategically important locations. To the south, the Elizabeth River provided access to the forts, shipyards, and ports of Norfolk and Portsmouth, as the Nansemond River did to the rich farm lands of Suffolk and eastern North Carolina. To the north, the Virginia Peninsula was formed by the James and York Rivers. To the north and west along the James was Richmond, soon to be the capital of the Confederacy. At the peninsula's tip was Union-controlled Fortress Monroe, whose guns commanded access to the other great Virginia and Maryland rivers—the Rappahannock with Fredericksburg at its fall line and the Potomac with Washington, Georgetown, and Alexandria near its fall line. "Not a barrel of flour, not a hogshead of tobacco, no article of commerce can float by" the forts' cannons, John Tyler warned.[3]

Superintendent Francis Smith brought Maury to the Virginia Military Institute to head the physical survey of the state, a necessary tool in trying to rebuild Virginia following the Civil War. The men had known each other for years. In the days following secession, they had served on the Governor's Advisory Council, a de facto war ministry that built up the Old Dominion's forces, trained and equipped its men, and laid the groundwork for the defense of the commonwealth when the Confederates came to Richmond (courtesy Virginia Military Institute Archives).

Letcher had more than Wise's firebrands to contend with. Delegates from the western part of the state, particularly those near the Ohio River, opposed this hush-hush rush to treason. Though pledged to silence, these men, long ill-treated by the plantocracy, trudged back to their homes along the runs of the Appalachians. They would hold their own convention, well out of the governor's sight and well before any May referendum on secession.[4]

The governor ordered Willoughby Light above Norfolk extinguished, commercial vessels on all waters seized, and Monroe isolated. As he issued those maritime commands, Letcher did not have a navy to enforce them.[5]

This was the maelstrom that Matthew Fontaine Maury entered when he arrived at the governor's mansion on Sunday, April 21. With Letcher was the superintendent of the Virginia Military

View from the Parade Ground of the main building at the Virginia Military Institute following the Civil War (courtesy Virginia Military Institute Archives).

Institute, Colonel Francis H. Smith. Maury had known Smith, an 1829 Military Academy graduate, for years. Also present was Judge John Allen, chief justice of the Virginia Supreme Court, who presided over the advisory council that became the state's de facto War and Navy departments.[6]

To that meeting Maury came armed with a theoretical understanding of nineteenth-century warfare. He knew the effect steam had on battle fleets, and he understood how John Dahlgren's heavier guns changed naval strategies and river and coastal defenses. Maury also was convinced that Robert F. Stockton and John Ericsson were on the right track with the design (small and maneuverable with their screw propellers) and armament (bigger and deadlier) of ill-fated *Princeton*. Most importantly, Maury was mastering the earlier works in mine warfare of Robert Fulton and Samuel Colt.[7]

While the four talked, Richmond was in panic. April 21 was as frantic a day as any in the capital since the British invasions of the Chesapeake in 1781 and 1814. Throughout the morning, rumors blew like tornadoes of an imminent attack by a federal warship. What probably started the panic was a telegraphed report from Alexandria saying sloop *Pawnee* had sailed from Washington to take back the naval shipyard. The report was dead wrong. *Pawnee* had left Washington with orders to relieve Sumter, but it arrived too late to help Major Robert Anderson and his troops.[8]

Alarm bells pealed as the tale turned from one of *Pawnee* steaming to Hampton Roads to an alarm that the Union Navy was about to shell Richmond. Male residents scurried from their churches and homes to the banks of the James, armed with whatever weapons they could muster. There, they waited resolutely like the Minutemen at Concord Bridge to hold invaders at bay, but no federal warship came through the Curles of the James that day. Indeed, Richmond's river defenses held through the course of the war. Maury saw to that.

As night doused the hysteria, Letcher ordered weapons moved from the Bellona Arsenal to the more easily defended state armory. If he was going to have to fight fellow Virginians or the federal Navy, he wanted to have the necessary guns, pikes, knives, and swords to control the city, defend the riverfront, and protect his government. Before they retired that evening, Letcher and his new council received the welcome news that Robert E. Lee had accepted command of Virginia's forces.[9]

Maury was energized and to work first thing Monday. Each day that followed was twenty-four hours devoted to building the state's defense. The overriding question in the minds of the governor, council, and convention delegates was: How long would the Black Republican government wait before attacking? For the council, the pause allowed them to assist the secessionists in Maryland in cutting off Washington. Encouraged by the riots in Baltimore on April 19, one of the council's first recommendations was to send one thousand rifles from Harper's Ferry and five thousand muskets from the arsenal at Lexington, as well as twenty-three naval guns from Gosport as "a loan to the Maryland troops ... to enable them to resist the passage of Northern troops." As it was in the observatory's earliest days, work was ceaseless. In addition to placing gun batteries on the York and the James, Maury intended to close the rivers to marauding gunships, sloops, and frigates with electrically detonated torpedoes or mines. In the confusion of the war's early days when old friends were not necessarily true friends, especially in trafficking arms and military materiel, Maury sent a merchant northward to buy insulated wire for the mines.[10]

The council next asked Professors Socrates Maupin and James Lawrence Cabell at the University of Virginia to create a special laboratory to research mine warfare. It also wanted Charlottesville's factories' and foundries' help in making percussion caps and other war material.[11]

Because housing was at a premium, Maury moved in with a banker cousin, Robert H. Maury, in a townhouse at 1105 East Clay Street, and this house became Maury's laboratory. Here he tested his ideas on electrical current, fuses, and gunpowder. Each success sent small geysers ceilingward from a humble bathtub. These tiny successes were becoming Virginia's river defenses.[12]

As Maury worked on defenses, the first news from Gosport was exhilarating. The hastily set fires by retreating federals had not substantially damaged the yard's buildings. Better yet, the militia had seized a "great deal of ordnance" and guns, including Dahlgrens with their long range and explosive power. As an added bonus, frigate *Merrimack* could be salvaged, and the repairs could be done in the yard's intact granite drydock.[13]

At noon on April 23, inside the House of Delegates' wing in the state Capitol, Maury and the other council members sat in places of honor with Letcher and Confederate Vice President Alexander Stephens as Virginia formally received Lee as the commanding officer of the commonwealth's forces. To the officials sitting for the ceremony, this was a day to savor.

The onetime Whig John Janney, who as president of the convention twice voted against secession, told Lee, "Yesterday, your mother Virginia, placed her sword in your hand upon the implied condition that we know you will keep to the letter and in spirit, that you will draw it only in her defense."[14]

That day, the Virginians who took the state out of the Union brimmed with confidence.

The *Richmond Daily Whig* trumpeted, "Maury is a sound familiar to all the voices of fame. Lee was the confessed hero of the Mexican War."[15]

Maury, who knew both the new commander and his family, said simply, "General Lee is clearheaded and cool."[16]

Any euphoria Maury enjoyed was tempered by a letter from Navy Secretary Gideon Welles demanding to know why the Virginian had resigned. Maury answered, "I desire to go with my people and with them to share the fortunes of our own state together. Such are the reasons for tendering my resignation, and I hope the president will consider them satisfactory." In sharing Virginia's fortune, he avoided giving any evidence for a future treason trial.[17]

Two weeks after Virginia seceded, former President John Tyler wrote his mother-in-law: "The whole state is clad in steel under the command of the most accomplished leaders.... In a week from this time, the James River will bristle with fortifications and Charles City will be far safer than Staten Island."[18]

Ordinances swam through the convention acting as the legislature, calling for volunteers; taking in officers from the Revenue Service and Coast Survey;

organizing a provisional army, a navy, and staff departments for the military forces; and creating commissaries, paymasters, terms of pay and enlistments, auditors, a medical department, an adjutant general department, an ordnance department, a chaplain corps, rules of war, distribution of arms, exemptions to military service, ways to pay for the state's defenses, and a flag. The raising and arming militia companies in the wake of John Brown's raid paled in comparison.[19]

At the same time, the governor and the council were inundated with requests. Some wanted commissions for themselves; for relatives, like the mother of Lieutenant J. E. B. Stuart; or for friends. A few offered their slaves' labor—for a price.

Letters and telegrams from out-of-work railroad men; miners; Mexican War veterans; engineers; graduates of West Point or VMI; old Army officers, like artilleryman Lieutenant Colonel John Bankhead Magruder; doctors; former revenue marines; mounted soldiers; and experienced naval officers, like Lieutenant J. S. Maury, told council members of their special skills.

A lighthouse service tender proudly informed the governor that he brought two small boats with him—a less potent navy than the gunboat flotillas in the War of 1812. "Free men of color" said they would throw up breastworks around the capital. Sewing circles pledged their aid to meet domestic needs. Sallie F. Crowder of Mecklenburg wrote, "I can shoot very accurately and feel quite sure that I could hit a Yankee," in asking for arms to defend herself, her family, her nation—Virginia.[20]

All of these mixed with pleadings such as this from Urbanna, a small community off the Rappahannock River, for protection: "There is not a musket or cannon or any other weapon in the hands of the people." To the north, women in Fauquier County wanted "Colts" to defend themselves now that their men were in the service of the state.[21]

From the seashore to the mountains, the telegrams clacked back to Richmond with news of events none could control. Union forces ordered families near Fortress Monroe out of their homes. Secessionists in the western part of the state warned of "this infernal plot to divide Virginia," as Union men prepared to meet in Wheeling on May 13.[22]

Letcher, Lee, and the council, now expanded to five members, knew there were few modern weapons in the arsenals and little they could do to protect the borders if the Union attacked. Their first priority was provisioning and training the volunteers.

In the round-the-clock pounding of rumors and fears, the state government needed calm thinking and organization, but the demands of do something, do anything, here and now were tempting. To their south, rash action was all that was wanted. Governor Francis Pickens offered five thousand South Carolina troops with the hopes that they and ten thousand others could march on Washington and "take it and the government." Instead of invading Washington, Letcher commanded all volunteers not in Richmond in late April or ordered to a training site to stay home until the state could provide food and shelter. Arms were still a question.[23]

To measure the caliber of those now in the state's service, the council sent the register of officers of the old Army and Navy to a special commission headed by Joseph E. Johnston, the former quartermaster general of the federal Army, and Samuel Barron, the former chief of the Bureau of Detail in the federal Navy, for evaluation. Maury left no record of seeing Barron's appointment or the choices of Captain Sidney Smith Lee, Robert E. Lee's older brother and former commandant of the Naval Academy, and Pegram to help with the review as another Plucking Board that threatened him, his friend William Francis Lynch, or his former boss, George Magruder.

The governor and the council turned to the iron industry for help. The Tredegar Works and other foundries, particularly in Richmond, geared for war production. By month's end, Harper's Ferry was back converting muskets into rifles. Boat builders in Norfolk offered to construct shallow draft vessels to protect rivers, bays, and harbors. Work also was underway on Richmond's waterfront to convert two seized paddlewheel steamers into warships. Additionally, the council gave the go-ahead to raise *Merrimack* from the mud. There were nine other warships in the yard when the Union abandoned it. But only three other than *Merrimack* were worth repairing when French Forrest, the senior naval officer in the state, took command.[24]

Ideas of how best to defend Virginia flooded into the governor's and council's offices. Concerned citizen D. G. Smith of Charlottesville suggested shopping abroad for materiel: "Select and send our best naval officer to Europe where vessels of the best class could be procured and no doubt upon favourable terms, including steel-plated frigates, gun boats armed with the heaviest metal and have these and all others fitted out and manned by English, Irish, French sailors of the best character, paying them the highest or extra wages." It was a suggestion adopted by the Confederate government. It proved a force in a much longer war.[25]

Without a real warship, Virginia's naval officers commanded the river batteries with captured Dahlgrens. Almost two thousand guns were seized at Gosport and brought to bear at strategic points along the state's one thousand miles of coastline and navigable rivers. At Maury's direction, heavy guns were placed at Aquia Creek, where it enters the Potomac, and at West Point, where the Pamunkey and Mattaponi form the York. The batteries were to block the landing of any invaders to attack Richmond. George Sinclair, an ordnance expert, warned Maury to "devote your strong mind" to strengthening defenses at Norfolk. Soon, seventy-five guns were there.[26]

Each night, more lighthouses along the ocean, the bay, and the tips of the rivers went dark, and channel markers in eastern Virginia were moved. For these acts of enlightened defense in the eyes of Virginians or sabotage in the eyes of Unionists, Maury, the pathfinder of the seas, was blamed.

"A price has been set upon my head in Boston. I thank them for the honor, for I do not forget that in other days a price was set upon the heads of the best men of that state, and the cause in which I fight is far more righteous than that which moved those great and good men to take up arms against their country," wrote Maury. The Marine Society of Salem—the "China hands" who so benefited from the charting work—struck Maury's name from its rolls and "voted the portrait of Commander Maury be reversed, and that the picture be hung in the society's room with the head downward." Likewise, the American Philosophical Society in Philadelphia took the "extraordinary" step of expelling Maury and Lynch, the leader of the Dead Sea expedition, from its membership, because they "have committed public and notorious acts of treason."[27]

As brave as his words were, Maury secretly sent a letter to his daughter Betty, still in Washington with her husband, Will, and their child, telling them to escape. The young family lied to a clerk that they were not related to the former superintendent of the observatory; and the man granted the pass. As always, the extended family fell back on Fredericksburg. Even S. Wellford Corbin, Maury's son-in-law who owned a plantation near the Potomac River, brought his wife, Diana, to stay with their cousin John Minor in the relative safety of Central Virginia. Ideas of evacuating all to Charlottesville, the final resting place of the Maury patriarch—the Rev. James Maury—were stayed, because Ann was too ill to travel.[28]

More and more warships patrolled the Chesapeake Bay to keep Fortress Monroe in Union hands and the waterways to the ocean closed. By May 1, no vessel could pass through Hampton Roads without clearance from the United States Navy. But so far, however, no federal ship had tried to pass Virginia's guns up its tidal rivers.[29]

Through this first spring of secession, Virginia hurriedly regularized its military training. A cavalry camp was established at Ashland, about fifteen miles north of Richmond. Green soldiers, like Lieutenant Richard Launcelot

Maury, one of Maury's sons, were trained in and around the capital. Other recruits drilled on college campuses under the tutelage of young men like John Herndon Maury. Another son in Charlottesville was sent to defend Harper's Ferry.

"This thing of officering and organizing an army out of the raw is working in the dark. You put in wheel after wheel, and pin after pin, you have to wait and try it and see whether it be good and fit. It is a hard business," Matthew Fontaine Maury wrote.[30]

Ideas on how best to defend the state rose like the incoming tide. Corbin and others in King George County offered to form a band of rangers to operate between the Potomac and Rappahannock Rivers. The rangers could strike wagon trains or troop columns from the thick woods that bordered the roads and then resume the appearance of quiet farmers or move from plantation barn to plantation house to escape Union patrols. From mountainous Monroe County came a similar scheme. There, one hundred mounted men wanted rifles instead of their old muskets to trap Union troops who might try to move through the region's rugged passes.[31]

Plans, plots, offers, and schemes were not confined to secessionists. Unionists in the western counties were also busy then raising their own volunteer units. They itched to fight the traitors in Richmond and Monroe County.

What kept Union forces at bay was not the state's hastily constructed defenses but the upcoming referendum on secession.

Waitman T. Willey, a pro–Union westerner, described the May 23 election day: "Thirty thousand glittering bayonets surrounded the polls from the Chesapeake to the summits of the Alleghenies." Not waiting for the official tally, Union troops crossed the Potomac and occupied Alexandria on May 24. Several days later and although twenty-seven counties had not reported, Letcher announced more than 125,000 Virginians had voted for secession and only slightly more than 20,000 against. The governor declared that the people had spoken, and Virginia was out of the Union.[32]

As Francis H. Pierpont, a later governor of Virginia, put it, "The time for voting is past; the time for fighting has arrived." He was on target. The Virginia government of Letcher guaranteed that when it invited the government of Jefferson Davis to move to Richmond.[33]

Five days later, at the convention's invitation, Davis arrived in Virginia's capital to make Richmond the new seat of the Confederacy. Over the next few weeks, on trains, in canal boats, in stage coaches, and on horseback, members of Davis's cabinet and the Confederate Congress trickled into the city. The Virginia Convention thought it fitting to welcome Davis and his secretaries. On a June evening, precisely at eight, a hundred or more "solid men" of Virginia gathered at the Capitol to parade to the Spotswood Hotel where Davis was staying.

Arm-in-arm, the two veterans of the William Henry Harrison campaign, Tyler and Janney, led the way to the hotel's private entrance. Once inside, the convention's president introduced its members to Davis; Robert Toombs, secretary of state; Stephen Mallory, secretary of the Navy; and C. G. Memminger, who had failed in tempting Virginia to follow South Carolina out of the Union the year before and was now secretary of the Treasury, each "one happy in that happiest of all reflections."[34]

The bonhomie did not last much beyond the evening's toasts. Mary Chesnut noted that "bickering and quarreling" was present from the start. Friction between the leaders of the Old Dominion and the Confederate government quickly developed. Nothing proved more fractious than control of Virginia's forces and control of the seized federal property, stores, arms, and vessels. In June, Maury, Allen, and Smith met with Davis to arrange the transfer of the state's army and navy to Confederate control and decide who was to control Harper's Ferry and Gosport.

Though the Confederate demand to turn over Harper's Ferry stuck in Letcher's craw, Davis had a more bitter pill for Virginians in uniform to swallow: "In relation to the proposition concerning officers who have left the service of the U. States and entered the Army or Navy of Virginia, I can only say that the Congress of the C. States secured by law to officers of the Army thus entering service, so far as they were of the same grade, they should have the same relative rank in this service as the one they left. The reason of the rule would equally apply to officers of the Navy, and I do not anticipate its being either disregarded or violated."[35]

In short, when the forces were transferred, Maury reverted to the rank of commander if he returned to uniform and Lee to colonel. For Maury there was the added bitter pill of having to serve under Mallory and Davis. None of the three could put aside the rancor that had engulfed the Senate over Maury's forced retirement six years earlier.

For a few days, the council advised Letcher to resist, and this delay magnified the Confederate government's disdain. Mary Chesnut scoffed that the Virginians were so many "vinegar cruets on pedestals." In his diary, Mallory wrote, "From all I can learn here, Gov. Letcher's conduct must be the result of lack of judgment. It is indefensible—a traitor or a fool might equally act as he does and he is not a traitor." Although confided to diaries, those two entries summed up relations between the two governments and their leaders.[36]

In the late spring and early summer, Maury bitterly wrote that the Confederate government was riddled with "small men." He went on to say, "Things do not look right to me. Where the wrong is, I am not so clear, but the biggest promotion seems to be on the other side. You may rely upon it; the Confederate States Government has come here feeling that there is between it and us something of an antagonism."[37]

When he could get away from the capital, Maury returned to Fredericksburg. William C. Hasbrouck, Maury's lifelong friend, found Betty before her family escaped and gave her letters for her father. She accepted them, but told Maury's former teacher, "I was proud of my father before, but I was a hundred times prouder of him now, that, if he had considered his own personal welfare, he would have remained with the North."[38]

Although Mallory sneered at Virginia's efforts, the state had done a remarkable job in an extremely turbulent time.

"Heavy cannon were moved to their destinations with dispatch; ammunition and projectiles provided; men instructed, and every other preparation made to repel an opposing force," Barron reported in discussing the naval defenses of the rivers. In addition, naval forces seized three hundred thousand pounds of powder and shells in Norfolk, raised *Merrimac* and planned to raise *Germantown* and *Plymouth* from the Elizabeth River, outfitted steamer *Teaser* with guns to patrol the James and were prepared to have steamer *Yorktown* on patrol by July 1.[39]

Lee, once superintendent of the Military Academy, estimated the state had in mid–June at least thirty-five thousand men under arms. The state colonel of ordnance had issued 2,054 rifles and 41,604 muskets, in addition to pistols and sabers. Arsenals in Richmond and Lexington also presented arms to volunteers from other states who came to Virginia's defense. The state, as well, provided 115 field guns. In addition to building the river batteries, he reported that field works were constructed in Norfolk and redoubts on Jamestown Island, Gloucester Point, Yorktown, and near Williamsburg.

"When it is remembered that this body of men was called from a state of profound peace to one of unexpected war, you will have reason to commend the alacrity with which they left their homes and families, and prepared themselves for the defense of the state," he wrote.

Lee signed his report to Letcher as "General Commanding."[40]

The reports were epitaphs to Maury. The heady days of cladding the state in steel were over. Maury's energies were burning red hot, but he, Lee, and all the others had been diminished in rank and power.

As proud as his family was of him, Maury's fate was back in the hands of two "small men." He also again awaited orders in Fredericksburg as he had for the great exploring expedition and while recovering from his crippling stagecoach injury. But it was in Fredericksburg that he rallied himself time and again. He had been born there, fell in love there, was married there, began a family there, and made himself a "useful man" there. Fredericksburg was a place where Maury took stock of himself.

It was also a place where he took stock of his achievements—recognized by scientists around the world, businessmen on both sides of the Atlantic, secretaries of the Navy, and presidents. Now, he heard his praises sung by the governor of his home state in a time of new danger.

For the five-member council, Letcher had special praise:

> The intercourse between the council and the executive has been of the most agreeable character. The journal, regularly kept, will show that their action has been characterized by a remarkable unanimity, and it is a source of satisfaction to me to know that I have rarely felt constrained to dissent from their advice. Their services have been appreciated by me and should be appreciated by the state.[41]

Maury rallied himself again.

20. At War with the Cotton Kings

In the early summer of 1861, Richmond, an inland river port, had more than its share of naval officers, like Matthew Fontaine Maury, looking for something to do. In a war just beginning, they were men without assignments or ships, having volunteered their services to a new nation that did not have a blue-water Navy and serving under a president who did not believe he needed one. Bracing for a land attack in Northern Virginia, President Jefferson Davis worried about how well the Confederacy's hastily raised army would fight.[1]

In Richmond's Spotswood Hotel then was George N. Hollins sharing an audacious scheme to capture a Union warship with Maury. Maury told the Baltimore-born officer that he might have better luck enlisting Governor John Letcher's support than risking Confederate Navy Secretary Stephen Mallory's rejection.[2]

The naval officer told Letcher he intended to buy arms surreptitiously in Baltimore, seize the steamer *St. Nicholas* on its nightly run to Washington, and use it to capture sloop-of-war *Pawnee*. For months, *Pawnee* had been a tempting target for Virginia and the Confederacy.[3]

At their meeting, Letcher agreed to provide one thousand dollars for the weapons and told Hollins to see Maury about working out other details. Maury detailed his oldest son, Richard; Robert D. Minor, formerly of the observatory and a cousin; and Jack Maury, another cousin and a survivor of the ill-starred 1854 mapping expedition of the Panamanian Isthmus, for the raid.[4]

For the ruse, Hollins's chief associate was Richard Thomas of Maryland. Thomas, a slight man, was a nineteenth-century romantic who said he had fought alongside Garibaldi in Italy. As Letcher was told, Thomas would be disguised as a French woman when boarding in Baltimore. The arms would be stored in trunks that Thomas would bring along. At Point Lookout on the Potomac, Hollins and the other Confederates posing as civilians would board and would attend the vivacious and veiled French woman.[5]

The first half of the scheme—capturing the steamer—unfolded exactly as planned. Then as the Confederates secured their prize, Hollins discovered a story in a discarded Baltimore newspaper, reporting the sloop would not be in the river that night because of a funeral.

Hollins wrote glumly: "Finding there was no chance of capturing the *Pawnee* and deeming it unsafe to remain where I was, in a steamer without guns, I resolved to go up to Fredericksburg and immediately run out in the Chesapeake." His luck brightened in the darkness. As he ordered the paddle-wheeler into the bay, Hollins first came on to, hailed, and captured a brig loaded with coffee, then a schooner loaded with ice, and finally another loaded with coal. Four prizes in all were not a bad catch, but, for all its flair, the scheme did not alter the naval situation where it mattered most to Virginia—in Hampton Roads.[6]

Maury focused on Hampton Roads, steaming ahead on his scheme to sink the fleet there. The commander arranged with the Tredegar Iron Works and Talbott Brothers foundry for tanks and casks, received batteries from the medical college in Richmond, and scrounged insulating wire for the mines he was building. Letcher provided the gunpowder. Nature was to do the rest.

The Maury plan was the same as David Bushnell's on the British fleet anchored in the Delaware River during the Revolution and Elijah Mix's on the British blockaders in the Chesapeake Bay in the War of 1812. But Maury had two distinct advantages over Bushnell and Mix: "the science of electricity" and chemical initiators to detonate the mines rather than flintlocks.[7]

For at least two nights, Maury and his small party scouted the Union fleet. The use of these "infernal machines" troubled Maury's family and many Confederate Army officers. Likewise, some raiders were disturbed to be using darkness and the cover of the Sabbath to wage war. Maury, brooking no qualms of conscience, stoutly defended the mission, declaring with the fervor of his grandfather James that President Abraham Lincoln had "set at naught our principles of honor and humanity."[8]

Electronically detonated mines first came to Maury's attention on April 13, 1844, when Samuel Colt successfully tested his in the Anacostia River. While greeted by "heartfelt plaudits, subsiding into long continuing murmurs of admiration," Colt's secretive ways about how the mines worked left many in the uniformed Navy cold.

A few officers, like Maury, remained intrigued by the mines' potential for coastal defense. They devoured reports on how the Russians had used them to ward off British and French sea and land assaults in the Crimean War.[9]

At 10 p.m., on July 7, 1861, the boats with five men in each shoved off from the Norfolk shore on such a calm night that the attackers could hear the anchored ships' bells. They rowed with muffled oars toward their targets using the light of Thatcher's Comet—the "War Comet of 1861"—as their guide.

When in position, Maury let the tide and current carry the powder-laden oak casks toward the ships. The pairs of casks were connected by a span of rope about six hundred feet long, and corks kept the span afloat. The explosives, contained in the barrels, were submerged, and the triggers were in the barrelheads.

The idea was this: As the span became entangled in the ship's hawse and the barrels were pulled alongside by the tidal wash, the tightening line would activate the triggers, setting off a fuse igniting the powder to explode below the vessels' waterlines.

When he thought he was in position, Maury ordered the first mines loaded with two hundred pounds of explosives released. Then the next set until all were off. The twenty-five Confederates tensed, waiting to hear the explosions. After about an hour, as they drew closer to safety, the Confederates heard only their muffled oars on a Tidewater summer night. There were no shattering blasts, secondary explosions, and alarm bells and trumpet calls.

Ashore, Maury "attributed it to the fact that such a fuse would not burn under a pressure of 20 feet of water" and vowed to try again. When Union forces found the washed ashore mines later, they had another explanation: wet powder. The *New York Times* prematurely declared the "submarine batteries" a "wretched failure."[10]

Torpedoes were deadly and cheap; for a government short of bullion, they could be a military godsend. To prove this point, Maury arranged to demonstrate the power of his hidden weapons to Mallory; Charles Conrad, a former secretary of war and now chair of the Confederate House's Naval Affairs Committee; and other congressmen.[11]

On a hot summer day, Maury and his son Richard rowed from Rockett's Wharf toward the middle of the James River and set out two kegs filled with rifle powder. The kegs floated down toward a buoy, where they became entangled, as they were supposed to do, in the raids at the mouth of the bay.

But again nothing happened.

Maury was unwilling to admit new defeat. He had his son row back toward the buoy. Again in the middle of the river, on his father's command, Richard pulled the rope connected to the mine's trigger. "Up went a column of water fifteen or twenty feet," Richard Maury wrote. "Many stunned or dead fish floated around." The jubilant Maurys were drenched in the baptismal water of modern mine warfare. They were warmed by the applause of the civilian officials on the shore.[12]

Although Mallory's priority was converting *Merrimack* into an ironclad warship, he requested fifty thousand dollars for more mines. The secretary also placed Maury in charge of coastal defenses and detailed a few men to work out of an office at Ninth and Bank streets to perfect the Confederacy's secret weapon.[13]

While Maury labored to obstruct the South's waterways, the road to Richmond for the Union Army in late July 1861 led through the rail junction at Manassas. There, with as much luck as skill and the courage of Thomas "Stonewall" Jackson's troops, the Confederates repulsed the first major Union thrust toward their capital. The West Point graduate and Mexican War commander Davis saluted his soldiers as "blood-stained victors on a hard-fought field."[14]

To Maury, the victory over ninety-day volunteers was a propaganda coup. He called the close-run win a major step toward independence. To political allies like Letcher, former Navy Secretary William Ballard Preston, and former President John Tyler, Maury sent letters with a proposal containing "the seed of peace" to plant in the North. Hadn't the Confederacy proven its mettle on the battlefield? he argued. At the end of the day, the Confederacy controlled almost 750,000 square miles of territory and eleven states.[15]

In August 1861, Maury sent the first of his "Why I Fight" letters to Britain: "Whenever we have met the enemy in the open field, we have beat him back, though he numbered three and in some cases even five to our one against us." He concluded, "I see no end to this wicked and savage war, as long as the arch spirits which surround Lincoln remain in power. Before and after every battle, we hold but the olive branch, demanding simply, 'LET US GO.'"

When *The South*, a pro–Confederate newspaper in Baltimore, reprinted Maury's letter, Union officials shut down the publication, arrested the city's pro–Confederate mayor and other sympathizers, and suspended the right of habeas corpus from Washington to Philadelphia.[16]

Alarmed Union officials were on the lookout for traitors and spies in their midst from the East Coast to California. Before the year was out, they arrested Maury's younger namesake cousin, a clerk for James Rareshide's cotton brokerage in New Orleans, at Fort Warren in Boston Harbor, and his brother Rutson, a clerk for Maury and Hogg in New Orleans, at Fort Lafayette in New York harbor as suspected spies. The arrests were made with cause. When the children of author Sarah Mytton Maury were arrested in Cleveland, they were carrying suspicious letters in concealed compartments in their baggage. Although the evidence appeared strong, the New York cotton-trading community and British consular officials bombarded the State Department with protests and inquiries. Clamor had its way in the cases of the Maurys. The British citizens were released in early 1862. Others, like the daring Thomas when he was captured following a second attempt to seize a warship, weren't so lucky.[17]

By September, Maury was in Albemarle County, visiting relatives and checking on war research at the university. When he returned to Richmond, Maury had the go-ahead from Mallory for a new attack on Union ships in Hampton Roads. This time, Minor, a participant in the *Pawnee* plot, was to command.

Instead of starting from shore as Maury's had, the raiders would launch from the Confederates' largest warship in Virginia waters, *Patrick Henry*. Iron sheathing protected the onetime packet steamer's boilers, and the 250-foot-long vessel carried eight guns. Commander John Randolph Tucker and the renamed steamer were ready.

Sometime on October 10, Minor, fellow lieutenants Thomas Dornin, the son of one of Maury's early Navy mentors, and Alexander M. Mason met up with the ship off Mulberry Island.

The rain and mist, as well as encroaching night, was a blessing. A darkened *Patrick Henry* proceeded slowly toward Newport News Point. There the fifty-two-gun sailing frigate *Congress* lay anchored, covering the entrance to Hampton Roads. About a mile and a half away from the anchorage, Tucker ordered *Patrick Henry* to stop.[18]

Minor reported:

> The [two raiding party] boats were then allowed to drift with the rapid ebb tide, while the end of the cork line was passed over to Mr. Dornin, and the line tightened by the boats pulling in opposite directions. The buoys were then thrown overboard, the guard lines on the triggers cut, the levers fitted and pinned, the trip line made fast to the bight at the end of the lever, the safety screw removed, the magazine carefully lowered in the water, where they were well supported by the buoys, the slack line (three fathoms of which was kept in hand for safety) thrown overboard and all set adrift within 800 yards of the ship.[19]

The boats were so close to the shore that voices could be heard from the land when they released the torpedoes. The Confederates waited for an explosion. Again, nothing happened. All Minor could report was that the magazines did not foul the ship lines "though planted fairly and in good drifting distances."[20]

The latest setback in Tidewater Virginia did not deter far-flung Confederate field officers from wanting mines to defend their positions. They had Maury's faith in their efficacy. Longtime Maury acquaintance Leonidas Polk, a Confederate general who had taken off his bishop's robes, wrote from Columbus, Kentucky, the day after Minor's attack, "I feel constrained to urge upon you the necessity of at once furnishing me an officer familiar with the subject of submarine batteries and capable of a practicable application of this species of defense to the Mississippi River."[21]

Polk's situation was deteriorating by the hour. Less than one day's ride away, the Union was completing its first gunboats to control the western rivers. Worse yet, Brigadier General U. S. Grant, in command at Cairo, took two regiments and an artillery battery to Paducah by steamboat accompanied by two "timber clad gunboats." The Union Army and Navy were afloat and attacking.[22]

Earlier, apparently outside of channels, Maury told Polk that he personally intended to take charge of mining the Mississippi. But it was December before Polk was helped in the way of mines, and it was not from Maury, but his trusted aide Confederate Navy Lieutenant Isaac Brown.[23]

By December, Maury again urged Confederate and Virginia officials to try more ambitious approaches to sinking the Union fleet. This time he touted mines, torpedo spars on gunboats, *Patrick Henry*'s guns, and the resurrected iron-sheathed *Merrimack* as key ingredients to an active defense. While his ideas held promise, Confederate civilian leaders were tired of Maury's prodding, even if *Merrimack* were ready to get underway, which it wasn't. He was back in the limelight, something they dreaded.

The news of the fighting at Manassas alarmed Maury's friends in Great Britain and on the continent. They promised him and his family haven. The czar of Russia offered Maury the superintendency of the St. Petersburg observatory. Maury politely said he could not leave Virginia when she was engaged in "a fierce and bloody war."[24]

The fierce and bloody war was turning against the Confederacy as Maury answered his Russian friends. Late 1861 and early 1862 was a time of repeated Confederate defeats in the West, along the Atlantic Coast, and in London and Paris. Noting that the South had ceded "all the Seaboard and the principal internal Rivers," British Prime Minister Palmerston cautioned, "We ought to know that their Separate Independence is a Truth and a Fact before we declare it be so." Maury's "LET US GO" did not resonate at Westminster.[25]

During this time, Maury saw himself as the man best equipped to create an almost impenetrable defense of ports, inlets, and waterways. As a member of the governor's advisory council, he had positioned Virginia's defenses to his

Maury lobbied tirelessly behind closed doors for his mine defenses and gunboats in the Capitol that served both the Virginia government and the Confederacy. His office at Ninth and Bank Streets was down the hill toward the river. Photograph by author.

liking—mines and obstructions to secure ports and waterways; well-placed coastal artillery, the heaviest guns with the longest range; and fast, maneuverable gunboats to sting invaders. Now as head of Confederate coastal defense, he intended to build the nation's layered defense.

At the time, Davis paid scant attention to Maury's plans, but Mallory saw the value in repositioning the guns seized at Gosport. Deploying mines could be done cheaply, although he and Maury's protégé John Mercer Brooke doubted their effectiveness and small gunboats' effectiveness. Even so the secretary approved the mining.[26]

While Mallory thought "small," in Maury's words, about coastal defense, ignoring the secretary's commitment to ironclad floating batteries, the commander dreamed large—as in the turf wars among the observatory, the Coast Survey, and the Smithsonian Institution. Maury anticipated a fight with Mallory over money to build the gunboats, and he worked his congressional allies, like Tyler and Conrad, for the upcoming clash through the press.

To prepare the way, Maury, writing as "Ben Bow," used the *Richmond Enquirer* for guerrilla strikes against Davis and Mallory. Starting in late September, he blasted the administration's naval defense spending as "mere makeshifts." He compared its two requests for naval appropriations to creating "a navy without vessels [to having] lamps without oil."[27]

As chairman of the Senate Naval Affairs Committee, Mallory had survived a war through the press and in Congress with Maury; and he was not about to countenance another with an officer directly under his control. In less than a week, the secretary ordered Maury to Cuba to buy weapons.

The reaction among the Virginians and in the Congress was instant outrage. With the powerful Tyler, Virginia's congressional delegation, and Conrad setting the tone, the Confederate Congress declared that the commander was too valuable where he was. Mallory for now backed down.[28]

Not trusting Mallory, Maury turned to good listener Letcher and his allies in the Virginia Convention, sitting as the legislature, with his "big gun and little ship" plan. Maury did not want a ship "stout enough to keep the sea," as "smart active steamers" could. Instead, he envisioned "steam launches each capable of carrying two rifled pivot guns and no more. Their structure should be simple and plain and as economical as possible; they should be literally nothing but floating gun carriages" with crews of forty men and no accommodations.[29]

The commander wanted to turn them loose on the Union fleet in the Chesapeake Bay and North Carolina sounds. Shipwrights in the bay counties of Mathews and Gloucester would be the primary builders, and they could do the work, along with soldier-artisans about to go into winter quarters, at half the cost of the naval yard. Yards in coastal North Carolina were also available.[30]

"Going out like a nest of hornets, they will especially, if the building and the fitting out be kept from the enemy, either sink, capture or drive away from the Chesapeake and its tributaries the whole fleet which the enemy now has or probably will in that time in these waters." Then the "nest of hornets" could close off the maritime traffic through the Virginia capes, starve out Fortress Monroe, inspire secessionists in Southern Maryland, and threaten Washington anew, Maury wrote.[31]

In late October, a Union fleet of more than twenty ships loaded with thousands of troops steamed to Port Royal, about halfway between Charleston, South Carolina, and Savannah, Georgia. With no gunboats to hinder them there and few coastal defenses of consequence, the Union Navy covered the beachhead that "would serve all the future needs of the army and navy," meaning the fleet had no need to return to Hampton Roads to refit or take on coal, historian Robert Browning noted. By the end of the year, 264 Union ships, the vast majority converted civilian steamers, were enforcing the blockade. Privation, hoarding, and inflation were moving into their ascendancy.[32]

Thomas Jefferson Page, a seasoned naval officer and battery commander at Gloucester Point in Virginia, wrote: "Suppose a fleet of twenty of these boats in the harbor of Port Royal at the time of late attack from the enemy, can any one fail to perceive that the result would have been vastly different."[33]

Following this latest debacle, Maury lobbied the Virginia Convention strenuously for his gunboats. The Virginians' renewed insistence, especially that of Tyler, and the tightening blockade moved the Confederate Congress to approve $2 million to build one hundred vessels. On Christmas Eve, Davis signed the bill putting Maury in charge of building the fleet that "shall present little more than a feather edge" to naval invaders. Like the money Mallory set aside to rebuild *Merrimack*, this was a high stakes roll of the dice.[34]

When members of the Virginia Convention approached Mallory about progress on the "Maury gunboats," the secretary replied that his agents were scouring the countryside for engines. He failed to say they were having little success in finding them. Tyler happily reported that Maury had "woven a proud chaplet around her brow by having won a name all over the world which reflects new luster on the name of Virginia" by advocating the state's strong defense.[35]

After resting during the holidays, Maury, with his son John, returned to Richmond to get the gunboats on the way. Over fears of new land attacks in Virginia, Maury's idea to free soldiers with carpentry skills from Army duties in the winter was rejected.

In spite of the setback, construction began on the Mattaponi and Pamunkey Rivers, near West Point, and also along the Rappahannock and at the naval yard. Talbott & Brothers, a large Richmond foundry, turned over its entire business to the Confederate Navy in February 1862 and announced the delivery of five double engines for the gunboats. At the same time, Maury advertised for "negro laborers to cut timber for the vessels."[36]

Thus a humble start for a major naval building project.

Ideas that flowed so easily from Maury's mind to his pen—like constructing one hundred gunboats, building charts for each ocean, cataloging every star, or determining the best crossing point on the Central American coast—again proved difficult to execute, even when the ideas had Mallory's wholehearted support. The "nest of hornets" project did not. It also was soon to lose its congressional support.

Mallory's wholehearted shipbuilding support at home remained in rebuilding an iron-sheathed *Merrimack* for Hampton Roads and eventually ironclads to defend other ports. What Mallory dreamed of was a class of ships "built exclusively for ocean speed, at a low cost, with a battery of one or two accurate guns of long range, with an ability to keep the sea upon a long cruise and to engage or to avoid an enemy at will." To him, building such a class of ships was a "matter of the first necessity."[37]

In CSS *Virginia*, Mallory received a cumbersome and deep-drafted vessel with historically defective engines, unable to face the sea, go far up rivers, or

The Brooke Rifle, designed by Maury protégé John Mercer Brooke, provided heavy artillery support for Confederate ships and fortifications. Photograph by author.

even to operate in many spots on the Chesapeake Bay. But on March 8, 1862, *Virginia*, covered in two-inch-thick, sharply angled armor plate from Tredegar and outfitted with four newly developed rifled and extremely heavy "Brooke guns" and six Dahlgren shell guns, succeeded where Maury had twice failed. *Minnesota* and three other Union ships were aground in Hampton Roads; *Congress* and *Cumberland* were destroyed.[38]

Maury exultantly wrote Alexander de La Marche of the French imperial navy, the "little ewe lamb" *Virginia* "overturned the 'wooden walls of Old England' and rendered effete the navies of the world."[39]

The Confederates only had one day to celebrate, because on March 9, the *Monitor*, designed by John Ericsson, arrived. Ericsson was the brilliant Swede who had come to the United States to work with Robert F. Stockton, Maury's ally, on the radically propelled and armed warship *Princeton*. For more than a decade after the tragic explosion of a gun aboard the ship, Ericsson's career had remained in the shadows in the United States. Undeterred, he took his screw propeller designs back to Europe, intriguing navies and shipbuilders there. It kept his business afloat.

On this day, Ericsson's radically designed an inexpensive "cheese box on a raft," pushed through the Navy bureaucracy by a relative of the Revolutionary War submarine hero David Bushnell, kept *Virginia* from finishing off the Union Navy in Hampton Roads.[40]

The "Ericsson Battery's" design might have been surprising, but the fact that the North was building ironclads using the Swede's plans was "old news." The *Dispatch* reported in late February that it had satisfactorily passed the Navy's test, and "a trial trip to Fortress Monroe is contemplated."[41]

After the March 1862 battle, the Confederate Congress wanted only floating fortress ironclads for harbor defense and Southern versions of Britain's *Warrior* and France's *Glorie* for commerce raiding and attacking Northern cities. Maury still believed gunboats with their shallow drafts were best suited for afloat coastal defense. This time he coupled the mine's power with the gunboat's speed—even one plated in iron. To attack, like CSS *Virginia*, the gunboat would ram a spar carrying a torpedo through the vessel's outer sheathing and detonate the charge as it backed away. This was potentially dangerous for the attacker and the attacked.[42]

In Hampton Roads, the Confederacy's military situation slowly crumbled as the ironclad stalemate wore on, and Union forces—more than 121,000 soldiers, with wagons, animals, ambulances, and artillery—landed safely on the Virginia Peninsula. Finally acting on Lincoln's incessant orders, McClellan recaptured the Old Navy's largest shipyard. The day after Norfolk and Portsmouth fell, CSS *Virginia*, which could not escape to Richmond, brave the ocean, or block the mouth of the James River, was scuttled near Craney Island. At a cost of more than $100,000, Mallory's hopes for ironclad floating fortresses went down with it.[43]

While Polk and Confederates in Richmond put their faith in Maury's mines in closing off rivers from attack, another Confederate Army officer, Gabriel Rains, knew from the Seminole Wars in Florida how effective hidden mines on land could be.

The North Carolinian and West Point graduate was covering the Con-

While in Great Britain during the Civil War, Maury clandestinely continued his work on electronically detonated mines, bought two commerce raiders, and tried but failed to have ironclad warships built in France. At the same time, he maintained a high profile as a propagandist and lobbyist for the Confederate cause (Valentine Richmond History Center).

federate retreat up the Virginia Peninsula, originally by mining the York River. Ignoring his superiors' concerns about using "deceptive devices," he argued with himself about placing subterranean shells on the roads leading to Yorktown. But with so many civilians on the few roads fleeing the Union advance, Rains decided against indiscriminately mining the march routes.

A few weeks later, following a fierce skirmish at Williamsburg, Rains changed his mind. He ordered his soldiers to bury four artillery shells on the main road connecting the last colonial capital with the new capital. They were set to explode on contact with a man's foot, a wagon's wheel, or a horse's hoof. As a lawyer, watching the Union cavalry abruptly halt when the shells exploded, noted, "They never moved a peg after hearing the report." Years later, Rains claimed "these 4 shells checkmated the advance of 115,000 men under Gen. McClellan and turned them from their line of march." It provided enough time so that officers like Maury's son Richard, then commanding the Twenty-Fourth Virginia Infantry, could reorganize to defend Richmond.[44]

Rains's success set off fierce debates inside the Confederate government on the ethics of using "weapons that wait" to maim or kill soldiers. Secretary of War George Randolph stepped in to cool the argument. Thomas Jefferson's grandson drafted a series of do's and don'ts covering their use on land and on water. His endorsement eased some consciences but didn't end the debate over ethics in total war.

"Each new invention in the material of war ... has taken the position by the universal consent of nations according to its efficiency in human slaughter," Rains later wrote.[45]

For all of Mallory's spending on ironclads, the Richmond press complained, "The enemy commands the water."[46]

The *Dispatch*, the *Examiner*, and the *Whig* demanded the James River be obstructed. They wondered what lessons, if any, had been learned from the defeats at Forts Donelson and Henry and Island Number 10, which fell in a combined naval and land attack and put much of Tennessee under Union control. Worse yet, the ironclads being built to defend New Orleans were not ready, and the Union Navy captured the South's largest city in a daring strike up river. Along the Atlantic coast, matters were no better. Fort Macon in North Carolina was taken in a combined sea and land assault, as was Fort Pulaski, defending the water approaches to Savannah, Georgia.

The *Whig* was scathing: "The amiable somnambulist who presides over naval affairs has contented himself ... without once putting his foot outside the city to see that work."[47]

Closer to the capital, Norfolk, Portsmouth, Yorktown, and Williamsburg had fallen or were being evacuated as Union forces advanced. Betty Herndon Maury worried about a slave uprising as the Union solders drew closer to Fredericksburg that spring. After a year of war, the Confederate government was in mortal danger.[48]

Having voted for a draft and given itself a pay raise, the Confederate Congress adjourned and its members fled Richmond. Davis sent his family to Raleigh. Robert E. Lee, as Davis's senior military adviser, castigated the provost marshal for issuing too many passports allowing citizens to leave Richmond. The remaining officials paused to put their spiritual and temporal affairs in order. Davis was "baptized [at home] and privately confirmed at St. Paul's." A little earlier Maury wrote out his will, requesting burial in a sailor's grave.[49]

J. B. Jones, a War Department clerk, wrote "as strong a letter as I could to the President, stating what I have every reason to believe would be the consequences of the abandonment of Richmond. There would be demoralization and even insubordination in the army." He was crying in a wilderness of fear.[50]

The Virginia legislature insisted that the Confederate government defend the city, as the Davis government's bullion was prepared for special rail shipment away from it. As Jones knew, the War Department archives also were being crated up to be sent to Columbia, South Carolina, and Lynchburg, Virginia. Heavy planks had been laid across the bridges to move artillery out of the city. The city's tobacco holdings, valued at $60 million, were consolidated in selected warehouses with other combustibles ready for the torch. Davis's and Letcher's denials of an evacuation rang hollow.[51]

On May 31 and June 1, the two armies collided in the tangled woods and rain-swollen swamps of the Chickahominy River. Uncharacteristically, Johnston attacked. Richard Maury's regiment, the hastily reorganized Twenty-Fourth Virginia Infantry, was integral to the strike.

Richard Maury's soldiers waded through knee-deep water at a pace so fast that they caught up with the skirmishers trying to determine where the Union forces were. At the edge of a tangled woods, they were stopped by abatis and fire from entrenched Union units. There, Maury, the regiment's only remaining field grade officer, fell wounded. By the Twenty-Fourth's side was the Twenty-Third North Carolina, who saw all its field grade officers, eight of ten company commanders, and seventeen of its twenty-nine officers either disabled or killed. The brigade commander, Samuel Garland, tried rallying his troops to continue the attack, but the men left standing couldn't move together. They held what ground they could.[52]

Back in the capital, Maury received word that Richard was injured. In a war where a wounded soldier's chance of survival was middling at best, Maury's worry mounted as he rushed over the muddied roads toward the aid stations outside the city. Was a makeshift battlefield hospital going to be any better than the slovenly Hotel Phoenix in Somerset, Ohio?

Maury was greatly relieved when he finally found Dick. Although Dick was smiling when his father arrived, a musket ball had shattered his right arm below the elbow; for now, the younger Maury was out of the fight. So too was

Johnston, having been wounded first in the shoulder by a musket ball and then in the chest and groin from an exploding artillery shell.

The beleaguered capital was unprepared for war so close. More than forty-seven hundred Confederate wounded overwhelmed Richmond's hospitals. As Jones wrote, "All day the wounded were borne past our boardinghouse in Third Street to the general hospital; and hundreds, with shattered arms and slight flesh wounds, came in on foot." Davis, who had strong doubts about Johnston as a fighter, put the wounded general's West Point classmate, Lee, in command of what was left of the sixty-thousand-man army.[53]

Maury's worries over his son mirrored his worries over his own service. From the time the Confederate government came to Richmond, Maury saw his influence erode. Sentences like "I find myself powerless" or "they cannot appreciate the importance of a Navy" appear often in his letters during this time.[54]

Nowhere did Maury better deliver his service to Virginia and the Confederacy than at Richmond. His torpedoes (mines) and coastal batteries ultimately forced the Union to keep to the land. The few poor roads, thick woods, and swamps to the east proved natural chokepoints. The fortuitous finding of miles of insulated telegraph cable along Willoughby Spit in Hampton Roads in February 1862 allowed Maury, not Davis or Mallory, to make the James River near the capital impenetrable by the summer of 1862, indeed for the remainder of the war. While the press clamored for stout defenses, Maury quietly provided them.

About six miles downstream of Rocketts Wharf, Maury and his assistants, notably Hunter Davidson, also with service at the observatory, placed the mines in midchannel at between 3½ and 7½ fathoms.[55]

"Ranges" were covered by guns on Drewry's Bluff on the south bank and Chaffin's farm on the north. "They were ignited by a bit of fine, platinum wire, heated by means of a galvanic current from a galvanic battery on shore. The conducting wire having been cut, the two terminals were then connected with the platinum wire making a span between the terminals of say one-half inch. They were then secured firmly in a small bag of rifle powder to serve as a bursting charge," Maury later lectured.[56]

By June, Maury and Davidson had fifteen casks in the river arranged in rows and spaced about thirty feet apart. The Confederates in Richmond made "submarine warfare an extremely important and feared tool of war." If the Navy or Letcher had more powder, Maury and Davidson would have deployed more mines.[57]

On July 4, during the lull in the fighting around Richmond following

Drewry's Bluff commanded the James River just below Richmond. Alongside the water, Maury placed his ranges of mines and heavy cannons, many taken from the Gosport Naval Shipyard, turning this stretch of the river into a death trap for the Union Navy. Photograph by author.

the "Seven Days," Davidson undertook another dangerous mission in his two-gun vessel *Teaser*. He carried additional telegraph wire to extend the mine fields further down the James, and a dress-silk balloon for aerial reconnaissance of City Point and Harrison's Landing, where the Union Army remained.

The *Teaser* ran aground on a mud bank. Steamer *Marantanza* spotted the former screw tug, built in Philadelphia, and fired a round that struck the boiler, crippling it. *Teaser* fired one shot back. Outgunned and stuck, the crew abandoned the vessel for the safety of the Charles City County shore. While the wire and balloon proved interesting novelties, Union Army officers were more interested in Maury's diagrams and memoranda. In the end, the information did McClellan little good, because by then the river was too tightly sealed.[58]

The Union Navy tried time and again, but could not run the obstructions, torpedoes, and gun batteries. Flag Officer Louis Goldsborough admitted the obstructions at Drewry's Bluff and the narrowness of the river there left the river "completely blocked up." The James River had become a death trap for the Union Navy.

Maury played a critical but unsung role in Lee's hammering McClellan's army into abandoning its siege. The Seven Days fighting on the land and the Union Navy's failure to attack Richmond from the river broke McClellan's nerve. News from the West further buoyed Confederate spirits. Raids by Nathan Bedford Forrest and John Hunt Morgan in Tennessee and Kentucky made it seem that "the star of the Confederacy was rising." The dread of the early spring lifted—for a time.

After the war Jefferson Davis noted the mines' effectiveness, but he never acknowledged Maury's contributions. In fact, by the summer of 1862, if Davis were honest, he would have said he and Mallory were totally exasperated by Maury. His penchant for sniping in the press or behind the closed doors of the Virginia legislature and the Confederate Congress could no longer be tolerated.[59]

Of what use to the "Cotton Kings" was Maury in Richmond? Their navy had few ships—its most formidable warship never made it to the James River. The naval shipyard was back in Union hands. Maury's "gunboat shipyards" along the rivers and near the coast were undermanned and endangered by marauding Union vessels.[60]

As hard as it was to do, Maury told Mallory that the gunboat plan was dead. The "useful man" asked the secretary what he wanted done. "He thought I would be of use doing nothing."[61]

A dejected Maury was stunned when a few days later Mallory approached him to take command of shipbuilding in Richmond. As Mallory laid it out, when enough vessels were ready, they were to head down the James and take Fortress Monroe. "Hurra for 'Mal'" was all Maury could say. Mallory's "plan" died aborning. Maury's freshly cut orders to Great Britain, however, stayed in place.

This time, the Confederate Congress was silent.[62]

This time, Maury stewed over the orders. Sure, as a naval officer, he could use his contacts in Great Britain, France, and the Netherlands either in ship buying or mine warfare. Sure, as a public man, he could write about the Confederate cause and organize Europeans' support. But these were not the acts of the warrior who laid his life on the line in Hampton Roads and closed the James River to invaders.

Maury, for the rest of his days, treated these orders for what they were: a decree of banishment.[63]

21. The Confederate European Crusade

Across Great Britain in 1862, Union agents shadowed Confederate spies and arms buyers as they made their rounds to shipyards, laboratories, newspaper offices, clubs, and banks. For both sides, at stake were thousands of lives on hundreds of American battlefields and treasures carried in scores of ships on the high seas. Matthew Fontaine Maury was now one of those Southern spies, but his profile was anything but low.[1]

When Maury was ordered to London, the Confederacy was triumphing on the battlefield. Lee's victory at Second Manassas put Washington in peril—and Baltimore, Harrisburg, Philadelphia, and the rail lines west. But by the time Maury took up his duties that fall, the pendulum of war had swung back. The limited Union victories at Antietam in Maryland and Perryville in Kentucky had blunted Confederate advances.

The pendulum more importantly had moved politically when the Union changed its war aims. With the Emancipation Proclamation, the Union gained a diplomatic edge over the Confederacy it never relinquished. Great Britain hadn't tolerated slavery on the island since the eighteenth century and in its Caribbean colonies since the 1830s.[2]

Ignoring Britain's hostility to slavery, the overseas Confederates took great heart when William Gladstone, the chancellor of the exchequer, said in a widely reported speech, "We may have our own opinions about slavery, we may be for or against the South, but there is no doubt that Jefferson Davis and other leaders of the South have made an army; they are making, it appears, a navy; and they have made what is more than either, they have made a nation."[3]

A realistic Maury wrote, "It is not that the sympathizers love us or our cause more, but they hate us less than they hate the Yankees, and as for the cause, they like ours less than they do the Yankee cause with its abolition and the like."[4]

For Maury, getting to Britain from "Davis's nation" was a trial. In fall 1862, he and his son Matthew journeyed from Richmond to Charleston to board a blockade-runner. Eighteen months after the firing on Fort Sumter, Charleston and Wilmington, North Carolina, were the only reliably "open" Confederate ports on the Eastern Seaboard.

When the blockade was announced, Great Britain and France protested that with so few ships and so many ports it could not be uniformly enforced and denounced the obstruction of shipping channels.

The Europeans demanded to know how a nation that claimed to be one state could blockade its own ports. This objection caught the Lincoln administration off guard, but it led all parties to accept belligerent status for the Confederacy. For the Union Navy it meant accessible prize courts almost anywhere, and for captured Confederate soldiers, treatment as combatants, rather than as traitors.[5]

After successful Union invasions at Roanoke Island and at Port Royal, the Europeans shifted their position to keeping the cotton-shipping port of New Orleans open. They failed there too. Napoleon III later admitted that he had "committed a great error" by not forcibly challenging the blockade early in the war. "But what ... can now be done?"[6]

From its founding, the Confederacy relied on British speculators for its international trade. Despite Gladstone's welcome words, the Confederacy didn't have a navy to speak of. It barely had a coastal merchant marine. Confederate international trade meant blockade running, a business done in stages. Smaller vessels often cloaked in worsening weather sailed to the Bahamas, Bermuda, or Cuba and unloaded passengers and cargo, primarily cotton, there to be placed in a ship flying the flag of a European nation to continue the voyage across the Atlantic. Then after a time, loaded with arms, munitions, cloth, medicines, provisions, iron rails, and plates, and too often luxury goods, the blockade runners headed back to the Southern coast to test their luck against the Union Navy, shoaly water, rocks, and obstructed channels.[7]

The Maury party's first try for the open sea aboard a ship named *Hero* had to be called off. On October 9, under a nighttime cover of clouds, a second vessel, *Herald*, with Maury aboard, tried to dash to the Atlantic, but as the sky cleared, a lookout on a Union warship spotted it. The warship fired a warning round. Luckily for Maury, thirteen-year-old Matthew, and newly minted teenage aide James Morris Morgan, the shot missed.[8]

Three days later, with the twin blessings of rain and high seas, *Herald* slipped out of Charleston, but in the race for the ocean it ran hard on the harbor's bar. Fortunately for the Maurys, no Union ship approached *Herald* in its struggle with the moving sands. When finally free, the twin blessings became double curses. One engine died, and the vessel was adrift. After the engine was fixed, the captain, Louis Coxetter, a coastal privateer, acknowledged he was lost and, putting all at risk, asked a passing ship for bearings. But soon enough, the veteran coastal trader was lost again on the open ocean.

What should have been a two-day journey had turned into a nerve-racking trial. The passengers grumbled, fearful of being chased down by a Union vessel. Then what? Habeas corpus was a memory in a martial-law nation and nonexistent to an aggressive naval officer.

As the seventh day dawned, the captain finally asked Maury's help. Maury said there was little he could do until ten at night, but if it were clear then, he could make the proper sightings and set the correct course.[9]

That night, sometimes lying on his back with sextant in hand, the roly-poly, balding man, who once had commanded the United States' observatory, took the astronomical fixes. Although he had not been ordered to sea for decades, he knew where the stars were in the heavens, and he soon found where *Herald* was on the ocean. He told Coxetter that if *Herald* kept to the course and speed he prescribed, the ship would be within sight of Port Hamilton light in Bermuda around 2 a.m.

To the passengers on the deck, each minute of the next four hours was filled with fear over failing engines, capture, or again being hopelessly lost. When the lookout at last shouted, "Light ho!" it was 2:10, and Maury was resting peacefully in his cabin.[10]

Maury's reputation as a naval officer and scientist had sailed with him. His exploits on *Herald* provided a light anecdote over dinner, but it was his pathfinding through the seas that gained him entry to the highest levels of British colonial society. Ashore, the island's governor, Sir Harry St. George Ord; the commandant of Fort St. George and commander of the Thirty-Ninth Regiment; and the commander of warship *Immortality* feted the Maury party during its stay.[11]

As they dined, the impetuous Charles Wilkes, longtime Maury antagonist and commander of the West Indies Squadron, patrolled off the coast. In November 1861, he stopped the British mail steamer *Trent* and removed at gunpoint former United States Senators James M. Mason and John Slidell and two of their aides from its deck. An outraged British government demanded the Confederate diplomats be freed; that Wilkes be punished; and that the United States apologize. The men later were freed and the United States apologized, but a year later Wilkes commanded a flotilla menacing famous Confederates, like Maury, who dared sail the high seas.[12]

Knowing Wilkes's history, "I must say I felt quite uneasy," Morgan remembered feeling as he boarded the British-flagged vessel bound for Nova Scotia. When the ship carrying the Maury party headed out to sea, a British man-of-war and sloop-of-war under Ord's orders fell into line as armed escorts. The Union vessels kept their distance.[13]

At Halifax, Maury and his entourage were again treated with "distinguished consideration." Conversations there were more direct than in Bermuda. The mayor of Halifax later reported that Maury "declared very publicly that he was visiting England to take command of a Confederate vessel-of-war." When they boarded the Cunard paddle-wheeler *Arabia* bound for Liverpool, the Maury party kept their distance from Northern passengers who came on in Boston. There were no more public discussions about a Confederate command at sea.[14]

The North Atlantic crossing was rough, and Morgan, the young Confederate naval officer, was amazed at Maury's ability to remain amiable even while sick. "I remember once entering his stateroom where he was seated with a Bible on his lap and a basin alongside of him. I told him that there was a ship in sight, and between paroxysms, he said, 'Sometimes we see a ship, and sometimes ship a sea!'"[15]

Upon landing in Liverpool, the Maury party went from the Cunard's terminal along miles of piers and quays toward the United States' Consulate on Steers Dock, long the domain of Maury's uncle James, a man who nourished the cotton trade in a port where "even the clergymen drove hard bargains over funeral costs." This was the Old Consul's city, his portrait still hanging in an honored place in the Town Hall. In this city of half a million, "Cotton had spread itself ... like Ahab's cloud over the realms of commerce."[16]

Buttressing Liverpool's cotton trade were shipyards and ironworks on the Mersey's banks. Their owners—Charles Cammell; the Laird brothers and their father John; George Wilson; and Lionel Hitchens—were industrial legends on both sides of the Atlantic. To United States officials in 1862, the Mersey men were war profiteers, aiding and abetting the pirates of the Confederacy.[17]

When the party reached 10 Rumford Place, they knocked on the door of the imposing three-story, block-long headquarters of Fraser, Trenholm & Co. Inside, the party didn't stop in the office of Charles K. Prioleau, the transplanted South Carolinian who managed the Trenholm company's trading in Great Britain.

During their service together in Great Britain starting in 1862, Maury and James D. Bulloch developed a professional and successful relationship unmarked by squabbles over rank that tainted the work of other Confederate agents overseas (courtesy the Naval History and Heritage Command).

Maury and the others kept going to another office where James Bulloch waited for them. Bulky, of medium height with long bushy whiskers, he was a man of singular importance to the Confederacy. Charged with buying cargo ships and commerce raiders, the vessels he really wanted were oceangoing ironclads, the would-be crown jewels of a Confederate fleet.[18]

Following his success in building *Alabama*, Bulloch, with fourteen years in the Navy and eight in merchant service, had just ordered two ironclad rams at Laird's Birkenhead yard, outraging United States officials across Great Britain. He appeared on his way to commanding one of them.[19]

At their first meeting, Maury told Bulloch exactly what he was sent to do from harbor defenses to torpedoes, predictable missions for the former commander of Confederate coastal defense. Maury added that if he had the chance he was to buy a commerce raider, not a surprise either. He had cotton certificates with him for the purchase. Other Confederate agents carried similar orders. Maybe left unsaid, Bulloch certainly surmised that the commander was to plead the Confederate cause publicly.

With Maury, there was no rancor over seniority, as there had been between James North, another Confederate naval agent, and Bulloch. By date of rank, Maury was then the senior naval officer in Europe. Not letting rank get in the way, the relationship between the two "best prepared of all Confederate agents" was cordial, respectful, and successful under trying circumstances, historian Amanda Foreman wrote.

Finances were crippling Confederate European war efforts. Major Caleb Huse, the Confederate Army's agent, had filled warehouses but lacked the money to ship the goods to North America. Likewise, Bulloch's rams, costing more than £94,000 apiece, were fast draining the Confederate funds that remained in Fraser, Trenholm's hands and its lines of credit. Worse, these were only the tip of the iceberg of agents spending and contracting across Europe.

At the same time, Bulloch picked up rumblings from his spies that the British government wanted no more embarrassing incidents like Number 290's being transformed into *Alabama*, the high-seas raider, after leaving one of its shipyards. The rams were potentially far more devastating to Union-British relations. In Confederate plans, the rams would attack Northern ports. The best he could hope for on the financial front was that James Spence, a talented polemicist and banker from Liverpool, and Member of Parliament William Lindsay's idea to sell bonds based on the delivery of cotton succeeded.[20]

Across the channel, Bulloch saw a flicker of light if his plans in Britain were thwarted. By early 1863, the French appeared willing to build oceangoing ironclads, like *La Gloire*, for the Confederacy in exchange for a free hand in Mexico—a very tempting possibility.

Tempering Confederate giddiness at the moment was French practice. Napoleon III, a "sleight-of-hand performer," possessed an extremely broad vision of new French imperial power in the Americas. Secretary of State Judah P. Benjamin became so incensed over the emperor's "vision" that he ordered the French consul in Galveston back to France for plotting Texas's secession from the Confederacy.[21]

How was the South to pay for all these European-built ships and arms? Cotton.

South Carolina's James Hammond proclaimed the gospel of cotton in an 1858 speech: "I will not stop to depict what every one can imagine, but this is certain: England would topple headlong and carry the whole civilized world with her, save the South. No, you dare not make war on cotton. No power on earth dares to make war upon it. Cotton is king." Northern cotton brokers and transatlantic shippers worshipped in the same temple.[22]

Early on, the Confederate government halted cotton exports and destroyed existing supplies. The political class's reasoning was twofold: As mills closed in Britain and France, workers and owners would pressure their governments to recognize the Confederacy so the cotton trade could resume. Second, because cotton was scarce, the price would rise when shipments resumed.[23]

As Rutson Maury, an expert in the trade, wrote before the fall of Fort Sumter, there was plenty of cotton already in Britain, some from India and Egypt, and all too quickly, the Confederacy's busiest port, New Orleans, shockingly fell to the Union Navy in May 1862. Getting cotton to the few ports still open taxed the Confederacy's railroads to the hilt, and getting it out was problematic, as the blockade tightened weekly.[24]

Rutson Maury explained to his cousin the secret of brokering cotton.

Brokers raised prices when commodities were scarce. When commodities were plentiful, they substituted volume to turn a profit. Profits were there either way.

When Matthew Fontaine Maury arrived in Liverpool, "King Cotton," the "Dagon of Dixie" as one Union diplomat called it, was a weakened monarch and but a minor god.[25]

Mallory, through Maury, demanded Commissioners James M. Mason and John Slidell give the Navy's spending priority over every other department's. Mason, who was authorized to sign the obligations, rightly saw chaos in Maury's certificates; he called a meeting in London of all the agents and Prioleau to coordinate Confederate arms and ship spending.[26]

While Spence and Lindsay scurried from banking house and trading firm and back again in the City of London and Liverpool, the immediate financial crisis was nearing a successful conclusion across the channel. Slidell, with Huse's assistance, was arranging with the Erlanger banking house for a transfusion of cash, secured upon future cotton deliveries using bonds not certificates. Erlanger was on a par with the Rothschilds and Barings in international finance. It was also more obtuse. The laws governing its transactions were not as familiar to Union diplomats and agents as those of Great Britain. The other factor was political. Like all successful French businesses of the era, the house's relationship with the emperor was strong.

Slidell also had a personal stake in the selection. His daughter, Mathilda, thoroughly enchanted Baron Rodolphe Erlanger at their first meeting in New Orleans, and their courtship was flowering in Paris. But Erlanger, in love as he was, remained a sharp businessman. In the first subscription, £6 million was raised, and the banking house collected its hefty 5 percent commission.

Having its own difficulties raising money overseas, the Lincoln government launched an all-out effort to undercut the bonds. Without the bonds' sale, the Confederacy lacked the hard currency to buy European arms and ships. Robert Walker, a former Treasury secretary, wrote blistering letters to British newspapers detailing "Davis, the Repudiator's" support of Mississippi's default on prewar bonds. He also met privately with London bankers to personalize the risk they took in holding Confederate bonds. The Union bears intended to chase the Confederate bulls from the European bond markets.

To counter Walker, the Confederacy secretly propped up the bonds by using early subscription funds to keep prices close to par. Peter was robbing Paul, who, in turn, was robbing Peter. The $15 million the Confederates hoped to generate through the bond sales was fantasy paper and some hard currency.[27]

Mason's meeting to coordinate spending was doomed as Mallory constantly hatched more complicated financial illusions to buy ships. For example, to cover the drain on the loan, Mallory promised to ship cotton to Europe using Confederate Navy–owned ships as blockade runners. This way, certificate holders were no longer responsible for moving cotton out of the Confederacy on their own or having to wait for war's end to receive it. Not to be outdone, the Army's Ordnance Bureau readied its own fleet. By the end of the war, the departments also competed with individual Confederate states' "volunteer navies" selling cotton abroad for their military needs.

If the cotton did not make it through, however, the Confederate bonds reverted to hard currency. Lacking that pledge, the certificate holders were left holding the bag. Prioleau was so concerned about the ballooning risks in the certificates and bonds that he urged George A. Trenholm, then secretary of the Treasury, to let the British company stop doing business with the Confederate government.[28]

For Maury, Confederate financial problems were also personal. The cost of living ate up his pay, and he was compelled to move to smaller quarters on the third floor of a house on Sackville Street. From this dwelling Maury, with his son and Morgan by his side, began his clandestine war; for it, he enlisted old friend Marin Jansen, the Dutch naval officer then touring British and French shipyards for his government.[29]

As he awaited news on ship-buying opportunities, Maury sent the pro–Confederate *Times* another "Why I Fight" letter. He told readers how Lincoln had subverted the Constitution with his proclamations of martial law and the Emancipation Proclamation. "Events now transpiring in America show that we are quite as able to keep the field as is the enemy and far more united."[30]

By the time the piece was published, Maury was after his first ship, an iron steamer with a screw propeller. Maury employed Bulloch's subterfuge lesson of naming false buyers and having one of his wife's relatives, Thomas Bold, a chandler, pay for the purchase.

Using cotton certificates to proceed, Jansen oversaw the work. By then, United States officials were tired of the Clyde and Mersey shipbuilders' assertions that these vessels were for the emperor of China or licensed traders. Nonetheless, for a time, they paid little attention to this ship. Their interest only rose as Lewis Maury rounded up known Confederate officers scattered around the island. What they didn't know was that Lewis Maury brought with him hard currency and new cotton certificates to buy more ships.[31]

Despite the nasty exchange of notes between Union diplomats and the Palmerston government over Confederate military spending, construction proceeded smoothly on the Clyde. For whatever reason—bribery, indolence, distraction—Crown officials didn't interfere. On January 10, 1863, a daughter of Confederate Commander North "officiated as princess and christened the craft *Virginia*." Pierside, it was still a merchantman. Inside and below decks, the compartments were "stronger than a jail," well suited for a commerce raider. Soon enough, it had a new identity to ward off suspicious Union agents or scrupulous crown inspectors. On Friday March 27, newly named *Japan*, registered in Bold's name, set out for Greenock to await crew and trials.[32]

The Maurys had pulled off a coup few Confederate agents matched. *Japan* left British waters legally as a cargo vessel. A British citizen bought the guns and stores and put them on another ship bound for who knows where. Best yet, from a British legal standpoint, the final transformation into a warship was made off France. The only niggling problem was the crew's nationalities.[33]

By December 1862, Maury looked for more than disguised cargo raiders from Jansen. "[N]ote any gunboats or ironclads that you may come across. In short make a note of all that comes under your observation upon a subject which you know is a hobby of mine," Maury wrote.[34]

What the other agents were to do to buy arms, ammunition, clothing, and gear was not Maury's concern. Maury insisted to Mason that quick approval was needed, especially if the Confederates were to buy ironclads from the French. Mason reluctantly agreed, but only after obtaining a promise not to put the certificates brought by Lewis Maury on the market for sixty days.

It was the sea, not a battlefield, that threw Bulloch and Maury off schedule. A vessel carrying more certificates went down off Charleston. "If I had money and officers, I could assume I now would have fitted out half a dozen just as good to prey upon Yankee commerce as is *Alabama*. I have had no money, but a small amount since I came here, and in a few weeks after it came to me I had an elegant cruiser at sea," Bulloch wrote.[35]

In October 1862 during a wide-ranging meeting, the emperor asked Slidell why the Confederacy didn't have a navy capable of breaking the blockade. The two discussed French advances in armoring ships, and Napoleon III dropped broad hints to look to private French yards. This was the flicker of light Bulloch saw.

Slidell told Bulloch and Mason that the emperor was very encouraging when their discussion turned to arms and ships. There were two private French shipyards close to Great Britain, where Bulloch and Maury were, and Paris, where Samuel Barron headquartered in the Grand Hotel. The two were Arman's in Bordeaux and Vorduz in Nantes with reputations for quality and capable technology. Like Erlanger, the owners were "solid with the emperor" and members of his parliament.[36]

Bulloch needed the French yards more than ever. The British had seized *Alexandra*, a suspected commerce raider, in a Liverpool yard, and pressure on the Lairds mounted over the rams. Foreign Minister John Russell told Palmerston privately it was time for a public investigation of the ship's ownership. Both understood that way their government's hands would be "clean" in a demonstration of neutrality. Bulloch knew that any investigation meant the rams were lost.

For Slidell, Bulloch, and Maury in dealing with the French, the rush was on. To speed the work at Arman's shipyard, Bulloch agreed in April 1863 to an elaborate fee system that retained but a hair's breadth of difference from bribery. There were to be four ships, ostensibly being built for private trading companies working in China and San Francisco, and they were to be armed "to ward off pirates."[37]

Maury's work with the French was patriotic and personal. As he told the mayor of Halifax, his mission was to command an oceangoing warship. If he did, Maury would best elderly Franklin Buchanan, a Plucking Board member and first commander of CSS *Virginia*, and the aged Josiah Tattnall, its last commander, as a sea-going warrior. This was his best chance to do that.

In late April and early May, drawings on the new class—called the "Cupola rams"—were exchanged among Bulloch, Maury, and Jansen. The three wanted ships drawing about fifteen feet that could smash through the Union *Monitors*, something the Birkenhead rams couldn't do. To make the vessels doubly deadly, Maury attached a spar torpedo on the bow, like the classic Athenian triremes and CSS *Virginia*.

When Union diplomats got word from bribed shipyard employees, they were stunned. Arman's ironclads "would have posed the gravest peril to which the American Union has ever been exposed." They would be the naval complement to Lee's Army of Northern Virginia. The diplomats rolled up their sleeves to sabotage the Confederate scheme.[38]

After Mallory gave the go-ahead to buy in France, Maury crossed the channel in early June 1863 to meet Arman. The Confederates envisioned a ship with "two screws—1,280 tons displacement—220 h.p.—eight guns—for 60,000 pounds." The two screws allowed the ship to turn in a river or harbor and direct fire at targets on water and ashore. Delivery was expected in seven months. An optimistic Slidell wrote Mason, "I have no doubt that he can build on as good terms as in England, but will have no difficulties in carrying his ship to sea."[39]

Because the money was to come from the Erlanger loan, Maury needed the Confederate commissioners' permission to proceed. After listening to his plea, Mason and Slidell, joined by former Mississippi Congressman L. Q. C. Lamar, now commissioner to Russia, put one condition on granting the money: The emperor openly acknowledge the ships were for the Confederacy. That acknowledgment would leave full diplomatic recognition a baby's step away. What the three diplomats did not grasp was how much the political situation in France pivoted. Great Britain's reluctance to recognize the Confederacy after the Emancipation Proclamation caused France's position to change again. The emperor would not go it alone in the American war.[40]

In the Tuileries on June 18, 1863, with the victory at Chancellorsville known, the nephew of the original Napoleon listened to Slidell, who at last got around to the meeting's real purpose: declaring the vessels on the ways in Bordeaux be built openly for the Confederacy. To Slidell's amazement, Napoleon III insisted construction could go ahead *only* if "their destination be concealed."[41]

While this did not bar the door to construction, it put a guard by it. The commissioners' conditions crippled what was the Confederacy's last best chance to take the naval war to Union ports. For Maury, try as he might, he could not get enough funds, even from sales of existing cotton certificates, to proceed.

By early 1864, the French Ministry of Marine declared Arman's ironclads could not go to any belligerent in the American war. A furious Bulloch wrote, "There never was any pretense of concealing them from the emperor's government, because, they were undertaken at its instigation."[42]

Arman and the Confederacy had gone too far together to let the ironclad program expire. Bulloch patched together an installment payment plan, and the yard was back at work on newly named *Cheops* and *Sphinx*, supposedly for the British viceroy of Egypt, a scam too similar to the one used for the rams. The ploy failed.

Union authorities in France prematurely breathed a sigh of relief after they heard the news that one ironclad was going to Prussia and the other to Denmark, two European nations at war with each other.[43]

A frustrated Bulloch explained if money were regularly appropriated, he could build twenty such ships. However, "our finances will not admit of my contract for more than two at this time." That one sentence summed up Confederate arms buying and shipbuilding abroad. There was never enough money to prolong the war until the North became too weary to fight.[44]

While Maury dreamed of building an oceangoing ironclad from the keel up, he actually next succeeded in buying another potential raider. The ship, HMS *Victor*, had been mustered out of active service; as an enticement to potential buyers, the Royal Navy offered its artisans and a yard to make the ship ready. Maury again used Bold to ease in and out of financial fronts. Supposedly being refitted for the China trade, the Royal Navy accepted a bid from a Gordon Coleman and Company, and the work started at Sheerness in July and continued through October 1863.[45]

For Maury the news from home in 1863 was painful. John, serving with his cousin Lieutenant General Dabney Maury near Vicksburg, was missing in action. He worried continuously about Ann and the children, now refugees in the infirmary of the University of Virginia. "My dreams are nightly of death," Maury wrote.[46]

Again doubting the value of what he was doing, Maury sank into depression. Was the young man still alive, wounded, a prisoner? He wrote his wife, "My heart is gone from me—my poor dear Davy—no purer nor better spirit has been given up in this war. If he had to die, I hope he died as nobly as he lived." To check his sadness in front of his youngest son, Maury sent Mat to study under J. M. D. Meiklejohn in Bowdon, near Manchester. Meiklejohn had taught the older boys in Washington.[47]

In his grief and staying at Bowdon, away from the crucible of London, Maury wrote to relatives in New York and to Hasbrouck, his former teacher, imploring them to help the family learn what had happened to John.

Although a career naval officer, Maury usually did not wear a uniform while working in the observatory or to most public functions (Valentine Richmond History Center).

Advertisements were placed in New York papers. Inquiries went directly to General U. S. Grant, commander of the Union Army at Vicksburg, and to David Dixon Porter, commanding the Union Navy on the Mississippi River, for their assistance. Agents for the family traveled to Midwestern prisoner-of-war camps. The aid of Chester A. Arthur, a rising New York politician, was obtained through his cousins there.[48]

Thirty years later, Dabney Maury wrote in his memoirs that "not once has the curtain which shrouds the actual facts in this pathetic drama of the war been lifted."[49]

To check his mounting worries, Maury rallied himself with work. He readied *Victor* in late November. But the tribulations in Maury's personal life mirrored his professional life that fall. The British Foreign Office ordered the ship detained. Ignoring the authorities, a young "Scot," but more likely a Confederate officer in civilian clothes with a Scot's surname, ran it down the Thames toward the English Channel.

In the river, the ship's brasses blew, and it drifted with its unsuspecting British crew of "engineers, riggers, carpenters, joiners and painters" toward the French coast flying a Confederate flag, anchoring off Calais. With the climate supposedly warm between imperial France and the Confederacy, Lieutenant William P. A. Campbell took it into port "without papers and in an unfinished condition."[50]

The British added their howls to the Union's about the ship. The finger-pointing about activities in French ports and shipyards involving Confederates made a bad situation worse. As if they were stopping prostitutes from leaving a brothel, the French placed a gunboat across the bow of CSS *Rappahannock*, formerly HMS *Victor*, to prevent it from going to sea.[51]

The Confederate Navy's senior officer, Samuel Barron, ignored that fact in ordering *Rappahannock* to rendezvous with *Georgia* to transfer that ship's armament to the Confederacy's newest warship.[52]

During these troubled months, Maury turned to Maximilian, now emperor of Mexico. The letters to the new emperor go beyond the congratulations on ascending the Mexican throne one might expect. Maury was in the job market. The naval officer was well aware of how lukewarm some California politicians were to the Union, especially former Senator William Gwin. Gwin had been detained earlier in the war for his Confederate sympathies. Maury told Maximilian, "It may become the policy of Mexico as it is already the interest of the Confederacy to see California withdrawn from her present political associations."

Maury advised the emperor that California could be brought under his control if a "few good ironclads were quietly sent around Cape Horn at an early day." Unsaid was the immense political advantage for the emperor in returning such a large territory to Mexican control. Unsaid for the Confederacy was recognition of its independence. Maury then added a paragraph that forever linked Maximilian with the Lost Cause: "Furthermore others of my countrymen and friends might be readily induced to accept service with me under the imperial flag of Mexico. Their example and influence would have a telling effect upon the Californians."[53]

To ensure Maximilian understood his sincerity, Maury wrote a few days later about an impounded ironclad—one of the Birkenhead rams. "We cannot get her out because of the foreign enlistment, and she will probably be sold on the stocks where she is now.... I think she might be transferred to the emperor of Mexico in preference to any other power" with Maury potentially commanding.[54]

Maury further unburdened himself to his wife: "The feeling that I have the ability to serve but am not permitted to have an opportunity that I am here in practical banishment, drawing pay that I do not earn, and so whether I will or not, helping to swell the gang to deprive the treasury and scramble for that? I am sure the very question has shocked you. What then? Seek other occupation. You know what that would involve. But as great as would be the sacrifice, I am equal to it, provided that by it the good of the cause be helped."[55]

Maury wanted her to sound out "the innocents," the children, about serving Maximilian, although he tells her "my own mind is made up."[56]

To J. B. Minor on Christmas Day, Maury offered no cheer. "For the want of real statesmen in our councils, we suffer and have suffered terribly. With true statesmanship to guide us, we would never have been where we are now [or] would our sufferings have been what they have."[57]

22. Winning Hearts and Minds

The Confederacy's most prominent propagandist, Matthew Fontaine Maury, was in the same dark place in the summer of 1863 as the sixty thousand readers of the *Times* of London and the subscribers to Paul Julius Reuter's news service were about the fighting in Virginia, in Tennessee, along the Mississippi, and at Charleston.

The *Times* ran numerous stories in late June and early July reporting the likely secession of the "Great State of New York" to restore its profitable cotton trade, imminent French recognition of the Confederacy, and "the impossible task before General Ulysses Grant at Vicksburg." A letter writer to the paper asserted that if Lee succeeded across the Potomac, "It will be absurd to deny the South has won its independence."[1]

That summer what was known in Europe about the war was about the same as what was known in Richmond.

Then came the news. Catastrophe!

Maury, the other Confederates in Great Britain, and their very rich and often aristocratic supporters were stunned by the Army of Northern Virginia's retreat from Pennsylvania, the see-saw fighting in Tennessee, and the fall of Vicksburg. Expectations for recognition were hurriedly scaled back.

Maury counterattacked. He selected the *Times* for a letter on the Confederacy's steadfastness in the face of adversity. For every Union advance, he had an answer: George Meade at bay behind Robert E. Lee; Ulysses Grant afraid of Joseph Johnston's decoy; William Rosecrans stymied in Tennessee; and "Charleston may be considered safe."

"The military tide which set in with so much federal promise on the young flood in July, and which has so damped the spirit of our English friends and depressed Southern securities, appears suddenly to have slackened, and to be on the point of again turning in our favor," he wrote. "All that we have to do is to maintain the defensive, watch our chances, and strike whenever there is an opportunity for a good stroke, either with the sword or with the pen." These words really were a hope, maybe a prayer, not a campaign, not a strategy.[2]

In Richmond, he selected the *Enquirer*, among "the most read and most admired newspapers in the South." Like the *Times*, its editorial model, the newspaper reached the influential.[3]

Much had changed in the ten months since Maury had left Virginia. The restored Union government controlled only a small arc of territory from Hampton Roads up the Potomac into the Appalachians, but it allowed the western forty-five counties to win admission to the Union as a new state.[4]

The crowding in Richmond that Maury experienced when he moved in with his cousin's family had worsened. The city's population more than doubled from the thirty-nine thousand living there in 1860. Adding to the strain on providing shelter and food for families piled on top of each other was caring for the thousands of wounded and invalided Confederate soldiers in hospitals all over the city and hundreds of Union prisoners confined in riverfront warehouses. Privation was visible in drawn faces and tattered clothes.

To Richmonders and Londoners in summer 1863, he wrote, "The war is become more and more unpopular in the North. In proof of this, I point to the conduct of the Pennsylvanians during Lee's invasion of that state, to the riots in New York, to the Organized resistance to the war in Iowa and to the circumstances which the English public has made acquaintance by the newspaper press."

Fight on![5]

Before Maury came to Europe as an exiled celebrity, he had ushered in the Confederate propaganda offensive. For decades, he played the media of his time—letters to the influential, reprinted in newspapers, magazines, circulars, pamphlets, and dramatized in lecture tours—to argue for naval reform, a national weather service, the riches awaiting a commercially independent South, and now a new North American republic.

Already noted were his letters celebrating the Confederate victory at First Manassas with its "LET US GO" message being reprinted in Southern newspapers and telegraphed to newspapers north and west, and carried abroad. There also was his letter in late October 1861 to Grand Duke Constantine of Russia declining to leave Virginia for safety in St. Petersburg, reprinted as a morale booster in at least two Richmond newspapers.[6]

But no letter that Maury wrote in the early stages of the Civil War had greater impact than the one to Rear Admiral Robert FitzRoy, the head of Great Britain's Board of Trade. Its timing was providential. Maury dated the long letter August 4, several weeks after First Manassas. The images—"a price upon my head" and threatened with a halter around the neck for siding with his state in "this nefarious war ... forced upon us"—are Maury at his most graphic. The *Times*, usually sympathetic to the Confederacy, reprinted it. In print, recognition of the insurgent government was moving from very possible that fall to very likely. In Whitehall, there was hesitation.[7]

Thurlow Weed, now a Union diplomat-propagandist, tried rebutting Maury in the London *Globe*. About Maury's claim of a "price" being put on his head, he said the assertion was wrong; about the halter charge, "The second should be true." In sum, weak parries to the powerful thrust.[8]

Maury's letter should have been forgotten in the daily grind of news, but for Charles Wilkes. He breathed life into the propaganda war and pushed Great Britain and the United States to the brink of a shooting war when he forcibly removed two Confederate diplomats from a British packet in international waters.

The editors of the *London Review*, the *Athenaeum*, and the *Edinburgh Review* saw Maury's letter as a godsend. A pamphlet form of the letter was printed and distributed in Berlin. The pamphlet spawned new published responses, including John Welsford Cowell's "A Letter Addressed to Captain M. T. Maury."[9]

As day follows night, Cowell's pamphlet sparked a new round of reviews in more periodicals. The theme, one Maury encouraged: The Confederacy was a North American Poland and Italy, fighting for its independence.

When he arrived in Great Britain in the fall of 1862, Maury was the Confederacy's stentorian voice. He was again in the *Times* as he settled into quarters on Sackville Street. Using Gladstone's speech about the Confederacy building a nation as a platform, he brushed aside the Emancipation Proclamation as cant. "Let the South stand Firm, and this is the beginning of the end" of the war and the Union was his message, one repeated by more writers and public figures in other publications, at rallies for the Confederacy, and in the drawing rooms of leading writers, politicians, businessmen, and industrialists. Karl Marx, writing for the *New York Herald* and reflecting on it all, found the "English press ... more Southern than the South itself."[10]

To understand Maury's diplomatic and propaganda efforts, we need to see how the Confederacy fought on these two fronts and the weaknesses and strengths of the men in this struggle.

The overseas propaganda and diplomatic fronts predated the Confederate government. Thomas Butler King, a Maury congressional ally and now representing an independent Georgia, and Dudley Mann, the first assistant secretary of State, had "been well received" by Prime Minister Palmerston and Foreign Minister John Russell in face-to-face meetings in London. The same was true when they met with Napoleon III. The two optimistically reported that both countries would recognize the Confederacy and establish commercial relations when the government was formed.[11]

When the Confederate government sent its first official commissioners abroad, Mann; William Lowndes Yancey, a fiery-tempered secessionist from Alabama; and Pierre Rost, a Bonapartist veteran and longtime friend of Jefferson Davis's older brother Joseph, the Europeans soon questioned its diplomatic competence. Yancey's nonstop, unapologetically proslavery rhetoric alienated Londoners. Rost, despite his imperial French background and "Cotton King" connections, turned out to be "inept and ineffective." Only Mann held his own, but he gained little.

The Confederacy was far better served by their replacements in London, Mason, and in Paris, Slidell, who earned respect for their ordeal in the "Trent Affair," and in both capitals unofficially by Maury.[12]

At the start of the war, propaganda was given short shrift in the Confederate government. The Treasury Department doubted the value of a war of words. It doled out $750 to newspaperman Henry Hotze, born in Zurich but who grew up in the United States, and $25,000 to Edwin DeLeon, a former American consul in Egypt and a journalist, to spread the "truth" about the Confederacy in Europe.[13]

DeLeon, with the stronger diplomatic credentials, was to grease editorial palms. After the money changed hands, "Papers that had violently opposed Jefferson Davis now became his most valiant champions"; he later was recalled after a bitter dispute with Slidell.

By default, Hotze became the retailer of Confederate overseas propaganda. Fortunately, his "sure grasp of English politics and European statesmen" in his newspaper, the *Index*, in London and British writer and banker James Spence's work in Liverpool kept the Confederate cause alive in British politics and journalism.[14]

From the start, Hotze's British-accented propaganda worked well for Maury, opening up a new range of contacts. Of particular importance was Spence, to a lesser degree Cowell, and to a greater degree Alexander James Beresford-Hope, and through him entrée to a broad array of influential men in journalism, Parliament, and the Anglican Church. Inside the church's walls was another key figure, the Rev. Francis W. Tremlett, in Confederate propaganda and diplomatic efforts overseas. As pro–Confederate as they and Gladstone were, all opposed slavery.

Most troubling to Confederates privately was Beresford-Hope, their principal backer in London. He denounced slavery as "a curse." Yet, here was a man who moved in the circles that Maury, the high-end propagandist, traveled in and Hotze, the retail propagandist, forayed in. What were Confederates to do about their antislavery British supporters? When it came to Beresford-Hope, fervent Anglican, Liberal-Conservative, the Confederates kept their mouths shut, as they did with Gladstone.

Beresford-Hope's three lectures on the Confederacy—"The Results of the American Disruption"—were gathered into monographs and widely distributed, often keyed to political and military developments in North America.

In his last lecture, Beresford-Hope ridiculed the Emancipation Proclamation for applying only to areas in rebellion. What was to happen to the slaves in areas not in revolt? As for slaves in the Confederacy, he quoted the "Pastoral of Confederate Episcopal Church" admonishing masters to treat their slaves "not merely as so much property, but ... a sacred trust," a salve for British antislavery consciences.

Following defeats in Tennessee and the Carolinas and Lee's retreat from Maryland in 1862, Beresford-Hope's address, like Maury's "prospects" published in December, gave the drive for recognition new but short-lived spirit in Britain.[15]

All the high-level private British support could not affect the fallout in the covert shipbuilding and arms-buying program from the Confederate defeats at Gettysburg and Vicksburg. Using the findings of its own investigation, Palmerston's government seized the Birkenhead rams in the summer of 1863. Whatever the motive for the seizure—"much more baseness than magnanimity"—the rams were not going to the Confederacy.

The seizure did not stop the rams from heating up the propaganda war, though.

Northern newspapers were publishing stories about a purported message from Mallory to C. G. Memminger, Confederate Treasure secretary, on plans to buy five ironclads in Great Britain and three in France and a plot to free Confederate prisoners held at a camp on Lake Erie.

Here's where Maury stepped in, branding the "report" first published in the *New York Sun* a hoax. His piece, like Weed's rebuttal to the FitzRoy letter, failed to "'nail to the counter' this spurious thing." The story refused to die.

It had too many juicy elements to chew over. The *New York Tribune* dismissed the rebuttal as another case of Maury doing his duty "to look sharply after Rebel interests" in London.

It took Weed to put the story to bed. With Adams pushing Russell in London, Seward's confidante Weed took up the matter with Moses Beach, the paper's editor. Because of Weed's long history in New York journalism and politics, the editor admitted the story was in large part conjecture, an effort to show that his paper had better connections in Richmond than his rivals. Instead of castigating the man for creating an international incident, a relieved Weed "laughed heartily."[16]

The final cost of this tempest was "the expenditure of a vast amount of printer's ink" in New York and London. Looking back at it all, Henry Raymond wrote, "The temptation of humbugging a whole nation and a government supposed to be omniscient is too great for human nature to resist."[17]

After the summer defeats in 1863, Confederate fortunes on the battlefield were sinking on all fronts. Confederate sympathizers and agents in Great Britain searched for new ways to keep the cause alive. The Southern Independence Association, started in Manchester, turned out to be a high-profile means to that end. The impetus for its founding came in a long letter from Maury to Lord Wharncliffe, reprinted in the *Times*.

Boiled down to its essence, Maury wrote, "The war has been more unpopular at the North than it is now." To its editors and Maury, war-weary Northerners were poised to throw the Lincoln dictatorship out of office. Like Maury, the association's message became: Hold firm.

In late December 1863, Beresford-Hope invited thirty Confederate sympathizers, many of them subscribers to the Erlanger loan, to his home on Connaught Place to build the association in London. When the association was fully organized in 1864, more than nine hundred names with luster signed on.

As busy and as sick as he was, Maury wrote and edited many of its pamphlets and circulars. Hotze dutifully covered the association's meetings.[18]

Looking at all this activity, Goldwin Smith, the regius professor of modern history and pro–Union, tartly described the association's signatories as being "men of title and family" but "not as strong in representation of the interests of the working class." He also could have asked: How committed were these influential men to getting their hands dirtied? They certainly didn't rush to William Lindsay's side when he announced plans to introduce another bill in the Commons to mediate the war. For many signers, the association was another club for like-minded Britons.[19]

For all his bluster in the 1840s, Maury moved easily among the British elite in the 1860s, the Confederacy's corps of support abroad. Beresford-Hope and Wharncliffe were among the journalistic and political elite. In late 1863, Maury visited Thomas Bold and his family and the Lairds in Liverpool, the business and maritime elite. From there Maury and his son went to the home of Lord Wrottesley and met with Sir Charles Wheatstone on a number of occasions, the scientific elite. Maury also journeyed to Stowe as the guests of the Duke and Duchess of Buckingham, true royalty. The duke had been Maury's guest at the observatory. Through almost all these connections, there was another invaluable tie—the Church of England. For Maury, this was as important as his bonds with the Rev. James Hervey Otey and the Episcopal Church of the United States. In London, the connection was the Newfoundland-born Tremlett.[20]

By the time he was thirty, Frank Tremlett had preached the Anglican gospel in the pulpit of one of the great shrines of American Puritanism, St. Botolph's in Boston, and Lincolnshire in Great Britain. Yankees could stand in the church where John Cotton once had preached their nonconformity and tour the town where John Foxe, the author of Foxe's *Book of Martyrs*, had been born. Just about the time that Beresford-Hope had donated a splendid baptismal font to the fourteenth-century church, the vestry, disapproving Tremlett's establishing a church for the town's poor without its permission, forced his resignation.

When Tremlett reemerged in the public record in 1859, he was the pastor of the new St. Peter's in Belsize Park, a fashionable London suburb. The cleric took with him into the vicarage, a house he owned, his mother and his much younger and flirtatious sister, Louise. Over a short period, Frank and Louise moved from sympathizers to Confederate zealots from the pulpit, in pamphlets, and in opening the doors of "Rebel's Roost," their home, to visiting Confederates. Captain Raphael Semmes tapped Tremlett as raider *Alabama*'s chaplain, and Louise anointed herself "cabin boy" of raider *Sumter*. Later, Maury called Tremlett "the best Confederate in England."[21]

Like other Anglican clerics, Tremlett's sermons called for an end to hostilities in North America. His sermon on "Christian Brotherhood" in November 1863, praising Southerners for "having Christianized that race" of black slaves, inspired Confederate propagandists to have his manna distributed in other British churches. The sermons were the cornerstone of his "Society for the Promotion of Cessation of Hostilities in America." Instead of laboring fruitlessly for independence, the society downplayed slavery and set its sights on rebuilding the cotton mill industry, a pressing domestic issue. Yet here again though, many of its founding members and largest contributors, like Beresford-Hope; Lord Cecil, his brother-in-law; Spence, the Confederate financial agent and writer; and Lindsay, parliamentarian and businessman, also were prominent in the Southern Independence Association. Again, as Smith noted about the independence association, too many of these men were the well-to-do.

By the summer, the society had thousands of names affixed to petitions calling on Palmerston's government to use its influence to obtain a cease-fire to alleviate the suffering of Southern families (and give the Confederacy breathing room to negotiate, rearm, and refit).[22]

As Grant slogged southward in Virginia, recording appalling casualties, and Sherman tramped eastward, trying to outmaneuver Joseph Johnston in Georgia in 1864, Maury and Tremlett produced a resolution for the society that said: "Looking upon the restoration of the Union as impossible and the independence of the Southern confederacy as virtually a fait accompli; any prolongation of the war can only result in mutual slaughter and in debt and in weakness to both belligerents."[23]

From then on, Tremlett sent Maury copies of petitions and other materials for review. When he wanted something toughened, Maury inserted his own wording that became the official line. The problem with the official line was that it was increasingly out of synchronization with events in North America.[24]

Maury and Spence met with the prime minister as members of Tremlett's society. In explaining why Great Britain remained neutral, Palmerston joked: "They who in quarrels interpose / will often wipe a bloody nose." As with Mason earlier, he promised the government wouldn't oppose a resolution calling for an end to hostilities, but it wouldn't introduce one either. For Maury, there was no satisfaction in knowing that he had been the only Confederate agent to have an audience with the prime minister.[25]

Maury's diary in spring 1864 revealed a man in deteriorating health. There were new worries over S. Wellford Corbin, a son-in-law who had been taken prisoner near Petersburg. Fifty-eight and old beyond his years, Maury complained of intestinal pains so severe a Confederate doctor was sent from Paris to treat him at Bowdon, and eventually he underwent kidney surgery. He also then noted he had tendered his resignation to Mallory and offered his services to Maximilian, but nothing came of the tender or offer. Maybe they were lost at sea like the cotton certificates to pay French shipbuilders.[26]

In his own gathering gloom, Maury looked to two weapons, which, if employed with the oceangoing ironclads, might stave off the final plunge to defeat. He wrote Jansen: "I must repeat my request that you will furnish me with any thing useful which you may find upon the use of submarines and submarine boats. We are, I am convinced, far ahead of the outside world with these devices, simply because our attention has been directed to their development while they encountered prejudices elsewhere."[27]

As commander of Confederate coastal defense, Maury had been intrigued by semisubmersible boats, armed with spars like his gunboats, as having a place in layered defense-shore batteries, electronically detonated mines, shallow-draft gunboats even when armored, and what became known as the "*Davids*" in Charleston to attack the blockading fleet. Before leaving for Great Britain in 1862, Maury is believed to have helped his professional acquaintance Dr. St. Julien Ravenel in designing prototypes of the *David* torpedo boat for Charleston's defense. How much information Maury brought from Richmond on work there on similar vessels is not known. At that time, Brigadier General P. G. T. Beauregard, as out of favor with the Davis administration as Maury, encouraged the Charleston experimenters to continue with their submersibles.

Maury, when writing Jansen, knew of the failed attack of CSS *David* on USS *New Ironsides* the previous October and the later successful attack in the new year of *H. L. Hunley*, a submarine, on *Housatonic* in Charleston. Did Jansen know a European Ravenel? More to Maury's taste, were there inventive officers like John Mercer Brooke and Hunter Davidson in European navies? If so, Maury wanted to meet the war-making scientist and the unorthodox officers.[28]

The Confederates' work in mine warfare resonated with the British. Royal Navy officers overcame their distaste about silent weapons from the Crimean War when they learned of the torpedoes' effectiveness. They were eager to learn more from Maury.

Because of the time spent in ship buying and propagandizing, Maury did not return actively to mine warfare research until August 1863. Maury then worked with the British telegraphy expert Wheatstone and Nathaniel Holmes on harbor defense.[29]

Charting the progress they made can be laborious and dissecting his notebooks of drawings and scribbles of ranges and mine placement tedious. There is one experiment—"the time gun"—that drew daily public attention at one o'clock each afternoon in Newcastle and Piazzi Smyth's Royal Observatory in Edinburgh. The demonstration of the power of electric current passing through stations caught Maury's attention.

Using Wheatstone's magneto-exploder and a chemical fuse developed by the Royal Laboratory at Woolwich, the wires of connected torpedoes could be tested without having them explode to see if they were still operable by having the current detected at a receiving station miles away like Smyth's observatory. If the current couldn't be detected, either an enemy had cut the wires intentionally or they had been broken accidentally. What was broken could be repaired.

Holmes then made the mines larger and deadlier for Maury's work in Great Britain. The mines, looking like steam-engine boilers, were packed with five hundred pounds of explosives. They were set sixteen feet below the surface, not easily detectable. When in range, the observer hidden from the vessel's lookouts' views detonated them using the magneto-exploder and the Royal Laboratory's fuse.[30]

Picking up on earlier work, Maury also successfully tested land mines to break up frontal assaults. In 1864, his letters to Confederate officials sounded like an overseas Gabriel Rains, a pioneer in the field. All they had to remember was the mines' success in the James River when a Union vessel tried to cross an electrically operated minefield: "The boiler, engine and smoke stack went up about 20 or 30 feet, the boiler bursting at the time, and the hull of the vessel was reduced to fragments. Strange to say a few of her people escaped alive." With his reports and pleas, he shipped torpedo equipment to Richmond.[31]

With the war winding down, Sir John Burgoyne, Great Britain's chief engineer in the Crimean War, delivered a cargo hold of good news to Maury. The siege of Sevastopol had convinced Burgoyne that frontal assaults on fortified positions were little short of murder. If siege guns were not enough to reduce an enemy, newer technologies could. The British government was willing to share information on torpedoes that it had, he said. More to the point, Burgoyne pledged money for "acid, batteries, insulated wire, and other necessary ingredients" for their form of "rarified warfare" and the skilled men to help Maury "in the cause of science." After that meeting, Maury met on the sly with the Russians, offering to teach them about mine warfare if they promised not to share this knowledge with "enemies of my country."[32]

Like the cessation of hostilities society, the pro–Confederate press now focused on the suffering of civilians and soldiers, especially prisoners of war. Many Britons remembered the horrors of typhus, cholera, and dysentery that killed their soldiers by the hundreds during the Crimean War. The ever-persistent Spence organized a four-day charity and propaganda event in the grand St. George's Hall to raise money to alleviate the prisoners' suffering.

Opening at noon on October 18 under the "real Confederate sunshine," twelve stalls representing the eleven states of the Confederacy plus Kentucky were inside. Mrs. James Bulloch worked at the Georgia stall, as did Mrs. John

Slidell at the Mississippi stall, Lady Wharncliffe and Mrs. Charles Prioleau at South Carolina, and Lady Beresford-Hope at Tennessee. They sold raffle chances on Robert E. Lee's pipe, crosses made from Fort Sumter's wreckage, autography of Davis, Lee, and Beauregard, and portraits. There were also silver castings, ceremonial swords, ship models, and a raffle for a Shetland pony.

Commissioner Mason, Maury, and *Alabama*'s crew mingled with the thousands who attended. Lord Wharncliffe, Beresford-Hope, and John Laird were among the British dignitaries present. Popular bands, opera singers, and classical organists entertained the throngs, who feasted on donated food and drink. More than £20,000 were raised.

The Union could afford to wait. Wharncliffe's petition to Seward to act as an "accredited agent" visiting the camps was denied, and the £20,000 disappeared. The Confederacy had a little more than six months to live.[33]

Back at work, Maury heard from Vice Admiral Octave de Chabannes, prefect of the French Marines, about his test of firing "torpedo rockets under water." He admitted that the French had not succeeded in having the torpedoes reach sufficient speed "to strike the enemy's ships' bottoms with enough force to explode."[34]

By spring 1865, Maury knew that further efforts in Europe were pointless, and he decided to help Confederate forces on the Texas Gulf Coast. Diehard commanders like John Bankhead Magruder, a longtime Maury acquaintance, and William Preston still fought there. By taking that as his next mission, he also was close to sanctuary in Mexico, if all else failed. In London, the would-be warrior arranged for a new edition of his *Physical Geography of the Sea* to be published in Great Britain and worked with Jansen in securing a new copyright for it in the Netherlands. In closing out Maury's accounts, Bold found the books in balance and added approvingly that Maury never "received shilling" in commissions for his arms and ship buying, money that his family certainly could have used.

As when he resigned his commission, the good officer squared accounts with Bulloch, who was remaining in Great Britain, and Barron, who was going to Cuba. The good secret agent met one more time with Mason, who handed Maury dispatches for the Confederate government. The commissioner was staying, awaiting further orders. Maury asked fellow agent James North, trying to return to Richmond, to tell his wife "to present to the Confederacy all of my medals except the three that were struck for me and Humboldt medal."

To the end, Maury kept up the fight. He worked with Bulloch and Barron before he left to get *Stonewall*, one of Arman's powerful warships, into Confederate hands and underway from Denmark. He assisted in another Confederate attempt to buy a steamer in Limerick, Ireland, and convert it into another raider. The United States minister to France was surprised that the Confederate Navy continued to put guns on ships and get them to sea that spring.[35]

What had Maury accomplished during these years? A great deal, in the opinions of historians Warren Spencer and Amanda Foreman. In addition to his propaganda work, buying two ships, and research into mines, Spencer credited Maury with introducing "an efficient and quick way to finance ship purchases ... consulted with and advised the Confederate diplomatic commissions [and] analyzed European political attitudes toward the American strife." Foreman thought him the best qualified Confederate to serve in a diplomatic post. Maury considered it exile.[36]

On May 2, Maury and son Matthew sailed from Great Britain. When they reached the West Indies, newspapers reported Lee's surrender at Appomattox and Davis's abandonment of Richmond. In Havana, the man who had given his health, reputation, skill, and intelligence to defend his beloved Virginia knew his war was over. Barron and a number of Confederate naval officers in Cuba planned to bide their time until a general amnesty was granted. Maury was not so sure there was going to be an immediate amnesty for "pirates" like themselves. He had his own plans for survival.

The Confederate secret agent did not want the new fuses and exploders to fall into Union hands, so he stored them in Bulloch's name. Over the course of the few days he spent in Cuba, Maury also decided to send his son to New York to stay with relatives there.[37]

Maury wrote to the commander of the Union Navy in the Gulf of Mexico on May 25:

> In peace as in war, I follow the fortunes of my old native state, Virginia. I read in the public prints that she has practically confessed defeat and laid down arms. In that mine were ground also. I am here without command, officially alone and bound on matters of private concern abroad. Nevertheless as I consider further resistance more than useless, I deem it proper formally so to confess, and to pledge you in words of honor that should I find myself before the final inauguration of peace within the jurisdiction of the United States to consider myself a prisoner of war, bound by the terms and conditions which have been or may be granted to General Lee and his officers.[38]

He asked that any answer be sent through his son, Richard, on parole in Richmond.

To Jansen two days later, he was more succinct: "All's lost—save individual honor."[39]

23. The Long Exile

The heaviest baggage Matthew Fontaine Maury carried with him from Cuba was his plan for building a "New Virginia" in imperial Mexico with two hundred thousand disaffected Southerners and his war experiences to defend its northern border. It was all he had. Although his cousin Rutson Maury thought the immigration proposition dubious, the businessman warned the former Confederate officer, "You would be sent to prison at once if you came here now." The Rev. Francis W. Tremlett, an ardent supporter of the Confederacy in Britain, had misgivings as well: "Can Max give you the feelings for Mexico that you have for Virginia? He can give you nothing else but land and that you have in Virginia or can buy and now perhaps, it's cheap enough."[1]

Maury landed at Veracruz and went by train to Mexico City to contact the minister of war, General Juan de Dios de la Peza. He wrote the minister and later Maximilian's French backers, "That the value of submarine mining as a means of defense has been fully proved by the late American war. That during that war and a cost altogether insignificant in comparison with the ends accomplished and the means usually adapted to those ends, more armed vessels were destroyed than by all the heavy forts and expensive fortifications put together, which lined the river and harbors of the Southern states."[2]

Back in Charlottesville less than a month after General Robert E. Lee's surrender, his daughter Diana Corbin wrote him and said Virginia was a living hell. Union forces "have freed all the negroes and ordered the masters what way to pay them."[3]

As he waited at the Hotel Iturbide for a nod from the emperor, more questions from Virginia descended: Stay in exile, but what about us here? There were no easy answers coming by return mail.[4]

When he saw Maximilian in late June, Maury told the emperor, "From such a wreck, Mexico may gather and transfer to her own borders, the very intelligence, skill and labour which made the South what she was in her palmy days—except bondage." He predicted newly freed blacks would voluntarily accompany their former masters southward.[5]

Marin Jansen, his ally, thought that ridiculous. "You have not seen the revolution in the black people of the South after the fall of Richmond."[6]

Maximilian and his wife, Carlota, wanted more details, and the Virginian complied. Maury called for a proclamation of religious toleration, free entry through customs, exemption from taxation and military service, rights of American citizens, unrestricted grants of land, offers of a bounty, and a clear statement of the immigrants' status on the land.

The *New York Times* noted, "All white immigrants are allowed certain privilege and immunities ... but 'people of color' will be subjected to a system which differs very little from serfdom."[7]

In exchange, Maury said the displaced Confederates would turn Mexico into a New Eden. "Cotton, sugar, coffee, tobacco, rice, indigo, cochineal, India rubber, hemp, corn and olives with flocks and herbs all do well." He was as enthusiastic as Raleigh in Elizabeth's time. By August, Maximilian named the former superintendent of the Naval Observatory the imperial commissioner of colonization at a salary of $5,000 per year.[8]

From Maury's family in Virginia, only Dick, lame from the war, intended to start over in Mexico. Both his family and the most prominent man in the state pressured Dick to stay.

Robert E. Lee wrote: "I have entertained the opinion that it would be better for them [immigrants to Mexico] and the country to remain at their homes and share the fate of their respective states. I hope however the efforts of your father will facilitate the wishes and promote the welfare of all who find it necessary or convenient to expatriate themselves but should sincerely regret that either he or his should be embraced in that number [of 200,000]."[9]

Lee repeated this counsel to Matthew Fontaine Maury. The crux for Lee came down to two sentences: "I shall be very sorry if your presence be lost to Virginia. She has now need for all her sons, and can ill afford to spare you."[10]

For Maury in Mexico, the task was to attract as many of those sons as he could. By doing this, he saw himself as an "honourable" man helping his fellow Southerners succeed in Mexico.[11]

As soon as Benito Juarez appealed to Americans to help free Mexico from French domination, his overthrown government's legation began supplying Secretary of State William Seward with every scrap of information they could find on French intentions and forces, Maximilian's decrees, and the colonization effort. Matias Romero, the Mexican minister to the United States, early on wrote that Maury "has been declared a subject of the usurper" and appointed "an honorary councilor," showing his privileged position with the throne. Accompanying the letter was a list of the ex–Confederate arrivals in Mexico published in the *Mexico Times*.[12]

Maximilian's court and the French influence also disturbed Maury's family. One relative wrote, "Although it will shock you, you will see that the South will in this, as in all other things, support the United States in overrunning Mexico."[13]

Maury answered defiantly: "As for me, I regard Virginia now very much in the light of my own dead; rescue the spirit, but let the body be put out of sight. Her spirit resides in her people and not in her hills and streams. I invite her people while that spirit yet glows within them to come away and help found here in this lovely land a 'new Virginia.'"[14]

As brave as those words were, the Confederate in exile was unwilling to risk his posterity in Maximilian's Mexico. He sent his wife and family to tranquil Britain. Then, Maury stepped up efforts to lure other Confederate families across the border. In newspaper advertisements and handbills, Maury told prospective immigrants how the emperor governed "mildly and wisely." Unmentioned were forty years of revolution and a country where the people found their "energies paralyzed, haciendas neglected and industry itself at a standstill."[15]

At the palace, Maury was end-running ministers directly to the emperor and the empress, whom he found "very clever, practical and business-like." As he rose in favor, their highnesses rewarded Maury with another honor, head of the unbuilt national observatory.[16]

Support for immigration depended on Maximilian's mood. Napoleon III's ideal immigrant was a European talented in agriculture, finance, engineering, administration, and trade. The former Confederates were a different breed. How far to trust former soldiers, especially those who had waged the guerrilla war in the West, like the Missourian Jo Shelby? At a meeting in the palace with Maury, Shelby, and the French military commander, Maximilian blanched "when the talk was of bloodshed and provinces held by the bayonet."[17]

Confederates found local officials unwilling to talk or openly hostile. Editor Henry Watkins Allen warned, "I fear there will be much misery among the colonists who come without money." A glum Maury added, "I now almost despair of seeing it well in motion before this time next year."[18]

Spurred by Romero's one-man campaign and their own reports from Mexico, American officials feared New Virginia's success might spread guerrilla warfare into the Southwest. General Philip Sheridan wrote from New Orleans, "The scheme for emigration to Mexico is now fully organized in the city of Mexico, with Captain Maury, Sterling Price and General J. B. Magruder as the prominent men. They hold titles and honors from Maximilian and are now officers of his majesty's government.... This information is without question, and is a premonitory symptom of what I have for some time believed—that we can never have a fully restored union and give a total and final blow to all malcontents until the French leave Mexico."[19]

Sheridan posted soldiers at border crossings and ordered all ships leaving New Orleans inspected. He stepped up running guns and shipping food to Juarez to keep the pressure on Maximilian and the French. In addition, Seward required Southerners departing for Mexico to swear an oath never to return.[20]

In his quest for a throne, the Habsburg monarch ignored reality at his own peril. The Mexican military told Maximilian that he controlled about three-quarters of the land and four-fifths of the people. If he were lucky, his government controlled about one-third of the country, concentrated around the capital. When he looked at what all those foreign soldiers cost, he should have "proclaimed [himself] insolvent before his reign began," but as a Habsburg, he wanted to rule.[21]

Maximilian was writing his own fairy tale with bloody consequences. In accepting the crown, he pointed to his lineage to Emperor Charles V, the first European ruler of Mexico. Most Mexicans found his comments insulting.[22]

In Paris, Napoleon III felt pressure about the deployment of so many soldiers so far away from Metropolitan France. American saber rattling and doubts about the Mexicans' ability to pay for those soldiers and their war debts raised red flags in sectors of the French body politic. Aiming at the American administration but talking to the Assembly, the emperor told the United States it had nothing to fear from his army's presence in Mexico. All that was needed was Mexico to set a time for withdrawal, he added soothingly, knowing that Prussia was threatening France in Europe.[23]

Ignoring American harassments, Maury covered the South with New Virginia circulars, reading, "The best time for coming is the dry season from October to May when the new comer may live in tents, put his seed into the ground, have till June to build and get his family comfortably housed by the time the rains set in." He also worked on keeping spirits high among the American arrivals. In Mexico City, Maury and Dick were "a light, as it were, in the night of the exiles." Maury delighted listeners with "the sparkle of salt water [which] ran through his conversation."[24]

The story he told his son-in-law, S. Wellford Corbin, was more honest:

"As I have always said if colonization fails, Mexico is no place for me. But before I set about to hunt up a place to die, I wish to make the experiment." For a change, Maury's finances were "now in a condition to support my family again in their wanted comfort." For Ann, the "wanted comfort" was not in Mexico or even Britain; she wanted to be with the people she had known all her life.[25]

Ever the public optimist as 1866 began, Maury found encouraging signs. Confederate immigrants, like Shelby, farmed the Carlota colony. Maury pointed to that five hundred thousand–acre tract on the rail line to Mexico City as a success. It was propaganda with a twist. He was shilling land this time, not a cause.[26]

Soon, the emperor put former Confederates into colonizing Sonora in northwest Mexico, to protect mining interests there. Its silver would reimburse the French and its allies for their soldiers' deployment.[27]

For a time prominent Confederates continued crossing the Rio Grande. Engineers such as Andrew Talcott, Daniel Leadbetter, and Thomas C. Reynolds came to build spectacular railroads like the 350-mile line from Veracruz to the capital. Generals such as Jubal A. Early, David S. Terry, Manning Kimmel, and William Hardeman also were establishing new lives in imperial Mexico. As Maury reported, "They are well mounted and armed and in case of an emergency would be very useful to the commander of the department." That was music to Shelby's ears. "This Commodore Maury seems to sail as well upon the land as upon the water."[28]

Yet the favoritism shown the Americans, like Maury and Shelby, undermined support for the emperor with the very people who should have been his staunchest allies. Within a year, Mexican landholders, Indians, the church, the press, and the French were criticizing the immigration policy.[29]

Maury went to Carlota with a request to visit his family in London and to buy the instruments for the observatory. To demonstrate his intention of returning, Maury left Dick in charge of "New Virginia," and Maximilian granted Maury's request at a time when Juarez and Diaz were on a rampage.[30]

In his letters to his family during the war and from Mexico, Maury tried to brace them for the physical changes he had undergone. Slipping health, worry over them in Virginia, the mystery surrounding John's disappearance in Mississippi, Dick's crippling wounds, Corbin's capture, his own exile in Europe, and now Mexico had aged him greatly.

"The old man with a white beard" and iron gray hair was how his youngest daughter, Lucy, remembered her father on his arrival in London late on March 29, 1866. But the shock of his appearance evaporated quickly. The separation of three and a half years ended in long embraces with his wife and children in a house on Harley Street in Cavendish Square.

Seeing his children—now adolescents and young adults—after so long was a shock. Lucy was fourteen, Mary was twenty-one, and Eliza was seventeen. Brave, Maury's son Matthew, was enrolled again at Rose Hill, the school he attended when he came to Britain in 1862. Maury moved easily into his role as paterfamilias and made his daughters' education his first order of business. Maury didn't want any "Boarding School Misses" in his household.[31]

By late April, Maury dashed off letters to dozens of diplomats about opening a school on mine warfare and meeting again with engineer and telegraphy expert Nathaniel Holmes. Finally, Maury made the observatory purchases and met briefly with former Confederate Commissioner James M. Mason, who was interested in going to Mexico. Maury gave all appearances of returning to the emperor's court.[32]

In Mexico, Maximilian, listening anew to opponents of immigration, wrote Maury on April 19, saying he was "impelled by motives of economy and convenience to abolish the Imperial Commission of Colonization." Not closing the door completely, he added, "If your talents cannot for the present be made available in that way, I am convinced that they will be eminently useful in the direction of the Observatory which station I formerly conferred on you."[33]

The decision's suddenness stunned Maury. The back-channel comments about his concerns to family members had played out. "Colonization being suspended, I fear that my return to Mexico would tend rather to increase the embarrassments than to smooth any difficulties by which your majesty is surrounded," Maury wrote.[34]

When the news arrived from Mexico, Maury's enemies gloated: "The grand Mexican emigration campaign has turned out to be a huge imposture."[35]

Maury's prospects in Britain and Europe, on the other hand, appeared promising. He was hailed for his charting work, the laying of the transatlantic cable, and surveys of the Isthmus of Panama for a future canal. After all, he had parlayed that acclaim into cooperation with the British in mine warfare as the American war wound down.[36]

Across the channel, Napoleon III talked at length with Maury about "my position." The French emperor told him, "In a year they will let you back to your place. They [the United States] are proud of you. And if I can serve you let me know." He remained intrigued by Maury's shipbuilding proposals and his thoughts on the "infernal machines." Mines, submersibles, submarines, and ironclads were revolutionizing naval warfare and harbor defense, areas that tantalized Napoleon. With the emperor's encouragement, Maury grabbed the low-hanging fruit, a "torpedo school," to sell to the French. For £500, students could learn the latest developments during a month's intensive study.[37]

As the exile looked around Britain for new ventures like a Central American canal project and another transatlantic cable attempt, the *Richmond Whig* on the day after Maximilian's letter was written, slapped Maury for being an "ornament to the court."

"We certainly feel that we are discharging our duty when we condemn all efforts to drain the South of its capital and population."[38]

The newspaper was beating a dead horse.

By January 1866, the French refused any more credit to Maximilian's government: "If Mexico cannot pay the troops which we maintain in its territory, it will be impossible for us to keep them there." Then there were the Juaristas. The regime's hold in the cities was weakening. Inside the court, intrigues soon drove out other Confederate refugees—"the men of intelligence." Richard Maury wrote "gloomy and desponding" letters to his father in London. New Virginia became another piece of lost baggage in a fast-collapsing papier-mâché empire.[39]

That news was not enough to shift Maury's hostility away from the Union occupiers. The unreconstructed Confederate rebuked his nephew Dabney for aiding the new despots in crossing "off the map the very name Virginia, blot out all former state lines, make new provinces and called a part of what was VIRGINIA the state of Winnepesscoggee."[40]

With that off his chest, Maury returned in earnest to selling his torpedo school. He used "testimonials" from an exasperated Union Secretary of the Navy Gideon Welles describing the deadliness of Confederate torpedoes to promote the school.[41]

In his sales pitch, Maury wrote: "In 1862, I mined the James River with them and that so effectively, as not only to prevent any further attack by ironclads upon the defenses of Richmond, but so to paralyze the powerful fleet of the federals as to render it of no avail in the siege of that city by General Grant."[42]

Maury reached out to his Confederate contacts like Thomas Jefferson Page, now in Argentina working with its navy. Page, citing the advances in torpedo warfare made by "a learned professor in London," urged the commander of the Argentine armed forces to buy these "completely effective" weapons already in the hands of "France, England, Russia, and all the principal powers in Europe."[43]

At the same time, Maury expanded his study of shipbuilding, including mine-carrying submarines. The good teacher was a good student.

To arouse more interest in the school, Holmes, whom Maury entrusted with his patents on torpedoes in 1865, took to the road. But his journeying, meeting, and talking were not producing revenue. Instead of reexamining the school, he and Holmes plowed onward, building bile.[44]

When asked by Maury how business was going, Holmes reported frustrating failure. Without proof, Maury suspected Holmes was lining his own pockets. He wrote in exasperation years later: "Why don't I come out and prevent people from stealing my brains, torpedoes and all.... Didn't Queen Vice [Victoria] her own dear self steal my torpedoes right before my face."[45]

Maury was too harsh with Holmes. The former Confederate ignored the strong probability that French and Scandinavian officers who attended the school spread what they learned for a price or a promotion or for patriotism among colleagues and allies. The Royal Corps of Engineers published its own accounts of submarine mines in 1866. Also, other Confederates, including Viktor Ernst Karl Rudolf, knowledgeable about mine warfare were as willing as Maury to sell their expertise.

The torpedo school went out of business by summer 1866.[46]

While Maury's value as a clandestine warrior was of declining worth, his reputation as a scientist remained substantive abroad. He and his family needed that. They needed money. It was the Rev. Francis Tremlett's idea, first proposed in early 1865, to defray Maury's medical expenses from wartime surgery and resurrected after the war to ease the financial pinch. In the clergyman's first try, Member of Parliament John Laird pledged funds and said his sons would do likewise, but John Polito, representing Lloyd's, wished Tremlett well but promised no funds. That didn't stop Tremlett.

The cleric plugged away for about a year until he had enough money and guests to honor Maury. Wearing his medals and decorations, the old Confederate was celebrated by senior naval officers from Europe, like Marin Jansen, and Latin America; leaders of the Royal Institution, Laird; Confederate sympathizers like Tremlett, Alexander Beresford-Hope, James Spence, and Sir Charles Wheatstone; and former Confederate officers like P. G. T. Beauregard. One hundred eighty men gathered in his honor at the very popular Willis's Rooms in St. James, London, in early June 1866. Sir John Pakington, twice first lord of the Admiralty, chaired the gala.

Pakington drew cheers when citing Maury's decision to take "the part worthy of his character and his career" in siding with the Confederacy. The loudest applause erupted when he listed the contributions in cash from Holland, Russia, and Great Britain and handed the silver casket with more than £3,000 in it to Maury.

Maury was almost speechless. In looking back over his career, he called turning merchantmen into "temples of science" his proudest achievement. But his climax of thankfulness in his short speech was marked by "sealed lips and the eloquence of silence," creating the loudest applause of the evening. While toasts and salutes provided a warm glow for a night, the £3,000 was desperately needed.[47]

The financial gift provided only a temporary reprieve. The royalties from his earlier works had dried up. As Harper publishers told William C. Hasbrouck when he inquired about money due Maury from *The Physical Geography of the Sea*, "Mr. Maury's retirement from the service of the United States under the circumstances accompanying such retirement seems literally to have killed the sale of the book." To make matters worse, the funds he left in Britain when he came from Mexico were lost in a bank collapse. As a result, the family moved twice that summer to cheaper lodgings.[48]

The Maurys' prospects narrowed dangerously.[49]

Through Rutson Maury's intercession, Charles B. Richardson, the New York publisher of the *Historical Magazine* and the pro–Union military *United States Service Magazine*, expressed an interest in working with Matthew Fontaine Maury on a series of geography textbooks. It was part of a series of textbooks that Richardson envisioned "to exploit the local patriotism of the South."[50]

Richardson figured Maury's name in the region could still sell books. Also by aiming the books at children, Richardson hoped to avoid resentments in publishing the work of an exile who had taken up arms against his country.

There was other baggage about Maury that Richardson hoped to discard. His refusal to go silently into the night by scheming to lure disillusioned Southerners to Mexico and willingness to sell everything he knew about naval warfare to any nation but the one of his birth was not easily forgotten.[51]

Richardson ignored the whole kit and caboodle. For the series, Maury was to be paid $10,000 in gold. So his pen scribbled, trying to carry the family across the bar of hard times.[52]

The geographies arose from Maury's experiences as a young man, traveling to distant lands and meeting people so different from his family and friends. As he wrote his son-in-law in August 1866, "I suppose I shall stay here and write school books for a New York publisher." In their London home, Eliza and Mary transcribed his rough notes into legible copy; his son Matthew drew the maps. It was the kind of work the older children had done on the *Physical Geography of the Sea*.[53]

Their combined talents changed geographic narrative. It was an achievement as large as *Physical Geography*'s. In *Physical Geography*, the public had been shown the link between the oceans, atmosphere, and changing weather. In the geography series, children were shown in an entertaining way how people differed in places they likely would never see. Alexander Dallas Bache, the head of the Coast Survey, in castigating "popularizers" more than a decade before, had been far too narrow in his view of science—especially for the general public and for children. Maury's view may have been too broad. But in these works, he again answered the question: *Cui bono?*

Opening the *First Lessons in Geography* with a description of a trip around the world, Maury was back aboard *Vincennes*—full of dreams, looking for wonders.[54]

After receiving the first volume, a pleased Richardson offered to increase the gold payment if Maury returned to the United States. Probably after talking with Rutson Maury, Richardson sweetened the enticement with an offer to endow the University of Virginia with money for an observatory—if the former Confederate headed it; but the leery old rebel felt the political climate with its "test oaths" of loyalty was not yet right for his return.

Richardson then proposed meeting in Toronto, and that intrigued Maury. Shortly thereafter, Maury, describing himself as an "unpardoned rebel," wrote the governor general of Canada, offering to lecture on the electric torpedo's ability to enhance his defenses.

In the late 1860s, the governor general sat on an international powder keg. Irish nationalists—Fenians—crossed and recrossed the northern border attacking symbols and representatives of British authority where they found them, but for his own reasons, the governor general did not respond.[55]

Although he was safe in Britain, events in Mexico again pressed upon Maury. Carlota was in Paris, imploring Napoleon III for the military aid he had promised the archduke. "Mexican affairs are so complicated," his son-in-law wrote in explaining that Maury had no plans to return to Central America. Carlota next turned to the pope for other than spiritual assistance, but neither he nor any other crowned head of Europe helped the tottering empire militarily. Maury, sensing Maximilian was doomed, told his son Richard to flee.

The end came with a volley of rifle shots in a Mexican courtyard away from the capital. In June 1867, Napoleon III burst into tears when he heard the news; when the French emperor told his wife, she collapsed. Maximilian's wife, Carlota, went mad.[56]

Across the channel, Maury coldly wrote: "Our people would have formed the cement that is indispensable to give to the Mexicans the elements of nationality, which is the very thing the United States does not want that country to have." To Jack Maury, who had helped mine Virginia waters, he counted his luck in being exiled to Great Britain by President Jefferson Davis and Navy Secretary Stephen Mallory and having "Mexican villains intrigue me out of Mexico, you see the rocks that but for enemies, and I should have split upon."[57]

While Maury's official relations with the emperor were severed, they had continued corresponding. In the last exchange Maximilian congratulated Maury on reestablishing the transatlantic telegraph cable, but in truth, Maury had no connection with Field's 1866 success. To the New England–born businessman, the Virginian was a traitor.[58]

Field might be through with him, but Maury was not finished with submarine telegraphy. In a letter, Holmes told Maury that Baring Brothers, the large investment banking firm, was launching a transatlantic cable enterprise. The company planned first to lay cable between Norway and Denmark. Additionally, cable would be laid between the Faroe Islands, Iceland, and Greenland, and from there to North America, a route similar to one Maury had urged on Field.[59]

If he was not willing to take money from Field in the 1850s, Maury definitely hoped to profit from Barings' in the 1860s. "I am willing to pledge my reputation to the success of the enterprise and to superintend the construction and laying of the cable and to make any fee contingent upon success."[60]

As with Field, Maury cited the lack of currents on the ocean floor and the need for a slack light cord for success. By using the lighter cord, he also estimated that he could cut the cost to about 150 pounds per mile, half of Field's, in laying a competing cable.

For all of this correspondence, Maury did not channel his ideas into the concrete proposals that investment bankers of any century needed to breed confidence that this project would succeed. Shades of his Southern Commercial Convention addresses were present, offering only vision.[61]

Ann said often she longed to return to Virginia to be with family and friends. By spring he looked at crossing the Atlantic himself. What to do, not if, when he returned was now the question. Maury was well on his way by mid–1867 with the geography series, but how much money that would bring in was questionable. After all, he had seen the American royalties dry up from his once hugely successful *Physical Geography of the Sea*.

Although he was soon to be celebrated at Cambridge for his accomplishments, where did Maury stand as a man of American science during his years in British exile? His critics in the United States continued in power and were untainted by being on the losing side of the Civil War. Alexander Dallas Bache, broken physically and mentally, died on February 17, 1867, only to be replaced by Harvard's Benjamin Peirce as superintendent of the Coast Survey. A few miles from the survey's Capitol Hill offices, Joseph Henry remained like a monument at the Smithsonian Institution.

How did the Navy view Maury then? To them he was a traitor, an officer who took up arms against his country, a man who fought a cowardly war with mines, and a pirate master with his commerce raiders. James Gilliss, twice snubbed by secretaries rooted in Virginia for Maury, immediately collaborated with the Coast Survey upon becoming superintendent of the observatory in 1861. When he died on February 8, 1865, Charles Davis, now an admiral and the instigator of the "Steamer Plan," took over the duties.

From the moment Davis became chief of the Bureau of Navigation in 1863, the former editor of the *Nautical Almanac* began purging all traces of Maury's work. He turned to Bache in his role as the first president of the National Academy of Science to review the *Wind and Current Charts* and the *Sailing Directions* to determine if they were "prolix and faulty."

To do the dirty work, Bache named F. A. P. Barnard, who supervised the survey's publication of maps and charts, to chair the twelve-member committee of "hydrographers and scientific men," which included Davis's brother-in-law Peirce. It was as rigged a review as the Navy's of *Arctic*'s deep sea soundings.

The Lazzaroni tore into Maury's work as "fanciful." Their report challenged Maury's grandest assertion that the charts saved time. They cited changes in naval architecture as a key but overlooked factor in reduced sailing time. In sum, they recommended suspending publication of both works. Davis happily complied.[62]

Maury's old, known places in American science and the Navy were forever gone. Yet sharing knowledge was an integral part of his life. His strong views on education were as deeply held as those of his grandfather, the Rev. James Maury. It was to be the final chapter in the book of Matthew Fontaine Maury's life.

Maury's most appealing prospects lay in higher education, a "useful field of labor." While Richardson mentioned the University of Virginia, Rutson Maury discussed possible positions for his cousin with Francis H. Smith at the Virginia Military Institute and the bishops who oversaw the unfinished University of the South in Tennessee, places where he was well known in peace and war. They importantly were safe places where the shibboleth "traitor" would never be uttered.[63]

All in all from London, the ten thousand-acre "Domaine" on a Tennessee mountaintop looked to be the right place to start over. Topping his own interest was the courting he was receiving from the bishops who oversaw the institution and likely with prodding from Tremlett and Beresford-Hope in London. The Southern bishops sent an envoy with long ties to Otey to court Maury.

For Maury, there remained an obstacle. As attentive as he was to his children's religious instruction, Maury, like Robert E. Lee and Davis, had held off making the last commitment an adult makes to the church. At Tremlett's urging and with two of his children, Lucy and Matthew, Maury was confirmed in the faith of his grandfather in London's Saint James Church.[64]

Only then did Maury feel ready to take up the rest of his life's work. "I shall hold myself ready to go over in the spring (1868) if they are ready for me then. It's in a wilderness on the top of a mountain," he wrote Jansen.[65]

In the South, after the Civil War, Maury's name retained an heirloom's value in a region searching its soul for a new identity. The old Southern nationalist, the champion of its needs, wanted to bring to another generation his vision of a new life under old principles. If he and others, such as Lee now at Washington College, could not forge a new Zion, or even a "New Virginia," they could through practical education stressing moral values lead the young out of the wilderness of defeat.[66]

Institutions such as Otey's and now Bishop Charles Quintard's University of the South, Thomas Jefferson's University of Virginia, Benjamin Crozet's Virginia Military Institute, and the benighted University of Alabama all saw in Maury the mixture of science and religiosity they wanted. He, like their boards of visitors, were on a voyage of faith—one of a better tomorrow coming from the ruins of today. In the ruins of a disastrous war, they wanted that better tomorrow for their children.

For Maury, a career in education was as natural as throwing open the shutters at the observatory and greeting each new day as special. The slogans of his life, *cur non* and *cui bono*, were particularly appropriate now. He again posed those very questions in a historic setting—Cambridge.[67]

For all the medals, decorations, and honorary degrees he had received, there was none as satisfying as the doctorate in civil law he received on May 28, 1868, from Cambridge University. That day in the university's Senate House, he was honored alongside two of the preeminent scholars of his time, Friedrich Max Muller, the classicist from Oxford, and William Wright, translator of Egyptian manuscripts and hieroglyphics at the British Museum.

Accompanied by his wife, two of their daughters—Mary and Lucy—and Tremlett, Maury was "rigged up in 'died garments from Bozra' in a gown and cap and a beautiful red silk cowl and hear myself all done up in Latin."

Like his testimonial in London, he was praised for his decision to forsake "all the goods and gifts of fortune" by siding with Virginia and the Confederacy. By doing this, he "held his faith pure and unblemished even at the price of poverty and exile."[68]

Then, Maury delivered a lecture-sermon—"Science and the Bible: Educational Ideals of the South"—that he wanted preached from Lexington, Virginia, to Sewanee, Tennessee, to Tuscaloosa, Alabama. He decried the North's secular school system, which spawned Mormonism, Millinialism, Spiritualism, and free love. In Great Britain, he found the firmly Protestant religious education he believed the South alone treasured. "We of the South have observed these things and we have longed for a university to do for us what yours have done for you."[69]

The long exile was ending, but he did not ascend a Tennessee mountaintop as expected. Instead Maury returned to his native Virginia—this time to its Shenandoah Valley and a military institute where Otey had sent his son William. For Maury, the choice came down to money—money to fund the vision of the education he extolled to the Cambridge dons.[70]

24. At Peace in the Ruins of War

The final chapter of Matthew Fontaine Maury's life unfolded in a familiar way. It began with the lifelong influence that James Hervey Otey had on Maury and rested upon continuing help by his extended family, especially the children of the Old Consul, James Maury. Through these bonds, he ended his exile. Immediately before Maury was Bishop Charles Todd Quintard. Otey's successor, pleaded with him to become the University of the South's academic head.[1]

Quintard, a chaplain with the Confederate Army, was not the only Episcopal prelate wanting Maury to come to Sewanee. Bishop William Mercer Green was an optimistic man who believed the Episcopal Church could build a premier university in the postwar South. He convinced himself money would flow from conscience-stricken Northerners and fellows in the worldwide Anglican communion, like Alexander Beresford-Hope, if Maury became chancellor. Green's unbridled enthusiasm caused Maury to examine the offer more closely.

Maury knew that the Rev. Francis Tremlett's appeal to American Episcopal bishops to support the university drew little response. He realized his name was synonymous with "traitor" in many quarters. Far from America, the former naval officer viewed the university's vice chancellorship as a Flying Dutchman, a lost ship forever wandering the Southern seas, and turned down the position.[2]

Maury could afford to do that. Virginia Military Institute looked, from a transatlantic distance, very appealing. He knew Superintendent Francis H. Smith more intimately than he had Green. In 1861, Virginia's hurried rush to defend its borders brought the two more closely together than ever before.

The politically astute Smith wanted VMI to produce a physical survey of the state. Agents were to use it to attract immigrants and capital to re-lay twisted rails, clear detritus from canals, relight foundries' fires, and plant grain and tobacco to cover scarred battlefields.[3]

Once bitten, twice cautious Maury wrote Smith April 21, 1868:

> I should lack the courage to undertake a regular course of lectures as one of the faculty, simply because it would lead me into an untried line of life; and as my rule is to put my heart into whatever I attempt to do and try my best. I should have to work very much—especially at the beginning; and I am afraid of that.[4]

Smith assured Maury he had no plans for him in the classroom. That was enough for Maury.[5]

Maury's son-in-law S. Wellford Corbin brought even more welcome news when he greeted the arriving family in New York. President Andrew Johnson had extended amnesty to all Confederates not indicted for treason. Maury, while called a traitor, was never indicted as one. Upon debarking, the summer heat and the excitement weakened him, but following a doctor's examination and rest, the former Confederate was able to leave for his cousins' Manhattan home.[6]

Life's unpredictability caught up with Maury again that eventful day. Two letters tempered the family's joy. From Central America, Dick reported the death of his young son Richard Launcelot, and from Richmond, Betty said she was too ill to travel. Yet, in Rutson Maury's home, the old rebel tried to relax with his relatives and to visit old friends, including William Hasbrouck, but ever restless, it was "On to Richmond!"[7]

When Maury reached the Virginia capital, "The absence in the streets of well-dressed gentlemen, the multitude of idle Negroes there, many of them more dandily rigged than the whites" stunned him. For a few days, he limped around the city, using the connections of his cousin Robert H. Maury, in reintroducing himself to bankers, industrialists, and merchants, and outlining his plans for Smith and the institute's survey. From there, Maury traveled to the cool mountain resorts to rub elbows with some of the most powerful men of the old Confederacy.[8]

In the summer of 1868, former Union General William S. Rosecrans was at the White Sulphur Springs resort, long a gathering place for the elite, to meet with Robert E. Lee, former Confederate Vice President Alexander Stephens, former Governor John Letcher, Virginia Central Railroad President Edward Fontaine, Joseph R. Anderson of the Tredegar Iron Works, Maury, and other Southern leaders. Rosecrans, then a Democratic Party operative, and the others

The Tredegar Iron Works, just above the James River and Kanawha Canal, proved to be the arsenal of the Confederacy, supplying war needs to its Army and Navy. Photograph by author.

strained to bring the militarily occupied South back into the Union as civilian-run states out of the hands of Radical Republicans and freed slaves.[9]

From those discussions came the "White Sulphur Springs Manifesto," with its moderately toned opening. "The important fact that the two races are, under existing circumstances, necessary to each other is gradually becoming apparent to both." Men like Lee, Maury, P. G. T. Beauregard, Letcher, Anderson, Fontaine, and Stephens urged Southerners to treat the freed slaves with kindness, an out-of-date repeat of former President James Madison's warnings in the 1830s.

These men feared for their future. The "Loyal Leagues," promoting solidarity among former slaves, worked hand-in-glove with Virginia's Republicans at the 1867 constitutional convention to cage former Confederate leaders. Only intervention by General John Schofield, Virginia's military governor, spared them from permanent disenfranchisement.[10]

The Southerners wrote, "Above all, they would appeal to their countrymen for the re-establishment in the Southern states of that which has justly been regarded as the birth-right of every American—the right of self-government."

If they were almost on their knees, their backs were stiff. Virginia's former white political leaders wanted power back in their hands. "The Negroes have neither the intelligence nor the qualifications which are necessary to make the safe disposition of political power." They rejected the Thirteenth, Fourteenth, and Fifteenth amendments, the very price of readmission. To Radical Republicans, the manifesto brought to mind the slaveholder's prewar congressional demands of "Do it on our terms or else."[11]

While the others signed willingly, Maury did not, claiming he wanted "to avoid the possibility of having his name appear in northern newspapers."[12]

As reasonable as the manifesto sounded to white Southerners and many Democrats, neither the Radical Republicans in Congress nor the more temperate and soon-to-be president, Ulysses S. Grant, wanted to pursue its agenda.[13]

The war had been fought too long to forgive and forget so quickly.[14]

To Smith and Maury, the manifesto was a commitment by men of stature to look beyond the ruins of home, farms, churches, and courthouses to create a new dominion. For all its faults, it became grist for their salesmen's mill.[15]

As the family traveled from the springs through Goshen Pass, Maury fell in love with its rough-hewn natural beauty. The moss-covered rocky gorge, with its swift-flowing stream and glistening rhododendron, laurel, and ferns became for him a special place of peace as he moved into the final chapter of his life.

The family went to a "cheap, cool, pleasant watering place in the mountains not far from Lexington" while their war-damaged quarters at VMI were rebuilt. At the Rockbridge Baths Inn, eleven miles from town, he and Smith developed a draft survey to be sent out quickly.[16]

At 5 p.m., on September 10, in front of Robert E. Lee, president of neighboring Washington College; Letcher, president of VMI's Board of Visitors; other board members; citizens of Lexington; and the corps of cadets, Smith officially welcomed Maury. To the gathering, Maury explained, "The main object of this survey is to make known the natural resources of Virginia; to invite enterprise; to stimulate industry; encourage commerce; promote immigration and advance the material prosperity of the people."[17]

These were broad goals, but unlike the Southern Commercial Convention movement with big ideas and little meaningful work, Maury needed data as he had from "public cruisers and merchantmen." This time he would produce investors' guides for a phoenix rising. Over the coming weeks, Maury refined the questions. In Tidewater, for example, he wanted details about fish and waterfowl, how much land a family could cultivate and gather on a truck farm, etc.[18]

As before, Maury had Marin Jansen's assistance, prodding the Dutch to start a steamer line to Norfolk. He wrote Maury: "My task is more difficult to get the money out of the pockets of people that don't know anything more about Virginia than your people know about Holland.... Slow but sure is our motto."[19]

Maury was so taken by the beauty of Goshen Pass that he asked that his remains be taken through it before final burial in Richmond's Hollywood Cemetery (courtesy Library of Virginia).

To Maury, speed was of the essence: First, to ward off other institutions, like Washington College, from undertaking such a study, and second, to give battle-weary Virginia a leg up over other Southern states. He had little choice. For the survey, he only had his $2,000 salary, passes from the state's railroads, and the able John Mercer Brooke, also at VMI, as an aide.[20]

The Maury family had to remain in an inn for a time after returning from Great Britain until their quarters, shown here, could be repaired (courtesy Virginia Military Institute Archives).

In a temporary office in Richmond, Maury pored over Pennsylvania's coal and oil report and Ohio's agricultural statistics. He sent Brooke to Memphis with circulars explaining Virginia's survey and had Smith promise governors in the Mississippi Valley copies of the preliminary report as soon as they were ready.[21]

In an October address at Staunton, Maury stressed the theme that internal improvements were imperative if Virginia were to prosper again. It was Maury's gospel of commercial expansion, not industrialization.[22]

Smith and Maury knew that if Washington College proceeded, VMI could lose more than control of the "state survey." They wanted the institute to be named Virginia's land grant college. Before the war, Southern congressmen and senators fought tooth and nail to defeat the land grant college and Western homestead legislation. When they failed in Congress to block the bills' passage, President James Buchanan vetoed both.

But with only a handful of Southern Unionists remaining, Congress passed both bills in 1862. In a concession to wartime reality, the bill's sponsor, Senator Justin Morrill of Vermont, amended the land grant college bill to include teaching military science. Lincoln signed them.[23]

Then five years later to the legislature, Smith and Maury pointed to VMI's history in engineering and military science as reasons to select it as the land grant college. But the General Assembly remained divided over too many issues to choose one institution, so let the decision slip.[24]

In November, Maury rallied railroad men who had rechristened the Virginia Central the Chesapeake and Ohio Railroad, and businessmen in Norfolk, Petersburg, Richmond, and West Point to complete the physical survey. He demanded the printers hurry to preempt any rival. "Our hands are now fully to the plough and we must not draw back, but truthfully and hopefully go forward. I am only anticipating 'breakers ahead' by providing 'ways and means' by 'hook and by crook' and I throw out the suggestion for you to cogitate on," Maury wrote Smith.[25]

By late December the preliminary report was in the mail. "The Railway and Canal men have been watching the press and literally devouring the sheets as fast as they were printed," he told his son-in-law. Soon enough, Midwestern and Southern governors, bankers in Cincinnati, and the Tennessee River Improvement Committee took their turns hailing the work. But the far more important capital expected from Northern and Western bankers and investors was slow in coming. The results in that regard were as dismal as the Rev. Francis Tremlett's postwar appeals to Northern Episcopalians to support the University of the South.[26]

That wasn't all that frustrated Maury.

Maury knew that some data came when slave labor was used, facts that troubled potential investors and observant editors. The *Southern Review* in its critique noted that slavery "produced the *satisfied* state and not the entrepreneurial society" that Virginia needed now. In addition, cooperation in gathering the information was less than expected. Shades of "New Virginia" foot-dragging also were appearing in the Old Dominion.[27]

"Farmers don't respond. I am proposing to try them on another tack and have asked Shields to print me 500 copies of the new appeal which I will send with 'Preliminary' No. 1 to picked men in each of our 99 counties. If anything will bring us immigration, it is our climate and productions and the noising of them abroad and for this, nibbling won't do."

If this didn't work, Maury wanted to hire agents. "We must go at them 'hammer and tongs' and keep at them with might and main as we have commenced else we shall labor in vain."[28]

The problem was the lack of seed money for projects large and small. In Norfolk, for example, the city government wrangled over how best to spend its scant resources: on education, rebuilding businesses, or expanding the port. All competed for pieces of a very small pie. The reality was the state's seven hundred thousand whites and five hundred thousand blacks were staggering under a half a billion dollars of war debt.[29]

Maury and Smith wanted the survey to appear annually like the *Wind and Current Charts* and *Sailing Directions*, but they needed underwriting. The state's railroads, with the most at stake in trying to attract capital, were to pay for the second report.[30]

The railroads themselves were in financial turmoil. Inside the boardroom of the state's largest line one of the highest business dramas in postwar Virginia unfolded. To Maury's cousin Robert H. Maury, completing the Chesapeake and Ohio Railroad from Covington, Virginia, to a terminus on the river was critical to building a strong competitor to the Baltimore and Ohio.

For decades, the legislature split over building a railroad to cross the mountains or completing the James River and Kanawha Canal to connect Virginia harbors with the Ohio River valley. When the Civil War began, the canal reached the Allegheny foothills and the separate, competing railroads only a little further. "Internal improvements" were political footballs that found transportation interests linking with sectional interests inside the state's borders to undercut each other.

To Robert Maury, the arguments for the canal were as circular as an old hoop, but the railroads, by constantly warring against each other and the canal company, could never grow. Consolidation was needed, and with it, new leadership. By late 1868, Robert Maury plotted to oust Fontaine from the presidency of the Virginia Central line.[31]

Behind the scenes, Robert Maury tried but failed to lure Lee from Washington College to head the new line. That did not stop Maury on his long walk through the shadows. For a successful coup, Maury needed to win the directors who voted the government's share of the road's stock, Fontaine's base of power.[32]

One minute, Fontaine was in charge of a likely eastern link in the transcontinental line, and the next, he was dumped in the name of progress.[33]

The usurpers moved to solidify their control. Maury enticed New York bond salesmen to put on the market $10 million in the railroad's securities, and installed a new board, with Matthew Fontaine Maury a member. The new board soon approved selling the bonds and mortgaging the rolling stock and tracks from Richmond to Clifton Forge to bring in more money.[34]

Robert Maury proved that in tightened financial times there were ways to raise capital, but at a dear price. Seeing his chance after all these moves, Collis P. Huntington with his "Big Four" stake in the Central Pacific railroad and his money-hunting history in New York and Washington, leapt into the boardroom. By fall 1869, Huntington was president, and shortly after he took the railroad and the port of Norfolk out of Virginia's and Virginians' hands.[35]

This loss of control over their own affairs—from railroads to the port of Norfolk to the "French Enterprise" on the canal—troubled many Virginians, including Maury, who resigned his seat on the new road's board. Yet the economic engine for recovery demanded that Virginia bring in outside people and outside capital. That was Maury's charge as the head of the physical survey. For every Huntington and James Fisk with vision, capital, and enthusiasm, there were governments like Norfolk's hamstrung over race and control of their meager treasure. A sarcastic Maury wrote Tremlett, "Let's make the Pope infallible and then get him ... to rain dollars on Virginia for 24 hours."[36]

Then contradictory advice on how to resurrect Virginia's fortunes came from, of all people, Jansen. "Drive the blacks out of the state if you can, or put them altogether in a corner where they may rule just as they please but make a clear sweep of them as soon as possible."[37]

Maury must have understood that, with military occupation and the Freedmen's Bureau in place, it was impossible to remove the blacks, as whites had removed the Indians east of the Mississippi. Nevertheless, in the second preliminary report, he wrote that many blacks were leaving the state for "the sunny climes of the Gulf." He added the time was near when "Virginia will be relieved of this thriftless class." Invest now![38]

Maury's frustrations were temporarily put aside on July 2, when, at the cadets' invitation, he delivered their commencement address. That day in Lexington, Maury, a nineteenth-century Nehemiah, electrified the cadets with a hymn to the myth of the noble fight. Slavery was never mentioned.

> Are you not heirs of the Lost Cause, with its noble examples and Christian memories? Its traditions make us very proud. Are you not sons of the Sunny South? Do you not now, in the day of your youth, tread the soil of Virginia, breathe her atmosphere and drink at the fountains from which the bravest of men and noblest of women have drawn inspiration? In them you have the most heroic fortitude and of the gentlest graces that have ever arrayed themselves on the side of right. They are trumpet-tongued. Their silent teachings are far more effective, with their mute eloquence, than my poor powers of speech can make them. Treasure them up. They are a special legacy—heirlooms of inestimable value in the eyes of every true man among us![39]

When students begged for copies of the speech, the institute published it as a pamphlet. He was back in demand. Other institutions now came hunting for him. Leading the way was the University of Alabama. Maury liked what he heard from Tuscaloosa, but he was not yet ready to move. VMI was safe. As he had with Maximilian before and during the war, he did not bolt the door closed to future offers.[40]

Although the present state of Virginia did not offer much succor, it was not as grim as his fortunes four years earlier. Maury, for now, stayed at VMI, where he took up its cause. Bigger, better, more was the order of the day. The men who headed institutions of higher education—like Smith and Maury—thought the same way. During the last half of 1869, Maury and Smith worked with the Educational Association of Virginia again to push the legislature to establish a polytechnic school at VMI.[41]

In a December 1869 speech, Maury said, "No change in our system of education can answer the demands of this necessity short of a Polytechnic School, where all the life-sciences are taught in the most complete manner, and to which all who will, in any Southern state, may resort free of charge, and in which each may, according to his fancy, drink at this or that fountain, and learn all that is known, including the most recent discoveries covering the laws of nature and the properties of matter."[42]

"The College" in Williamsburg and Mr. Jefferson's university in Charlottesville had their proponents in the legislature. Private colleges also made their cases in the corridors of the state Capitol. So the bull rush for a decision that Smith and Maury started failed. The reasons were the tired ones of sectional interests, economic priorities, and race. The legislature was in stalemate.

As another winter arrived between the Virginia mountains, Maury's strength ebbed like the daylight. Old leg injuries plagued him, and he used crutches to hobble around his quarters. His fingers were swollen, and his handwriting too shaky to be legible.[43]

Demands on Maury did not end as the snows fell. Jansen urged him to work with the state government to get its credit restored: "Without credit, you can't do anything and few wealthy immigrants will trust their money to such a state."[44]

When the state finally ratified the Thirteenth, Fourteenth, and Fifteenth Amendments in 1870, Virginia's formal military occupation ended. But Maury had little cause for joy. He stood beside Lee's casket in the tiny Washington College Chapel that October. In the same month, Maury glumly reported on the survey that "I am pained to say that instead of securing reports from each of the 99 counties left to the state, I had returns from only about 30."

Not even the offer of the presidency of St. John's College in Annapolis brightened Maury's spirits. He requested a leave to visit his sister Betsy in Mississippi and nephew Dabney in New Orleans, and friends like General Joseph E. Johnston in Savannah. For Maury, it was a chance to escape the accompanying illnesses of the changing seasons.[45]

Without new money the survey remained on hold when Maury returned with the warmer weather to Lexington. To fill his time, he lectured on the physical sciences and contributed his thoughts to the cadets' publication. The lectures and writings were mere glimmerings of Maury's earlier life when he spoke before prestigious scientific gatherings and his articles appeared in the day's leading periodicals. His high hopes for Virginia and his children's future were dimmed.[46]

The University of Alabama's board was back with a sweeter offer than a $5,000 salary to become its president. The regents offered Maury the power to hire faculty, establish the curriculum, provide him with a home, and not require him to teach. This time, he accepted.[47]

Tuscaloosa seemed to offer the opportunity to build the kind of institution he long espoused, the one he might have built at Sewanee and one that drew on the lessons of VMI. Alabama then was a shell of a university. The faculty was largely unqualified; there were few students; and the grounds and buildings were as scarred as a Confederate veteran. What Maury didn't see was a portent of problems to come. He believed he could move the legislature to rubber stamp his plans for its university. Hadn't he done this at the observatory and in the voyages of exploration? Hadn't he done this with the Virginia secession convention on the state's defenses and Confederate Congress with the "Maury gunboat" plan? He ignored his more recent experience with Virginia's legislature.[48]

In his inaugural address on August 23 at Alabama, Maury sounded optimistic: "The aim is to build up and improve this institution until it attains to the proportions of a real university, complete in all its appointments, and to crown it with a polytechnic school of a high order in the halls, galleries, museums, laboratories and workshops, to which Southern youth, of whatever state, may come and without fail qualify themselves for any one of the mechanical arts or industrial callings."[49]

To do this, Maury wanted an endowment of at least $10,000 to open the school in early 1872 with one hundred students. By then, he expected to have hired good faculty, bought the proper equipment, and repaired its buildings. Through the summer of 1871, Maury, settling affairs in Lexington and seeking advice from Smith, exchanged letters with the regents on the "launching fund," as he called the endowment. With each exchange, Maury's patience grew shorter when promises were not backed with cash. He wrote: "I wish I had your happy knack of getting over difficulties. It seems that you have had to pooh, pooh them and they go." The legislature was not moved.[50]

By late August, Maury was looking for a dignified way out. Tuscaloosa, like Sewanee, had turned into another Flying Dutchman. "Being ignorant of the currents and counter currents and the political undertow which may be besetting you, I feel no small degree of embarrassment in finding my way harmlessly out of an awkward position into which I have been so innocently brought." The next month, he submitted his resignation, asking it be backdated to July 1.[51]

Maury had little choice but to return to VMI, even if his return was not hat in hand. Soon he was back ritually lobbying the Virginia legislature on designating VMI as the land grant institution.

"There are but two institutions of learning in the state in which the legislature has the power to prescribe either the subjects to be taught or the manner of teaching them. These are the University and her Military Institute and therefore it is meet and proper that she should endow one or both of them with that fund."[52]

Words to little avail.

At last tired of bickering among the twenty-four colleges in the state, the legislature established the Virginia Agricultural and Mechanical College on the grounds of the Preston and Olin Institute at Blacksburg, far up the valley and hundreds of miles from the capital, Williamsburg, Lexington, and Charlottesville. Maury and Smith had lost out to a foundering school with scant academic reputation and no history of success in any study. It was a sobering blow.[53]

In 1871, Maury gravitated once more to the scientific project dearest to his heart, building a national weather reporting system. *The Physical Survey of Virginia* again showed how vital this information was. In such an effort, he relighted the fires of his crusade to have farmers do on the land what mariners did on the sea in recording the weather. He also rekindled the ancient antagonisms with Joseph Henry, who was still in charge of the Smithsonian.

As infirm as he was, Maury took to the road in late spring 1871, speaking at agricultural fairs as close as Rockbridge County, the county that surrounds Lexington, and as far away as Shelby County, Tennessee, and St. Louis, Missouri. He wrote his daughter Nannie, "Tell Corbin I am going to carry that plan: i.e., do my best and to *roll* that ball [of a national weather service] over Henry & the rest of them. But the rascals they'll catch it up as soon as they see it rolling along finely and say it was theirs."[54]

In a smaller way, it was like those days before the war when Maury had orchestrated a campaign. Support was guaranteed in the South, and was drawing approval from the North as well.[55] The influential *Prairie Farmer* editorialized:

> Commodore Maury proposes to make himself much more useful to the world (if the world will let him) than he has been during the past ten years. He proposes to-wit, to organize an international system of crop reporting in connection with the Weather Signal Service, already in operation in this country. The reports the world has been able thus far to obtain have, he shows, been of the most desultory and imperfect character, besides being usually made up in the interest of the buyers.[56]

Support, too, poured in from abroad. The poet-astronomer Quetelet, who had chaired the maritime conference in Belgium, invited Maury to speak at the one-hundredth anniversary of the Royal Academy of Science, Letters, and Fine Arts in Brussels. The International Congress of Geographical, Cosmographical, and Commercial Sciences endorsed Maury's proposal at its meeting in St. Petersburg.[57]

If Maury believed domestic and international support was enough to carry the day in Washington, he was wrong. Instead of the cooperation of Secretary of State Hamilton Fish in contacting foreign governments, as Daniel Webster had provided two decades before, Maury found his proposal bounced around Washington offices like a child's ball. Not even the commissioner of agriculture endorsed it.[58]

A frustrated Maury lashed out. Before the National Agricultural Association meeting in St. Louis, he denounced the scientifics as servants of the greedy: "To lift you up from under the heels of the speculator and to place merchants, producers and consumer side by side, all upon the same level, and on the same platform in this knowledge as to supply and demand is surely a noble aim and a consummation devoutly to be wished."[59]

After that speech, Maury was so enfeebled that he broke off the fight—for then. During the spring, he submitted his resignation to Smith, but the superintendent and the board of visitors, led by Letcher, refused it. It was a question of how much more time did he have.[60]

As he tried to recoup his vigor, Maury was intrigued by a newspaperman's offer to speak to the farmers of Norfolk County, Massachusetts. He made a "to do" list of people and places he needed to visit. He also knew he should see his publisher in New York about revising the geographies, and there was another invitation to speak in St. Louis in October 1872. Last, he was wanted for an address in Norfolk. As he saw it, with one long extended trip he could tie up many loose ends in his life. And from it, he might realize the dream of launching the national weather service. *Cui bono? Cur non?*[61]

Speaking in Massachusetts, he praised John Quincy Adams for elevating American science, while omitting how for three years as a member of the Confederate Secret Service he had bedeviled Adams's son. His stay in New York was debilitating, and his daughter Eliza, traveling with Maury, wanted him to return home. He stubbornly pressed on.[62]

The journey by train to St. Louis was the first tolling of the death knell. He was barely able to make himself heard when he addressed the St. Louis agricultural fair. On October 10, 1872, he wrote, "I am too poorly to undertake the long journey east and propose going tomorrow to Jefferson City to General James Minor's to recuperate." This was the second tolling of the death knell.[63]

If only he could get to Norfolk, obsessed Maury until he and Eliza could go no further than Fredericksburg. At sixty-six, he could give no more. He staggered back to the hillside campus of the Virginia Military Institute.

Ann Herndon Maury, photographed in 1877, often found herself separated for months and years from her husband before and after the Civil War (Valentine Richmond History Center).

As winter crept over the Blue Ridge, Matthew Fontaine Maury told his beloved wife, Ann Herndon Maury: "My dear, I am come home to die."[64]

Yes, he had come home to die.

So much had passed between them in thirty-eight years of marriage: the nagging worries after he was crippled in a stage coach accident, the raging anger over being forcibly pushed out of the Navy, the heart-stopping fears as the Union Army swept through the family's Virginia refuge, the anguish over the grave wounds suffered by one son at Seven Pines and Petersburg, and the soul-wrenching loss of another at Vicksburg, followed by years of exile.

Now bedridden in his house on VMI's parade ground, Maury's once-sparkling blue eyes were clouded with sickness and pain. Depression came upon him in waves. His daughter Mary wrote, "He likes his room as dark as he can get it, only allowing the shutters to be opened early in the morning or at night when the stars are out."[65]

Corbin, his son-in-law, brought Maury's daughter Nannie and their family to Lexington as the end neared. Richard, the son so savagely wounded in the war, came down from West Virginia, and Betty and her children traveled up from Richmond. They joined the four children still at home.

The dying man gave his family one last command. Before burial in Richmond, he wanted his body to be carried through lovely Goshen Pass, near Lexington, and "you must pluck the rhododendrons and the mountain ivy and lay them upon me."[66]

Ann Herndon Maury lay down in the bed with him.

"When I am dead, lay me out in the library."[67]

She pointed directly across the frozen fastness of the parade ground to a gray turreted building on a small bluff overlooking the quiet college town. "Over there dear?"

"Yes."

Psalm 130 came often to his lips:

> Out of the depths I cry to you, O Lord;
> Lord, hear my voice![68]

Maury told Mary a few days before his death, "If that monster who comes to all were to come in that door, I would not fear him."

"Ah not a monster, Papa," she said, "But an angel to take you to your rest."

Maury turned in his deathbed to a picture of his son John, forever missing in action, and nodded to it. "And to him, and to John," his brother who had died at sea.[69]

On Thursday, January 30, the grandson of one of the colonial era's most important educators taught all his children the prayer he had said every day since his crippling accident in Ohio:

> Lord God, thou redeemer of the world and ransomer of my soul, have mercy upon me, pardon my sins and teach me the errors of my ways; give me a new heart and a right mind. Teach me and all mine to do thy will, and in all things to keep thy law. Teach me also to ask those things necessary for eternal life. Lord, pardon me for all my sins, for thine is the kingdom and the power and the glory, for ever and ever. Amen.

He then ordered his son-in-law: "Put this in Betty's mouth and in Nanny's mouth and in Will's mouth and let them say, 'Glory be to God for his mercies.'"[70]

The night before he died, Maury said for all his family to hear, "The peace of God which passeth all understanding be with you all—all!"[71]

February 1, 1873, was a Saturday. Matthew Fontaine Maury, a man who exulted in studying the heavens and plotting the stars, did not see another sunset or sunrise.

Maury asked Dick, his oldest son, "Are my feet growing cold? Do I drag my anchors?" The thirty-four-year-old Confederate veteran answered, "They are firm and secure." As if from the deck of a warship, the commander said, "All's well." He asked his wife and daughters to leave. Only young Diana disobeyed, but stayed out of sight. She saw her father "lift his hands toward Heaven like a little child who wants to be taken up."[72]

He died at 12:40 p.m.

On learning of the death, Henry wrote: "Maury a man of talent but vain, boastful, vindictive with but little scientific capacity ... and still suggestive and capable of doing work of value as the basis of other men's investigations."[73]

The *New York Herald* was kinder:

> As the founder and most successful prosecutor of the benign system of oceanic researches which has illuminated the perilous paths of the mariner and taught commerce how to make the winds and currents of the sea do its bidding, his labors will long be gratefully remembered. As a marked type of an American scientist his career deserves careful study.[74]

From February 3 to February 5, 1873, an honor guard of cadets stood watch over Matthew Fontaine Maury's mortal remains. Already, Superintendent Smith issued orders honoring Maury and

JOHN TYLER
PRESIDENT
OF THE
UNITED STATES
1841 1845
BORN
IN CHARLES CITY COUNTY VA
MARCH 29 1790
DIED
IN THE CITY OF RICHMOND
JANUARY 18 1862

Former president John Tyler, as a member of the Confederate Congress, provided Maury staunch support in his plans to defend Virginia's waterways with mines and gunboats. Tyler's support kept President Jefferson Davis and Navy Secretary Stephen Mallory at bay. Maury is buried close to Tyler, his strongest political ally. Photograph by author.

Maury is buried near James Monroe (within the wrought iron enclosure), who was president when Maury entered the Navy, and John Tyler, Maury's champion while president and later a member of the Confederate Congress (courtesy Library of Virginia).

calling for reflection. Then, the solemn words of the English church in marking a life's final chapter were read.[75]

In the spring, his body was removed from its temporary burial site in Lexington; and as he requested, taken through Goshen Pass and on to Richmond.

The surge of the James over its falls resonates through the capital's Hollywood Cemetery. There, the scientist-warrior is at rest, in the immediate company of two Virginia presidents: John Tyler, who did so much for Maury's career in and out of the service of two navies, and James Monroe, who was in office when Maury received his midshipman's warrant.

Down a small hill from Maury's grave, overlooking the river, is the tomb of Jefferson Davis and his second wife, Varina. Now they are only names with which Maury's life was so intimately intertwined.

And in a glade near the cemetery's entrance are the graves of hundreds of Confederate soldiers, who preceded them all in death. Today and then, the ruins of an old war cannot be seen in the glade or even from the hills overlooking the falls.

All are finally at peace there.

Chapter Notes

Abbreviations: AOR, Appointments, Orders, and Resignations; **LC**, Library of Congress; **MFM**, Matthew Fontaine Maury; **MP**, Maury Papers; **MS**, Manuscript Collection; **NAN**, National Archives Navy; **NOLR**, National (later Navy) Observatory Letters Received; **NOLS**, National (later Navy) Observatory Letters Sent; **NR**, Naval Records; **RG**, Record Group

Prologue

1. Rutson Maury to Marin H. Jansen, Mar. 25, 1873, Maury Papers (hereafter cited as MP), vol. 44, Library of Congress (hereafter cited as LC). Address reported in *St. Louis Democrat*, Oct. 10, 1872; manuscript in MP, vol. 51, fols. 10143–72, LC.

2. Manuscript in MP, vol. 51, fols. 10143–72, LC.

3. As Frances Leigh Williams noted in her biography of Maury, *Matthew Fontaine Maury: Scientist of the Sea* (hereafter cited as Williams, *Maury Scientist;* New Brunswick: Rutgers University Press, 1963), the division of science into the elites and the popularizers is a common thread running through the correspondence of Joseph Henry, maintained in the Smithsonian Institution Archives and the Bache Papers in the Manuscript Collection (hereafter cited as MS), LC, pp. 173–75. A. D. Bache letter to Joseph Henry, Dec. 4, 1846, quoted in Merle Middleton Odgers, *Alexander Dallas Bache: Scientist and Educator, 1806–1867* (hereafter cited as Odgers, *Bache;* Philadelphia: University of Pennsylvania Press, 1947), 165. It is the premise of Patricia Jahns's book, *Matthew Fontaine Maury and Joseph Henry: Scientists of the Civil War* (New York: Hastings House, 1961). Other interesting documents on this split exist in the Samuel F. DuPont Papers, both in the MS Collection, LC, and the Hagley Museum and Library in Wilmington, Del.

4. Williams, *Maury Scientist*, 173–75.

5. Bache to Henry, Nov. 28, 1850, Smithsonian Institution Archives.

6. Kenneth J. Hagan, *This People's Navy: The Making of American Sea Power* (hereafter cited as Hagan, *People's*; New York: Free Press, 1991), 115, 158; Stephen Howarth, *To Shining Sea: A History of the United States Navy, 1775–1991* (New York: Random House, 1991), 148.

7. *Man on the Hill* came to be the term many of his critics used to describe Maury. They were referring to the observatory's location on a bluff above the Potomac. Correspondence between Bache and Henry, both in Smithsonian Institution Archives and LC, use the phrase. Correspondence of S. F. DuPont contains the same phrase.

8. Early examples include these: Jefferson Davis, who served as a board member for the Smithsonian Institution, was an intimate of Henry and Bache, who used the Mississippian's influence to protect the Coast Survey, notably documented in Davis to A. D. Bache, Oct. 27 and 28, 1858, Bache Papers, vol. 10, MS, LC; Cong. Globe, 34th Cong., 1st Sess. 405 (1856) (Mallory remarks). Benjamin was a New Orleans businessman keenly interested in exploiting the Tehautepec route to connect Atlantic and Pacific traffic to the California gold fields.

9. Armistead B. Gordon, *Virginia Portraits* (Staunton, Va.: McClure, 1924), 38.

10. Cong. Globe, 34th Cong., 1st Sess. appendix, 12 (Apr. 28 and 29, 1856) and 244, 245, 248 (Mar. 18, 1856) (speech of Sen. John Bell of Tennessee on the Naval Retiring Board), published as a monograph and found at the Library of Virginia, Richmond.

11. Ps. 107:23–24 (Revised Standard Edition).

Chapter 1

1. Virginia County Records, Deed Book P, Spotsylvania County, 1797–1802, deed of sale, Aug. 31, 1797, pp. 6–8, microfilm 01000, reel 8, Library of Virginia; Lease, Deed Book P, Spotsylvania County, 1797–1802, with plat, pp. 9–11, microfilm 01000, reel 8, Library of Virginia. Maury's home is on the edge of the Virginia Wilderness, within a few miles of a tavern once owned by the Chancellor Family. During the Civil War Battle of Chancellorsville, J. E. B. Stuart used the abandoned homestead as his headquarters.

2. Francis Leigh Williams, *Matthew Fontaine Maury: Scientist of the Sea* (hereafter cited as Williams, *Maury Scientist*), 8; Hildegarde Hawthorne, *Matthew Fontaine Maury: Trail Maker of the Seas* (hereafter cited as Hawthorne, *Trail;* New York: Longmans Green, 1943), 13; Jaquelin Ambler Caskie, *Life and Letters of Matthew Fontaine Maury* (hereafter cited as Caskie, *Life*; Richmond: Richmond, 1928), 15; John Hastings Gwathmey, *Twelve Virginia Counties: Where the Western Migration Began* (hereafter cited as Gwathmey, *Twelve Counties;* Richmond: Genealogical, 1937), 210, 211, 273, 345; *Virginia Magazine of History and Biography* (hereafter cited as *Va. Mag.*) 27 (1919): 375–76.

3. Ann Maury, *Memoirs of a Huguenot Family, Translated and Compiled from the Original Autobiography of the Rev. James Fontaine and Other Family Manuscripts, Comprising an Original Journal of Travels in Virginia, New York, etc., in 1715 and 1716* (hereafter cited as Maury, *Memoirs;* New York: George P. Putnam, 1853; 2nd ed., 1872). "Pure reformed" is on page 14, second edition.

4. James Fontaine, *A Tale of the Huguenots; or, Memoirs of a French Refugee Family*, trans. and comp. Ann Maury (New York: John S. Taylor, 1838); reprinted in a collection of Maury material as *Memoirs of a Huguenot Family* (hereafter cited as Fontaine, *Tale;* Baltimore: Genealogical, 1973), 142–229.

5. Fontaine, *Tale*, 271–87; Virginius Dabney, *Virginia: The New Dominion* (hereafter cited as Dabney, *Virginia;* Garden City, N.Y.: Doubleday, 1971), 73–77; Carl Bridenbaugh, *Seat of Empire: The Political Role of Eighteenth Century Williamsburg* (hereafter cited as Bridenbaugh, *Seat;* Williamsburg, Va.: Colonial Williamsburg Foundation, 1963), 27.

6. John Hammond Moore, *Albemarle: Jefferson's County, 1727–1976* (Charlottesville: University Press of Virginia for the Albemarle County Historical Society, 1976), 8; David Hackett Fischer and James C. Kelly, *Bound Away: Virginia and the Western Movement* (hereafter cited as Fischer and Kelly, *Bound;* Charlottesville: University Press of Virginia, 2000), 98–103; R. A. Broad, *The Official Letters of Alexander Spotswood, Lieutenant Governor of the Colony of Virginia, 1710–1722* (Richmond: Virginia Historical Society, 1932), 1:167; "Governor's Palace," Colonial Williamsburg Foundation, accessed Aug. 21, 2013, http://www.history.org/almanack/places/hb/hbpal.cfm; Henry Mayer, *A Son of Thunder: Patrick Henry and the American Revolution* (hereafter cited as Mayer, *Son*; New York: Grove, 1991), 19–21.

7. Fontaine, *Tale*, 271–87; Fischer and Kelly, *Bound*, 98–103; Edwin Wiley and Irving F. Rine, eds., "Progress of Virginia, Maryland, and the Carolinas, 1690–1748" (hereafter cited as Wiley and Rine, "Progress"), vol. 2, pt. 1, chap. 19 in *Lecture on the Growth and Development of the United States* (New York: American Educational Alliance, 1916), 26–27.

8. Wiley and Rine, "Progress," 26–27.

9. Fontaine, *Tale*, 271–87; Dabney, *Virginia*, 79; Fischer and Kelly, *Bound*, 98–103.

10. D. W. Meinig, *The Shaping of America: Atlantic America, 1492–1800* (New Haven: Yale University Press, 1983), 1:154; letters of the Rev. James Maury quoted in Fontaine, *Tale*, and specifically on p. 379; Clifford Dowdey, *The Virginia Dynasties* (hereafter cited as Dowdey, *Dynasties;* New York: Little, Brown, 1969), 309.

11. Williams, *Maury Scientist*, 5–6; Fairfax Harrison, *Landmarks of Old Prince William*, 2 vols. (Richmond: privately printed, 1924), 1:133, 166, 233.

12. Bishop William Meade, *Old Churches, Ministers, and Families of Virginia* (Philadelphia: J. B. Lippincott, 1861), 1:315; Genealogical Account, *Va. Mag.* 11 (1901): 289–304; Richard L. Maury, *The Huguenots in Virginia* (Richmond: Huguenot Society of America, n.d.), 113.

13. *Va. Mag.* 27 (1919): 376–77; *Va. Mag.* 26 (1918): 325. Both genealogical accounts.

14. Letters of the Rev. James Maury as quoted in Fontaine, *Tale*, 379; Dowdey, *Dynasties*, 309; Thomas Jefferson Randolph, ed., *Memoir, Correspondence, and Miscellanies from the Papers of Thomas Jefferson* (Charlottesville, Va.: F. Carr, 1829), 1:1.

15. James Maury to Robert Jackson, July 17, 1762, Albemarle County (Va.) Historical Society Records; Dumas Malone, *Jefferson: The Virginian* (hereafter cited as Malone, *Jefferson;* Boston: Little, Brown, 1948), 42–45; Maury, *Memoirs*, 386–88.

16. "Loyal Company Grant, July 12, 1749," *Exploring the West from Monticello: A Perspective in Maps from Columbus to Lewis and Clark;* An Exhibition of Maps and Navigational Instruments on View in the Tracy W. McGregor Room, Alderman Library, University of Virginia, July 10 to Sept. 26, 1995, last modified Dec. 16, 2009, http://www2.lib.virginia.edu/exhibits/lewis_clark/exploring/ch3-16.html.

17. William Goetzmann, *New Lands, New Men: America and the Second Great Age of Dis-*

covery (hereafter cited as Goetzmann, *New Men;* New York: Viking Penguin, 1987), 144; Fischer and Kelly, *Bound,* 152–53.

18. *Encyclopedia Virginia,* Virginia Foundation for the Humanities, s.v. "John Camm," last modified Aug. 12, 2013, http://www.encyclopedia virginia.org/Camm_John_bap_1717-1779; Mayer, *Son,* 59–61.

19. William Wirt, *Sketches of the Life and Character of Patrick Henry* (hereafter cited as Wirt, *Sketches;* Philadelphia: James Webster, 1817), 24; Mayer, *Son,* 26–31, 34, 35, 62–66; Arthur Scott Pearson, "The Constitutional Aspects of the Parson's Cause," *Political Science Quarterly* (New York) 31 (1916): 558–77; Dabney, *Virginia,* 120–21; William Wirt Henry, ed., *Patrick Henry: Life, Correspondence, and Speeches* (New York: Scribner's, 1891), 38, 41; Genealogical Account, *Va. Mag.* 27 (1919): 375–76; Malone, *Jefferson,* 44n19.

20. John B. Minor, *The Minor Family* (hereafter cited as Minor, *Family;* Lynchburg, Va.: privately printed, 1923); Williams, *Maury Scientist,* 9; Hawthorne, *Trail,* 13; Caskie, *Life,* 15; William W. Hening, ed., *The Statutes at Large: Being a Collection of All the Laws of Virginia from the First Session of the Legislature in the Year 1819* (Vols. 1–2, New York: R., W., and G. Barlow, 1825; Vol. 3, Richmond: Samuel Shepherd, 1823), 2:308–9, 3:479.

21. Minor, *Family;* Williams, Hawthorne, and Caskie, as cited in note 20 above.

22. Gwathmey, *Twelve Counties,* 210–11, 273, 345; Williams, *Maury Scientist,* 8–10; Minor, *Family.*

23. Ann Maury of New York to Mary H. Maury, Aug. 8, 1873, MP, vol. 44, LC.

24. Lease Deed Book P, Spotsylvania County, 1797–1802, with plat, pp. 9–11, microfilm 01000, reel 8, Library of Virginia.

25. Spotsylvania County Records, Deed Book R, 1806–1809, deed of sale, Feb. 13, 1808, p. 411, microfilm 01000, reel 9, Library of Virginia; Williams, *Maury Scientist,* 12; Fischer and Kelly, *Bound,* 199.

26. Spotsylvania County Records, Deed Book R, 1806–1809, deed of sale, Aug. 1, 1808, pp. 399–400, microfilm 01000, reel 9, Library of Virginia.

27. Naval Records (hereafter cited as NR), Letters to Officers, Ships of War, 8:9, 242; National Archives, Navy Records Branch, National Archives naval (hereafter cited as NAN); NR, Acceptances G–N, 1804–1823, NAN.

28. Walter W. Faw, "Boyhood Home of MFM" (hereafter cited as Faw, "Boyhood"), Tennessee State Library and Archives, photocopy sent to author; Paul Leicester Ford, ed., *The Writings of Thomas Jefferson, 1816–1826* (New York: G. P. Putnam, 1899), 10:372; Meyer Jacobstein, *The South in the Building of the Nation* (Richmond: Southern Historical Publication Society, 1909), 5:163–64.

29. Fischer and Kelly, *Bound,* 199.

30. Spotsylvania County Deed Book S, microfilm, Library of Virginia, pp.159–61.

31. Otis K. Rice, *The Allegheny Frontier* (Lexington: University Press of Kentucky, 1970), 2–5; Edward Bull, *Sketch of Western Virginia* (London, 1837), Library of Virginia; letter to author from Ron Vineyard, master wheelwright, Colonial Williamsburg, Oct. 10, 1991; Diana Fontaine Maury Corbin, *A Life of Matthew Fontaine Maury, U.S.N. and C.S.N., Compiled by His Daughter* (hereafter cited as Corbin, *Maury;* London: Sampson, Low, Marston, Searles, and Rivington, 1888), 7; Norwood C. Middleton, *Salem: A Virginia Chronicle* (Salem, Va.: Salem Historical Society, 1986); François André Michaux, *Early Western Travels* (Cleveland: Arthur H. Clark, 1904), 3:261–62; Auguste Levasseur, *Lafayette in America in 1824 and 1825; or, A Journal of a Voyage to the U.S.,* trans. John D. Godman (hereafter cited as Levasseur, *Lafayette;* Philadelphia: Carey and Lea, 1829), 1–2:52, 55.

Chapter 2

1. Virginia Bowman, *Historic Williamson County* (hereafter cited as Bowman, *Williamson;* Franklin, Tenn.: Williamson County Historical Society, 1989), 1–2; Michaux, *Early Western Travels,* 94; Francis Leigh Williams, *Matthew Fontaine Maury: Scientist of the Sea* (hereafter cited as Williams, *Maury Scientist*), 18–19.

2. Diana Fontaine Maury Corbin, *A Life of Matthew Fontaine Maury, U.S.N. and C.S.N., Compiled by His Daughter* (hereafter cited as Corbin, *Maury*), 7–8.

3. Dabney H. Maury to Mary H. Maury, concerning his father, John M. Maury, Aug. 7, 1873, MP, vol. 44, LC; Corbin, *Maury,* 10–12; Williams, *Maury Scientist,* 22–25; Hildegarde Hawthorne, *Matthew Fontaine Maury: Trail Maker of the Seas* (hereafter cited as Hawthorne, *Trail*), 15–20; Jaquelin Ambler Caskie, *Life and Letters of Matthew Fontaine Maury,* 16–17; Christopher McKee, *A Gentlemanly and Honorable Profession: The Creation of the U.S. Naval Officer Corps, 1794–1815* (hereafter cited as McKee, *Honorable;* Annapolis: Naval Institute, 1991), 161; Ian Toll, *Six Frigates: The Epic History of the Founding of the United States Navy* (hereafter cited as Toll, *Six;* New York: W. W. Norton, 2006), 232–53.

4. Stephen Budiansky, *Perilous Fight: America's Intrepid War with Britain on the High Seas, 1812–1815* (hereafter cited as Budiansky, *Perilous;* New York: Alfred A. Knopf, 2011), 51; Toll, *Six,* 270–71; Eric Jay Dolin, *Fur, Finance, and Empire: The Epic History of the Fur Trade in America* (New York: W. W. Norton, 2010), 189–222; William

H. Goetzmann, *When the Eagle Screamed: The Romantic Horizon in American Expansionism, 1800–1816* (Norman: University of Oklahoma Press, 2000), 94.

5. Robert V. Remini, *Henry Clay: Statesman for the Union* (hereafter cited as Remini, *Clay;* New York: W. W. Norton, 1991), 89–93; Gordon S. Wood, *Empire of Liberty: A History of the Early Republic, 1789–1815* (hereafter cited as Wood, *Empire;* New York: Oxford University Press, 2009), 670–73; Gordon S. Brown, *The Captain Who Burned His Ships: Captain Thomas Tingey, USN, 1750–1829* (hereafter cited as Brown, *Tingey;* Annapolis: Naval Institute, 2011), 163.

6. Harry Ammon, *James Monroe: The Quest for American Identity* (Charlottesville: University of Virginia Press, 1990), 301, 306; Toll, *Six*, 139–40, 270–73, 284–86, 325.

7. Budiansky, *Perilous*, 97; Brown, *Tingey*, 163.

8. Remini, *Clay*, 89–93; Wood, *Empire*, 670–73; Stephen Howarth, *To Shining Sea*, 107; McKee, *Honorable*, 341–47; Kenneth J. Hagan, *This People's Navy*, 65–66, 76–77.

9. Williamson County, Tenn., Deed Book C, Tennessee State Library, pp. 459–60.

10. Bowman, *Williamson*, 5–7; Mary H. Maury Werth to her children (hereafter cited as Werth, Reminiscence), July 26, 1879, MP, vol. 42, LC; Corbin, *Maury*, 12–13.

11. Dabney H. Maury to Mary H. Maury, Aug. 7, 1873, MP, vol. 44, LC; Williams, *Maury Scientist*, 22.

12. David Dixon Porter, *Memoir of Commodore David Porter of the United States Navy* (hereafter cited as Porter, *Memoir;* Albany, N.Y.: J. Munsell, 1875), 214; David Porter, *Journal of a Cruise Made to the Pacific Ocean in U.S. Frigate* Essex, *1812–14* (hereafter cited as Porter, *Journal Cruise;* New York: Wiley and Halsted, 1822), 2:19–163; NR, Logs of the *Essex* and *Essex Junior* of David Porter, David G. Farragut, and John M. Maury, NAN; Col. James Edmonds Saunders, *Early Settlers of Alabama*, with notes and genealogies by his granddaughter Elizabeth Saunders Blair Stubbs, part 1, *Dabney Maury Contribution* (New Orleans: Graham and Sons, 1899), 317.

13. J. C. Beaglehole, *Life of Captain James Cook* (Palo Alto, Calif.: Stanford University Press, 1974), 110–11; David F. Long, *Nothing Too Daring* (hereafter cited as Long, *Daring;* Annapolis: Naval Institute, 1987), 130–31; Porter, *Journal Cruise*, 303, 311; Benson J. Lossing, *The Pictorial Field-Book of the War of 1812* (hereafter cited as Lossing, *Pictorial;* New York: Harper and Brothers, 1869), 727.

14. See note 13 above.

15. Archibald Douglas Turnbull, *Commodore David Porter, 1780–1843* (New York: Century, 1929), 176–237; Budiansky, *Perilous*, 322–23; Porter, *Journal Cruise*, 311–12; Long, *Daring*, 131; Lossing, *Pictorial*, 732; Porter, *Memoir*, 214, 220–21; William H. Goetzmann, *New Lands, New Men: America and the Second Great Age of Discovery*, 230, 240.

16. Porter, *Memoir*, 192–214.

17. Sir Charles Oman, *A History of the Peninsular War* (London: Greenhill Books, 2004), 3:1–36, 105–27, 153–96; Charles Ingersoll, *History of the Second War Between the United States and Great Britain*, 2nd ser. (Philadelphia: Lippincott, Grambo, 1852), 1:19–20; Irene Nicholson, *The Liberators: A Study of Independence Movements in Spanish America* (hereafter cited as Nicholson, *Study;* New York: Praeger, 1969), 80–84.

18. See note 17 above.

19. Nicholson, *Study*, 124–25, 133–36; Thomas Hart Benton, *Thirty Years' View; or, A History of the Working of the American Government for Thirty Years from 1820 to 1850* (New York: D. Appleton, 1873), 2:493.

20. Porter, *Journal Cruise*, 145; Dudley W. Knox, *A History of United States Navy* (New York: Putnam's, 1948), 103–7.

21. Loyall Farragut, *The Life of David Glasgow Farragut, First Admiral of the United States Navy, Embodying His Journals and Letters* (hereafter cited as Farragut, *Life;* New York: D. Appleton, 1879), 41; see note 20 above.

22. Budiansky, *Perilous*, 328; see note 21.

23. H[ezekiah] Niles, "Defense of Baltimore," in *The Weekly Register* (Baltimore: Franklin Press, 1814), cover page.

24. Werth, Reminiscence; Walter W. Faw, "Boyhood Home of MFM" (hereafter cited as Faw, "Boyhood"); Bowman, *Williamson*, 98; Joseph F. Kett, *Rites of Passage: Adolescence in America, 1790 to the Present* (New York: Basic Books, 1977), 19.

25. Werth, Reminiscence; Faw, "Boyhood"; Bowman, *Williamson*, 98.

26. Cornelius J. Heatwole, *A History of Education in Virginia* (New York: Macmillan, 1916), 59, 127, 131; MFM to daughter Elizabeth H. Maury, June 14, 1863, MP, vol. 18, LC; MFM to W. C. S. Ventress, Feb. 6, 1825, MP, vol. 1, LC; Charles Lee Lewis, *Matthew Fontaine Maury: The Pathfinder of the Seas* (hereafter cited as Lewis, *Maury;* Annapolis: Naval Institute, 1927), 3.

27. MFM to Rutson Maury, Aug. 31, 1840, MP, vol. 2, LC; Lewis, *Maury*, 6.

28. MFM to W. C. S. Ventress, Feb. 6, 1825, MP, vol. 1, LC.

29. MFM to Rutson Maury, Aug. 31, 1840, MP, vol. 2, LC.

30. Memorial to John M. Maury, St. George's Episcopal Church, Fredericksburg, Va.; Werth, Reminiscence; Dabney H. Maury, John M. Maury's son, note to MFM attached to material Jan. 25, 1872, MP, vol. 44, LC; Corbin, *Maury*, 133.

31. MFM to Rutson Maury letter cited in note 27 above.

32. Ibid.

33. MFM to W. C. S. Ventress, Feb. 6, 1825, MP, vol. 1, LC; NR, Appointments, Orders, and Resignations (hereafter cited as AOR), 13:235, NAN.

34. See note 27 above.

35. See note 27 above.

Chapter 3

1. Matthew Fontaine Maury to Rutson Maury, Aug. 31, 1840, MP, vol. 2, LC; Brodie S. Herndon to Mary H. Maury, Aug. 8, 1873, MP, vol. 44, LC; Diana Maury Corbin, *A Life of Matthew Fontaine Maury, U.S.N. and C.S.N., Compiled by His Daughter* (hereafter cited as Corbin, *Maury*), 14–15; Mary H. Maury Werth to her children (hereafter cited as Werth, Reminiscence), July 26, 1879, MP, vol. 42, LC.

2. Ronald E. Shibley, *Fredericksburg* (Fredericksburg, Va.: Historic Fredericksburg Foundation, 1977), 7–8; Werth, Reminiscence.

3. Col. James Edmonds Saunders, *Early Settlers of Alabama*, with notes and genealogies by his granddaughter Elizabeth Saunders Blair Stubbs, p. 318.

4. *Dictionary of American Biography*, s.v. Samuel L. Southard; *Biographical Directory of the United States Congress*, 1774–Present, http://bioguide.congress.gov/biosearch/biosearch.asp; U.S. Department of the Navy, *Rules, Regulations, and Instructions for the Naval Service of the United States, 1818* (hereafter cited as *Navy Regulations 1818*; Washington, D.C.: U.S. Department of the Navy, 1818), 18–66; Charles Oscar Paullin, "Washington City and the Old Navy," in *Columbia Historical Society Records* (Washington, D.C.: Columbia Historical Society, 1932), vols. 33–34, pp. 174–75; MFM to Rutson Maury, Aug. 31, 1840, MP, vol. 2, LC.

5. Order to MFM July 8, 1825, NR, AOR, vol. 13, p. 266, NAN; Daniel Walker Howe, *What Hath God Wrought: The Transformation of America, 1815–1848* (New York: Oxford University Press, 2007), 304–5; Harry Ammon, *James Monroe: The Quest for American Identity*, 541–43; George Jones, *Sketches of the Naval Life with Notices of Men, Manners, and Scenery on the Shores of the Mediterranean in a Series of Letters from the* Brandywine *and* Constitution *Frigates* (hereafter cited as Jones, *Naval Life*; New Haven: H. Howe, 1829), 2:271.

6. Howard I. Chappelle, *The History of the American Sailing Navy: The Ships and Their Development* (New York: Norton, 1949), 356, 534; NR, Log No. 1, U.S.S. *Brandywine*, NAN (various entries in summer 1825 on rating and condition of ship); Auguste Levasseur, *Lafayette in America in 1824 and 1825; or, A Journal of a Voyage to the U.S.*, 2:256.

7. Richard B. Maury to W. C. S. Ventress, Nov. 4, 1825, MP, vol. 1, LC.

8. Jones, *Naval Life*, 2:271; Charles Nordhoff, *Man-of-War Life: A Boy's Experience in the United States Navy, During a Voyage around the World, in a Ship of the Line*, Classics of Naval Literature (Cincinnati: Moore, Wilstach, Keys, 1855; reprint, Annapolis: Naval Institute, 1985), 25. Citation refers to the 1985 edition.

9. Francis Leigh Williams, *Matthew Fontaine Maury: Scientist of the Sea*, 44.

10. Christopher McKee, *A Gentlemanly and Honorable Profession: The Creation of the U.S. Naval Officer Corps, 1794–1815*, 69, 115, 131; Enoch Cobb Wines, *Two Years and a Half in the Navy; or, Journal of a Cruise in the Mediterranean and Levant, on Board of the U.S. Frigate* Constellation, *in the Years 1829, 1830, and 1831* (hereafter cited as Wines, *Two Years*; Philadelphia: Carey and Lea, 1832), 1:28–37; *Navy Regulations 1818*, 68; NR *Brandywine* Log, Aug. 21, 1825, NAN.

11. Wines, *Two Years*, 34–35; *Navy Regulations 1818*, 68; NR, *Brandywine* Log, Aug. 21, 1825, NAN.

12. NR, *Brandywine* Log, Sept. 5, 1825, NAN.

13. NR, *Brandywine* Log, Sept. 8, 1825, NAN; Levasseur, *Lafayette*, 2:255–56; Jones, *Naval Life*, 1:15.

14. Levasseur, *Lafayette*, 2:257; Corbin, *Maury*, 17.

15. Corbin, *Maury*, 17; Williams, *Maury Scientist*, 50.

16. Wines, *Two Years*, 40–43; McKee, *Honorable*, 153–55.

17. Jones, *Naval Life*, 2:261; MFM, "Scraps from the Lucky Bag," *Southern Literary Messenger* (hereafter cited as *SLM*) 6, no. 4 (May 1840): 316.

18. *The Book of Common Prayer and Administration of the Sacraments and Other Rites and Ceremonies of the Church* (New York: Church Pension Fund, 1945), 42; Jones, *Naval Life*, 1:34–90, 2:90, 2:240–41.

19. NR, *Brandywine* Log, Oct. 3–5, 1825, NAN; Levasseur, *Lafayette*, 2:261.

20. NR, *Brandywine* Log, Oct. 8, 1825, NAN; MFM to W. C. S. Ventress, Nov. 13, 1825, MP, vol. 1, LC.

21. McKee, *Honorable*, 404.

22. Corbin, *Maury*, 16; NR, *Brandywine* Log, Nov. 17, 28, Dec. 6, 1825, Feb. 21, 1826, NAN; Jones, *Naval Life*, 1:58, 1:85–86; McKee, *Honorable*, 201, 403, 447–57; Loyall Farragut, *The Life of Glasgow David Farragut*, 59.

23. MFM to Rutson Maury, Aug. 31, 1840, MP, vol. 2, LC; Farragut, *Life*, 104; John Spencer Bassett, *The Life of Andrew Jackson* (New York: Macmillan, 1925), 165; Robert V. Remini, *The Battle of New Orleans: Andrew Jackson and Amer-*

ica's First Military Victory (New York: Viking, 1999), 71–72, 126, 136, 161–64; Gene Allen Smith, "Preventing the 'Eggs of Insurrection' from Hatching: The U.S. Navy and Control of the Mississippi River, 1806–1815," *Northern Mariner* (Ottawa, Ontario, Canada), July/Oct. 2008, 90–91.

24. MFM, "Scraps from the Lucky Bag," *SLM*, 6, no. 4 (May 1840): 316; Farragut, *Life*, 104.

25. MFM to Secretary Southard, May 2, 1826, NR, AOR, 13:303.

Chapter 4

1. Walter Havighurst, *Long Ships Passing* (New York: Macmillan, 1943), 77–79; MFM (but unsigned), "A Scheme for Rebuilding Southern Commerce: Direct Trade with the South," *Southern Literary Messenger* (hereafter cited as *SLM*) 5, no. 1 (Jan. 1839): 3–12; MFM, "Direct Foreign Trade of the South: Commercial Conventions," *DeBow's Review* (hereafter cited as *DeBow's*) 12, no. 2 (Feb. 1852): 126–48; MFM, "The Commercial Prospects of the South: An Address Reprinted from the Proceedings of the Virginia Mercantile Convention," Sept. 10–11, 1851, Richmond, *SLM* 17, nos. 10–11 (Oct.–Nov. 1851): 686–98; Richard C. McKay, *South Street: A Maritime History of New York* (Riverside, Conn.: Seven Seas, 1934), 66, 90, 144; Christopher McKee, *A Gentlemanly and Honorable Profession: The Creation of the U.S. Naval Officer Corps, 1794–1815*, 468; Howard I. Chappelle, *The History of the American Sailing Navy: The Ships and Their Development*, 278–81.

2. NR, Letters of Officers, Ships of War, vol. 17, Orders to Commodore Jacob Jones, Aug. 21, 23, and 26, 1826. Adding to Jones's irritation was the discovery that shortly before *Brandywine* was to sail many water casks were empty.

3. Harry Ammon, *James Monroe: The Quest for American Identity*, 409, 480–81.

4. H. W. V. Temperley, *Life of Canning* (London: James Finch, 1903), 180; Daniel Walker Howe, *What Hath God Wrought: The Transformation of America, 1815–1848*, 11.

5. MFM, "Scraps from the Lucky Bag," *SLM* 6, no. 4 (May 1840): 315.

6. NR, Commodore Jacob Jones to Secretary of the Navy Southard, Oct. 30, 1826, Captains Letters, Sept.–Oct. 1826; *Brandywine* Log, Sept. 15, 1826, NAN; Thomas Dornin, personal journal kept on board U.S.S. *Brandywine*, 1826–1830, p. 1; John Tackett Goolrick, *Historic Fredericksburg: The Story of an Old Town* (Richmond: Whitteley and Shepperson, 1922), 98–132.

7. NR, *Brandywine* Log, Oct. 25–27, 1826, NAN; Charles S. Stewart, *A Visit to the South Seas in the U.S. Ship* Vincennes *During the Years 1829–1830* (hereafter cited as Stewart, *South Seas*; New York: John P. Haven, Sleight, and Robinson, 1831 and 1832), 1:47–51; Fisher, Son and Jackson, London edition of Stewart's accounts, edited and abridged by William Ellis, 1833, p. 57.

8. Stewart, *South Seas*, London edition, 47–51; MFM writing as "Inca," three-part series "Valley of the Amazon," *DeBow's*, vol. 14, no. 5 (May 1853): 449–60; vol. 14, no. 6 (June 1853): 556–67; vol. 15, no. 1 (July 1853): 36–43.

9. NR, Captains Letters, Oct.–Nov. 1826, NAN; NR, Letter Collection no. 82, Condy Raguet to Commodore Jacob Jones, Nov. 14, 1826, NAN; NR, Commodore Jacob Jones to Condy Raguet, Nov. 14, 1826, NAN; Gardener Weld Allen, ed., Letter from Condy Raguet to Commodore Hull, in *Papers of Commodore Hull* (Boston: Athenaeum, 1929), 58–59; NR, Condy Raguet to Commodore Jacob Jones, Nov. 17, 1826, NAN.

10. See note 9 above.

11. MFM, "On the Navigation of Cape Horn," *American Journal of Science and Arts* 26, art. 5 (July 1834): 54.

12. NR, *Brandywine* Log entries for Dec. 26, 1826, to Jan. 8, 1827, NAN.

13. NR, *Brandywine* Log, entry Jan. 9 and subsequent days, 1827, NAN.

14. MFM to the Rev. James H. Otey, Feb. 18, 1829, MP, vol. 1, LC.

15. Diana Fontaine Maury Corbin, *A Life of Matthew Fontaine Maury, U.S.N. and C.S.N., Compiled by His Daughter*, 19.

16. Irene Nicholson, *The Liberators: A Study of Independence Movements in Spanish America*: on study, 142–47; on fall of Callao, 194–95; on Lima under San Martin and Bolivar, 202–3; Basil Hall, *Hall's Voyages*, vol. 3, *Constables Miscellany* (Edinburgh, U.K.: Constable, 1827), 53–54, 65–66.

17. MFM to W. C. S. Ventress, June 18, 1829, MP, vol. 1, LC; Edwin Hall, "Samuel Lewis Southard, 16 Sept. 1823–Mar. 1829," in *American Secretaries of the Navy, 1775–1913*, ed. Paolo E. Coletta (hereafter cited as name of chapter author, name of secretary, *American Secretaries*; Annapolis: Naval Institute, 1980), 1:135–36.

18. William B. Whiting to Capt. John M. Brooke, May 31, 1873, MP, vol. 44, LC; McKee, *Honorable*, 462.

19. Stewart, *South Seas*, 1:209–10; Gene Allen Smith, *Thomas ap Catesby Jones: Commodore of Manifest Destiny* (hereafter cited as Smith, *Jones*; Annapolis: Naval Institute, 2000), 59–60; "Society Islands," in "For the Admiralty," *The Nautical Magazine: A Journal of Papers* 3 (1834): 545–46.

20. NR, *Vincennes* Log, July 28–29, 1829, NAN; Robert L. Browning, Lt. USN, "Notes on the South Sea Islands," (hereafter cited as Browning, "Notes"), MS Collection, LC.

21. Stewart, *South Seas*, 1:196, 1:277–81.

22. Browning, "Notes," MS Collection, LC.

23. MFM to John Minor, Sept. 18, 1859, and N. P. Willis to MFM, Sept. 24, 1859, MP, both vol. 8, LC.

24. Stewart, *South Seas*, 1:352; Charles Lee Lewis, *Matthew Fontaine Maury: The Pathfinder of the Seas*, 17.

25. Smith, *Jones*, 54–55.

26. Stewart, *South Seas*, 2:44.

27. David F. Long, *Mad Jack: The Biography of Captain John Percival, USN, 1779–1862*, Contributions in Military Studies (hereafter cited as Long, *Mad Jack*; Westport, Conn.: Greenwood, 1993), 68–69; NR, Captain Finch's Cruise in U.S.S. *Vincennes*, 1826–30, NAN; Stewart, *South Seas*, 2:115; William H. Goetzmann, *New Lands, New Men: America and the Second Great Age of Discovery* (hereafter cited as Goetzmann, *New Men*), 36–39; Stewart, *South Seas*, 2:104.

28. Hiram Bingham, *A Residence of Twenty-One Years in the Sandwich Islands* (hereafter cited as Bingham, *Residence*; Hartford, Conn.: Hezekiah Huntington; New York: Sherman Converse, 1847), 335.

29. Kathleen Dickson Mellen, *The Gods Depart: A Saga of the Hawaiian Kingdom, 1832–73* (New York: Hastings House, 1936), 3–15; NR, Captain Finch's Cruise in U.S.S. *Vincennes*, NAN; Stewart, *South Seas*, 2:171–234, 2:249–83.

30. See note 29 above.

31. Bingham, *Residence*, 284–88; Long, *Mad Jack*, 70.

32. S. T. Shulman, D. L. Shulman, and R. H. Sims, "The Tragic 1824 Journey of the Hawaiian King and Queen to London: History of Measles in Hawaii," Abstract, *Pediatric Infectious Disease Journal* 28, no. 8 (Aug. 2009): 728–33, doi:10.1097/INF.0b013e31819c9720.

33. Goetzmann, *New Men*, 248; Rufus Anderson, *A Heathen Nation Evangelized: History of the Mission of the American Board for Foreign Missions to the Sandwich Islands*, 3rd ed. (London: Hodder and Stoughton, 1872), 91–93; William Richards account in the *Religious Intelligencer* (New Haven, Conn.) 11 (June 1826): 22.

34. NR, Captain Finch's Cruise in U.S.S. *Vincennes*, NAN; Smith, *Jones*, 64–66.

35. NR, Captain Finch's Cruise in U.S.S. *Vincennes*, NA; Bingham, *Residence*, 302.

36. Finch as cited in note 35 above; Bingham, *Residence*, 361.

37. MFM, *Sailing Directions* (Washington, D.C.: C. Alexander, 1854), 45.

38. NR, *Vincennes* Log, Dec. 19–30, 1829, and Jan. 1, 1830, NAN.

39. Ibid.

40. Charles Oscar Paullin, *Diplomatic Negotiations of American Naval Officers, 1778–1883* (hereafter cited as Paullin, *Diplomatic Negotiations*; Baltimore: Johns Hopkins University Press, 1912), 182–85.

41. Stewart, *South Seas*, 2:294; Paullin, *Diplomatic Negotiations*, 170–72, 183–85; NR, *Vincennes* Log, Jan. 21–22, 1830, NAN.

42. Browning, "Notes"; MFM (but unsigned), "A Scheme for Rebuilding Southern Commerce: Direct Trade with the South," *SLM* 5, no. 1 (Jan. 1839): 3–12; Stewart, South Seas, 2:171–234, 2:249–83, as cited in note 29 above; Paullin, *Diplomatic Negotiations*, as cited in note 40 above; "Flower Boat" exhibit in the Marine Room of the Peabody Museum, Salem, Mass.

43. Paullin, *Diplomatic Negotiations*, 183; Kenneth Scott Latourette, *The History of the Early Relations Between the United States and China, 1784–1844*, Transactions of the Connecticut Academy of Arts and Sciences (New Haven: Yale University Press, 1917), 81n34; John Foord, "Old Canton Days," *Asia: Journal of the American Asiatic Association* 17 (Mar.–Dec. 1918): 191–95.

44. Emory Johnson, T. W. Van Metre, G. G. Huebner, and D. S. Hanchett, *History of Domestic and Foreign Commerce of the United States*, vols. 1 and 2 in one volume (Washington, D.C.: Carnegie Institution of Washington, 1915; repr., 1922), 108, 185, accessed Nov. 2, 2013, http://books.google.com/books?id=1tUxAQAAMAAJ; *Message from the President of the United States Communicating the Letter of Mr. Prevost, and Other Documents, Relating to an Establishment Made at the Mouth of the Columbia River, Jan. 27, 1823* (Washington, D.C.: Gales and Seaton, 1823), accessed Nov. 3, 2013, http://books.google.com/books?id=TbG2k_TsZmcC; *letter from John Jacob Astor to the secretary of State*, U.S. Department of State (Washington, D.C.: Gales and Seaton, 1823), 45; Eric Jay Dolin, *Fur, Finance, and Empire: The Epic History of the Fur Trade in America*, 155–56.

45. R. B. Forbes, *Remarks on China and the China Trade* (Boston: Samuel N. Dickinson, 1844), 19.

46. Society for the Diffusion of Useful Knowledge, *Penny Cyclopedia of the Society for the Diffusion of Useful Knowledge* 18 (London: Charles Knight, 1839), s.v. "Philippines," p. 90.

47. See note 44 above; NR, *Vincennes* Log, entries Apr. 7, 8, 1830, NAN.

48. William Leigh to Mary Maury, 1873, MP, vol. 44, LC; Stewart, *South Seas*, 2:300–16.

49. Corbin, *Maury*, 17.

50. Adrian Desmond and James Moore, *Darwin's Sacred Cause: How Darwin's Hatred of Slavery Shaped Darwin's Views on Evolution* (New York: Houghton Mifflin, 2009), 106; Stewart, *South Seas*, 2:323–27.

51. Stewart, *South Seas*, 2:323–27.

52. Stewart, *South Seas*, 2:334–47; Browning, "Notes," MS Collection, LC; B. B. Edwards, comp., *American Quarterly Register* (Boston: Congregational Education Society, 1833), 5:51.

53. NR, Captain Finch's Cruise in U.S.S. *Vincennes*, 1826–30, NAN.

54. Herman Melville, *Moby Dick; or, The White Whale* (Boston: St. Adolph Society, 1892), http://books.google.com/books?id=XV8XAAAAYAAJ.

55. Samuel P. Huntington, *The Soldier and the State: The Theory and Politics of Civil-Military Relations* (Cambridge, Mass.: Belknap Press of Harvard University Press, 1957), 216.

56. NR, *Vincennes* log, June 8, 1830, NAN.

Chapter 5

1. MFM to Richard L. Maury, Apr. 10, 1833, MP, vol. 1, LC; Samuel R. Franklin, *Memories of a Rear Admiral: Life in the United States Sailing from Hampton Roads to Pacific Squadron* (Washington, D.C.: Navy Department Library, Microfilm Collection, n.d.); NR, Bureau of Navigation, Record of Officers, Sept. 1825–Dec. 1831, vol. G, p. 55, NAN.

2. Dabney H. Maury to Mary H. Maury, Aug. 7, 1873, MP, vol. 44, LC; Mary H. Maury Werth to her children (hereafter cited as Werth, Reminiscence), July 26, 1879, MP, vol. 42, LC; MFM to Richard L. Maury, July 3, 1830, MP, vol. 1, LC.

3. Werth, Reminiscence.

4. MFM to Rutson Maury, Aug. 31, 1840, MP, vol. 2, LC.

5. Charles Lee Lewis, *Admiral Franklin Buchanan: Fearless Man of Action* (Baltimore: Norman Remington, 1929), 44–45; Charles Lee Lewis, *Matthew Fontaine Maury: The Pathfinder of the Seas* (hereafter cited as Lewis, *Maury*), 21; Christopher McKee, *A Gentlemanly and Honorable Profession: The Creation of the U.S. Naval Officer Corps, 1794–1815* (hereafter cited as McKee, *Honorable*), 169; Howard I. Chappelle, *The History of the American Sailing Navy: The Ships and Their Development*, 278–81.

6. Dabney Maury letter cited in note 2 above; NR, Bureau of Navigation, Record of Officers, Sept. 1825–Dec. 1831, vol. G, p. 337, NAN.

7. MFM, "Scraps from the Lucky Bag," *Southern Literary Messenger*, Dec. 1840, p. 120; NR, Bureau of Navigation, Record of Officers, Sept. 1825–Dec. 1831, vol. G, p. 351, NAN; MFM to Diana Maury Corbin, quoted in Diana Fontaine Maury Corbin, *A Life of Matthew Fontaine Maury, U.S.N. and C.S.N., Compiled by His Daughter* (hereafter cited as Corbin, *Maury*), 164.

8. Lewis, *Maury*, 21; NR, Bureau of Navigation, Record of Officers, Sept. 1825–Dec. 1825, vol. G, p. 361, NAN.

9. Corbin, *Maury*, 164.

10. MFM to Richard L. Maury, Apr. 10, 1833, MP, vol. 1, LC.

11. Corbin, *Maury*, p. 20.

12. Donald Chisholm, *Waiting for Dead Men's Shoes: Origins and Development of the U.S. Navy's Officer Personnel System, 1793–1941* (Stanford, Calif.: Stanford University Press, 2001), 116; McKee, *Honorable*, 289; NR, Falmouth Master Roll, June 1831, NAN; Corbin, *Maury*, 23.

13. NR, Dornin Papers, vol. 1, 1826–36, Jan. 1, 1830 entry, NAN.

14. NR, Dornin Papers, vol. 1, 1826–36, n.d. [likely late Sept. 1830], NAN.

15. MFM, "On the Navigation of Cape Horn," *American Journal of Science and the Arts* 26, art. 5 (July 1834): 60–61.

16. Ibid.

17. Nathaniel Bowditch, *Memoir of Nathaniel Bowditch* (Boston: James Munroe, 1841), 78–90, http://books.google.com/books?id=iwcEAAAAYAAJ.

18. MFM to Richard L. Maury, Apr. 10, 1833, MP, vol. 1, LC; MFM to T. Averett Berkeley, May 28, 1853, MP, vol. 4, LC.

19. MFM to Richard L. Maury, Nov. 17, 1831, MP, vol. 1, LC.

20. Francis Warriner, *Cruise of the United States Frigate* Potomac *Round the World, During the Years 1831–34, Embracing the Attack on Quallah Battoo, with Notices of Scenes, Manners, etc., in Different Parts of Asia, South America, and the Islands of the Pacific* (New York: Leavitt, Lord, 1835), 75–118; NR, Journal of U.S.S. *Potomac*, John Downes commanding, NAN; NR, Potomac Log entries from May 19, 1833, to July 7, 1834, NAN; NR, Potomac Muster Roll, 1831–33, p. 27, NAN; MFM to Richard Maury, Nov. 17, 1831, MP, vol. 1, LC; Jon Meacham, *American Lion: Andrew Jackson in the White House* (New York: Random House, 2008), 213–15.

21. "On the Expediency and Importance of Authorizing a Naval Expedition to Explore the Pacific Ocean and South Seas, including Letters from Passed Midshipmen Maury and Gordon," Feb. 7, 1835, Doc. No. 578, in *American State Papers, Documents Legislative and Executive of the Congress of the United States from the Second Session of the Twenty-First to the First Session of the Twenty-Fourth Congress, Commencing March 1, 1831, and Ending June 15, 1836*, vol. 4, *Naval Affairs*, ed. Asbury Dickens and John W. Forney (Washington, D.C.: Gales and Seaton, 1861); MFM to J. N. Reynolds with extracts from his note-books of 1832, Dec. 26, 1834, part of the preceding work edited by Dickens and Forney, "On the Expediency and Importance..."; Jeremiah N. Reynolds, *Voyage of the United States Frigate* Potomac *Under the Command of Commodore John Downes During the Circumnavigation of the Globe, 1831–34* (New York: Harper and Brothers, 1835), particularly the appendix with details on the orders received, the attack, its aftermath, and medical conditions aboard the ship (hereafter cited as Reynolds, *Voyage*); Jerimiah N. Reynolds, "Mocha Dick: Or the White Whale of the Pa-

cific," *Knickerbocker Magazine* (New York) 13, no. 5 (May 1839): 377–92.

22. William B. Whiting to Capt. John M. Brooke, May 31, 1873, MP, vol. 44, LC.

23. NR, *Potomac* log entries from May 19, 1833, to July 7, 1834, NAN.

24. Whiting letter cited in note 22 above; Reynolds, *Voyage*, 520–21.

Chapter 6

1. Dabney H. Maury to Mary H. Maury, Aug. 7, 1873, MP, vol. 44, LC; MFM to Mrs. William Maury, Liverpool, Nov. 14, 1846, MP, vol. 3, LC.

2. MFM to Richard L. Maury, Sept. 24, 1834, MP, vol. 1, LC.

3. MFM to Secretary Southard, January 1835, Princeton University Library MS Collection.

4. MFM to James Maury, Nov. 19, 1834, MP, vol. 1, LC; MFM, preface to *A New Theoretical and Practical Treatise on Navigation, in Which the Auxiliary Branches of Mathematics and Astronomy Are Treated of the Theory and Most Simple Methods of Finding Time, Longitude, and Latitude* (hereafter cited as Maury, *Navigation*; Philadelphia: Key and Biddle, 1836), title page imprinted with the motto "*Cur non?*"

5. Robert V. Remini, *Andrew Jackson: The Course of American Democracy, 1833–1845* (hereafter cited as Remini, *Jackson:* Baltimore: Johns Hopkins University Press, 1984), 227; Daniel Walker Howe, *What Hath God Wrought: The Transformation of America, 1815–1848* (hereafter cited as Howe, *Wrought*), 433.

6. David Hackett Fischer and James C. Kelly, *Bound Away: Virginia and the Western Movement*, 137, 203.

7. Charles H. Ambler, *The Life and Diary of John Floyd, Governor of Virginia, an Apostle of Secession, and the Father of the Oregon County* (hereafter cited as Ambler, *Floyd*; Richmond: Richmond, 1918), 62.

8. William Goetzmann, *New Lands, New Men: America and the Second Great Age of Discovery* (hereafter cited as Goetzmann, *New Men*), 108–10; Eric Jay Dolin, *Fur, Finance, and Empire: The Epic History of the Fur Trade in America* (hereafter cited as Dolin, *Fur*), 147–54, 166–75.

9. Howe, *Wrought*, 395–410, 534–39.

10. Howe, *Wrought*, 214.

11. MFM [but unsigned], "A Scheme for Rebuilding Southern Commerce: Direct Trade with the South," *Southern Literary Messenger* (hereafter cited as *SLM*) 5, no. 1 (Jan. 1839).

12. Robert V. Remini, *Henry Clay: Statesman for the Union* (hereafter cited as Remini, *Clay*), 231; Howe, *Wrought*, 117–20; Marie Tyler McGraw, *At the Falls: Richmond, Virginia, and Its People* (hereafter cited as McGraw, *Falls*; Chapel Hill: University of North Carolina Press, 1994), 110–11; Jean Edward Smith, *John Marshall: Definer of a Nation* (New York: Henry Holt, 1996), 411–16; *Journal of the House of Delegates, Session 1843–1844* (Richmond: Samuel Shepherd, 1846), 12; MFM [but unsigned], "A Scheme for Rebuilding Southern Commerce: Direct Trade with the South," *SLM* 5, no. 1 (Jan. 1839); Fischer and Kelly, *Bound*, 284.

13. Virginius Dabney, *Virginia: The New Dominion* (hereafter cited as Dabney, *Virginia*), 183.

14. Howe, *Wrought*, 563.

15. Remini, *Jackson*, 4; McGraw, *Falls*, iii.

16. Ann Fontaine Maury, *Intimate Virginiana: A Century of Maury Travels by Land and Sea* (Richmond: Dietz, 1941), 15–21, 162–209; Jon Meacham, *American Lion: Andrew Jackson in the White House*, 82.

17. William S. Drewry, *The Southampton Insurrection* (hereafter cited as Drewry, *Insurrection*; Washington, D.C.: Neale, 1900), 80–81, 87; Howe, *Wrought*, 323; Dabney, *Virginia*, 224; Anthony Santoro, "The Prophet in His Own Words: Nat Turner's Biblical Construction," *Virginia Magazine of History and Biography* 116, no. 2 (Spring 2008): 123.

18. Drewry, *Insurrection*, 77, 88; Charles Ambler, ed., *Branch Papers of Randolph-Macon College*, vol. 5, June 1918 (hereafter cited as Ambler, *Branch*; Ashland, Va.: Randolph-Macon College, 1918), 152–53; Howe, *Wrought*, p. 323.

19. See note 18 above.

20. Craig L. Symonds, *Joseph E. Johnston: A Civil War Biography* (hereafter cited as Symonds, *Johnston*; New York: W. W. Norton, 1994), 23–24; Robert W. Coakley, *The Role of Military Forces in Domestic Disorders, 1789–1878* (hereafter cited as Coakley, *Role*; Washington, D.C.: Center of Military History, United States Army, 1988), 93, http://books.google.com/books?id=SMmJsJLKmvoC.

21. Dabney, *Virginia,* 226; MFM to Richard L. Maury, Sept. 9, 1836, MP, vol. 1, LC; Launcelot Minor Blackford, *Mine Eyes Have Seen the Glory* (hereafter cited as Blackford, *Mine Eyes*; Cambridge, Mass.: Harvard University Press, 1954), 16–47, 84–87; Ambler, *Floyd,* 159; Symonds, *Johnston,* 24.

22. Drewry, *Insurrection*, 101.

23. Ibid.

24. Howe, *Wrought*, 184n58, 399, 425; Ambler, *Branch,* 155.

25. William Lee Miller, *Arguing About Slavery: The Great Battle in the United States Congress* (New York: Alfred P. Knopf, 1996), 67–68; Drewry, *Insurrection*, 144; Howe, *Wrought,* 423–24; Blackford, *Mine Eyes*; Cambridge, Mass.: Harvard University Press, 1954).

26. Ambler, *Floyd,* 89, 91; Blackford, *Mine Eyes,* 16–47; Howe, *Wrought,* 437; Charles H. Ambler, *Sectionalism in Virginia from 1776 to 1861* (Chicago: University of Chicago Press, 1910), 190–91; Dumas Malone, *Jefferson and His Time: The Sage of Monticello* (hereafter cited as Malone, *Sage*; Boston: Little, Brown, 1970), 336.

27. Gordon S. Wood, *Empire of Liberty: A History of the Early Republic, 1789–1815,* 268–71; Gaillard Hunt, ed., *Writings of Madison, 1790–1802,* vol. 6 (New York: G. P. Putnam, 1906), 312–13; Harry Ammon, *James Monroe: The Quest for American Identity,* 184, 193, 338, 340, 455.

28. Ammon, *Monroe,* 193.

29. Ammon, *Monroe,* 184, 193; Wood, *Empire,* 268–71; Dumas Malone, *Jefferson and the Ordeal of Liberty* (hereafter cited as Malone, *Ordeal*; New York: Little, Brown, 1962), 406.

30. Malone, *Ordeal,* 505.

31. William Gardner Bell, *Secretaries of War and Secretaries of the Army: Portraits and Biographical Sketches* (Washington, D.C.: Center of Military History, United States Army, 1992), 3; Dabney, *Virginia,* 283.

32. Ambler, *Floyd,* 114; William W. Freehling, *The Road to Disunion: Secessionists at Bay, 1776–1854* (New York: Oxford University Press, 1990), 253–57; Coakley, *Role,* 95.

33. Coakley, *Role,* 95–99.

34. Coakley, *Role,* 97–101; Thomas Hart Benton, *Thirty Years' View; or, A History of the Working of the American Government for Thirty Years from 1820 to 1850,* 1:343.

35. Ambler, *Branch,* 110, 113; Ambler, *Floyd,* 113.

36. Mark O. Hatfield, "William Rufus King (1853)," in *Vice Presidents of the United States,* with the Senate Historical Office (Washington, D.C.: Government Printing Office, 1997), 181–87; Coakley, *Role,* 97–101.

37. Coakley, *Role,* 100.

38. Remini, *Clay,* 427.

39. Mary H. Maury Werth to her children (hereafter cited as Werth, Reminiscence), July 26, 1879, MP, vol. 42, LC.

40. MFM to Richard L. Maury, Oct. 29, 1835, MP, vol. 1, LC.

41. Frances Leigh Williams, *Matthew Fontaine Maury: Scientist of the Sea* (hereafter cited as Williams, *Maury Scientist*), 106; MFM to Richard L. Maury, Sept. 9, 1835, MP, vol. 1, LC; Werth, Reminiscence.

42. MFM to Richard L. Maury, Oct. 20, 1835, MP, vol. 1, LC.

43. Copyright Copy, Apr. 29, 1836, MP, vol. 1, LC.

44. Williams, *Maury Scientist,* 119.

45. Edgar Allan Poe, *SLM* 2, no. 7 (June 1836): 454–55; letters of recommendation included in 3rd ed., Maury, *Navigation*; "Description of an Alembic for Distilling Amalgam of Gold," *American Journal of Science and Arts* (hereafter cited as *Am. Journ. Science*) 32, no. 1 (July 1837): 208; Alexander Dallas Bache to MFM in "Opinions of Navigators and Professors," p. 1, in Maury, *Navigation.*

46. Bache to MFM in "Opinions" cited in note 45 above, pp. 1–5.

47. Samuel F. DuPont Papers, 1855, Hagley Museum and Library, Wilmington, Del.

48. Maury, *Navigation,* preface.

49. MFM to Ann Maury, June 18, 1836, MP, vol. 1, LC; MFM address before the Geological and Mineralogical Society of Fredericksburg, Va., May 13, 1836, published in *Fredericksburg Political Arena,* May 20 and 24, 1836 (MS in MP, vol. 1, LC).

50. Johnston Family Papers, Oct. 2, 1835, on board meeting of the U.S. Mining Company, University of Virginia Library Special Collections; Palmer C. Sweet and David Trimble, *Virginia Gold: Resource Data* (Charlottesville, Va.: Virginia Department of Mineral Resources, 1983); James Furman Kemp, *The Ore Deposits of the United States and Canada,* 3rd ed. (New York: Scientific, 1900), 382n.

51. George P. Fisher, *Life of Benjamin Silliman, M.D., LL.D., Late Professor of Chemistry, Mineralogy, and Geology at Yale College* (New York: Scribner's, 1966), 1:377–79; MFM, "Notice of the Gold Veins of the United States Mine near Fredericksburg, Virginia," *Am. Journ. Science* 32, no. 2, art. 14 (July 1837): 98–109, 117, 126.

52. MFM, "Description of an Alembic for Distilling Amalgam of Gold, Contrived by M.F. Maury, U.S.N.," *Am. Journ. Science* 33, no. 2, art. 5 (Jan. 1838): 66.

53. Johnston Family Papers, U.S. Mining Company, University of Virginia Library Special Collections.

Chapter 7

1. John Dryden Kazar, Jr., "The United States Navy and Scientific Exploration, 1837–1860" (hereafter cited as Kazar, "Exploration"; PhD diss., University of Massachusetts, 1973), 10, photocopy in Smithsonian Institution Archives, Washington, D.C.; John Quincy Adams, "First Annual Message," Dec. 6, 1825, online by Gerhard Peters and John T. Woolley, American Presidency Project, accessed Dec. 16, 2013, http://www.presidency.ucsb.edu/ws/?pid=29467; Charles Francis Adams, ed., *Memoirs of John Quincy Adams, Comprising Portions of His Diary from 1795–1848* (hereafter cited as Adams, *Memoirs*; Philadelphia: J. B. Lippincott, 1866), 6:518–524.

2. Kazar, "Exploration," 30; Paolo Coletta, "Samuel Lewis Southard, 16 Sept. 1823–3 Mar. 1829," in Coletta, *American Secretaries of the Navy, 1775–1913,* 1:135.

3. William Goetzmann, *New Lands, New Men: America and the Second Great Age of Discovery* (hereafter cited as Goetzmann, *New Men*), 281; MFM to Richard L. Maury, Oct. 29, 1835, MP, vol. 1, LC.

4. Titian Ramsey Peale, "The South Sea Surveying and Exploring Expedition," in *American Historical Record and Repertory of Notes and Queries*, ed. Benson J. Lossing (hereafter cited as Peale, "South Seas"; Philadelphia: John E. Potter, 1874), 145.

5. Elizabeth Green Musselman, "Science as a Landed Activity: Scientifics and Seamen aboard the U.S. Exploring Expedition," in *Surveying the Record: North American Scientific Exploration to 1930*, ed. Edward Carlos Cater II (hereafter cited as Musselman, "Science"; Philadelphia: American Philosophical Society, 1999), 80–81; *Exploring Expedition: Correspondence Between John N. Reynolds and Hon. Mahlon Dickerson Under Signatures of Citizen and Friend to the Navy, New York, 1838; Report on the Exploring Expedition, 1838*, 25th Cong., 2d Sess., House Executive Document 147 (hereafter cited as *Exploring Expedition*; Washington, D.C.: United States Congress, 1838), 74; Goetzmann, *New Men*, 271.

6. See note 5 above; Gene A. Smith, *Thomas ap Catesby Jones: Commodore of Manifest Destiny*, 52.

7. Musselman, "Science," 81; Goetzmann, *New Men*, 263, 277; *Exploring Expedition*, House Executive Document 147, p. 74.

8. See note 6 above.

9. MFM to Richard L. Maury, Sept. 9, 1839, MP, vol. 1, LC.

10. MFM to Thomas A. Dornin, Sept. 24, 26, Oct. 9, Nov. 8, 1836, MP, vol. 1, LC. From October 1836 through March 1837, Maury wrote often to a wide circle of readers of the problems surrounding the Exploring Expedition, all in MP, vol. 1, LC.

11. Herman J. Viola and Carolyn Margolis, eds., *Magnificent Voyagers: The U.S. Exploring Expedition, 1838–1842* (Washington, D.C.: Smithsonian Institution Press, 1983), 9–23; MFM to Richard L. Maury, Sept. 9, 1839, MP, vol. 1, LC.

12. MFM to Dornin, as cited in note 10 above.

13. MFM to Ann Maury of New York, Jan. 25, 1872, MP, vol. 42, LC; "South Sea Expedition: A Report of the House Naval Affairs Committee," *Southern Literary Messenger* 2, no. 9 (Aug. 1836): 589; Goetzmann, *New Men*, 271.

14. MFM to Thomas A. Dornin, Sept. 24 and 26, 1836, MP, vol. 1, LC.

15. MFM to Thomas A. Dornin, Sept. 19, 1837, MP, vol. 1, LC; Peale, "South Seas," 246; Musselman, "Science," 88; *Exploring Expedition*, House Executive Document 194, p. 347; House Executive Document 138, p. 303; House Executive Document 147, pp. 327, 503, 560–61, 583–585; House Executive Document 255, p. 328.

16. MFM to Thomas A. Dornin, Sept. 29, 1837, MP, vol. 1, LC.

17. MFM to Secretary Dickerson, Oct. 23, 1837, *Exploring Expedition*, House Executive Document 147, pp. 498–99.

18. Comm. Thomas ap Catesby Jones to Secretary Dickerson, Nov. 4, 1837, *Exploring Expedition*, House Executive Document 147, pp. 562–64; Musselman, "Science," 78; Peale, "South Seas," 246.

19. Kazar, "Exploration," 40, 42–43.

20. Kazar, "Exploration," 44; Comm. Thomas ap Catesby Jones to Secretary Dickerson, Nov. 14, 1837, *Exploring Expedition*, House Executive Document 147, pp. 562–64.

21. Comm. Thomas ap Catesby Jones to Secretary Dickerson, Nov. 14, 1837, *Exploring Expedition*, House Executive Document 147, pp. 562–64.

22. Secretary Dickerson to Comm. Thomas ap Catesby Jones, Dec. 6, 1837, *Exploring Expedition*, House Executive Document 147, pp. 600–601.

23. Kazar, "Exploration," 47; *Exploring Expedition*, House Executive Document 147, pp. 10, 603.

24. *Exploring Expedition*, House Executive Document 147, pp. 10, 603; Adams, *Memoirs*, 9:491.

25. MFM to Ann Maury, June 20, 1838, MP, vol. 2, LC; Musselman, "Science," 81.

26. Charles Lee Lewis, *Matthew Fontaine Maury: The Pathfinder of the Seas*, 33.

27. MFM letter to Ann Maury, as cited in note 25 above.

28. Ibid.

29. MFM to F. R. Hassler, Feb. 11 and Aug. 12, 1839, F. R. Hassler Papers, New York Public Library, Manuscripts and Archives Section. The superintendent of the Coast Survey was a civilian, Ferdinand R. Hassler, and was under the control of the secretary of the Treasury. The officers, crews, and ships that were used by the survey usually came from the Navy.

30. Charles Wilkes, *Western America, Including California and Oregon, with Maps of Those Regions and the Sacramento Valley* (Philadelphia: Lea and Blanchard, 1849), 13–18.

31. MFM to Ann Maury, Sept. 27, 1839, MP, vol. 1, LC; Corbin, *Maury*, 30–31.

32. M. F. Maury v. D. Talmadge, *U.S. Circuit Court Reports, 1829–55* (Columbus, Ohio: H. W. Derby and H. S. Allen, 1843), 2:157–67.

33. MFM to Ann Maury, Nov. 6 and Dec. 7, 1839, MP, vol. 2, LC; MFM to M. Maury, Nov. 26, 1839, MP, vol. 2, LC.

34. See note 33 above.

35. MFM to Ann Maury, Dec. 25, 1839, MP, vol. 2, LC.

36. MFM to Ann Maury, Jan. 18, 1840, MP, vol. 2, LC.

Chapter 8

1. Harry Bluff articles, *Richmond Whig and Public Advertiser* (hereafter cited as Harry Bluff, *Richmond Whig*) Aug. 10, 13, 14, 17, 18, 25, 27, and 28, 1838; and Sept. 4, 1838; Will Watch, same newspaper, Dec. 21, 25, and 28, 1838.

2. Claude H. Hall, *Abel Parker Upshur* (hereafter cited as Hall, *Upshur*; Madison: State Historical Society of Wisconsin, 1964), 86–89; "Right of Instruction," *Southern Literary Messenger* (hereafter cited as *SLM*) 2, no. 7 (July 1836): 530–35; John Tyler, "Oration," *SLM* 3, no. 12 (Dec. 1837): 744; Abel Parker Upshur, "Domestic Slavery as It Exists in Southern States with Reference to Its Influence upon Free Government," *SLM* 5, no. 10 (Oct. 1839): 677–87.

3. MFM as Harry Bluff, *Richmond Whig*, Aug. 10, 1838; Joel C. Poinsett to Francis H. Gregory, Feb. 19, 1838, Joel C. Poinsett Papers, p. 10:43, Historical Society of Pennsylvania, Philadelphia; Mr. Mallory of Virginia remarks on Why the Delay in Exploring Expedition, Dec. 21, 1837 (Washington, D.C.: Gales and Seaton, 1837).

4. See note 1 above.

5. See note 3 above.

6. Harry Bluff, *Richmond Whig*, Aug. 14, 1838.

7. Will Watch, *Richmond Whig*, Dec. 28, 1838.

8. MFM [but unsigned], "A Scheme for Rebuilding Southern Commerce: Direct Trade with the South," *SLM* 5, no. 1 (1839): 3.

9. Will Watch, *Richmond Whig*, Dec. 21, 25, and 28, 1838, offers a litany of complaints.

10. MFM to Ann Maury, Jan. 18 and Mar. 3, 1840, letters, MP, vol. 2, LC. One of MFM's most penetrating analyses of the officer corps appeared in "Scraps from the Lucky Bag," *SLM* 7, no. 1 (Jan. 1841): 3–25; MFM, "Scraps from the Lucky Bag," *SLM* 6, no. 4 (1840): 724–29. Several historians claim that from 1840 to 1843 Maury edited the *Southern Literary Messenger*. If this view is correct, then Thomas White, who carried the title editor, was actually the publisher, making sure the periodical's finances were in sufficient order to continue printing and mailing. See particularly Edward R. Rogers, *Four Southern Magazines*, PhD diss. (Charlottesville: University of Virginia Studies in Southern Literature, 1902), 104–5; Donald Chisholm, *Waiting for Dead Men's Shoes: Origins and Development of the U.S. Navy's Officer Personnel System, 1793–1941* (hereafter cited as Chisholm, *Waiting*), 170.

11. See note 9 above.

12. MFM, "Scraps from the Lucky Bag," *SLM* 6, no. 5 (May 1840): 306–11; Christopher McKee, *A Gentlemanly and Honorable Profession: The Creation of the U.S. Naval Officer Corps, 1794–1815*, 195.

13. MFM, "More Scraps from the Lucky Bag," *SLM* 7, nos. 5 and 6 (May–June 1841): 345–79; Chisholm, *Waiting*, 172.

14. MFM "Scraps from the Lucky Bag," *SLM* 7, no. 1 (Jan. 1841): 12–25, and the same series, *SLM* 7, nos. 5–6 (May–June 1841): 345–79, and no. 10 (Oct. 1841): 724–29.

15. See note 14 above.

16. MFM as Union Jack in "Letters to Mr. Clay," *SLM* 7, no. 10 (Oct. 1840): 724–29, and under his own name, *SLM* 9, no. 1 (Jan. 1843): 1–5.

17. See note 16 above.

18. Frances Leigh Williams, *Matthew Fontaine Maury: Scientist of the Sea*, 131.

19. William Freehling, *The Road to Disunion: Secessionists at Bay, 1776–1854* (hereafter cited as Freehling, *Bay*), 357.

20. See note 19 above; Hatfield, "John Tyler (1841)," in *Vice Presidents of the United States*, 137–46; Freehling, *Bay*, 360.

21. Daniel Walker Howe, *What Hath God Wrought: The Transformation of America, 1815–1848* (hereafter cited as Howe, *Wrought*), 349; Gordon S. Wood, *Empire of Liberty: A History of the Early Republic*, 674–79; David Hackett Fischer and James C. Kelly, *Bound Away: Virginia and the Western Movement*, 173.

22. Howe, *Wrought*, 579; Launcelot Minor Blackford, *Mine Eyes Have Seen the Glory*, xii; Elizabeth Varon, *We Mean to Be Counted: White Women and Politics in Antebellum Virginia* (Chapel Hill: University of North Carolina Press, 1998), 80.

23. MFM to Ann Maury of New York, May 4, 1840, MP, vol. 2, LC; Hatfield, *Vice Presidents of the United States*, 137–46; Howe, *Wrought*, p. 579; MFM to his mother, Diana Minor Maury, Nov. 10, 1840, MFM Papers, Virginia Military Institute Archives.

24. Hatfield, *Vice Presidents*.

25. Ibid.

26. Paolo Coletta, "George F. Badger, 6 Mar. 1841–11 Sept. 1841" (hereafter cited as Coletta, "Badger"), in Coletta, *American Secretaries of the Navy, 1775–1913*, 1:173–75.

27. "A Brother Officer," *SLM* 7, no. 7 (July 1841): 560–63.

28. Paolo Coletta, "Abel Parker Upshur, 11 Oct. 1841–23 July 1843" (hereafter cited as Coletta, "Upshur"), in Coletta, *American Secretaries of the Navy, 1775–1913*, 1:178; Coletta, "Badger," 1:173–75; Chisholm, *Waiting*, 174.

29. MFM to Lucian Minor, Nov. 8, Dec. 14, 1840, MP, vol. 2, LC; Coletta, "Upshur," 1:178.

30. Receipt from Hustings Court, Fredericksburg, Va., for bond by MFM, filed under May 10, 1842, MP, vol. 2, LC; Verdict, M. F. Maury v. D. Talmadge, U.S. Circuit Court, Columbus, Ohio, *McLeans Records, United States Circuit Court Reports, 1829–1855* (Columbus, Ohio: H. W. Derby and H. S. Allen, 1843), 2:167.

31. NR, MFM to Secretary of the Navy Paulding, Feb. 24, 1840; Records of the Office of the Judge Advocate General (Navy): Courts of Inquiry, Act of Jan. 16, 1857, vol. 21.

32. Hall, *Upshur*, 120–45; Freehling, *Bay*, 401; MFM to Lucian Minor, Nov. 8, Dec. 14, 1840, MP, vol. 2, LC.

33. Hall, *Upshur*, 120–45.

34. Report of the Secretary of the Navy, Dec. 4, 1841, in collected reports, Department of the Navy Library, Washington, D.C.; "Judge Abel Parker Upshur," *SLM* 7, no. 12 (Dec. 1841): 865–72; MFM, "Our Navy: Judge Abel Parker Upshur and His Report (Review)," *SLM* 8, no. 1 (Jan. 1842), 89–97. On a variety of reform issues, *Naval Magazine*, Jan. 1836–Jan. 1837; Matthew C. Perry et al. were writers-editors for this publication from the New York Navy Yard. See also Freehling, *Bay*, 401.

35. Louis M. Goldsborough to his wife, 1841, Louis M. Goldsborough Papers, MS Collection, LC.

36. MFM to Secretary Badger, June 10, 1841, MP, vol. 2, LC.

37. NR, Judge John Tayloe Lomax to Secretary Upshur, Nov. 11, 1841; Miscellaneous Records of the Hydrographic Office, NAN.

38. Secretary of the Navy A. P. Upshur to MFM, Nov. 15, 1841, MP, vol. 2, LC; MFM to Secretary Upshur, Nov. 18, 1841, MP, vol. 2, LC; Diana Fontaine Maury Corbin, *A Life of Matthew Fontaine Maury, U.S.N. and C.S.N., Compiled by His Daughter*, p. 39, quoting letter from MFM to Rutson Maury.

39. MFM to Ann Maury, Feb. 15, 1840, MP, vol. 2, LC.

Chapter 9

1. "Report of the Secretary of the Navy, Dec. 4, 1841," in collected reports, Department of the Navy Library, Washington, D.C.; MFM, "Our Navy: Judge Abel Parker Upshur and His Report (Review)," *Southern Literary Messenger* (hereafter cited as *SLM*) 8, no. 1 (Jan. 1842): 89–97; on a variety of reform issues, *Naval Magazine*, Jan. 1836–Jan. 1837; Secretary A. P. Upshur to MFM, Nov. 15, 1841, MP, vol. 2, LC; MFM to Secretary Upshur, Nov. 18, 1841, MP, vol. 2, LC; Diana Fontaine Maury Corbin, *A Life of Matthew Fontaine Maury, U.S.N. and C.S.N., Compiled by His Daughter*, p. 39, quoting a letter from MFM to Rutson Maury; "Letters to Mr. Clay," *SLM* 7, no. 10 (Oct. 1841): 724–29; "The Right of Search," *SLM* 8, no. 4 (Apr. 1842): 289–301; "Our Relations with England," *SLM* 8, no. 6 (June 1842): 381–96; Francis Markoe, Jr., ed., *Proceedings of the National Institution for the Promotion of Science*, Bulletin No. 1, and later collected in fifteen pamphlets and produced in a single volume, "MFM, to National Institution for the Promotion of Science," Dec. 5, 1840, in the institution's *Proceedings*. See also the Constitution of the National Institution for the Promotion of Science, 1841; Maury's name appears on p. 16.

2. MFM to Rutson Maury, Feb. 1842, MP, vol. 2, LC.

3. Jan Herman, *A Hilltop in Foggy Bottom* (Washington, D.C.: Naval Medical Command, 1984), 7.

4. Charles Francis Adams, ed., *Memoirs of John Quincy Adams, Comprising Portions of His Diary from 1795–1848* (hereafter cited as Adams, *Memoirs*; Philadelphia: J. B. Lippincott, 1866), 7:55; Steven J. Dick, "John Quincy Adams: The Smithsonian Bequest and the Founding of the U.S. Naval Observatory" (hereafter cited as Dick, "Founding"), *Journal for the History of Astronomy* 22 (Feb. 1991): 31–44; J. M. Gilliss, *Report of the Secretary of the Navy Communicating a Report of the Plan and Construction of the Depot of Charts and Instruments with a Description of the Instruments* (hereafter cited as Gillis, *Depot of Charts and Instruments*), 28th Cong., 2d Sess., Senate Document 114, pamphlet (Washington, D.C., 1844–45); Gilliss to Board of Navy Commissioners, included in Upshur's *1841 Secretary of the Navy Report*, Dec. 4, 1841 (hereafter cited as Gillis to Navy Commissioners 1841; Washington, D.C.); Benjamin A. Gould, Jr., "Gilliss Memoir," *National Academy of Sciences Annual*, pamphlet (Washington, D.C.: National Academy of Sciences, 1866), 27.

5. Steven J. Dick, *Sky and Ocean Joined: The United States Naval Observatory, 1830–2000* (London: Cambridge University Press, 2003), 55–56; Dick, "Founding," 37.

6. Frances Leigh Williams, *Matthew Fontaine Maury: Scientist of the Sea* (hereafter cited as Williams, *Maury Scientist*), 141.

7. MFM to Lucian Minor, Nov. 8, Dec. 14, 1840, MP, vol. 2, LC; MFM to Rutson Maury, Feb. 20, 1842, MP, vol. 2, LC; MFM to Professor John B. Minor, Jan. 28, 1856, MP, vol. 5, LC; Williams, *Maury Scientist*, 141.

8. Gilliss, *Depot of Charts and Instruments*; Gilliss to Navy Commissioners 1841.

9. NR, Captain Finch's Cruise in U.S.S. *Vincennes*, 1826–30, NAN; Matthew J. Karp, "The Navalist Impulse in the Antebellum South," *Journal of Southern History* 77, no. 2 (May 2011): 297–322.

10. "Report of the Secretary of the Navy, Dec. 4, 1841," in collected reports, Department of the Navy Library, Washington, D.C.; MFM, "Our Relations with England," *SLM* 9, no. 6 (June 1842): 381–96.

11. William H. Goetzmann, *Exploration and Empire: The Explorer and the Scientist in the Winning of the American West* (hereafter cited as Goetzmann, *Exploration*; Austin: Texas State His-

torical Association, 1993), 32–33; Samuel Eliot Morison, *The Maritime History of Massachusetts, 1783–1860* (Boston: Houghton Mifflin, 1922), 45–48; see note 10 above.

12. Thomas Hart Benton, *Thirty Years' View; or, A History of the Working of the American Government for Thirty Years from 1820 to 1850* (hereafter cited as Benton, *Thirty*), 2:460; James C. Carter, *Fur-Seal Arbitration: Oral Argument of James C. Carter, Esq., on Behalf of the United States Before the Tribunal of Arbitration Convened at Paris* (Washington, D.C.: Government Printing Office, 1895), 123–24; W. Patrick Strauss, "James Kirke Paulding, 1 July 1838–3 Mar. 1841," in Coletta, *American Secretaries of the Navy, 1775–1913*, 1:167.

13. Fred Lockley, *Oregon Trail Blazers* (New York: Knickerbocker, 1909), 276–81, on interest of New England missionaries in Oregon; F. G. Young, ed., *Sources of the History of Oregon*. Vol. 1, Pts. 3–6, *The Correspondence and Journals of Captain Nathaniel J. Wyeth, 1831–6: A Record of Two Expeditions for the Occupation of the Oregon Country, with Maps, Introduction, and Index* (Eugene, Ore.: University, 1899), 290, on first foray into Willamette Valley; *Report of the Committee on Foreign Affairs, to Which Was Referred a Message from the President of the United States in Relation to the Territory of the United States beyond the Rocky Mountains*, Feb. 16, 1839, 25th Cong., 3d Sess., H.R. Rep. 101 (Washington, D.C., 1835), 1–24, accessed Apr. 13, 2014, http://books.google.com/books?id=E7YTAAAAYAAJ; Goetzmann, *Exploration*, 169, 244; Howe, *Wrought*, 914; Benton, *Thirty*, 2:478–82.

14. Goetzmann, *Exploration*, 169, 244.

15. NR, MFM to Commodore William M. Crane, Chief, Bureau of Ordnance and Hydrography, Mar. 22, 1845, Naval Observatory Letters Sent (hereafter cited as NOLS), vol. 1, NAN.

16. Alfred Friendly, introduction to *Beaufort of the Admiralty: The Life of Sir Francis Beaufort, 1774–1857* (hereafter cited as Friendly, *Beaufort*; New York: Random House, 1977).

17. Friendly, *Beaufort*, 144–47.

18. Friendly, *Beaufort*, 244–66.

19. Ibid.

20. The drive and energy that Maury had is probably best encapsulated in his letter to Rutson Maury, Aug. 31, 1840, MP, vol. 2, LC. That letter set the stage for his writing in *SLM*, public speaking, and drive to succeed inside and outside the Navy.

21. Explained by MFM in "Blank Charts on Board Public Cruisers," *SLM* 9, no. 8 (Aug. 1843): 458–61.

22. Williams, *Maury Scientist*, 151.

23. NR, MFM to Crane, Sept. 25, 1843, NOLS, vol. 1, NAN.

24. *Army and Navy Chronicle and Scientific Repository* (Washington, D.C.), Jan. 19, 1843, 58.

25. Helen M. Rozwadowski, *Fathoming the Ocean: The Discovery and Exploration of the Deep Sea* (Cambridge, Mass.: Belknap Press of Harvard University Press, 2005), 18; MFM to Ann Maury, Feb. 11, 1843, MP, vol. 2, LC, on the workload at the observatory; MFM to William M. Blackford, Nov. 19, 1843, MP, vol. 3, LC; Corbin, *Maury*, 53.

26. NR, MFM to Capt. William Crane, Nov. 9, 1842, NOLS, vol. 1, NAN.

27. MFM to Ann Maury, Feb. 11, 1843, MP, vol. 2, LC; gravestone, Hollywood Cemetery, Richmond.

28. A number of letters in MP, vol. 3, LC, including MFM to Lucian Minor, July 29, 1843; letters to MFM from Thomas N. Fiquers, Aug. 31, 1844, and Matilda Maury Guthrie, Mar. 27, 1845, vol. 3, MP, LC; gravestone, Hollywood Cemetery, Richmond.

29. MFM, "Blank Charts on Board Public Cruisers, *SLM* 9, no. 8 (Aug. 1843): 458.

30. Ibid.

31. NR, MFM to Capt. F. H. Gregory, Aug. 29, 1843, NOLS, vol. 1, NAN; NR, "Suggestions for the Home Squadron in Observing Gulf Stream and Other Currents," Oct. 30, 1843, NOLS, vol. 1, NAN.

32. Blank charts in note 29 above; suggestions in note 31 above.

33. NR, MFM to Blunt Co. (engravers), Oct. 19, 1843, NOLS, vol. 1, NAN.

Chapter 10

1. *Bulletin of the Proceedings of the National Institute* 1, nos. 1–3 (Washington, D.C.: Gales and Seaton, 1841), 424.

2. Rexmond C. Cochrane, *The First Hundred Years, 1863–1963* (hereafter cited as Cochrane, *First Hundred*; Washington, D.C.: National Academy of Sciences, 1978), 13–14; *Bulletin of the Proceedings of the National Institution for the Promotion of Science* (Washington, D.C.: Gales and Seaton, 1841), 17–18.

3. Cochrane, *First Hundred*, 14.

4. Peter Booth Wiley, *Yankees in the Lands of the Gods: Commodore Perry and the Opening of Japan*, with Korogi Ichiro (New York: Viking, 1990), 37.

5. James Fenimore Cooper, *Cruise of the* Somers (New York: J. Winchester, 1844), accessed Feb. 24, 2014, http://cdm16099.contentdm.oclc.org/cdm/ref/collection/p15241coll1/id/18.

6. Dudley Knox, *History of United States Navy*, 167; Judith A Nientimp, "The Somers Mutiny," *University of Rochester Library Bulletin* 20, no. 1 (Autumn 1964), accessed Dec. 17, 2013, http://www.lib.rochester.edu/index.cfm?PAGE=2477.

7. Tyler to Senate and House of Representa-

tives, Feb. 29, 1844, *A Compilation of the Messages and Papers of the Presidents, 1789–1897*, comp. James D. Richardson (Washington, D.C.: U.S. Congress, 1897), 4:206–16, accessed Dec. 17, 2013, http://books.google.com/books?id=8jcPAAAAYAAJ; K. Jack Bauer, "Thomas Walker Gilmer, 10 Feb. 1844–28 Feb. 1844," in Coletta, *American Secretaries of the Navy, 1775–1913*, 1:203–4; Franklin Institute, "Report on the Explosion of the Gun on Board the Steam Frigate 'Princeton,'" *Journal of the Franklin Institute* (Franklin Institute of Pennsylvania, Philadelphia), 3rd ser., 3 (1844): 206–16; Paulo E. Coletta, "Abel Parker Upshur, 11 Oct. 1841–23 July 1843," in Coletta, *American Secretaries of the Navy, 1775–1913*, 1:194; Robert J. Schneller, Jr., *A Quest for Glory: A Biography of Rear Admiral John A. Dahlgren* (hereafter cited as Schneller, *Dahlgren*; Annapolis: Naval Institute, 1996), 68. As Alexander Slidell changed his name to Alexander Slidell MacKenzie, William Bolton Finch had his name changed to William Bolton following his command of *Vincennes*.

8. "Proceedings of the Meeting of April 1844," *Proceedings of the National Institute for the Promotion of Science*, Bulletin No. 3, Papers Relating to the National Institute (hereafter cited as *National Institute Proceedings*; Washington, D.C.: William Q. Force, 1845), 430, 442, accessed Dec. 17, 2013, http://books.google.com/books?id=sRK5AAAAIAAJ; William Jay Youmans, ed., *Pioneers of Science in America: Sketches of Their Lives and Scientific Work* (New York: D. Appleton, 1896), 436–37.

9. MFM, "The Gulf Stream and Currents of the Seas," *Southern Literary Messenger* (hereafter cited as *SLM*) 10, no. 7 (July 1844): 393–409. Pamphlet reproducing an article found in the Library of Virginia.

10. *National Institute Proceedings*, 431.

11. Marc Rothenberg et al., eds., *The Papers of Joseph Henry*, vol. 6, *January 1844–December 1846: The Princeton Years* (hereafter cited as Rothenberg, *Henry*; Washington, D.C.: Smithsonian Institution Press, 1992), 76; Youmans, *Pioneers*, 360.

12. *Proceedings of Association of American Geologists and Naturalists, 1844* (Washington, 1844), 86.

13. John H. Schroeder, *Shaping a Maritime Empire* (Westport, Conn.: Greenwood, 1985), 60; "The Narrative of the Exploring Expedition," *SLM* 11, no. 6 (June 1845): 388–89.

14. Geologists, *American Journal of Science and Arts* (hereafter cited as *Am. Journ. Science*) 67 (Oct. 1844): 161–81.

15. "Abstract of the Proceedings of the Association of American Geologists and Naturalists," *Am. Journ. Science* 67 (Oct. 1844): proceedings, pp. 161–81, MFM address in annex, pp. 94–134; MFM, "On the Currents of the Sea as Connected with Meteorology," paper presented May 14, 1844, in *Proceedings of the Association of American Geologists and Naturalists, 1844*, and published in *Army and Navy Chronicle*, June 1, 1844, p. 699. MFM lectured and wrote extensively on the division of responsibility for collecting weather data. One early work was "On the Establishment of a Universal System of Meteorological Observations by Sea and Land," in *Compilation of Correspondence* (including Maury), comp. MFM (Washington, D.C.: C. Alexander, 1851), 2–3.

16. K. Jack Bauer, "David Henshaw, 24 July 1843–18 Feb. 1844," in Coletta, *American Secretaries of the Navy, 1775–1913*, 1:199–201.

17. K. Jack Bauer, "John Young Mason, 16 Mar. 1844–10 Mar. 1845" (hereafter cited as Bauer, "Mason"), in Coletta, *American Secretaries of the Navy, 1775–1913*, 1:107.

18. Frank M. Bennett, *The Steam Navy of the United States: A History of the Growth of the Steam Vessel of War in the U.S. Navy and Naval Engineer Corps* (Pittsburgh: Warren, 1896), 69–70; Kenneth J. Hagan, *This People's Navy: The Making of American Sea Power*, 122; Schneller, *Dahlgren*, 169; Paolo Coletta, "Abel Parker Upshur, 11 Oct. 1841–13 July 1843," in Coletta, *American Secretaries of the Navy, 1775–1913*, 1:194; K. Jack Bauer, "Thomas Walker Gilmer, 19 Feb. 1844–28 Feb. 1844," in Coletta, *American Secretaries of the Navy, 1775–1913*, 1:204.

19. John Tyler, "Third Annual Message," Dec. 5, 1843, online by Gerhard Peters and John T. Woolley, *American Presidency Project*, University of California, Santa Barbara, http://www.presidency.ucsb.edu/ws/?pid=29647; Bauer, "Mason," in Coletta, *American Secretaries of the Navy, 1775–1913*, 1:211–13; Hagan, *People's*, 123; Schneller, *Dahlgren*, 67–71.

20. Bauer, "Mason," in Coletta, *American Secretaries of the Navy, 1775–1913*, 209, 1:211–13.

21. Steven J. Dick, "John Quincy Adams: The Smithsonian Bequest and the Founding of the U.S. Naval Observatory," *Journal for the History of Astronomy* 22 (Feb. 1991): 31–44; Edwin Holden, "The United States Naval Observatory, Washington," (hereafter cited as Holden, "Observatory"), *Science: A Weekly Journal of Scientific Papers* (New York) 21, no. 2 (July 3, 1880): 1; Raymond Charles Archibald, *Biographical Sketch of Benjamin Peirce* (Oberlin, Ohio: Mathematical Association of America, 1925), 8–20.

22. MFM to Ann Maury, Sept. 11, 1844, MP, vol. 3, LC.

23. NR, MFM to Commodore William M. Crane, Chief, Bureau of Ordnance and Hydrography, Oct. 12, 1844, NOLS, vol. 1, NAN; Dick, "Founding," 31–45.

24. *Man on the Hill* came to be the term used to describe Maury by many of his critics. They were referring to the observatory's location on a

bluff above the Potomac. Correspondence between Bache and Henry, both in Smithsonian Institution Archives and Library of Congress Manuscript Collection, use the phrase. Correspondence of S. F. DuPont contains the same phrase.

25. Tour of the old observatory, then headquarters of the Naval Medical Command, Washington, D.C. Jan Herman, command historian, conducted the tour.

26. NR, MFM to Crane, Oct. 12, 1844, NOLS, vol. 1, NAN.

27. Ibid.

28. Ibid.

29. NR, MFM to Crane, Oct. 20, 1844, NOLS, vol. 2, and Apr. 17, 1845, NOLS, vol. 2, NAN. A summary of problems in same volume at archives; several letters to city officials asking for assistance in controlling spectators and dampness problems.

30. NR, MFM to Crane, Oct. 12, 1844, NOLS, vol. 1, NAN.

31. NR, MFM to Crane, Apr. 17, 1845, NOLS, vol. 2, NAN.

32. Ibid.

33. NR, MFM to F. A. P. Barnard, University of Alabama, Dec. 23, 1844, NOLS, vol. 1, NAN; NR, MFM to Benjamin Peirce, Cambridge, Mass., Mar. 20, 1845, NOLS, vol. 1, NAN; and NR, MFM to Lt. Col. Sabine, Feb. 22, 1845, NOLS, vol. 1, NAN, on improved compasses and study of magnetism, are examples.

34. MFM, "On the Probable Relation between Magnetism and the Circulation of the Atmosphere," *Sailing Directions*, 3rd ed. (1851), 143–72; see the letter to Sabine in note 33 above.

35. John Dryden Kazar, Jr., "The United States Navy and Scientific Exploration, 1837–1860," 414; Elizabeth Green Musselman, "Science as a Landed Activity: Scientifics and Seamen aboard the U.S. Exploring Expedition," in *Surveying the Record: North American Scientific Exploration to 1930*, 119; Charles Francis Adams, ed., *Memoirs of John Quincy Adams* (hereafter cited as Adams, *Memoirs*), 7:55, 12:189, 12:193; Simon Newcomb, *Reminiscences of an Astronomer* (hereafter cited as Newcomb, *Astronomer*; Boston: Riverside Press of Houghton Mifflin, 1903), 160.

36. MFM, "National Observatory," *SLM* 14, no. 1 (Jan. 1848): 5–6; MFM to George Bancroft, July 28, 1846, and MFM to J. Q. Adams, Nov. 17, 1847, NOLS, both vol. 2, NAN; Adams, *Memoirs*, 12:189, 12:192.

37. Holden, "Observatory," 1; Steven J. Dick, *Sky and Ocean Joined: The United States Naval Observatory, 1830–2000*, 56; Gould, "Gilliss Memoir," 27.

38. Newcomb, *Astronomer*, 98; MFM, "National Observatory," *SLM* 14, no. 1 (Jan. 1848): 4–6; NR, MFM to Crane, Nov. 3, 1845, NOLS, vol. 2, NAN; Clyde N. Wilson, *Carolina Cavalier* (Athens: University of Georgia Press, 1990), 20; Frances Leigh Williams, *Matthew Fontaine Maury: Scientist of the Sea*, 161.

39. MFM to William M. Blackford, Jan. 1, 1847, MP, vol. 3, LC; Rothenberg, *Henry*, 592n.

40. MFM, "National Observatory," *SLM* 14, no. 1 (Jan. 1848): 4–6; Musselman, "Science," 100; K. Jack Bauer, "George Bancroft, 11 Mar. 1845–9 Sept. 1846," in Coletta, *American Secretaries of the Navy, 1775–1913*, 1:228–29.

41. See note 39 above.

42. NR, MFM report on Biela contained in letters to Crane, Jan. 13, 15, and 19, 1846, and to Secretary of the Navy Bancroft, Feb. 19, 1846, NOLS, both vol. 2, NAN.

43. See note 39 above.

44. Article on MFM and quotation from mayor of Halifax, Nova Scotia, on Maury's intentions in Europe, *Richmond Daily Dispatch*, Dec. 5, 1862.

45. Mary H. Maury Werth to her children (hereafter cited as Werth, Reminiscence), July 26, 1879, MP, vol. 42, LC.

46. MFM to Mrs. William M. Blackford, Apr. 15, 1844, MP, vol. 3, LC; MFM to Prof. Charles Piazzi Smyth, Edinburg, Oct. 28, 1853, NOLS, vol. 10, NAN; MFM to his wife, Jan. 1 and Apr. 15, 16, and 19, 1863, MP, vol. 17, LC; Diana Maury Corbin, *A Life of Matthew Fontaine Maury, U.S.N. and C.S.N., Compiled by His Daughter*, 150–51; Werth, Reminiscence. While MFM loved mottoes, including *Cur non?* on the title page of his book on navigation, his most revealing insights into how he viewed his life work is contained in his letter to Rutson Maury, Aug. 31, 1840, MP, vol. 2, LC.

47. MFM to Mrs. William Blackford, Apr. 2, 1849, MP, vol. 3, LC.

48. See note 46 above.

49. MFM to A. Hamilton Lieber, May 30, 1850, Caroliana Room, University of South Carolina Library; Werth, Reminiscence.

Chapter 11

1. William Freehling, *The Road to Disunion: Secessionists at Bay, 1776–1854* (hereafter cited as Freehling, *Bay*), 449; Hatfield, "John Tyler (1841)," *Vice Presidents of the United States*, 137–46.

2. "The Annexation of Texas," *Southern Literary Messenger* (hereafter cited as *SLM*) 10, no. 4 (Apr. 1844): 325.

3. K. Jack Bauer, *The Mexican War, 1846–1848* (hereafter cited as Bauer, *Mexican*; Lincoln: University of Nebraska Press, 1974), 5.

4. Freehling, *Bay*, 437, 448–49; Daniel Walker Howe, *What Hath God Wrought: The Transformation of America, 1815–1848* (hereafter cited as Howe, *Wrought*), 699; Daniel J. Boorstin,

The Americans: The National Experience (New York: Vintage Books, 1965), 272.

5. Linda Arnold, "The Mexican-American War and the Media, 1845–1848," Department of History, Virginia Polytechnic Institute and State University, 2005, http://www.history.vt.edu/MxAmWar/INDEX.HTM; Dudley Knox, *History of United States Navy*, 164–65; Kenneth J. Hagan, *This People's Navy: The Making of American Sea Power*, 125; Bauer, *Mexican*, 9.

6. Anson Jones, *Memoranda and Official Correspondence Relating to the Republic of Texas, Its History, and Annexation* (hereafter cited as Jones, *Memoranda*; New York: D. Appleton, 1859), 41.

7. Milo Milton Quaife, ed., *The Diary of James K. Polk During His Presidency, 1845–1849*, 4 vols. (hereafter cited as Polk, *Diary:* Chicago: A. C. McClurg, 1910): Biographical Sketch, 1:xxi–xxxii; "Aug. 20, 1845," 1:9; "Aug. 30, 1845," 1:12; Howe, *Wrought*, 750; Jones, *Memoranda*, 46.

8. Polk, "May 13, 1845," *Diary*, 1:398; Bauer, *Mexican*, 239, 350–51.

9. Dabney H. Maury, *Recollections of a Virginian in the Mexican, Indian, and Civil Wars* (hereafter cited as D. Maury, *Recollections*; New York: Scribner's, 1894), 32; Bauer, *Mexican*, 236, 243–44.

10. Sarah Mytton Maury, *The Statesmen of America in 1846*, American ed. (Philadelphia: Carey and Hart, 1847), 167–68, accessed Nov. 3, 2013, http://books.google.com/books?id=lt0DAAAAYAAJ; Polk, *Diary*, 3:183; Bauer, *Mexican*, 339; *Proceedings of the New York Historical Society for the Year 1847* (New York: Press of the Historical Society, 1847), 164.

11. NR, MFM to Prof. Benjamin Peirce, Jan. 26, 1846, NOLS, vol. 2, NAN.

12. Ian R. Bartky, *Selling the True Time: Nineteenth Century Timekeeping in America* (hereafter cited as Bartky, *Selling*; Stanford, Calif.: Stanford University Press, 2001), 34n13; NR, MFM to Secretary of the Navy Bancroft, Feb. 28, 1846, NOLS, vol. 2, NAN; William Jay Youmans, ed., *Pioneers of Science in America: Sketches of Their Lives and Scientific Work* (hereafter cited as Youmans, *Pioneers*), 428–31.

13. "Bache and Maury: The Attack of 1849," *NOAA History: A Science Odyssey*, NOAA Central Library, U.S. National Oceanographic and Atmospheric Administration, last modified Nov. 30, 2007, http://www.lib.noaa.gov/noaainfo/heritage/coastsurveyvol1/BACHE2.html#MAURY.

14. Bartky, *Selling*, 34.

15. NR, MFM to Secretary of the Navy Bancroft, Feb. 28, 1846, NOLS, vol. 2, NAN; Youmans, *Pioneers*, 428–31.

16. See note 15 above.

17. NR, MFM to Secretary of the Navy Mason, Feb. 8, 18, and 26 and Mar. 25, 1847, NOLS, vol. 2, NAN; Youmans, *Pioneers*, 431.

18. See MFM letters in note 17 above, particularly Feb. 8 and Mar. 25, 1847.

19. NR, MFM to Prof. Loomis, Union College, Apr. 20, 1847, NOLS, vol. 2, NAN.

20. Steven J. Dick, *Sky and Ocean Joined: The United States Naval Observatory, 1830–2000* (hereafter cited as Dick, *Sky*), 85; Steven J. Dick, "John Quincy Adams, the Smithsonian Bequest, and the Founding of the U.S. Naval Observatory," 41.

21. NR, MFM to Joseph Henry, Sept. 20, 1847, NOLS, vol. 2, NAN; Youmans, *Pioneers*, 431.

22. See note 21 above; NR, MFM to Henry, Oct. 20, 1847, NOLS, vol. 2, NAN.

23. A copy of an article from *Astronomische Nachrichten* is filed in NR, Oct. 1847, NOLS, vol. 2, NAN.

24. Ibid.

25. NR, MFM to Joseph Henry, Oct. 20, 1847, NOLS, vol. 2, NAN.

26. NR, MFM to Joseph Henry, Nov. 15, 1847, NOLS, vol. 2, NAN.

27. Bessie Jones, *Golden Age of Science* (New York: Simon & Schuster, 1966), 308–315, provides an excellent description of Bache and Henry as power brokers. John W. Oliver, *History of American Technology* (Ann Arbor, Mich.: University Microfilms, 1980), 108–9, 240–44; Varina Howell Davis, *Jefferson Davis, Ex-President of the Confederate States of America: A Memoir by His Wife* (Baltimore: Nautical and Aviation, 1990), 1:262.

28. Merle Middleton Odgers, *Alexander Dallas Bache: Scientist and Educator, 1806–1867*, 165.

29. Richard Stachurski, *Longitude by Wire: Finding North America* (Columbia: University of South Carolina Press, 2009), 69; Odgers, *Bache*, 204.

30. See note 29 above.

31. Thomas Coulson, *Joseph Henry: His Life and Work* (Princeton: Princeton University Press, 1950), 153–54; Marc Rothenberg et al., eds., *The Papers of Joseph Henry*, vol. 6, *January 1844–December 1846: The Princeton Years* (hereafter cited as Rothenberg, *Henry*), 438n.

32. "Meteorology for Farmers," *American Farmer* 11, no. 2 (Aug. 1855): 1–2; Dick, *Sky*, 95. One of many calls for a national weather service.

33. Wendell W. Huffman, "The United States Naval Astronomical Expedition (1849–52) for the Solar Parallax," *Journal for the History of Astronomy* 22 (Feb. 1991): 209, 214–15, indicating Peirce's views of Maury's work at the observatory.

34. MFM, "National Observatory," *SLM* 15, no. 5 (May 1849): 304–8, reprint of address, Virginia Historical Society, Richmond, Dec. 14, 1848.

35. MFM, "A Railroad from the Atlantic to the Pacific," *Hunt's Merchants' Magazine* 18, no. 6 (June 1848): 592–601; MFM, "The Isthmus Line to the Pacific," *SLM* 15, no. 8 (Aug. 1849):

253–66; MFM as Harry Bluff, "Lake Defenses and Western Interests," *SLM* 11, no. 2 (Feb. 1845): 83–91.

36. William Goetzmann, *New Lands, New Men: America and the Second Great Age of Discovery*, 267.

37. MFM to the Rev. James Curley, July 11 and Oct. 18, 1847, correspondence, Curley Papers, box 2, Georgetown University Archives, Washington, D.C.; Edward Leon Towle, "Science, Commerce, and the Navy on the Seagoing Frontier: The Role of M. F. Maury and the U.S. Naval Hydrographic Office in Naval Exploration, Commercial Expansion, and Oceanography before the Civil War" (PhD diss., University of Rochester, 1966), 106 (copy read at the Department of the Navy Library, Washington, D.C.).

38. Kemp P. Battle, *History of the University of North Carolina from Its Beginning to the Death of President Swain, 1789–1868* (hereafter cited as Battle, *History;* Raleigh, N.C.: Edwards and Broughton, 1907), 1:508–9; Polk, *Diary*, 3:41, 47, 177; Kemp P. Battle, "Commodore Maury and General Pettigrew," *North Carolina University Magazine* (Chapel Hill) 12 (1892–1893): 273–80.

39. Polk, *Diary*, 3:48.

40. Harold D. Langley, "William Alexander Graham, 1 Aug. 1850–30 June 1852," in Coletta, *American Secretaries of the Navy, 1775–1913*, 1:260–61.

41. Battle, *History*, 508–9.

42. Battle, *History*, 546–48.

43. MFM to William Blackford, July 12, 1847, MP, vol. 3, LC; MFM to Ann Maury, Sept. 30 and Oct. 31, 1847, MP, vol. 3, LC; MFM to John Quincy Adams, Nov. 14, 1847, *SLM* 14, no. 1 (Jan. 1847): 9–10; Rothenberg, *Henry*, 264n.

44. NR, MFM to George Bancroft, Nov. 1, 1847, NOLS, vol. 2, NAN; Simon Newcomb, *Reminiscences of an Astronomer*, 103–4; Abel Parker Upshur, "Domestic Slavery," *SLM* 5, no. 10 (Oct. 1839): 677.

45. David M. Potter, *The Impending Crisis, 1848–1861*, completed and edited by Don E. Fehrenbacher (hereafter cited as Potter, *Impending;* New York: Harper Colophon, 1976), 21–22; Bauer, *Mexican*, 250, 369.

46. Howe, *Wrought*, 276; Potter, *Impending*, 48.

47. MFM to Mrs. Kemp S. Holland, Jan. 10, 1847, MP, vol. 3, LC; Dunbar Rowland, ed., *Encyclopedia of Mississippi History* (Madison, Wis.: Selwyn A. Brant, 1907), 2:259–60; D. Maury, *Recollections*, 36–37; Robert V. Remini, *Henry Clay: Statesman for the Union*, 684–85; Bauer, *Mexican*, 307.

Chapter 12

1. William Whiting to John M. Brooke, May 31, 1873, MP, vol. 44, LC.

2. Andrew Foote Papers, MS Collection, LC, including "Instructions to British Fleet off Africa"; letter to Foote from Cmdr. John Tudor, Mar. 1850, on right to search; Secretary of the Navy Preston, June 1850, order barring overnight stays in Africa, the Cape Verde islands, or traveling up river from the coast. Foote collected some of this material into a manuscript entitled, "Africa and the American Flag," dated 1854.

3. Simon Newcomb, *Reminiscences of an Astronomer*, 103–4.

4. "The Gulf Stream and Currents of the Sea" as read before the National Institute Annual Meeting, Apr. 2, 1844, *Southern Literary Messenger* (hereafter cited as *SLM*) 10, no. 7 (July 1844): 393–409.

5. Edward Leon Towle, "Science, Commerce, and the Navy on the Seagoing Frontier: The Role of M. F. Maury and the U.S. Naval Hydrographic Office in Naval Exploration, Commercial Expansion, and Oceanography before the Civil War," 337–38; Whiting to Brooke letter cited in note 1 above.

6. MFM, *Sailing Directions*, 4th ed. (1852), 41; see note 1 above.

7. Explanatory notes on sheets 2 and 3 of the *Wind and Current Charts of the North Atlantic* (1848), from the information book at the U.S. Naval Observatory (now the vice president's residence), Washington, D.C.

8. MFM to John Q. Adams, Nov. 14, 1847, *SLM* 14, no. 1 (Jan. 1848): 9–10.

9. William Goetzmann, New Lands, New Men: America and the Second Great Age of Discovery (hereafter cited as Goetzmann, New Men), 310; "Secretary of the Navy Annual Report," in *Message from the President of the United States to the Two Houses of Congress at the Commencement of 2d Session of the 29th Congress, Dec. 8, 1846* (Washington, D.C.: Ritchie and Heiss, 1846), accessed Jan. 14, 2014, http://books.google.com/books?id=D7UTAAAAYAAJ; MFM, "The National Observatory," SLM 14, no. 1 (Jan. 1848): 9–10. The best collections of the charts are in the present Naval Observatory in northwest Washington, D.C., now the vice president's residence. Because many of these charts were from the earliest work, they are not as cluttered as the ones produced immediately before the Civil War.

10. NR, MFM to Robert Walsh, Jan. 24, 1848, NOLS, vol. 2, NAN.

11. MFM letter to Walsh cited in note 10 above. See also NR, MFM to Robert Bennet Forbes on Nantucket Whalers, Jan. 27, Feb. 11, 18, 20, 1848, NOLS, vol. 2, NAN; MFM to William M. Blackford, Mar. 12, 1849, MP, vol. 3, LC; MFM to Baron Alexander von Humboldt, Sept. 6, 1849, MP, vol. 3, LC.

12. MFM, "The Routes to Rio" and "Comparison of Passages by Old and New Route," in *Sailing Directions* (1852), 288–91; NR, MFM to Sec-

retary of the Navy Isaac Toucey, Oct. 29, 1858, NOLS, vol. 16, NAN.

13. MFM to Secretary of the Navy Toucey cited in note 12 above.

14. MFM to William Blackford, July 17, 1848, MP, vol. 3, LC. Contemporary monograph on Robert Bennet Forbes available in the Library of Virginia details his life as an early China trader and standing in New England maritime trade circles.

15. MFM, *Proceedings, American Association for the Advancement of Science (AAAS), First Meeting* (Philadelphia: American Association for the Advancement of Science, 1849), 64–67; Elizabeth Green Musselman, "Science as a Landed Activity: Scientifics and Seamen aboard the U.S. Exploring Expedition," in *Surveying the Record, North American Scientific Exploration to 1930*, 100.

16. MFM, "The Cruise of the Taney," *Sailing Directions* (1858), 125–27; NR, MFM to J. C. Walsh, Lieut., Commanding, U.S. Schooner *Taney*, Oct. 3, 1849, NOLS, vol. 4, NAN.

17. NR, MFM to A. Vattaman, Mar. 1, 1848, NOLS, vol. 2, NAN; MFM, *Sailing Directions* (1858), 13.

18. Daniel Walker Howe, *What Hath God Wrought: The Transformation of America, 1815–1848* (hereafter cited as Howe, *Wrought*), 809.

19. Felix Driver and Luciana Martin, *Tropical Visions in an Age of Empire* (Chicago: University of Chicago Press, 2005), 121–25.

20. Charles Bateson, *Gold Fleet for California: Forty-Niners from Australia and New Zealand* (East Lansing: Michigan State University, 1963), 14–21; Carl C. Cutler, *Greyhounds of the Sea* (New York: G. P. Putnam, 1930), 149, 240, 299–300; A. B. C. Whipple, *The Challenge* (New York: William Morrow, 1987), 14, 20, 140, 144, 183; MFM, *The Physical Geography of the Sea*, 2nd ed. (London: Sampson Low, 1855), 568, accessed Dec. 17, 2013, http://books.google.com/books?id=_I05AAAAcAAJ.

21. James P. Delgado, *To California by Sea: A Maritime History of the California Gold Rush* (hereafter cited as Delgado, *California*; Columbia: University of South Carolina Press, 1990), 19; Hagan, *People's*, 146; MFM, *The Physical Geography of the Sea*, 270.

22. NR, MFM to T. Butler King, Chairman, House Naval Affairs Committee, Feb. 29, 1848, NOLS, vol. 2, NAN; similar letter to John C. Calhoun, Mar. 27, 1848, same volume. In both Maury recommends Monterey for the naval base.

23. H. W. Brands, *The Age of Gold: The California Gold Rush and the New American Dream* (New York: Doubleday, 2002), 61; Howe, *Wrought*, 814–15.

24. Delgado, *California*, 24.

25. Ibid.

26. T. J. Stiles, *The First Tycoon: The Epic Life of Cornelius Vanderbilt* (hereafter cited as Stiles, *Vanderbilt*; New York: Random House, 2009), 173; William H. Goetzmann, *Army Exploration in the American West, 1803–1863* (Austin: Texas State Historical Association, 1991), 262–304.

27. Delgado, *California*, 47.

28. Delgado, *California*, 70–71; Kenneth J. Hagan, *This People's Navy: The Making of American Sea Power*, 146; Bateson, *Gold Fleet for California*, 20–21, 39.

29. John H. Schroeder, *Shaping a Maritime Empire*, 89.

30. Edwin Hall, "Samuel Lewis Southard, 18 Sept. 1823–3 Mar. 1829," in Coletta, *American Secretaries of the Navy, 1775–1913*, 1:134; MFM letter against Mexican railroad, *DeBow's Review* 7, no. 1 (July 1849): 16–17; MFM, "Panama Railway and the Gulf of Mexico," *SLM* 15, no. 8 (Aug. 1849): 441–57.

31. "Crossing the Isthmus in 1852," *Panama Canal Record*, vol. 1, Sept. 4, 1907–Aug. 26, 1908 (Ancon, Panama Canal Zone: Isthmian Canal Commission, 1908), 347–48; Delgado, *California*, 53, 58–59; Stiles, *Vanderbilt*, 183; David M. Potter, *The Impending Crisis 1848–1861*, completed and edited by Don E. Fehrenbacher, 192.

32. MFM, *Sailing Directions* (1859), 2:585–605; NR, MFM to Secretary of the Navy John Y. Mason, Nov. 18, 1844, NOLS, vol. 1, NAN; MFM, "National Observatory," SLM 14, no. 1 (Jan. 1848): 4–19.

33. MFM, *Sailing Directions* (1854), 845.

34. MFM to Com. C. Morris, *Executive Documents Printed by Order of the House of Representatives*, pt. 3, 13th Congress, 2d Sess., House Document 2 (Washington, D.C.: A. O. P. Nicholson, 1854, but mistakenly dated July 12, 1855), 1:245; "Literary and Scientific Intelligence: New Grinnell Arctic Expedition," *Journal of Education, Upper Canada* (Toronto) 6, no. 1 (Jan. 1853): 63; Frances Leigh Williams, *Matthew Fontaine Maury: Scientist of the Sea*, 182–83.

Chapter 13

1. John Dryden Kazar, Jr., "The United States Navy and Scientific Exploration, 1837–1860" (hereafter cited as Kazar, "Exploration"), 140.

2. David Graham Burnett, *Matthew Fontaine Maury's "Sea of Fire"* (Chicago: University of Chicago Press, 2005), 129; NR, MFM to Commodore William M. Crane, Oct. 12, 1844, NOLS, vol. 1, NAN; MFM, "National Observatory," *Southern Literary Messenger* (hereafter cited as *SLM*) 14, no. 1 (Jan. 1848): 6–10.

3. MFM to J. E. Knight, June 9, 1848, NOLS, vol. 3, NAN, gives Maury's views on internal improvements, foreign trade, isthmian crossing, etc. See also MFM, "Valley of the Amazon" series in

DeBow's Review, vol. 14, nos. 5–6, and vol. 15, no. 1 (May–July 1853); MFM, "The Dead Sea Expedition: Lieut. Lynch's Circumnavigation of the Sea," *SLM* 14, no. 9 (Sept. 1848): 547–53. James Gilliss's astronomical expedition to Chile was a partial exception. In his "Science, Commerce, and the Navy on the Seagoing Frontier: The Role of M. F. Maury and the U.S. Naval Hydrographic Office in Naval Exploration, Commercial Expansion, and Oceanography before the Civil War," Edward Leon Towle noted that Maury did not mention once Perry's expedition as being sponsored by the observatory, and this could have been related to Perry's service on the "Plucking Board," p. 436. See also Kenneth J. Hagan, *This People's Navy: The Making of American Sea Power*, 158; Harold B. Gill, Jr. and Joanne Young, eds., *Searching for the Franklin Expedition: The Arctic Journal of Robert Randolph Carter* (hereafter cited as Carter, *Arctic*; Annapolis: Naval Institute, 1998), 5; NR, MFM to Dr. Elisha Kent Kane, Oct. 7, 1856, NOLS, vol. 11, NAN; M. F. Maury, "Progress of Geography," *DeBow's Review* 17, no. 6 (Dec. 1854): 569–93.

4. NR, MFM to J. D. B. DeBow, Dec. 19, 1849, NOLS, vol. 4, NAN; Vincent Ponko, Jr., prologue to *Ships, Seas, and Scientists* (Annapolis: Naval Institute, 1974).

5. MFM, "The Dead Sea Expedition: Lieut. Lynch's Circumnavigation of the Sea," *SLM* 14, no. 9 (Sept. 1848): 547; William Francis Lynch, introduction to *Narrative of the U.S. Expedition to the River Jordan and the Dead Sea* (hereafter cited as Lynch, *Dead Sea*; Philadelphia: Lea and Blanchard, 1849).

6. Lynch, *Dead Sea*, 18–26.

7. MFM in *SLM* as cited in notes 3 and 5 above; Edward Leon Towle, "Science, Commerce, and the Navy on the Seagoing Frontier: The Role of M. F. Maury and the U.S. Naval Hydrographic Office in Naval Exploration, Commercial Expansion, and Oceanography before the Civil War" (hereafter cited as Towle, "Scientific"), 160.

8. Ponko, *Ships*, 55–58; Towle, "Scientific," 160; MFM in *SLM*, as cited in notes 3 and 5 above.

9. David Howard Bain, prelude to *Bitter Waters: America's Forgotten Naval Mission to the Dead Sea* (New York: Overlook, 2011); Ponko, *Ships*, 55–58.

10. See note 8 above.

11. Lynch, *Dead Sea*, tables and charts; W. F. Lynch, "Lieut. Lynch's Expedition to the Jordan and Dead Sea," *Am. Journ. Science*, 2nd ser., 6 (Nov. 1848): 317–33, accessed Feb. 24, 2014, http://books.google.com/books?id=emEWAAAAYAAJ.

12. Lynch, *Dead Sea*, 18.

13. Lynch, *Dead Sea*, 25–26.

14. William Goetzmann, *New Lands, New Men: America and the Second Great Age of Discovery* (hereafter cited as Goetzmann, *New Men*), 342; Ponko, *Ships*, 58.

15. Towle, "Scientific," 355–56; "The Arctic Expedition," *Stryker's American Register and Magazine* (Philadelphia) 4 (July 1850): 414; Melba Potter Hay, ed., and Carol Reardon, assoc. ed., *Henry Clay Papers: Candidate, Compromiser, Elder Statesman, January 1844–June 29, 1852* (Lexington: University Press of Kentucky, 1991), 10:695; Carter, *Arctic*, 6–7.

16. Towle, "Scientific," 366–70; American Philosophical Society description of Elisha Kent Kane Papers in its collection (hereafter cited as Philosophical, Kane Papers), Philadelphia; "The Life of Dr. Kane," *New York Times*, Jan. 23, 1858.

17. Towle, "Scientific," 371–72.

18. Philosophical, Kane Papers; Towle, "Scientific," 355.

19. Philosophical, Kane Papers; William H. Goetzmann, *Army Exploration in the American West, 1803–1863*, 61.

20. Philosophical, Kane Papers.

21. Ibid.; Harold D. Langley, "John Pendleton Kennedy, 26 July 1852–3 Mar. 1853" (hereafter cited as Langley, "Kennedy"), in Coletta, *American Secretaries of the Navy, 1775–1913*, 1:371.

22. Philosophical, Kane Papers; Towle, "Scientific," 378; William Elder, *Biography of Elisha Kent Kane* (Philadelphia: Childs and Petersen; Boston: Phillips Sampson, 1858), 2:159–60; "Death of Lieut. E. J. DeHaven," *New York Times*, May 6, 1865.

23. MFM, *The Physical Geography of the Sea*, 146.

24. MFM, "The Open Polar Sea in the Arctic Ocean," *Sailing Directions* (1854), 190–213; MFM, "People's Lectures: The Sea and Circulation of its Water," *New York Times*, Jan. 1, 1853; MFM, "The Sea and Circulation of its Water," *Hunt's Merchants' Magazine and Commercial Review* 28 (Apr. 1853): 416–19.

25. MFM, "The Open Polar Sea in the Arctic Ocean," *Sailing Directions* (1854), 190–213; Walter Barrett, *The Old Merchants of New York City* (New York: Carleton, 1863), 9. Kane's book was published in 1856.

26. MFM, "The Open Polar Sea in the Arctic Ocean," *Sailing Directions* (1854), 190–213.

27. Towle, "Scientific," 384–85, 391, 393; "The Search for Sir John Franklin," *New York Times*, Feb. 14, 1852; Langley, "Kennedy," in Coletta, *American Secretaries of the Navy, 1775–1913*, 1:271.

28. MFM, *Sailing Directions* (1854), 867; Elisha Kent Kane, *Arctic Exploration: The Second* Grinnell *Expedition in Search of Sir John Franklin in 1853, '54, '55* (Philadelphia: Childs and Petersen, 1856), 1:297–302.

29. See note 28 above.

30. MFM, "Progress of Geography," *DeBow's Review* 17, no. 6 (Dec. 1854): 569–93; Peter

Boothe Wiley, *Yankees in the Lands of the Gods*, with Korogi Ichiro, 39, 92–94.

31. William Lewis Herndon, *Exploration of the Valley of the Amazon, Made Under Direction of the Navy Department*, vol. 1 (hereafter cited as Herndon, *Amazon*; Washington, D.C.: Taylor and Maury, 1854).

32. MFM to William Lewis Herndon, July 1, 1850, NOLS, vol. 5, NAN. Followed earlier correspondence with Secretary of the Navy Ballard, particularly MFM letter Mar. 29, 1850, on goals of exploration and subsequent memo on cost, NOLS, NAN. At the same time, MFM was corresponding with Henry Grinnell on expeditions to the Arctic to search for the remains of Sir John Franklin and his crew. All contained in NOLS, vol. 5, NAN. See also David M. Potter, *The Impending Crisis 1848–1861*, completed and edited by Don E. Fehrenbacher (hereafter cited as Potter, *Impending*), 197.

33. J. D. B. DeBow, "Cotton and Its Prospects," *DeBow's Review* 9, no. 2 (Aug. 1850): 168; Potter, *Impending*, 197.

34. MFM to Ballard as cited in note 32 above; Goetzmann, *New Men*, 337; Kazar, "Exploration," 141.

35. NR, MFM to William Lewis Herndon, Feb. 16, 1851, NOLS, vol. 6, NAN.

36. Herndon, *Amazon*, 111.

37. Herndon, *Amazon*, 180.

38. "Trade of the Amazon: An Interesting Document," *New York Times*, May 25, 1852; Helen M. Rozwadowski, *Fathoming the Ocean: The Discovery and Exploration of the Deep Sea*, 24, 55, 69.

39. *DeBow's Review* series as cited in note 3 above; MFM, writing under the pseudonym "Inca," *The Amazon and the Atlantic Slopes of South America: Collected Letters That Appeared in the* National Intelligencer *in Fall 1852* (Washington, D.C.: Franck Taylor, 1853).

40. NR, MFM to A. C. Robinson, Apr. 3, 1852, NOLS, vol. 7, NAN.

41. NR, MFM to T. Gilmore Simms, June 25, 1852, NOLS, vol. 8, NAN.

42. Goetzmann, *New Men*, 337–38; Robert V. Remini, *Henry Clay: Statesman for the Union*, 755.

43. NR, MFM to T. Gilmore Simms, June 25, 1852, NOLS, vol. 8, NAN. "Questions of the day" and "question of the age" were phrases MFM used repeatedly in describing the Amazon.

44. Geoffrey Sutton Smith, "The Navy before Darwinism: Science, Exploration, and Diplomacy in Antebellum America," *American Quarterly* 28, no. 1 (Spring 1976): 47.

45. Diana Fontaine Maury Corbin, *A Life of Matthew Fontaine Maury, U.S.N. and C.S.N., Compiled by His Daughter*, 104–5; MFM [but unsigned], "A Scheme for Rebuilding Southern Commerce: Direct Trade with the South," *SLM* 5, no. 1 (Jan. 1839): 3–12; Potter, *Impending*, 147.

46. Herbert Wender, *Southern Commercial Conventions* (Baltimore: Johns Hopkins University Press, 1930), 24; Robert Royal Russel, *Economic Aspects of Southern Sectionalism* (hereafter cited as Russel, *Economic*; Urbana: University of Illinois, 1923), 13, 118–19.

47. NR, MFM, draft resolutions for Southern Commercial Convention in Memphis, Tenn., contained in NOLS, written in June 1848, NAN.

48. Russel, *Economic*, 145; see NR cited in note 47 above; MFM to William Blackford, Sept. 20, 1849, MP, vol. 3, LC; MFM as Inca, "Inca," *National Intelligencer*, Nov. 29 and Dec. 1, 1849; "Panama Railway and the Gulf of Mexico: Great Commercial Advantages of the Gulf of Mexico," *SLM* 15, no. 8 (Aug. 1849): 441–57; NR, MFM to J. D. B. DeBow, Apr. 30, 1849, NOLS, vol. 4, NAN; MFM letter on Tehuantepec, *DeBow's Review* 7, no. 1 (July 1849): 16–17; Eli N. Evans, *Judah P. Benjamin: The Jewish Confederate* (New York: Free Press, 1988), 44–45.

49. See note 48 above.

50. Cong. Globe, 32nd Cong., 2d Sess., appendix 238–39 (Mar. 18, 1853) (statement of Mr. Dodge of Iowa on Railroad to the Pacific).

51. MFM, "Direct Foreign Trade of the South: Commercial Conventions," *DeBow's Review* 12, no. 2 (Feb. 1852): 126–48.

52. NR, MFM writings from April through June 1852, including Memorial to Congress in May that year, covers much of this ground, NOLS, NAN; *Memorial*, May 3, 1852, 32nd Cong., 1st Sess., Senate Miscellaneous Document 83, ser. 629, vol. 1; *DeBow's* articles as cited in note 3 above and "Inca" collection as cited in note 48 above.

53. "Maury on South America and Amazonia," *Southern Quarterly Review* (Charleston, S.C.) 8 (Oct. 1853): 412–49.

54. Maury is most directly connected with immigration to Mexico following the Civil War. Brazil, Venezuela, Cuba, and Chile were other havens for defeated Southerners in the Western Hemisphere.

55. Cong. Globe, 34th Cong., 1st Sess. pt. 2, 1594 (July 10, 1856); NR, MFM to Sen. John Bell, Feb. 25, 1856, Miscellaneous (Maury and Plucking Board) No. 54, NAN; Langley, "Kennedy," in Coletta, *American Secretaries of the Navy, 1775–1913*, 274; Goetzmann, *New Men*, 1:315.

56. "Astronomical Observatories," *DeBow's Review* 12 (June 1852): 597.

Chapter 14

1. Mary H. Maury Werth to her children, July 26, 1879, MP, vol. 42, LC; NR, Logbooks, USS *Brandywine*, 1825–27, *Dolphin*, 1833, *Falmouth*, 1831–33, *Macedonian*, 1825–26, *Potomac*, 1833–34, and (most importantly) *Vincennes*,

1827–30; MFM, *Explanations and Sailing Directions to Accompany the Wind and Current Charts*, 1851 to 1858–59 (Washington, D.C.: C. Alexander, 1851–53; Philadelphia: E. L. and J. Biddle, 1854; Washington, D.C.: William A. Harris, 1855 to vol. 1, 1858; Washington, D.C.: Cornelius Wendell, vol. 2, 1858); NR, MFM to Lieut. Marin Jansen, May 7, 1853, NOLS, vol. 8, NAN; NR, MFM to Capt. Henry James, Apr. 19, 1853, and to Secretary of the Navy John P. Kennedy, Nov. 6, 1852, NOLS, vol. 8, NAN.

2. MFM, "An Appeal to the Agricultural Interests of Virginia," *Southern Planter and Farmer* 15, no. 6 (June 1855): 161–63; MFM, "Meteorology for the Farmers," *American Farmer* 11, no. 2 (Aug. 1855): 33–35.

3. A. D. Bache, *Address of the President of the Association*, AAAS, Albany, N.Y., Aug. 1851 (Washington, D.C.: American Association for the Advancement of Science, 1852), 31–40.

4. NR, MFM to Commodore Charles Morris, Chief, Bureau of Ordnance and Hydrography, Nov. 21, 1851, NOLS, vol. 7, NAN; MFM, "On the Establishment of a Universal System of Meteorological Observations by Sea and Land," in *Compilation of Correspondence*, comp. MFM (Washington, D.C.: C. Alexander, 1851), 1–8; *Report of the Fifteenth Meeting of the British Association for the Advancement of Science: Held at Cambridge in June 1845* (London: John Murray, 1846), xxvi–xxx.

5. NR, MFM to Commodore Charles Morris, Chief, Bureau of Ordnance and Hydrography, Nov. 28, 1851, NOLS, vol. 7, NAN. (Included copies of correspondence that followed and plans for wide-ranging conference.)

6. NR, MFM to Peter S. Parker, Dec. 31, 1851, NOLS, vol. 7, NAN; letter to J. C. Walsh the same day in NOLS.

7. NR, MFM to George Manning, Jan. 10, 1852, NOLS, vol. 7, NAN, followed in succeeding days through Jan. 20 by circular letters under instruction of the secretary of the Navy to other cabinet members.

8. NR, MFM to Baron von Humboldt, Apr. 1, 1851, NOLS, vol. 7, NAN.

9. NR, MFM to Joseph Henry, Smithsonian Institution, Jan. 14, 1852, NOLS, vol. 7, NAN, followed in succeeding days through Jan. 20 by letters to other scientists. Second letter to Henry, dated Jan. 22, 1852, NOLS, vol. 7, NAN.

10. Joseph Henry Journal, May 6, 1852, Smithsonian Institution Archives, Washington, D.C.

11. A. D. Bache to Henry, May 30, 1853, Smithsonian letters, Smithsonian Institution Archives.

12. NR, Reply of the Surgeon General of the Army to MFM, Feb. 18, 1851, Naval Observatory Letters Received (hereafter cited as NOLR), NAN.

13. Joseph Henry Journal, May 6, 1852, Smithsonian Institution Archives.

14. NR, MFM to Adolphe Quetelet, Director, Royal Observatory, Brussels, Belgium, Dec. 7, 1860, NOLS, vol. 18, NAN.

15. NR, MFM to Secretary of the Navy John P. Kennedy, Nov. 6, 1852, NOLS, vol. 8, NAN; NR, MFM to ministers of Russia, England, France, Holland, Russia, Denmark, and Brazil, Mar.–Apr. 1853, NOLS, vol. 9, NAN.

16. NR, MFM to Capt. Henry James, Apr. 19, 1853, NOLS, vol. 9, NAN.

17. NR, reference to an April 26, 1853, speech on Maury's work in the House of Lords by Lord Wrottesley, president of the Royal Society, in several letters in spring 1853; especially note May 7 correspondence with Lt. Marin Jansen, NOLS, vol. 9, NAN; Roger H. Charlier, "Fratres in Maribus: 150 Years Ago, the First International Ocean-Science Conference," *Journal of Coastal Research* (West Palm Beach, Fla.) *20*, no. 1 (2010): 48–51.

18. Charlier, "Fratres in Maribus," 48–51.

19. MFM, *Sailing Directions* (1859), 2:591; NR, Lieut. George Minor to MFM, Sept. 8, 1853, NOLS, vol. 9, NAN; NR, MFM in London to Lieut. George Minor, Aug. 14, 1853, NOLR, vol. 9, NAN; Charlier, "Fratres in Maribus," 48–51; NR, Notice of Thomas Challis, Mansion House, London, to Shipowners of London, Aug. 18, 1853, NOLS, vol. 9, NAN.

20. MFM, *Sailing Directions* (1858), 1:330.

21. NR, Lieut. George Minor to Cadwallader Ringgold, Sept. 15, 1853, NOLS, vol. 9, NAN; MFM, *Sailing Directions* (1854), 58; "Obituary: Admiral Jansen," *Geographical Journal* (Royal Geographical Society) 2 (July–Dec. 1893): 465–68.

22. See note 21 above.

23. NR, MFM to Adolphe Quetelet, Nov. 10, 1853; MFM to Francis Lieber and Baron von Humboldt Oct. 27 and Nov. 10, 1853, respectively, NOLS, vol. 10, NAN; Charlier, "Fratres in Maribus," 48–51.

24. MFM, *Sailing Directions* (1854), 49, 58.

25. NR, MFM to the Earl of Rosse, July 27, 1854, NOLS, vol. 11, NAN; MFM, *Sailing Directions* (1858), 1:ix, xiii.

26. MFM, "Meteorology for the Farmers," *American Farmer* 11, no. 2 (Aug. 1855): 33–35.

27. NR, MFM to Lieut. Marin H. Jansen, Mar. 9, 1854, NOLS, vol.10, NAN.

28. NR, MFM to Adolphe Quetelet, Director, Royal Observatory, Brussels, Dec. 7, 1860, NOLS, vol. 18, NAN.

29. NR, MFM to Maryland Agricultural Society, Nov. 14, 1855, NOLS, vol. 12, NAN; MFM, "An Appeal to the Agricultural Interests of Virginia," *Southern Planter and Farmer* 15, no. 6 (June 1855): 11–163. An administrative board recommended to the secretary of the Navy, who passed on the recommendation to the president, that a number of officers be removed from active service. Maury was among the officers ordered retired, but retained as head of the observatory.

30. MFM, letter to editor, *New York Tribune*, Dec. 25, 1855.

31. MFM, "Agricultural Meteorology," Jan. 10, 1856, *Journal of 41st Annual Meeting of the United States Agricultural Society*, pt. 1, vol. 4 (Jan. 1856): 39–53.

32. Ibid.

33. Ibid.

34. MFM to B. Franklin Minor, Jan. 11, 1856, MP, vol. 5, LC.

35. Copy of Senate Report 292, Dec. 18, 1856, On Behalf of Senate Committee on Agriculture, 34th Cong., 3d sess., found in MP, vol. 46, LC.

36. X, letter to the editor, *Boston Atlas*, Feb. 18, 1857; Frances Leigh Williams, *Matthew Fontaine Maury: Scientist of the Sea*, 321; Hildegarde Hawthorne, *Matthew Fontaine Maury: Trail Maker of the Seas*, 138–39; Jaquelin Ambler Caskie, *Life and Letters of Matthew Fontaine*, 81–90.

37. NR, MFM to Capt. E. P. Dorr, Buffalo, N.Y., Dec. 28, 1858, NOLS, vol. 16, NAN; Capt. E. P. Dorr to Thompson Maury, Feb. 25, 1873, MP, vol. 43, LC.

38. MFM to daughter Diana Maury Corbin, Sept. 12, 1858; MFM to his wife Ann Herndon Maury, Nov. 10, 1858, and Dec. 1, 1858, all in MFM Papers, Virginia Military Institute Archives.

39. NR, MFM to Secretary Toucey, Nov. 10, 1858, NOLS, vol. 16, NAN; MFM to John Minor, Fredericksburg, Va., Nov. 15, 1858, MP, vol. 7, LC; MFM, letters to his wife, Nov. 20–Dec. 1, 1859, MP, vol. 7, LC; MFM, address delivered before North Alabama Mechanical and Agricultural Society, Oct. 19, 1859, MP, vol. 47, LC; Diana Fontaine Maury Corbin, *A Life of Matthew Fontaine Maury, U.S.N. and C.S.N., Compiled by His Daughter*, 96–97.

40. MFM to John B. Minor, July 4, 1859; to William C. Hasbrouck, July 14, 1859, both MP, vol. 8, LC.

41. NR, MFM to Gov. Dennison of Ohio, June 5, 1860, NOLS, vol. 17, NAN.

42. *Annual Report of the Board of Regents of the Smithsonian Institution, 1861* (Washington, D.C.: Government Printing Office, 1862), 35.

43. NR, MFM to Adolphe Quetelet, Director, Royal Observatory, Brussels, Dec. 7, 1860, NOLS, vol. 18, NAN.

44. MFM, introduction, *Sailing Directions* (1858), vol. 1; William Goetzmann, *New Lands, New Men: America and the Second Great Age of Discovery*, 315. Among the nations and societies recognizing Maury were Great Britain's Royal Astronomical Society, the Great Gold Medal from France; the Kosmos Medal from Prussia at intercession of Baron von Humboldt; and jeweled pins from the czar of Russia and Archduke Ferdinand Maximilian.

Chapter 15

1. Best exemplified in NR, MFM to Secretary of the Navy Dobbin, Oct. 1, 1855, NOLS, vol. 12, NAN; MFM to Ann Maury, June 21, 1854, MP, vol. 4, LC.

2. MFM, "Lanes for the Steamers Crossing the Atlantic," twelve-page pamphlet, Board of Underwriters of New York, 1855, scrapbook, MP, LC; MFM, *Sailing Directions* (1859), 2:71–73.

3. NR, MFM to Commodore Charles Morris, Chief of Bureau of Ordnance and Hydrography, May 18, 1855, NOLS, vol. 11, NAN.

4. NR, MFM to Boston Board of Trade, June 5, 1855, NOLS, vol. 11, NAN; NR, Robert H. Fitzroy to MFM, undated but placed in the region of 1856 correspondence, NOLR, NAN. European nations did not accept the Maury steamer lanes until 1898.

5. Dabney H. Maury to Mary Maury, Aug. 7, 1873, MP, vol. 44, LC; Diana Fontaine Maury Corbin, *A Life of Matthew Fontaine Maury, U.S.N. and C.S.N., Compiled by His Daughter* (hereafter cited as Corbin, *Maury*), 149–50.

6. See note 5 above.

7. See note 5 above.

8. MFM, introduction to *Physical Geography* (1855).

9. MFM, letter to William C. Hasbrouck in introduction to *Physical Geography* (New York: Harper, 1868).

10. MFM, *Physical Geography* (1868), 146–47, 153–54. Post–Civil War editions stressed work on the cable, because Cyrus Field refused to acknowledge the work of John Mercer Brooke and Maury, who fought for the Confederacy.

11. MFM, *Physical Geography* (1855), 53.

12. Hasbrouck letter cited in note 9 above.

13. E. F. Jomard to MFM, Nov. 18, 1855, MP, vol. 5, LC; Corbin, *Maury*, 70–72. Five printings of *The Physical Geography of the Sea*, called editions, appeared in 1855. It was revised and enlarged in 1856, 1857, 1859, and 1871.

14. *New York Herald*, Feb. 3, 1873; John Leighly, ed., introduction to *Physical Geography of the Sea and Its Meteorology*, by M. F. Maury (Cambridge, Mass.: Belknap Press of Harvard University Press, 1963); William Goetzmann, *New Lands, New Men: America and the Second Great Age of Discovery*, 326–27. The 1861 edition of *Physical Geography* mentions early critics of the work.

15. Senator Mallory in Senate on S. 567, 33rd Cong., 2d Sess., S. Rep. No. 443, at 6 (Jan. 29, 1855).

Chapter 16

1. Samuel Carter III, *Cyrus Field: Man of Two Worlds* (hereafter cited as Carter, *Field*; New York: G. P. Putnam, 1968), 30.

2. William O. Stoddard, *Men of Business: Men of Achievement* (hereafter cited as Stoddard, *Men*; New York: Scribner's, 1893), 133; Walter Barrett, *The Old Merchants of New York City* (New York: John W. Lovell, 1885; repr. electronically, Ann Arbor, Mich.: University of Michigan Library, 2006), 3:195, accessed Nov. 5, 2013, http://quod.lib.umich.edu/g/genpub/4610558.0003.001.

3. Carter, *Field*, 39–47; Kenneth J. Silverman, *Lightning Man: The Accursed Life of Samuel F. B. Morse* (hereafter cited as Silverman, *Morse*; New York: Alfred P. Knopf, 2003), 327.

4. Carter, *Field*, 65, 72–92; MFM as "Inca," *The Amazon and the Atlantic Slopes of South America: Collected Letters That Appeared in the* National Intelligencer *in Fall 1852* (Washington, D.C.: Franck Taylor, 1853). See also the "Valley of the Amazon" series in *DeBow's Review*, vol. 14, nos. 5 and 6, and vol. 15, no. 1 (May–July 1853); Silverman, *Morse*, 216.

5. NR, MFM to Cyrus W. Field, Nov. 3, 1853, NOLS, vol. 10, NAN; NR, MFM to Samuel F. B. Morse, Feb. 23, 1854, NOLS, vol. 10, NAN; Atlantic Telegraph Co., *The Atlantic Telegraph: A History of Preliminary Experimental Proceedings and a Descriptive Account of the Present State and Prospects of the Undertaking* (London: Atlantic Telegraph Co., July 1857), 5–7.

6. Silverman, *Morse*, 216; K. Jack Bauer, "John Young Mason, 10 Sept.–7 Mar. 1849," in Coletta, *American Secretaries of the Navy, 1775–1913*, 1:208.

7. NR, MFM to Cyrus W. Field, Nov. 3, 1853, NOLS, vol. 10, NAN; NR, MFM to Samuel F. B. Morse, Feb. 23, 1854, NOLS, vol. 10, NAN; Carter, *Field*, 92, 94–95.

8. Carter, *Field*, 92–100; NR, MFM to Secretary of the Navy Isaac Toucey, Sept. 4, 1858, NOLS, vol. 16, NAN; MFM, *Sailing Directions* (1858), 1:113–79; NR, MFM to Samuel F. B. Morse, Feb. 23, 1854, NOLS, vol. 10, NAN.

9. MFM, *Sailing Directions* (1858), 1:113–79; MFM letter to Morse cited in note 7 above.

10. NR, MFM to Otway Berryman, Lieut., Commanding USS *Dolphin*, Mar. 14, 1853, NOLS, vol. 12, NAN.

11. NR, MFM to Cyrus W. Field, Nov. 3, 1853, NOLS, vol. 10, NAN; NR, MFM to Samuel F. B. Morse, Feb. 23, 1854, NOLS, vol. 10, NAN; Frances Leigh Williams, *Matthew Fontaine Maury: Scientist of the Sea*, 140.

12. NR, MFM to Secretary Dobbin, Feb. 23, 1854, NOLS, vol. 10, NAN.

13. NR, MFM to Cyrus W. Field, Feb. 24, 1854, NOLS, vol. 10, NAN; William Goetzmann, *New Lands, New Men: America and the Second Great Age of Discovery*, 322; Silverman, *Morse*, 327.

14. Stoddard, *Men*, 137–39; Carter, *Field*, 94–106; Silverman, *Morse*, 339.

15. NR, MFM to Cyrus W. Field, Apr. 21, 1854, NOLS, vol. 10, NAN.

16. Ibid.

17. Ibid.

18. "The 'American Method' of Longitude Determination," *The Coast Survey, 1807–1867*, NOAA Central Library, National Oceanographic and Atmospheric Administration, last modified Nov. 30, 2007, http://www.lib.noaa.gov/noaainfo/heritage/coastsurveyvol1/BACHE2.html#AMERICAN; copy of resolution, Board of Directors, New York, Newfoundland, and London Telegraphy Co., June 22, 1855, NOLS, vol. 12, NAN; MFM to B. Franklin Minor, July 25, 1855, and to J. B. Minor, July 28, 1855, MP, both vol. 4, LC.

19. Commodore Charles Morris, Chief of Bureau of Ordnance and Hydrography, to MFM, Jan. 9, 1855, "From Sea to Sandy Hook," *Sailing Directions* (1855), 848–54; MFM, *Sailing Directions* (1855), 848; NR, MFM to Morris and R. B. Forbes, Jan. 11 and Mar. 5, 1855, respectively, NOLS, vol. 11, NAN; "Our Harbor Entrances: Sandy Hook and Hell Gate," *New York Times*, July 14, 1869; Harold D. Langley, "William Ballard Preston, 8 Mar. 1849–22 July 1850," in Coletta, *American Secretaries of the Navy, 1775–1913*, 1:260.

20. Samuel F. DuPont to J. S. Biddle, Oct. 11, 1855, S. F. DuPont Papers, Hagley Museum and Library, Wilmington, Del.

21. Marc Rothenberg et al., eds., *The Papers of Joseph Henry*, vol. 6, *January 1844–December 1846: The Princeton Years*, 264n.

22. NR, MFM to Charles H. Davis, Cambridge, Mass., Feb. 9, 1853, NOLS, vol. 8, NAN.

23. Alexander D. Bache to Commander Charles Henry Davis, Nov. 9, 1855, Bache Papers, MS, vol. 1, LC.

24. NR, Secretary of the Navy Dobbin to O. H. Berryman, New York, July 10, 1856, Letters to Officers, Ships of War, vol. 53, NAN; NR, Secretary of the Navy Dobbin to Secretary of the Treasury Guthrie, June 23, 1856, Executive Letter Book, no. 10, NAN.

25. NR, MFM to Cyrus W. Field, June 13, 1856, NOLS, vol. 13, NAN.

26. Samuel Phillips Lee, *Report on the Cruise of the U.S. Brig* Dolphin (Washington, D.C.: Beverly Tucker, Printer to the Senate, 1854), 180.

27. Order to Berryman cited in note 24 above.

28. NR, MFM to Secretary of the Navy Dobbin, Oct. 30, 1856, NOLS, vol. 14, NAN; NR, MFM to Secretary of the Navy Dobbin, Nov. 8, 1856, NOLS, vol. 14, NAN; MFM, *Sailing Directions* (1858), 1:147–54.

29. NR, MFM to editor, *Union* (Washington, D.C.), Dec. (date unknown, possibly Nov. 29) 1856, NOLS, vol. 14, NAN.

30. MFM to Dobbin, Nov. 8, 1856, as cited in note 28 above.

31. Carter, *Field*, 106–33; NR, MFM to Cyrus W. Field, Mar. 28, 1857, NOLS, vol. 14, NAN; MFM, *Sailing Directions* (1858), 1:147–54; Helen M. Rozwadowski, *Fathoming the Ocean: The Discovery and Exploration of the Deep Sea*, 89–92.

32. NR, MFM to Cyrus W. Field, Apr. 28, 1857, NOLS, vol. 14, NAN.

33. NR, MFM to Secretary of the Navy Isaac Toucey, May 11, 1857, NOLS, vol. 14, NAN; MFM, *Sailing Directions* (1858), 1:165–66.

34. MFM manuscript, "Atlantic Cable: 1857," MP, vol. 47, LC; NR, Atlantic Telegraph Co. to MFM, Sept. 2, 1857, NOLR, NAN.

35. Richard Stachurski, *Longitude by Wire*, 147; MFM, *Sailing Directions* (1858), 1:147–54; see note 34 above.

36. MFM, *Sailing Directions* (1858), 1:147–54.

37. Silverman, *Morse*, 368.

38. NR, Cyrus W. Field to MFM, Dec. 12, 1856, and Apr. 27, 1857, NOLR, NAN; Henry M. Field, *The Story of the Atlantic Telegraph* (hereafter cited as Henry Field, *Telegraph*; New York: Scribner's, 1892), 142–43.

39. MFM, *Sailing Directions* (1858), 1:147–66.

40. NR, MFM to Cyrus W. Field, July 21, 1858, NOLS, vol. 15, NAN; NR, MFM to Adolphe Quetelet, July 9, 1857, NOLS, vol. 14, NAN; Silverman, *Morse*, 330; Stachurski, *Longitude*, 221.

41. NR, MFM to Benjamin Silliman, Sept. 15 and 21, 1858, NOLS, vol. 16, NAN; NR, copy of address of W. P. Trowbridge, Oct. 8, 1858, NOLR, NAN, which contains some of the assertions of Trowbridge's earlier address to the American Association for the Advancement of Science and was reprinted as "The Telegraphic Plateau: Remarkable Discrepancies in the Published Statement of Soundings," *American Journal of Science and Arts* (hereafter cited as *Am. Journ. Science*), 2nd ser., 26 (Sept. 1858): 219–25.

42. W. H. Russell, *Atlantic Telegraph* (Dublin: Nonsuch, 2005), 24, 37; MFM, *Sailing Directions* (1858), 1:147–66; Maury endorsement in Appendix, "Scientific Testimony Received December 1865," in *Great North Atlantic Telegraph Route* (London: William Clowes and Sons, 1866), 35.

43. MFM, *Sailing Directions* (1858), 1:147–54.

44. Carter, *Field*, 106–36.

45. NR, MFM to C. Piazzi Smyth, Aug. 2, 1858, NOLS, vol. 15, NAN.

46. Henry Field, *Telegraph*, 174.

47. Henry Field, *Telegraph*, 198.

48. *New York Times*, Sept. 2 and 3, 1858; Thomas Coulson, *Joseph Henry: His Life and Work*, 128–29.

49. NR, MFM to Augustus Maverick, *Daily Times*, New York, Sept. 9, 1858, NOLS, vol. 16, NAN; W. P. Trowbridge, "On Deep Sea Soundings," *Am. Journ. Science*, 2nd ser., 26, no. 77, art. 17 (Sept. 1858): 219–25.

50. NR, MFM to editors, *Am. Journ. Science*, Sept. 15, 1858, and follow-up letter Sept. 21, 1858, NOLS, vol. 16, NAN.

51. NR, MFM to Secretary of the Navy Toucey, Sept. 24 and 28, 1858, and to Secretary of the Treasury Howell Cobb, Sept. 20, 1858, both NOLS, vol. 16, NAN.

52. Alexander Dallas Bache to Secretary of the Treasury Howell Cobb, Oct. 1, 1858, vol. 10, Bache Papers, MS Collection, LC.

53. Jefferson Davis to Alexander Dallas Bache, Oct. 27, 1858, Bache Papers, MS, vol. 10, LC.

54. NR, MFM to Secretary of the Navy Isaac Toucey, Nov. 10, 1858, NOLS, vol. 16, NAN.

55. NR, B. Franklin Minor to MFM, Nov. 8, 1858, NOLR, NAN.

56. Silverman, *Morse*, 377.

57. Joseph Henry to A. D. Bache, Sept. 13, 1859, Smithsonian Institution Archives.

58. NR, MFM to Cyrus W. Field, Aug. 8, 12, 26, 1859, NOLS, vol. 17, NAN.

59. NR, Cyrus W. Field to MFM, Sept. 6, 1859, NOLR, NAN.

60. NR, Henry B. Rogers to MFM, Dec. 8, 1859, NOLR, NAN.

61. Anon., clipping, undated 1867, MP, vol. 47, LC.

Chapter 17

1. NR, B. Franklin Minor to MFM, Mar. 8, 1849, NOLR, NAN; NR, William F. Lynch to MFM, Mar. 25, 1850, NOLR, NAN; NR, Lieut. George Minor to George Manning, Oct. 8, 1853, NOLS, vol. 9, NAN.

2. Act to Promote the Efficiency of the Navy, 32nd–33rd Cong., 1851–55, *U.S. Statutes at Large*, 10:616–17.

3. Marion Mills Miller, ed., *Great Debates in American History: Departments of Government* (New York: Current Literature, 1913), 9:226, 236, accessed Dec. 18, 2013, http://books.google.com/books?id=ZAghAAAAMAAJ; *The State of the Union: Being a Complete Documentary History of the Public Affairs for the United States, Foreign and Domestic, for the Year 1854* (Washington, D.C.: Taylor and Maury, 1855), 99; NR, James C. Dobbin, Report of the Secretary of the Navy to the President, Dec. 1853, as collected at the Department of the Navy Library, Washington, D.C.

4. MFM to Capt. S. F. DuPont, Nov. 1, 1850, NOLS, vol. 6, NAN; NR, MFM to Lieut. Stephen R. Rowan, Jan. 15, 1851, NOLS, vol. 8, NAN.

5. S. F. DuPont to Sophie DuPont, Jan. 14, 1855, S. F. DuPont Papers, Hagley Museum and Library.

6. Report with Draft of a Bill Submitted to the Sec. of the Navy, January 1855, S. F. DuPont

Papers, Hagley Museum and Library; Donald Chisholm, *Waiting for Dead Men's Shoes: Origins and Development of the U.S. Navy's Officer Personnel System, 1793–1941* (hereafter cited as Chisholm, *Waiting*), 236.

7. S. F. DuPont to C. H. Davis, Apr. 3, 1855, S. F. DuPont Papers, Hagley Museum and Library; Chisholm, *Waiting*, 237.

8. Cong. Globe, 34th Cong., 1st Sess. 386–87, 711, and appendix, 242–43 (1855–56); letter to C. H. Davis as cited in note 7 above; Craig L. Symonds, *Confederate Admiral: The Life and Wars of Franklin Buchanan* (Annapolis: Naval Institute, 1999), 116–17.

9. S. F. DuPont to C. H. Davis, Apr. 16, 1855, S. F. DuPont Papers, Hagley Museum and Library.

10. James C. Dobbin, Report of the Secretary of the Navy, 1855, as collected at the Department of the Navy Library, Washington, D.C.

11. S. F. DuPont to Sophie DuPont, July 5, 1855, S. F. DuPont Papers, Hagley Museum and Library.

12. MFM to B. Franklin Minor, Oct. 16, 1855, MP, vol. 5, LC.

13. James M. Merrill, *DuPont: The Making of an Admiral; A Biography of Samuel Francis DuPont* (New York: Dodd Mead, 1986), 220–21.

14. Ibid.

15. Secretary of the Navy Dobbin to MFM, Sept. 17, 1855, MP, vol. 4, LC.

16. See note 9 above.

17. NR, MFM to Secretary of the Navy Dobbin, Sept. 20, 1855, and Robert Hatton, Dec. 10, 1855, both in NOLS, vol. 12, NAN; more specifically, MFM to William M. Blackford, Sept. 23 and Oct. 17, 1855, and to the Rev. James H. Otey, Sept. 21, 1855, all in MP, vol. 5, LC. *Grievous error* is a phrase MFM used repeatedly.

18. See note 17 above.

19. See note 17 above.

20. NR, MFM to Secretary of the Navy Dobbin, Oct. 11, 1855, and MFM to Marin Jansen, Oct. 24, 1855, NOLS, both vol. 12, NAN.

21. Samuel F. DuPont to J. S. Biddle, Oct. 11, 1855, S. F. DuPont Papers, Hagley Museum and Library.

22. Dudley Taylor Cornish and Virginia Jeans Lass, *Lincoln's Lee* (Lawrence: University Press of Kansas, 1986), 79.

23. MFM to B. Franklin Minor, Nov. 3, 1855, MP, vol. 5, LC; all responses in NR, Nov.–Dec. 1855, NOLR, NAN.

24. NR, MFM to Secretary of the Navy Dobbin, Oct. 29, 1855, NOLS, vol. 12, NAN.

25. NR, MFM to Adm. Beechey, Oct. 28, 1855, NOLS, vol. 12, NAN.

26. NR, MFM to Neill S. Brown, Nov. 29, 1855, NOLS, vol. 12, NAN.

27. Samuel F. DuPont to C. H. Davis, Nov. 21, 1855, and to J. S. Biddle, Dec. 16, 1855, both in S. F. DuPont Papers, Hagley Museum and Library; MFM to B. Franklin Minor, Jan. 16, 1856, MP, vol. 5, LC.

28. Bell's championship of Maury could be understood from his long acquaintance with MFM and his family. MFM's letter to Brown, as cited in note 26 above, would help the legislature formulate a memorial for a senator it elected. MFM continued to support Bell, including his 1860 bid for the presidency.

29. Cong. Globe, 34th Cong., 1st Sess. 386–87, 711, and appendix, 242–43 (1855–56).

30. Cong. Globe, 34th Cong., 1st Sess. 1589 (Feb. 26, 1855) (remarks of Sen. Stephen Mallory).

31. Cong. Globe, 34th Cong., 1st Sess. 204–10 (Jan. 10, 1856) (remarks of Sen. Judah P. Benjamin).

32. Remarks of Sen. John Bell in Cong. Globe, as cited in note 29 above.

33. Mallory remarks, as cited in note 30 above; Samuel F. DuPont to Garrett Pendergrast, Mar. 20, 1856, S. F. DuPont Papers, Hagley Museum and Library.

34. Remarks of Bell, Mallory, and others in pamphlet published by Cong. Globe, 34th Cong., 1st Sess. 274–75 (Jan.21, 1856), Washington, D.C., found among S. F. DuPont Papers, Hagley Museum and Library; Cong. Globe, 34th Cong., 1st Sess. 272–74 (Jan. 21, 1856); Cong. Globe, 34th Cong., 1st Sess. 386–87, 711, and appendix, 242–43, 248 (1855–56).

35. Samuel F. DuPont to Garrett Pendergrast, Mar. 20, 1856, S. F. DuPont Papers, Hagley Museum and Library; Chisholm, *Waiting*, 252–53.

36. Cong. Globe, 34th Cong., 1st Sess. appendix 245–50 (Mar. 18, 1856); DuPont to Pendergrast, as cited in note 35 above.

37. Cong. Globe, 34th Cong., 1st Sess. appendix 245–50 (Mar. 18, 1856).

38. Ibid.

39. Samuel F. DuPont to J. S. Biddle, Apr. 3, 1856, S. F. DuPont Papers, Hagley Museum and Library.

40. Samuel F. DuPont to C. H. Davis, undated but in 1856 correspondence file, S. F. DuPont Papers, Hagley Museum and Library.

41. NR, MFM to A. Delamarche and to Thomas Dornin, both Feb. 13, 1856, NOLS, vol. 13, NAN.

42. Cong. Globe, 34th Cong., 1st Sess., pt. 2, 1594, 1638 (July 10 and 15, 1856).

43. S. F. DuPont to Garrett Pendergrast, July 18, 1856, and S. F. DuPont to J. S. Biddle, July 29, 1856, S. F. DuPont Papers, Hagley Museum and Library.

44. S. F. DuPont to J. S. Biddle, July 29, 1856, S. F. DuPont Papers, Hagley Museum and Library.

45. Ibid.

46. Ibid.

47. The phrase *courts of old men* appears regularly, including Samuel F. DuPont to C. H. Davis, May 4, 1857, S. F. DuPont Papers, Hagley Museum and Library.

48. NR, MFM to Prof. John B. Minor, Feb. 25, 1857, NOLS, vol. 14, NAN.

49. Ibid.

50. Secretary of the Navy Isaac Toucey, Report to the President 1857, as collected at the Department of the Navy Library, Washington, D.C.

51. MFM to B. Franklin Minor, June 27, 1857, MP, vol. 7, LC.

52. T. J. Stiles, *The First Tycoon: The Epic Life of Cornelius Vanderbilt* (hereafter cited as Stiles, *Vanderbilt*), 309.

53. "Report of Lt. Matthew F. Maury on the Loss of the United States Mail Steamer *Central America* under the Command of William Lewis Herndon," written Oct. 19, 1857, MP, vol. 7, LC; "Storybook Treasure Found Off South Carolina; Salvagers Rescue 90% of Treasure, Insurers 10%," *New York Times*, Apr. 4, 1990; "Central America Treasure," Associated Press (Virginia wire), Apr. 13, 1990; *Treasures of a Lost Voyage*, broadcast Sept. 15, 1990 (Silver Spring, Md.: Discovery Channel, 1992), VHS; Stiles, *Vanderbilt*, 309. Recovery and possession of *Central America*'s cargo was a subject of interest in the 1990s.

54. NR, MFM to C. Piazzi Smyth, Sept. 28, 1857, NOLS, vol. 15, NAN.

55. NR, MFM to Secretary of the Navy Isaac Toucey, Oct. 15, 1857, NOLS, vol. 15, NAN; Diana Fontaine Maury Corbin, *A Life of Matthew Fontaine Maury, U.S.N. and C.S.N., Compiled by His Daughter*, 133–41.

56. NR, "The Case of Lieut. M. F. Maury, Naval Court of Inquiry, No. 1," RG 125: Records of the Office of the Judge Advocate General (Navy): "Courts of Inquiry, Act of Jan. 16, 1857," vol. 21, NAN.

57. Ibid.

58. All responses in NR, NOLR, NAN; Samuel F. DuPont correspondence, in particular, 1856–1857, S. F. DuPont Papers, Hagley Museum and Library; *Journal of Executive Proceedings of the Senate of the United States of America from Dec. 3, 1855, to Aug. 16, 1858*, 34th Cong., 1st Sess. (Washington, D.C.: Government Printing Office, 1887), 10:268, 277, 285, and 291.

59. MFM to William M. Blackford, Dec. 17, 1857, MP, vol. 7, LC; Secretary of the Navy Isaac Toucey, *Report to the President 1857*, as collected at the Department of the Navy Library, Washington, D.C.

60. Secretary of the Navy Toucey to MFM, Jan. 29, 1858, MP, vol. 7, LC; commission in Misc. File, MP, LC.

61. Chisholm, *Waiting*, 261.

Chapter 18

1. NR, William C. Hasbrouck to MFM, Jan. 7, 1860, NOLR, NAN; MFM, Home Journal, undated, where MFM uses the term *Old Brown* extremists to describe abolitionists of New England, MP, LC; MFM to Bishop James H. Otey, Dec. 30, 1859, MP, vol. 8, LC, where MFM uses the term *madcaps* to describe Brown's followers; Charles H. Ambler, ed., "Correspondence of Robert M. T. Hunter," in *Annual Report of the American Historical Association for 1916* (Washington, D.C.: American Historical Association, 1918), 281.

2. NR, MFM to B. Franklin Minor, Dec. 30, 1859, NOLS, vol. 17, NAN.

3. John Tyler to Edward Ruffin, Feb. 18, 1860, Francis H. Smith Collection, Virginia Military Institute Archives; Philip Gerald Auchampaugh, *Robert Tyler: Southern Rights Champion* (hereafter cited as Auchampaugh, *Champion*; Duluth, Minn.): Himan Stein, 1934), 320–21.

4. MFM to Bishop James H. Otey, Jan. 16, 1860, NOLS, vol. 17, NAN; MFM address, Oct. 10, 1860, at the laying of the cornerstone of the University of the South, text in microfilm archives, University of the South, Sewanee, Tenn.

5. *Journal of the House of Delegates of the State of Virginia for the Extra Session, 1861* (Richmond: William F. Ritchie, 1861), 10; David M. Potter, *The Impending Crisis 1848–1861*, completed and edited by Don E. Fehrenbacher (hereafter cited as Potter, *Impending*), 432, 437–38.

6. C. G. Memminger, *Address of the Hon. C. G. Memminger, Special Commissioner from the State of South Carolina, Before the Assembled Authorities of the State of Virginia, Jan. 19, 1860* (Richmond, 1860), Library of Virginia, Richmond, accessed Nov. 3, 2013, http://books.google.com/books?id=MFK0BxIwlpcC.

7. "Message of the Governor of Virginia," *Richmond Daily Dispatch*, Jan. 8, 1861; speech by John C. Rutherfoord in the House of Delegates, Feb. 21, 1860, in Favor of Conference of Southern States, p. 10, Rutherfoord Family Papers, Virginia Historical Society, Richmond; for insight into Virginia secessionist thinking, see Beverley D. Tucker, *Nathaniel Beverley Tucker: Prophet of the Confederacy, 1784–1851* (Tokyo: Nan'undo, 1979), 457; for insight into conditional unionist thinking, see Shearer Davis, "Conditional Unionism," *Virginia Magazine of History and Biography* 96, no. 1 (Jan. 1988): 31–54.

8. MFM to Commodore Robert F. Stockton, Dec. 14 and 24, 1860; William M. Blackford, Dec. 16, 1860; the Rt. Rev. James H. Otey, Dec. 17, 1860; B. Franklin Minor, Dec. 21 and 24, 1860, MP, all vol. 10, LC; Daniel W. Crofts, *Reluctant Confederates* (Chapel Hill: University of North Carolina Press, 1989), 17–18, 58–59; Henry T. Shanks, *The Secession Movement in Virginia, 1847–61* (hereafter cited as Shanks, *Secession*; New York: AMS, 1934), 109; MFM to B. Franklin Minor, May 12, 1860, MP, vol. 10, LC; William W. Freehling, *The Road to Disunion: Secessionists Triumphant, 1854–1861* (New York: Oxford University Press, 2007), 369.

9. NR, MFM to Lord Wrottesley, May 10, 1860, NOLS, vol. 18, NAN.

10. Harold C. Langley, "Isaac Toucey, 7 Mar. 1857–6 Mar. 1861," in Coletta, *American Secretaries of the Navy, 1775–1913*, 305, 316; Simon Newcomb, *Reminiscences of an Astronomer*, 1: 103–4.

11. Ferdinand Maximilian to MFM, June (year unknown) and Dec. (year unknown), MP, vol. 10, LC; in early 1861, MFM wrote several letters to B. Franklin Minor and acquaintances in the "Republic of Alabama," telling them to "keep their eye" on Mexico, all in MP, vols. 11 and 12, LC.

12. MFM address, Oct. 10, 1860, at the laying of the cornerstone of the University of the South, text in microfilm archives, University of the South, Sewanee, Tenn.; James McGrath Morris, *Pulitzer: A Life in Politics, Print, and Power* (New York: HarperCollins, 2010), 146.

13. MFM to S. Welford Corbin, Oct. 1 and Oct. 20, 1860, MFM Papers, Virginia Military Institute Archives.

14. NR, MFM to the Rt. Rev. James H. Otey, Oct. 22, 1860, and "At Sea" letter to Otey, NOLS, both vol. 18, NAN.

15. NR, MFM to Lord Wrottesley, Nov. 30, 1860, NOLS, vol. 18, NAN.

16. MFM to Robert F. Stockton, as cited in note 8 above; MFM to Rutson Maury, Jan. 24, 1861, MP, vol. 11, LC.

17. Rutson Maury to MFM, Jan. 27, 1861, MP, vol. 11, LC.

18. Collection of the Washington (District of Columbia) Historical Society.

19. Diana Fontaine Maury Corbin, *A Life of Matthew Fontaine Maury, U.S.N. and C.S.N., Compiled by His Daughter* (hereafter cited as Corbin, *Maury*), 183–84; MFM letters to Rutson Maury, Jan. 24, 1861; John Tyler, Jan. 26, 1861; Joseph Seddon, Jan. 28, 1861; and Lord Wrottesley, Jan. 28, 1861, all in MP, vol. 10, LC; Auchampaugh, *Champion*, 317, 324–25.

20. Robert Gray Gunderson, *The Old Gentleman's Convention* (hereafter cited as Gunderson, *Gentleman*; Madison: University of Wisconsin Press, 1961), 38–45; Margaret Leech, *Reveille in Washington* (Alexandria, Va.: Time-Life Books, 1980), 21–24.

21. Gunderson, *Gentleman*, 38–45; F. N. Boney, *John Letcher of Virginia* (hereafter cited as Boney, *Letcher*; Tuscaloosa: University of Alabama Press, 1966), 103–4; L. E. Chittenden, comp., *A Report of the Debates and Proceeding in the Secret Sessions of the Conference Convention for Proposing Amendments to the Constitution of the United States, Held at Washington, D.C., in February, A.D. 1861* (hereafter cited as Chittenden, *Peace*; New York: D. Appleton, 1864; repr., New York: DaCapo, 1971), 8–102, citations refer to the 1864 edition, accessed Jan. 1, 2014, http://books.google.com/books?id=cGwFAAAAQAAJ; Potter, *Impending*, 546; Crofts, preface to *Reluctant Confederates*; Henry Adams, *Henry Adams: Selected Letters*, ed. Ernest Samuels (Boston: Massachusetts Historical Society, 1982), 37; Ernest B. Furgurson, *Freedom Rising: Washington in the Civil War* (New York: Random House, 2005), 37; William Warner Hoppen, *The Peace Conference of 1861 at Washington, D.C.*, pt. 3 (Providence, R.I.: Standard, 1891), 4–13, accessed Dec. 18, 2013, http://books.google.com/books?id=YKJYAAAAMAAJ; Benson J. Lossing, *Pictorial History of the Civil War in the United States of America* (Hartford, Conn.: T. Belknap, 1868; repr., Carlisle, Mass.: Applewood Books, 2010), 1:235–39, citations refer to 1868 edition, accessed Nov. 2, 2013, http://books.google.com/books?id=clWOWqQmu5kC; MFM to Mrs. Mary Minor Blackford, Dec. 2, 1851, MP, vol. 4, LC; Roy W. Curry, "James A. Seddon: A Southern Prototype," *Va. Mag.* 63, no. 2 (Apr. 1955): 123–50.

22. See note 21 above.

23. MFM to B. Franklin Minor, Jan. 28, 1861, and proposal on ultimatum, both in MP, vol. 11, LC; Chittenden, *Peace*, 82, 91, 146–55, 581; Jesse L. Kenner, *The Peace Convention of 1861* (Tuscaloosa, Ala.: Confederate, 1961), 54; Gunderson, *Gentleman*, 84–85, 91; Potter, *Impending*, p. 307.

24. *Report of the Kentucky Commissioners to the Late Peace Conference Held at Washington City, Made to the Legislature of Kentucky* (Frankfort, Ky.: Yeoman Office, 1861), 89.

25. Gunderson, *Gentleman*, 84–85; Boney, *Letcher*, 104; Auchampaugh, *Champion*, 324–25; Shanks, *Secession*, 149; John M. Coski, "A Navy Department: Hitherto Unknown to Our State Organization" (hereafter cited as Coski, "Navy"), in *Virginia at War: 1861*, ed. William C. Davis and James I. Robertson, Jr. (Lexington: University Press of Kentucky, 2005), 69, 72.

26. MFM to the delegates of the Virginia Convention, Feb. 5 and 6, 1861, MP, vol. 12, LC (letters on Virginia's and Border States' situation appear in vols. 10, 11, and 12 as well as addresses to the convention); for a statement on earlier positions, NR, MFM to the Rt. Rev. James H. Otey, Jan. 16, 1860, NOLS, vol. 17, NAN; MFM letters to Jubal Early, Jan. 17 and Jan. 24, 1861, vol. 2, Jubal Early Papers, MS Collection, LC.

27. Boney, *Letcher*, 107–14; "Memorial from Albemarle," Nov.–Dec. 1860, in John B. Minor Papers, University of Virginia; *Journal and Papers of the Virginia State Convention of 1861* (hereafter cited as *Journ. Va. Convention*; Richmond: Virginia State Library, 1966), 1:50; Coski, "Navy," 75–77.

28. Gunderson, *Gentleman*, 91; Chittenden, *Peace*, 581; Potter, *Impending*, 550; MFM to B. Franklin Minor, MP, vol. 11, LC.

29. See note 28 above.

30. Abraham Lincoln, inaugural address, Mar. 4, 1861, accessed Dec. 19, 2013, http://avalon.law.yale.edu/19th_century/lincoln1.asp; Charles P. Stone, "Washington on the Eve of the War," *Century Magazine* 26, no. 3 (July 1883): 458–66.

31. Frances Leigh Williams, *Matthew Fontaine Maury: Scientist of the Sea*, 359.

32. MFM to B. Franklin Minor, Mar. 8, 1861, MP, vol. 11, LC; Corbin, *Maury*, 186; Charles Lee Lewis, *Matthew Fontaine Maury: The Pathfinder of the Seas*, 124–25.

33. MFM to B. Franklin Minor, Mar. 26, 1861, MP, vol. 11, LC.

34. Howard K. Beale, ed., *Diary of Gideon Welles* (New York: W. W. Norton, 1960), 1:19, 43.

35. MFM to the Rt. Rev. James H. Otey, Feb. 23, 1861, MP, vol. 13, LC; James Hervey Otey, "Trust in God: The Only Safety of Nations," Transcript of Sermon Delivered Jan. 1, 1860, in *Memoir of Rt. Rev. James Hervey Otey, D.D., LL.D.*, ed. the Rt. Rev. William Mercer Green (New York: James Pott, 1885), 336.

36. "Return of the Commissioners—Serenade and Speeches," *Richmond Dispatch*, Mar. 1, 1861.

37. *Journ. Va. Convention*, 141–43; *Interview Between President Lincoln and Col. John B. Baldwin, Apr. 4, 1861: Statements and Evidence* (Staunton, Va.: "Spectator" Job Office, 1866), http://openlibrary.org/books/OL6540951M/Interview_between_President_Lincoln_and_Col._John_B._Baldwin_April_4th_1861.

38. Diary of Edmund Ruffin, MS Collection, 4:797–98, LC; William W. Freehling, *The Road to Disunion: Secessionists Triumphant, 1854–1861*, 517–24; Avery Odell Craven, *Edmund Ruffin: Southerner* (Baton Rouge: Louisiana State University Press, 1932), 224–25.

39. Boney, *Letcher*, 107–17; "Memorial from Albermarle," Nov.–Dec. 1860, in John B. Minor Papers, University of Virginia; *Journ. Va. Convention*, 50; Executive Correspondence 1861, Library of Virginia, contains undated handwritten rough drafts of ordinance of secession from convention meeting of Apr. 17, 1861, along with notes to Gov. John Letcher.

40. MFM to Mrs. B. Franklin Minor, Apr. 17, 1861, MP, vol. 14, LC; MFM, *Maury's Nautical Monographs: No. 2; The Barometer at Sea* (Washington, D.C.: U.S. Naval Observatory, Mar. 1861), accessed Dec. 19, 2013, http://books.google.com/books?id=0z1DAAAAYAAJ; MFM, *Maury's Nautical Monographs: No. 3; The Southeast Trade-Winds of the Atlantic* (Washington, D.C.: U.S. Naval Observatory, May 1861), accessed Dec. 19, 2013, http://books.google.com/books?id=0z1DAAAAYAAJ; Corbin, *Maury*, 190.

41. Gideon Welles, Diary and Narratives, Welles Papers, reel 2, MS Collection, LC.

42. NR, MFM to His Excellency Abraham Lincoln, Apr. 20, 1861, NOLS, vol. 18, NAN; MFM to William C. Hasbrouck, Apr. 29, 1861, MP, vol. 14, LC.

43. J. M. Gilliss, introduction to *Astronomical and Meteorological Observations Made at the United States Naval Observatory During the Year 1861* (Washington, D.C.: Secretary of the Navy, 1862), x; Gideon Welles Diary and Narratives, Welles Papers, reel 2, MS Collection, LC.

Chapter 19

1. Craig Michael Simpson, *Henry A. Wise in Antebellum Politics, 1850–61*, PhD diss. (Ann Arbor, Mich.: University Microfilms, 1979), 290–91, 302–303; "Letter from Ex. Gov. Wise," *Richmond Daily Dispatch*, Jan. 8, 1861.

2. See note 1 above.

3. Philip Gerald Auchampaugh, *Robert Tyler: Southern Rights Champion*, 324; Executive Correspondence, Gov. John Letcher to Gen. William B. Taliaferro, Apr. 18, 1861, Library of Virginia; to Capt. Robert B. Pegram, same day; T. T. Cropper to Letcher, Apr. 17, 18, 1861, on situation at Gosport and Norfolk; F. N. Boney, *John Letcher of Virginia* (hereafter cited as Boney, *Letcher*), 114–17.

4. Charles H. Ambler, *Francis H. Pierpont* (hereafter cited as Ambler, *Pierpont*; Chapel Hill: University of North Carolina Press, 1937), 69–92.

5. Executive Correspondence, 1861, Library of Virginia. Specifically, G. W. Richardson to John Letcher, Apr. 17, 1861, announcing vote of secession and approval to call up volunteers to defend the state; message of Gov. John Letcher to the Virginia Convention, Apr. 21, 1861, *Journal and Papers of the Virginia State Convention of 1861* (hereafter cited as *Journ. Va. Convention*), 1:179.

6. Message of Gov. John Letcher to the Virginia Convention, Apr. 21, 1861, *Journ. Va. Convention*, 1:179.

7. MFM address in France, May 21, 1866, MP, vol. 25, fols. 4552–59, LC.

8. T. C. De Leon, *Four Years in Rebel Capitals: An Inside View of Life in the Southern Confederacy from Birth to Death* (Mobile, Ala.: Gossip Printing, 1890), 104; *The War of the Rebellion: A Compilation of the Official Records of the Union and Confederate Armies*, vol. 41, pt. 2 (Washington, D.C.: Government Printing Office, 1880–1901), p. 24.

9. Executive Correspondence, Apr. 21, 1861, Library of Virginia.

10. Colonel Richard L. Maury, *Notes: Southern Historical Society Papers* (Richmond, Va.: Southern Historical Society, 1903), 326–28. Richard L. Maury's reminiscence on torpedoes (hereafter cited as R. Maury, Torpedoes), published as an undated pamphlet and in Library of

Virginia collection, refers to washtub for the tests. The house where the testing was done has been demolished. A marker has been placed on a building across the street, attesting to Maury's development of electronically detonated mines. Additionally, in the Letcher executive correspondence from Apr. 21 to June 12, 1861, at the Library of Virginia, there are intriguing letters to MFM from inventors such as Arthur Parbarin in New Orleans on how to use mines to thwart infantry and naval assaults. Some of MFM's later war correspondence from Great Britain and Confederate practice on the battlefield showed how CSA and CSN forces employed these secret weapons.

11. Minutes for May 27, 1861, *Proceedings of the Advisory Council of Virginia, 1861* (hereafter cited as *Proceedings Advisory Council*); MFM to James L. Cabell, May 31, 1861, MP, vol. 14, LC.

12. R. Maury, Torpedoes, 326–32.

13. Executive Correspondence, Apr. 23, 1861, Library of Virginia. Included were telegraph dispatches from Norfolk and acknowledgments from the governor.

14. *Journ. Va. Convention*, Apr. 23, 1861, 186–87.

15. "Glorious Rebels," editorial, *Richmond Daily Whig*, Apr. 23, 1861.

16. MFM to B. Franklin Minor, May 9, 1861, MP, vol. 14, LC.

17. NR, MFM to Secretary of the Navy Welles, Apr. 26, 1861, Executive Letters Received, NAN.

18. Lyon Gardiner Tyler, comp., *The Letters and Times of the Tylers*, vol. 2, pt. 2 (Richmond: Whittet and Shepperson, 1885), 644, accessed Dec. 19, 2013, https://ia600406.us.archive.org/33/items/cu31924092903917/cu31924092903917.pdf.

19. Ordinances, *Journ. Va. Convention*, vol. 2.

20. Executive Correspondence, Apr.–June 1861, Library of Virginia, Sallie F. Crowder letter to Letcher, Apr. 24, 1861.

21. Executive Correspondence, Apr.–June 1861, Library of Virginia; Urbanna letter to Letcher, Apr. 22, 1861; ladies of Ingleside, Fauquier County, letter to Letcher, Apr. 25, 1861.

22. Executive Correspondence, Apr.–June 1861, Library of Virginia; Ambler, *Pierpont*, 69–92.

23. *Proceedings Advisory Council*, May 15, 1861, on how to drill mounted troops was representative of what the Virginia government was trying to do in its defense, as was *Journ. Va. Convention*, 1861, ordinances covering military forces and navy, Apr. 26–27, 1861, 1:197–207; *Journ. Va. Convention*, 1861, Ordinances, Apr. 30, 1861, for "Better Regulation of the Departments of the Army and Navy of Virginia," 2:221; Executive Correspondence, Apr.–June 1861, Library of Virginia: Pickens began telegramming Letcher Apr. 22, 1861, with offers of troops to defend Norfolk and the Gosport Navy Yard.

24. Executive Correspondence, Apr.–June 1861, Library of Virginia; Letcher to Virginia Convention, June 17, 1861.

25. Executive Correspondence, Apr.–June 1861, Library of Virginia; D. G. Smith to Letcher, May 18, 1861.

26. Executive Correspondence, Apr.–June 1861, Library of Virginia, Report on River Defenses, Apr. 24, first of series on naval defenses. This one names commanders and placement of guns. Telegram reports on military situations, particularly in Hampton Roads, almost daily.

27. MFM to William C. Hasbrouck, May 10, 1861, MP, vol. 14, LC; *Richmond Daily Dispatch*, July 1, 1861; "Stated Meeting, March 21, 1862," *Proceedings of the American Philosophical Society* 9, no. 67 (1863): 12.

28. Brodie S. Herndon to MFM, May 29, 1861, MP, vol. 14, LC; June 3, 1861, entry, *Betty Herndon Maury Diary*, 2 vols., vol. 1, MP, LC.

29. Executive Correspondence, Apr.–June 1861, Library of Virginia, Letcher report to Virginia Convention, June 17, 1861.

30. MFM to William Blackford, May 20, 1861, MP, vol. 14, LC.

31. Executive Correspondence, Apr.–June 1861, Library of Virginia; W. Lively of Monroe County to Letcher, June 7, 1861, and S. Welford Corbin et al. to Letcher May 29, 1861.

32. Ambler, *Pierpont*, 88–92.

33. Ibid.

34. Varina Howell Davis, *Jefferson Davis, Ex-President of the Confederate States of America: A Memoir by His Wife*, 2:74–76; John S. Pierson as Personne, *Marginalia; or, Gleanings from an Army Note-Book* (Columbia, S.C.: F. G. deFontaine, 1864), 27.

35. Executive Correspondence, Apr.–June 1861, Library of Virginia, Jefferson Davis to Letcher, June 1, 1861.

36. June 4, 1861, entry, *Stephen R. Mallory Diary*, Southern Historical Collection, Wilson Library, University of North Carolina; Minutes for June 3 and 7, 1861, *Proceedings of Advisory Council*; Mary Boykin Chesnut, *A Diary from Dixie*, ed. Isabelle D. Martin and Mytrta Locket Avary, facsimile (New York: Portland House, 1905; repr., New York: Random House, 1997), 79, citations refer to 1997 edition.

37. MFM to B. Franklin Minor, June 11, 1861, MP, vol. 14, LC; July 9, 1861, entry, *Mallory Diary*.

38. June 3, 1861, entry, *Betty Herndon Maury Diary*, vol. 1, MP, LC.

39. Report of Capt. Samuel Barron to Gov. John Letcher, date included in Letcher report to the Virginia Convention, June 17, 1861, Executive Correspondence, Apr.–June 1861, Library of Virginia; Report of Maj. Gen. R. E. Lee to Gov. John Letcher, June 17, 1861, Executive Correspondence, Apr.–June 1861, Library of Virginia,.

40. Letcher to Virginia Convention, June 17, 1861, Executive Correspondence, Apr.–June 1861, Library of Virginia.

41. Ibid.

Chapter 20

1. MFM to B. Franklin Minor, June 11, 1861, MP, vol. 14, LC; Aug. 1, 1862, entry and Mallory letter, June 24, 1862, *Stephen R. Mallory Diary*, both in Mallory Papers, Southern Historical Collection, Wilson Library, University of North Carolina; June 21, 1861, letter, Mallory Papers, Southern Historical Collection, Wilson Library, University of North Carolina; Jefferson Davis, *The Rise and Fall of the Confederate Government* (hereafter cited as Davis, *Rise and Fall*; New York: DaCapo, 1990), 1:295–99. As an example of Confederate government thinking at the time, Mallory wrote, "Virginians as a people are supine and inert and seem hardly to realize the state of things around them."

2. MFM to B. Franklin Minor, June 26, 1861, MP, vol. 14, LC; *Official Records of the Union and Confederate Navies in the War of the Rebellion* (hereafter cited as *ORN*), ser. 1 (Washington, D.C.: Government Printing Office, 1894–1922), 4:553–55.

3. George W. Bagby, "Pawnee War," in *Selections from the Miscellaneous Writings of Dr. George W. Bagby* (Richmond: Whittet and Shepperson, 1884), 1:324–32, accessed Dec. 19, 2013, http://books.google.com/books?id=PhdEAAAAYAAJ.

4. MFM letter cited in note 2 above.

5. George N. Hollins, "Autobiography of Commodore George N. Hollins," *Maryland Historical Magazine* 34 (Sept. 1938): 235–43, standalone item, Maryland Historical Society, Baltimore; MFM letter cited in note 2 above.

6. See note 5 above.

7. Richard L. Maury, *Brief Sketch of the Work of Matthew F. Maury*, pamphlet (hereafter cited as R. L. Maury, *Brief*; Richmond: Whittel and Stephenson, 1915), 6–12; MFM to B. Franklin Minor, June 26, July 8 and 19, 1861, MP, vol. 14, LC; July 10, 1861, entry, *Betty Herndon Maury's Diary*, vol. 1, MP, LC; Stephen Budiansky, *Perilous Fight: America's Intrepid War with Britain on the High Seas, 1812–1815*, 348; Ian Toll, *Six Frigates: The Epic History of the Founding of the United States Navy*, 422–23; Gregory K. Hartman, *Weapons That Wait: Mine Warfare in the United States Navy*, with Scott Truver (hereafter cited as Hartman, *Wait*; Annapolis: Naval Institute, 1991), 19, 24, 34.

8. Milton F. Perry, *Infernal Machines* (Baton Rouge: Louisiana State University Press, 1965), 3–4; Betty Herndon entry as cited in note 7 above; MFM to Dr. Brodie S. Herndon, Apr. 22, 1863, MP, vol. 18, LC.

9. Gabriel J. Rains and Peter S. Michie, *Confederate Torpedoes: Two Illustrated 19th Century Works with New Appendices and Photographs*, ed. Herbert Schiller (hereafter cited as Rains and Michie, *Torpedoes*; Jefferson, N.C.: McFarland, 2011), 56; Gordon S. Brown, *The Captain Who Burned His Ships: Captain Thomas Tingey, USN, 1750–1829*, 109–10; Alan Rems, "Man of War," *Naval History* (Annapolis, Md.) 25, no. 4 (Aug. 2011): 38–45; Philip K. Lundenberg, *Samuel Colt's Submarine Battery: The Secret and the Enigma* (Washington, D.C.: Smithsonian Institution Press, 1974), 10; "Affairs in the Upper Potomac," *New York Times*, Dec. 8, 1861; see notes 7 and 8 above.

10. Maury, *Brief*, 6–12.

11. Ibid.

12. Ibid.

13. MFM to B. Franklin Minor, July 19, 1861, MP, vol. 14, LC; see note 10 above.

14. Jefferson Davis, *The Rise and Fall of the Confederate Government*, 1:297–332.

15. James McPherson, *Antietam: Crossroads of Freedom; The Battle That Changed the Course of the Civil War* (hereafter cited as McPherson, *Antietam*; Oxford: Oxford University Press, 2004), 11.

16. Frank Freidel, ed., *Union Pamphlets of the Civil War* (Cambridge, Mass.: Belknap Press of Harvard University Press, 1967), 1:166–86; Sidney T. Matthews, "Control of the Baltimore Press during the Civil War," *Maryland Historical Magazine* 36 (June 1941): 150.

17. "Case of Matthew Fontaine Maury and Rutson Maury," *The War of the Rebellion: A Compilation of the Official Records of the Union and Confederate Armies*, ser. 2 (hereafter cited as *OR*), 2:1041–76.

18. MFM to B. Franklin Minor, Oct. 8, 1861, MP, vol. 15, LC.

19. Ibid.; R. L. Maury, *Brief*, 9–12.

20. R. L. Maury, *Brief*, 9–12.

21. MFM to Maj. Gen. Leonidas Polk, Dec. 4, 1861, *Official Records of the Union and Confederate Navies in the War of the Rebellion*, ser. 1 (hereafter cited as *ORN*), 22:793, 806.

22. Edward C. Bearrs, *Receding Tide: Vicksburg and Gettysburg; The Campaigns That Changed the Civil War*, with J. Parker Hills (Washington, D.C.: National Geographic, 2010), 22.

23. Ibid.

24. Edward de Stoeckl to MFM, Sept. 18, 1861, MP, vol. 14, LC; MFM to Grand Duke Constantine, Oct. 29, 1861, MP, vol. 15, LC.

25. McPherson, *Antietam*, 40.

26. MFM to B. Franklin Minor, Aug. 11, 19, 21, 1861, MP, Vol. 15, LC; John Beauchamp Jones, *A Rebel War Clerk's Diary at the Confederate States Capital* (hereafter cited as Jones, *Clerk*; Philadelphia: J. P. Lippincott, 1866), 1:137; McPherson, *Antietam*, 40; Warren F. Spencer, *The Confederate*

Navy in Europe (Tuscaloosa: University of Alabama Press, 1983), 131.

27. MFM as Ben Bow, *Richmond Enquirer:* "Ought We Have a Navy," Sept. 27, 1861; "Navy Big Gun, Small Ships," Oct. 3, 1861. Maury's relationship with Tyler extended back at least to MFM's writing on direct trade with Europe from Southern ports in the *Southern Literary Messenger* in 1839. For an excellent description of what the Confederacy was doing in shipbuilding, see Robert Holcome's "Type of Ships" in *The Confederate Navy: The Ships, Men, and Organization, 1861–1965*, ed. William N. Still, Jr. (Annapolis: Naval Institute, 1997), 57–61.

28. *OR*, ser. 1, vol. 51, pt. 2, pp. 416–18; Oct. 21 and 24, 1861, entries, *Betty Herndon Maury's Diary*, vol. 1, MP, LC.

29. *OR*, ser. 1, vol. 51, pt. 2, p. 49; MFM to Gov. John Letcher, Oct. 15, 1861, MP, vol. 15, LC; Permanent Fortifications and Sea Coast Defense [To Accompany H.R. 416], 37th Cong., 2d Sess., Apr. 23, 1862, H.R. Rep. 86, 449–78, accessed Dec. 19, 2013, http://books.google.com/books?id=G_DHuvB5YugC; Harold Langley, "Isaac Toucey, 7 Mar. 1857–6 Mar. 1861," in Coletta, *American Secretaries of the Navy, 1775–1913*, 1: 305.

30. MFM to Letcher, as cited in note 29 above.

31. MFM to Letcher, as cited in note 29 above; MFM in correspondence with Lt. Marin Jansen of the Dutch Navy, especially NR, Dec. 3, 1859, NOLS, vol. 17, NAN, a letter and others in the two years preceding the outbreak of the Civil War in which MFM offered ideas on how such a fleet might operate in coastal waters.

32. Robert M. Browning, Jr., *From Cape Charles to Cape Fear: The North Atlantic Blockading Squadron During the Civil War* (Tuscaloosa: University of Alabama Press, 1993), 8, 11.

33. Thomas Jefferson Page, *OR*, vol. 51, ser. 1, pt. 2, enclosure no. 3, p. 423; James M. Merrill, *DuPont: The Making of an Admiral*, 264–74; Robert M. Browning, Jr., *Success Is All That Was Expected: The South Atlantic Blockading Squadron During the Civil War* (Washington, D.C.: Potomac Books, 2002), 27.

34. *ORN*, ser. 2, vol. 1, pp. 447–51.

35. See note 34 above.

36. Advertisement, *Richmond Daily Dispatch*, Feb. 26, 1862; "Great Naval Battle! The Iron Marine Battle; Virginia Engages the Federal War Ship," *Richmond Daily Dispatch*, Mar. 10, 1862; MFM to Letcher in note 29 above on availability of shipwrights; Aug. 1, 1862, entry, *Mallory Diary*; William F. Martin Papers, Oct. 3–Nov. 15, 1861, on gunboats, both at Southern Historical Collection, Wilson Library, University of North Carolina; MFM to Secretary of the Navy Mallory, Jan. 25, 1862, *ORN*, ser. 2, vol. 2, p. 138.

37. Stephen C. Small, "The Ship That Couldn't Be Built," *Naval History* (Annapolis, Md.) 22, no. 5 (Oct. 2008): 69–74; Stephen W. Sears, "The Rise and Fall of CSS *Virginia:* Did a Radical New Confederate Gunship Foil McClellan's Plan to End the Civil War in 1862?," *MHQ: Quarterly Journal of Military History* (Leesburg, Va.) 21, no. 3 (Spring 2009): 82–93; Stephen Mallory to Jefferson Davis, Apr. 26, 1861, *ORN*, ser. 2, vol. 2, p. 51; James D. Bulloch to Mallory, Oct. 24 and Oct. 27, 1864, *ORN*, ser. 2, vol. 2, pp. 740–43; Testimony of John Mercer Brooke to Confederate Congress, Feb. 26, 1863, *ORN*, ser. 2, vol. 1, pp. 783–85; George M. Brooke, Jr., *John M. Brooke: Naval Scientist and Educator* (Charlottesville: University Press of Virginia, 1980), 231–37, for early construction details and objectives; William N. Still, *Iron Afloat* (Nashville, Tenn.: Vanderbilt University Press, 1971), 96–195, for an excellent description of plating and guns for CSS *Virginia*; Raimondo Luraghi, *A History of the Confederate Navy* (hereafter cited as Luraghi, *Confederate*), trans. Paolo E. Coletta (Annapolis: Naval Institute, 1996), 1:98.

38. See note 37 above.

39. MFM to A. de La Marche, Mar. 15, 1862, MP, vol. 15, LC.

40. William N. Still, *Ironclad Captains: The Commanding Officers of the U.S.S.* Monitor (Washington, D.C.: Marine and Estuarine Management Division, National Oceanic and Atmospheric Administration, 1988), details each commander's perspective on the Battle of Hampton Roads and immediate aftermath; Catesby ap R. Jones, "Services of the *Virginia* (*Merrimack*)," *Southern Historical Society Papers* 11, no. 2 (1883): 65–74.

41. *Richmond Dispatch*, Feb. 26, 1862.

42. MFM to B. Franklin Minor, Apr. 1, 1862, MP, vol. 15, LC; April and May entries, *Betty Herndon Maury's Diary*, vol. 2, MP, LC; R. L. Maury, *Brief*, 18; MFM Prospectus on Torpedo School, 1866, MP, vol. 47, LC.

43. *ORN*, ser. 1, vol. 7, pp. 787–99. As part of his duties with the Confederate Navy, MFM served on the court-martial board of Josiah Tattnall, the last commander of CSS *Virginia*. *Richmond Enquirer*, May 19, 1862, editorial questioning destruction of *Virginia*; "A Reply to Commodore Tatnall's Report," *Richmond Daily Dispatch*, May 24, 1862; John M. Coski, *Capital Navy: The Men, the Ships, and Operations of the James River Squadron* (hereafter cited as Coski, *Capital*; Campbell, Calif.: Savas Woodbury, 1996), 29.

44. Coski, *Capital*, 29; Rains and Michie, *Torpedoes*, 56, 59.

45. Luraghi, *Confederate*, 240–41, 245; see note 44 above.

46. "The Peril of Richmond," editorial, *Richmond Dispatch*, May 15, 1862.

47. "River Defenses—Common Sense," editorial, *Richmond Daily Whig*, Apr. 19, 1862.

48. Donald J. Meyers, *And the War Came: The Slavery Quarrel and the American Civil War* (New York: Algora, 2005), 136.

49. MFM will, MP, vol. 16, LC; Jones, *Clerk*, 1:123–27.

50. Jones, *Clerk*, as cited in note 49 above.

51. Emory M. Thomas, *The Confederate State of Richmond: A Biography of the Capital* (Baton Rouge: Louisiana State University Press, 1971), 90; Jones, *Clerk*, as cited in note 49 above.

52. Luther S. Dickie, *History of the Eighty-Fifth Regiment Pennsylvania Volunteer Infantry, 1861–1865* (New York: J. C. and W. F. Powers, 1915), 157–58; James D. Bulloch, *The Secret Service of the Confederate States in Europe; or, How the Confederate Cruisers Were Equipped*, 2 vols. (London: Bentley and Son, 1883; repr. with introduction by Philip Van Doren Stern, New York: Sagamore, 1959), 1:53 (page references are to the 1883 edition). Bulloch credited Charles K. Prioleau and Major Caleb Huse in Great Britain for providing the materiel the Confederates needed to stymie the Peninsula campaign.

53. MFM to B. Franklin Minor, June 1, 1862, MP, vol. 16, LC; May 17 to 22, 1862, entries, *Betty Herndon Maury Diary*, vol. 2, MP, LC; Jones, *Clerk*, 128–32; Craig L. Symonds, *Joseph E. Johnston: A Civil War Biography*, 172.

54. MFM to B. Franklin Minor, June 5 and Aug. 5, 1862, MP, both vol. 16, LC.

55. Acting Master Rogers to Acting Rear Adm. Lee, Sept. 16 and 17, 1862, *ORN*, ser. 1, vol. 8, pp. 72–73; MFM remarks before the French Commission, May 21, 1866, MP, vol. 25, LC; MFM lectures to Dutch, Swedish, and Norwegian officers in MP, vol. 67, fols. 9192–331, 9332–55, LC.

56. MFM lectures, as cited in note 55 above.

57. MFM to Secretary Mallory, June 19, 1862, *ORN*, ser. 1, pp. 544–46; Flag Officer Samuel F. DuPont, Apr. 22, 1863, *ORN*, ser. 1, vol. 14, pp. 54–55; Hartman, *Wait*, 30–32; Luraghi, *Confederate*, 234.

58. MFM lectures, as cited in note 55 above; Williams, *Maury Scientist*, 393; Charles Lee Lewis, *Matthew Fontaine Maury: The Pathfinder of the Seas*, 205–8; "The Capture of the Confederate Gunboat Teaser—Escape of All on Board," *Richmond Daily Dispatch*, July 7, 1862.

59. *Journal of the Congress of Confederate States of America, 1861–1865*, 58th Cong., 2d sess., Senate Document No. 234, Session Aug. 28, 1862 (Washington, D.C.: Government Printing Office, 1905), 5:322, accessed Nov. 16, 1013, http://memory.loc.gov/cgi-bin/query/r?ammem/hlaw:@field(DOCID+@lit(cc00569)). The antagonism between Davis and Mallory toward MFM was best expressed in MFM to his wife, Oct. 12, 1862, MP, vol. 17, LC; Davis, *Rise and Fall*, 2:152–223; MFM to John Minor Maury, July 24, 1867, MP, vol. 26, LC.

60. Letters as cited in note 59 above; MFM describing meeting with the secretary of the Navy before leaving Richmond for duty in Great Britain to Lieut. Robert D. Minor, C.S.N., Apr. 21, 1863, MP, vol. 18, LC.

61. MFM to B. Franklin Minor, June 5 and 8, 1862, MP, vol. 16, LC.

62. Ibid.

63. MFM to his wife, Oct. 6, 1862, MP, vol. 17, LC.

Chapter 21

1. Glyndon G. Van Deusen, *William Henry Seward* (New York: Oxford University Press, 1967), 292–93; James D. Bulloch, *The Secret Service of the Confederate States in Europe* (hereafter cited as Bulloch, *Secret Service*), 1:54–55; James Morris Morgan, *Recollections of a Rebel Reefer* (hereafter cited as Morgan, *Rebel Reefer*; Boston: Houghton Mifflin, 1917), 17, 111.

2. James McPherson, *Tried by War: Abraham Lincoln as the Commander in Chief*, 160; Jefferson Davis, *The Rise and Fall of the Confederate Government* (hereafter cited as Davis, *Rise and Fall*), 2:151–62; Spencer Walpole, *The Life of Lord John Russell* (London: Longmans Green, 1891), 2: 350–52; Edward Dicey, *Six Months in the Federal States* (London: Macmillan, 1863), 199; Adrian Desmond and James Moore, *Darwin's Sacred Cause: How Darwin's Hatred of Slavery Shaped Darwin's Views on Evolution*, 334–35; Worthington Chauncey Ford, *A Cycle of Adams Letters* (Boston: Houghton Mifflin, 1920), 243.

3. Frank J. Merli, *Great Britain and the Confederate Navy* (Bloomington: Indiana University Press, 1970), 100, quoting Gladstone Oct. 7, 1862, speech.

4. MFM to B. Franklin Minor, Jan. 21, 1863, MP, vol. 17, LC.

5. James Morton Callahan, *The Diplomatic History of the Southern Confederacy* (hereafter cited as Callahan, *Diplomatic*; Baltimore: Johns Hopkins University, 1901), 204; Warren F. Spencer, *The Confederate Navy in Europe* (hereafter cited as Spencer, *Navy in Europe*), 212–13; Judith W. McGuire, *Diary of a Southern Refugee During the War*, 3rd ed. (Richmond: J. W. Randolph and English, 1889), 91.

6. John Bigelow, *Retrospections of an Active Life, 1817–1863* (hereafter cited as Bigelow, *Retrospections*; New York: Baker and Taylor, 1909–10), 1:380–81; Morgan, *Rebel Reefer*, 93–97; Amanda Foreman, *A World on Fire: Britain's Crucial Role in the American Civil War* (hereafter cited as Foreman, *World*; New York: Random House, 2010), 80–81.

7. Spencer, *Navy in Europe*, 193; Michael Clark, "Alexander Collie: The Ups and Downs of Trading with the Confederacy," *Northern Mari-*

ner, Apr. 2009, 125–48; Davis, *Rise and Fall*, 1:402–3.

8. Morgan, *Rebel Reefer*, 93–96; Ethel S. Nepveux, *George Alfred Trenholm and the Company That Went to War, 1861–1865* (hereafter cited as Nepveux, *Company*; Charleston, S.C.: Comprint, 1973), 61.

9. Morgan, Rebel Reefer, 98–105; Robert Browning, Jr., *Success Is All That Was Expected: The South Atlantic Blockading Squadron During the Civil War*, 20; William H. Roberts, *Now for the Contest: Coastal and Oceanic Naval Operations in the Civil War*, Great Campaigns of the Civil War (Lincoln: University of Nebraska Press, 2004), 105.

10. Morgan, *Rebel Reefer*, 98–105.

11. MFM to his wife, Oct. 12, 1862; MFM to B. Franklin Minor, Oct. 24, 1862, all in MP, vol. 17, LC; Morgan, *Rebel Reefer*, 98–105.

12. See note 9 above.

13. Morgan, *Rebel Reefer*, 98–105.

14. Morgan, *Rebel Reefer*, 98–105; "Capt. M. F. Maury," *Richmond Daily Dispatch*, Dec. 5, 1862.

15. Morgan, *Rebel Reefer*, 98–105.

16. MFM (unsigned), "Maritime Interests of the South and West," *Southern Quarterly* 4, no. 8 (Oct. 1849): 323; Nathaniel Hawthorne, *Passages from the English Note-Books* (Boston: Mifflin, 1870 and 1890), 1:12; Morgan, *Rebel Reefer*, 106; Thomas Ellison, *The Cotton Trade of Great Britain, Including a History of the Liverpool Cotton Market and the Liverpool Cotton Brokers Association* (London: Effingham Wilson, 1886), 188; Graeme J. Milne, *Trade and Traders in Mid-Victorian Liverpool: Mercantile Business and the Making of a World Port* (Liverpool, U.K.: Liverpool University Press, 2000), 3.

17. Kenneth Warren, *Steel, Ships, and Men: Cammell Laird, 1824–1993* (Liverpool, U.K.: Liverpool University Press, 1998), 2, 26, 34, 36.

18. Bulloch, *Secret Service*, 1:314–17, for a description of the aims of the Confederacy in overseas arms and ship buying; Raimondo Luraghi, *A History of the Confederate Navy* (hereafter cited as Luraghi, *Confederate*), 201, 205; Foreman, *World*, 141–44; Wesley Loy, "10 Rumford Place: Doing Confederate Business in Liverpool" (hereafter cited as Loy, "10 Rumford"), *South Carolina Historical Magazine* 98, no. 4 (Oct. 1997): 349–74.

19. Spencer, *Navy in Europe*, 127, 147–48.

20. Spencer, *Navy in Europe*, 38–39, 134–35; Luraghi, *Confederate*, 76; Bulloch, *Secret Service*, 1:272, 2:261; Morgan, *Rebel Reefer*, 106; Stephen R. Wise, *Lifeline of the Confederacy: Blockade Running During the Civil War*, paperback ed. (hereafter cited as Wise, *Lifeline*; Columbia: University of South Carolina Press, 1991), 49, 67; Foreman, *World*, 404–5.

21. "The State Department: Mr. Benjamin to Mr. Slidell," *New York Times*, Jan. 19, 1863; Orlando Figes, *The Crimean War: A History* (New York: Henry Holt, 2010), 433–39; Karl Marx, *The Eighteenth Brumaire of Louis Bonaparte*, trans. Daniel de Leon (Chicago: Charles H. Kerr, 1907), 73; *Times* (London) scrapbook in Library of Virginia.

22. L. B. Schmidt, "The Influence of Wheat and Cotton on Anglo-American Relations during the Civil War," paper presented to American Historical Association in Philadelphia, *Iowa Journal of History and Politics* (Des Moines) 16 (1918): 400–411; Frank L. Owsley, *King Cotton Diplomacy*, 2nd ed. (Chicago: University of Chicago Press, 1959), 12–15; Frank E. Vandiver, ed., *Confederate Blockade Running Through Bermuda* (Austin: University of Texas Press, 1947), xii–xxvii; Samuel B. Thompson, *Confederate Purchasing Operations Abroad* (hereafter cited as Thompson, *Purchasing*; Chapel Hill: University of North Carolina Press, 1935), 18–20; Harriet Chappel Owsley, "Henry Shelton Sanford and Federal Surveillance Abroad, 1861–1865," *Mississippi Valley Historical Review* 48, no. 2 (Sept. 1961): 211–28.

23. See note 22 above.

24. Rutson Maury to MFM, Jan. 27, 1861, MP, vol. 11, LC; Craig L. Symonds, *Lincoln and His Admirals* (Oxford: Oxford University Press, 2008), 283–86.

25. Morgan, *Rebel Reefer*, 106; Nepveux, *Company*, 1, 35; Bigelow, *Retrospections*, 2:256.

26. *The War of the Rebellion: A Compilation of the Official Records of the Union and Confederate Armies* (hereafter cited as *OR*), ser. 4, 2:557, 909.

27. Burton J. Hendrick, *Statesmen of the Lost Cause: Jefferson Davis and His Cabinet* (New York: Literary Guild of America, 1939), 225–28; Spencer, *Navy in Europe*, 142; Thompson, *Purchasing*, 31–47; Foreman, *World*, 405–7; John Douglass Van Horne, *Jefferson Davis and Repudiation in Mississippi* (Baltimore: Sun, 1915), http://archive.org/details/jeffersondavisre00vanh.

28. Wise, *Lifeline*, 94–106; Josiah Gorgas, *The Journals of Josiah Gorgas, 1857–1878*, ed. Sarah Woolfolk Wiggins (hereafter cited as Gorgas, *Journals*; Tuscaloosa: University of Alabama Press, 1995), 139, 152; Loy, "10 Rumford," 349–74. Mallory really had little other choice. His assessment of naval needs was correct and supported by an experienced naval officer and merchant mariner, Bulloch. The Confederate government eventually sent Colin McRae to represent the Treasury Department to sort out the competing claims on the Erlanger loan funds.

29. Morgan, *Rebel Reefer*, 107; MFM to Marin H. Jansen, Dec. 13, 1862, and MFM to his wife, Nov. 30, 1862, both in MP, vol. 17, LC.

30. MFM, letter to the editor, *Times* (London), Dec. 22, 1862, reprinted in *New York Times*, Jan. 8, 1863; Rutson Maury to MFM, July 30, 1863, vol. 18, MP, LC.

31. *The Case of the United States, Laid Before the Tribunal of Arbitration, Convened at Geneva Under the Provisions of the Treaty Between the United States of America and Her Majesty the Queen of Great Britain, Concluded at Washington, May 8, 1871* (Leipzig, Germany: F. A. Brockhaus, 1872), 156–57, accessed Nov. 9, 2013, http://books.google.com/books?id=ZgEdAAAAYAAJ; Joseph McKenna, British Ships in the Confederate Navy (Jefferson, N.C.: McFarland, 2010), 162–63; "Deposition of Benjamin Conolly," Correspondence concerning Claims against Great Britain Transmitted to the Senate of the United States (Washington, D.C.: Philp and Solomons, 1869), 2:689–91; Foreman, World, 409.

32. Morgan, *Rebel Reefer*, 113–17; Luraghi, *Confederate*, 77; Bulloch, *Secret Service*, 2:261–62.

33. See note 32 above.

34. MFM to Marin H. Jansen, Dec. 20, 1862, MP, vol. 17, LC.

35. Walter Chandler, "Diplomatic History of the Southern Confederacy," *Confederate Veteran* (Nashville, Tenn.) 30, no. 13 (Dec. 1922): 454; James Daniel Richardson, *A Compilation of the Messages and Papers of the Confederacy* (Nashville, Tenn.: United States, 1905), 2:338–51; James D. Bulloch to Secretary of the Navy Mallory, July 20, 1863, pp. 468–69, and Oct. 20, 1863, *ORN*, ser. 2, vol. 2, pp. 507–11.

36. Spencer, *Navy in Europe*, 146–51; Bulloch, *Secret Service*, 2:24; "The State Department: Mr. Benjamin to Mr. Slidell," *New York Times*, Jan. 19, 1863.

37. Spencer, *Navy in Europe*, 150–51, 153–55.

38. MFM Diary, entries June 4 and 25, Nov. 3, all 1863, MP, vol. 57, LC; Bigelow, *Retrospections*, 2:150–51, 284; Louis Martin Sears, "A Confederate Diplomat at the Court of Napoleon III," *American Historical Review* 26, no. 2 (Jan. 1921): 255–81.

39. MFM Diary, entries June 4 and 25, Nov. 3, all 1863, MP, vol. 57, LC.

40. Spencer, *Navy in Europe*, 145, 157–60; Callahan, *Diplomatic*, 205, 210.

41. Spencer, *Navy in Europe*, 157–160.

42. Bulloch, *Secret Service*, 2:58.

43. James D. Bulloch to Secretary of the Navy Mallory, July 20, 1863, pp. 468–69, and Oct. 20, 1863, *ORN*, ser. 2, vol. 2, pp. 507–11; MFM to Secretary of the Navy Mallory, July 6, 1863, MP, vol. 18, LC; Bigelow, *Retrospections*, 2:150–51, 284; John Thomas Scharf, *History of the Confederate States Navy: From Its Organization to the Surrender of Its Last Vessel* (hereafter cited as Scharf, *Confederate*; New York: Rodgers and Sherwood, 1887; repr., New York: Random House/Value Publishing, 1996), 804–5.

44. Bulloch to Mallory July 20, 1863, letter cited in note 43 above.

45. MFM to Secretary of the Navy Mallory, July 6, 1863, MP, vol. 18, LC; MFM Diary, entries Oct. 6, 1863, and Nov. 23, 25, 26, 1863, MP, LC; Bulloch, *Secret Service*, 2:265–67; Scharf, *Confederate*, 802.

46. MFM to B. Franklin Minor and to his wife, both Jan. 23, 1863, MP, vol. 17, LC; Lovelle Reeve, *Portraits of Men of Eminence in Literature, Science, and Art* (Covent Garden, U.K.: Reeve, 1864), 2:118.

47. Related to the disappearance of John Maury: Gen. Dabney H. Maury to Dr. Brodie S. Herndon, Feb. 3, 1863; William A. Maury and Betty Herndon to Mrs. Ann Herndon Maury, Mar. 3 and 20, 1863, all in MP, vol. 17, LC; MFM to his wife, Apr. 15, 1863, MP, vol. 17, LC; MFM Diary, entries Nov. 7 and 24, 1863, Dec. 1 and Dec. 15, 1863; Jan. 20 and 27, 1864; Mar. 13 and 18, 1864, MP, LC.

48. MFM Diary, entries Nov. 24, 1863, MP, LC; Ann Maury to MFM, Mar. 30, 1863, MP, vol. 18, LC. After the Civil War, Dabney Maury continued placing advertisements in a number of newspapers to learn what happened to John Maury at Vicksburg, Miss. MFM placed the date of disappearance as Jan. 27, 1863.

49. Dabney H. Maury, *Recollections of a Virginian in the Mexican, Indian, and Civil Wars*, 185.

50. Scharf, *Confederate*, 802; Bigelow, *Retrospections*, 2:29; Morgan, *Rebel Reefer*, 169–70.

51. Charles C. Beaman, *The National and Private* Alabama *Claims and the Final Amicable Settlement* (Washington, D.C.: W. T. Moore, 1871), 237–38.

52. Orders from Flag Officer Samuel Barron to Lieut. Evans, Jan. 29, 1864, *ORN*, ser. 1, vol. 2, p. 810.

53. MFM to Maximilian, Nov. 8, 1863, MP, vol. 19, LC.

54. MFM to Maximilian, Nov. 25, 1863, MP, vol. 19, LC.

55. MFM to his wife, Dec. 16, 1863, MP, vol. 19, LC.

56. Ibid.

57. MFM to J. B. Minor, Dec. 25, 1863, MP, vol. 19, LC.

Chapter 22

1. Mitchel Roth, *Historical Dictionary of War Journalism* (Westport, Conn.: Greenwood, 1997), 4–5; K. M. Shrivastava, *News Agencies from Pigeon to Internet* (Elgin, Ill.: New Dawn, 2007), 2–5; Sir John R. Robinson, *Fifty Years of Fleet Street: Being the Life and Recollections of Sir John R. Robinson*, ed. Frederick Moy Thomas (London: Macmillan, 1904), 165; John D. Bennett, "General Jackson's Statue," *American Civil War Round Table UK*, 2004, originally published in *Crossfire: The Magazine of the ACWRT (UK)*, no. 75 (Dec. 2004), accessed Nov. 9, 2013, http://

www.acwrt.org.uk/uk-heritage_General-Jacksons-Statue.asp; Richard D. Fulton, "Now Only the *Times* Is on Our Side: The London *Times* and America before the Civil War," *Victorian Review* (University of Victoria, Victoria, B.C.) 16, no. 1 (Summer 1990): 48–59; John D. Bennett, *The London Confederates: The Officials, Clergy, Businessmen, and Journalists Who Backed the American South During the Civil War* (hereafter cited as Bennett, *London Confederates*; Jefferson, N.C.: McFarland, 2008), 49, 144; George Henderson, *Stonewall Jackson and the Civil War* (London: Longmans Green, 1906), 2:478; Charles M. Hubbard, *Burden of Confederate Diplomacy* (hereafter cited as Hubbard, *Burden*; Knoxville: University of Tennessee Press, 2000), 142–43; Frances Leigh Williams, *Matthew Fontaine Maury: Scientist of the Sea* (hereafter cited as Williams, *Maury Scientist*), 403; Charles Francis Adams, Jr., *Charles Francis Adams, by His Son* (Boston: Houghton Mifflin, 1900; Rye Brook, N.Y.: Elibron Classics/Adamant Media, 2006), 335; *Times* (London) Scrapbook in Library of Virginia.

2. Frank Moore, ed., *The Rebellion Record: A Diary of American Events* (New York: D. Van Nostrand, 1862), 10:482–483; Amanda Foreman, *A World on Fire: Britain's Crucial Role in the American Civil War* (hereafter cited as Foreman, *World*), 394.

3. Ted Tunnell, "Confederate Newspapers in Virginia during the Civil War," *Encyclopedia Virginia*, Virginia Foundation for the Humanities, last modified May 18, 2011, http://www.EncyclopediaVirginia.org/Newspapers_in_Virginia_During_the_Civil_War_Confederate; "The Position of Gov. Wise: Speech of O. Jennings Wise at Norfolk," *New York Times*, Aug. 6, 1860; Orlando Figes, *The Crimean War: A History* (hereafter cited as Figes, *Crimean*), 122–23, 146, 412–13, 433.

4. "Message of Gov. Letcher," *Richmond Dispatch*, Jan. 8, 1863; "Reporting on the Emancipation Proclamation," *Richmond Dispatch*, Jan. 7, 1863; "Voting on West Virginia Officials," *Richmond Dispatch*, July 3, 1863; Richard Orr Curry, *A House Divided: A Study of Statehood Politics and the Copperhead Movement in West Virginia* (Pittsburgh: University of Pittsburgh Press, 1964), 74–78.

5. MFM letter to the editor, Aug. 17, 1863, on "Prospects of the Confederacy," MP, vol. 18, LC; MFM Diary, entry on *Times* (London) article, Aug. 23, 1863, MP, LC; Mary DeCredico, "Richmond Bread Riot," *Virginia Encyclopedia*, Virginia Foundation for the Humanities, last modified Feb. 10, 2012, http://www.encyclopediavirginia.org/bread_riot_richmond; J. B. Jones, *A Rebel War Clerk's Diary at the Confederate States Capital* (hereafter cited as Jones, *Diary*), 1:230; Virginius Dabney, *Virginia: The New Dominion*, 129; "Bread Riot," *Harper's Weekly*, Apr. 18, 1863; "Bread Riots," *Harper's Weekly*, Apr. 25, 1863; "Bread Riot in Richmond," *New York Times*, Apr. 8, 1863; "Bread Riot Again," *Richmond Dispatch*, Jan. 20, 1889; "Pardon and Reprieves," *Richmond Whig*, Jan. 16, 1864; Jones, *Diary*, 284–87.

6. "Interesting Correspondence between Grand Duke Constantine and Commander M. F. Maury," *Richmond Dispatch*, Oct. 29, 1861, originally appeared in the Richmond *Enquirer* the day before.

7. MFM to Rear Admiral Robert FitzRoy, MP, vol. 16, LC; Fulton, "*Times*," 48–59; Figes, *Crimean*, 148–49.

8. Thurlow Weed, *Life of Thurlow Weed, Including His Autobiography and a Memoir*, ed. Harriet A. Weed (Boston: Houghton Mifflin, 1884), 2:369–75; "The Truth About Lieut. Maury," *New York Times*, Jan. 26, 1862.

9. John Welsford Cowell, *Letter to M. T. Maury* (typographical error on pamphlet jacket; London: Robert Hardwicke, 1862), 99; "The American Revolution," *Edinburgh Review* 116 (Oct. 1862): 550; "Southern Secession," *London Review* 4 (1862): 170; "Our Library Table," *Athenaeum*, Dec. 17, 1862, 846; Bennett, *London Confederates*, 143; MFM, "Letter to Chabannes," *Edinburgh Review* (American ed., Leonard Scott, New York) 116–17 (July–Oct. 1862): 298.

10. From *Richmond Whig*, Jan. 13, 1863, letter from Commander Matthew Fontaine Maury to the editor of the *Times* (London), *ORN*, ser. 2, vol. 2, pp. 335–36; John D. Bennett, *The London Confederates: The Officials, Clergy, Businessmen, and Journalists Who Backed the American South During the Civil War*, 143.

11. Hubbard, *Burden*, 31–32; Foreman, *World*, 86–95, 403.

12. Burton J. Hendrick, *Statesmen of the Lost Cause: Jefferson Davis and His Cabinet* (hereafter cited as Hendrick, *Statesmen*), 390; Jefferson Davis, *Papers of Jefferson Davis, 1861*, ed. Mary Seaton Dix and Linda Criswell Crist (Baton Rouge: Louisiana State University Press, 1991), 378n21; Ferdinand de Lesseps, *Recollections of Forty Years*, trans. C. B. Pitman (London: Chapman and Hall, 1887), 1:189; Bennett, *London Confederates*, 41.

13. James M. Mason to Judah P. Benjamin, May 2, 1862, *ORN*, ser. 2, vol. 3, p. 48; Judah P. Benjamin to James M. Mason, Apr. 12, 1862, *ORN*, ser. 2, vol. 3, p. 385.

14. Hendrick, *Statesmen*, 395; "The American War in London," *Saturday Review*, Aug. 2, 1862, 135.

15. Lovelle Reeve, *Portraits of Men of Eminence in Literature, Science, and Art*, 2:103–6; Charles Priestley, "'Batavian Grace': Alexander Beresford Hope," *American Civil War Round Table UK*, originally published as "Batavian Grace" in *Crossfire: The Magazine of the ACWRT (UK)*, no. 69 (Aug. 2002), http://www.acwrt.org.

uk/uk-heritage_Batavian-Grace—Alexander-Beresford-Hope.asp; Alexander Beresford Hope, *The Social and Political Bearings of the American Disruption* (London: Ridgway, 1863), 6, 13, 18.

16. Hubbard, *Burden*, 127; John Bigelow, "The Confederate Diplomatists," *The Century* 42 (May–Oct. 1891): 122; James Spence, *The American Union: Its Effect on National Character and Policy*, 3rd ed. (London: Richard Bentley, 1862), 304–5; Hendrick, *Statesmen*, 81; "Foreign," *Record of News, History, and Literature* (Richmond) 1, no. 21 (Nov. 5, 1863): 196; Bigelow, *Retrospections*, 1:618; Ernest H. Baldwin, "The 'Mallory Report' and Its Consequences," *National Magazine: An Illustrated American Monthly* (Boston) 9, no. 6 (Mar. 1899): 155–60; Bulloch to Mallory, *ORN*, ser. 2, vol. 2, p. 602; Weed, *Life*, 369–75.

17. See *National Magazine* in note 16 above.

18. "France and the United States; The Mission of Gen. Forey; Capt. Maury Again; Lord Brougham Again; The Sir William Peel; The Texan Blockade," *New York Times*, Nov. 21, 1863; MFM letter to the editor, Aug. 17, 1863, on "Prospects of the Confederacy," MP, vol. 18, LC; Ephraim Douglass Adams, "The Southern Independence Association," chap. 15 in *Great Britain and the American Civil War* (New York: Longmans Green, 1925), Project Gutenberg e-book no. 13789, released Oct. 18, 2004, http://www.gutenberg.org/files/13789/13789-h/13789-h.htm#CHAPTER_XV; Statement on Cessation of Hostilities in America, June 11, 1864, MP, vol. 20, LC. MP, vol. 20, LC, contained rough and edited versions of a statement on ending hostilities in America. Index of incomplete collection, originals in rare book section, Library of Virginia; some originals in rare book collection, Massachusetts Historical Society, Boston; Raphael Semmes, *Service Afloat; or, The Remarkable Career of the Confederate Cruisers* Sumter *and* Alabama *During the War Between the States* (Baltimore: Kelly, Piet, 1869; repr., London: Sampson Low, Marston, Searle, and Rivington, 1887), 789; MFM Diary, entries May 31, June 2 and 9, 1864, MP, LC.

19. Brooks Adams, *Seizure of the Rams at Birkenhead: Proceedings of Massachusetts Historical Society* (Boston: Massachusetts Historical Society, 1914), 47:264–65, 269; Goldwin Smith, *Letter to a Whig Member of the Southern Independence Association*, American ed. (Boston: Ticknor and Fields, 1864), 32; "The American Prospects," *Saturday Review*, Aug. 23, 1862; "The Confederate Congress," *Saturday Review*, Sept. 6, 1862; "Another Revelation: How British Sympathy with Rebellion Was Manipulated; History of the Southern Independence Association," *New York Times*, Oct. 2, 1865; John Bigelow, *Lest We Forget: Gladstone, Morley, and the Confederate Loan of 1863* (New York, 1905), accessed Nov. 9, 2013, https://archive.org/details/lestweforgetconf00bige.

20. MFM to his wife, Dec. 25, 1863, MP, vol. 19, LC.

21. 193 Parl. Deb. (3d ser.) (1868), 262–83 (Cornelius Buck); Lytton Strachey, *Eminent Victorians* (San Diego, Calif.: Harvest Book, 1969), 7, 11–58; Shannon Ryan, *The Ice Hunters: A History of Newfoundland Sealing to 1914*, Newfoundland History Series 8 (St. John's, Newfoundland, Canada: Breakwater Books, 1994), 126; "From the *Richmond Times-Dispatch*, Sept. 26, 1915," *Confederate Veteran* 25, no. 5 (May 1917): 201–2; Bennett, *London Confederates*, 144.

22. Statement on Cessation of Hostilities in America, June 11, 1864, MP, vol. 20, LC; MFM Diary, entries May 31, June 2 and 9, 1864, MP, LC; Josiah Gorgas, *The Journals of Josiah Gorgas, 1857–1878*, ed. Sarah Woolfolk Wiggins, 139.

23. Statement cited in note 22 above.

24. MFM Diary, entries June 10 and July 1, 1864, MP, vol. 20, LC.

25. Foreman, *World*, 667.

26. MFM to his wife and children, June 28, 1864, and to his brother Richard, June 28, 1864, MP, vol. 20, LC.

27. MFM to Marin Jansen, June 18, 1864, MP, vol. 20, LC; "Additional Report of Captain Barnes, U.S. Navy, Transmitting a Drawing of Torpedo Boat," May 24, 1864, *ORN*, ser. 1, vol. 9, pp. 601, 604.

28. See note 27 above; Richard L. Maury, *Brief Sketch of the Work of Matthew F. Maury*, 18; "First Day, Tuesday, Mar. 21, 1850," *Proceedings of the American Association for the Advancement of Science* (Charleston, S.C.: Walker and James, 1850), 4:v; David Stephen and Jeanne T. Heilder, eds., and David Coles, assoc. ed., *American Civil War Encyclopedia: A Political, Social, and Military History*, s.v. "P. G. T. Beauregard" (New York: W. W. Norton, 2000), 199.

29. "The Electrical Torpedoes," Correspondence, *Mechanics Magazine* (London), July 7, 1865, 676; William S. Powell, ed., *Dictionary of North Carolina Biography*, s.v. "Gabriel Rains" (Chapel Hill: University of North Carolina Press, 1994), 5:163–65.

30. "Proceedings of Societies: Society of Telegraph Engineers," *Telegraphic Journal of Electrical Review* (London: Henry Gillman, 1874) 2 (Dec. 1873–Dec. 1874): 121–25; J. H. Pepper, ed., "The Electric Torpedo," *Cyclopedia Science Simplified* (London: Frederick Warne, 1869), 223–24.

31. MFM to Marin H. Jansen, Apr. 24, 1864, MP, vol. 20, LC; MFM to John Mercer Brooke and Secretary of the Navy Mallory, Mar. 1864, MP, vol. 20, LC.

32. MFM to Marin Jansen, Aug. 9, Aug. 20, Aug. 29, Sept. 10, Sept. 28, Oct. 12, Oct. 21, Nov. 17, and Nov. 27, 1864, MP, vols. 20 and 21, LC; MFM to Nathaniel Holmes, Apr. 11, 1865, MP, vol. 21, LC; MFM, letter the editor, Aug. 17, 1863,

on "Prospects of the Confederacy," MP, vol. 18, LC.

33. John D. Bennett, "The Confederate Bazaar at Liverpool," *American Civil War Round Table UK*, originally published in *Crossfire: The Magazine of the American Civil War Round Table (UK)*, no. 61 (Dec. 1999), accessed Nov. 9, 2013, http://www.acwrt.org.uk/uk-heritage_The-Confederate-Bazaar-at-Liverpool.asp; Foreman, *World*, 704–5; MFM Diary, entries Aug. 2 and 11, 1864, MP, LC.

34. Vice Admiral Octave de Chabannes to MFM, Apr. 10, 1865, Maury Wartime Correspondence, Museum of the Confederacy, Richmond; Figes, *Crimean*, 235–41; Foreman, *World*, 704n.

35. M. F. Maury to J. H. North, Apr. 2, 1865, *ORN*, ser. 2, vol. 2, p. 810; Bigelow, *Retrospections*, 2:406–7, 431–32.

36. Warren F. Spencer, *Confederate Navy in Europe*, 133; Foreman, *World*, 403.

37. Rutson Maury to the Rev. Francis W. Tremlett, June 1, 1865, MP, vol. 21, LC; MFM to his wife, Oct. 15, 1865, MP, vol. 23, LC.

38. MFM to Officer in Command, Naval Forces Gulf of Mexico, May 25, 1865, *ORN*, ser. 1, vol. 3, pp. 546–47; MFM to S. Welford Corbin, off San Domingo, May 19, 1865, MFM Papers, Virginia Military Institute Archives.

39. MFM to Marin H. Jansen, May 27, 1865, MP, vol. 21, LC.

Chapter 23

1. MFM to Maximilian, Nov. 10 and 25, 1863, MP, vol. 19, LC; MFM Diary, entry Apr. 1, 1864, MP, vol. 20, LC; MFM to S. Welford Corbin, May 19, 1865, MFM Papers, Virginia Military Institute Archives; Rutson Maury to MFM, June 13, 1865, MP, vol. 22, LC; the Rev. Francis W. Tremlett to MFM, July 30, 1865, MP, vol. 22, LC, written on paper with letterhead "Maury Testimonial Fund." When it was obvious the war was over, MFM had sent his namesake son from Havana to New York to stay with relatives there. MFM stored in James D. Bulloch's name the torpedo equipment he had brought from Great Britain in the Cuban capital.

2. MFM to General de la Peza, June 6, 1865, MP, vol. 21, LC.

3. Diana Maury Corbin to MFM, May 7, 1865, Maury Papers, Wartime Correspondence, Museum of the Confederacy, Richmond.

4. William A. Maury to Rutson Maury, May 19, 1865, MP, vol. 21, LC; Richard L. Maury to MFM, May 21, 1865, MP, vol. 21, LC; Elizabeth Herndon Maury to MFM, June 19, 1865, MP, vol. 21, LC.

5. MFM to Octave de Chabannes, June 9, 1865, MP, vol. 22, LC; Octave de Chabannes to MFM, July 27, 1865, MP, vol. 22, LC; MFM to his wife, Sept. 23, 1865, MP, vol. 23, LC; MFM draft letter to Maximilian, Aug. 8, 1865, MP, vol. 22, LC.

6. Marin H. Jansen to MFM, July 1, July 22, and Aug. 19, 1865, MP, vol. 22, LC.

7. MFM Diary entry, Sept. 8, 1865, MP, vol. 57, LC; draft copies of various imperial decrees on immigration in MP, vols. 22, 23, and 24, LC; "Mexican Affairs," *New York Times*, Oct. 17, 1865.

8. MFM circular letter used in response to queries from interested immigrants, Jan. 22, 1865, MP, vol. 23, LC. Similar wording occurs in a pamphlet MFM prepared for prospective immigrants, Nov. 1865, MP, vol. 23, LC. Maximilian decree on immigration classes dated Sept. 5, 1865, MFM Papers, Virginia Military Institute Archives; MFM to his wife, Sept. 23, 1865, MP, vol. 23, LC; MFM to S. Welford Corbin, Oct. 31, 1865, MP, vol. 23, LC; *Times* (London) scrapbook, Library of Virginia.

9. R. E. Lee to Richard L. Maury, July 30, 1865, MP, vol. 21, LC.

10. R. E. Lee to MFM quoted in Diana Fontaine Maury Corbin, *A Life of Matthew Fontaine Maury, U.S.N. and C.S.N., Compiled by His Daughter* (hereafter cited as Corbin, *Maury*), 238–39.

11. Corbin, *Maury*, 239–40. Although MFM had trumpeted the Amazon for development for decades, he was now in the employ of the Habsburg emperor of Mexico. MFM described the differences between the two for prospective immigrants in January letters, MP, vol. 24, LC.

12. U.S. Congress, *Papers Related to Foreign Affairs, Accompanying the Annual Message of the President*, pt. 3, 39th Cong., 1st sess. (Washington, D.C.: Government Printing Office, 1866), 522–25.

13. John B. Minor to MFM, Aug. 25, 1865, MP, vol. 22, LC.

14. MFM Parting Letter to Virginia, likely in response to a letter from R. E. Lee to MFM and Richard L. Maury, n.d., MP, vol. 22, LC. Similar wording appeared in his circular letter and pamphlet for prospective immigrants, as cited in note 8 above.

15. Pamphlet cited in note 8 above; MFM to S. Welford Corbin, Oct. 31, 1865, MP, vol. 23, LC; MFM to his wife, Nov. 27, 1865, MFM Papers, Virginia Military Institute Archives.

16. MFM to his wife, Sept. 12 and 27, 1865, MP, vol. 23, LC.

17. John N. Edwards, *Shelby's Expedition to Mexico: An Unwritten Leaf of the War*, compiled by Edwards's wife, Jennie Edwards (hereafter cited as Edwards, *Shelby's*; Kansas City, Mo.: Jennie Edwards, 1889), 362.

18. MFM to S. Welford Corbin, Oct. 31, 1865, MP, vol. 23, LC; Lawrence F. Hill, "The Confederate Exodus to Latin America" (hereafter cited as Hill, "Exodus"), *Southwestern Historical Quar-*

terly Online 39, no. 2 (Oct. 1935): 100–34, accessed Feb. 24, 2014, http://texashistory.unt.edu/ark:/67531/metapth101095/m1/114/; Sarah A. Davis, ed., *Recollections of Henry Winthrop Allen, Brig. Gen., CSA, and Ex-Governor of Louisiana* (New York: M. Doolady; New Orleans: James Gresham, 1866), 341.

19. P. H. Sheridan telegram to U. S. Grant, Nov. 26, 1865, in *Papers of Ulysses S. Grant*, ed. John Y. Simon (Carbondale: Southern Illinois University Press, 1988), 15:425; P. H. Sheridan, *Personal Memoirs* (New York: C. L. Webster, 1888), 2:205–28, for a complete description of Sheridan's mission along the border with Mexico and the situation in New Orleans; William H. Seward correspondence to Sheridan, Dec. 26, 1866, Seward Papers, MS Collection, LC.

20. See note 19 above.

21. Alfred J. Hanna and Kathryn A. Hanna, *Napoleon III and Mexico* (Chapel Hill: University of North Carolina Press, 1971), 232; Sarah Yorke Stevenson, *Maximilian in Mexico: A Woman's Reminiscences of the French Intervention* (New York: Century, 1889), 168; "Marshal Bazaine Dead," *New York Times*, Aug. 15, 1888.

22. "Marshal Bazaine Dead," *New York Times*, Aug. 15, 1888; Anthony Arthur, *General Jo Shelby's March* (New York: Random House, 2010), 101; John Bigelow, *Retrospections of an Active Life*, 2:382–83, 385, 417.

23. Editorial Notes, *United States Service Magazine* (Charles B. Richardson, New York) 5 (Mar. 1866): 260; "Marshal Bazaine Dead," *New York Times*, Aug. 15, 1888; Foreman, *World*, 798; Spencer, *Confederate Navy in Europe*, 175–76; Bigelow, as cited in note 22 above.

24. Pamphlet cited in note 8 above; Edwards, *Shelby's*, 357.

25. MFM to Corbin cited in note 18 above; MFM to his wife, Sept. 23 and Oct. 24, 1865, MP, vol. 23, LC.

26. MFM to his wife, Nov. 27, 1865, MP, vol. 23, LC.

27. John Ross Brown, *Resources of the Pacific Slope: A Statistical and Descriptive Summary* (San Francisco: H. H. Bancroft, 1869), 618–19; William M. Gwin, "Senator Gwin's Plan for the Colonization of Sonora," ed. Evan J. Coleman (hereafter cited as Gwin, "Senator Gwin's"), *Overland Monthly* (San Francisco), 2nd ser., no. 102 (June 1891): 598–607.

28. Edwards, *Shelby's*, 342–43; "Marshal Bazaine Dead," *New York Times*, Aug. 15, 1888.

29. Undated report of the Office of Colonization, presumably late 1865 or early 1866, MP, vol. 24, LC; Bigelow, *Retrospections*, 2:508; Gwin, "Senator Gwin's," 598–607; Edwards, *Shelby's*, 341; "A Great Railroad Enterprise," *Scientific American* (New York) 15, no. 2 (July 7, 1866): 18.

30. Field Agent Report to Richard L. Maury, Office of Colonization, Apr. 10, 1866, MP, vol. 24, LC; Hill, "Exodus," 100–34; Maximilian to MFM, Jan. 29, 1866, MP, vol. 24, LC. MFM proposed and approved a plan to bring back the cinchona tree to Mexico. The tree's bark produces quinine, proven effective in fighting malaria, and would benefit not only the Mexicans, but also could be exported.

31. Corbin, *Maury*, 257; unsigned, "Female Education: Young Ladies Seminary at Prince Edward Court House," *Southern Literary Messenger* 1, no. 9 (May 1835): 529–30.

32. MFM Diary, numerous entries in May 1866, especially May 21, on meetings with Ministry of Marine on "electrical torpedoes" in Paris; Virginia Mason, comp., *The Public Life and Diplomatic Correspondence of James Murray Mason* (New York: Neale, 1906), 582–83, accessed Nov. 3, 2013, https://archive.org/details/publiclifediplom00masonva; MFM to William C. Hasbrouck, Apr. 14, 1866, MP, vol. 24, LC; MFM letters to various government officials in Europe about his plans for lectures on mine warfare are in MP, vol. 24, LC.

33. Maximilian to MFM, Apr. 19, 1866, MP, vol. 25, LC.

34. MFM to Maximilian, July 1, 1866, MP, vol. 25, LC.

35. "Collapse of an Emigration Scheme," *Anglo-American Times* (London) 2 (May 5, 1866), 9.

36. Commodore Bedford Pim, Royal Navy, *The Gate of the Pacific*, brochure (London: Lovell Reed, 1863); MFM Diary, entry May 25, 1866, MP, vol. 57, LC.

37. MFM Diary, letter to MFM from French government after May 28, 1866, entry, indicating new interest in recruiting Maury, "if he was to find arrangement or occupation in conformity with his favorite studies," MP, vol. 57, LC.

38. "Mexico and the South and Captain Maury," *Richmond Whig*, Apr. 20, 1866.

39. MFM Diary, entries Aug. 9 and 11, 1866, MP, vol. 57, LC; John Bigelow, *Retrospections of an Active Life*, vol. 3, *1865–1866* (New York: Doubleday, 1909–10), 315–16.

40. MFM to Dabney H. Maury, Mar. 1, 1866, MFM Papers, Virginia Military Institute Archives.

41. MFM remarks before the French Commission, May 21, 1866, MP, vol. 25, LC; MFM lectures to Dutch, Swedish, and Norwegian officers in MP, vol. 67, fols. 9192–331, 9332–55, LC.

42. MFM lectures to Swedes, Norwegians, and Dutch officers, July and Aug. 1866, MP, vol. 47, LC; "Obituary: Admiral Jansen," *Geographical Journal* (Royal Geographical Society) 2 (July–Dec. 1893): 465–68.

43. T. J. Page to Gen. Jose J. D. Urquiza, Page Family Collection (1800–1869), Virginia Historical Society, Richmond.

44. MFM Diary, MP, vol. 57, LC. MFM's in-

terest in military science was constant. For example, as his diary notes, on his way from Mexico to Great Britain to meet his family, he made sure that the torpedo equipment he stored in Bulloch's name was still secure. See November 1866 entries on Holmes's continuing experiments with mines and visits to European capitals.

45. MFM to Diana Maury Corbin, Apr. 10, 1872, MFM Papers, Virginia Military Institute Archives.

46. MFM to Rutson Maury, July 8, 1866, and to Richard L. Maury, July 10, 1866, both MP, vol. 25, LC; Victor Ernst Karl Rudolf Von Scheliha, *A Treatise on Coast Defence: Based on the Experience Gained by Officers of the Corps of Engineers of the Army of the Confederate States, and Compiled from Official Reports of Officers of the Navy of the United States, Made During the Late North American War from 1861 to 1865* (London: E. and F. N. Spon, 1868); Captain E. Hardin Stewart, "Notes on the Employment of Submarine Mines (Commonly Called Torpedoes) in America during the Late Civil War," *Papers on Subjects Connected with the Duties of the Corps of Royal Engineers* (Woolwich, U.K.), n.s., 15 (1866): 1–28.

47. Copy of *Illustrated London News*, June 23, 1866, MP, vol. 25, fols. 4578–79, LC; Corbin, *Maury*, 257–58; MFM Folder, Correspondence re. Maury Testimonial File, Maury Papers, Museum of the Confederacy, Richmond; "Testimonial to Capt. Maury," *Anglo-American Times* 2 (June 9, 1866): 79.

48. William C. Hasbrouck to MFM, Jan. 31, 1866, MP, vol. 24, LC.

49. MFM to Dabney H. Maury, Feb. 23, 1867, MP, vol. 25, LC.

50. Gonzalez Lodge, ed., *Gildersleve's Latin Grammar* (Wauconda, Ill.: Bolchazy-Carducci, 1997), xiii; "Miscellany," *Historical Magazine and Notes and Queries* (John G. Shea, New York) 8 (Jan. 1864): 48.

51. Ibid.

52. Copy of agreement between MFM and Charles B. Richardson, Sept. 20, 1866, MP, vol. 25, LC.

53. MFM to S. Welford Corbin, Aug. 11, 1866, MFM Papers, Virginia Military Institute Archives; Corbin, *Maury*, 266.

54. MFM, *First Lessons in Geography* (New York: Richardson, 1868; 2nd ed., New York: University, 1871); MFM, *New Elements of Geography* (New York: New American Books, 1922); Frances Leigh Williams, *Matthew Fontaine Maury: Scientist of the Sea* (hereafter cited as Williams, *Maury Scientist*), 466; Jaquelin Ambler Caskie, *Life and Letters of Matthew Fontaine Maury*, 172–73.

55. MFM to C. B. Richardson, June–Sept. 1867 (especially Sept. 2), and C. B. Richardson to MFM, June–Sept. 1867 (especially Aug. 10, Sept. 2, Sept. 11, and Sept. 18), MP, vol. 26, LC; Charles Lee Lewis, *Matthew Fontaine Maury: The Pathfinder of the Seas* (hereafter cited as Lewis, *Maury*), 208; Thomas Keneally, *The Great Shame and the Triumph of the Irish in the English-Speaking World* (New York: Nan A. Talese, 1999), 437–46.

56. Alyn Brodsky, *Imperial Charade: A Biography of Emperor Napoleon III and Empress Eugenie, Nineteenth-Century Europe's Most Successful Adventurers* (Indianapolis: Bobbs-Merrill, 1978), 267–68; MFM Diary, entry Aug. 9, 1866, MP, vol. 57, LC.

57. MFM Diary, entry May 25, 1866, MP, vol. 57, LC; MFM to John Minor Maury, July 24, 1867, MP, vol. 26, LC.

58. Maximilian to MFM, Aug. 16, 1866, MP, vol. 25, LC; MFM to Francis H. Smith, Feb. 21, 1867, MFM Papers, Virginia Military Institute Archives.

59. Nathaniel Holmes to MFM, Oct. 5, 1866, MP, vol. 25, LC.

60. MFM to Brooks (of Baring Brothers), July 3, 1867, MP, vol. 26, LC; MFM to Baring Brothers, July 2, 1867, MP, vol. 26, LC.

61. *Bradshaw's Railway Manual and Shareholder's Guide and Official Directory* (London: W. J. Adams, 1867), 421; Captain Bedford Pim, "The Panama Canal," Dec. 19, 1879, *Journal of the Society of the Arts* (London) 28 (Nov. 21, 1879–Nov. 12, 1880): 70.

62. *Report of the National Academy of Sciences for Year 1863* (Washington, D.C.: Government Printing Office, 1864), 98–112.

63. Rutson Maury to Francis H. Smith, Feb. 23, 1868, MFM Papers, Virginia Military Institute Archives.

64. Charles Todd Quintard Diary, entry Mar. 15, 1868, luncheon with MFM in Cambridge, U.K., vol. 5, University of the South Archives, Sewanee, Tenn.; Francis W. Tremlett to Charles Todd Quintard, Jan. 4, 1868, University of the South Archives; Charles Todd Quintard Diary, copy of letter from Francis W. Tremlett, undated 1873, University of the South Archives.

65. MFM to Marin H. Jansen, Apr. 13, 1868, MP, vol. 26, LC.

66. MFM to Richard L. Maury, Nov. 16, 1834, MP, vol. 1, LC.

67. MFM to James M. Minor, May 10, 1868, MP, vol. 26, LC.

68. Williams, *Maury Scientist*, 452; Lewis, *Maury*, 215–16; Cambridge Senate speech, translated from Latin by J. M. D. Meicklejohn, MP, vol. 26, fol. 4999, LC.

69. MFM lecture, "Science and the Bible Educational Ideals of the South," delivered at Cambridge University, June 1868, MP, vol. 47, fols. 9451–81, LC.

70. Francis H. Smith to the Rt. Rev. J. H. Otey, Tennessee, Outgoing Correspondence, Aug. 5, 1859, Virginia Military Institute Archives.

Chapter 24

1. MFM to Marin H. Jansen, Dec. 19, 1867; to William A. Maury, Jan. 12, 1868, both in MP, vol. 26, LC; MFM to the Rt. Rev. Charles T. Quintard, Jan. 4, 1868, University of the South Archives, Sewanee, Tenn.

2. Minutes of the Executive Committee, University of the South, Apr. 4, 1868, University of the South Archives; MFM to the Rt. Rev. W. M. Green, Apr. 21, 1868, University of the South Archives; MFM to Rutson Maury, Apr. 6, 1868, MP, vol. 26, LC; MFM to William Maury, Apr. 22, 1868, MP, vol. 26, LC; MFM to James B. Minor, May 10 and June 7, 1868, both MP, vol. 26, LC.

3. "French Enterprise in Virginia," *Anglo-American Times*, May 26, 1866, 9.

4. MFM to Francis H. Smith, Apr. 21, 1868, MP, vol. 26, LC.

5. MFM to Rutson Maury, Apr. 22, 1868, MP, vol. 26, LC; Rutson Maury to MFM, May 1, 1868, MP, vol. 26, LC; Rutson Maury to Francis H. Smith, June 18 and July 28, 1868, MFM Papers, Virginia Military Institute Archives.

6. MFM to Marin H. Jansen, July 17, 1868, MP, vol. 27, LC; letter of MFM appointment to Virginia Military Institute faculty originally as professor of meteorology, but struck through and replaced with physics, signed by John Letcher, Feb. 22, 1868, MFM Papers, Virginia Military Institute Archives.

7. See note 6 above.

8. MFM to addressee unknown, written summer 1868, saved by the Rev. Francis Tremlett, MP, vol. 27, LC; Diana Fontaine Maury Corbin, *A Life of Matthew Fontaine Maury, U.S.N. and C.S.N., Compiled by His Daughter* (hereafter cited as Corbin, *Maury*), 269–72; *The History of the Greenbrier: America's Resort* (Greenbrier, W. Va.: privately printed by the Greenbrier, n.d.), 66–69, for a description of the meeting with Rosecrans and the writing of the "White Sulphur Springs Manifesto."

9. Corbin, *Maury*, and *History of the Greenbrier*, as cited in note 8 above.

10. Brian A. Conley, comp., *Return to Union: Fairfax County's Role in the Adoption of the Virginia Constitution of 1870* (Fairfax, Va.: Fairfax County Public Library, 2000), 8–11.

11. Ibid.

12. Peter C. Thomas, "Matthew Fontaine Maury and the Problem of Virginia's Identity" (hereafter cited as Thomas, "Maury"), *Virginia Magazine of History and Biography* 90 (Oct. 1982): 214–16; Virginius Dabney, *Virginia: The New Dominion*, 373.

13. *Richmond Enquirer*, Aug. 24, 26, 27, and 30, 1868, for description of meetings with Rosecrans; manifesto was published by the *Richmond Enquirer*, Sept. 5, 1868; Rosecrans acknowledged letter to R. E. Lee, *Richmond Enquirer*, Sept. 7, 1868; Thomas, "Maury," 221–23.

14. Hamilton James Eckenrode, *The Political History of Virginia During the Reconstruction* (hereafter cited as Eckenrode, *Political*; Baltimore: Johns Hopkins University Press, 1904; repr., Gloucester, Mass.: Peter Smith, 1966), 95–101. Citations refer to the 1904 edition.

15. Francis H. Smith to MFM, July 30, 1868, MP, vol. 27, LC.

16. MFM to B. Franklin Minor, Sept. 1, 1868, MP, vol. 27, LC; MFM to Diana Maury Corbin, Sept. 4, 1868, MFM Papers, Virginia Military Institute Archives. On his deathbed, Maury made his family promise to carry his body through Goshen before final burial in Richmond's Hollywood Cemetery.

17. Francis H. Smith, *Annual Report to the Board of Visitors*, June 25, 1869, Virginia Military Institute Archives; MFM address, Sept. 10, 1868, MFM Papers, Virginia Military Institute Archives.

18. Copies of rough survey forms, MP, vol. 27, LC, and forms at Virginia Military Institute Archives.

19. Marin H. Jansen to MFM, Sept. 14 1868, MP, vol. 27, LC.

20. Francis H. Smith to MFM, Sept. 24 and Oct. 14, 1868, MP, vol. 27, LC; MFM to Col. Edmund Fontaine, president of the Chesapeake and Ohio Railroad, Sept. 17, 1868, MP, vol. 27, LC. Brooke was not the only Virginia Military Institute faculty member involved. Notably Gen. George Washington Custis Lee was participating, but Brooke was mentioned more often with specific aspects of the survey in the next year.

21. MFM to Francis H. Smith, Sept. 23 and 24, 1868, MFM Papers, Virginia Military Institute Archives; MFM to Francis H. Smith, Nov. 14, 1868, MFM Papers, Virginia Military Institute Archives. Copies of Report on Pennsylvania Coal and Oil and Ohio Agriculture are maintained at the Virginia Military Institute Archives.

22. MFM, "Augusta County Fair Speech of Commodore M. F. Maury," *Southern Planter and Farmer* 2, no. 11 (Nov. 1868): 698–704; Thomas, "Maury," 223.

23. James McPherson, *Battle Cry of Freedom: The Civil War Era* (Oxford: Oxford University Press, 1988), 451.

24. Francis H. Smith, letter to his wife, July 20, 1858, letterbook of 1858, no. 2, Virginia Military Institute Archives.

25. MFM to Francis H. Smith, Nov. 14, 1868, MFM Papers, Virginia Military Institute Archives. MFM letters to presidents of railroads in Virginia, and responses of Richmond and Danville, Seaboard and Roanoke to assist in physical survey, MP, vol. 27, LC.

26. *The Physical Survey of Virginia: Geographical Position of Its Commercial Advantages and*

National Importance, Preliminary Report No. 1, 1st ed., 1868, Virginia Military Institute Archives; M. F. Maury to S. Welford Corbin, Jan. 14, 1869, MFM Papers, Virginia Military Institute Archives.

27. "Virginia: Her Geographical Position," *Southern Review* (John Taylor Bledsoe, Baltimore) 6 (Oct. 1869): 458.

28. MFM to Francis H. Smith, Dec. 28, 1869, MFM Papers, Virginia Military Institute Archives.

29. MFM to S. Welford Corbin, Jan. 14, 1869, MFM Papers, Virginia Military Institute Archives. Jansen and Maury's chief agent, Thomas Ellis, repeatedly wrote MFM (particularly note Mar. 4, 9, and 15, 1869) about problems of Norfolk Borough Council in financing its end of the steamer line, improving waterfront facilities, and racial relations in the Tidewater municipality, MP, vols. 29 and 30, LC.

30. Thomas Ellis to MFM, Mar. 15, 1869, MP, vol. 30, LC. Richmond, Fredericksburg, and Potomac Railroad subscribed to 260 copies of Preliminary Report No. 2.

31. MFM draft report to Francis H. Smith on both preliminary reports, Oct. 1870, MP, vol. 48, LC; John Fitzpatrick, ed., entry Apr. 12, 1792, *The Diaries of George Washington*, vol. 5 (New York: Houghton Mifflin, 1925; repr., New York: Kraus Reprint, 1971), 131; J. C. Hanes and J. M. Morgan, *History and Heritage of Civil Engineering in Virginia* (Richmond: Virginia Section of the American Society of Civil Engineers, 1973), 43–54; MFM to Francis H. Smith, Dec. 28, 1868, MP, vol. 53, LC; MFM to Marin H. Jansen, Dec. 14, 1869, MP, vol. 54, LC; Robert H. Maury Papers, particularly letters to Morton, Sept. 18, Oct. 24, and Nov. 14, 1868, Virginia Historical Society, Richmond.

32. Charles W. Turner, "Chesapeake and Ohio Railroad in Reconstruction," *North Carolina Historical Review* 31, no. 2 (1954): 150–72; James Poyntz Nelson, special engineer, *The Chesapeake and Ohio Railroad* (Richmond: Lewis, Feb. 24, 1927), 254.

33. Nelson as cited in note 32 above; *Chesapeake and Ohio Railroad Prospectus for Investors* (Richmond: W. A. Nye, 1868), Virginia Historical Society; *The Chesapeake and Ohio Railroad: Its Advantage as a Through Passenger and Freight Route Between the Seaboard and the West; Prospectus for Investors* (New York: Fisk and Hatch, 1873), Virginia Historical Society, includes MFM's Physical Surveys; see note 25 above.

34. Merchants and Mechanics Exchange invitation to MFM, Feb. 22, 1869, MP, vol. 29, LC; Portsmouth Borough Council Resolution, Apr. 6, 1869, MP, vol. 39, LC; see Ellis correspondence, note 29 above; H. W. Brands, *The Age of Gold: The California Gold Rush and the New American Dream*, 424.

35. Robert Binford to MFM, in response to a plea for aid in new survey and with survey form, June 1869, MP, vol. 30, LC.

36. Thomas, "Maury," 229–30.

37. Marin H. Jansen to MFM, July 12 and 19, 1869, MP, vol. 32, LC; undated but with July correspondence, Jansen to William Lamb, Norfolk Chamber of Commerce, MP, vol. 32, LC.

38. Thomas, "Maury," 235.

39. MFM, "Address to the Graduating Class of the Virginia Military Institute, July 2, 1869, by Commodore M. F. Maury," MFM Papers, Virginia Military Institute Archives.

40. MFM to Francis Tremlett, Jun 13, 1869, MP, vol. 31, LC; H. L. Owen to MFM, July 16, 1869, MP, vol. 32, LC.

41. Eckenrode, *Political*, 125–27; MFM, MS memorial signed by Smith for Academic Board of Virginia Military Institute on using a portion of land grant, Dec. 18, 1871, MP, vol. 50, fols. 10084–126, LC.

42. MFM, "Address Before the Educational Society of Virginia," manuscript in MP, vol. 48, LC, and printed version, *Educational Journal of Virginia* 1, no. 10 (Aug. 1870): 304–13.

43. MFM to Mrs. Elizabeth Maury Holland, Dec. 22, 1869, MP, vol. 33, LC.

44. Marin H. Jansen to MFM, April 1870, MP, vol. 35, LC; Marin H. Jansen to MFM, June 16 and July 7, 1870, MP, vol. 33, LC.

45. "Funeral Obsequies for General Lee," Oct. 15, 1870, MP, vol. 36, LC; MFM to Francis H. Smith, Oct. 1870, MFM Papers, Virginia Military Institute Archives; Francis H. Smith to MFM, Nov. 29, 1870, MP, vol. 36, LC; Virginius Dabney, *Virginia: The New Dominion*, 358–59.

46. MFM to Francis W. Tremlett, Dec. 7, 1870, MP, vol. 36, LC; MFM to Brodie S. Herndon, Jan. 6, 1871, MP, vol. 36, LC; Brodie S. Herndon to Ann Herndon Maury (MFM's wife), Jan. 6, 1871, MP, vol. 36, LC; MFM, "Man's Power-Giving Knowledge," manuscript, MP, vol. 48, LC.

47. Board of Regents, University of Alabama, to MFM, Apr. 15 and June 21, 1871, MP, vol. 37, LC.

48. "The State University," *Southern Argus* (Selma, Ala.), Apr. 28, 1871; "University of Alabama," *Alabama Journal* (Montgomery, Ala.), June 16, 1871; "A Week's Doings in Tuscaloosa," *Independent Monitor* (Tuscaloosa, Ala.), June 21, 1871; "The Newly Elected Faculty of the State University," *Independent Monitor* (Tuscaloosa, Ala.), June 21, 1871; "The State University," *Independent Monitor* (Tuscaloosa, Ala.), (n.d., ca. 1871); "The University," *Alabama Journal* (Montgomery, Ala.), June 23, 1871; all typed manuscripts, University of Alabama Archives.

49. MFM, "Inaugural Address of the President of the University of Alabama," n.d., ca. 1871, University of Alabama Archives.

50. MFM to Joseph Hodgson, July 31, 1871, reference to telegram MFM sent earlier accepting the position, MP, vol. 37, LC; MFM to Executive Committee, problems with "launching fund," Aug. 5, 1871, Aug. 5, 1871, MP, vol. 37, LC.

51. *Journal of the Board of Education and Board of Regents*, specifically sessions June 15, 16, 17, 19, 20, 1871, on university organization, hiring of new faculty, and financial problems, University of Alabama Archives; MFM to Col. Joseph Hodgson, Sept. 11, 1871, University of Alabama Archives; MFM to Hodgson, Aug. 30, Sept. 6, and another formal letter of resignation dated Sept. 20, 1871, MP, vol. 55, LC; MFM to Executive Committee, problems with "launching fund," Aug. 5, 1871; to Professor of Latin Wyman, Aug. 8 and Aug. 23, 1871, MP, vol. 55, LC.

52. MFM, draft remarks for delivery to the General Assembly of Virginia, Dec. 18, 1871, MP, vol. 50, LC.

53. Clara B. Cox, "Looking Back at Virginia Tech's 125th Year: The Rocky Beginning," *Virginia Tech Magazine* 19, no. 3 (Spring 1997), accessed Nov. 9, 2013, http://www.vtmag.vt.edu/spring97/feature2.html.

54. MFM, Address before Congress of the National Agricultural Association, St. Louis, manuscript, MP, vol. 51, LC; MFM, Address before the Fair of the Agricultural and Mechanical Society of Memphis, pamphlet, Oct. 17, 1871, MP, LC; M. F. Maury to Diana Maury Corbin, Nov. 11, 1871, MFM Papers, Virginia Military Institute Archives.

55. Copies of resolutions and letters from state legislatures, governors, and others supporting MFM's call for a National Weather Service, MP, vols. 39, 43, 51, LC. States represented include Connecticut, New York, Tennessee, and Missouri. Publicity for the campaign exemplified by a letter from the owners of Advocate Publishing Co., Jackson, Tenn., Feb. 2, 1872, MP, vol. 38, LC.

56. Copy of *Prairie Farmer* editorial, n.d., MP, vol. 38, LC.

57. Records of officials of Scottish Meteorological Society, MP, vol. 39, LC; Adolphe Quetelet to MFM, Sept. 28, 1872, MP, vol. 41, LC.

58. Sen. John W. Johnston to MFM, Mar. 18, 1872, MP, vol. 39, LC; Sen. Johnston to MFM, Apr. 25, 1872, MP, vol. 40, LC.

59. MFM address in St. Louis cited in note 54 above.

60. MFM to Mary Maury, May 5, 1872, MP, vol. 40, LC; MFM to Marin H. Jansen, July 4, 1872, MP, vol. 40, LC.

61. William F. Rowland to MFM, June 5, 1872, MP, vol. 40, LC; Rutson Maury to Marin H. Jansen, Mar. 25, 1873, MP, vol. 44, LC.

62. Rutson Maury letter cited in note 61 above.

63. MFM to S. Welford Corbin, Oct. 10, 1871, MP, vol. 38, LC.

64. Corbin, *Maury*, 284.

65. Mary Maury notes on Maury death, MP, vol. 47, LC; Corbin notes on Maury death, MP, vol. 63, LC. All the children kept accounts of Maury's last days. The accounts are in accord on major events in the weeks leading up to his death. The accounts are contained in MP vol. 43, LC, fols. 8426–38, LC.

66. Mary Maury notes on Maury death, MP, vol. 47, LC.

67. Mary Maury notes on Maury death, Jan. 27, 1873, MP, vol. 43, LC.

68. Ps. 130:1–2 (Revised Standard Edition).

69. Mary Maury notes on Maury death, Jan. 28, 1873, MP, vol. 43, LC.

70. Ibid.

71. Ibid.

72. Recollections of Lucy M. Maury, MP, vol. 42, fol. 8258, LC; others in MP, vol. 43, LC; Corbin, *Maury*, 285.

73. Joseph Henry, Desk Diary, entry Feb. 7, 1873, Smithsonian Institution Archives.

74. "The Late Commodore Maury—His Eminent Service to Humanity," *New York Herald*, Feb. 3, 1873.

75. Corbin, *Maury*, 286; General Order No. 5, Feb. 1, 1873, MFM Papers, Virginia Military Institute Archives; "Obituary: Mathew F. Maury," *Richmond Dispatch*, Feb. 6, 1873.

Bibliography

Abbreviations: ***Am. Journ. Science***, *American Journal of Science and the Arts*; ***SLM***, *Southern Literary Messenger*; ***Va. Mag.***, *Virginia Magazine of History and Biography*

Federal Collections

Library of Congress: Manuscript Division

Papers of Alexander Dallas Bache
Papers of Robert Browning
Papers of Jefferson Davis
Papers of Jubal Early
Papers of Andrew Foote
Papers of Louis M. Goldsborough
Papers of Matthew Fontaine Maury
Papers of Thomas O. Selfridge
Papers of William Seward
Papers of Robert W. Shufeldt, including Writings of George E. Belknap
Papers of Gideon Welles

National Archives: Navy Records, Navy and Military Service Branch

Record Group 45
Acceptance, 1809–61
Applications for Appointments, 1808–61
Appointments, Orders, and Resignations, 1809–61
Captains' Letters, 1822–61
Thomas A. Dornin, Lieut., U.S.N.—Journal kept on board USS *Brandywine*, 1826–30
William Bolton Finch, Lieut. Commanding USS *Vincennes*, reports and letters to United States
Miscellaneous Records—Correspondence relating to Lieut. M. F. Maury, U.S.N., and the "Plucking Board," 1855, 1 vol., and press clippings

Record Group 37
Records of the Bureau of Ordnance and Hydrography, 1842–61
Hydrographic Surveys, 1854–61
Letters Sent; Letters Received

Record Group 125
Records of the Office of the Judge Advocate General (Navy), "The Case of Lieut. M. F. Maury, Naval Court of Inquiry, No. 1," Courts of Inquiry, Act of Jan. 16, 1857, vol. 21, 68 pages (not with microfilm records of JAG proceedings; separate bound volume)

Record Group 78
Records of the U.S. Naval Observatory
Abstract Logs Received, 1848–61, in bound volumes and index
Naval Observatory Letters Received, 1842–61
Naval Observatory Letters Sent, 1842–61

Record Group 45
Secretary of the Navy: Executive Letter Books
Correspondence with Executive Group
Records of the Office of the Secretary of the Navy, Personnel Records, 1809–61

Record Group 24
Ships' Records—Journals, Logbooks, Muster Rolls, Pay Rolls of:
- USS *Brandywine*, 1825–27
- USS *Dolphin*, 1833
- USS *Falmouth*, 1831–33
- USS *Macedonian*, 1825–26
- USS *Potomac*, 1833–34
- USS *Vincennes*, 1827–30

Other Collections

Duke University, Durham, N.C.

Papers of John Rutherfoord

Georgetown University, Washington, D.C.

Papers of the Rev. James Curley
Records of the Observatory

Hagley Museum and Library, Wilmington, Del.

Papers of Samuel F. DuPont

Library of Virginia, Richmond

County records: Court orders, deeds, inventories, and marriages of Caroline, Louisa, and Spotsylvania Counties and Fredericksburg, Va., on microfilm.
Governor's Executive Correspondence, 1861.
Journal of the House of Delegates of Virginia, Session, 1843–44. Richmond: Samuel Shepherd, 1844.
Proceedings of the Advisory Council of Virginia, 1861. 2 vols. Executive correspondence. Richmond: Library of Virginia, 1977.

Maryland Historical Society, Baltimore

Letter Collection of John Pendleton Kennedy, Secretary of the Navy, 1852–53

Museum of the Confederacy, Richmond

Matthew Fontaine Maury

New York Public Library

Maury Collection, Letters of Maury to F. R. Hassler, Coast Survey, Feb. 11 and Aug. 12, 1839

Philadelphia Historical Society

Papers of Joel Poinsett

Smithsonian Institution Archives, Washington, D.C.

Letters Sent and Letters Received: Joseph Henry, Secretary of the Smithsonian Institution
Journals of Joseph Henry

Tennessee State Library and Archives, Nashville

County Records: Deeds of Williamson County, Tenn.
Faw, Walter W. "Boyhood Home of Matthew Fontaine Maury" and "Historical Sketch of Harpeth Academy."

University of Alabama, William Hoole Special Collections, Tuscaloosa

Typescript papers surrounding appointment and later resignation of Matthew Fontaine Maury as president of the university. Includes meetings of university board of regents, correspondence, and newspaper accounts.

University of North Carolina, Southern Historical Collection, Chapel Hill

Papers of Edward Clifford Anderson
Papers of Stephen R. Mallory
Papers of William F. Martin

University of South Carolina, South Caroliniana Library, Columbia

Papers of Matthew Fontaine Maury
Papers of Ravenel Family

University of the South, Sewanee, Tenn.

Diary of the Rt. Rev. Charles Todd Quintard, Bishop of Tennessee, Vice Chancellor of the University of the South, Aug. 1867–May 1868
Letters of Matthew Fontaine Maury to the Rt. Rev. Charles Todd Quintard, Jan. 4, 1868; to the Rt. Rev. W. M. Green, Bishop of Mississippi, Chancellor of the University of the South, Apr. 21, 1868
Minutes of the Board of Trustees of the University of the South, meeting Aug. 13, 1868
Minutes of the Executive Committee of the University of the South, meetings Apr. 4 and May 28, 1868

University of Virginia, Alderman Library, Charlottesville

Papers of Johnston Family
Papers of John B. Minor
The Rev. James Maury–The Rev. John Camm Letterbook
"Loyal Company Grant, July 12, 1749." *Exploring the West from Monticello: A Perspective in Maps from Columbus to Lewis and Clark.* An Exhibition of Maps and Navigational Instruments on View in the Tracy W. McGregor Room, Alderman Library, University of Virginia, July 10 to

Sept. 26, 1995. Last modified Dec. 16, 2009. http://www2.lib.virginia.edu/exhibits/lewis_clark/exploring/ch3-16.html.

Vanderbilt University, Nashville, Tenn.

Collection of letters from Matthew Fontaine Maury to Gen. William Giles Harding of Nashville, on loan by Mrs. Mary Harding Ragland

Virginia Historical Society, Richmond

Papers of Matthew Fontaine Maury
Papers of Page Family (1800–69)
Papers of Maury Family
Papers of Rutherfoord Family

Virginia Military Institute, Lexington

Letters, papers, and lectures of Matthew Fontaine Maury, Professor of Physics
Letters and papers of Gen. Francis H. Smith, Superintendent, V.M.I., General Order No. 41, Sept. 26, 1873

Printed and Electronic Sources—Official Documents

United States Congress

Act to Promote the Efficiency of the Navy. [Public Law number?]. 32d–33d Cong. 1851–55. *Statutes at Large of the United States of America, 1789–1873*. Vol. 10, pp. 616–17.

Biographical Directory of the United States Congress, 1774–Present. http://bioguide.congress.gov/biosearch/biosearch.asp.

Cong. Globe. 34th Cong., 1st Sess. 203, 343, 344, 346, 367, 388, 400–5, 407, 409, 487 (1856). Debate on Naval Retiring Board.

Cong. Globe. 34th Cong., 1st Sess. Appendix, 170–73, 244–45, 248, 250, 266–70, 310–25, 333–36, 487, 510, 572–74, 577, 584–87, 589 (1856). Debate on Naval Retiring Board.

Cong. Globe. 34th Cong., 1st Sess. Pt. 2. 1594, 1638, 1795–96, 2159–60 (1856). Debate on Naval Retiring Board and Vote on S. 113.

Cong. Globe. 34th Cong., 3d Sess. 301–2 (1857). Final debate and vote on S. 113 in House.

"Deposition of Benjamin Conolly." *Correspondence Concerning Claims Against Great Britain Transmitted to the Senate of the United States*. Vol. 2. Washington, D.C.: Philp and Solomons, 1869.

Dickens, Asbury, and John W. Forney, eds. *American State Papers: Documents Legislative and Executive of the Congress of the United States from the Second Session of the Twenty-First to the First Session of the Twenty-Fourth Congress, Commencing March 1, 1831, and Ending June 15, 1836*. Vol. 4. *Naval Affairs*. "On the Expediency and Importance of Authorizing a Naval Expedition to Explore the Pacific Ocean and South Seas." Including Letters from Passed Midshipmen Maury and Gordon. Feb. 7, 1835. Doc. No. 578. Washington, D.C.: Gales and Seaton, 1861.

Hatfield, Mark O. *Vice Presidents of the United States*. With the Senate Historical Office. Washington, D.C.: Government Printing Office, 1997. http://www.senate.gov/artandhistory/history/common/briefing/Vice_President.htm.

Message from the President of the United States Communicating the Letter of Mr. Prevost, and Other Documents, Relating to an Establishment Made at the Mouth of the Columbia River, Jan. 27, 1823. Washington, D.C.: Gales and Seaton, 1823. Accessed Nov. 3, 2013. http://books.google.com/books?id=TbG2k_TsZmcC.

Message from the President of the United States to the Two Houses of Congress at the Commencement of 2d Session of the 29th Congress, Dec. 8, 1846. Washington, D.C.: Ritchie and Heiss, 1846. Accessed Jan. 14, 2014. http://books.google.com/books?id=D7UTAAAAYAAJ.

Tyler, John. John Tyler to Senate and House of Representatives, Feb. 29, 1844. *A Compilation of the Messages and Papers of the Presidents, 1789–1897*. Vol. 4. Washington, D.C.: Government Printing Office, 1897. Accessed Dec. 19, 2013. http://books.google.com/books?id=3iNKAAAAMAAJ.

U.S. Congress. House. *A Compilation of the Messages and Papers of the Presidents, 1789–1897*. Compiled by James D. Richardson. 53rd Cong., 2d Sess. H.R. Misc. Doc. No. 210. Ser. 3265. Washington, D.C.: Government Printing Office, 1897.

_____. *Exploration of the Valley of the Amazon*. By Lardner Gibbon. Feb. 1854. Vol. 2. 33d Cong., 1st Sess., 1854. H.R. Exec. Doc. No. 53. Ser. 722.

_____. *General Regulations for Navy and Marine Corps*. For Joint Resolution of Congress of 24 May 1842. 27th Cong., 2d Sess., 1842. H.R. Doc. No. 148. Ser. 421.

_____. *Papers Related to Foreign Affairs, Accompanying the Annual Message of the President*. Pt. 3. 39th Cong., 1st Sess. H.R. Exec. Doc. No. 7. Washington, D.C.: Government Printing Office, 1866.

_____. *Report of the Committee on Foreign Affairs, to Which Was Referred a Message from the President of the United States in Relation to the Territory of the United States beyond the Rocky

Mountains, Feb. 16, 1839. 25th Cong., 3d Sess., H.R. Rep. No. 101. Washington, D.C., 1835. Accessed Apr. 13, 2014. http://books.google.com/books?id=E7YTAAAAYAAJ.
_____. *Report on Exploring Expedition.* (1838). 25th Cong., 2d Sess., 1838. H.R. Exec Doc. No. 147. Ser. 327.
_____. *Report Recommending Construction of Naval Observatory.* 27th Cong., 2d Sess., 1842. H.R. Rep. No. 449. Ser. 408.
_____. *Rules and Regulations.* Prepared by the Board of Revision for the Government of the Navy. 23rd Cong. 1st Sess., Dec. 23, 1833. H.R. Exec. Doc. Nos. 20 and 375. Ser. 254, 258.
U.S. Congress. Senate. *Exploration of the Valley of the Amazon.* By William Lewis Herndon. 32d Cong., 2d Sess., 1852. S. Exec. Doc. No. 1. Ser. 659.
_____. *Journal of the Executive Proceedings of the Senate of the United States of America, December 3, 1855–June 16, 1858.* 34th Cong., 2d Sess., and 35th Cong., 1st and 2d Sess. Vol. 10, pp. 268, 277, 285, 291.
_____. *Report of the Secretary of the Navy Communicating a Report of the Plan and Construction of the Depot of Charts and Instruments with a Description of the Instruments.* By J. M. Gilliss. 28th Cong., 2d Sess., 1845. S. Doc. 114.
_____. *Report on Senate Committee on Agriculture in Support of S. 481 to Extend to the Land the System of Observations Carried On at the National Observatory.* Presented by Senator James Harlan, Dec. 18, 1856. 34th Cong., 2d Sess., 1856. S. Rep. No. 292. Ser. 891. Vol. 1.
U.S. Department of the Navy. *Laws of the United States in Relation to the Navy and the Marine Corps to the Close of the Second Session of the 26th Congress.* Compiled by Benjamin Homans. Washington, D.C.: Government Printing Office, 1841.

United States Navy

U.S. Department of the Navy. *Astronomical and Meteorological Observations Made at the United States Naval Observatory, During the Year 1861.* Washington, D.C.: Gales and Seaton, 1862.
_____. *Official Report of the U.S. Expedition to Explore the Dead Sea and the River Jordan.* By William Francis Lynch, USN, Lieut., Commanding. Washington, D.C.: U.S. Naval Observatory, 1852.
_____. *Regulations, Circulars, Orders, and Decisions for Guide of Officers of Navy, 1851.* Washington, D.C.: Gales and Seaton, 1851.
_____. *Regulations for Uniform and Dress, 1841.* Washington, D.C.: Gales and Seaton, 1841.
_____. *Report on the Work of the Naval Observatory from July 1, 1846, to Jan. 1, 1850.* Washington, D.C.: Gales and Seaton, 1851.
_____. *Rules, Regulations, and Instructions for the Naval Service of the United States, 1818.* Washington, D.C.: E. DeKraaft, 1898.
_____. *U.S. Navy Register,* 1824–61. Washington, D.C.: Gales and Seaton, 1861.
_____. *U.S. Secretary of the Navy's Annual Report,* 1824–61. Washington, D.C., 1824–61.

Miscellaneous

Fur-Seal Arbitration. Washington, D.C.: Government Printing Office, 1895.
Smithsonian Institution. *Documents Relative to Its Origin and History, 1835–1899.* Edited and compiled by William J. Rhees. 12 vols. Washington, D.C.: Smithsonian Institution, 1901.
_____. *Journal of the Board of Regents; Report of Committees, Statistics, Etc.* Edited and compiled by William J. Rhees. Washington, D.C.: Smithsonian Institution, 1879.
Tyler, John. "Third Annual Message," Dec. 5, 1843. Online by Gerhard Peters and John T. Woolley. *American Presidency Project,* University of California, Santa Barbara. http://www.presidency.ucsb.edu/ws/?pid=29647.
U.S. Coast and Geodetic Survey. *Annual Reports, 1844–1910.* NOAA Central Library. U.S. National Oceanographic and Atmospheric Administration. Last modified Dec. 7, 2007. http://www.lib.noaa.gov/researchtools/subjectguides/cgsreports.html.

Virginia

Acts of the Virginia General Assembly of 1857–58. Richmond: William Ritchie, Public Printer, 1858.
Constitution of Virginia, Framed by the Convention That Met in Richmond on Tuesday, Dec. 3, 1867. Passed Apr. 17, 1868. Richmond: New Nation, 1868.
Flournoy, H. W., ed. *Calendar of Virginia State Papers and Other Manuscripts: Preserved in the Capitol at Richmond.* Vol. 11. Richmond: Secretary of the Commonwealth, 1895.
Hening, William W., ed. *The Statutes at Large: Being a Collection of All the Laws of Virginia from the First Session of the Legislature in the Year 1819.* Vols. 1–2, New York: Printed by the Editor, 1825. Vol. 3, Philadelphia: Printed by the Editor, 1825. Vols. 4–13, Richmond: Printed by the Editor, 1819–27.
Journal of the Acts and Proceedings of a General Convention of the State of Virginia, 1861. Richmond: Virginia State Library, 1861.
Journal of the Committee of the Whole, Virginia Convention. Richmond: Virginia State Library, 1966.
Journal of the House of Delegates of the State of Virginia for the Extra Session, 1861. Richmond: William F. Ritchie, 1861.

War 1861–65

Journal of the Congress of the Confederate States of America, 1861–65. Washington, D.C.: Government Printing Office, 1904–5.

Official Records of the Union and Confederate Navies in the War of the Rebellion. 30 vols. Washington, D.C.: Government Printing Office, 1894–1922.

The War of the Rebellion: A Compilation of the Official Records of the Union and Confederate Armies. 70 vols. in 128 parts. Washington, D.C.: Government Printing Office, 1880–1901.

Newspapers

Alexandria (Va.) Gazette
Anglo-American Times (London)
Army-Navy Chronicle and Scientific Repository (Washington, D.C.)
Baltimore American
Boston Atlas
Buffalo (N.Y.) Commercial Advertiser
Charleston (S.C.) Daily Courier
Charleston (S.C.) Mercury
Daily Evening Traveller (Boston)
Fredericksburg (Va.) Political Arena
Illustrated London News
Index (London)
London Review and Journal
National Intelligencer (Washington, D.C.)
New York Herald
New York Journal of Commerce
New York Times
Niles' Weekly Register (Baltimore)
Panama Canal Record
Religious Intelligencer (New Haven, Conn.)
Richmond (Va.) Daily Times
Richmond (Va.) Daily Whig
Richmond (Va.) Dispatch
Richmond (Va.) Enquirer and Examiner
Richmond (Va.) Semi-weekly Whig
Richmond (Va.) Whig and Public Advertiser
South (Baltimore)
Times (London)
Washington (D.C.) Star
Washington (D.C.) Post
Washington (D.C.) Times

Books, Pamphlets, and Periodicals

Abbot, Willis J. *The Naval History of the United States: Blue-Jackets of '61*. New York: Dodd Mead, 1886.

Abernethy, Thomas P. *From Frontier to Plantation in Tennessee*. Chapel Hill, N.C.: University of North Carolina, 1932.

_____. "Thomas Walker." In *Dictionary of American Biography*. Edited by Dumas Malone, 19:360–61. New York: Scribner's, 1936.

Abridgement of the Debates of Congress from 1789 to 1856. Vol. 16. New York: D. Appleton, 1863.

Adams, Brooks. *Seizure of the Rams at Birkenhead: Proceedings of Massachusetts Historical Society*. Boston: Massachusetts Historical Society, 1914.

Adams, Charles Francis. *Memoirs of John Quincy Adams*. 12 vols. Philadelphia: J. B. Lippincott, 1876–77.

_____. "The Seizure of the Laird Rams." In *Proceedings of Massachusetts Historical Society*, vol. 45: 246–333. Boston: Massachusetts Historical Society, 1912.

_____. *Studies Military and Diplomatic, 1775–1865*. New York: Macmillan, 1911.

Adams, Charles Francis, Jr. *Charles Francis Adams, by His Son*. Boston: Houghton Mifflin, 1900; Rye Brook, N.Y.: Elibron Classics/Adamant Media, 2006.

Adams, Ephraim Douglass. "The Southern Independence Association." Chap. 15 in *Great Britain and the American Civil War*. New York: Longmans Green, 1925. Reprint, Project Gutenberg e-book no. 13789, Oct. 18, 2004. http://www.gutenberg.org/files/13789/13789-h/13789-h.htm#CHAPTER_XV.

Adams, Herbert B., ed. *The Life and Writings of Jared Sparks: Comprising Selections from His Journals and Correspondence*. Vol. 1. Boston: Houghton Mifflin, 1893.

Adams, Henry. *The Education of Henry Adams: An Autobiography*. 1918. Reprint, Hong Kong: Forgotten Books, 2013. http://www.forgottenbooks.org/books/The_Education_of_Henry_Adams_1000037123.

_____. *Henry Adams: Selected Letters*. Edited by Ernest Samuels. Boston: Massachusetts Historical Society, 1982.

Adams, John Quincy. "First Annual Message," Dec. 6, 1825. Online by Gerhard Peters and John T. Woolley, American Presidency Project. Accessed Dec. 16, 2013. http://www.presidency.ucsb.edu/ws/?pid=29467.

Adkins, Roy, and Lesley Adkins. "Don't Give Up the Ship." *MHQ: The Quarterly Journal of Military History* (Leesburg, Va.) 20, no. 4 (Summer 2008). Accessed Dec. 19, 2013. http://www.historynet.com/dont-give-up-the-ship.htm.

Allen, Gardener Weld, ed. *Papers of Commodore Hull*. Boston: Athenaeum, 1929.

Ambler, Charles H., ed. "Correspondence of Robert M. T. Hunter." In *Annual Report of the American Historical Association for 1916*, 281. Washington, D.C.: American Historical Association, 1918).

_____. *Francis H. Pierpont*. Chapel Hill: University of North Carolina Press, 1937.

_____, ed. *John P. Branch Papers of Randolph-*

Macon College. Vol. 5. Ashland, Va.: Randolph-Macon Historical Society, 1918.
_____. *The Life and Diary of John Floyd, Governor of Virginia, an Apostle of Secession, and the Father of the Oregon County*. Richmond: Richmond, 1918.
_____. *Sectionalism in Virginia from 1776 to 1861*. Chicago: University of Chicago Press, 1910.
American Association for the Advancement of Science. *Proceedings and Reports, 1848–51*. Washington, D.C.: American Association for the Advancement of Science, 1852.
American Journal of Science and Arts. Issues from 1834 through 1873. New Haven, Conn.
American Philosophical Society. Elisha Kent Kane Papers. Accessed Dec. 19, 2013. http://amphilsoc.org/mole/view?docId=ead/Mss.B.K132-ead.xml.
_____. *Proceedings*. Vol. 9. Philadelphia: [Publisher?], 1862.
Ammen, Daniel. *The Atlantic Coast: The Navy in the Civil War*. New York: Scribner's, 1905.
_____. *The Old Navy and the New: Personal Reminiscences*. Philadelphia: J. B. Lippincott, 1891.
Ammon, Harry. *James Monroe: The Quest for American Identity*. Charlottesville: University of Virginia Press, 1990.
Anderson, Dice Robins. *William Branch Giles: A Study in the Politics of Virginia and the Nation from 1790 to 1830*. Menasha, Wis.: George Banta, 1914.
Anderson, Joseph R., Jr. *The Virginia Military Institute and Her Sons: In the Past*. Lexington, Va.: Virginia Military Institute, 1904.
Anderson, Rufus. *A Heathen Nation Evangelized: History of the Mission of the American Board for Foreign Missions to the Sandwich Islands*. 3rd ed. London: Hodder and Stoughton, 1872.
_____. *A History of the Mission of the American Board of Commissioners for Foreign Missions to the Sandwich Islands*. 3rd ed. Boston: Congressional Publishing Society, 1872.
Archibald, Raymond Charles. *Biographical Sketch of Benjamin Peirce*. Oberlin, Ohio: Mathematical Association of America, 1925.
Arthur, Anthony. *General Jo Shelby's March*. New York: Random House, 2010.
Atlantic Telegraph Co. *The Atlantic Telegraph: A History of Preliminary Experimental Proceedings and a Descriptive Account of the Present State and Prospects of the Undertaking*. London: Atlantic Telegraph Co., July 1857.
Auchampaugh, Philip Gerald. *Robert Tyler: Southern Rights Champion*. Duluth, Minn.: Himan Stein, 1934.
Bache, Alexander Dallas. *Address of Professor Alexander Dallas Bache, President of the American Association for the Advancement of Science for the Year 1851, on Retiring from the Duties of President*. Reprinted from the *American Association for the Advancement of Science Proceedings, 6th Meeting Held at Albany, N.Y., August 1851*. Washington, D.C.: American Association for the Advancement of Science, 1852.
_____. *Notes on the Coast of the United States: Memoir for the Blockade Strategy Board*. Washington, D.C.: Government Printing Office, 1861. Accessed Nov. 2, 2013. http://www.nauticalcharts.noaa.gov/nsd/hcp_notesoncoast.html.
"Bache and Maury: The Attack of 1849." *NOAA History: A Science Odyssey*. NOAA Central Library. U.S. National Oceanographic and Atmospheric Administration. Last modified Nov. 30, 2007. http://www.lib.noaa.gov/noaainfo/heritage/coastsurveyvol1/BACHE2.html#MAURY.
Bagby, George W. "Pawnee War." In *Selections from Miscellaneous Writings of Dr. George W. Bagby*, 322–32. Vol. 1. Richmond: Whittet and Shepperson, 1884. Accessed Dec. 19, 2013. http://books.google.com/books?id=PhdEAAAAYAAJ.
Bain, David Howard. *Bitter Waters: America's Forgotten Naval Mission to the Dead Sea*. New York: Overlook, 2011.
Baldwin, Ernest H. "The 'Mallory Report' and Its Consequences." *National Magazine: An Illustrated American Monthly* (Boston) 9, no. 6 (Mar. 1899): 155–60.
Baldwin, John B. *Interview Between President Lincoln and Col. John B. Baldwin, Apr.4, 1861: Statements and Evidence*. Staunton, Va.: "Spectator" Job Office, 1866. http://openlibrary.org/books/OL6540951M/Interview_between_President_Lincoln_and_Col._John_B._Baldwin_April_4th_1861.
Ball, Benjamin Lincoln. *Rambles in Eastern Asia, Including China and Manilla, During Several Years Residence*. Boston: James French, 1856.
Bancroft, George. *History of the United States*. Rev. ed. 6 vols. Boston: Little, Brown, 1876.
Bancroft, Hubert Howe. *The New Pacific*. Rev. ed. New York: Bancroft, 1912.
Barnard, John G. *Notes of Sea Coast Defense: Consisting of Sea-Coast Fortifications, the Fifteen-inch Gun, and Casemate Embrasures*. New York: D. Van Nostrand, 1861.
Barnes, J. S. *Submarine Warfare: Offensive and Defensive*. New York: D. Van Nostrand, 1869.
Barrett, Walter. *The Old Merchants of New York City*. New York: Carleton, 1863.
Bartky, Ian R. *Selling the True Time: Nineteenth Century Timekeeping in America*. Stanford, Calif.: Stanford University Press, 2001.
Bartlett, Irving H. *John C. Calhoun: A Biography*. New York: W. W. Norton, 1994.
Bassett, John Spencer. *The Life of Andrew Jackson*. New York: Macmillan, 1925.
Bateson, Charles. *Gold Fleet for California: Forty-Niners from Australia and New Zealand*. East Lansing: Michigan State University, 1963.
Battle, Kemp P. "Commodore Maury and General

Pettigrew." *North Carolina University Magazine* (Chapel Hill) 12 (1892–1893): 273–80.

______. *History of the University of North Carolina from Its Beginning to the Death of President Swain, 1789–1868*. Raleigh, N.C.: Edwards and Broughton, 1907.

Bauer, K. Jack. *The Mexican War, 1846–1848*. New York: Macmillan, 1974; Lincoln: University of Nebraska Press, 1992.

Bayard, Samuel John, and Robert F. Stockton. *A Sketch of the Life of Com. Robert F. Stockton with an Appendix*. New York: Derby and Jackson, 1856.

Beach, Edward L. *The United States Navy: A 200-Year History*. Boston: Houghton Mifflin, 1986.

Beaglehole, J. C. *Life of Captain James Cook*. Palo Alto, Calif.: Stanford University Press, 1974.

Beale, Howard K., ed. *Diary of Gideon Welles*. Vol. 1. New York: W. W. Norton, 1960.

Beaman, Charles C. *The National and Private* Alabama *Claims and the Final Amicable Settlement*. Washington, D.C.: W. T. Moore, 1871.

Bearrs, Edward C. *Receding Tide: Vicksburg and Gettysburg; The Campaigns That Changed the Civil War*. With J. Parker Hills. Washington, D.C.: National Geographic, 2010.

Bell, John. *Lieut. M. F. Maury: Speech of Hon. John Bell, of Tennessee, on the Naval Retiring Board, Delivered in the Senate of the United States, April 28–29, 1856*. Pamphlet. Washington, D.C.: Congressional Globe, 1856.

Bell, William Gardner. *Secretaries of War and Secretaries of the Army: Portraits and Biographical Sketches*. Washington, D.C.: Center of Military History, United States Army, 1992.

Bennett, Frank M. *The Steam Navy of the United States: A History of the Growth of the Steam Vessel of War in the U.S. Navy and Naval Engineer Corps*. Pittsburgh: Warren, 1896.

Bennett, John D. "The Confederate Bazaar at Liverpool." *American Civil War Round Table UK*. Originally published in *Crossfire: The Magazine of the American Civil War Round Table (UK)*, no. 61 (Dec. 1999). Accessed Nov. 2, 2013. http://www.acwrt.org.uk/uk-heritage_The-Confederate-Bazaar-at-Liverpool.asp.

______. "General Jackson's Statue." *American Civil War Round Table UK*, 2004. Originally published in *Crossfire: The Magazine of the ACWRT (UK)*, no. 75 (Dec. 2004). Accessed Nov. 2, 2013. http://www.acwrt.org.uk/uk-heritage_General-Jacksons-Statue.asp.

______. *The London Confederates: The Officials, Clergy, Businessmen, and Journalists Who Backed the American South During the Civil War*. Jefferson, N.C.: McFarland, 2008.

Benton, Thomas Hart. *Thirty Years' View; or, A History of the Working of the American Government for Thirty Years from 1820 to 1850*. 2 vols. New York: D. Appleton, 1873.

Beresford Hope, Alexander. *The Social and Political Bearings of the American Disruption*. London: Ridgway, 1863.

Berube, Claude, and John Rodgaard. *A Call to the Sea: Captain Charles Stewart of the USS* Constitution. Dulles, Va.: Potomac, 2005.

Bidwell, W. H., ed. "Astronomy in America." *The Eclectic Magazine of Foreign Literature, Science, and Art* (New York), n.s., 25 (Dec. 1876): 682–87.

Bigelow, John. "The Confederate Diplomatists." *The Century* 42 (May–Oct. 1891): 122.

______. *France and the Confederate Navy: An International Episode*. New York: Century, 1888.

______. *Lest We Forget: Gladstone, Morley, and the Confederate Loan of 1863*. New York: [Bigelow?], 1905.

______. *Retrospections of an Active Life*. Vols. 1 and 2, *1817–63*. Vol. 3, *1865–66*. New York: Baker and Taylor, 1909–10.

Bigelow, John, Jr. *The Campaign of Chancellorsville: A Strategic and Tactical Study*. New Haven: Yale University Press, 1910.

Bill, Alfred Hoyt. *The Beleaguered City: Richmond, 1861–65*. New York: Knopf, 1946.

Bingham, Hiram. *A Residence of Twenty-One Years in the Sandwich Islands*. Hartford, Conn.: Hezekiah Huntington; New York: Sherman Converse, 1847.

Blackford, Launcelot Minor. *Mine Eyes Have Seen the Glory*. Cambridge, Mass.: Harvard University Press, 1954.

Blumenthal, Henry. "Confederate Diplomacy: Popular Notions and International Realities." *Journal of Southern History* 32, no. 2 (May 1966): 151–71.

Boney, F. N. *John Letcher of Virginia*. Tuscaloosa: University of Alabama Press, 1966.

The Book of Common Prayer and Administration of the Sacraments and Other Rites and Ceremonies of the Church. New York: Church Pension Fund, 1945.

Boorstin, Daniel J. *The Americans: The National Experience*. New York: Vintage Books, 1965.

Bowditch, Nathaniel. *Memoir of Nathaniel Bowditch*. Boston: James Munroe, 1841. Accessed Dec. 19, 2013. http://books.google.com/books?id=iwcEAAAAYAAJ.

______. *The New American Practical Navigator: An Epitome of Navigation and Nautical Astronomy*. Newburyport, Mass.: Proprietor, 1802.

Bowman, Virginia. *Historic Williamson County*. Franklin, Tenn.: Williamson County Historical Society, 1989.

Boyd, William H. *Boyd's Washington and Georgetown Directory, 1860: Containing a Business Directory of Washington, Georgetown, and Alexandria*. Washington, D.C.: William H. Boyd, 1860.

Boynton, Charles B. *The History of the Navy During the Rebellion*. 2 vols. New York: D. Appleton, 1867.

Bradshaw, George. *Bradshaw's Railway Manual and Shareholder's Guide and Official Directory.* London: W. J. Adams, 1867.

Brady, William N. *The Kedge-Anchor; or, Young Sailors' Assistant.* New York: R. L. Shaw, 1848.

Brands, H. W. *The Age of Gold: The California Gold Rush and the New American Dream.* New York: Doubleday, 2002.

Brent, John Carroll, ed. *Letters on the National Institute, Smithsonian Legacy, and the Fine Arts.* Washington, D.C.: J. and G. S. Gideon, 1844.

Bridenbaugh, Carl. *Seat of Empire: The Political Role of Eighteenth Century Williamsburg.* Williamsburg, Va.: Colonial Williamsburg Foundation, 1963.

Briggs, Charles, and Augustus Maverick. *The Story of the Telegraph and a History of the Great Atlantic Cable.* New York: Rudd and Carleton, 1858.

Broad, R. A. *The Official Letters of Alexander Spotswood, Lieutenant Governor of the Colony of Virginia, 1710–1722.* Richmond: Virginia Historical Society, 1932.

Brock, Robert Alonzo. *Documents Chiefly Unpublished Relating to the Huguenot Emigration to Virginia and to the Settlement at Manakin-Town.* Richmond: Virginia Historical Society, 1886.

_____. *Virginia and Virginians.* 2 vols. Richmond: Virginia Historical Society, 1888.

Brodine, Charles E., Jr. "'Children of the Storm': Life at Sea in the First Six Frigates," *Naval History* 23, no. 4 (Aug. 2009). Accessed Nov. 2, 2013. http://www.usni.org/magazines/navalhistory/2009-08/children-storm-life-sea-first-six-frigates.

Brodsky, Alyn. *Imperial Charade: A Biography of Emperor Napoleon III and Empress Eugenie, Nineteenth-Century Europe's Most Successful Adventurers.* Indianapolis: Bobbs-Merrill, 1978.

Brooke, George M., Jr. *Ironclads and Big Guns of the Confederacy: The Journal and Letters of John M. Brooke.* Studies in Maritime History. Columbia: University of South Carolina Press, 2002.

_____. *John M. Brooke: Naval Scientist and Educator.* Charlottesville: University Press of Virginia, 1980.

Brown, Gordon S. *The Captain Who Burned His Ships: Captain Thomas Tingey, USN, 1750–1829.* Annapolis: Naval Institute, 2011.

Brown, John Howard, ed. *Lamb's Biographical Dictionary of the United States.* Vol. 5. Boston: Federal Book, 1903.

Brown, John Ross. *Resources of the Pacific Slope: A Statistical and Descriptive Summary.* San Francisco: H. H. Bancroft, 1869.

Browning, Robert M., Jr. *From Cape Charles to Cape Fear: The North Atlantic Blockading Squadron During the Civil War.* Tuscaloosa: University of Alabama Press, 1993.

_____. "Go Ahead, Go Ahead." *Naval History* 23, no. 6 (Dec. 2009). http://www.usni.org/magazines/navalhistory/2009-12/go-ahead-go-ahead.

_____. "More Than Just Blockade Duty." *Naval History* 23, no. 6 (Dec. 2009). http://www.usni.org/magazines/navalhistory/2009-12/more-just-blockade-duty.

_____. *Success Is All That Was Expected: The South Atlantic Blockading Squadron During the Civil War.* Washington, D.C.: Potomac Books, 2002.

Bruce, Kathleen. *Virginia Iron Manufacture in the Slave Era.* New York: Century, 1931.

Bruce, Philip Alexander. *History of the University of Virginia, 1819–1919.* Vol. 3. New York: Macmillan, 1921.

Brydon, George MacLaren. *Virginia's Mother Church and the Political Conditions Under Which It Grew.* Philadelphia: Virginia Historical Society, 1952.

Budiansky, Stephen. *Perilous Fight: America's Intrepid War with Britain on the High Seas, 1812–1815.* New York: Alfred A. Knopf, 2011.

Bull, Edward. *Sketch of Western Virginia.* London: E. Bull, 1837

Bulletin of the Proceedings of the National Institute 1, nos. 1–3. Washington, D.C.: Gales and Seaton, 1841.

Bulletin of the Proceedings of the National Institution for the Promotion of Science. Washington, D.C.: Gales and Seaton, 1841.

Bulloch, James D. *The Secret Service of the Confederate States in Europe; or, How the Confederate Cruisers Were Equipped.* London: Bentley and Son, 1883. Reprinted with introduction by Philip Van Doren Stern. 2 vols. New York: Sagamore, 1959. Page references are to the 1883 edition.

Burnett, David Graham. *Matthew Fontaine Maury's "Sea of Fire."* Chicago: University of Chicago Press, 2005.

Burns, E. Bradford. *A History of Brazil.* 3rd ed. New York: Columbia University Press, 1993.

Cajori, Florian. *The Chequered Career of Ferdinand Rudolph Hassler.* Boston: Christopher, 1929.

Callahan, James Morton. *The Diplomatic History of the Southern Confederacy.* Baltimore: Johns Hopkins University, 1901.

Campbell, John Archibald. "Papers of Hon. John A. Campbell, 1861–65." *Southern Historical Society Papers*, n.s., 4, no. 42 (Oct. 1917): 30–38.

Carter, James C. *Fur-Seal Arbitration: Oral Argument of James C. Carter, Esq., on Behalf of the United States Before the Tribunal of Arbitration Convened at Paris.* Washington, D.C.: Government Printing Office, 1895.

Carter, Samuel, III. *Cyrus Field: Man of Two Worlds.* New York: G. P. Putnam, 1968.

Case, Lynn M., and Warren Spender. *The United*

States and France: Civil War Diplomacy. Philadelphia: University of Pennsylvania Press, 1970.

The Case of the United States, Laid Before the Tribunal of Arbitration, Convened at Geneva Under the Provisions of the Treaty Between the United States of America and Her Majesty the Queen of Great Britain, Concluded at Washington, May 8, 1871. Leipzig, Germany: F. A. Brockhaus, 1872. Accessed Dec. 19, 2013. https://archive.org/details/cihm_34251.

Caskie, Jaquelin Ambler. *Life and Letters of Matthew Fontaine Maury.* Richmond: Richmond, 1928.

Cater, Edward Carlos, II, ed. *Surveying the Record: North American Scientific Exploration to 1930.* Philadelphia: American Philosophical Society, 1999.

Catton, Bruce. *The Coming Fury: The Centennial History of the Civil War.* Vol. 1. New York: Doubleday, 1959.

_____. *A Stillness at Appomattox.* Garden City, N.Y.: Doubleday, 1953.

Chandler, Algernon B., Jr. "Matthew Fontaine Maury: An Appreciation." Address delivered at Louisa County Fair, Louisa Courthouse, Va., June 22, 1922. *Bulletin, State Normal School for Women* 8, no. 5 (Jan. 1923): 23.

Chandler, Walter. "Diplomatic History of the Southern Confederacy." *Confederate Veteran* (Nashville, Tenn.) 30 (1922): 453–57.

Chapelle, Howard Irving. *The History of American Sailing Ships.* New York: W. W. Norton, 1935.

_____. *The History of the American Sailing Navy: The Ships and Their Development.* New York: Norton, 1949.

Charlier, Roger H. "Fratres in Maribus: 150 Years Ago, the First International Ocean-Science Conference." *Journal of Coastal Research* (West Palm Beach, Fla.) 19, no. 1 (2004): 48–51.

The Chesapeake and Ohio Railroad: Its Advantage as a Through Passenger and Freight Route Between the Seaboard and the West; Prospectus for Investors. New York: Fisk and Hatch, 1873.

Chesapeake and Ohio Railroad Prospectus for Investors. Richmond: W. A. Nye, 1868.

Chesnut, Mary Boykin. *A Diary from Dixie.* Edited by Isabella D. Martin and Myrta Locket Avary. Facsimile. New York: Portland House, 1905. Reprint, New York: Random House, 1997. Page references are to the 1997 edition.

Chisholm, Donald. *Waiting for Dead Men's Shoes: Origins and Development of the U.S. Navy's Officer Personnel System, 1793–1941.* Stanford, Calif.: Stanford University Press, 2001.

Chisholm, Hugh, ed. "Queen Victoria." *Encyclopedia Brittanica.* 11th ed. Vol. 28. London: Encyclopedia Brittanica, 1910–11.

Chittenden, L. E., comp. *A Report of the Debates and Proceedings in the Secret Sessions of the Conference Convention for Proposing Amendments to the Constitutions of the United States Held at Washington, D.C., in February, A.D. 1861.* New York: D. Appleton, 1864. Reprint, New York: Da Capo, 1971. Accessed Jan. 1, 2014. http://books.google.com/books?id=cGwFAAAAQAAJ.

Chitty, Arthur Benjamin. *Reconstruction at Sewanee: The Founding of the University of the South and Its First Administration, 1857–72.* Sewanee, Tenn.: University of the South, 1954.

Church, William Constant. *The Life of John Ericsson.* Vol. 1. London: Scribner's, 1890.

Clark, Michael, and Clark Collie. "The Ups and Downs of Trading with the Confederacy." *Northern Mariner*, Apr. 2009.

Clayton, John M. *Speech of Hon. John M. Clayton of Delaware in the U.S. Senate, March 31 and April 1, 1856, in Reply to Senator Houston of Texas and in Defense of the Naval Board.* Pamphlet. Washington, D.C.: Congressional Globe, 1856.

Cleaver, Anne Hoffman, and E. Jeffrey Stann, eds. *Voyage to the Southern Ocean: The Letters of Lieutenant William Reynolds from the U.S. Exploring Expedition.* Annapolis: Naval Institute, 1988.

Coakley, Robert W. *The Role of Military Forces in Domestic Disorders, 1789–1878.* Washington, D.C.: Center of Military History, United States Army, 1988. Accessed Nov. 2, 2013. http://books.google.com/books?id=SMmJsJLKmvoC.

Cochrane, Rexmond C. *The First Hundred Years, 1863–1963.* Washington, D.C.: National Academy of Sciences, 1978.

Cohn, David L. *The Life and Times of King Cotton.* New York: Oxford University Press, 1956.

Coker, P. C. *Charleston's Maritime Heritage, 1670–1865.* Charleston, S.C.: Craft, 1987.

Coletta, Paolo E., ed. *American Secretaries of the Navy, 1775–1913.* Vol. 1. Annapolis: Naval Institute, 1980.

Colton, Calvin, ed. *Private Correspondence of Henry Clay.* New York: A. S. Barnes, 1855.

Comegys, Joseph P. *Memoir of John M. Clayton.* Wilmington, Del.: Historical Society of Delaware, 1882.

"Commodore Matthew Fontaine Maury." Obituary. *Educational Journal of Virginia* 4 (Mar. 1873): 189–90.

"Commodore Maury and Immigration." Obituary. *Southern Planter and Farmer*, Mar. 1873, 113.

Conklin, Edwin G. "Alexander Dallas Bache and His Connection with the American Philosophical Society." *American Philosophical Journal Proceedings* 34, no. 2 (Feb. 14–15, 1941): 125–44.

Conley, Brian A., comp. *Return to Union: Fairfax County's Role in the Adoption of the Virginia*

Constitution of 1870. Fairfax, Va.: Fairfax County Public Library, 2000.
Conot, Theodore. *Adventures of a Slaver*. Cornwall, U.K.: Albert and Charles Bone, 1928.
Cooper, James Fenimore. *Cruise of the* Somers. New York: J. Winchester, 1844.
Corbin, Diana Fontaine Maury. *A Life of Matthew Fontaine Maury, U.S.N. and C.S.N., Compiled by His Daughter*. London: Sampson, Low, Marston, Searles, and Rivington, 1888.
Cornish, Dudley Taylor, and Virginia Jeans Lass. *Lincoln's Lee*. Lawrence: University Press of Kansas, 1986.
Coski, John M. "A Navy Department: Hitherto Unknown to Our State Organization." In *Virginia at War: 1861*, edited by William C. Davis and James I. Robertson, Jr., 65–88. Lexington: University Press of Kentucky, 2005.
_____. *Capital Navy: The Men, the Ships, and Operations of the James River Squadron*. Campbell, Calif.: Savas Woodbury, 1996.
Coulson, Thomas. *Joseph Henry: His Life and Work*. Princeton: Princeton University Press, 1950.
Coulter, Ellis Martin. *The Confederate States of America, 1861–1865*. Baton Rouge: Louisiana State University Press, 1950.
Cowell, John Welsford. *Letter to M. T. Maury* [typographical error on pamphlet jacket]. London: Robert Hardwicke, 1862.
Cowen, Robert C. *Frontiers of the Sea: The Story of Oceanographic Exploration*. With an introduction by Roger R. Revelle. New York: Doubleday, 1950.
Cox, Clara B. "Looking Back at Virginia Tech's 125th Year: The Rocky Beginning." *Virginia Tech Magazine* 19, no. 3 (Spring 1997). Accessed Nov. 2, 2013. http://www.vtmag.vt.edu/spring97/feature2.html.
Cralle, Richard. *Works of John C. Calhoun: Reports and Public Letters*. New York: A. Appleton, 1867.
Craven, Avery Odell. *The Coming of the Civil War*. 2nd ed. Chicago: University of Chicago Press, 1957.
_____. *Edmund Ruffin: Southerner*. Baton Rouge: Louisiana State University Press, 1932
_____. *The Growth of Southern Nationalism, 1848–61*. Baton Rouge: Louisiana State University Press, 1953.
Crofts, Daniel W. *Reluctant Confederates*. Chapel Hill: University of North Carolina Press, 1989.
Crowley, R. O. "The Confederate Torpedo Service," *Century Magazine*, June 1898.
Cullop, Charles P. *Confederate Propaganda in Europe, 1861–1865*. Coral Gables, Fla.: University of Miami Press, 1969.
Curry, Richard Orr. *A House Divided: A Study of Statehood Politics and the Copperhead Movement in West Virginia*. Pittsburgh: University of Pittsburgh Press, 1964.
Curry, Roy W. "James A. Seddon: A Southern Prototype." *Va. Mag.* 63, no. 2 (Apr. 1955): 123–50.
Curtis, Christopher M. "Can These Be the Sons of Their Fathers? The Defense of Slavery in Virginia, 1831–1832." Master's thesis, Virginia Polytechnic Institute and State University, 1997. Accessed Nov. 2, 2013. http://scholar.lib.vt.edu/theses/available/etd-4744152149731401/unrestricted/ETD.PDF.
Cutler, Carl C. *Greyhounds of the Sea*. New York: G. P. Putnam, 1930.
Dabney, Virginius. *Virginia: The New Dominion*. Garden City, N.Y.: Doubleday, 1971.
Darlington, William, ed. *Christopher Gist's Journals with Historical, Geographical, and Ethnological Notes*. Pittsburgh: J. R. Weldin, 1893.
Davidson, Hunter. "Electrical Torpedoes as a System of Defence." *Southern Historical Society Papers* 2, no. 1 (1876): 1–6.
Davies, Phil. "The Rise and Fall of Nicholas Biddle." The Federal Reserve Bank of Minneapolis. Ninth Federal Reserve District. Sept. 1, 2008. Accessed Nov. 2, 2013. http://www.minneapolisfed.org/publications_papers/pub_display.cfm?id=4047.
Davis, Burke. *Gray Fox: Robert E. Lee and the Civil War*. New York: Fairfax, 1956.
Davis, Charles Henry. *Life of Charles Henry Davis, Rear-Admiral, 1807–77, by His Son*. Boston: Houghton Mifflin, 1899.
Davis, Charles. *Colin McRae: Confederate Financial Agent*. Tuscaloosa, Ala.: Confederate, 1961.
Davis, Jefferson. *Papers of Jefferson Davis, 1861*. Edited by Mary Seaton Dix and Linda Criswell Crist. Baton Rouge: Louisiana State University Press, 1991.
_____. *The Rise and Fall of the Confederate Government*. 2 vols. New York: DaCapo, 1990.
Davis, Sarah A., ed. *Recollections of Henry Winthrop Allen, Brig. Gen., CSA, and Ex-Governor of Louisiana*. New York: M. Doolady; New Orleans: James Gresham, 1866.
Davis, Shearer. "Conditional Unionism." *Va. Mag.* 96, no. 1 (Jan. 1988): 43–52.
Davis, Varina Howell. *Jefferson Davis, Ex-President of the Confederate States of America: A Memoir by His Wife*. 2 vols. Baltimore: Nautical and Aviation, 1990.
Davis, William C., and James I. Robertson Jr., eds. *Virginia at War: 1861*. Lexington: University Press of Kentucky, 2005.
_____, eds. *Virginia at War: 1864*. Lexington: University Press of Kentucky, 2009.
DeCredico, Mary. "Richmond Bread Riot." *Virginia Encyclopedia*. Virginia Foundation for the Humanities. Last modified Feb. 10, 2012. http://www.encyclopediavirginia.org/bread_riot_richmond.
De Leon, T. C. *Four Years in Rebel Capitals: An Inside View of Life in the Southern Confederacy*

from Birth to Death. Mobile, Ala.: Gossip Printing, 1890.

de Lesseps, Ferdinand. *Recollections of Forty Years*. Translated by C. B. Pitman. Vol. 1. London: Chapman and Hall, 1887.

Delgado, James P. *To California by Sea: A Maritime History of the California Gold Rush*. Columbia: University of South Carolina Press, 1990.

Denney, Robert E. *Civil War Medicine: Care and Comfort of the Wounded*. New York: Sterling, 1994.

Desmond, Adrian, and James Moore. *Darwin's Sacred Cause: How Darwin's Hatred of Slavery Shaped Darwin's Views on Evolution*. New York: Houghton Mifflin, 2009.

de Tocqueville, Alexis. *Democracy in America*. Translated by Henry Reeve. Vol. 2. New York: D. Appleton, 1904.

DeVoto, Bernard. *The Year of Decision: 1846*. Boston: Little, Brown, 1943.

Dicey, Edward. *Six Months in the Federal States*. London: Macmillan, 1863.

Dick, Steven J. "John Quincy Adams: The Smithsonian Bequest and the Founding of the U.S. Naval Observatory." *Journal for the History of Astronomy* 22 (Feb. 1991): 31–44.

_____. *Sky and Ocean Joined: The United States Naval Observatory, 1830–2000*. London: Cambridge University Press, 2003.

Dickens, Asbury, and John W. Forney, eds. "On the Expediency and Importance of Authorizing a Naval Expedition to Explore the Pacific Ocean and South Seas, including Letters from Passed Midshipmen Maury and Gordon," Feb. 7, 1835. Doc. No. 578. In *American State Papers, Documents Legislative and Executive of the Congress of the United States from the Second Session of the Twenty-First to the First Session of the Twenty-Fourth Congress, Commencing March 1, 1831, and Ending June 15, 1836*. Vol. 4. *Naval Affairs*, 707–15. Washington, D.C.: Gales and Seaton, 1861.

Dickie, Luther S. *History of the Eighty-Fifth Regiment Pennsylvania Volunteer Infantry, 1861–1865*. New York: J. C. and W. F. Powers, 1915.

Dolin, Eric Jay. *Fur, Finance, and Empire: The Epic History of the Fur Trade in America*. New York: W. W. Norton, 2010.

Dowdey, Clifford. *Experiment in Rebellion*. New York: Books in Libraries, 1946.

_____. *The Virginia Dynasties*. New York: Little, Brown, 1969.

Drewry, William S. *The Southampton Insurrection*. Washington, D.C.: Neale, 1900.

Driver, Felix, and Luciana Martin. *Tropical Visions in an Age of Empire*. Chicago: University of Chicago Press, 2005.

du Bellet, Louise Perquet. *Some Prominent Virginia Families*. Lynchburg: J. P. Bell, 1907.

Dudley, Thomas H. "Three Critical Periods in Our Diplomatic Relations during the Late War." *Pennsylvania Magazine of History and Biography* 17, no. 1 (1893): 34–54.

Dufour, Charles L. *Nine Men in Gray*. Lincoln, Neb.: University of Nebraska Press, 1993.

Dunaway, Wayland Fuller. *History of the James River and Kanawha Company*. New York: Columbia University Press, 1922.

Dunn, Susan. *Dominion of Memories: Jefferson, Madison, and the Decline of Virginia*. New York: Basic Books, 2007.

Dupree, A. Hunter. *Science in the Federal Government: A History of Policies and Activities to 1940*. Cambridge, Mass.: Belknap Press of Harvard University Press, 1957.

Durham, Roger S., ed. *High Seas and Yankee Gunboats: A Blockade-Running Adventure from the Diary of James Dickson*. Columbia, S.C.: University of South Carolina Press, 2005.

Durkin, Joseph Thomas. *Stephen Russell Mallory: Confederate Navy Chief*. Chapel Hill, N.C.: University of North Carolina Press, 1954.

Eaton, Clement. *A History of the Southern Confederacy*. New York: Collier Books, 1966.

Eckenrode, Hamilton James. *The Political History of Virginia During the Reconstruction*. Baltimore: Johns Hopkins University Press, 1904. Reprint, Gloucester, Mass.: Peter Smith, 1966. Page references are to the 1904 edition.

Edinburgh Review 116–17 (July–Oct. 1862).

"Editorial Notes." *United States Service Magazine* 5 (June 1866): 563.

Educational Association of Virginia. *Minutes of the Fourth Annual Session, Held in Lexington, Va., July 13–15, 1869*. Lynchburg, Va.: Educational Journal, 1870.

_____. *Minutes of the Fifth Annual Session, Held in Warrenton, Va., July 12–15, 1870*. Lynchburg, Va.: Educational Association of Virginia, 1871.

Edwards, B. B., comp. *American Quarterly Register* 5. Boston: Congregational Education Society, 1833.

Edwards, John N. *Shelby's Expedition to Mexico: An Unwritten Leaf of the War*. Compiled by Jennie Edwards. Kansas City, Mo.: Jennie Edwards, 1889.

Eisenhower, John S. D. *Agent of Destiny: The Life and Times of General Winfield Scott*. New York: Free Press, 1997.

Elder, William. *Biography of Elisha Kent Kane*. Vol. 2. Philadelphia: Childs and Petersen; Boston: Phillips Sampson, 1858.

"The Electrical Torpedoes." Correspondence. *Mechanics Magazine* (London), July 7, 1865.

Ellison, Thomas. *The Cotton Trade of Great Britain, Including a History of the Liverpool Cotton Market and the Liverpool Cotton Brokers Association*. London: Effingham Wilson, 1886.

Exploring Expedition: Correspondence Between John N. Reynolds and Hon. Mahlon Dickerson

Under Signatures of Citizen and Friend to the Navy, New York, 1838; Report on the Exploring Expedition, 1838. 25th Cong., 2d Sess. House Executive Document 147. Washington, D.C.: United States Congress, 1838.

Evans, Eli N. *Judah P. Benjamin: The Jewish Confederate.* New York: Free Press, 1988.

Farragut, Loyall. *The Life of David Glasgow Farragut, First Admiral of the United States Navy, Embodying His Journals and Letters.* New York: D. Appleton, 1879.

Field, Henry M. *The Story of the Atlantic Telegraph.* New York: Scribner's, 1892.

Figes, Orlando. *The Crimean War: A History.* New York: Henry Holt, 2010.

Fischer, David Hackett, and James C. Kelly. *Bound Away: Virginia and the Western Movement.* Charlottesville: University Press of Virginia, 2000.

Fisher, George P. *Life of Benjamin Silliman, M.D., LL.D., Late Professor of Chemistry, Mineralogy, and Geology at Yale College.* New York: Scribner's, 1966.

Fitzpatrick, John, ed. *The Diaries of George Washington.* Vol. 4. New York: Houghton Mifflin, 1925. Reprint, New York: Kraus Reprint, 1971.

Fleming, Fergus. *Barrow's Boys: The Original Extreme Adventurers.* New York: Grove/Atlantic, 1998.

Foltz, J. M. "Medical Statistics of the United States Frigate *Potomac*, Commodore John Downes, Commander, During a Three Years' Voyage of Circumnavigation of the Globe." *New York Journal of Medicine and the Collateral Sciences* 1 (Sept. 1843): 189–207.

Foord, John. "Old Canton Days." *Asia: Journal of the American Asiatic Association* 17 (Mar.–Dec. 1918): 191–95.

Fontaine, James. *A Tale of the Huguenots; or, Memoirs of a French Refugee Family.* Translated and compiled by Ann Maury. New York: John S. Taylor, 1838.

Forbes, R. B. *Remarks on China and the China Trade.* Boston: Samuel N. Dickinson, 1844.

Ford, Paul Leicester, ed. *The Writings of Thomas Jefferson, 1816–1826.* Vol. 10. New York: G. P. Putnam, 1899.

Ford, Worthington Chauncey. *A Cycle of Adams Letters.* Boston: Houghton Mifflin, 1920.

Foreman, Amanda. *A World on Fire: Britain's Crucial Role in the American Civil War.* New York: Random House, 2010.

Fowler, William M. *Under Two Flags: The American Navy in the Civil War.* New York: W. W. Norton, 1990.

Franklin Institute. "Report on the Explosion of the Gun on Board the Steam Frigate 'Princeton.'" *Journal of the Franklin Institute* (Franklin Institute of Pennsylvania, Philadelphia), 3rd ser., 3, no. 8 (1844): 206.

Franklin, Samuel R. *Memories of a Rear Admiral: Life in the United States Sailing from Hampton Roads to Pacific Squadron.* Washington, D.C.: Navy Department Library, Microfilm Collection, n.d.

Freehling, William W. *The Road to Disunion: Secessionists at Bay, 1776–1854.* New York: Oxford University Press, 1990.

_____. *The Road to Disunion: Secessionists Triumphant, 1854–1861.* New York: Oxford University Press, 2007.

Freeman, Douglas Southall. *George Washington: A Biography.* 6 vols. Clifton, N.J.: A. M. Kelley, 1948–57.

_____. *Lee's Lieutenants: A Study in Command.* 3 vols. New York: Scribner's, 1942–44.

_____. *R. E. Lee: A Biography.* 4 vols. New York: Scribner's, 1936.

Freidel, Frank, ed. *Union Pamphlets of the Civil War.* Cambridge, Mass.: Belknap Press of Harvard University Press, 1967.

Friendly, Alfred. *Beaufort of the Admiralty: The Life of Sir Francis Beaufort, 1774–1857.* New York: Random House, 1977.

Fulton, Richard D. "Now Only the *Times* Is on Our Side: The London *Times* and America before the Civil War." *Victorian Review* (University of Victoria, Victoria, B.C.) 16, no. 1 (Summer 1990): 48–59.

Furgurson, Ernest B. *Freedom Rising: Washington in the Civil War.* New York: Random House, 2005.

George III. *The Royal Proclamation*, Oct. 7, 1763. The Avalon Project: Documents in Law, History, and Diplomacy. Yale Law School, New Haven, Conn. Accessed Nov. 2, 2013. http://avalon.law.yale.edu/18th_century/proc1763.asp.

Gill, Harold B., Jr., and Joanne Young, eds. *Searching for the Franklin Expedition: The Arctic Journal of Robert Randolph Carter.* Annapolis: Naval Institute, 1998.

Gilliss, J. M. *Astronomical and Meteorological Observations Made at the United States Naval Observatory During the Year 1861.* Washington, D.C.: Government Printing Office, 1862.

Goetzmann, William H. *Army Exploration in the American West, 1803–1863.* Austin: Texas State Historical Association, 1991.

_____. *Exploration and Empire: The Explorer and the Scientist in the Winning of the American West.* Austin: Texas State Historical Association, 1993.

_____. *New Lands, New Men: America and the Second Great Age of Discovery.* New York: Viking Penguin, 1987.

_____. *When the Eagle Screamed: The Romantic Horizon in American Expansionism, 1800–1816.* Norman: University of Oklahoma Press, 2000.

Goode, George Brown. *The Origin of the National Scientific and Educational Institutions of the United States*. Washington, D.C.: Smithsonian Institution, 1890.

_____. *The Smithsonian Institution, 1846–96: The History of Its First Half Century*. Washington, D.C.: Smithsonian Institution, 1897.

Goolrick, John Tackett. *Historic Fredericksburg: The Story of an Old Town*. Richmond: Whitteley and Shepperson, 1922.

Gordon, Armistead B. *Virginia Portraits*. Staunton, Va.: McClure, 1924.

Gorgas, Josiah. *The Journals of Josiah Gorgas, 1857–1878*. Edited by Sarah Woolfolk Wiggins. Tuscaloosa: University of Alabama Press, 1995.

Gould, Benjamin A., Jr. "Gilliss Memoir." In *National Academy of Sciences Annual*, 135–80. Pamphlet. Washington, D.C.: Home Secretary, 1866.

"Governor's Palace." Colonial Williamsburg Foundation. Accessed Aug. 21, 2013. http://www.history.org/almanack/places/hb/hbpal.cfm.

Graham, John Remington. *A Constitutional History of Secession*. Gretna, La.: Pelican, 2002.

Grant, Alfred. *The American Civil War and the British Press*. Jefferson, N.C.: McFarland, 2000.

Grant, Ulysses S. *Papers of Ulysses S. Grant*. Edited by John Y. Simon. Carbondale: Southern Illinois University Press, 1988.

Great North Atlantic Telegraph Route. London: William Clowes and Sons, 1866.

"A Great Railroad Enterprise." *Scientific American* (New York) 15, no. 2 (July 7, 1866): 18.

Greeley, Horace. "The Exploring Expedition." Four articles. Edited by Park Benjamin. *New Yorker*, Mar.–Sept. 1839.

Green, William Mercer. *Memoir of Rt. Rev. James Hervey Otey, D.D., LL.D.* New York: James Pott, 1885.

Greiner, James M., Janet L. Coryell, and James R. Smither, eds. *A Surgeon's Civil War: The Letters and Diary of Daniel M. Holt, M.D.* Kent, Ohio: Kent State University Press, 1994.

Griffis, William Elliot. "Our Navy in Asiatic Waters." *Harper's New Monthly Magazine* 17 (June–Nov. 1898): 738–59.

Gunderson, Robert Gray. *The Old Gentleman's Convention*. Madison: University of Wisconsin Press, 1961.

Guyot, Arnold. *A Collection of Meteorological Tables*. Washington, D.C.: Smithsonian Institution, 1852.

Guyot, Arnold, and Joseph Henry. *Circular of Instructions to Meteorological Observers*. Washington, D.C.: Smithsonian Institution, 1850.

Gwathmey, John Hastings. *Twelve Virginia Counties: Where the Western Migration Began*. Richmond: Genealogical, 1937.

Gwin, William M. "Senator Gwin's Plan for the Colonization of Sonora." Edited by Evan J. Coleman. *Overland Monthly* (San Francisco), 2nd ser., no. 102 (June 1891): 598–607.

Hagan, Kenneth J. *This People's Navy: The Making of American Sea Power*. New York: Free Press, 1991.

Hall, Basil. *Hall's Voyages*. Vol. 3. *Constables Miscellany*. Edinburgh, U.K.: Constable, 1827.

Hall, Claude H. *Abel Parker Upshur*. Madison: State Historical Society of Wisconsin, 1964.

Hanes, J. C., and J. M. Morgan. *History and Heritage of Civil Engineering in Virginia*. Richmond: Virginia Section of the American Society of Civil Engineers, 1973.

Hanna, Alfred J. "The Role of Matthew Fontaine Maury in the Mexican Empire." *Va. Mag.* 45, no. 2 (Apr. 1947): 102–25.

Hanna, Alfred J., and Kathryn A. Hanna. *Napoleon III and Mexico*. Chapel Hill: University of North Carolina Press, 1971.

Hansard Parliamentary Debates. 3d ser. Vol. 193. London, 1868.

Harper's Weekly. "Bread Riot." Apr. 18, 1863.

_____. "Bread Riots." Apr. 25, 1863.

Harrison, Fairfax. *Landmarks of Old Prince William*. 2 vols. Richmond: privately printed, 1924.

Hartman, Gregory K. *Weapons That Wait: Mine Warfare in the United States Navy*. With Scott Truver. Annapolis: Naval Institute, 1991.

Harvey, Robert. *Liberators: Latin America's Struggle for Independence*. Woodstock, N.Y.: Overlook, 2002.

Hatfield, Mark O. *Vice Presidents of the United States*. With the Senate Historical Office. Washington, D.C.: Government Printing Office, 1997.

Havighurst, Walter. *Long Ships Passing*. New York: Macmillan, 1943.

Hawthorne, Hildegarde. *Matthew Fontaine Maury: Trail Maker of the Seas*. New York: Longmans Green, 1943.

Hawthorne, Nathaniel. *Passages from the English Note-Books*. Vol. 1. Boston: Mifflin, 1870 and 1890.

Headley, Joel Tyler. "Darien Exploring Expedition." *Harper's New Monthly Magazine* 10, 3 installments (Dec. 1854–May 1855).

Hearn, Chester G. *Ellet's Brigade: The Strangest Outfit of All*. Baton Rouge: Louisiana State University Press, 2000.

Heatwole, Cornelius J. *A History of Education in Virginia*. New York: Macmillan, 1916.

Henderson, George. *Stonewall Jackson and the Civil War*. 2 vols. London: Longmans Green, 1906.

Hendrick, Burton J. *Statesmen of the Lost Cause: Jefferson Davis and His Cabinet*. New York: Literary Guild of America, 1939.

Henry, Joseph. "The Coast Survey." *Princeton Review*, Apr. 1845. Accessed Nov. 2, 2013. http://books.google.com/books?id=bDlYAAAAYAAJ.

_____. "Meteorology in Its Connection with Agriculture." In *Scientific Writings of Joseph*

Henry. 2 vols. bound as one. Washington, D.C.: Smithsonian Institution, 1886.

Henry, William Wirt, ed. *Patrick Henry: Life, Correspondence, and Speeches*. Vol. 1. New York: Scribner's, 1891.

Herman, Jan. *A Hilltop in Foggy Bottom*. Washington, D.C.: Naval Medical Command, 1984.

Herndon, William Lewis, and Lardner Gibbon. *Exploration of the Valley of the Amazon, Made Under Direction of the Navy Department*. 2 vols. Washington, D.C.: Taylor and Maury, Vol. 1, by Herndon, 1853; Vol. 2, by Gibbon, 1854.

Hill, Lawrence F. "The Confederate Exodus to Latin America." *Southwestern Historical Quarterly Online* 39, no. 4 (July 1935–April 1936): 100–34. Accessed Feb. 24, 2014. http://texashistory.unt.edu/ark:/67531/metapth101095/m1/114/.

The History of the Greenbrier: America's Resort. Greenbrier, W.Va.: privately printed by the Greenbrier, n.d. Photocopies sent to author in 1991.

Hodgson, D. D., ed. *Reprints of the Documents and Proceedings of the Board of Trustees of the University of the South*. University of the South Papers, ser. A, no. 1. Sewanee, Tenn.: University of the South, 1888.

Holcome, Robert. "Type of Ships." In *The Confederate Navy: The Ships, Men, and Organization, 1861–1965*, edited by William N. Still Jr., 57–61. Annapolis: Naval Institute, 1997.

Holden, Edwin. "The United States Naval Observatory, Washington." *Science: A Weekly Journal of Scientific Papers* (New York) 1, no. 1 (July 3, 1880): 1–3.

Hollins, George N. "Autobiography of Commodore George N. Hollins." *Maryland Historical Magazine* 34 (Sept. 1938): 235–43. Article contained in separate photocopy holding at Maryland Historical Society, Baltimore.

Holt, Michael E. *The Rise and Fall of the Whig Party: Jacksonian Politics and the Onset of the Civil War*. New York: Oxford University Press, 1999.

Honduras Interoceanic Railway: With Maps of the Line and Ports. London: Trubner, 1857.

Hoppen, William Warner. *The Peace Conference of 1861 at Washington*. Pt. 3. Providence, R.I.: Standard, 1923. Google e-Book. Accessed Dec. 19, 2013. http://books.google.com/books?id=YKJYAAAAMAAJ.

Hotze, Henry. *Henry Hotze: Confederate Propagandist; Selected Writings on Recognition and Revolution*. Edited by Lonnie A. Burnett. Tusca loosa: University of Alabama Press, 2008.

Howarth, Stephen. *To Shining Sea: A History of the United States Navy, 1775–1991*. New York: Random House, 1991.

Howe, Daniel Walker. *What Hath God Wrought: The Transformation of America, 1815–1848*. New York: Oxford University Press, 2007.

Howe, Octavius T., and Frederick C. Matthews. *American Clipper Ships, 1833–1858*. 2 vols. Salem, Mass.: Marine Research Society, 1926–27.

Hubbard, Charles M. *Burden of Confederate Diplomacy*. Knoxville: University of Tennessee Press, 2000.

Huffman, Wendell W. "The United States Naval Astronomical Expedition (1849–52) for the Solar Parallax." *Journal for the History of Astronomy* 22 (Feb. 1991): 208–20.

Hughes, Sarah Forbes. *Letters and Recollections of John Murray Forbes*. Vol. 1. Boston: Houghton Mifflin, 1900.

Hunt, Gaillard, ed. *Writings of Madison, 1790–1802*. Vol. 6. New York: G. P. Putnam, 1906.

Huntington, Samuel P. *The Soldier and the State: The Theory and Politics of Civil-Military Relations*. Cambridge, Mass.: Belknap Press of Harvard University Press, 1957.

Hunt's Merchants' Magazine and Commercial Review 20, no. 2 (Feb. 1849); no. 6 (June 1849); and 24, no. 6 (June 1853).

Illustrated London News. "Account of Testimonial Dinner to Matthew Fontaine Maury: Willis' Rooms, June 5, 1866." June 23, 1866.

Ingersoll, Charles J. *History of the Second War Between the United States and Great Britain*. 2nd ser. Vol. 1. Philadelphia: Lippincott, Grambo, 1852.

In Memoriam: Matthew Fontaine Maury. Lexington, Va.: Virginia Military Institute, 1873.

Jackson, C. Ian. "Three Puzzles from Early Nineteenth Century Exploration." *Northern Mariner*, July 2007.

Jacobstein, Meyer. *The South in the Building of the Nation*. Vol. 5. Richmond: Southern Historical Publication Society, 1909.

Jahns, Patricia. *Matthew Fontaine Maury and Joseph Henry: Scientists of the Civil War*. New York: Hastings House, 1961.

Jeffrey, Walter. *A Century of Our Sea Story*. London: G. P. Putnam's Sons, 1900.

Jenkins, Stephen. *The Greatest Street in the World: The Story of Broadway Old and New*. New York: G. P. Putnam's Sons, 1911.

Johnson, Allen, Dumas Malone, et al., eds. *Dictionary of American Biography*. 22 vols. New York: Scribner's, 1928–43.

Johnson, Emory R., T. W. Van Metre, G. G. Huebner, and D. S. Hanchett. *History of Domestic and Foreign Commerce of the United States*. Vols. 1 and 2 in one volume. Washington, D.C.: Carnegie Institution of Washington, 1915. Reprint, 1922. Accessed Nov. 2, 2013. http://books.google.com/books?id=1tUxAQAAMAAJ.

Johnson, Robert Underwood, and C. C. Buel, eds. *Battles and Leaders of the Civil War*. 4 vols. New York: Century, 1887.

Johnson, Rossiter, ed. *Twentieth Century Biogra-*

phical Dictionary of Notable Americans. Vol. 8. Boston: Biographical Society, 1904.

Jones, Anson. *Memoranda and Official Correspondence Relating to the Republic of Texas, Its History, and Annexation*. New York: D. Appleton, 1859.

Jones, Bessie. *Golden Age of Science*. New York: Simon & Schuster, 1966.

Jones, Catesby ap R. "Services of the *Virginia* (*Merrimack*)." *Southern Historical Society Papers* 11, no. 2 (1883): 65–74.

Jones, Charles C., Jr. *Life and Services of Commodore Josiah Tattnall*. Savannah, Ga.: Morning News, 1878.

Jones, Frederick. "Charles Blackman." In *Dictionary of Canadian Biography*. Vol. 8. University of Toronto/Université Laval, 2003–. Accessed Sept. 26, 2013. http://www.biographi.ca/en/bio/blackman_charles_8E.html.

Jones, George. *Sketches of the Naval Life with Notices of Men, Manners, and Scenery on the Shores of the Mediterranean in a Series of Letters from the* Brandywine *and* Constitution *Frigates*. 2 vols. New Haven: H. Howe, 1829.

Jones, Howard. *Blue and Gray Diplomacy: A History of Union and Confederate Foreign Relations*. Chapel Hill: University of North Carolina Press, 2010.

Jones, John Beauchamp. *A Rebel War Clerk's Diary at the Confederate States Capital*. 2 vols. Philadelphia: J. P. Lippincott, 1866.

Jones, J. William. *Personal Reminiscences, Anecdotes, and Letters of General Robert E. Lee*. New York: D. Appleton, 1875.

Kane, Elisha Kent. *Arctic Exploration: The Second* Grinnell *Expedition in Search of Sir John Franklin in 1853, '54, '55*. 2 vols. Philadelphia: Childs and Petersen, 1856.

_____. *The United States* Grinnell *Expedition in Search of Sir John Franklin: A Personal Narrative*. New York: Harper and Brothers, 1854.

Karp, Matthew J. "The Navalist Impulse in the Antebellum South." *Journal of Southern History* 77, no. 2 (May 2011): 297–322.

Kazar, John Dryden, Jr. "The United States Navy and Scientific Exploration, 1837–1860." PhD diss., University of Massachusetts, 1973. Photocopy in Smithsonian Institution Archives, Washington, D.C.

Kemp, James Furman. *The Ore Deposits of the United States and Canada*. 3rd ed. New York: Scientific, 1900.

Keneally, Thomas. *The Great Shame and the Triumph of the Irish in the English-Speaking World*. New York: Nan A. Talese, 1999.

Kennedy, Elijah H. *The Contest for California in 1861*. Boston: Riverside, 1912.

Kenner, Jesse L. *The Peace Convention of 1861*. Tuscaloosa, Ala.: Confederate, 1961.

Kett, Joseph F. *Rites of Passage: Adolescence in America, 1790 to the Present*. New York: Basic Books, 1977.

Klapp, Orrin E. "Matthew Fontaine Maury, Naval Scientist." *Naval Institute Proceedings* 71, no. 11 (Nov. 1945): 1315–25.

Knox, Dudley W. *A History of United States Navy*. New York: G. P. Putnam's Sons, 1948.

Langley, Harold D. *Social Reform in the United States Navy, 1798–1862*. Urbana, Ill.: University of Illinois Press, 1967.

Lankford, Nelson. *Cry Havoc! The Crooked Road to Civil War, 1861*. New York: Penguin Books, 2007.

Latimore, Carey H. "Surviving War and the Underground: Richmond Free Blacks and Criminal Networks During the Civil War." *Va. Mag.* 117, no. 1 (Winter 2009): 2–31.

Latourette, Kenneth Scott. *The History of the Early Relations Between the United States and China, 1784–1844*. Transactions of the Connecticut Academy of Arts and Sciences. New Haven: Yale University Press, 1917.

Lauridsen, Peter. *Vitus Bering: The Discovery of Bering Strait*. Translated by Julius E. Olson. Chicago: S.C. Griffs, 1889.

Laut, Agnes C. *Canada: The Empire of the North, Being the Romantic Story of the New Dominion's Growth from Colony to Kingdom*. Boston: Ginn, 1909.

Lee, Samuel Phillips. *Report on the Cruise of the U.S. Brig* Dolphin. Washington, D.C.: Beverly Tucker, Printer to the Senate, 1854.

Leech, Margaret. *Reveille in Washington*. Alexandria, Va.: Time-Life Books, 1980.

Leighly, John, ed. *Physical Geography of the Sea and Its Meteorology*. By M. F. Maury. Cambridge, Mass.: Belknap Press of Harvard University Press, 1963.

"Letting the Cat Out." *Living Age*, Jan.–Mar., 1863.

Levasseur, Auguste. *Lafayette in America in 1824 and 1825; or, A Journal of a Voyage to the U.S.* Translated by John D. Godman. 2 vols. Philadelphia: Carey and Lea, 1829.

Lewis, Charles Lee. *Admiral Franklin Buchanan: Fearless Man of Action*. Baltimore: Norman Remington, 1929.

_____. *David Glasgow Farragut: Admiral in the Making*. 2 vols. Annapolis: Naval Institute, 1941–43.

_____. *Matthew Fontaine Maury: The Pathfinder of the Seas*. Annapolis: Naval Institute, 1927.

"Literary and Scientific Intelligence: New Grinnell Arctic Expedition." *Journal of Education, Upper Canada* (Toronto) 6, no. 1 (Apr. 1853): 63.

Lloyd, Christopher. *The Navy and the Slave Trade*. London: Taylor and Francis, 1968.

Lockley, Fred. *Oregon Trail Blazers*. New York: Knickerbocker, 1909.

Lodge, Gonzalez, ed. *Gildersleve's Latin Grammar*. Wauconda, Ill.: Bolchazy-Carducci, 1997.

London Review and Journal, 1861–65. London.
Long, David F. *Mad Jack: The Biography of Captain John Percival, USN, 1779–1862*. Contributions in Military Studies. Westport, Conn.: Greenwood, 1993.
_____. *Nothing Too Daring*. Annapolis: Naval Institute, 1987.
Loomis, Elias. "Astronomical Observatories in the United States." *Harpers New Monthly Weekly*, June 1856.
Lossing, Benson J. *The Pictorial Field-Book of the War of 1812*. New York: Harper and Brothers, 1869.
_____. *Pictorial History of the Civil War in the United States of America*. Hartford, Conn.: T. Belknap, 1868. Reprint, Carlisle, Mass.: Applewood Books, 2010. Accessed Nov. 2, 2013. http://books.google.com/books?id=clWOWqQmu5kC.
Lovette, Leland P. *Naval Customs, Traditions, and Usage*. Annapolis: Naval Institute, 1939.
Lundenberg, Phillip K. *Samuel Colt's Submarine Battery: The Secret and the Enigma*. Washington, D.C.: Smithsonian Institution Press, 1974.
Luraghi, Raimondo. *A History of the Confederate Navy*. Translated by Paolo E. Coletta. Annapolis: Naval Institute, 1996.
Lynch, William Francis. *Narrative of the U.S. Expedition to the River Jordan and the Dead Sea*. Philadelphia: Lea and Blanchard, 1849.
_____. *Naval Life; or, Observations Afloat and on Shore; The Midshipman*. New York: Scribner's, 1851.
Mabee, Carleton. *The American Leonardo: The Life of Samuel F. B. Morse*. New York: Knopf, 1943.
MacKenzie, Alexander Slidell. *Commodore Oliver Hazard Perry: Famous American Naval Hero*. Akron, Ohio: Werner, 1910.
Mackesy, Piers. *The War for America: 1775–1783*. Lincoln: University of Nebraska Press, 1992.
Mahan, Alfred Thayer. *From Sail to Steam: Recollections of Naval Life*. New York: Harper and Brothers, 1907.
_____. *Great Commanders: Admiral Farragut*. New York: D. Appleton, 1892.
_____. *Sea Power in Its Relation to the War of 1812*. 2 vols. Boston: Little, Brown, 1905.
Malone, Dumas. *Jefferson and His Time: The Sage of Monticello*. Boston: Little, Brown, 1970.
_____. *Jefferson and the Ordeal of Liberty*. New York: Little, Brown, 1962.
_____. *Jefferson the President: Second Term, 1805–1809*. Boston: Little, Brown, 1974.
_____. *Jefferson: The Virginian*. Boston: Little, Brown, 1948.
Marx, Karl. *The Eighteenth Brumaire of Louis Bonaparte*. Translated by Daniel de Leon. Chicago: Charles H. Kerr, 1907.
Mason, Virginia, comp. *The Public Life and Diplomatic Correspondence of James Murray Mason*. New York: Neale, 1906. Accessed Nov. 3, 2013. https://archive.org/details/publiclifediplom00masonva.
"Matthew Fontaine Maury: A Sketch." *Southern Magazine*, 1872.
Matthews, Sidney T. "Control of the Baltimore Press During the Civil War." *Maryland Historical Magazine* 36 (June 1941): 150–71.
Maude, H. E. *Slavers in Paradise: The Peruvian Slave Trade in Polynesia*. Palo Alto, Calif.: Stanford University Press, 1981.
Maury, Ann. *Memoirs of a Huguenot Family, Translated and Compiled from the Original Autobiography of the Rev. James Fontaine and Other Family Manuscripts, Comprising an Original Journal of Travels in Virginia, New York, etc., in 1715 and 1716*. New York: George P. Putnam, 1853; 2nd ed., 1872.
_____, comp. *A Tale of Huguenots; or, Memoirs of a French Refugee Family, Translated from James Fontaine Manuscript*. New York: John S. Taylor, 1832. Reprint, Baltimore: Genealogical, 1967.
Maury, Anne Fontaine. *Intimate Virginiana: A Century of Maury Travels by Land and Sea*. Richmond: Dietz, 1941.
Maury, Dabney H. "How the Confederacy Changed Naval Warfare." *Southern Historical Society Papers* 22 (Jan.–Dec. 1894): 75–81.
_____. "Maury on South America and Amazonia." *Southern Quarterly Review* (Charleston, S.C.) 8 (Oct. 1853): 412–49.
_____. *Recollections of a Virginian in the Mexican, Indian, and Civil Wars*. New York: Scribner's, 1894.
Maury, Richard Launcelot. *A Brief Sketch of the Work of Matthew Fontaine Maury During the War, 1861–65*. Richmond: Whittet and Shepperson, 1915.
_____. "The First Marine Torpedoes." *Southern Historical Society Papers* 32 (Jan.–Dec. 1903): 326–34.
Maury, Sarah Mytton. *The Statesmen of America in 1846*. American ed. Philadelphia: Carey and Hart, 1847. Accessed Nov. 3, 2013. http://books.google.com/books?id=lt0DAAAAYAAJ.
Mayer, Henry. *A Son of Thunder: Patrick Henry and the American Revolution*. New York: Grove, 1991.
McCullough, David. *The Path Between the Seas: The Creation of the Panama Canal, 1870–1914*. New York: Simon & Schuster, 1977.
McGraw, Marie Tyler. *At the Falls: Richmond, Virginia, and Its People*. Chapel Hill: University of North Carolina Press, 1994.
McGuire, Judith W. *Diary of a Southern Refugee During the War*. 3rd ed. Richmond: J. W. Randolph and English, 1889.
McKay, Richard C. *South Street: A Maritime History of New York*. Riverside, Conn.: Seven Seas, 1934.

McKee, Christopher. *A Gentlemanly and Honorable Profession: The Creation of the U.S. Naval Officer Corps, 1794–1815*. Annapolis: Naval Institute, 1991.

McKenna, Joseph. *British Ships in the Confederate Navy*. Jefferson, N.C.: McFarland, 2010.

McNeil, Jim. *Charleston's Navy Yard: A Picture History*. Charleston, S.C.: Coker Craft, 1985.

McPherson, Edward. *The Political History of the United States of America During the Great Rebellion from November 6, 1860, to July 4, 1864*. New York: Philp and Solomons, 1865.

McPherson, James. *Antietam: Crossroads of Freedom; The Battle That Changed the Course of the Civil War*. Oxford: Oxford University Press, 2004.

_____. *Battle Cry of Freedom: The Civil War Era*. Oxford: Oxford University Press, 1988.

_____. *Tried by War: Abraham Lincoln as the Commander in Chief*. New York: Penguin, 2008.

Meacham, Jon. *American Lion: Andrew Jackson in the White House*. New York: Random House, 2008.

Meade, Robert Douthat. *Judah P. Benjamin*. New York: Oxford University Press, 1943.

Meade, William. *Old Churches, Ministers, and Families of Virginia*. 2 vols. Philadelphia: J. B. Lippincott, 1872.

Mellen, Kathleen Dickinson. *The Gods Depart: A Saga of the Hawaiian Kingdom, 1832–73*. New York: Hastings House, 1936.

Melville, Herman. *Moby Dick; or, The White Whale*. Boston: St. Adolph Society, 1892. Accessed Dec. 19, 2013. http://books.google.com/books?id=XV8XAAAAYAAJ.

Meinig, D. W. *The Shaping of America: Atlantic America, 1492–1800*. 2 vols. New Haven: Yale University Press, 1983.

Memminger, C. G. *Address of the Hon. C. G. Memminger, Special Commissioner from the State of South Carolina, Before the Assembled Authorities of the State of Virginia, Jan. 19, 1860*. Richmond, 1860. Library of Virginia, Richmond. Accessed Nov. 3, 2013. http://books.google.com/books?id=MFK0BxIwlpcC.

Merk, Frederick. *Manifest Destiny and Mission*. New York: Alfred A. Knopf, 1970.

_____. *The Oregon Question*. Cambridge, Mass.: Harvard University Press, 1967.

Merli, Frank J. *Great Britain and the Confederate Navy*. Bloomington: Indiana University Press, 1970.

Merrill, James M. *DuPont: The Making of an Admiral; A Biography of Samuel Francis DuPont*. New York: Dodd Mead, 1986.

Mesick, Jane Louise. *The English Traveller in America, 1785–1835*. New York: Columbia University Press, 1922.

Message from the President of the United States Communicating the Letter of Mr. Prevost, and Other Documents, Relating to an Establishment Made at the Mouth of the Columbia River, Jan. 27, 1823. Washington, D.C.: Gales and Seaton, 1823. Accessed Nov. 3, 2013. http://books.google.com/books?id=TbG2k_TsZmcC.

Message from the President of the United States to the Two Houses of Congress at the Commencement of 2d Session of the 29th Congress, Dec. 8, 1846. Washington, D.C.: Ritchie and Heiss, 1846. Accessed Jan. 14, 2014. http://books.google.com/books?id=D7UTAAAAYAAJ.

Meyers, Donald J. *And the War Came: The Slavery Quarrel and the American Civil War*. New York: Algora, 2005.

Michaux, François André. *Early Western Travels*. Cleveland: Arthur H. Clark, 1904.

_____. *Travels to the Westward of the Allegany Mountains, in the States of the Ohio, Kentucky, and Tennessee, in the Year 1802*. London: Barnard and Sultzer, 1805. Accessed Nov. 3, 2013. http://books.google.com/books?id=AV4VAAAAYAAJ.

Middleton, Norwood C. *Salem: A Virginia Chronicle*. Salem, Va.: Salem Historical Society, 1986.

Miller, Marion Mills, ed. *Great Debates in American History: Departments of Government*. 9 vols. New York: Current Letter, 1913.

Miller, William Lee. *Arguing About Slavery: The Great Battle in the United States Congress*. New York: Alfred P. Knopf, 1996.

Milne, Graeme J. *Trade and Traders in Mid-Victorian Liverpool: Mercantile Business and the Making of a World Port*. Liverpool, U.K.: Liverpool University Press, 2000.

Minor, Benjamin Blake. *The Southern Literary Messenger, 1834–1864*. New York: Neale, 1905.

Minor, John B. *The Minor Family of Virginia*. Lynchburg, Va.: privately printed, 1923.

_____. "Miscellany." *Historical Magazine and Notes and Queries* (John G. Shea, New York) 8 (Jan. 1864): 48.

Montgomery, H. *Life of Major General William H. Harrison: 9th President of the United States*. New York: C. M. Saxton, 1860.

Moore, Frank, ed. *The Rebellion Record: A Diary of American Events*. New York: D. Van Nostrand, 1862.

Moore, John Hammond. *Albemarle: Jefferson's County, 1727–1976*. Charlottesville: University Press of Virginia for the Albemarle County Historical Society, 1976.

Morgan, James Morris. *Recollections of a Rebel Reefer*. Boston: Houghton Mifflin, 1917.

Morison, Samuel Eliot. *John Paul Jones: A Sailor's Biography*. Boston: Little, Brown, 1959.

_____. *Life and Letters of Harrison Gray Otis, Federalist, 1765–1848*. Vol. 2. Boston: Houghton Mifflin, 1913.

_____. *The Maritime History of Massachusetts, 1783–1860*. Boston: Houghton Mifflin, 1922.

Morris, Charles. *The Autobiography of Commodore Charles Morris, U.S. Navy*. Annapolis: Naval Institute, 1914.
Morris, James McGrath. *Pulitzer: A Life in Politics, Print, and Power*. New York: HarperCollins, 2010.
Morse, Charles Fesseden. *Letters Written During the Civil War*. Kansas City, Mo.: privately printed, 1898.
Morse, Edward L. *Samuel F. B. Morse: His Letters and Journals*. Boston: Houghton Mifflin, 1914.
Mullaly, John. *The Laying of the Cable; or, The Ocean Telegraph*. New York: D. Appleton, 1858.
Munford, Beverly B. *Virginia's Attitude toward Slavery and Secession*. Richmond: L. H. Jenkins, 1914.
Musicant, Ivan. *Divided Waters: The Naval History of the Civil War*. New York: HarperCollins, 1995.
Musselman, Elizabeth Green. "Science as a Landed Activity: Scientifics and Seamen aboard the U.S. Exploring Expedition." In *Surveying the Record: North American Scientific Exploration to 1930*, edited by Edward Carlos Cater II, 77–102. Philadelphia: American Philosophical Society, 1999.
National Academy of Sciences. *Annual of the National Academy of Sciences for 1863–1864*. Cambridge, Mass.: Welch and Bigelow, 1865.
_____. *Annual of the National Academy of Sciences for 1866*. Cambridge, Mass.: Welch and Bigelow, 1867.
_____. *Biographical Memoirs of the National Academy of Sciences*. Vol. 1. Washington, D.C.: National Academy of Sciences, 1877.
"National Agricultural Association Congress, May 27–30, 1872." In *Proceedings*, 1, 7–72. Indianapolis: Sentinel, 1872.
National Institute for the Promotion of Science. *Papers Relating to the National Institute, Collected and Arranged by Francis Markoe, Corresponding Secretary*. 15 Pamphlets in One Volume. Washington, D.C.: National Institute for the Promotion of Science, n.d.
_____. *Proceedings, Washington, 1855–57*. Washington, D.C.: Smithsonian Institution, 1858.
National Oceanic and Atmospheric Administration. NOAA Central Library. *The Coast Survey, 1807–1867*. Last modified Nov. 30, 2007. http://www.lib.noaa.gov/noaainfo/heritage/coastsurveyvol1/CONTENTS.html.
_____. "The 'American Method' of Longitude Determination." *The Coast Survey, 1807–1867*. Last modified Nov. 30, 2007. http://www.lib.noaa.gov/noaainfo/heritage/coastsurveyvol1/BACHE2.html#AMERICAN.
Naval Magazine (New York), 1836–37.
Nelson, James Poyntz. *The Chesapeake and Ohio Railroad*. Richmond: Lewis, Feb. 24, 1927.
Nelson, Stewart B. *Oceanographic Ships: Fore and Aft*. Washington, D.C.: Office of the Oceanographer of the Navy, 1982.
Nepveux, Ethel S. *George Alfred Trenholm and the Company That Went to War, 1861–1865*. Charleston, S.C.: Comprint, 1973.
Newcomb, Simon. *Reminiscences of an Astronomer*. Boston: Riverside Press of Houghton Mifflin, 1903. Reprint, Boston: Houghton Mifflin, 1991. Page references are to the 1903 edition.
Newell, Layton, Charles Schroeder, and Edwin Coffin. *Of Duty Well and Faithfully Done: A History of the Regular Army in the Civil War*. Lincoln: University of Nebraska Press, 2011.
Nicholson, Irene. *The Liberators: A Study of Independence Movements in Spanish America*. New York: Praeger, 1969.
Nicolay, John G., and John Hay. *Abraham Lincoln: A History; The Border States*. New York: Century, 1888.
Nientimp, Judith A. "The Somers Mutiny." *University of Rochester Library Bulletin* 20, no. 1 (Autumn 1964). Accessed Dec. 17, 2013. http://www.lib.rochester.edu/index.cfm?PAGE=2477.
Niles, H[ezekiah]. "Defense of Baltimore." In *The Weekly Register*, back cover. Baltimore: Franklin Press, 1814.
Nordoff, Charles. *Man-of-War Life: A Boy's Experience in the United States Navy, During a Voyage around the World, in a Ship of the Line*. Classics of Naval Literature. Cincinnati: Moore, Wilstach, Keys, 1855. Reprint, Annapolis: Naval Institute, 1985. Page references are to the 1985 edition.
"Obituary: Admiral Jansen." *Geographical Journal* (Royal Geographical Society) 2 (July–Dec. 1893): 465–68.
Odgers, Merle Middleton. *Alexander Dallas Bache: Scientist and Educator, 1806–1867*. Philadelphia: University of Pennsylvania Press, 1947.
Ohio Historical Society. "Ohio Medical History." *Ohio History*. Columbus, Ohio: Ohio Historical Society, 2003.
Oliver, John W. *History of American Technology*. Ann Arbor, Mich.: University Microfilms, 1980.
Oman, Charles. *A History of the Peninsular War*. Vol. 3. London: Greenhill Books, 2004.
Oren, Michael. *Power, Faith, and Fantasy: The Middle East and Antebellum America*. New York: W. W. Norton, 2007.
Otey, James Hervey. "Trust in God: The Only Safety of Nations." Transcript of Sermon Delivered Jan. 1, 1860. In *Memoir of Rt. Rev. James Hervey Otey, D.D., LL.D*. Edited by William Mercer Green, 323–50. New York: James Pott, 1885.
Owsley, Frank L. *King Cotton Diplomacy*. 2nd ed. Chicago: University of Chicago Press, 1959.

Quarstein, John V. *CSS* Virginia*: Sink Before Surrender*. Charleston, S.C.: History, 2012.
Page, Thomas Jefferson. *La Plata: The Argentine Confederation and Paraguay Under Orders of the U.S. Government*. New York: Harper and Brothers, 1859.
Paine, Albert Bigelow. *A Sailor of Fortune: Personal Memorials of Albert Bigelow Paine*. New York: McClure Phillips, 1906.
Parker, William Harwar. *Recollections of a Naval Officer, 1841–65*. New York: Scribner's, 1883.
Parramore, Thomas C., Peter C. Stewart, and Tommy L. Bogger. *Norfolk: The First Four Centuries*. Charlottesville: University of Virginia Press, 1994.
Paullin, Charles Oscar. *Diplomatic Negotiations of American Naval Officers, 1778–1883*. Baltimore: Johns Hopkins University Press, 1912.
_____. *Naval Administration Under the Navy Commissioners, 1815–1842*. Reprinted from Naval Institute *Proceedings*. Annapolis: Naval Institute, 1907.
_____. "Washington City and the Old Navy." In *Columbia Historical Society Records*. Vols. 33–34. Washington, D.C.: Columbia Historical Society, 1932.
Peale, Titian Ramsey. "The South Sea Surveying and Exploring Expedition." In *American Historical Record and Repertory of Notes and Queries*. Edited by Benson S. Lossing, 243–51. Philadelphia: John E. Potter, 1874.
Pearson, Arthur Scott. "The Constitutional Aspects of the Parson's Cause." *Political Science Quarterly* (New York) 31 (1916): 558–77.
Pepper, J. H., ed. "The Electric Torpedo." In *Cyclopedia Science Simplified*, 305–11. London: Frederick Warne, 1869.
Perry, Milton F. *Infernal Machines*. Baton Rouge: Louisiana State University Press, 1965.
Petra, Francis Loraine. *Simon Bolivar: "El Libertador."* London: Lane, 1910.
Phillips, Ulrich Bonnell. *American Negro Slavery*. New York: D. Appleton, 1918.
_____. *The Life of Robert Toombs*. New York: Macmillan, 1913.
Pierson, John S. [Personne, pseud.]. *Marginalia; or, Gleanings from an Army Note-Book*. Columbia, S.C.: F. G. deFontaine, 1864.
Pim, Bedford. *The Gate of the Pacific*. Brochure. London: Lovell Reed, 1863.
_____. "The Panama Canal," Dec. 19, 1879. *Journal of the Society of the Arts* (London) 28 (Nov. 21, 1879–Nov. 12, 1880): 70.
Pollard, Edward A. *Jefferson Davis: With a Secret History of the Confederacy*. Philadelphia: National, 1869.
Ponko, Vincent, Jr. *Ships, Seas, and Scientists*. Annapolis: Naval Institute, 1974.
Poole, Ben Perley. *Perley's Reminiscences of Sixty Years in the National Metropolis*. Vol. 1. Philadelphia: Hubbard Brothers, 1886.
Porter, David. *Journal of a Cruise Made to the Pacific Ocean in U.S. Frigate* Essex*, 1812–14*. 2 vols. New York: Wiley and Halsted, 1822.
Porter, David Dixon. *Memoir of Commodore David Porter of the United States Navy*. Albany, N.Y.: J. Munsell, 1875.
_____. *The Naval History of the Civil War*. New York: Sherman, 1886.
Potter, David M. *The Impending Crisis, 1848–1861*. Completed and edited by Don E. Fehrenbacher. New York: Harper Colophon, 1976.
Potter Hay, Melba, ed., and Carol Reardon, assoc. ed. *Henry Clay Papers: Candidate, Compromiser, Elder Statesman, January 1844–June 29, 1852*. Vol. 10. Lexington: University Press of Kentucky, 1991.
Powell, William S., ed. "Gabriel Rains." In *Dictionary of North Carolina Biography*. Vol. 5. Chapel Hill: University of North Carolina Press, 1994.
Pratt, Fletcher. *The Navy: A History; The Story of a Service in Action*. Garden City, N.Y.: Garden City, 1941.
Priestley, Charles. "'Batavian Grace': Alexander Beresford Hope." *American Civil War Round Table UK*. Originally published as "Batavian Grace" in *Crossfire: The Magazine of the ACWRT (UK)*, no. 69 (Aug. 2002). Accessed Nov. 5, 2013. http://www.acwrt.org.uk/uk-heritage_Batavian-Grace—Alexander-Beresford-Hope.asp.
"Proceedings of Societies: Society of Telegraph Engineers." *Telegraphic Journal of Electrical Review* (London: Henry Gillman, 1874) 2 (Dec. 1873–Dec. 1874): 121–25.
Proceedings of the American Association for the Advancement of Science. Charleston, S.C.: Walker and James, 1850.
Proceedings of the New York Historical Society for the Year 1847. New York: Press of the Historical Society, 1847.
Pryor, Sally A. *Reminiscences of Peace and War*. New York: Grosset and Dunlap, 1904.
Putnam, Sallie Ann. *Richmond During the War: Four Years of Personal Observation*. New York: G. W. Carleton, 1867.
Quaife, Milo Milton, ed. *The Diary of James K. Polk During His Presidency, 1845–1849*. 4 vols. Chicago: A. C. McClurg, 1910.
Rains, Gabriel J., and Peter S. Michie. *Confederate Torpedoes: Two Illustrated 19th Century Works with New Appendices and Photographs*. Edited by Herbert Schiller. Jefferson, N.C.: McFarland, 2011.
Randolph, Thomas Jefferson, ed. *Memoir, Correspondence, and Miscellanies from the Papers of Thomas Jefferson*. Vol. 1. Charlottesville, Va.: F. Carr, 1829.
Rapport, Mike. *1848: Year of Revolution*. New York: Basic Books, 2009.

Record of News History and Literature. Richmond: West and Johnson, 1863.
Reeve, Lovelle. *Portraits of Men of Eminence in Literature, Science, and Art*. Covent Garden, U.K.: Reeve, 1864.
Reid, Whitelaw. *After the War: A Southern Tour*. Cincinnati: Moore, Wilstack, and Baldwin, 1866.
Remini, Robert V. *Andrew Jackson: The Course of American Democracy, 1833–1845*. Baltimore: Johns Hopkins University Press, 1984.
_____. *The Battle of New Orleans: Andrew Jackson and America's First Military Victory*. New York: Viking, 1999.
_____. *Daniel Webster: The Man and His Time*. New York: W. W. Norton, 1997.
_____. *Henry Clay: Statesman for the Union*. New York: W. W. Norton, 1993.
Report of the Fifteenth Meeting of the British Association for the Advancement of Science: Held at Cambridge in June 1845. London: British Association for the Advancement of Science, 1846.
Report of the Kentucky Commissioners to the Late Peace Conference Held at Washington City, Made to the Legislature of Kentucky. Frankfort, Ky.: Yeoman Office, 1861.
Report of the National Academy of Sciences for Year 1863. Washington, D.C.: Government Printing Office, 1864.
Reynolds, Clark G. *Command of the Seas*. New York: Krieger, 1974.
Reynolds, David S. *John Brown: Abolitionist*. New York: Vintage Books, 2005.
Reynolds, Jeremiah N. "Mocha Dick: Or the White Whale of the Pacific." *Knickerbocker Magazine* (New York) 13, no. 5 (May 1839): 377–92.
_____. *Voyage of the United States Frigate* Potomac *Under the Command of Commodore John Downes During the Circumnavigation of the Globe, 1831–34*. New York: Harper and Brothers, 1835.
Rice, Otis K. *The Allegheny Frontier*. Lexington: University Press of Kentucky, 1970.
Richardson, James Daniel. *A Compilation of the Messages and Papers of the Confederacy*. Vol. 2. Nashville, Tenn.: United States, 1905.
Roberts, Steven. "Nathaniel John Holmes (1824–1888)." *History of the Atlantic Cable and Undersea Communications: From the First Submarine Cable of 1850 to the Worldwide Fiber Optic Network*. Last modified Feb. 12, 2010. http://atlantic-cable.com/CablePioneers/Holmes/index.htm.
Roberts, William H. *Now for the Contest: Coastal and Oceanic Naval Operations in the Civil War*. Great Campaigns of the Civil War. Lincoln: University of Nebraska Press, 2004.
Robinson, John R. *Fifty Years of Fleet Street: Being the Life and Recollections of Sir John R. Robinson*. Edited by Frederick Moy Thomas. London: Macmillan, 1904.
Rogers, Edward R. *Four Southern Magazines*. PhD diss. Charlottesville: University of Virginia Studies in Southern Literature, 1902.
Roth, Mitchel. *Historical Dictionary of War Journalism*. Westport, Conn.: Greenwood, 1997.
Rothenberg, Marc, ed., and Kathleen W. Dennison, John C. Rumm, and Paul Theerman, asst. eds. *The Papers of Joseph Henry*. Vol. 6, *January 1844–December 1846: The Princeton Years*. Washington, D.C.: Smithsonian Institution Press, 1992.
Rowland, Dunbar, ed. *Encyclopedia of Mississippi History*. Vol. 2. Madison, Wis.: Selwyn A. Brant, 1907.
Royal Astronomical Society. *Monthly Notes*, Nov. 12, 1858. London: Royal Astronomical Society, 1859.
Royster, Charles. *The Fabulous History of the Dismal Swamp Company: A Story of George Washington's Times*. New York: Alfred A. Knopf, 1999.
Rozwadowski, Helen M. *Fathoming the Ocean: The Discovery and Exploration of the Deep Sea*. Cambridge, Mass.: Belknap Press of Harvard University Press, 2005.
Ruffin, Edward. *Diary*. Baton Rouge: Louisiana State University Press, 1977.
_____, ed. "On Improvement by Rail-Roads and Canals." Extract from an article in the *New York Review* for Apr. 1840. *Farmer's Register*, a monthly publication (Petersburg, Va.) 8, no. 9 (Sept. 30, 1840): 543–45.
Russel, Robert Royal. *Economic Aspects of Southern Sectionalism*. Urbana: University of Illinois, 1923.
Russell, W. H. *Atlantic Telegraph*. Dublin: Nonsuch, 2005.
Ryan, Shannon. *The Ice Hunters: A History of Newfoundland Sealing to 1914*. Newfoundland History Series 8. St. John's, Newfoundland, Canada: Breakwater Books, 1994.
Santoro, Anthony. "The Prophet in His Own Words: Nat Turner's Biblical Construction." *Va. Mag.* 116, no. 2 (Spring 2008): 115–19.
Saturday Review. "The Americans in London." Aug. 2, 1862.
_____. "The American Prospects." Aug. 23, 1862.
_____. "The Confederate Congress." Sept. 6, 1862.
Saunders, James Edmonds. *Early Settlers of Alabama*. With notes and genealogies by his granddaughter Elizabeth Saunders Blair Stubbs. New Orleans: Graham and Sons, 1899.
Scharf, John Thomas. *History of the Confederate States Navy: From Its Organization to the Surrender of Its Last Vessel*. New York: Rodgers and Sherwood, 1887. Reprint, New York: Random House/Value Publishing, 1996.
Schmidt, L. B. "The Influence of Wheat and Cot-

ton on Anglo-American Relations during the Civil War." Paper presented to American Historical Association in Philadelphia. *Iowa Journal of History and Politics* (Des Moines) 16 (1918): 400–411.

Schneller, Robert J., Jr. *A Quest for Glory: A Biography of Rear Admiral John A. Dahlgren*. Annapolis: Naval Institute, 1996.

Schroeder, John H. *Shaping a Maritime Empire*. Westport, Conn.: Greenwood, 1985.

Sears, Stephen W. *Landscape Turned Red: The Battle of Antietam*. New York: Houghton Mifflin, 2003.

_____. "The Rise and Fall of CSS *Virginia:* Did a Radical New Confederate Gunship Foil McClellan's Plan to End the Civil War in 1862?" *MHQ: Quarterly Journal of Military History* (Leesburg, Va.) 21, no. 3 (Spring 2009): 82–93.

Semmes, Raphael. *Service Afloat and Ashore During the Mexican War*. Cincinnati: William H. Moore, 1851.

_____. *Service Afloat; or, The Remarkable Career of the Confederate Cruisers* Sumter *and* Alabama *During the War Between the States*. Baltimore: Kelly, Piet, 1869. Reprint, London: Sampson Low, Marston, Searle, and Rivington, 1887.

Senior, Elinor. "Edward Feild." In *Dictionary of Canadian Biography*. Vol. 10. University of Toronto/Université Laval, 2003–. Accessed Sept. 26, 2013. http://www.biographi.ca/en/bio/feild_edward_10E.html.

Shanks, Henry T. *The Secession Movement in Virginia, 1847–61*. New York: AMS, 1934.

Sheridan, P. H. *Personal Memoirs*. Vol. 2. New York: C. L. Webster, 1888.

Shibley, Ronald E. *Fredericksburg*. Fredericksburg, Va.: Historic Fredericksburg Foundation, 1977.

Shrivastava, K. M. *News Agencies from Pigeon to Internet*. Elgin, Ill.: New Dawn, 2007.

Siegenthaler, John K. *James K. Polk*. New York: Macmillan, 2003.

Silliman, Benjamin. "Remarks on Some of the Gold Mines and on Parts of the Gold Region of Virginia Founded on Personal Observation, 1836. *Am. Journ. Science* (New Haven, Conn.) 32, no. 1, art. 10 (1837): 98–130.

Silliman, Benjamin, Jr. "Sears C. Walker." *Am. Journ. Science* (New Haven, Conn.) 2nd ser., 15, no. 44 (May 1853): 293–96.

Silverberg, Robert. *Stormy Voyager*. Philadelphia: Lippincott, 1968.

Silverman, Kenneth J. *Lightning Man: The Accursed Life of Samuel F. B. Morse*. New York: Alfred P. Knopf, 2003.

Simmons, R. C. *The American Colonies: From Settlement to Independence*. New York: W. W. Norton, 1976.

Simpson, Craig Michael. *Henry A. Wise in Antebellum Politics, 1850–61*. PhD diss. Ann Arbor, Mich.: University Microfilms, 1979.

Small, Stephen C. "The Ship That Couldn't Be Built." *Naval History* (Annapolis, Md.) 22, no. 5 (Oct. 2008): 69–74.

Smith, Francis Henney. *The Virginia Military Institute: Its Building and Rebuilding*. Lynchburg, Va.: J. P. Bell, 1912.

_____. "West Point Fifty Years Ago." Address before the Association of Graduates. New York: D. Van Nostrand, 1879.

Smith, Gene Allen. "A Most Unprovoked, Unwarrantable, and Dastardly Attack: James Buchanan, Paraguay, and the Water Witch Incident of 1855." With Larry Bartlett. *Northern Mariner* (Ottawa, Ontario, Canada), July 2009.

_____. "Preventing the 'Eggs of Insurrection' from Hatching: The U.S. Navy and Control of the Mississippi River, 1806–1815." *Northern Mariner* (Ottawa, Ontario, Canada), July/Oct. 2008.

_____. *Thomas ap Catesby Jones: Commodore of Manifest Destiny*. Annapolis: Naval Institute, 2000.

Smith, Geoffrey Sutton. "The Navy before Darwinism: Science, Exploration, and Diplomacy in Antebellum America." *American Quarterly* 28, no. 1 (Spring 1976): 41–55.

Smith, Goldwin. *Letter to a Whig Member of the Southern Independence Association*. American ed. Boston: Ticknor and Fields, 1864.

Smith, Jean Edward. *John Marshall: Definer of a Nation*. New York: Henry Holt, 1996.

Smithsonian Institution. *Annual Report of the Board of Regents of the Smithsonian Institution, 1861*. Washington, D.C.: Government Printing Office, 1862.

Society for the Diffusion of Useful Knowledge. *Penny Cyclopedia of the Society for the Diffusion of Useful Knowledge*. Vol. 18. London: Charles Knight, 1840.

Soley, James Russell. *Historical Sketch of the U.S. Naval Academy*. Washington, D.C.: Government Printing Office, 1876.

_____. *The Navy in the Civil War: The Blockades and the Cruisers*. New York: Scribner's, 1890.

Southern Historical Society Papers. 47 vols. Richmond: Southern Historical Society, 1876–1930.

Southern Literary Messenger. Richmond: 1834–64.

Spence, James. *The American Union: Its Effect on National Character and Policy*. 3rd ed. London: Richard Bentley, 1862.

Spencer, Warren F. *The Confederate Navy in Europe*. Tuscaloosa: University of Alabama Press, 1983.

Stachurski, Richard. *Longitude by Wire: Finding North America*. Columbia: University of South Carolina Press, 2009.

Stampp, K. M. *America in 1857: A Nation on the Brink*. Oxford: Oxford University Press, 1990.

The State of the Union: Being a Complete Docu-

mentary History of the Public Affairs for the United States, Foreign and Domestic, for the Year 1854. Washington, D.C.: Taylor and Maury, 1855.

Stephen, David, and Jeanne T. Heilder, eds., and David Coles, assoc. ed. "P. G. T. Beauregard." In *American Civil War Encyclopedia: A Political, Social, and Military History*. New York: W. W. Norton, 2000.

Stephen, Leslie, and Sidney Lee, eds. *Dictionary of National Biography*. London: Harrison, 1885–1900; supplementary vols., 1901.

Stephens, Alexander Hamilton. *A Constitutional View of the Late War Between the States: Its Causes, Character, Conduct, and Results*. 2 vols. Philadelphia: National, 1868 and 1870.

Stevenson, Sarah Yorke. *Maximilian in Mexico: A Woman's Reminiscences of the French Intervention*. New York: Century, 1889.

Stewart, Charles S. *A Visit to the South Seas in the U.S. Ship* Vincennes *During the Years 1829–1830*. 2 vols. New York: John P. Haven, Sleight, and Robinson, 1831 and 1832.

Stewart, E. Hardin. "Notes on the Employment of Submarine Mines (Commonly Called Torpedoes) in America During the Late Civil War." *Papers on Subjects Connected with the Duties of the Corps of Royal Engineers* (Woolwich, U.K.), n.s., 15 (1866): 1–28.

Stewart, George. *Curiosities of Glasgow Citizenship as Exhibited Chiefly in the Business Center of the Old Commonwealth Aristocracy*. Glasgow, U.K.: James MacLehose, 1881.

Stiles, Robert. *Reconstruction in Virginia*. Baltimore: R. H. Woodward, 1890.

Stiles, T. J. *The First Tycoon: The Epic Life of Cornelius Vanderbilt*. New York: Random House, 2009.

Still, William N. *Iron Afloat*. Nashville, Tenn.: Vanderbilt University Press, 1971.

_____. *Ironclad Captains: The Commanding Officers of the U.S.S.* Monitor. Washington, D.C.: Marine and Estuarine Management Division, National Oceanic and Atmospheric Administration, 1988.

Stoddard, William O. *Men of Business: Men of Achievement*. New York: Scribner's, 1893.

Stone, Charles P. "Washington on the Eve of the War." *Century Magazine* 26, no. 3 (July 1883): 458–66.

Strachey, Lytton. *Eminent Victorians*. San Diego, Calif.: Harvest Book, 1969.

Strode, Hudson. *Jefferson Davis: American Patriot, 1808–1861*. New York: Harcourt, Brace, 1955.

_____. *Jefferson Davis: Confederate President*. New York: Harcourt, Brace, and World, 1959.

Sweet, Palmer C., and David Trimble. *Virginia Gold: Resource Data*. Charlottesville, Va.: Virginia Department of Mineral Resources, 1983.

Symonds, Craig L. *Confederate Admiral: The Life and Wars of Franklin Buchanan*. Annapolis: Naval Institute, 1999.

_____. "Confluence of Careers at Mobile Bay." *Naval History*, Dec. 2009.

_____. *Decision at Sea*. Oxford: Oxford University Press, 2005.

_____. *Lincoln and His Admirals*. Oxford: Oxford University Press, 2008.

_____. *Joseph E. Johnston: A Civil War Biography*. New York: W. W. Norton, 1994.

"A Talk with a President's Son." *Lippincott's Monthly Magazine*, Jan.–June, 1888.

Taylor, John M. *Confederate Raider: Raphael Semmes of the* Alabama. Washington, D.C.: Potomac Books, 1994.

Temperley, H. W. V. *Life of Canning*. London: James Finch, 1903.

Thomas, Emory M. *The Confederate State of Richmond: A Biography of the Capital*. Baton Rouge: Louisiana State University Press, 1971.

_____. *Robert E. Lee: A Biography*. New York: W. W. Norton, 1997.

Thomas, Peter C. "Matthew Fontaine Maury and the Problem of Virginia's Identity." *Va. Mag.* 90 (Oct. 1982): 214–16.

Thompson, Samuel B. *Confederate Purchasing Operations Abroad*. Chapel Hill: University of North Carolina Press, 1935.

Todd, Richard Cecil. *Confederate Finance*. Athens: University of George Press, 1954.

Toll, Ian. *Six Frigates: The Epic History of the Founding of the United States Navy*. New York: W. W. Norton, 2006.

"Torpedoes: Naval, Military, and Gunnery Items." *Mechanics Magazine* (London), July 7, 1865.

Towle, Edgar Leon. "Science, Commerce, and the Navy on the Seagoing Frontier: The Role of M. F. Maury and the U.S. Naval Hydrographic Office in Naval Exploration, Commercial Expansion, and Oceanography before the Civil War." PhD diss., University of Rochester, 1966. Photocopy at the Department of the Navy Library, Washington, D.C.

Trahan, Joseph V., III. *Knights of the Quill: Confederate Correspondents and their Civil War Reports*. West Lafayette, Ind.: Purdue University Press, 2010.

Trinkle, E. Lee. "Maury and the Confederate Navy: Address delivered by the governor of Virginia, June 22, 1922." *Bulletin, State Normal School for Women* 8, no. 5 (Jan. 1923): 3–7.

Trowbridge, W. P. "On Deep Sea Soundings." *Am. Journ. Science*, 2nd ser., 26, no. 77, art. 17 (Sept. 1858): 9–12.

Tucker, Beverley D. *Nathaniel Beverley Tucker: Prophet of the Confederacy, 1784–1851*. Tokyo: Nan'undo, 1979.

Tunnell, Ted. "Confederate Newspapers in Virginia During the Civil War." *Encyclopedia Virginia*. Virginia Foundation for the Humanities. Last modified May 18, 2011. http://www.Ency

clopediaVirginia.org/Newspapers_in_Virginia_During_the_Civil_War_Confederate.

Turnbull, Archibald Douglas. *Commodore David Porter, 1780–1843*. New York: Century, 1929.

Twombly, Alexander S. *Hawaii and Its People: The Land of Rainbow and Palm*. Boston: Silver Burdett, 1900.

Tyler, Lyon Gardiner. "John Moncure Daniel." *Encyclopedia of Virginia Biography*. Vol. 4. New York: Lewis Historical, 1915.

_____. *The Letters and Times of the Tylers*. 3 vols. Richmond: Whittet and Shepperson, 1884–86.

_____. *Men of Mark in Virginia: Ideals of American Life*. Vol. 1. Washington, D.C.: Men of Mark, 1906.

U.S. Agricultural Society. "Journal of 4th Annual Meeting," Jan. 1856, Boston. *Journal for 1856*. Pt. 1. Vols. 1–3. (1856).

U.S. Circuit Court Reports, 1829–55. Columbus, Ohio: H. W. Derby and H. S. Allen, 1843.

Vancouver, George. *Voyage of Discovery to the North Pacific Ocean and Round the World*. Vol. 3. London: A. J. Robinson, 1798 and 1801.

Van Deusen, Glyndon G. *William Henry Seward*. New York: Oxford University Press, 1967.

Vandiver, Frank E., ed. *Confederate Blockade Running Through Bermuda*. Austin: University of Texas Press, 1947.

Van Horne, John Douglass. *Jefferson Davis and Repudiation in Mississippi*. Baltimore: Sun, 1915. http://archive.org/details/jeffersondavisre00vanh.

Varon, Elizabeth. *Disunion! The Coming of the American Civil War, 1789–1859*. Chapel Hill: University of North Carolina Press, 2008.

_____. *We Mean to Be Counted: White Women and Politics in Antebellum Virginia*. Chapel Hill: University of North Carolina Press, 1998.

Viola, Herman J., and Carolyn Margolis, eds. *Magnificent Voyagers: The U.S. Exploring Expedition, 1838–1842*. Washington, D.C.: Smithsonian Institution Press, 1983.

"Virginia: Her Geographic Position." *Southern Review* (Baltimore) 6, no. 11 (Oct. 1869): 453–69.

von Holst, H. "Annexation of Texas: Compromise of 1850." In *The Constitutional and Political History of the United States, 1846–1850*. Translated by John J. Lalor and Paul Shorey. Chicago: Callaghan Tex, 1881.

Von Scheliha, Viktor Ernst Karl Rudolf. *A Treatise on Coast Defence: Based on the Experience Gained by Officers of the Corps of Engineers of the Army of the Confederate States, and Compiled from Official Reports of Officers of the Navy of the United States, Made During the Late North American War from 1861 to 1865*. London: E. and F. N. Spon, 1868.

Waddell, Hope Masterton. *Twenty-Nine Years in the West Indies and Central Africa: A Review of Missionary Work and Adventure, 1829–1858*. London: T. Nelson and Sons, 1863. Reprinted, London: Frank Cass, 1970.

Walder, David. *Nelson: A Biography*. New York: Dial, 1978.

Wallace, Edward S. *Destiny and Glory*. New York: J. Wade, Coward-McCann, 1957.

Walpole, Spencer. *The Life of Lord John Russell*. Vol. 2. London: Longmans Green, 1891.

Warren, Kenneth. *Steel, Ships, and Men: Cammell Laird, 1824–1993*. Liverpool, U.K.: Liverpool University Press, 1998.

Warriner, Francis. *Cruise of the United States Frigate* Potomac *Round the World, During the Years 1831–34, Embracing the Attack on Quallah Battoo, with Notices of Scenes, Manners, etc., in Different Parts of Asia, South America, and the Islands of the Pacific*. Boston: Leavitt, Lord, 1835.

Wayland, John Walter. *The Pathfinder of the Seas: The Life of Matthew Fontaine Maury*. Richmond: Garret and Massie, 1930.

Weber, Gustavus A. *The Coast and Geodetic Survey: Its History, Activities, and Organization*. Service Monograph of the U.S. Government No. 16. Baltimore: Institute for Government Research, 1923.

_____. *The Naval Observatory: Its History, Activities, and Organization*. Service Monograph of the U.S. Government No. 39. Baltimore: Institute for Government Research, 1926.

_____. *The Weather Bureau: Its History, Activities, and Organization*. New York: D. Appleton, 1922.

Weed, Thurlow. *Life of Thurlow Weed, Including His Autobiography and a Memoir*. Edited by Harriet A. Weed. Vol. 2. Boston: Houghton Mifflin, 1884.

Wender, Herbert. *Southern Commercial Conventions*. Baltimore: Johns Hopkins University Press, 1930.

Whipple, A. B. C. *The Challenge*. New York: William Morrow, 1987.

White, James T., ed. *National Cyclopaedia of America Biography*. Vol. 6. New York: National Institute for the Promotion of Science, 1892.

Wild, Anthony. *The East India Company: Trade and Conquest from 1600*. New York: HarperCollins, 2000.

Wiley, Edwin, and Irving F. Rine, eds. "Progress of Virginia, Maryland, and the Carolinas, 1690–1748." Vol. 2, pt. 1, chap. 19 in *Lecture on the Growth and Development of the United States*. New York: American Educational Alliance, 1916.

Wiley, Peter Booth. *Yankees in the Lands of the Gods: Commodore Perry and the Opening of Japan*. With Korogi Ichiro. New York: Viking, 1990.

Wilkes, Charles. *Narrative of the U.S. Exploring Expedition, 1838–42*. 5 vols. Philadelphia: Lea and Blanchard, 1845.

_____. *Western America, Including California and Oregon, with Maps of Those Regions and the Sacramento Valley*. Philadelphia: Lea and Blanchard, 1849.

Williams, Frances Leigh. *Matthew Fontaine Maury: Scientist of the Sea*. New Brunswick: Rutgers University Press, 1963.

_____. *They Faced the Future: A Saga of Growth*. Richmond: Whittet and Shepperson, 1951.

Williamson, George. *Old Greenock: From the Earliest Time to the Early Part of the Nineteenth Century*. London: Alexander Gardner, 1886.

Wilson, Clyde N. *Carolina Cavalier*. Athens: University of Georgia Press, 1990.

Wilson, James Grant, ed. *Cyclopaedia of American Biography*. New York: D. Appleton, 1885.

Wilson, Thomas. *Biography of American Military and Naval Heroes: Comprehending Details of Their Achievements During the Revolutionary and Late War*. 2nd ed. Revised vol. 2. New York: John Low, 1821.

Wines, Enoch Cobb. *Two Years and a Half in the Navy; or, Journal of a Cruise in the Mediterranean and Levant, on Board of the U.S. Frigate* Constellation, *in the Years 1829, 1830, and 1831*. Philadelphia: Carey and Lea, 1832.

Wirt, William. *Sketches of the Life and Character of Patrick Henry*. Philadelphia: James Webster, 1817.

Wise, Barton H. *The Life of Henry A. Wise of Virginia, 1806–1876*. New York: Macmillan, 1899.

Wise, Jennings C. *The Long Arm of Lee; or, The History of the Artillery of the Army of Northern Virginia*. Vol. 1. Lynchburg, Va.: J. P. Bell, 1915.

_____. *The Military History of the Virginia Military Institute from 1839 to 1865*. Lynchburg, Va.: J. P. Bell, 1915.

Wise, Stephen R. *Lifeline of the Confederacy: Blockade Running During the Civil War*. Paperback ed. Columbia: University of South Carolina Press, 1991.

Withey, Lynne. *Voyages of Discovery*. Berkeley: University of California Press, 1989.

Wood, Gordon S. *Empire of Liberty: A History of the Early Republic, 1789–1815*. New York: Oxford University Press, 2009.

Wood, John Taylor. "The First Fight of the Iron-Clads." In *Battles and Leaders of the Civil War*, edited by Robert Underwood Johnson and C. C. Buel, 692–711. Vol. 1. New York: Century, 1887.

Youmans, William Jay, ed. *Pioneers of Science in America: Sketches of Their Lives and Scientific Work*. New York: D. Appleton, 1896.

Young, F. G., ed. *Sources of the History of Oregon*. Vol. 1, pts. 3–6, *The Correspondence and Journals of Captain Nathaniel J. Wyeth, 1831–6: A Record of Two Expeditions for the Occupation of the Oregon Country, with Maps, Introduction, and Index*. Eugene, Ore.: University, 1899.

Youngblood, Norman. *The Development of Mine Warfare: A Most Murderous and Bloody Conduct*. Westport, Conn.: Praeger Security International, 2006.

Online Resources

Arnold, Linda. "The Mexican-American War and the Media, 1845–1848." Department of History, Virginia Polytechnic Institute and State University, 2005. http://www.history.vt.edu/MxAmWar/INDEX.HTM.

Biographical Directory of the United States Congress, 1774–Present. http://bioguide.congress.gov/biosearch/biosearch.asp.

Colonial Williamsburg Foundation. http://www.history.org.

Encyclopedia Virginia. Virginia Foundation for the Humanities. http://www.encyclopediavirginia.org.

Shulman, S. T., D. L. Shulman, and R. H. Sims. "The Tragic 1824 Journey of the Hawaiian King and Queen to London: History of Measles in Hawaii." Abstract. *Pediatric Infectious Disease Journal* 28, no. 8 (Aug. 2009): 728–33. doi:10.1097/INF.0b013e31819c9720.

University of Virginia Library. http://www.library.virginia.edu.

Selected Published Works of Matthew Fontaine Maury
(Arranged Chronologically in Subject Section)

Navigation and Oceanography

"On the Navigation of Cape Horn." *Am. Journ. Science* 26 (July 1834): 54–63.

"Plan for an Instrument for Finding the True Lunar Distance." *Am. Journ. Science* 26 (July 1834): 63–65.

A New Theoretical and Practical Treatise on Navigation, in Which the Auxiliary Branches of Mathematics and Astronomy are Treated of the Theory and Most Simple Methods of Finding Time, Longitude, and Latitude. Philadelphia: Key and Biddle, 1836.

"Blank Charts on Board Public Cruisers." *SLM* 9, no. 8 (Aug. 1843): 458–61.

"The Gulf Stream and Currents of the Sea." *SLM* 10, no. 10 (July 1844): 161–81.

Elementary, Practical, and Theoretical Treatise on Navigation. Philadelphia: E. C. and J. Biddle, 2nd ed., 1843; rev. 3rd ed., 1845.

Steam Navigation to China: Circular Address to the People of the United States. Memphis, Tenn.: Twyman and Tannehill, 1849.

Charts and Maps

"Contributions of the Navy to Science and Commerce." *DeBow's Review* 5, no. 1 (Jan. 1848): 64–68.

"On the Winds and Currents of the Ocean." *Am. Journ. Science*, 2nd ser., 6, no. 19 (Nov. 1848): 399–401.

"Southern Commerce as Influenced by the Gulf Stream." *DeBow's Review* 9, no. 4 (Oct. 1850): 439–49.

"On the Influence Arising from the Discovery of the Gulf Stream on the Commerce of Charleston." In *Sailing Directions*, 25–37. Washington, D.C.: C. Alexander, 3rd ed., 1851; 4th ed., 1852.

Letter Stressing Advantages of Wind and Current Charts to Vessels Sailing from Atlantic to Pacific. 32d Cong., 1st Sess., 1852. Senate Executive Document 1.

Report on the Harbor of Charleston, S.C. Prof. A. D. Bache, Lieuts. C. H. Davis, J. N. Maffitt, M. F. Maury, U.S.N., S. D. Kurtz, U.S.E. Charleston, S.C: Councell and Daggett, 1852.

"The Cruise of the *Taney*." In *Sailing Directions*, 125–38. Washington, D.C.: C. Alexander, 3rd ed., 1851; 4th ed., 1853.

Chart of Cruise of American Expedition in Search of Sir John Franklin in 1850 and 1851. Washington, D.C.: Division of Maps and Charts, Library of Congress, ca. 1853.

Abstract Log for the Merchant Service: Wind and Current Charts. Philadelphia: E. C. and J. Biddle, 1854.

"Bathymetical Map of the North Atlantic Basin with Contour Lines Drawn In at 1,000, 2,000, 3,000, and 4,000 Fathoms." In *Explanations and Sailing Directions to Accompany the Wind and Current Charts*, 240. 5th ed. Washington, D.C.: C. Alexander, 1853. Revised in *Physical Geography of the Sea*, 1st ed. New York: Harper and Brothers, 1855.

Abstract Log for Men of War. Philadelphia: E. C. and J. Biddle, 1855.

Chart Showing Two Steamer Lanes Each Twenty Miles Wide, North Atlantic. New York: Board of Underwriters, 1855.

Sailing Directions from the Sea to Sandy Hook. Philadelphia: E. C. and J. Biddle, May 1855.

"Orographic Profiles Showing Telegraphic Plateau Along Maury's Proposed Route." In *Sailing Directions*, plates 11 and 12. 8th ed. Vol. 1. Washington, D.C.: William A. Harris, 1858.

Physical Geography of the Sea. New York: Harper and Brothers, 1st–5th ed., 1855; rev., 1856, 1857, 1858, 1859, 1861, 1871. Reprint of 1861 ed., Cambridge, Mass.: Harvard University Press, 1963. Accessed Dec. 19, 2013 (1858 edition). http://books.google.com/books?id=hlxDAAAAIAAJ.

Meteorology of Sea and Land

"The Currents of the Sea as Connected with Meteorology." In *Proceedings of the Association of American Geologists and Naturalists.* Boston: Association of American Geologists and Naturalists, May 14, 1844.

"On the Establishment of a Universal System of Meteorological Observations by Sea and Land." In *Compilation of Correspondence.* Compiled by MFM. Washington, D.C.: C. Alexander, 1851. Includes works by MFM and others.

"On the General Circulation of the Atmosphere." In *Sailing Directions*, 42–57. Washington, D.C.: C. Alexander, 3rd ed., 1851; 4th ed., 1852.

"On the Probable Relation Between Magnetism and the Circulation of the Atmosphere." In *Sailing Directions*, 441–57. Washington, D.C.: C. Alexander, 3rd ed., 1851; 4th ed., 1852.

"An Appeal to the Agricultural Interests of Virginia." *Southern Planter and Farmer* 15, no. 6 (June 1855): 161–62.

"Meteorology for the Farmers." *American Farmer* 11, no. 2 (Aug. 1855): 33–35.

"Agricultural Meteorology." In *The Year-Book of Agriculture*, 221–23. Philadelphia: Childs and Peterson, 1856.

Nautical Monographs

No. 1, *The Winds at Sea.* Washington, D.C.: U.S. Naval Observatory, 1859.

No. 2, *The Barometer at Sea.* Washington, D.C.: U.S. Naval Observatory, 1861.

No. 3, *The Southeast Trade Winds of the Atlantic.* Washington, D.C.: U.S. Naval Observatory, 1861.

"Address on Crop and Weather Forecasts." In *Twelfth Annual Report of St. Louis Agricultural and Mechanical Association.* Jefferson City, Mo.: Regan and Custer, 1873.

Navy Reform

As Harry Bluff: Nine articles. *Richmond Whig and Public Advertiser*, Aug. 10, 13, 14, 17, 18, 25, 27, and 28; Sept. 4, 1838.

Letter from Will Watch to Harry Bluff. *Richmond Whig and Public Advertiser*, Dec. 21, 25, and 28, 1838.

"Scraps from the Lucky Bag" series by Harry Bluff. *SLM*, vol. 6, nos. 4, 5, and 12 (1840); vol. 7, nos. 4, 5, and 6 (1841).

"Letters to Mr. Clay" by Union Jack. *SLM* 7, no. 10 (Oct. 1841): 577–602.

"The Navy and the West." *SLM* 9, no. 1 (Jan. 1843): 90–91.

"Another Scrap from the Lucky Bag: Lake Defenses and Western Interests." *SLM* 11, no. 2 (Feb. 1845): 4–10.

"To the Memphis Convention." *SLM* 11, no. 10 (Oct. 1845): 1–5.

Astronomy

Astronomical Observations Made During the Year 1845 at the National Observatory, Washington, D.C. Vol. 1. Washington, D.C.: J. and G. S. Gideon, 1846.
"Duplicity of Biela's Comet." *Royal Astronomical Society Monthly Notices* (London) 7 (1845–47): 90–91.
"National Observatory." *SLM* 14, no. 1 (Jan. 1848): 4–10.
Circular Prepared by the Direction of the Hon. William Ballard Preston, Secretary of the Navy, in Relation to the Astronomical Expedition to Chile, by Lt. M. F. Maury, U.S.N., Superintendent of the National Observatory, Washington. Washington, D.C.: C. Alexander, 1849.
"National Observatory." *SLM* 15, no. 5 (May 1849): 304–8.

Atlantic Cable

"Submarine Telegraph Across the Atlantic." *DeBow's Review* 16, no. 6 (June 1854): 626–28.
Physical Geography of the Sea. 1st ed. New York: Harper and Brothers, 1855.
The Annual Address Delivered Before the Maryland Institute for the Promotion of the Mechanic Arts, Maryland Agricultural Society, Baltimore, 1856. Baltimore: Maryland Agricultural Society, 1856.
Sailing Directions. Vols. 1 and 2. Washington, D.C.: C. Alexander, 4th ed., 1852; 6th ed., 1854; 8th ed., 1858.
"Scientific Testimony Received, December 1865." Appendix containing MFM endorsement. In *Great North Atlantic Telegraph Route*, 35. London: William Clowes and Sons, 1866.

Geography

"Geography of Commerce." *DeBow's Review* 15, no. 4 (Oct. 1853): 385–400.
"Progress of Geographical Science." *DeBow's Review* 17, no. 6 (Dec. 1854): 569–94.
First Lessons in Geography. New York: Richardson, 1868; 2nd ed., New York: University, 1871.
The World We Live In. New York: Richardson, 1868. 2nd ed., New York: University, 1871.
New Complete Geography. New York: University, 1907.
New Elements of Geography. New York: New American Books, 1922.

Education

"Naval." *SLM* vol. 6, nos. 5 and 12 (1840); vol. 7, no. 10 (1841).
Address Delivered Before the Literary Societies of the University of Virginia. Richmond: H. K. Ellyson, 1855.
Annual Address to the Graduating Class of the Virginia Military Institute, Lexington, Va., 1869. N.p.: Dispatch Steam Power Press, 1840.
"Introductory Address before the Educational Association of Virginia" [on Establishing a Polytechnic School]. *Educational Journal of Virginia* 1, no. 10 (Aug. 1870): 303–13.
"What We Owe to Science." *Cadet* (Virginia Military Institute), Jan. 1872.
"Address on the Study of Physical Geography." In *Documents and Proceedings, University of the South, Prior to 1860, Sewanee, Tenn., 1888*, 63–68. Sewanee, Tenn.: University of the South, 1888.

Exploration and Transportation

"A Scheme for Rebuilding Southern Commerce: Direct Trade with the South." *SLM* 5, no. 1 (Jan. 1839): 3–12.
"Lakes Defenses and Western Interests." *SLM* 11, no. 2 (Feb. 1845): 83–91.
"To the Memphis Convention." *SLM* 11, no. 11 (Nov. 1845): 547–600.
"The Dead Sea Expedition: Lieut. Lynch's Circumnavigation of Sea." *SLM* 14, no. 9 (Sept. 1848): 547–53.
"Letter to the Hon. John C. Calhoun." *DeBow's Review* 6, no. 3 (Sept. 1848): 195–226.
"The Isthmus Line to the Pacific." *SLM* 15, no. 5 (May 1849): 259–77.
Letter Opposing the Tehuantepec Railroad. *DeBow's Review* 7, No. 1 (July 1849): 16–17.
"Panama Railway and the Gulf of Mexico: Great Commercial Advantages of the Gulf of Mexico." *SLM* 15, no. 8 (Aug. 1849): 259–66.
"Maritime Interests of the South and West." *Southern Quarterly Review* 4, no. 8 (Oct. 1849): 309–46.
"The Commercial Prospects of the South: Proceedings of the Virginia Mercantile Convention, Richmond, 1851." *SLM* 17, no. 10 (Oct. 1851): 686–98.
"Direct Foreign Trade of the South: Commercial Conventions." *DeBow's Review* 12, no. 2 (Feb. 1852): 126–48.
Letter to Henry Grinnell requesting suggestions about Ringgold Expedition to Bering Straits. In *American Geographical and Statistical Society Bulletin* 1 (1852): 82–83.
"On Extending the Commerce of the South and West by Sea." *DeBow's Review* 12, no. 4 (Apr. 1852): 381–99.
The Amazon and the Atlantic Slopes of South America: Collected Letters That Appeared in the National Intelligencer *in Fall 1852*, by MFM, writing under the pseudonym "Inca." Washington, D.C.: Franck Taylor, 1853.

"Valley of the Amazon." 3 articles. *DeBow's Review*, vol. 14, nos. 5 and 6 (May and June 1853) and vol. 15, no. 1 (July 1853).

"Report to Richmond and York River Railroad Co. Concerning the Harbor of West Point, Va." No place or date given, but following MFM's assumption of position at Virginia Military Institute in 1868.

Civil War

"Ben Bow" series on Confederate naval problems. *Richmond Enquirer*, Sept. and Oct., 1861.

Captain Maury's Letter on American Affairs. Baltimore, 1862. Accessed Nov. 26, 2013. http://books.google.com/books?id=JwMk9HNWS_oC.

Letter on conditions in the Confederate States. *Times* (London), Dec. 22, 1862.

"A Vindication of the South and of Virginia." *Southern Historical Society Papers* 1, no. 2 (Feb. 1876): 49–61.

Letter to Grand Duke Constantine, St. Petersburg. *Southern Historical Society Papers* 2 (July 1876): 51–53.

Mexico

Decrees for the Encouragement of Immigration and Colonization. Mexico City, 1865. MP, vol. 23, LC.

Letter in response to inquiries about Mexico. *DeBow's Review* 32, no. 6 (June 1866): 624–30.

Virginia Military Institute

Address at installation as professor of physics. *Southern Planter and Farmer* 28, no. 10 (Oct. 1868): 633–38.

"An Appeal to the Public for Information on Virginia." *Richmond Whig*, Sept. 28, 1868.

"The Augusta County Fair and Speech." *Southern Planter and Farmer* 38, no. 11 (Nov. 1868): 698–704.

Physical Survey of Virginia: Her Resources, Climates, and Productions; Preliminary Report, No. 1. Richmond: W. A. R. Nye, 1869. 2nd ed., New York: D. Van Nostrand, 1869.

Physical Survey of Virginia: Her Resources, Climates, and Productions; With Notes and Additions by His Son, Richard L. Maury. Richmond: N. V. Randolph, 1878.

Miscellaneous

"Notice of the Gold Veins of the United States Mine Near Fredericksburg." *Am. Journ. Science* 32 (July 1837): 325–30.

"Description of an Alembic for Distilling Amalgam of Gold." *Am. Journ. Science* 33 (Jan. 1838): 289–301.

"Our Relations with England." *SLM* 8, no. 6 (June 1842): 381–96.

"The Right of Search." *SLM* 8, no. 4 (Apr. 1842): 211–52.

"The Bible and Science." *Southern Churchman*, Jan. 22, 1855.

Petition of Matthew Fontaine Maury to the Senate and House of Representatives in Congress Assembled. Washington, D.C., Jan. 1856.

"Report of Lt. Matthew F. Maury on the Loss of the United States Mail Steamer *Central America* Under the Command of William Lewis Herndon," written Oct. 19, 1857, MP, vol. 7, LC.

Index

Numbers in ***bold italics*** indicate pages with photographs.